A HUNDRED ENGLISH ESSAYS

A HUNDRED ENGLISH ESSAYS

Edited by
ROSALIND VALLANCE

Essay Index Reprint Series

 BOOKS FOR LIBRARIES PRESS
FREEPORT, NEW YORK

First Published 1936
Reprinted 1972

Library of Congress Cataloging in Publication Data

Vallance, Rosalind, ed.
    A hundred English essays.

    (Essay index reprint series)
    1. English essays. I. Title.
PR1363.V3 1972   824'.008   72-5806
ISBN 0-8369-7282-1

CONTENTS

viii   CONTENTS

INTRODUCTION

THE essay is a form of writing more easily recognized than defined. The very term " essay " suggests that something is being " tried out," and therefore is capable of development, both by the individual writer and by succeeding generations. Our modern conception of the essay differs considerably from that held by Francis Bacon, who, being the first Englishman to apply the title to his prose writings, is popularly regarded as the father of the art in this country. But the English essay in its later developments owes more to Montaigne, his great French contemporary, than to Bacon, and it was Montaigne, whose "Essaies" were published in 1580, seventeen years previously to Bacon's, who made the first recorded attempt to define the essay :

" Reader, loe here a well-meaning Booke. It doth at the first entrance forewarne thee, that in contriving the same, I have proposed unto my selfe no other than a familiar and private end : I have no respect or consideration at all, either to thy service, or to my glory : my forces are not capable of any such desseigne. I have vowed the same to the particular commodity of my kinsfolks and friends : to the end, that losing me (which they are likely to doe ere long) they may therein find some lineaments of my conditions and humours, and by that meanes reserve more whole, and more lively foster the knowledge and acquaintance they have had of me. Had my intention beene to forestal and purchase the worlds opinion and favour, I would surely have adorned my selfe more quaintly, or kept a more grave and solemne march. I desire therein to be delineated in mine owne genuine, simple and ordinarie fashion, without contention, art or study : for it is my selfe I pourtray. My imperfections shall therein be read to the life, and my naturall forme discerned, so farre-forth as publike reverence hath permitted me. For if my fortune had beene to have lived among those nations, which yet are said to live under the sweet liberty of Natures first and uncorrupted lawes, I assure thee, I would most willingly have pourtrayed my selfe fully and naked. Thus gentle Reader my selfe am the groundworke of my booke : It is then no reason thou shouldst employ thy time about so frivolous and vaine a Subject. Therefore farewell.—From *Montaigne*, the first of March, 1580." [1]

Nearly two hundred years later, when he should have known better, Dr. Johnson committed one of those famous blunders which have given so much amusement to schoolboys and others when he described the essay as " a loose sally of the mind, an irregular, undigested piece." Sir Edmund Gosse was kinder. He defined it as " a composition of moderate length, usually in prose, which deals in an easy cursory way with a subject, and, in strictness, with that subject only as it affects the writer."

But Mr. J. B. Priestley goes to the heart of the matter when he says simply, " An essay is the kind of composition written by an essayist."

Now no one would dream of defining a drama as " something written by a dramatist," or a novel as " something written by a novelist," though certainly the only right description of a poem is that it is written by a poet. In these two forms, the poem (by which we mean the only true poetry, the lyrical) and the essay, what counts

[1] From Florio's translation, 1603.

supremely is not the thing written about, but the personality of the writer and his power to convey to his reader a sense of contact with that personality.

This is what we in our time have come to look for as the distinctive quality of the essay. We feel that it belongs definitely to the class of writing which De Quincey described as "the literature of power" rather than to "the literature of knowledge." This point is elaborated by Alexander Smith in his essay "On the Writing of Essays," which appears in this book. The integrity of the essay, he says, depends upon its adherence to "some central mood" in the mind of the writer. "Give the mood, and the essay, from the first sentence to the last, grows around it as the cocoon grows around the silkworm."

Obviously a writer may have some moods, a vindictive one, for example, or a fit of moral indignation, round which sentences could never do anything so peaceful as to grow, but would dart off like sparks from a Catherine-wheel, and the resulting composition will be a diatribe or a sermon ; or having won the truth from the heart of a collection of data, he may be glowing with triumph, and will write a brilliant scientific treatise. But none of these can be called essays, for the essay at its best is a quiet commentary on life that does not seek, except indirectly, to rouse the critical faculties or the moral judgment, but rather to soothe, delight, or amuse. The essayist is of that pleasant company who know how to fleet the time carelessly, as they did in the golden world, enriching the mind and spirit, if only by an airy bubble of fantasy.

The essay, for reasons inherent in its nature, was never more flourishing than it is to-day ; but those who delight in the free and intimate style of our contemporaries must remember that this modern flexibility has been acquired by the efforts of writers who, generation by generation, have shaken off the verbal conventions and mental limitations of their time. For every advance, however, the price must be paid, and if we have gained in subtilty we have lost somewhat in richness, elegance, and a certain static charm that the older writers had.

The hundred essays in this book have been chosen from the work of outstanding writers from the time of Bacon to our own day. The greater number of them are acknowledged masterpieces, and there are none, we hope, that do not deserve to be described as " something written by an essayist."

Because Bacon is the first represented here, we do not mean to imply that no previous writer has given us anything in the spirit of the essay. On the contrary, there are passages in Malory, Caxton, Richard de Bury and Thomas Nashe, to name but four, which do foreshadow the intimate style of the true essayist. But these writers, like the gentleman in Molière who had been " talking prose all his life," wrote scraps of essays " without knowing it," and such passages cannot properly be taken from their context and printed in a book of this kind.

Upon the work of Bacon little comment is necessary, since his influence upon the development of the language has been duly acknowledged in every history of literature. But it may be noted here as a curious paradox that his fame as a great essayist has been won, not as Lamb's, by the intimacy of his style, but by its precise opposite. Bacon's famous " impersonality " is the most truly personal quality shown in his work. One may not be attracted by his character, but it is impossible in reading his " Essays " not to be conscious of it. But for the reader to be merely conscious of the personality of an essayist is not enough ; to-day the true essayist goes further—he makes a friend, or at least a relation, of the reader in his first few sentences, and that is what Lord Bacon could never do, and why it was left for a later and lesser writer to be " the father of the English essay."

The process of time has given new dimensions to our conception of the possibilities of the essay, and the work of seventeenth- and eighteenth-century writers seems flat in comparison. But each of these has added his own particular facet. The seventeenth century saw the flowering of English prose into many new forms ; some were extravagantly silly, some were exquisite, and some had great significance in relation to the future. The essays which follow Bacon's in this book have been chosen not only for their intrinsic interest, but as representing different aspects of thought and of style which have influenced the history of the essay.

Thomas Dekker's *Gul's Horn-Book*, from which has been taken " How a Gallant should behave in Paul's Walk," is a notable contribution to English satiric writing, which has always been an important feature of the essay. One can imagine how Thackeray must have relished this pungent commentary upon London life, this earlier version of his own *Book of Snobs*.

Then there are the character-writers, Overbury, Earle, and Lamb's " dear silly angel " Thomas Fuller. They are typical of a fashion that saw great developments in the work of Addison, Steele, and Goldsmith, and after them of Lamb and the novelists. This is a point which is touched upon later in these notes.

Beside Fuller are two more idols of Lamb—his " fantastic old great man," Sir Thomas Browne, and that other metaphysical fantastic, Robert Burton of *The Anatomy of Melancholy*, the astonishing tome from which Lamb shook the dust of a century's neglect. No compilation such as ours may ignore these two great writers, if for no other reason than for their influence upon *The Essays of Elia*. But they are also, of course, themselves essentially essayists, though, most annoyingly for editors, there is no single short piece of work by which they may be worthily represented in a book of this kind. The only possibility was bold dismemberment, and, in the case of Burton, abridgment also, and for this the compiler must offer apology.

In spite of Lamb's devotion to Browne and Burton, their names are not among the four that he was wont to say " sounded sweetest in his ears." Those names were " Kit Marlowe, Drummond of Hawthornden, Drayton, and Cowley." " It was no more than filial piety in Lamb," says Mr. Priestley, " to praise Cowley," for Cowley is regarded, by consent now almost general, as the father of the English essay. His little volume, *Several Discourses by way of Essays*, published in 1668, holds a place in our affections perhaps disproportionate to its merits, indisputable as these are. One can hardly touch that faded little book in the British Museum without feeling a faint, sweet thrill, for Cowley was the first to make an exquisite small bouquet of the random flowers of intimate thought, and tie them with the unmistakable knot of his own personality. " It is a hard and nice subject," he says, " for a man to write of himself," and at once proceeds, in " a composition of moderate length," to do so with the utmost grace and charm.

And so the essay at last really began.

In the work of the eighteenth-century essayists the character-study reappears, with a difference. It is no longer the portrait of a type, but of an individual, not " The Gentleman," but Sir Roger de Coverley, not " The Gallant," but Beau Tibbs. Narrative makes its first appearance, and at once raises that really " hard and nice " question, " What is the difference between an essay and a short story ? " May not one merge into the other ? Why, for example, is " Sir Roger in Church " an essay, and Katherine Mansfield's " Life of Ma Parker " a story ? Where do Goldsmith's " Distresses of a Common Soldier," his " Adventures of a Strolling Player " come in—and Lamb's " Captain Jackson " ?

The answer may be found by putting another question : After you have read this essay or story, whose personality remains the more vividly impressed upon your consciousness, that of the author, or that of the character he describes ?

If, with this question before him, the reader will turn again to " The Coverley Papers " he will see why, in spite of their narrative quality, they are not to be classed as " stories." For it is not with Sir Roger alone that we go to church, talk with the gipsies, or stroll round his estate ; the shade of Addison, courteous, tolerant, benignly amused, moves discreetly beside the old knight. At the end of the finely ironic " Distresses of a Common Soldier " it is not so much that poor battered old man but the ever-charitable, warm-hearted Goldsmith himself who remains to sweeten the memory. Captain Jackson is a delightful character *seen through Lamb's eyes*, but it is Lamb, not the captain, whose experience we share the more deeply.

" Ma Parker," however, is indubitably a story, for the author, in creating her, lost the sense of her own personality. In one of her letters she discusses this very question of losing oneself to find oneself in the creation of another being. " When I write about ducks I swear that I am a white duck with a round eye, floating on a pond fringed with yellow-blobs and taking an occasional dart at the other duck with the round eye, which floats upside down beneath me." This is what the essayist never does. It does not follow, of course, that the essayist may not also be story-writer. By the early death of Katherine Mansfield it may be that we have missed a fine essayist ; here were all the necessary qualities, except peace of mind ; she always had to school herself into " that inner calm necessary to writing " before she could begin. That calm must be an acquired, if not a temperamental possession of the essayist.

The essay may treat of any subject or of none. (Have

not Fielding and Mr. Belloc both written with great conviction upon " Nothing " ?)   But the perfect essay, such a one as " Old China," or " First Acquaintance with Poets," does not leave the reader without having given him at least a glimpse of the wide lands of thought and the dim-discovered spires of imagination. Thus far the essayist and the poet go side by side. But, to reverse Keats's famous axiom of poetry, the essay *should* surprise by singularity rather than by a fine excess ; it need not, as Keats thought poetry should, " strike the reader as a wording of his own highest thoughts," rather should it delight him as the altogether unpredictable thoughts of another. This quality of unexpectedness is, of course, most characteristic of the satirists and nonsense-writers, who are able, like the comic actor, in the twinkling of an eye to appear upon the stage in some unimagined attitude. Lamb's " Roast Pig " is a famous example of this engaging originality, but his other essays abound in surprises. Perhaps one of the most memorable is his story of the traveller who boasted of having sailed through the legs of the Colossus of Rhodes, and, upon being informed that the statue was destroyed long since, bethought himself that now, of course, he remembered having noticed that " one of the legs *was* a little mutilated."

No reader could possibly anticipate either this story or Father Ronald Knox's solemn " discovery " that *In Memoriam* was really written by Queen Victoria in memory of Lord Melbourne ; and who but the late G. K. Chesterton would have thought of reflecting sadly that lying in bed could never be perfect happiness until some one gave him a pencil long enough to write upon the ceiling ?

The essay does not always march breast forward, but often employs a kind of crab-wise walk, as Hazlitt complained that Coleridge was apt to do when lost in the mazes of an argument, to the great disconcerting of his fellow-traveller. Hazlitt himself, one of our best and most

(4,316)

engaging essayists, often seems to ramble, regardless of the relation between his starting-point and his destination, but where he leads the reader is content to follow, for if ever a writer "lived in gusto, be it fair or fine," it is Hazlitt. With the work of Lamb and Hazlitt the personal essay reached a pinnacle that no modern writer aspires to pass. Of Lamb himself it seems that nothing remains to be written. He is the prince of essayists, and is so by virtue of his power to draw his own portrait from many different angles. There is no figure in literature so familiar and so dear to us as "Elia," who, while capable of heavenly flights of imagination, as in "The Child Angel," and of the delicious nonsense of "Roast Pig" and "All Fools' Day," is ever sane with the sanity of true genius.

Yet, as a modern critic has pointed out, "Elia" is not, perhaps, so truly "the real Lamb" as we have always allowed him to be, but a Lamb heightened, Lamb intensified for the sake of effect. If he were living in the present day he would be considered a *poseur*. There is no doubt that the genius of the present age, if it has one, lies in our power to express the subtleties of life and character in a way the writers of the last century, even at their most intimate, never imagined. It may be there is another pinnacle ahead of us, a master of the intimate essay as far removed from Lamb as Lamb is from Bacon.

We cannot tell. Meanwhile, we rejoice in Elia.

R. V.

A HUNDRED ENGLISH ESSAYS

OF TRUTH

FRANCIS BACON

" WHAT is truth ? " said jesting Pilate, and would not stay
for an answer. Certainly there be that delight in giddi-
ness, and count it a bondage to fix a belief—affecting free-
will in thinking, as well as in acting—and, though the
sects of philosophers of that kind be gone, yet there remain
certain discoursing wits which are of the same veins,
though there be not so much blood in them as was in those
of the ancients. But it is not only the difficulty and labour
which men take in finding out of truth ; nor again, that,
when it is found, it imposeth upon men's thoughts, that
doth bring lies in favour ; but a natural, though corrupt
love of the lie itself. One of the later schools of the
Grecians examineth the matter, and is at a stand to think
what should be in it, that men should love lies, where
neither they make for pleasure, as with poets, nor for
advantage, as with the merchant, but for the lie's sake.
But I cannot tell ; this same truth is a naked and open
daylight, that doth not show the masques, and mummeries, and triumphs of the world, half so stately and
daintily as candlelights. Truth may perhaps come to the
price of a pearl, that showeth best by day ; but it will not
rise to the price of a diamond or carbuncle, that showeth
best in varied lights. A mixture of a lie doth ever add
pleasure. Doth any man doubt, that if there were taken
out of men's minds vain opinions, flattering hopes, false
valuations, imaginations as one would, and the like, but

3

it would leave the minds of a number of men poor
shrunken things, full of melancholy and indisposition, and
unpleasing to themselves ?   One of the fathers, in great
severity, called poesy " vinum dæmonum," because it
filleth the imagination, and yet is but with the shadow of
a lie. But it is not the lie that passeth through the mind,
but the lie that sinketh in and settleth in it that doth the
hurt, such as we spake of before. But howsoever these
things are thus in men's depraved judgments and affections,
yet truth, which only doth judge itself, teacheth that the
inquiry of truth, which is the love-making, or wooing of
it—the knowledge of truth, which is the presence of it—
and the belief of truth, which is the enjoying of it—is the
sovereign good of human nature. The first creature of
God, in the works of the days, was the light of the sense,
the last was the light of reason, and his Sabbath work, ever
since, is the illumination of his spirit. First he breathed
light upon the face of the matter, or chaos, then he
breathed light into the face of man ; and still he breatheth
and inspireth light into the face of his chosen. The poet,
that beautified the sect, that was otherwise inferior to the
rest, saith yet excellently well, " It is a pleasure to stand
upon the shore, and to see ships tost upon the sea ;
a pleasure to stand in the window of a castle, and to see a
battle, and the adventures thereof below ; but no pleasure
is comparable to the standing upon the vantage ground of
truth (a hill not to be commanded, and where the air is
always clear and serene), and to see the errors, and wanderings, and mists, and tempests, in the vale below ; " so
always that this prospect be with pity, and not with swelling or pride. Certainly it is heaven upon earth to have a
man's mind move in charity, rest in providence, and turn
upon the poles of truth.

  To pass from theological and philosophical truth to the
truth of civil business, it will be acknowledged, even by
those that practise it not, that clear and round dealing is the

honour of man's nature, and that mixture of falsehood is like alloy in coin of gold and silver, which may make the metal work the better, but it embaseth it ; for these winding and crooked courses are the goings of the serpent, which goeth basely upon the belly, and not upon the feet. There is no vice that doth so cover a man with shame as to be found false and perfidious ; and therefore Montaigne saith prettily, when he inquired the reason why the word of the lie should be such a disgrace, and such an odious charge, " If it be well weighed, to say that a man lieth, is as much as to say that he is brave towards God, and a coward towards man ; for a lie faces God, and shrinks from man." Surely the wickedness of falsehood and breach of faith cannot possibly be so highly expressed as in that it shall be the last peal to call the judgments of God upon the generations of men : it being foretold, that when " Christ cometh," he shall not " find faith upon earth."

Essays. 1597.

OF MASQUES AND TRIUMPHS

FRANCIS BACON

THESE things are but toys to come amongst such serious observations ; but yet, since princes will have such things, it is better they should be graced with elegancy than daubed with cost. Dancing to song is a thing of great state and pleasure. I understand it that the song be in quire, placed aloft, and accompanied with some broken music, and the ditty fitted to the device. Acting in song, especially in dialogues, hath an extreme good grace—I say acting, not dancing (for that is a mean and vulgar thing) ; and the voices of the dialogue would be strong and manly (a bass and a tenor, no treble), and the ditty high and tragical, not nice or dainty. Several quires placed one over against another, and taking the voice by catches, anthem-wise, give great pleasure. Turning dances into figure is a childish curiosity ; and generally let it be noted, that those things which I here set down are such as do naturally take the sense, and not respect petty wonderments. It is true, the alterations of scenes, so it be quietly and without noise, are things of great beauty and pleasure ; for they feed and relieve the eye before it be full of the same object. Let the scenes abound with light, especially coloured and varied, and let the masquers, or any other that are to come down from the scene, have some motions upon the scene itself before their coming down ; for it draws the eye strangely and makes it with great pleasure to desire to see that it cannot perfectly discern. Let the songs be loud and cheerful, and not chirpings or pulings ; let the music likewise be sharp and loud, and well placed. The colours that show best by candlelight are white, carnation, and a kind of sea-water green ; and ouches,[1] or spangs, as they are of no great cost, so they are of most glory. As for rich embroidery, it is lost and not discerned. Let the suits of the masquers be graceful, and such as become the person when the vizards are off, not after examples of known attires, Turks, soldiers, mariners, and the like. Let anti-masques not be long ; they have been commonly of fools, satyrs, baboons, wild men, antics, beasts, sprites, witches, Æthiopes, pigmies, turquets, nymphs, rustics, Cupids, statues moving, and the like. As for angels, it is not comical enough to put them in anti-masques ; and anything that is hideous, as devils, giants, is, on the other side, as unfit ; but chiefly, let the music of them be recreative, and with some strange changes. Some sweet odours suddenly coming forth, without any drops falling, are, in such a company, as there is steam and heat, things of great pleasure and refreshment. Double masques, one of men, another of ladies, addeth state and variety ; but all is nothing except the room be kept clear and neat.

For justs, and tourneys, and barriers, the glories of them are chiefly in the chariots, wherein the challengers make their entry, especially if they be drawn with strange beasts, as lions, bears, camels, and the like ; or, in the devices of their entrance, or in bravery of their liveries, or in the goodly furniture of their horses and armour. But enough of these toys.

Essays. 1597.

[1] Jewelled clasps or buckles.

OF GARDENS

Francis Bacon

GOD ALMIGHTY first planted a garden, and, indeed, it is the purest of human pleasures ; it is the greatest refreshment to the spirits of man, without which buildings and palaces are but gross handyworks : and a man shall ever see, that when ages grow to civility and elegancy, men come to build stately, sooner than to garden finely ; as if gardening were the greater perfection. I do hold it, in the royal ordering of gardens, there ought to be gardens for all the months in the year, in which, severally, things of beauty may be then in season. For December and January, and the latter part of November, you must take such things as are green all winter ; holly, ivy, bays, juniper, cypress-trees, yew, pines, fir-trees, rosemary, lavender ; periwinkle, the white, the purple, and the blue ; germander, flag, orange-trees, lemon-trees, and myrtles, if they be stoved ; and sweet marjoram, warm set. There followeth, for the latter part of January and February, the mezereon-tree, which then blossoms ; crocus vernus, both the yellow and the grey ; primroses, anemones, the early tulip, hyacinthus orientalis, chamaïris, fritellaria. For March, there come violets, especially the single blue, which are the earliest ; the early daffodil, the daisy, the almond-tree in blossom, the peach-tree in blossom, the cornelian-tree in blossom, sweetbriar. In April, follow the double white violet, the wallflower, the stock-gilliflower, the cowslip, flower-de-luces, and lilies of all natures ; rosemary-flowers, the tulip, the double peony, the pale daffodil, the French honeysuckle, the cherry-tree in blossom, the damascene and plum-trees in blossom, the white thorn in leaf, the lilac-tree. In May and June come pinks of all sorts, especially the blush pink ; roses of all kinds, except the musk, which comes later ; honeysuckles, strawberries, bugloss, columbine, the French marigold, flos Africanus, cherry-tree in fruit, ribes, figs in fruit, rasps, vine flowers, lavender in flowers, the sweet satyrian, with the white flower ; herba muscaria, lilium convallium, and apple-tree in blossom. In July come gilliflowers of all varieties, musk roses, the lime-tree in blossom, early pears, and plums in fruit, gennitings, quodlins. In August come plums of all sorts in fruit, pears, apricocks, barberries, filberds, musk melons, monks-hoods, of all colours. In September come grapes, apples, poppies of all colours, peaches, melocotones, nectarines, cornelians, wardens, quinces. In October and the beginning of November come services, medlars, bullaces, roses cut or removed to come late, hollyoaks, and suchlike. These particulars are for the climate of London ; but my meaning is perceived, that you may have *ver perpetuum*, as the place affords.

And because the breath of flowers is far sweeter in the air (where it comes and goes, like the warbling of music) than in the hand, therefore nothing is more fit for that delight, than to know what be the flowers and plants that do best perfume the air. Roses, damask and red, are fast flowers of their smells ; so that you may walk by a whole row of them, and find nothing of their sweetness, yea, though it be in a morning's dew. Bays, likewise, yield no smell as they grow, rosemary little, nor sweet marjoram ; that which, above all others, yields the sweetest smell in the air is the violet ; especially the white double violet, which comes twice a-year—about the middle of April, and about Bartholomew-tide. Next to that is the musk rose ; then the strawberry leaves dying,

with a most excellent cordial smell ; then the flower of the
vines—it is a little dust like the dust of a bent, which
grows upon the cluster in the first coming forth—then
sweetbriar, then wallflowers, which are very delightful
to be set under a parlour or lower chamber window ;
then pinks and gilliflowers, especially the matted pink
and clove gilliflowers ; then the flowers of the lime-tree ;
then the honeysuckles, so they be somewhat afar off.   Of
bean-flowers I speak not, because they are field flowers ;
but those which perfume the air most delightfully, not
passed by as the rest, but being trodden upon and crushed,
are three, that is, burnet, wild thyme, and water-mints ;
therefore, you are to set whole alleys of them, to have the
pleasure when you walk or tread.

For gardens (speaking of those which are, indeed,
prince-like, as we have done of buildings), the contents
ought not well to be under thirty acres of ground, and to
be divided into three parts : a green in the entrance, a
heath or desert in the going forth, and the main garden
in the midst, besides alleys on both sides ; and I like well
that four acres of ground be assigned to the green, six to
the heath, four and four to either side, and twelve to the
main garden.   The green hath two pleasures : the one,
because nothing is more pleasant to the eye than green
grass kept finely shorn ; the other, because it will give you
a fair alley in the midst, by which you may go in front
upon a stately hedge, which is to enclose the garden :
but because the alley will be long, and, in great heat of the
year, or day, you ought not to buy the shade in the garden
by going in the sun through the green, therefore you are,
of either side the green, to plant a covert alley, upon
carpenters' work, about twelve feet in height, by which
you may go in shade into the garden.   As for the making
of knots, or figures, with divers-coloured earths, that they
may lie under the windows of the house on that side on
which the garden stands, they be but toys ; you may see

as good sights many times in tarts. The garden is best to
be square, encompassed on all the four sides with a stately
arched hedge ; the arches to be upon pillars of carpenters'
work, of some ten feet high, and six feet broad, and the
spaces between of the same dimensions with the breadth of
the arch. Over the arches let there be an entire hedge of
some four feet high, framed also upon carpenters' work ;
and upon the upper hedge, over every arch, a little turret,
with a belly enough to receive a cage of birds : and over
every space between the arches some other little figure,
with broad plates of round coloured glass gilt, for the sun
to play upon : but this hedge I intend to be raised upon a
bank, not steep, but gently slope, of some six feet, set all
with flowers. Also, I understand that this square of the
garden should not be the whole breadth of the ground,
but to leave on either side ground enough for diversity
of side alleys, unto which the two covert alleys of the green
may deliver you ; but there must be no alleys with hedges
at either end of this great enclosure—not at the hither
end, for letting your prospect upon this fair hedge from
the green—nor at the farther end, for letting your prospect
from the hedge through the arches upon the heath.

For the ordering of the ground within the great hedge,
I leave it to variety of device, advising, nevertheless, that
whatsoever form you cast it into first, it be not too busy,
or full of work ; wherein I, for my part, do not like
images cut out in juniper or other garden stuff—they be
for children. Little low hedges, round like welts, with
some pretty pyramids, I like well ; and in some places
fair columns, upon frames of carpenters' work. I would
also have the alleys spacious and fair. You may have
closer alleys upon the side grounds, but none in the main
garden. I wish, also, in the very middle, a fair mount,
with three ascents and alleys, enough for four to walk
abreast, which I would have to be perfect circles, without
any bulwarks or embossments ; and the whole mount to

be thirty feet high, and some fine banqueting-house, with some chimneys neatly cast, and without too much glass.

For fountains they are a great beauty and refreshment; but pools mar all, and make the garden unwholesome, and full of flies and frogs. Fountains I intend to be of two natures, the one that sprinkleth or spouteth water ; the other a fair receipt of water, of some thirty or forty feet square, but without any fish, or slime, or mud. For the first, the ornaments of images, gilt, or of marble, which are in use, do well ; but the main matter is so to convey the water as it never stay, either in the bowls or in the cistern—that the water be never by rest discoloured, green or red, or the like, or gather any mossiness or putre-faction ; besides that, it is to be cleansed every day by the hand—also some steps up to it, and some fine pavement about it do well. As for the other kind of fountain, which we may call a bathing pool, it may admit much curiosity and beauty, wherewith we will not trouble ourselves : as, that the bottom be finely paved, and with images ; the sides likewise ; and withal embellished with coloured glass, and such things of lustre, encompassed also with fine rails of low statuas ; but the main point is the same which we mentioned in the former kind of fountain, which is, that the water be in perpetual motion, fed by a water higher than the pool, and delivered into it by fair spouts, and then discharged away under ground, by some equality of bores, that it stay little ; and for fine devices of arching water without spilling, and making it rise in several forms (of feathers, drinking glasses, canopies, and the like), they be pretty things to look on, but nothing to health and sweetness.

For the heath, which was the third part of our plot, I wished it to be framed as much as may be to a natural wildness. Trees I would have none in it, but some thickets made only of sweetbriar and honeysuckle, and some wild vines amongst, and the ground set with violets, strawberries, and primroses ; for these are sweet, and prosper in the shade, and these are to be in the heath here and there, not in any order. I like also little heaps, in the nature of mole-hills (such as are in wild heaths), to be set, some with wild thyme, some with pinks, some with germander, that gives a good flower to the eye ; some with periwinkle, some with violets, some with strawberries, some with cowslips, some with daisies, some with red roses, some with lilium convallium, some with sweet-williams red, some with bear's-foot, and the like low flowers, being withal sweet and sightly—part of which heaps to be with standards of little bushes pricked upon their top, and part without—the standards to be roses, juniper, holly, berberries (but here and there, because of the smell of their blossom), red currants, gooseberries, rosemary, bays, sweetbriar, and suchlike, but these standards to be kept with cutting, that they grow not out of course.

For the side grounds, you are to fill them with variety of alleys, private to give a full shade ; some of them wheresoever the sun be. You are to frame some of them likewise for shelter, that, when the wind blows sharp, you may walk as in a gallery ; and those alleys must be likewise hedged at both ends, to keep out the wind, and these closer alleys must be ever finely gravelled, and no grass, because of going wet. In many of these alleys, likewise, you are to set fruit-trees of all sorts, as well upon the walls as in ranges ; and this should be generally observed, that the borders wherein you plant your fruit-trees be fair, and large, and low, and not steep, and set with fine flowers, but thin and sparingly, lest they deceive the trees. At the end of both the side grounds I would have a mount of some pretty height, leaving the wall of the enclosure breast-high, to look abroad into the fields.

For the main garden, I do not deny but there should be some fair alleys ranged on both sides, with fruit-trees, and some pretty tufts of fruit-trees and arbours with seats, set in some decent order ; but these to be by no means set too thick, but to leave the main garden so as it be not close, but the air open and free. For as for shade, I would have you rest upon the alleys of the side grounds, there to walk, if you be disposed, in the heat of the year or day ; but to make account, that the main garden is for the more temperate parts of the year, and, in the heat of summer, for the morning and the evening, or overcast days.

For aviaries, I like them not, except they be of that largeness as they may be turfed, and have living plants and bushes set in them, that the birds may have more scope and natural nestling, and that no foulness appear on the floor of the aviary. So I have made a platform of a princely garden, partly by precept, partly by drawing—not a model, but some general lines of it—and in this I have spared for no cost ; but it is nothing for great princes, that, for the most part, taking advice with workmen, with no less cost, set their things together, and sometimes add statues and such things, for state and magnificence, but nothing to the true pleasure of a garden.

Essays. 1597.

OF ADVERSITY

Francis Bacon

It was a high speech of Seneca (after the manner of the Stoics), that the " good things which belong to prosperity are to be wished, but the good things that belong to adversity are to be admired "—" Bona rerum secundarum optabilia, adversarum mirabilia." Certainly, if miracles be the command over nature, they appear most in adversity. It is yet a higher speech of his than the other (much too high for a heathen), " It is true greatness to have in one the frailty of a man, and the security of a God "— " Vere magnum habere fragilitatem hominis, securitatem Dei." This would have done better in poesy, where transcendencies are more allowed ; and the poets, indeed, have been busy with it—for it is in effect the thing which is figured in that strange fiction of the ancient poets, which seemeth not to be without mystery ; nay, and to have some approach to the state of a Christian, " that Hercules, when he went to unbind Prometheus (by whom human nature is represented), sailed the length of the great ocean in an earthen pot or pitcher," lively describing Christian resolution, that saileth in the frail bark of the flesh through the waves of the world. But to speak in a mean, the virtue of prosperity is temperance, the virtue of adversity is fortitude, which in morals is the more heroical virtue. Prosperity is the blessing of the Old Testament, adversity is the blessing of the New, which carrieth the greater benediction, and the clearer revelation of God's favour. Yet even in the Old Testament, if you listen to David's harp, you shall hear as many hearse-like airs as carols ; and the pencil of the Holy Ghost hath laboured more in describing the afflictions of Job than the felicities of Solomon. Prosperity is not without many fears and distastes ; and adversity is not without comforts and hopes. We see in needleworks and embroideries, it is more pleasing to have a lively work upon a sad and solemn ground, than to have a dark and melancholy work upon a lightsome ground : judge, therefore, of the pleasure of the heart by the pleasure of the eye. Certainly virtue is like precious odours, most fragrant where they are incensed, or crushed ; for prosperity doth best discover vice, but adversity doth best discover virtue.

Essays. 1597.

HOW A GALLANT SHOULD BEHAVE IN PAUL'S WALK

Thomas Dekker

THAT true humorous gallant that desires to pour himself
into all fashions (if his ambition be such to excel even
compliment itself) must as well practise to diminish his
walks, as to be various in his sallets, curious in his tobacco,
or ingenious in the trussing up of a new Scotch-hose. All
which virtues are excellent and able to maintain him,
especially if the old worm-eaten farmer (his father) be
dead, and left him five hundred a year, only to keep an
Irish hobby, an Irish horse-boy, and himself (like a gentleman). He therefore that would strive to fashion his legs
to his silk stockings, and his proud gait to his broad garters,
let him whiff down these observations ; for, if he once get
to walk by the book (and I see no reason but he may, as
well as fight by the book) Paul's may be proud of him,
Will Clarke shall ring forth encomiums in his honour,
John in Paul's Churchyard shall fit his head for an excellent block, whilst all the Inns of Court rejoice to behold
his most handsome calf.

Your Mediterranean Aisle, is then the only gallery,
wherein the pictures of all your true fashionate and com-
plemental gulls are, and ought to be hung up : into that
gallery carry your neat body, but take heed you pick out
such an hour, when the main Shoal of Islanders are swimming up and down. And first observe your doors of
entrance, and your exit, not much unlike the players at

the theatres, keeping your decorums, even in phantasti-
cality. As for example : if you prove to be a Northern
gentleman, I would wish you to pass through the north
door, more often (especially) than any of the other ; and
so, according to your countries, take note of your entrances.

Now for your venturing into the Walk, be circumspect
and wary what pillar you come in at, and take heed in any
case (as you love the reputation of your honour) that you
avoid the Serving-man's log, and approach not within
five fathom of that pillar ; but bend your course directly
in the middle line, that the whole body of the church
may appear to be yours ; where, in view of all, you may
publish your suit in what manner you affect most, either
with the slide of your cloak from the one shoulder, and
then you must (as 'twere in anger) suddenly snatch at the
middle of the inside (if it be taffeta at the least) and so by
that means your costly lining is betrayed, or else by the
pretty advantage of compliment. But one note by the way
do I especially woo you to, the neglect of which makes
many of our gallants cheap and ordinary, that by no means
you be seen above four turns ; but in the fifth make yourself away, either in some of the sempsters' shops, the new
tobacco-office, or amongst the booksellers, where, if you
cannot read, exercise your smoke, and inquire who has writ
against this divine weed, etc. For this withdrawing yourself a little will much benefit your suit, which else, by
too long walking, would be stale to the whole spectators ;
but howsoever if Paul's Jacks be once up with their
elbows, and quarrelling to strike eleven, as soon as ever
the clock has parted them, and ended the fray with his
hammer, let not the Duke's gallery contain you any
longer, but pass away apace in open view. In which
departure, if by chance you either encounter, or aloof off
throw your inquisitive eye upon any knight or squire,
being your familiar, salute him not by his name of Sir
such a one, or so, but call him *Ned*, or *Jack*, etc. This will

set off your estimation with great men ; and if (though there be a dozen companies between you, 'tis the better) he call aloud to you (for that's most genteel), to know where he shall find you at two o'clock, tell him at such an ordinary, or such, and be sure to name those that are dearest ; and whither none but your gallants resort. After dinner you may appear again, having translated yourself out of your English cloth cloak into a light turkey-grogram (if you have that happiness of shifting), and then be seen (for a turn or two) to correct your teeth with some quill or silver instrument, and to cleanse your gums with a wrought handkerchief : it skills not whether you dined or no (that's best known to your stomach) or in what place you dined, though it were with cheese (of your own mother's making), in your chamber or study.

Now if you chance to be a gallant not much crossed among citizens, that is a gallant in the mercers' books, exalted for satins and velvets, if you be not so much blessed to be crossed (as I hold it the greatest blessing in the world, to be great in no man's books) your Paul's Walk is your only refuge : the Duke's Tomb is a sanctuary, and will keep you alive from worms and land-rats, that long to be feeding on your carcass : there you may spend your legs in winter a whole afternoon : converse, plot, laugh, and talk anything, jest at your creditor, even to his face, and in the evening, even by lamplight, steal out, and so cozen a whole covey of abominable catch-polls. Never he seen to mount the steps into the choir, but upon a high festival day, to prefer the fashion of your doublet, and especially if the singing-boys seem to take note of you : for they are able to buzz your praises above their Anthems, if their voices have not lost their maidenheads : but be sure your silver spurs dog your heels, and then the boys will swarm about you like so many white butterflies, when you in the open choir shall draw forth a perfumed em-broidered purse (the glorious sight of which will entice

many countrymen from their devotion to wondering)
and cast silver into the boys' hands, that it may be heard
above the first lesson, although it be read in a voice as big
as one of the great organs.

This noble and notable act being performed, you are to
vanish presently out of the choir, and to appear again in
the Walk : but in any wise be not observed to tread there
long alone : for fear you be suspected to be a gallant
cashiered from the society of captains and fighters.

Suck this humour up especially. Put off to none, unless
his hatband be of a newer fashion than yours, and three
degrees quainter : but for him that wears a trebled cipers
about his hat (though he were an Alderman's son), never
move to him : for he's suspected to be worse than a gull,
and not worth the putting off to, that cannot observe the
time of his hatband, nor know what fashioned block is
most kin to his head : for, in my opinion, the brain that
cannot choose his felt well (being the head ornament) must
needs pour folly into all the rest of the members, and be
an absolute confirmed fool in *Summâ Totali*.

All the diseased horses in a tedious siege cannot show so
many fashions, as are to be seen for nothing, every day,
in Duke Humphrey's Walk. If therefore you determine
to enter into a new suit, warn your tailor to attend you
in Paul's, who, with his hat in his hand, shall like a spy
discover the stuff, colour, and fashion of any doublet, or
hose that dare be seen there, and stepping behind a pillar
to fill his table-books with those notes, will presently send
you into the world an accomplished man : by which
means you shall wear your clothes in print with the first
edition. But if fortune favour you so much as to make you
no more than a mere country gentleman, or but some
three degrees removed from him (for which I should be
very sorry, because your London experience will cost
you dear before you shall have the wit to know what you
are) then take this lesson along with you : the first time

that you venture into Paul's, pass through the body of the
church like a porter, yet presume not to fetch so much as
one whole turn in the middle aisle, no, nor to cast an eye
to *Si quis* door (pasted and plastered up with Serving-
men's supplications) before you have paid tribute to the
top of Paul's steeple with a single penny : and when you
are mounted there, take heed how you look down into
the yard ; for the rails are as rotten as your great-grand-
father ; and thereupon it will not be amiss if you inquire
how Kit Woodroffe durst vault over, and what reason he
had for it, to put his neck in hazard of reparations. From
hence you may descend, to talk about the horse that went
up, and strive, if you can, to know his keeper : take the
day of the month, and the number of the steps, and suffer
yourself to believe verily that it was not a horse, but something else in the likeness of one : which wonders you may
publish, when you return into the country, to the great
amazement of all farmers' daughters, that will almost
swound at the report, and never recover till their banns
be asked twice in the church.

But I have not left you yet. Before you come down
again, I would desire you to draw your knife, and grave
your name (or, for want of a name, the mark which you
clap on your sheep) in great characters upon the leads,
by a number of your brethren (both citizens and country
gentlemen), and so you shall be sure to have your name
lie in a coffin of lead, when yourself shall be wrapped in
a winding-sheet : and indeed the top of Paul's contains
more names than Stowe's Chronicle. These lofty tricks
being played, and you (thanks to your feet) being safely
arrived at the stair's foot again, your next worthy work is,
to repair to my lord Chancellor's Tomb (and, if you can
but reasonably spell) bestow some time upon the reading
of Sir Philip Sidney's brief Epitaph; in the compass of an
hour you may make shift to stumble it out. The great dial
is your last monument : there bestow some half of the

threescore minutes, to observe the sauciness of the Jacks that are above the man in the moon there; the strangeness of the motion will quit your labour. Besides, you may here have fit occasion to discover your watch, by taking it forth, and setting the wheels to the time of Paul's, which, I assure you, goes truer by five notes than St. Sepulchre's Chimes. The benefit that will arise from hence is this, that you publish your charge in maintaining a gilded clock; and withal the world shall know that you are a time-pleaser. By this I imagine you have walked your bellyful, and thereupon being weary, or (which rather I believe) being most gentlemanlike hungry, it is fit that I brought you into the Duke; so (because he follows the fashion of great men, in keeping no house, and that therefore you must go seek your dinner) suffer me to take you by the hand, and lead you into an ordinary.

Gul's Horn-Book. 1608.

A GOOD WIFE

Sir Thomas Overbury

A GOOD WIFE is a man's best movable, a scion incorporate with the stock, bringing sweet fruit ; one that to her husband is more than a friend, less than a trouble : an equal with him in the yoke. Calamities and troubles she shares alike ; nothing pleaseth her that doth not him. She is relative in all, and he without her, but half himself. She is his absent hands, eyes, ears, and mouth : his present and absent all. She frames her nature unto his howsoever : the hyacinth follows not the sun more willingly. Stubbornness and obstinacy are herbs that grow not in her garden. She leaves tattling to the gossips of the town, and is more seen than heard. Her household is her charge ; her care to that makes her seldom non-resident. Her pride is but to be cleanly, and her thrift not to be prodigal. By her discretion she hath children, not wantons ; a husband without her is a misery in man's apparel ; none but she hath an aged husband, to whom she is both a staff and a chair. To conclude, she is both wise and religious, which makes her all this.

Characters. 1614.

A FAIR AND HAPPY MILKMAID

Sir Thomas Overbury

A FAIR AND HAPPY MILKMAID is a country wench that is so
far from making herself beautiful by art, that one look of
hers is able to put all face-physic out of countenance. She
knows a fair look is but a dumb orator to commend virtue,
therefore minds it not. All her excellences stand in her so
silently, as if they had stolen upon her without her knowledge. The lining of her apparel (which is herself) is far
better than outsides of tissew ; for though she be not
arrayed in the spoil of the silkworm, she is decked in
innocency, a far better wearing. She doth not, with
lying long a-bed, spoil both her complexion and conditions ; Nature hath taught her too immoderate sleep
is rust to the soul ; she rises therefore with chaunticleare,
her dame's cock, and at night makes the lamb her curfew.
In milking a cow, and straining the teats through her
fingers, it seems that so sweet a milk-press makes the milk
the whiter or sweeter ; for never came almond glove, or
aromatic ointment on her palm to taint it. The golden
ears of corn fall and kiss her feet when she reaps them, as if
they wished to be bound and led prisoners by the same
hand that felled them. Her breath is her own, which
scents all the year long of June, like a new-made haycock.
She makes her hand hard with labour, and her heart soft
with pity : and when winter evenings fall early (sitting at
her merry wheel) she sings a defiance to the merry wheel
of fortune. She doth all things with so sweet a grace, it
seems ignorance will not suffer her to do ill, being her

mind is to do well. She bestows her year's wages at next
fair ; and in choosing her garments, counts no bravery
i' th' world like decency.   The garden and beehive are all
her physic and chirurgery ; and she lives the longer for't.
She dares go alone and unfold sheep i' th' night, and fears
no manner of ill, because she means none : yet to say
truth, she is never alone, for she is still accompanied with
old songs, honest thoughts, and prayers, but short ones ;
yet they have their efficacy, in that they are not palled with
ensuing idle cogitations.   Lastly, her dreams are so chaste
that she dare tell them ; only a Friday's dream is all her
superstition : that she conceals for fear of anger.   Thus
lives she, and all her care is she may die in the spring-time
to have store of flowers stuck upon her winding-sheet.

Characters. 1614.

ON MELANCHOLY CAUSED BY POVERTY

Robert Burton

[EDITOR'S NOTE.—It was not without misgiving that the editor decided to include as " essays " (which they certainly are) these two chapters from Burton's famous book, abridged and modernized to meet the requirements of such a collection as this.

Lovers of Burton, who may very properly feel that *The Anatomy of Melancholy* is a carefully constructed treatise which it is sacrilege thus to dismember, are asked to suspend judgment until they have read the Introduction.]

POVERTY and want are so violent oppugners, so unwelcome guests, so much abhorred of all men, that I may not omit to speak of them apart. Poverty, although (if considered aright, to a wise, understanding, truly regenerate, and contented man) it be Donum Dei, a blessed estate, the way to Heaven, as Chrysostom calls it, God's gift, the mother of modesty, and much to be preferred before riches (as shall be showed in his place) yet, as it is esteemed in the world's censure, it is a most odious calling, vile and base, a severe torture, a most intolerable burden. We shun it all, we abhor the name of it, as being the fountain of all other miseries, cares, woes, labours, and grievances whatsoever. To avoid which, we will take any pains, we will leave no haven, no coast, no creek of the world unsearched, though it be to the hazard of our lives ; we will dive to the bottom of the sea, to the bowels of the earth, five, six, seven, eight, nine hundred fathom deep, through all five Zones, and both extremes of heat and cold : we will turn parasites and slaves, prostitute ourselves, swear and lie, damn our bodies and souls, forsake God, abjure Religion, steal, rob, murder, rather than endure this unsufferable yoke of Poverty, which doth so tyrannize, crucify, and generally depress us.

For look into the world, and you shall see men most part esteemed according to their means, and happy as they are rich. In the vulgar opinion, if a man be wealthy, no matter how he gets it, of what parentage, how qualified, how virtuously endowed, or villainously inclined ; let him be a bawd, a gripe, an usurer, a villain, a Pagan, a Barbarian, a wretch, Lucian's Tyrant, on whom you may look with less security than on the Sun ; so that he be rich (and liberal withal) he shall be honoured, admired, adored, reverenced, and highly magnified. He shall be accounted a gracious Lord, a Mæcenas, a benefactor, a wise, discreet, a proper, a valiant, a fortunate man, of a generous spirit, a hopeful, a good man, a virtuous honest man. All honour, offices, applause, grand titles, and turgent epithets, are put upon him ; all men's eyes are upon him, God bless his good Worship ! his Honour ! every man speaks well of him, every man presents him, seeks and sues to him for his love, favour and protection, to serve him, belong unto him ; every man riseth to him, as to Themistocles in the Olympicks ; if he speak, as of Herod, vox Dei, non hominis ! [it is] the voice of God, not of man ! All the graces, Veneres, pleasures, elegances attend him, golden Fortune accompanies and lodgeth with him. He may sail as he will himself, and temper his estate at his pleasure ; jovial days, splendour and magnificence, sweet musick, dainty fare, the good things and fat of the land, fine clothes, rich attires, soft beds, down pillows, are at his command ; all the world labours for him ; thousands of artificers are his slaves, to drudge for him, run, ride, and post for him : Divines, Lawyers, Physicians, Philosophers, Scholars, are his, wholly devote to his service. Every man seeks his acquaintance, his kindred, to match with him ;

though he be an auf, a ninny, a monster, a goosecap, he is an excellent match for my son, my daughter, my niece, etc. Let him go whither he will, trumpets sound, bells ring, etc., all happiness attends him, every man is willing to entertain him, he sups in Apollo wheresoever he comes ; what preparation is made for his entertainment, fish and fowl, spices and perfumes, all that sea and land affords ! What cookery, masking, mirth, to exhilarate his person ! What dish will your good Worship eat of ?

> Sweet apples, and whate'er thy fields afford,
> Before thy Gods be served, let serve thy Lord.

What sport will your Honour have ? hawking, hunting, fishing, fowling, bulls, bears, cards, dice, cocks, players, tumblers, fiddlers, jesters, etc., they are at your good Worship's command. Fair houses, gardens, orchards, terraces, galleries, cabinets, pleasant walks, delightsome places, they are at hand ; wine, wenches, etc., a Turkey Paradise, an Heaven upon earth. Though he be a silly soft fellow, and scarce have common sense, yet if he be born to fortunes (as I have said), he must have honour and office in his course : none so worthy as himself : he shall have it. Get money enough, and command Kingdoms, Provinces, Armies, hearts, hands, and affections ; thou shalt have Popes, Patriarchs, to be thy Chaplains and Parasites ; thou shalt have (Tamerlane-like) Kings to draw thy coach, Queens to be thy Laundresses, Emperors thy footstools, build more Towns and Cities than great Alexander, Babel Towers, Pyramids and Mausolean Tombs, etc., command Heaven and Earth, and tell the World it is thy vassal. We have no Aristocracies but in contemplation, all Oligarchies, wherein a few rich men domineer, do what they list, and are privileged by their greatness. They may freely trespass, and do as they please, no man dare accuse them, no not so much as mutter against them, there is no notice taken of it, they may securely do it, live after their own laws, and for their money get Pardons, Indulgences, redeem their souls from Purgatory and Hell itself. Let them be Epicures, or Atheists, Libertines, Machiavelians (as often they are), they may go to heaven through the eye of a needle, if they will themselves, they may be canonized for Saints, they shall be honourably interred in Mausolean Tombs, commended by Poets, registered in Histories, have Temples and Statues erected to their names. If he be bountiful in his life, and liberal at his death, he shall have one to swear, as he did by Claudius the Emperor in Tacitus, he saw his soul go to Heaven, and be miserably lamented at his funeral. These prerogatives do not usually belong to rich men, but to such as are most part seeming rich ; let him have but a good outside, he carries it, and shall be adored for a God, as Cyrus was amongst the Persians, for his gay tires. Now most men are esteemed according to their clothes. In our gullish times, whom you peradventure in modesty would give place to, as being deceived by his habit, and presuming him some great Worshipful man, believe it, if you shall examine his estate, he will likely be proved a serving man of no great note, my Lady's Tailor, his Lordship's Barber, or some such gull, a Fastidious Brisk, [a] Sir Petronel Flash, a mere outside. Only this respect is given him, that, wheresoever he comes, he may call for what he will, and take place by reason of his outward habit.

But on the contrary, if he be poor, Prov. xv. 15, all his days are miserable, he is under hatches, dejected, rejected, and forsaken, poor in purse, poor in spirit ; money gives life and soul. Though he be honest, wise, learned, well deserving, noble by birth, and of excellent good parts : yet, in that he is poor, unlikely to rise, come to honour, office, or good means, he is contemned, neglected. If once poor, we are metamorphosed in an instant, base slaves, villains, and vile drudges ; for to be

poor is to be a knave, a fool, a wretch, a wicked, an
odious fellow, a common eyesore ; say poor and
say all : they are born to labour, to misery, to carry
burdens like juments with Ulysses' companions, and,
as Chremylus objected in Aristophanes [to] lick salt, to
empty jakes, fay channels, carry out dirt and dunghills,
sweep chimneys, rub horse-heels, etc. I say nothing of
Turks' Galley-slaves, which are bought and sold like
juments, or those African Negroes, or poor Indian drudges,
ugly to behold, and, though erst spruce, now rusty and
squalid, because poor. Others eat to live, but they live to
drudge, a servile generation, that dare refuse no task.

Sirrah, blow wind upon us while we wash ; and bid your
fellow get him up betimes in the morning ; be it fair or
foul, he shall run fifty miles a foot to-morrow, to carry me
a letter to my mistress ; Sosia shall tarry at home and grind
malt all day long ; Tristan [shall] thresh. Thus are they
commanded, being indeed some of them as so many footstools for rich men to tread on, blocks for them to get on
horseback. They are commonly such people, rude, silly,
superstitious, idiots, nasty, unclean, lousy, poor, dejected,
slavishly humble, base by nature, and no more esteemed
than dogs ; no learning, no knowledge, no civility, scarce
common sense, nought but barbarism amongst them ; like
rogues and vagabonds, they go bare-footed and bare-
legged, the soles of their feet being as hard as horse hoofs,
leading a laborious, miserable, wretched, unhappy life,
like beasts and juments, if not worse (for a Spaniard in
Yucatan sold three Indian boys for a cheese, and an hundred
Negro slaves for an horse) : their discourse is scurrility,
their *summum bonum* a pot of Ale. There is not any slavery
which these villains will not undergo ; like those people
that dwell in the Alps, chimney-sweepers, jakes-farmers,
dirt-daubers, vagrant rogues, they labour hard some, and
yet cannot get clothes to put on, or bread to eat. For what
can filthy poverty give else, but beggary, fulsome nastiness,

squalor, contempt, drudgery, labour, ugliness, hunger and
thirst, fleas and lice, rags for his raiment, and a stone for his
pillow ? He sits in a broken pitcher, or on a block, for a
chair ; he drinks water, and lives on wort leaves, pulse, like
a hog, or scraps like a dog, as we poor men live nowadays,
who will not take our life to be infelicity, misery, and
madness.

If they be of [a] little better condition than those base
villains, hunger-starved beggars, wandering rogues, those
ordinary slaves, and day-labouring drudges, yet they are
commonly so preyed upon by polling officers for breaking
laws, by their tyrannizing landlords, so flead and fleeced by
perpetual exactions, that, though they do drudge, fare hard,
and starve their Genius, they cannot live in some countries ;
but what they have is instantly taken from them ; the
very care they take to live, to be drudges, to maintain their
poor families, their trouble and anxiety, takes away their
sleep, it makes them weary of their lives : when they have
taken all pains, done their utmost and honest endeavours,
if they be cast behind by sickness, or overtaken with years,
no man pities them ; hard-hearted and merciless, un-
charitable as they are, they leave them so distressed, to beg,
steal, murmur, and rebel, or else starve. The feeling and
fear of this misery compelled those old Romans, whom
Menenius Agrippa pacified, to resist their governors : out-
laws, and rebels, in most places, to take up seditious arms ;
and in all ages hath caused uproars, murmurings, seditions,
rebellions, thefts, murders, mutinies, jars and contentions,
in every commonwealth : grudging, repining, complaining, discontent, in each private family, because they want
means to live according to their callings, bring up their
children ; it breaks their hearts they cannot do as they
would. No greater misery than for a Lord to have a
Knight's living, a Gentleman a Yeoman's, not to be able
to live as his birth and place requires ! Poverty and want
are generally corrosives to all kinds of men, especially to

such as have been in good and flourishing estate, are suddenly distressed, nobly born, liberally brought up, and by some disaster and casualty miserably dejected. For the rest, as they have base fortunes, so have they base minds correspondent, like beetles, as they were obscurely born and bred, so they delight and live in obscenity ; they are not so thoroughly touched with it. Yea, that which is no small cause of their torments, if once they come to be in distress, they are forsaken of their fellows, most part neglected, and left unto themselves by Scipio, Lælius, and Furius, his great and noble friends. All flee from him as from a rotten wall, now ready to fall on their heads.

> Whilst fortune favour'd, friends, you smiled on me,
> But when she fled, a friend I could not see.

Which is worse yet, if he be poor every man contemns him, insults over him, oppresseth him, scoffs at, aggravates his misery.

> When once the tottering house begins to shrink,
> Thither comes all the weight by an instinct.

Nay, they are odious to their own brethren and dearest friends. Which is most grievous, poverty makes men ridiculous, they must endure jests, taunts, flouts, blows, of their betters, and take all in good part to get a meal's meat. He must turn parasite, jester, fool, slave, villain, drudge, to get a poor living, apply himself to each man's humours, to win and please, etc., and be buffeted, when he hath all done, be reviled, baffled, insulted over, and may not so much as mutter against it. He must turn rogue and villain, for, as the saying is, poverty alone makes men thieves, rebels, murderers, traitors, assassinates, swear and forswear, bear false witness, lie, dissemble, anything, as I say, to advantage themselves, and to relieve their necessities ; when a man is driven to his shifts, what will he not do ? he will betray his father, Prince, and Country, turn Turk, forsake Religion, abjure God and all. Plato therefore calls poverty thievish, sacrilegious, filthy, wicked, and mischievous, and well he might ; for it makes many an upright man otherwise, had he not been in want, to take bribes, to be corrupt, to do against his conscience, to sell his tongue, heart, hand, etc., to be churlish, hard, unmerciful, uncivil, to use indirect means to help his present estate. It makes Princes to exact upon their subjects, Great men tyrannize, Landlords oppress, Justice mercenary, Lawyers vultures, Physicians Harpies, friends importunate, tradesmen liars, honest men thieves, devout assassinates, great men to prostitute their wives, daughters, and themselves, middle sort to repine, commons to mutiny, all to grudge, murmur, and complain. A great temptation to all mischief, it compels some miserable wretches to counterfeit several diseases, to dismember, make themselves blind, lame, to have a more plausible cause to beg, and lose their limbs to recover their present wants. And, that which is the extent of misery, it enforceth them, through anguish and wearisomeness of their lives, to make away themselves. They had rather be hanged, drowned, etc., than to live without means.

> Much better 'tis to break thy neck,
>   Or drown thyself i' th' sea,
> Than suffer irksome poverty :
>   Go make thyself away.

A Sybarite of old, as I find it registered in Athenæus, supping in Phiditiis in Sparta, and observing their hard fare, said it was no marvel if the Lacedæmonians were valiant men ; for his part he would rather run upon a sword point (and so would any man in his wits) than live with such base diet, or lead so wretched a life. In Japan 'tis a common

thing to stifle their children if they be poor, or to make an
abort, which Aristotle commends. In that civil commonwealth of China, the mother strangles her child, if she be
not able to bring it up, and had rather lose than sell it, or
have it endure such misery as poor men do. If we may
give credit to Munster, amongst us Christians in Lithuania
they voluntarily mancipate and sell themselves, their wives
and children, to rich men, to avoid hunger and beggary :
many make away themselves in this extremity. Apicius
the Roman, when he cast up his accounts, and found but
100,000 Crowns left, murdered himself for fear he should
be famished to death. P. Forestus, in his medicinal
observations, hath a memorable example of two brothers
of Louvain, that, being destitute of means, became both
melancholy, and in a discontented humour massacred
themselves ; another of a merchant, learned, wise otherwise and discreet, but, out of a deep apprehension he had
of a loss at seas, would not be persuaded but, as Ummidius
in the Poet, he should die a beggar. In a word, thus much
I may conclude of poor men, that, though they have good
parts, they cannot show or make use of them : 'tis hard
for a poor man to rise, the wisdom of the poor is despised,
and his words are not heard, Eccles. ix. 16 : his works are
rejected, contemned, for the baseness and obscurity of the
author ; though laudable and good in themselves, they
will not likely take.

> No poems can please long or live that are
> Written by water-drinkers.

Poor men cannot please, their actions, counsels, con-
sultations, projects, are vilified in the world's esteem.
This common misery of theirs must needs distract, make
them discontent and melancholy, as ordinarily they are,
wayward, peevish, like a weary traveller, still murmuring
and repining. If they be in adversity, they are more sus-

picious and apt to mistake ; they think themselves scorned by reason of their misery ; and therefore many generous spirits in such cases withdraw themselves from all company, as that Comedian Terence is said to have done ; when he perceived himself to be forsaken and poor, he voluntarily banished himself to Stymphalus, a base town in Arcadia, and there miserably died. Neither is it without cause, for we see men commonly respected according to their means, and vilified if they be in bad clothes. Philopæmen the Orator was sent to cut wood, because he was so homely attired. Terentius was placed at the lower end of Cæcilius' table, because of his homely outside. Dante, that famous Italian Poet, by reason his clothes were but mean, could not be admitted to sit down at a feast. Gnatho scorned his old familiar friend because of his apparel. Carolus Pugnax, that great Duke of Burgundy, made H. Holland, late Duke of Exeter, exil'd, run after his horse like a lackey, and would take no notice of him : 'tis the common fashion of the world. So that such men as are poor may justly be dis-content, melancholy, and complain of their present misery, and all may pray with Solomon, Give me, O Lord, neither riches nor poverty, feed me with food con-venient for me.

The Anatomy of Melancholy. 1621.

ON THE CURE OF MELANCHOLY CAUSED BY POVERTY

ROBERT BURTON

ONE of the greatest miseries that can befall a man, in the world's esteem, is poverty or want, which makes men steal, bear false witness, swear, forswear, contend, murder and rebel, which breaketh sleep, and causeth death itself. οὐδεν πενίας βαρύτερόν ἐστιφορίον, no burden (saith Menander) so intolerable as poverty : it makes men desperate, it erects and dejects ; money makes, but poverty mars, etc., and all this in the world's esteem : yet, if considered aright, it is a great blessing in itself, an happy estate, and yields no such cause of discontent, or that men should therefore account themselves vile, hated of God, forsaken, miserable, unfortunate. Christ himself was poor, born in a manger, and had not a house to hide his head in all his life, lest any man should make poverty a judgment of God, or an odious estate. And as he was himself, so he informed his Apostles and Disciples, they were all poor, Prophets poor, Apostles poor (Acts iii. [6] Silver and gold have I none). As sorrowing (saith Paul) and yet alway rejoicing ; as having nothing, and yet possessing all things, 2 Cor. vi. 10. Your great Philosophers have been voluntarily poor, not only Christians, but many others. Crates Thebanus was adored for a god in Athens, a nobleman by birth, many servants he had, an honourable attendance, much wealth, many Manors, fine apparel ; but when he saw this, that all the wealth of the world was but brittle, uncertain, and no whit availing to live well, he flung his burden into the sea, and renounced his estate. Those Curii and Fabricii will be ever renowned for contempt of these fopperies, wherewith the world is so much affected. Amongst Christians I could reckon up many Kings and Queens, that have forsaken their Crowns and fortunes, and wilfully abdicated themselves from these so much esteemed toys ; many that have refused honours, titles, and all this vain pomp and happiness, which others so ambitiously seek, and carefully study to compass and attain. Riches, I deny not, are God's good gifts, and blessings ; and *honor est in honorante*, honours are from God ; both rewards of virtue, and fit to be sought after, sued for, and may well be possessed ; yet no such great happiness in having, or misery in wanting of them. Good men have wealth that we should not think it evil ; and bad men that they should not rely on or hold it so good ; as the rain falls on both sorts, so are riches given to good and bad, but they are good only to be godly. But confer both estates, for natural parts they are not unlike ; and a beggar's child, as Cardan well observes, is no whit inferior to a Prince's, most part better ; and for those accidents of fortune, it will easily appear there is no such odds, no such extraordinary happiness in the one, or misery in the other. He is rich, wealthy, fat ; what gets he by it ? pride, insolency, lust, ambition, cares, fears, suspicion, trouble, anger, emulation, and many filthy diseases of body and mind. He hath indeed variety of dishes, better fare, sweet wine, pleasant sauce, dainty musick, gay clothes, lords it bravely out, etc., and all that which Micyllus admired in Lucian, but with them he hath the gout, dropsies, apoplexies, palsies, stone, pox, rheums, catarrhes, crudities, oppilations, Melancholy, etc. Lust enters in, anger, ambition. According to Chrysostom, the sequel of riches is pride, riot, intemperance, arrogancy, fury, and all irrational courses.

A poor man takes more delight in an ordinary meal's meat, which he hath but seldom, than they do with all their exotick dainties, and continual viands ; 'tis the rarity and necessity that makes a thing acceptable and pleasant. Darius, put to flight by Alexander, drank puddle water to quench his thirst, and it was pleasanter, he swore, than any wine or mead. All excess, as Epictetus argues, will cause a dislike ; sweet will be sour, which made that temperate Epicurus sometimes voluntarily fast. But they, being always accustomed to the same dishes (which are nastily dressed by slovenly cooks, that after their obscenities never wash their bawdy hands), be they fish, flesh, compounded, made dishes, or whatsoever else, are therefore cloyed ; nectar's self grows loathsome to them, they are weary of all their fine palaces, they are to them as so many prisons. A poor man drinks in a wooden dish, and eats his meat in wooden spoons, wooden platters, earthen vessels, and such homely stuff ; the other in gold, silver, and precious stones ; but with what success ? Fear of poison in the one, security in the other. A poor man is able to write, to speak his mind, to do his own business himself ; a rich man employs a parasite, and, as the Mayor of a City, speaks by the Town-clerk, or by Mr. Recorder, when he cannot express himself. Nonius the Senator had a purple coat as stiff with Jewels, as his mind is full of vices, rings on his fingers worth 20,000 sesterces, and as Perozes, the Persian King, an union in his ear worth 100 pound weight of gold : Cleopatra hath whole boars and sheep served up to her table at once, drinks jewels dissolved, 40,000 sesterces in value ; but to what end ?

Doth a man that is a dry, desire to drink in gold ? Doth not a cloth suit become him as well, and keep him as warm, as all their silks, satins, damasks, taffeties and tissues ? Is not home-spun cloth as great a preservative against cold, as a coat of Tartar Lambs' wool, dyed in grain, or a gown of Giants' beards ? Nero, said Suetonius, never put on one garment twice, and thou hast scarce one to put on ; what's the difference ? one's sick, the other sound : such is the whole tenor of their lives, and that which is the consummation and upshot of all, death itself makes the greatest difference. One like an hen feeds on the dunghill all his days, but is served up at last to his Lord's table ; the other as a Falcon is fed with Partridge and Pigeons, and carried on his master's fist, but when he dies, is flung to the muckhill, and there lies. The rich man lives, like Dives, jovially here on earth, *temulentus divitiis*, make the best of it ; and boasts himself in the multitude of his riches, Ps. xlix. 6, 11, he thinks his house, called after his own name, shall continue for ever ; but he perisheth like a beast, v. 12, his way utters his folly, v. 13, *malè parta, malè dilabuntur ;* like sheep they lie in the grave, 14. *Puncto descendunt ad infernum,* They spend their days in wealth, and go suddenly down to Hell, Job xxi. 13. For all Physicians and medicines enforcing nature, a swooning wife, family's complaints, friends' tears, Dirges, Masses, nænias, funerals, for all Orations, counterfeit hired acclamations, Elogiums, Epitaphs, hearses, heralds, black mourners, solemnities, obelisks, and Mausolean tombs, if he have them at least, he like a hog, goes to Hell with a guilty conscience and a poor man's curse ; his memory stinks like the snuff of a candle when it is put out ; scurrile libels, and infamous obloquies accompany him ; when as poor Lazarus is Dei Sacrarium, the Temple of God, lives and dies in true devotion, hath no more attendants but his own innocency, the Heaven a tomb, desires to be dissolved, buried in his Mother's lap, and hath a company of Angels ready to convey his soul into Abraham's bosom, he leaves an everlasting and a sweet memory behind him.

But consider all those other unknown, concealed happinesses, which a poor man hath (I call them unknown, because they be not acknowledged in the world's esteem, or so taken) *O fortunatos nimium, bona si sua norint;* happy they are in the meantime, if they would take notice of it, make use or apply it to themselves. A poor man wise is better than a foolish King, Eccles. iv. 13. Poverty is the way to heaven, the mistress of philosophy, the mother of religion, virtue, sobriety, sister of innocency, and an upright mind. How many such encomiums might I add out of the Fathers, Philosophers, Orators ! It troubles many that are poor, they account of it as a great plague, curse, a sign of God's hatred, damn'd villainy itself, a disgrace, shame and reproach ; but to whom, or why ? If fortune hath envied me wealth, thieves have robbed me, my father have not left me such revenues as others have, that I am a younger brother, basely born, of mean parentage, a dirt-dauber's son, am I therefore to be blamed ? an Eagle, a Bull, a Lion, is not rejected for his poverty, and why should a man ? 'Tis fortune's fault, not mine. Good Sir, I am a servant (to use Seneca's words) howsoever your poor friend ; a servant, and yet your chamber-fellow, and, if you consider better of it, your fellow-servant. I am thy drudge in the world's eyes, yet in God's sight peradventure thy better, my soul is more precious, and I dearer unto him. Thou art an Epicure, I am a good Christian : thou art many parasangs before me in means, favour, wealth, honour, Claudius his Narcissus, Nero's Massa, Domitian's Parthenius, a favourite, a golden slave ; thou coverest thy floors with marble, thy roofs with gold, thy walls with statues, fine pictures, curious hangings, etc., what of all this ? what's all this to true happiness ? I live and breathe under that glorious Heaven, that august Capitol of nature, enjoy the brightness of Stars, that clear light of Sun and Moon, those infinite creatures, plants, birds, beasts, fishes, herbs, all that sea and land affords, far surpassing all that art and opulentia can give. I am free, and which Seneca said of Rome, *culmus liberos texit, sed marmore et auro postea servitus habitavit*, thou hast *Amaltheæ cornu*, plenty, pleasure, the world at will, I am despicable and poor ; but a word over-shot, a blow in choler, a game at tables, a loss at Sea, a sudden fire, the Prince's dislike, a little sickness, etc., may make us equal in an instant ; howsoever, take thy time, triumph and insult a while, death will equalize us all at last. I live sparingly in the meantime, am clad homely, fare hardly ; is this a reproach ? am I the worse for it ? am I contemptible for it ? am I to be reprehended ? Happy he, in that he is freed from the tumults of the world, he seeks no honours, gapes after no preferment, flatters not, envies not, temporizeth not, but lives privately, and well contented with his estate ; he is not troubled with state matters, whether Kingdoms thrive better by succession or election ; whether Monarchies should be mixt, temperate, or absolute ; the house of Ottomon's and Austria is all one to him ; he inquires not after Colonies or new discoveries ; whether Peter were at Rome, or Constantine's donation be of force ; what comets or new stars signify, whether the earth stand or move, there be a new world in the Moon, or infinite worlds, etc. He is not touched with fear of invasions, factions or emulations.

A secure, quiet, blissful state he hath, if he could acknowledge it. But here is the misery, that he will not take notice of it ; he repines at rich men's wealth, brave hangings, dainty fare, as Simonides objecteth to Hiero, he hath all the pleasures of the world, he knows not the affliction of Joseph, stretching himself on ivory beds, and singing to the sound of the viol ; and it troubles him that he hath not the like ; there is a difference (he grumbles) between Laplolly and Phesants, to tumble i' th' straw and lie in a down-bed, betwixt wine and water, a cottage and a palace. He hates nature (as Pliny characterizeth him) that she hath made him lower than a God, and is angry with the Gods that any man goes before him ; and although he hath received much, yet (as Seneca follows it) he thinks it an injury that

he hath no more, and is so far from giving thanks for his
Tribuneship, that he complains he is not Prætor ; neither
doth that please him, except he may be Consul. Why is
he not a Prince, why not a Monarch, why not an Emperor ?
Why should one man have so much more than his fellows,
one have all, another nothing ? Why should one man be
a drudge or slave to another ? one surfeit, another starve,
one live at ease, another labour, without any hope of better
fortune ? Thus they grumble, mutter, and repine : not
considering that inconstancy of human affairs, judicially
conferring one condition with another, or well weighing
their own present estate. What they are now, thou mayest
shortly be ; and what thou art, they shall likely be.
Expect a little, confer future and times past with the present,
see the event, and comfort thyself with it.

Do (I say) as Christ himself did, when he lived here on
earth, imitate him as much as in thee lies. How many
great Cæsars, mighty Monarchs, Tetrarchs, Dynasts,
Princes, lived in his days, in what plenty, what delicacy,
how bravely attended, what a deal of gold and silver,
what treasure, how many sumptuous palaces had they,
what Provinces and Cities, ample territories, fields, rivers,
fountains, parks, forests, lawns, woods, cells, etc. ! Yet
Christ had none of all this, he would have none of this,
he voluntarily rejected all this, he could not be ignorant,
he could not err in his choice, he contemned all this, he
chose that which was safer, better, and more certain, and
less to be repented, a mean estate, even poverty itself ;
and why dost thou then, doubt to follow him, to imitate
him, and his Apostles, to imitate all good men ? So do
thou tread in his divine steps, and thou shalt not err eternally, as too many worldlings do, that run on in their own
dissolute courses, to their confusion and ruin, thou shalt
not do amiss. Whatsoever thy fortune is, be contented
with it, trust in him, rely on him, refer thyself wholly to
him. For know this, in conclusion, it is not as men, but

as God will. The Lord maketh poor, and maketh rich, bringeth low, and exalteth. (1 Sam. ii. 7, 8) he lifteth the poor from the dust, and raiseth the beggar from the dunghill, to set them amongst Princes, and make them inherit the seat of glory ; 'tis all as he pleaseth, how, and when, and whom ; he that appoints the end (though to us unknown) appoints the means likewise subordinate to the end.

Yea, but their present estate crucifies and torments most mortal men, they have no such forecast to see what may be, what shall likely be, but what is, though not wherefore, or from whom their present misfortunes grind their souls, and an envious eye which they cast upon other men's prosperities, how rich, how fortunate, how happy is he ! But in the meantime he doth not consider the other's miseries, his infirmities of body and mind, that accompany his estate, but still reflects upon his own false conceived woes and wants, whereas, if the matter were duly examined, he is in no distress at all, he hath no cause to complain, he is not poor, [since] he is not in need. Nature is content with bread and water ; and he that can rest satisfied with that, may contend with Jupiter himself for happiness. In that golden age the trees gave wholesome shade to sleep under, and the clear rivers drink. The Israelites drank water in the wilderness ; Sampson, David, Saul, Abraham's servant when he went for Isaac's wife, the Samaritan woman, and how many besides might I reckon up, Egypt, Palestine, whole countries in the Indies, that drink pure water all their lives. The Persian Kings themselves drank no other drink than the water of [the] Choaspes that runs by Susa, which was carried in bottles after them, whithersoever they went. Jacob desired no more of God, but bread to eat, and clothes to put on in his journey, Gen. xxviii. 20. *Bene est cui deus obtulit Parca quod satis est manu ;* bread is enough to strengthen the heart. And if you study Philosophy aright, saith Madaurensis, whatsoever is beyond this moderation, is not useful, but troublesome. S. Hierome esteems him rich. It was no Epicurean speech of an Epicure, " He that is not satisfied with a little will never have enough ; " and very good counsel of him in the Poet, O my son, mediocrity of means agrees best with men ; too much is pernicious. And, if thou canst be content, thou hast abundance, *nihil est, nihil deest*, thou hast little, thou wantest nothing. 'Tis all one to be hanged in a chain of gold, or in a rope ; to be filled with dainties, or coarser meat. Socrates in a Fair, seeing so many things bought and sold, such a multitude of people convened to that purpose, exclaimed forthwith, O ye Gods, what a sight of things do not I want ! It is thy want alone that keeps thee in health of body and mind, and that which thou persecutest and abhorrest as a feral plague is thy Physician and chiefest friend, which makes thee a good man, an healthful, a sound, a virtuous, an honest, and happy man. For when Virtue came from Heaven (as the Poet feigns) rich men kicked her up, wicked men abhorred her, Courtiers scoffed at her, Citizens hated her, and that she was thrust out of doors in every place, she came at last to her sister Poverty, where she had found good entertainment. Poverty and Virtue dwell together.

If adversity hath killed his thousand, prosperity hath killed his ten thousand : therefore adversity is to be preferred ; *hæc fræno indiget, illa solatio ; illa fallit, hæc instruit :* the one deceives, the other instructs : the one miserably happy, the other happily miserable : and therefore many Philosophers have voluntarily sought adversity, and so much commend it in their precepts. Demetrius in Seneca esteemed it a great infelicity, that in his life time he had no misfortune, *miserum cui nihil unquam accidisset adversi.* Adversity then is not so heavily to be taken, and we ought not in such cases so much to macerate ourselves : there is no such odds in poverty and riches. To conclude in Hierom's words, I will ask our Magnificoes, that build with Marble, and bestow a whole Manor on a thread, what difference betwixt them and Paul the Eremite, that bare old man ? they drink in jewels, he in his hand : he is poor, and goes to Heaven, they are rich, and go to Hell.

The Anatomy of Melancholy. 1621.

A CHILD

John Earle

Is a man in a small letter, yet the best copy of Adam before he tasted of Eve or the apple ; and he is happy whose small practice in the world can only write his character. He is nature's fresh picture newly drawn in oil, which time, and much handling, dims and defaces. His soul is yet a white paper unscribbled with observations of the world, wherewith, at length, it becomes a blurred note-book. He is purely happy, because he knows no evil, nor hath made means by sin to be acquainted with misery. He arrives not at the mischief of being wise, nor endures evils to come, by foreseeing them. He kisses and loves all, and, when the smart of the rod is past, smiles on his beater. Nature and his parents alike dandle him, and tice him on with a bait of sugar to a draught of wormwood. He plays yet, like a young prentice the first day, and is not come to his task of melancholy. His hardest labour is his tongue, as if he were loath to use so deceitful an organ ; and he is best company with it when he can but prattle. We laugh at his foolish sports, but his game is our earnest ; and his drums, rattles, and hobby-horses, but the emblems and mocking of man's business. His father hath writ him as his own little story, wherein he reads those days of his life that he cannot remember, and sighs to see what innocence he hath outlived. The elder he grows, he is a stair lower from ·God ; and, like his first father, much worse in his breeches. He is the Christian's example, and the old man's relapse ; the one imitates his pureness, and the other falls into his simplicity. Could he put off his body with his little coat, he had got eternity without a burden, and exchanged but one heaven for another.

Microcosmography. 1628.

A CARRIER

John Earle

Is his own hackney-man ; for he lets himself out to travel
as well as his horses. He is the ordinary ambassador
between friend and friend, the father and the son, and
brings rich presents to the one, but never returns any back
again. He is no unlettered man, though in show simple ;
for questionless, he has much in his budget, which he can
utter too in fit time and place. He is [like] the vault
in Gloster church, that conveys whispers at a distance, for
he takes the sound out of your mouth at York, and makes
it be heard as far as London. He is the young student's
joy and expectation, and the most accepted guest, to whom
they lend a willing hand to discharge him of his burden.
His first greeting is commonly, *Your friends are well ;*
then in a piece of gold delivers their blessing. You
would think him a churlish blunt fellow, but they
find in him many tokens of humanity. He is a great
afflictor of the highways, and beats them out of measure ;
which injury is sometimes revenged by the purse-taker,
and then the voyage miscarries. No man domineers
more in his inn, nor calls his host unreverently with more
presumption, and this arrogance proceeds out of the
strength of his horses. He forgets not his load where he
takes his ease, for he is drunk commonly before he goes to
bed. He is like the prodigal child, still packing away and
still returning again. But let him pass.

Microcosmography. 1628.

OF THE DIGNITY OF SPEECH

BEN JONSON

SPEECH is the only benefit man hath to express his excellency of mind above other creatures. It is the instrument of society ; therefore Mercury, who is the president
of language, is called *deorum hominumque interpres.* In all
speech, words and sense are as the body and the soul.
The sense is as the life and soul of language, without which
all words are dead. Sense is wrought out of experience,
the knowledge of human life and actions, or of the liberal
arts, which the Greeks called Ἐγκυκλοταιδείαν. Words
are the people's, yet there is a choice of them to be made ;
for *verborum delectus origo est eloquentiæ.* They are to be
chosen according to the persons we make speak, or the
things we speak of. Some are of the camp, some of the
council-board, some of the shop, some of the sheepcote,
some of the pulpit, some of the Bar, etc. And herein is
seen their elegance and propriety, when we use them fitly
and draw them forth to their just strength and nature by
way of translation or metaphor. But in this translation we
must only serve necessity (*nam temerè nihil transfertur à
prudenti*) or commodity, which is a kind of necessity :
that is, when we either absolutely want a word to express
by, and that is necessity ; or when we have not so fit a
word, and that is commodity ; as when we avoid loss by
it, and escape obsceneness, and gain in the grace and
property which helps significance. Metaphors far-
fetched hinder to be understood ; and affected, lose their
grace. Or when the person fetcheth his translations from

a wrong place : as if a privy councillor should at the table take his metaphor from a dicing-house, or ordinary, or a vintner's vault ; or a justice of peace draw his similitudes from the mathematics, or a divine from a bawdy-house, or taverns ; or a gentleman of Northamptonshire, Warwickshire, or the Midland, should fetch all the illustrations to his country neighbours from shipping, and tell them of the main-sheet and the bowline. Metaphors are thus many times deformed, as in him that said, *Castratam morte Africani rempublicam ;* and another, *Stercus curiæ Glauciam,* and *Canâ nive conspuit Alpes.* All attempts that are new in this kind are dangerous, and somewhat hard, before they be softened with use. A man coins not a new word without some peril and less fruit ; for if it happen to be received, the praise is but moderate ; if refused, the scorn is assured. Yet we must adventure ; for things at first hard and rough are by use made tender and gentle. It is an honest error that is committed, following great chiefs.

*Consuetudo.—Perspicuitas, Venustas.—Authoritas.—Virgil. —Lucretius.—Chaucerism.—Paronomasia.—*Custom is the most certain mistress of language, as the public stamp makes the current money. But we must not be too frequent with the mint, every day coining, nor fetch words from the extreme and utmost ages ; since the chief virtue of a style is perspicuity, and nothing so vicious in it as to need an interpreter. Words borrowed of antiquity do lend a kind of majesty to style, and are not without their delight sometimes ; for they have the authority of years, and out of their intermission do win themselves a kind of grace like newness. But the eldest of the present, and newness of the past language, is the best. For what was the ancient language, which some men so dote upon, but the ancient custom ? Yet when I name custom, I understand not the vulgar custom ; for that were a precept no less dangerous to language than life, if we should speak or live after the manners of the vulgar : but that I call custom of speech, which is the consent of the learned ; as custom of life, which is the consent of the good. Virgil was most loving of antiquity ; yet how rarely doth he insert *aquai* and *pictai* ! Lucretius is scabrous and rough in these ; he seeks them : as some do Chaucerisms with us, which were better expunged and banished. Some words are to be culled out for ornament and colour, as we gather flowers to strew houses or make garlands ; but they are better when they grow to our style ; as in a meadow, where, though the mere grass and greenness delight, yet the variety of flowers doth heighten and beautify. Marry, we must not play or riot too much with them, as in Paronomasies ; nor use too swelling or ill-sounding words ! *Quæ per salebras, altaque saxa cadunt.* It is true, there is no sound but shall find some lovers, as the bitterest confections are grateful to some palates. Our composition must be more accurate in the beginning and end than in the midst, and in the end more than in the beginning ; for through the midst the stream bears us. And this is attained by custom, more than care or diligence. We must express readily and fully, not profusely. There is difference between a liberal and prodigal hand. As it is a great point of art, when our matter requires it, to enlarge and veer out all sail, so to take it in and contract it, is of no less praise, when the argument doth ask it. Either of them hath their fitness in the place. A good man always profits by his endeavour, by his help, yea, when he is absent ; nay, when he is dead, by his example and memory. So good authors in their style : a strict and succinct style is that where you can take away nothing without loss, and that loss to be manifest.

De Stylo.—Tacitus.—The Laconic.—Suetonius.—Seneca and Fabianus.—The brief style is that which expresseth much in little ; the concise style, which expresseth not enough, but leaves somewhat to be understood ; the abrupt style, which hath many breaches, and doth not seem to end, but

fall.   The congruent and harmonious fitting of parts in a
sentence hath almost the fastening and force of knitting
and connection ;   as in stones well squared, which will
rise strong a great way without mortar.

   Periodi.—Obscuritas offundit tenebras.—Superlatio.—Periods
are beautiful when they are not too long ;   for so they
have their strength too, as in a pike or javelin.   As we must
take the care that our words and sense be clear, so if the
obscurity happen through the hearer's or reader's want of
understanding, I am not to answer for them, no more
than for their not listening or marking ;   I must neither
find them ears nor mind.   But a man cannot put a word
so in sense but something about it will illustrate it, if the
writer understand himself ;   for order helps much to
perspicuity, as confusion hurts.   (*Rectitudo lucem adfert ;
obliquitas et circumductio offuscat.*)   We should therefore
speak what we can the nearest way, so as we keep our gait,
not leap ;   for too short may as well be not let into the
memory, as too long not kept in.   Whatsoever loseth the
grace and clearness, converts into a riddle ;   the obscurity
is marked, but not the value.   That perisheth, and is passed
by, like the pearl in the fable.   Our style should be like a
skein of silk, to be carried and found by the right thread,
not ravelled and perplexed ;   then all is a knot, a heap.
There are words that do as much raise a style as others can
depress it.   Superlation and over-muchness amplifies ;
it may be above faith, but never above a mean.   It was
ridiculous in Cestius, when he said of Alexander :

"Fremit Oceanus, quasi indignetur, quod terras relinquas."

But propitiously from Virgil :

   "Credas innare revulsas Cycladas."

   He doth not say it was so, but seemed to be so.   Although it be somewhat incredible, that is excused before
it be spoken.   But there are hyperboles which will become

one language, that will by no means admit another. As
Eos esse P. R. *exercitus, qui cœlum possint perrumpere*, who
would say with us, but a madman ? Therefore we must
consider in every tongue what is used, what received.
Quintilian warns us, that in no kind of translation, or
metaphor, or allegory, we make a turn from what we
began ; as if we fetch the original of our metaphor from
sea and billows, we end not in flames and ashes : it is a
most foul inconsequence. Neither must we draw out our
allegory too long, lest either we make ourselves obscure,
or fall into affectation, which is childish. But why do
men depart at all from the right and natural ways of
speaking ? sometimes for necessity, when we are driven,
or think it fitter, to speak that in obscure words, or by
circumstance, which uttered plainly would offend the
hearers. Or to avoid obsceneness, or sometimes for
pleasure, and variety, as travellers turn out of the highway,
drawn either by the commodity of a footpath, or the
delicacy or freshness of the fields. And all this is called
ἐσχηματισμένη, or figured language.

Oratio imago animi.—Language most shows a man :
Speak, that I may see thee. It springs out of the most
retired and inmost parts of us, and is the image of the
parent of it, the mind. No glass renders a man's form
or likeness so true as his speech. Nay, it is likened to a
man ; and as we consider feature and composition in a
man, so words in language ; in the greatness, aptness,
sound structure, and harmony of it.

Structura et statura, sublimis, humilis, pumila.—Some men
are tall and big, so some language is high and great. Then
the words are chosen, their sound ample, the composition
full, the absolution plenteous, and poured out, all grave,
sinewy, and strong. Some are little and dwarfs ; so of
speech, it is humble and low, the words poor and flat, the
members and periods thin and weak, without knitting or
number.

Mediocris plana et placida.—The middle are of a just stature. There the language is plain and pleasing ; even without stopping, round without swelling : all well-turned, composed, elegant, and accurate.

Vitiosa oratio, vasta—tumens—enormis—affectata—abjecta. —The vicious language is vast and gaping, swelling and irregular : when it contends to be high, full of rock, mountain, and pointedness ; as it affects to be low, it is abject, and creeps, full of bogs and holes. And according to their subject these styles vary, and lose their names : for that which is high and lofty, declaring excellent matter, becomes vast and tumorous, speaking of petty and inferior things ; so that which was even and apt in a mean and plain subject, will appear most poor and humble in a high argument. Would you not laugh to meet a great councillor of State in a flat cap, with his trunk hose, and a hobby-horse cloak, his gloves under his girdle, and yond haberdasher in a velvet gown, furred with sables ? There is a certain latitude in these things, by which we find the degrees.

Figura.—The next thing to the stature is the figure and feature in language—that is, whether it be round and straight, which consists of short and succinct periods, numerous and polished ; or square and firm, which is to have equal and strong parts everywhere answerable, and weighed.

Cutis sive cortex. Compositio.—The third is the skin and coat, which rests in the well-joining, cementing, and coagmentation of words ; whenas it is smooth, gentle, and sweet, like a table upon which you may run your fingers without rubs, and your nail cannot find a joint ; not horrid, rough, wrinkled, gaping, or chapped : after these, the flesh, blood, and bones come in question.

Carnosa—adipata—redundans.—We say it is a fleshy style, when there is much periphrasis, and circuit of words ; and when with more than enough, it grows fat and corpulent : *arvina orationis*, full of suet and tallow. It hath blood and juice when the words are proper and apt, their sound sweet, and the phrase neat and picked—*oratio uncta, et benè pasta*. But where there is redundancy, both the blood and juice are faulty and vicious :—*Redundat sanguine, quia multo plus dicit, quam necesse est.* Juice in language is somewhat less than blood ; for if the words be but becoming and signifying, and the sense gentle, there is juice ; but where that wanteth, the language is thin, flagging, poor, starved, scarce covering the bone, and shows like stones in a sack.

Jejuna, macilenta, strigosa.—*Ossea, et nervosa.*—Some men, to avoid redundancy, run into that ; and while they strive to have no ill blood or juice, they lose their good. There be some styles, again, that have not less blood, but less flesh and corpulence. These are bony and sinewy ; *Ossa habent, et nervos.*

Notæ domini Sti. Albani de doctrin. intemper.—*Dictator.*—*Aristoteles.*—It was well noted by the late Lord St. Albans, that the study of words is the first distemper of learning ; vain matter the second ; and a third distemper is deceit, or the likeness of truth : imposture held up by credulity. All these are the cobwebs of learning, and to let them grow in us is either sluttish or foolish. Nothing is more ridiculous than to make an author a dictator, as the schools have done Aristotle. The damage is infinite knowledge receives by it ; for to many things a man should owe but a temporary belief, and suspension of his own judgment, not an absolute resignation of himself, or a perpetual captivity. Let Aristotle and others have their dues ; but if we can make further discoveries of truth and fitness than they, why are we envied ? Let us beware, while we strive to add, we do not diminish or deface ; we may improve, but not augment. By discrediting falsehood, truth grows in request. We must not go about, like men anguished and perplexed, for vicious affectation of praise, but calmly study the separation of opinions, find the errors have intervened, awake antiquity, call former times into question ; but make no parties with the present, nor follow any fierce undertakers, mingle no matter of doubtful credit with the simplicity of truth, but gently stir the mould about the root of the question, and avoid all digladiations, facility of credit, or superstitious simplicity, seek the consonancy and concatenation of truth ; stoop only to point of necessity, and what leads to convenience. Then make exact animadversion where style hath degenerated, where flourished and thrived in choiceness of phrase, round and clean composition of sentence, sweet falling of the clause, varying an illustration by tropes and figures, weight of matter, worth of subject, soundness of argument, life of invention, and depth of judgment. This is *monte potiri*, to get the hill ; for no perfect discovery can be made upon a flat or a level.

Discoveries.   1640.

OF FOLLY

Ben Jonson

WHAT petty things they are we wonder at, like children that esteem every trifle, and prefer a fairing before their fathers ! What difference is between us and them but that we are dearer fools, coxcombs at a higher rate ? They are pleased with cockle-shells, whistles, hobby-horses, and such like ; we with statues, marble pillars, pictures, gilded roofs, where underneath is lath and lime, perhaps loam. Yet we take pleasure in the lie, and are glad we can cozen ourselves. Nor is it only in our walls and ceilings, but all that we call happiness is mere painting and gilt, and all for money. What a thin membrane of honour that is ! and how hath all true reputation fallen, since money began to have any ! Yet the great herd, the multitude, that in all other things are divided, in this alone conspire and agree—to love money. They wish for it, they embrace it, they adore it, while yet it is possessed with greater stir and torment than it is gotten.

Discoveries. **1640.**

OF MYSELF AND MY DREAMS

SIR THOMAS BROWNE

Now for my life, it is a miracle of thirty years, which to relate were not a history but a piece of poetry, and would sound to common ears like a fable ; for the world, I count it not an inn but an hospital ; and a place not to live, but to die in. The world that I regard is myself ; it is the microcosm of my own frame that I cast mine eye on, for the other, I use it but like my globe, and turn it round sometimes for my recreation. Men that look upon my outside, perusing only my condition and fortunes, do err in my altitude, for I am above Atlas his shoulders. The earth is a point, not only in respect of the heavens above us, but of that heavenly and celestial part within us ; that mass of flesh that circumscribes me limits not my mind ; that surface that tells the heaven it hath an end cannot persuade me I have any. I take my circle to be above three hundred and sixty. Though the number of the arc do measure my body it comprehendeth not my mind. Whilst I study to find how I am a microcosm, or little world, I find myself something more than the great. There is surely a piece of divinity in us, something that was before the elements, and owes no homage unto the sun. Nature tells me I am the image of God, as well as Scripture. He that understands not thus much hath not his introduction, or first lesson, and is yet to begin the alphabet of man. Let me not injure the felicity of others, if I say I am as happy as any ; *Ruat cælum, fiat voluntas tua,* salveth all ; so that whatsoever happens it is but what our daily prayers desire. In brief, I am content, and what should Providence add more ? Surely this is it we call happiness, and this do I enjoy ; with this I am happy in a dream, and as content to enjoy a happiness in a fancy, as others in a more apparent truth and reality. There is surely a nearer apprehension of anything that delights us in our dreams, than in our waking senses ; without this I were unhappy ; for my awaked judgment discontents me, ever whispering unto me that I am from my friend, but my friendly dreams in night requite me, and make me think I am within his arms. I thank God for my happy dreams, as I do for my good rest, for there is a satisfaction unto reasonable desires, and such as can be content with a fit of happiness. And surely it is not a melancholy conceit to think we are all asleep in this world, and that the conceits of this life are as mere dreams to those of the next, as the phantasms of the night, to the conceits of the day. There is an equal delusion in both, and the one doth but seem to be the emblem or picture of the other. We are somewhat more than ourselves in our sleeps, and the slumber of the body seems to be but the waking of the soul. It is the ligation of sense, but the liberty of reason, and our waking conceptions do not match the fancies of our sleeps. At my nativity my ascendant was the watery sign of Scorpio. I was born in the planetary hour of Saturn, and I think I have a piece of the leaden planet in me. I am no way facetious, nor disposed for the mirth and galliardize of company ; yet in one dream I can compose a whole comedy, behold the action, apprehend the jests, and laugh myself awake at the conceits thereof. Were my memory as faithful as my reason is then fruitful, I would never study but in my dreams ; and this time also would I choose for my devotions ; but our grosser memories have then so little hold of our abstracted understandings that they forget the story, and can only relate to our awaked souls a confused and broken tale of that that hath passed. Aristotle, who hath written a singular tract of sleep, hath not, methinks, thoroughly defined it ; nor yet Galen, though he seem to have corrected it ; for those noctambuloes and night-walkers, though in their sleep, do yet enjoy the action of their senses. We must therefore say, that there is something in us that is not in the jurisdiction of Morpheus, and that those abstracted and ecstatic souls do walk about in their own corpses as spirits with the bodies they assume, wherein they seem to hear and feel, though indeed the organs are destitute of sense, and their natures of those faculties that should inform them. Thus it is observed, that men sometimes, upon the hour of their departure, do speak and reason above themselves ; for then the soul, beginning to be freed from the ligaments of the body, begins to reason like herself, and to discourse in a strain above mortality.

We term sleep a death, and yet it is waking that kills us and destroys those spirits that are the house of life. It is indeed a part of life that best expresseth death ; for every man truly lives, so long as he acts his nature, or some way makes good the faculties of himself : Themistocles, therefore, that slew his soldier in his sleep, was a merciful executioner ; it is a kind of punishment the mildness of no laws hath invented ; I wonder the fancy of Lucan and Seneca did not discover it. It is that death by which we may be literally said to die daily ; a death which Adam died before his mortality ; a death whereby we live a middle and moderating point between life and death ; in fine, so like death, I dare not trust it without my prayers, and a half adieu unto the world, and take my farewell in a colloquy with God.

Religio Medici. 1642.

ON IMMORTALITY

Sir Thomas Browne

Now, since these dead bones have already outlasted the
living ones of Methuselah, and in a yard under ground,
and thin walls of clay, outworn all the strong and spacious
buildings above it ; and quietly rested under the drums
and tramplings of three conquests : what prince can promise such diuturnity unto his relics, or might not gladly say,

Sic ego componi versus in ossa velim ?

Time, which antiquates antiquities, and hath an art to
make dust of all things, hath yet spared these minor
monuments. In vain we hope to be known by open and
visible conservatories, when to be unknown was the
means of their continuation, and obscurity their protection.
If they died by violent hands, and were thrust into their
urns, these bones become considerable, and some old
philosophers would honour them, whose souls they conceived most pure, which were thus snatched from their
bodies, and to retain a stronger propension unto them :
whereas they weariedly left a languishing corpse, and with
faint desires of reunion. If they fell by long and aged decay,
yet wrapt up in the bundle of time, they fall into indis-
tinction, and make but one blot with infants. If we begin
to die when we live, and long life be but a prolongation
of death, our life is a sad composition ; we live with
death, and die not in a moment. How many pulses made

up the life of Methuselah, were work for Archimedes :
common counters sum up the life of Moses his man. Our
days become considerable like petty sums by minute
accumulations ; where numerous fractions make up but
small round numbers ; and our days of a span long make
not one little finger.

If the nearness of our last necessity, brought a nearer
conformity unto it, there were a happiness in hoary hairs,
and no calamity in half senses. But the long habit of living
indisposeth us for dying ; when avarice makes us the sport
of death, when even David grew politically cruel, and
Solomon could hardly be said to be the wisest of men.
But many are too early old, and before the date of age.
Adversity stretcheth our days, misery makes Alcmena's
nights, and time hath no wings unto it. But the most
tedious being is that which can unwish itself, content to
be nothing, or never to have been, which was beyond the
malcontent of Job, who cursed not the day of his life,
but his nativity ; content to have so far been, as to have
a title to future being, although he had lived here but in an
hidden state of life, and as it were, an abortion.

What song the Syrens sang, or what name Achilles
assumed when he hid himself among women, though
puzzling questions, are not beyond all conjecture. What
time the persons of these ossuaries entered the famous
nations of the dead, and slept with princes and counsellors,
might admit a wide solution. But who were the proprie-
taries of these bones, or what bodies these ashes made up,
were a question above antiquarianism ; not to be resolved
by man, nor easily perhaps by spirits, except we consult
the provincial guardians, or tutelary observators. Had
they made as good provision for their names as they have
done for their relics, they had not so grossly erred in the
art of perpetuation. But to subsist in bones, and be but
pyramidally extant, is a fallacy in duration. Vain ashes,
which in the oblivion of names, persons, times, and sexes,

have found unto themselves a fruitless continuation, and only arise unto late posterity, as emblems of mortal vanities, antidotes against pride, vainglory, and madding vices. Pagan vainglories, which thought the world might last for ever, had encouragement for ambition, and finding no Atropos unto the immortality of their names, were never damped with the necessity of oblivion. Even old ambitions had the advantage of ours, in the attempts of their vainglories, who acting early, and before the probable meridian of time, have by this time found great accomplishment of their designs, whereby the ancient heroes have already outlasted their monuments, and mechanical preservations. But in this latter scene of time we cannot expect such mummies unto our memories, when ambition may fear the prophecy of Elias, and Charles the Fifth can never hope to live within two Methuselahs of Hector.

And therefore, restless inquietude for the diuturnity of our memories unto present considerations, seems a vanity almost out of date, and superannuated piece of folly. We cannot hope to live so long in our names as some have done in their persons. One face of Janus holds no proportion unto the other. It is too late to be ambitious. The great mutations of the world are acted, or time may be too short for our designs. To extend our memories by monuments, whose death we daily pray for, and whose duration we cannot hope, without injury to our expectations, in the advent of the last day, were a contradiction to our beliefs. We, whose generations are ordained in this setting part of time, are providentially taken off from such imaginations ; and, being necessitated to eye the remaining particle of futurity, are naturally constituted unto thoughts of the next world, and cannot excusably decline the consideration of that duration, which maketh pyramids pillars of snow, and all that is past a moment.

Circles and right lines limit and close all bodies, and the

mortal right-lined circle must conclude and shut up all.
There is no antidote against the opium of time, which
temporally considereth all things. Our fathers find their
graves in our short memories, and sadly tell us how we may
be buried in our survivors. Gravestones tell truth scarce
forty years. Generations pass while some trees stand, and
old families last not three oaks. To be read by bare
inscriptions like many in Gruter, to hope for eternity by
enigmatical epithets, or first letters of our names, to be
studied by antiquaries who we were, and have new names
given us, like many of the mummies, are cold consolations
unto the students of perpetuity, even by everlasting
languages.

To be content that times to come should only know there
was such a man, not caring whether they knew more of
him, was a frigid ambition in Cardan ; disparaging his
horoscopal inclination and judgment of himself. Who
cares to subsist, like Hippocrates's patients, or Achilles's
horses, in Homer, under naked nominations, without
deserts and noble acts, which are the balsam of our
memories, the *entelechia* and soul of our subsistences ? To
be nameless in worthy deeds exceeds an infamous history.
The Canaanitish woman lives more happily without a
name than Herodias with one. And who had not rather
have been the good thief, than Pilate ?

But the iniquity of oblivion blindly scattereth her poppy,
and deals with the memory of men without distinction to
merit of perpetuity. Who can but pity the founder of the
pyramids ? Herostratus lives that burnt the temple of
Diana ; he is almost lost that built it : time hath spared
the epitaph of Adrian's horse, confounded that of himself.
In vain we compute our felicities by the advantage of our
good names, since bad have equal durations ; and Ther-
sites is like to live as long as Agamemnon. Who knows
whether the best of men be known ? or, whether there
be not more remarkable persons forgot, than any that

stand remembered in the known account of time ? Without the favour of the everlasting register the first man had been as unknown as the last, and Methuselah's long life had been his only chronicle.

Oblivion is not to be hired : the greater part must be content to be as though they had not been, to be found in the register of God, not in the record of man. Twenty-seven names make up the first story before the flood, and the recorded names ever since contain not one living century. The number of the dead long exceedeth all that shall live. The night of time far surpasseth the day, and who knows when was the equinox? Every hour adds unto that current arithmetic, which scarce stands one moment. And, since death must be the Lucina of life, and even Pagans could doubt whether thus to live were to die ; since our longest sun sets at right descensions, and makes but winter arches, and therefore it cannot be long before we lie down in darkness, and have our light in ashes ; since the brother of death daily haunts us with dying mementoes, and time, that grows old itself, bids us hope no long duration ;—diuturnity is a dream and folly of expectation.

Darkness and light divide the course of time, and oblivion shares with memory a great part even of our living beings ; we slightly remember our felicities, and the smartest strokes of affliction leave but short smart upon us. Sense endureth no extremities, and sorrows destroy us or themselves. To weep into stones are fables. Afflictions induce callosities, miseries are slippery, or fall like snow upon us, which, notwithstanding, is no unhappy stupidity. To be ignorant of evils to come, and forgetful of evils past, is a merciful provision in nature, whereby we digest the mixture of our few and evil days, and our delivered senses not relapsing into cutting remembrances, our sorrows are not kept raw by the edge of repetitions. A great part of antiquity contented their hopes of subsistency with a transmigration of their souls. A good way to continue their memories, while, having the advantage of plural successions, they could not but act something remarkable in such variety of beings, and, enjoying the fame of their passed selves, make accumulation of glory unto their last durations. Others, rather than be lost in the uncomfortable night of nothing, were content to recede into the common being, and make one particle of the public soul of all things, which was no more than to return into their unknown and divine original again. Egyptian ingenuity was more unsatisfied, contriving their bodies in sweet consistences, to attend the return of their souls. But all was vanity, feeding the wind, and folly. The Egyptian mummies, which Cambyses or time hath spared, avarice now consumeth. Mummy is become merchandise ; Mizraim cures wounds, and Pharaoh is sold for balsams.

In vain do individuals hope for immortality, or any patent from oblivion, in preservations below the moon : men have been deceived even in their flatteries above the sun, and studied conceits to perpetuate their names in heaven. The various cosmography of that part hath already varied the names of contrived constellations : Nimrod is lost in Orion, and Osiris in the Dog-star. While we look for incorruption in the heavens, we find they are but like the earth ; durable in their main bodies, alterable in their parts : whereof, beside comets and new stars, perspectives begin to tell tales, and the spots that wander about the sun, with Phaeton's favour, would make clear conviction.

There is nothing strictly immortal but immortality ; whatever hath no beginning may be confident of no end ; —which is the peculiar of that necessary essence that cannot destroy itself ; and the highest strain of omnipotency, to be so powerfully constituted as not to suffer even from the power of itself. All others have a dependent being, and within the reach of destruction, but the sufficiency of

Christian immortality frustrates all earthly glory, and the quality of either state after death makes a folly of posthumous memory. God, who can only destroy our souls, and hath assured our resurrection, either of our bodies or names hath directly promised no duration. Wherein there is so much of chance, that the boldest expectants have found unhappy frustration ; and to hold long subsistence seems but a scape in oblivion. But man is a noble animal, splendid in ashes, and pompous in the grave, solemnizing nativities and deaths with equal lustre, nor omitting ceremonies of bravery in the infamy of his nature.

Life is a pure flame, and we live by an invisible sun within us. A small fire sufficeth for life, great flames seemed too little after death, while men vainly affected precious pyres, and to burn like Sardanapalus ; but the wisdom of funeral laws found the folly of prodigal blazes, and reduced undoing fires, unto the rule of sober obsequies, wherein few could be so mean as not to provide wood, pitch, a mourner, and an urn.

Five languages secured not the epitaph of Gordianus. The man of God lives longer without a tomb than any by one, invisibly interred by angels, and adjudged to obscurity, though not without some marks directing human discovery. Enoch and Elias, without either tomb or burial, in an anomalous state of being, are the great examples of perpetuity, in their long and living memory, in strict account being still on this side death, and having a late part yet to act upon this stage of earth. If in the decretory term of the world we shall not all die but be changed, according to received translation, the last day will make but few graves ; at least quick resurrections will anticipate lasting sepulchres. Some graves will be opened before they be quite closed, and Lazarus be no wonder. When many that feared to die shall groan that they can die but once, the dismal state is the second and living death, when life puts despair on the damned ; when men shall wish the coverings of mountains, not of monuments, and annihilation shall be courted.

While some have studied monuments, others have studiously declined them ; and some have been so vainly boisterous, that they durst not acknowledge their graves ; wherein Alaricus seems most subtle, who had a river turned to hide his bones at the bottom. Even Sylla, that thought himself safe in his urn, could not prevent revenging tongues, and stones thrown at his monument. Happy are they whom privacy makes innocent, who deal so with men in this world, that they are not afraid to meet them in the next, who, when they die, make no commotion among the dead, and are not touched with that poetical taunt of Isaiah.

Pyramids, arches, obelisks, were but the irregularities of vainglory and wild enormities of ancient magnanimity. But the most magnanimous resolution rests in the Christian religion, which trampleth upon pride, and sits on the neck of ambition, humbly pursuing that infallible perpetuity, unto which all others must diminish their diameters, and be poorly seen in angles of contingency.

Pious spirits who passed their days in raptures of futurity, made little more of this world than the world that was before it, while they lay obscure in the chaos of preordination and night of their forebeings. And if any have been so happy as truly to understand Christian annihilation, ecstasies, exolution, liquefaction, transformation, the kiss of the spouse, gustation of God, and ingression into the divine shadow, they have already had a handsome anticipation of heaven ; the glory of the world is surely over, and the earth in ashes unto them.

To subsist in lasting monuments, to live in their productions, to exist in their names, and predicament of chimeras, was large satisfaction unto old expectations, and made one part of their Elysiums. But all this is nothing in the metaphysics of true belief. To live indeed is to be again ourselves, which being not only a hope but an evidence in noble believers, it is all one to lie in St. Innocent's churchyard, as in the sands of Egypt ; ready to be anything, in the ecstasy of being ever, and as content with six foot as the *moles* of Adrianus.

——Tabesne cadavera solvat
An rogus haud refert.—*Lucan.*

Urn-Burial.   1658.

THE GOOD SCHOOLMASTER

Thomas Fuller

There is scarce any profession in the commonwealth more necessary, which is so slightly performed. The reasons whereof I conceive to be these : First, young scholars make this calling their refuge ; yea, perchance, before they have taken any degree in the university, commence schoolmasters in the country, as if nothing else were required to set up this profession but only a rod and a ferula. Secondly, others who are able, use it only as a passage to better preferment, to patch the rents in their present fortune, till they can provide a new one, and betake themselves to some more gainful calling. Thirdly, they are disheartened from doing their best with the miserable reward which in some places they receive, being masters to their children and slaves to their parents. Fourthly, being grown rich, they grow negligent, and scorn to touch the school but by the proxy of the usher. But see how well our schoolmaster behaves himself.

His genius inclines him with delight to his profession. Some men had as well be schoolboys as schoolmasters, to be tied to the school, as Cooper's Dictionary and Scapula's Lexicon are chained to the desk therein ; and though great scholars, and skilful in other arts, are bunglers in this. But God, of His goodness, hath fitted several men for several callings, that the necessity of Church and State, in all conditions, may be provided for. So that he who beholds the fabric thereof, may say, God hewed out the stone, and appointed it to lie in this very place, for it would fit none other so well, and here it doth most excellent. And thus God mouldeth some for a schoolmaster's life, undertaking it with desire and delight, and discharging it with dexterity and happy success.

He studieth his scholars' natures as carefully as they their books; and ranks their dispositions into several forms. And though it may seem difficult for him in a great school to descend to all particulars, yet experienced schoolmasters may quickly make a grammar of boys' natures, and reduce them all—saving some few exceptions—to these general rules:

1. Those that are ingenious and industrious. The conjunction of two such planets in a youth presage much good unto him. To such a lad a frown may be a whipping, and a whipping a death; yea, where their master whips them once, shame whips them all the week after. Such natures he useth with all gentleness.

2. Those that are ingenious and idle. These think with the hare in the fable, that running with snails—so they count the rest of their schoolfellows—they shall come soon enough to the post, though sleeping a good while before their starting. Oh, a good rod would finely take them napping.

3. Those that are dull and diligent. Wines, the stronger they be, the more lees they have when they are new. Many boys are muddy-headed till they be clarified with age, and such afterwards prove the best. Bristol diamonds are both bright, and squared, and pointed by nature, and yet are soft and worthless; whereas orient ones in India are rough and rugged naturally. Hard, rugged, and dull natures of youth, acquit themselves afterwards the jewels of the country, and therefore their dullness at first is to be borne with, if they be diligent. That schoolmaster deserves to be beaten himself who beats nature in a boy for a fault. And I question whether all the whipping in the world can

make their parts which are naturally sluggish rise one minute before the hour nature hath appointed.

4. Those that are invincibly dull, and negligent also. Correction may reform the latter, not amend the former. All the whetting in the world can never set a razor's edge on that which hath no steel in it. Such boys he consigneth over to other professions. Shipwrights and boatmakers will choose those crooked pieces of timber which other carpenters refuse. Those may make excellent merchants and mechanics which will not serve for scholars.

He is able, diligent, and methodical in his teaching ; not leading them rather in a circle than forwards. He minces his precepts for children to swallow, hanging clogs on the nimbleness of his own soul, that his scholars may go along with him.

He is and will be known to be an absolute monarch in his school. If cockering mothers proffer him money to purchase their sons' exemption from his rod—to live, as it were, in a peculiar, out of their master's jurisdiction —with disdain he refuseth it, and scorns the late custom in some places of commuting whipping into money, and ransoming boys from the rod at a set price. If he hath a stubborn youth, correction-proof, he debaseth not his authority by contesting with him, but fairly, if he can, puts him away before his obstinacy hath infected others.

He is moderate in inflicting deserved correction. Many a schoolmaster better answereth the name *paidotribes* than *paidagogos*, rather tearing his scholars' flesh with whipping than giving them good education. No wonder if his scholars hate the muses, being presented unto them in the shape of fiends and furies.

Such an Orbilius mars more scholars than he makes. Their tyranny hath caused many tongues to stammer which spake plain by nature, and whose stuttering at first was nothing else but fears quavering on their speech at their master's presence ; and whose mauling them about their heads hath dulled those who in quickness exceeded their master.

He makes his school free to him who sues to him *in formâ pauperis*. And surely learning is the greatest alms that can be given. But he is a beast who, because the poor scholar cannot pay him his wages, pays the scholar in his whipping ; rather are diligent lads to be encouraged with all excitements to learning. This minds me of what I have heard concerning Mr. Bust, that worthy late school-master of Eton, who would never suffer any wandering begging scholar—such as justly the statute hath ranked in the forefront of rogues—to come into his school, but would thrust him out with earnestness—however privately charitable unto him—lest his schoolboys should be dis-heartened from their books, by seeing some scholars after their studying in the university preferred to beggary.

He spoils not a good school to make thereof a bad college, therein to teach his scholars logic. For, besides that logic may have an action of trespass against grammar for encroaching on her liberties, syllogisms are solecisms taught in the school, and oftentimes they are forced after-wards in the university to unlearn the fumbling skill they had before.

Out of his. school he is no way pedantical in carriage or discourse ; contenting himself to be rich in Latin, though he doth not gingle with it in every company wherein he comes.

To conclude, let this, amongst other motives, make schoolmasters careful in their place—that the eminences of their scholars have commended the memories of their schoolmasters to posterity, who, otherwise in obscurity, had altogether been forgotten. Who had ever heard of R. Bond, in Lancashire, but for the breeding of learned Ascham, his scholar ? or of Hartgrave, in Brundly School, in the same county, but because he was the first did teach worthy Dr. Whitaker ? Nor do I honour the memory of

Mulcaster for anything so much as his scholar, that gulf of learning, Bishop Andrews. This made the Athenians, the day before the great feast of Theseus, their founder, to sacrifice a ram to the memory of Conidas, his schoolmaster, that first instructed him.

The Holy State. 1648.

OF NATURAL FOOLS

Thomas Fuller

THEY have the cases of men, and little else of them besides speech and laughter. And indeed it may seem strange that *risible* being the property of man alone, they who have least of man should have most thereof, laughing without cause or measure.

1. *Generally nature hangs out a sign of simplicity in the face of a fool;* and there is enough in his countenance for a hue and cry to take him on suspicion : or else it is stamped on the figure of his body ; their heads sometimes so little, that there is no room for wit, sometimes so long, that there is no wit for so much room.

2. *Yet some by their faces may pass current enough, till they cry themselves down by their speaking.* Thus men know the bell is cracked when they hear it tolled ; yet some that have stood out the assault of two or three questions, and have answered pretty rationally, have afterwards of their own accord betrayed and yielded themselves to be fools.

3. *The oaths and railing of fools is oftentimes no fault of theirs, but their teachers.* The Hebrew word *barac*, signifies to bless and to curse ; and it is the speaker's pleasure if he use it in the worst acceptation. Fools of themselves are equally capable to pray and to swear ; they therefore have the greater sin who, by their example or otherwise, teach them so to do.

4. *One may get wisdom by looking on a fool.* In beholding him, think how much thou art beholden to Him that

suffered thee not to be like him. Only God's pleasure put a difference betwixt you. And consider that a fool and a wise man are alike both in the starting-place, their birth, and at the post, their death ; only they differ in the race of their lives.

5. *It is unnatural to laugh at a natural.* How can the object of thy pity be the object of thy pastime ? I confess sometimes the strangeness, and, as I may say, witty simplicity of their actions, may extort a smile from a serious man, who at the same time may smile at them, and sorrow for them. But it is one thing to laugh at them *in transitu*, a snap and away, and another to make a set meal in jeering them, and as the Philistines, to send for Samson to make them sport.

6. *To make a trade of laughing at a fool, is the highway to become one.* Tully confesseth that whilst he laughed at one Hircus, a very ridiculous man, *dum illum rideo pene factus sum ille.* And one telleth us of Gallus Vibius, a man first of great eloquence, and afterwards of great madness, which seized not on him so much by accident as his own affectation, so long mimically imitating madmen, that he became one.

7. *Many have been the wise speeches of fools, though not so many as the foolish speeches of wise men.* Now the wise speeches of these silly souls proceed from one of these reasons : either because talking much, and shooting often, they must needs hit the mark sometimes, though not by aim, by hap : or else, because a fool's *mediocriter* is *optime* : sense from his mouth, a sentence ; and a tolerable speech cried up for an apophthegm : or lastly, because God may sometimes illuminate them, and, especially towards their death, admit them to the possession of some part of reason. A poor beggar in Paris being very hungry stayed so long in a cook's shop, who was dishing up of meat, till his stomach was satisfied with only the smell thereof. The choleric covetous cook demanded of him to pay for

his breakfast. The poor man denied it, and the controversy was referred to the decision of the next man that should pass by, who chanced to be the most notorious idiot in the whole city. He, on the relation of the matter, determined that the poor man's money should be put betwixt two empty dishes, and the cook should be recompensed with the jingling of the poor man's money, as he was satisfied with only the smell of the cook's meat. And this is affirmed by credible writers, as no fable, but an undoubted fact. More waggish was that of a rich landed fool, whom a courtier had begged and carried about to wait on him. He coming with his master to a gentleman's house where the picture of a fool was wrought in a fair suit of arras, cut the picture out with a penknife. And being chidden for so doing : *You have more cause,* said he, *to thank me, for if my master had seen the picture of the fool, he would have begged the hangings of the king, as he did my lands.* When the standers-by comforted a natural who lay on his death-bed, and told him that four proper fellows should carry his body to the church ; *Yea,* quoth he, *but I had rather by half go thither myself;* and then prayed God at his last gasp not to require more of him than he gave him.

As for a changeling, who is not one child changed for another, but one child on a sudden much changed from itself ; and for a jester, which some count a necessary evil in a court, an office which none but he that hath wit can perform, and none but he that wants wit will perform, I conceive them not to belong to the present subject.

The Holy State and Profane State. 1648.

OF FANCY

THOMAS FULLER

It is an inward sense of the soul, for a while retaining and examining things brought in thither by the common sense. It is the most boundless and restless faculty of the soul : for whilst the understanding and the will are kept as it were *in libera custodia* to their objects of *verum et bonum*, the fancy is free from all engagements : it digs without spade, sails without ship, flies without wings, builds without charges, fights without bloodshed, in a moment striding from the centre to the circumference of the world, by a kind of omnipotency creating and annihilating things in an instant : and things divorced in nature are married in fancy as in a lawful place. It is also most restless : whilst the senses are bound, and reason in a manner asleep, fancy, like a sentinel, walks the round, ever working, never wearied. The chief diseases of the fancy are, either they are too wild and high soaring, or else too low and grovelling, or else too desultory and over voluble. Of the first :

1. *If thy fancy be but a little too rank, age itself will correct it.* To lift too high is no fault in a young horse, because with travelling he will mend it for his own ease. Thus lofty fancies in young men will come down of themselves, and in process of time the overplus will shrink to be but even measure. But if this will not do it, then observe these rules.

2. *Take part always with thy judgment against thy fancy*

in anything wherein they shall dissent. If thou suspectest thy conceits too luxuriant, herein account thy suspicion a legal conviction, and damn whatsoever thou doubtest of. Warily Tully : *Bene moment, qui vetant quicquam facere, de quo dubitas, æquum sit an iniquum.*

3. *Take the advice of a faithful friend, and submit thy inventions to his censure.* When thou pennest an oration, let him have the power of *index expurgatorius*, to expunge what he pleaseth ; and do not thou, like a fond mother, cry if the child of thy brain be corrected for playing the wanton. Mark the arguments and reasons of his alterations ; why *that* phrase least proper, *this* passage more cautious and advised ; and after a while thou shalt perform the place in thine own person, and not go out of thyself for a censurer. If thy fancy be too low and humble,

4. *Let thy judgment be king, but not tryant over it, to condemn harmless, yea, commendable conceits.* Some for fear their orations should giggle, will not let them smile. Give it also liberty to rove, for it will not be extravagant. There is no danger that weak folks, if they walk abroad, will straggle far, as wanting strength.

5. *Acquaint thyself with reading poets, for there fancy is in her throne ;* and in time, the sparks of the author's wit will catch hold on the reader, and inflame him with love, liking, and desire of imitation. I confess there is more required to teach one to write than to see a copy : however, there is a secret force of fascination in reading poems to raise and provoke fancy. If thy fancy be over voluble, then

6. *Whip this vagrant home to the first object whereon it should be settled.* Indeed, nimbleness is the perfection of this faculty, but levity the bane of it. Great is the difference betwixt a swift horse and a skittish, that will stand on no ground. Such is the ubiquitary fancy, which will keep long residence on no one subject, but is so courteous to strangers, that it ever welcomes that conceit most which

comes last ; and new species supplant the old ones, before seriously considered. If this be the fault of thy fancy, I say whip it home to the first object whereon it should be settled. This do as often as occasion requires, and by degrees the fugitive servant will learn to abide by his work without running away.

7. *Acquaint thyself by degrees with hard and knotty studies,* as school-divinity, which will clog thy over nimble fancy. True, at the first it will be as welcome to thee as a prison, and their very solutions will seem knots unto thee. But take not too much at once, lest thy brain turn edge. Taste it first as a potion for physic, and by degrees thou shalt drink it as beer for thirst : practice will make it pleasant. Mathematics are also good for this purpose. If beginning to try a conclusion, thou must make an end, lest thou lose thy pains that are past, and must proceed seriously and exactly. I meddle not with those bedlam fancies, all whose conceits are antiques, but leave them for the physician to purge with hellebore.

8. *To clothe low-creeping matter with high-flown language is not fine fancy, but flat foolery.* It rather loads than raises a wren, to fasten the feathers of an ostrich to her wings. Some men's speeches are like the high mountains in Ireland, having a dirty bog in the top of them : the very ridge of them in high words having nothing of worth, but what rather stalls than delights the auditor.

9. *Fine fancies in manufactures invent engines rather pretty than useful;* and commonly one trade is too narrow for them. They are better to project new ways than to prosecute old, and are rather skilful in many mysteries than thriving in one. They affect not voluminous inventions, wherein many years must constantly be spent to perfect them, except there be in them variety of pleasant employment.

10. *Imagination, the work of fancy, hath produced real effects.* Many serious and sad examples thereof may be

produced : I will only insist on a merry one. A gentleman having led a company of children beyond their usual journey, they began to be weary, and jointly cried to him to carry them ; which, because of their multitude, he could not do, but told them he would provide them horses to ride on. Then cutting little wands out of the hedge as nags for them, and a great stake as a gelding for himself, thus mounted, fancy put metal into their legs, and they came cheerfully home.

11. *Fancy runs most furiously when a guilty conscience drives it.* One that owed much money, and had many creditors, as he walked London streets in the evening, a tenterhook caught his cloak. *At whose suit ?* said he, conceiving some bailiff had arrested him. Thus guilty consciences are afraid where no fear is, and count every creature they meet a serjeant sent from God to punish them.

The Holy State and Profane State. 1648.

SPIRITUAL ARTS OF LENGTHENING OUR DAYS

Jeremy Taylor

In the accounts of a man's life, we do not reckon that portion of days in which we are shut up in the prison of the womb ; we tell our years from the day of our birth ; and the same reason that makes our reckoning to stay so long, says also, that then it begins too soon. For then we are beholden to others to make the account for us ; for we know not of a long time whether we be alive or no, having but some little approaches and symptoms of a life. To feed, and sleep, and move a little, and imperfectly, is the state of an unborn child ; and when he is born he does no more for a good while ; and what is it that shall make him to be esteemed to live the life of a man ? and when shall that account begin ? For we should be loth to have the accounts of our age taken by the measures of a beast ; and fools and distracted persons are reckoned as civilly dead ; they are no parts of the commonwealth, not subject to laws, but secured by them in charity, and kept from violence as a man keeps his ox : and a third part of our life is spent before we enter into a higher order, into the state of a man.

Neither must we think that the life of a man begins when he can feed himself, or walk alone, when he can fight, or beget his like ; for so he is contemporary with a camel or a cow ; but he is first a man when he comes to a certain steady use of reason, according to his proportion : and when that is, all the world of men cannot tell precisely. Some are called at age at fourteen ; some at one-and-twenty ; some never ; but all men late enough ; for the life of a man comes upon him slowly and insensibly. But as, when the sun approaches towards the gates of the morning, he first opens a little eye of heaven, and sends away the spirits of darkness, and gives light to a cock, and calls up the lark to matins, and by-and-by gilds the fringes of a cloud, and peeps over the eastern hills, thrusting out his golden horns, like those which decked the brows of Moses when he was forced to wear a veil because himself had seen the face of God ; and still, while a man tells the story, the sun gets up higher, till he shows a fair face and a full light, and then he shines one whole day, under a cloud often, and sometimes weeping great and little showers, and sets quickly ; so is a man's reason and his life. He first begins to perceive himself to see or taste, making little reflections upon his actions of sense, and can discourse of flies and dogs, shells and play, horses and liberty ; but when he is strong enough to enter into arts and little institutions, he is at first entertained with trifles and impertinent things, not because he needs them, but because his understanding is no bigger, and little images of things are laid before him, like a cock-boat to a whale, only to play withal ; but before a man comes to be wise, he is half dead with gouts and consumptions, with catarrhs and aches, with sore eyes and a worn-out body. So that, if we must not reckon the life of a man but by the accounts of his reason, he is long before his soul be dressed ; and he is not to be called a man without a wise and an adorned soul, a soul at least furnished with what is necessary towards his well-being : but by that time his soul is thus furnished his body is decayed ; and then you can hardly reckon him to be alive, when his body is possessed by so many degrees of death.

But there is yet another arrest. At first he wants
strength of body, and then he wants the use of reason ;
and when that is come, it is ten to one but he stops by the
impediments of vice, and wants the strength of the spirit;
and we know that body, and soul, and spirit, are the constituent parts of every Christian man. And now let us
consider what that thing is which we call years of discretion. The young man is past his tutors, and arrived at
the bondage of a caitiff spirit ; he is run from discipline,
and is let loose to passion ; the man by this time hath wit
enough to choose his vice, to act his lust, to court his
mistress, to talk confidently, and ignorantly, and perpetually, to despise his betters, to deny nothing to his
appetite, to do things that, when he is indeed a man,
he must for ever be ashamed of ; for this is all the discretion
that most men show in the first stage of their manhood ;
they can discern good from evil ; and they prove their
skill by leaving all that is good, and wallowing in the evils
of folly and an unbridled appetite. And, by this time, the
young man hath contracted vicious habits, and is a beast
in manners, and therefore it will not be fitting to reckon the
beginning of his life ; he is fool in his understanding, and
that is a sad death ; and he is dead in trespasses and sins,
and that is sadder ; so that he hath no life but a natural,
the life of a beast or a tree ; in all other capacities he is
dead ; he neither hath the intellectual nor the spiritual
life, neither the life of a man nor of a Christian ; and this
sad truth lasts too long. For old age seizes upon most
men while they still retain the minds of boys and vicious
youth, doing actions from principles of great folly, and
a mighty ignorance, admiring things useless and hurtful,
and filling up all the dimensions of their abode with
businesses of empty affairs, being at leisure to attend no
virtue : they cannot pray because they are busy, and
because they are passionate ; they cannot communicate
because they have quarrels and intrigues of perplexed

causes, complicated hostilities, and things of the world, and therefore they cannot attend to the things of God ; little considering that they must find a time to die in ; when death comes they must be at leisure for that.   Such men are like sailors loosing from a port, and tossed immediately with a perpetual tempest lasting till their cordage crack, and either they sink or return back again to the same place ; they did not make a voyage, though they were long at sea. The business and impertinent affairs of most men steal all their time, and they are restless in a foolish motion : but this is not the progress of a man ; he is no further advanced in the course of a life, though he reckon many years ; [1] for still his soul is childish and trifling like an untaught boy.

Works.   1651.

[1] Bis jam consul trigesimus instat,
Et numerat paucos vix tua vita dies.—Mart. i. 16.

ON PRAYER

Jeremy Taylor

THERE is no greater argument in the world of our spiritual danger and unwillingness to religion, than the backwardness which most men have always, and all men have sometimes, to say their prayers—so weary of their length, so glad when they are done, so witty to excuse and frustrate an opportunity : and yet all is nothing but a desiring of God to give us the greatest and the best things we can need, and which can make us happy : it is a work so easy, so honourable, and to so great purpose, that in all the instances of religion and providence (except only the incarnation of his Son), God hath not given us a greater argument of his willingness to have us saved, and of our unwillingness to accept it, his goodness and our gracelessness, his infinite condescension and our carelessness and folly, than by rewarding so easy a duty with so great blessings.

MOTIVES TO PRAYER

. . . the prayers of men have saved cities and kingdoms from ruin : prayer hath raised dead men to life, hath stopped the violence of fire, shut the mouths of wild beasts, hath altered the course of nature, caused rain in Egypt, and drought in the sea ; it made the sun to go from west to east, and the moon to stand still, and rocks and mountains to walk ; and it cures diseases without

physic, and makes physic to do the work of nature, and
nature to do the work of grace, and grace to do the work
of God ; and it does miracles of accident and event :
and yet prayer, that does all this, is, of itself, nothing but
an ascent of the mind to God, a desiring things fit to be
desired, and an expression of this desire to God as we can,
and as becomes us. And our unwillingness to pray is
nothing else but a not desiring what we ought passionately
to long for ; or, if we do desire it, it is a choosing rather
to miss our satisfaction and felicity than to ask for it.

Holy Dying. 1651.

OF MYSELF

Abraham Cowley

It is a hard and nice subject for a man to write of himself;
it grates his own heart to say anything of disparagement,
and the reader's ears to hear anything of praise from him.
There is no danger from me of offending him in this kind;
neither my mind, nor my body, nor my fortune, allow
me any materials for that vanity. It is sufficient, for my
own contentment, that they have preserved me from being
scandalous, or remarkable on the defective side. But
besides that, I shall here speak of myself only in relation
to the subject of these precedent discourses, and shall be
likelier thereby to fall into the contempt, than rise up to
the estimation of most people. As far as my memory
can return back into my past life, before I knew or was
capable of guessing what the world, or glories, or business
of it were, the natural affections of my soul gave a secret
bent of aversion from them, as some plants are said to
turn away from others, by an antipathy imperceptible
to themselves, and inscrutable to man's understanding.
Even when I was a very young boy at school, instead of
running about on holidays, and playing with my fellows,
I was wont to steal from them, and walk into the fields,
either alone with a book, or with some one companion,
if I could find any of the same temper. I was then, too,
so much an enemy to constraint, that my masters could
never prevail on me, by any persuasions or encourage-
ments, to learn, without book, the common rules of
grammar, in which they dispensed with me alone, because

they found I made a shift to do the usual exercise out of
my own reading and observation. That I was then of the
same mind as I am now—which, I confess, I wonder at
myself—may appear at the latter end of an ode which
I made when I was but thirteen years old, and which was
then printed, with many other verses. The beginning of
it is boyish ; but of this part which I here set down, if a
very little were corrected, I should hardly now be much
ashamed.

> This only grant me, that my means may lie
> Too low for envy, for contempt too high.
>> Some honour I would have,
> Not from great deeds, but good alone ;
> Th' unknown are better than ill known.
>> Rumour can ope the grave ;
> Acquaintance I would have ; but when 't depends
> Not on the number, but the choice of friends.
>
> Books should, not business, entertain the light,
> And sleep, as undisturbed as death, the night.
>> My house a cottage, more
> Than palace, and should fitting be
> For all my use, no luxury,
>> My garden painted o'er
> With Nature's hand, not Art's ; and pleasures yield,
> Horace might envy in his Sabine field.
>
> Thus would I double my life's fading space,
> For he that runs it well, twice runs his race.
>> And in this true delight,
> These unbought sports, that happy state,
> I would not fear nor wish my fate,
>> But boldly say each night,
> To-morrow let my sun his beam's display,
> Or in clouds hide them ; I have lived to-day.

You may see by it I was even then acquainted with the poets, for the conclusion is taken out of Horace ; and perhaps it was the immature and immoderate love of them which stamped first, or rather engraved, the characters in me. They were like letters cut in the bark of a young tree, which, with the tree, still grow proportionably. But how this love came to be produced in me so early is a hard question : I believe I can tell the particular little chance that filled my head first with such chimes of verse, as have never since left ringing there ; for I remember when I began to read, and take some pleasure in it, there was wont to lie in my mother's parlour—I know not by what accident, for she herself never in her life read any book but of devotion—but there was wont to lie Spenser's works ; this I happened to fall upon, and was infinitely delighted with the stories of the knights, and giants, and monsters, and brave houses, which I found everywhere there—though my understanding had little to do with all this—and by degrees, with the tinkling of the rhyme, and dance of the numbers ; so that I think I had read him all over before I was twelve years old. With these affections of mind, and my heart wholly set upon letters, I went to the university ; but was soon torn from thence by that public violent storm, which would suffer nothing to stand where it did, but rooted up every plant, even from the princely cedars, to me, the hyssop. Yet I had as good fortune as could have befallen me in such a tempest ; for I was cast by it into the family of one of the best persons, and into the court of one of the best princesses in the world. Now, though I was here engaged in ways most contrary to the original design of my life ; that is, into much company, and no small business, and into a daily sight of greatness, both militant and triumphant—for that was the state then of the English and the French courts—yet all this was so far from altering my opinion, that it only added the confirmation of reason to that which was before but natural inclination. I saw plainly all the paint of that kind of life, the nearer I came to it ; and that beauty which I did not fall in love with, when, for aught I knew, it was real, was not like to bewitch or entice me when I saw it was adulterate. I met with several great persons, whom I liked very well, but could not perceive that any part of their greatness was to be liked or desired, no more than I would be glad or content to be in a storm, though I saw many ships which rid safely and bravely in it. A storm would not agree with my stomach, if it did with my courage ; though I was in a crowd of as good company as could be found anywhere, though I was in business of great and honourable trust, though I eat at the best table, and enjoyed the best conveniences for present subsistence that ought to be desired by a man of my condition, in banishment and public distresses ; yet I could not abstain from renewing my old schoolboy's wish, in a copy of verses to the same effect :

> Well, then, I now do plainly see
> This busy world and I shall ne'er agree, etc.

And I never then proposed to myself any other advantage from his majesty's happy restoration, but the getting into some moderately convenient retreat in the country, which I thought in that case I might easily have compassed, as well as some others, who, with no greater probabilities or pretences, have arrived to extraordinary fortunes. But I had before written a shrewd prophecy against myself, and I think Apollo inspired me in the truth, though not in the elegance of it—

> Thou neither great at court, nor in the war,
> Nor at the Exchange shalt be, nor at the wrangling bar ;
> Content thyself with the small barren praise
> Which thy neglected verse does raise, etc.

However, by the failing of the forces which I had expected, I did not quit the design which I had resolved on ; I cast myself into it a *corpus perditum*, without making capitulations, or taking counsel of fortune. But God laughs at man, who says to his soul, Take thy ease : I met presently not only with many little encumbrances and impediments, but with so much sickness—a new misfortune to me—as would have spoiled the happiness of an emperor as well as mine. Yet I do neither repent nor alter my course ; *Non ego perfidum dixi sacramentum.* Nothing shall separate me from a mistress which I have loved so long, and have now at last married ; though she neither has brought me a rich portion, nor lived yet so quietly with me as I hoped from her.

> Nec vos dulcissima mundi
> Nomina, vos musæ, libertas, otia, libri,
> Hortique, sylvæque, animâ remanente relinquam.

> Nor by me e'er shall you,
> You of all names the sweetest and the best,
> You muses, books, and liberty, and rest ;
> You gardens, fields, and woods forsaken be,
> As long as life itself forsakes not me.

Several Discourses. 1668.

OF THE DANGERS OF AN HONEST MAN IN MUCH COMPANY

Abraham Cowley

If twenty thousand naked *Americans* were not able to resist the assaults of but twenty well-armed *Spaniards*, I see little possibility for one honest man to defend himself against twenty thousand knaves, who are all furnished *cap-à-pie*, with the defensive arms of worldly prudence, and the offensive too of craft and malice. He will find no less odds than this against him, if he have much to do in humane affairs. The only advice therefore which I can give him, is, to be sure not to venture his person any longer in the open campaign, to retreat and entrench himself, to stop up all avenues, and draw up all bridges against so numerous an enemy. The truth of it is, that a man in much business must either make himself a knave, or else the world will make him a fool: and if the injury went no further than the being laughed at, a wise man would content himself with the revenge of retaliation; but the case is much worse, for these civil *cannibals* too, as well as the wild ones, not only dance about such a taken stranger, but at last devour him. A sober man cannot get too soon out of drunken company, though they be never so kind and merry among themselves, 'tis not unpleasant only, but dangerous to him. Do ye wonder that a virtuous man should love to be alone? It is hard for him to be otherwise; he is so, when he is among ten thousand: neither is the solitude so uncomfortable to be alone without any other

creature, as it is to be alone, in the midst of wild beasts.
Man is to man all kind of beasts, a fawning dog, a roaring
lion, a thieving fox, a robbing wolf, a dissembling crocodile, a treacherous decoy, and a rapacious vulture. The
civilest, methinks, of all nations, are those whom we
account the most barbarous, there is some moderation and
good nature in the *Toupinambaltians* who eat no men but
their enemies, whilst we learned and polite and Christian
Europeans, like so many pikes and sharks, prey upon everything that we can swallow. It is the great boast of eloquence and philosophy, that they first congregated men
dispersed, united them into societies, and built up the
houses and the walls of cities. I wish they could unravel
all they had woven ; that we might have our woods and
our innocence again instead of our castles and our policies.
They have assembled many thousands of scattered people
into one body : 'tis true, they have done so, they have
brought them together into cities, to cozen, and into
armies to murder one another ; they found them hunters
and fishers of wild creatures, they have made them
hunters and fishers of their brethren ; they boast to have
reduced them to a state of peace, when the truth is, they
have only taught them an art of war ; they have framed,
I must confess, wholesome laws for the restraint of vice,
but they raised first that devil which now they conjure
and cannot bind ; though there were before no punishments for wickedness, yet there was less committed
because there were no rewards for it. But the men who
praise philosophy from this topic are much deceived ;
let oratory answer for itself, the tinkling perhaps of that
may unite a swarm : it never was the work of philosophy
to assemble multitudes, but to regulate only, and govern
them when they were assembled, to make the best of an
evil, and bring them, as much as is possible, to unity again.
Avarice and ambition only were the first builders of towns,
and founders of Empire ; they said, *Go to, let us build us*

a city and a tower whose top may reach unto heaven, and let us
make us a name, lest we be scattered abroad upon the face of
the earth. What was the beginning of *Rome*, the *metropolis*
of all the word ? what was it, but a concourse of thieves,
and a sanctuary of criminals ? it was justly named by the
augury of no less than twelve vultures, and the founder
cemented his walls with the blood of his brother ; not
unlike to this was the beginning even of the first town too
in the world, and such is the original sin of most cities :
their actual increase daily with their age and growth ;
the more people, the more wicked all of them ; every one
brings in his part to inflame the contagion, which becomes
at last so universal and so strong, that no precepts can be
sufficient preservatives, nor anything secure our safety, but
flight from among the infected. We ought in the choice
of a situation to regard above all things the healthfulness
of the place, and the healthfulness of it for the mind rather
than for the body. But suppose (which is hardly to be
supposed) we had antidote enough against this poison ;
nay, suppose further, we were always and at all pieces
armed and provided both against the assaults of hostility,
and the mines of treachery, 'twill yet be but an uncomfortable life to be ever in alarms, though we were compassed
round with fire, to defend ourselves from wild beasts, the
lodging would be unpleasant, because we must always be
obliged to watch that fire, and to fear no less the defects of
our guard, than the diligences of our enemy. The sum
of this is, that a virtuous man is in danger to be trod upon
and destroyed in the crowd of his contraries, nay, which is
worse, to be changed and corrupted by them, and that 'tis
impossible to escape both these inconveniences without so
much caution, as will take away the whole quiet, that is,
the happiness of his life. Ye see then, what he may lose,
but, I pray, What can he get there ?   *Quid Romæ faciam ?*
Mentiri nescio. What should a man of truth and honesty
do at Rome ? he can neither understand, nor speak the

language of the place ; a naked man may swim in the sea, but 'tis not the way to catch fish there ; they are likelier to devour him, than he them, if he bring no nets, and use no deceits. I think therefore it was wise and friendly advice which *Martial* gave to *Fabian*, when he met him newly arrived at *Rome*.

Honest and poor, faithful in word and thought ;
What has thee, *Fabian*, to the city brought ?
Thou neither the buffoon, nor bawd canst play,
Nor with false whispers th' innocent betray :
Nor corrupt wives, nor from rich beldams get
A living by thy industry and sweat ;
Nor with vain promises and projects cheat,
Nor bribe or flatter any of the great.
But you're a man of learning, prudent, just ;
A man of courage, firm, and fit for trust.
Why you may stay, and live unenvied here ;
But (faith) go back, and keep you where you were.

Nay, if nothing of all this were in the case, yet the very sight of uncleanness is loathsome to the cleanly ; the sight of folly and impiety vexatious to the wise and pious.

Lucretius, by his favour, though a good poet, was but an ill-natured man, when he said, It was delightful to see other men in a great storm : And no less ill-natur'd should I think *Democritus*, who laughed at all the world, but that he retired himself so much out of it, that we may perceive he took no great pleasure in that kind of mirth. I have been drawn twice or thrice by company to go to *Bedlam*, and have seen others very much delighted with the fantastical extravagancy of so many various madnesses, which upon me wrought so contrary an effect, that I always returned, not only melancholy, but even sick with the sight, My compassion there was perhaps too tender, for I meet a thousand madmen abroad, without any perturbation ; though, to weigh the matter justly, the total loss of reason is less deplorable than the total depravation of it. An exact judge of human blessings, of riches, honours, beauty, even of wit itself, should pity the abuse of them more than the want.

Briefly, though a wise man could pass never so securely through the great roads of human life, yet he will meet perpetually with so many objects and occasions of compassion, grief, shame, anger, hatred, indignation, and all passions but envy (for he will find nothing to deserve that) that he had better strike into some private path ; nay, go so far, if he could, out of the common way, *Vt nec facta audiat Pelopidarum* ; that he might not so much as hear of the actions of the sons of *Adam*. But, whither shall we fly then ? into the deserts, like the ancient hermits ?

> Quia terra patet fera regnat Erynnis,
> In facinus jurasse putes.

One would think that all mankind had bound themselves by an oath to do all the wickedness they can ; that they had all (as the Scripture speaks) sold themselves to sin : the difference only is, that some are a little more crafty (and but a little God knows) in making of the bargain. I thought when I went first to dwell in the country, that without doubt I should have met there with the simplicity of the old poetical Golden Age ; I thought to have found no inhabitants there, but such as the shepherds of Sir *Phil. Sydney* in *Arcadia*, or of *Monsieur d'Vrfe* upon the banks of *Lignon* ; and began to consider with myself, which way I might recommend no less to posterity the happiness and innocence of the men of *Chertsea* : but to confess the truth, I perceived quickly, by infallible demonstrations, that I was still in Old *England*, and not in *Arcadia*, or *La Forrest* ; that if I could not content myself with anything less than exact fidelity in human conversation, I had almost as good go back and seek for it in the Court, or the Exchange, or Westminster Hall. I ask again then whither shall we fly, or what shall we do ? The world may so come in a man's way, that he cannot choose but salute it, he must take heed though not to go a whoring after it. If by any lawful vocation, or just necessity men happen to be married to it, I can only give them St. *Paul's* advice. *Brethren, the time is short, it remains that they that have wives be as though they had none. But I would that all men were even as I myself.*

In all cases they must be sure that they do *Mumdum ducere*, and not *Mundo nubere.* They must retain the superiority and headship over it : happy are they who can get out of the sight of this deceitful beauty, that they may not be led so much as into temptation ; who have not only quitted the metropolis, but can abstain from ever seeing the next market town of their country.

CLAUDIAN'S OLD MAN OF VERONA

Happy the man, who his whole time doth bound
Within th' enclosure of his little ground.
Happy the man, whom the same humble place,
(Th' hereditary cottage of his race)
From his first rising infancy has known,
And by degrees sees gently bending down,
With natural propension to that earth
Which both preserv'd his life, and gave him birth.
Him no false distant lights by fortune set,
Could ever into foolish wand'rings get.
He never dangers either saw, or fear'd :
The dreadful storms at sea he never heard.
He never heard the shrill alarms of war,
Or the worse noises of the lawyer's bar.
No change of consuls marks to him the year,
The change of seasons is his calendar.

The cold and heat, winter and summer shows,
Autumn by fruits, and spring by flow'rs he knows.
He measures time by landmarks, and has found
For the whole day the dial of his ground.
A neighbouring wood born with himself he sees,
And loves his old contemporary trees.
H'as only heard of near *Verona's* name,
And knows it like the *Indies*, but by fame.
Does with a like concernment notice take
Of the Red Sea, and of *Benacus* Lake.
Thus health and strength he to' a third age enjoys,
And sees a long posterity of boys.
About the spacious world let others roam,
The voyage life is longest made at home.

Several Discourses.   1668.

A CHILD'S VISION OF THE WORLD

Thomas Traherne

CERTAINLY Adam in Paradise had not more sweet and curious apprehensions of the world, than I when I was a child.

All appeared new, and strange at first, inexpressibly rare and delightful and beautiful. I was a little stranger, which at my entrance into the world was saluted and surrounded with innumerable joys. My knowledge was Divine. I knew by intuition those things which since my Apostasy, I collected again by the highest reason. My very ignorance was advantageous. I seemed as one brought into the Estate of Innocence. All things were spotless and pure and glorious : yea, and infinitely mine, and joyful and precious. I knew not that there were any sins, or complaints or laws. I dreamed not of poverties, contentions or vices. All tears and quarrels were hidden from mine eyes. Everything was at rest, free and immortal. I knew nothing of sickness or death or rents or exaction, either for tribute or bread. In the absence of these I was entertained like an Angel with the works of God in their splendour and glory, I saw all the peace of Eden ; Heaven and Earth did sing my Creator's praises, and could not make more melody to Adam, than to me. All Time was Eternity, and a perpetual Sabbath. Is it not strange, that an infant should be heir of the whole World, and see those mysteries which the books of the learned never unfold ?

The corn was orient and immortal wheat, which never

should be reaped, nor was ever sown. I thought it had stood from everlasting to everlasting. The dust and stones of the street were as precious as gold : the gates were at first the end of the world. The green trees when I saw them first through one of the gates transported and ravished me, their sweetness and unusual beauty made my heart to leap, and almost mad with ecstasy, they were such strange and wonderful things. The Men ! O what venerable and reverend creatures did the aged seem ! Immortal Cherubims ! And young men glittering and sparkling Angels, and maids strange seraphic pieces of life and beauty ! Boys and girls tumbling in the street, and playing, were moving jewels. I knew not that they were born or should die ; but all things abided eternally as they were in their proper places. Eternity was manifest in the Light of the Day, and something infinite behind everything appeared : which talked with my expectation and moved my desire. The city seemed to stand in Eden, or to be built in Heaven. The streets were mine, the temple was mine, the people were mine, their clothes and gold and silver were mine, as much as their sparkling eyes, fair skins and ruddy faces. The skies were mine, and so were the sun and moon and stars, and all the World was mine ; and I the only spectator and enjoyer of it. I knew no churlish proprieties,[1] nor bounds, nor divisions : but all proprieties and divisions were mine : all treasures and the possessors of them. So that with much ado I was corrupted, and made to learn the dirty devices of this world. Which now I unlearn, and become, as it were, a little child again that I may enter into the Kingdom of God.

Centuries of Meditation.

[1] Properties.

OF THE WORLD

George Savile, Lord Halifax

It is from the Shortness of Thought, that Men imagine there is any great Variety in the World.

Time hath thrown a Vail upon the Faults of former Ages, or else we should see the same Deformities we condemn in the present Times.

When a Man looketh upon the Rules that are made, he will think there can be no Faults in the World ; and when he looketh upon the Faults, there are so many he will be tempted to think there are no Rules.

They are not to be reconciled, otherwise than by concluding that which is called *Frailty* is the uncurable *Nature* of Mankind.

A Man that understandeth the World must be weary of it ; and a Man who doth not, for that Reason ought not to be pleased with it.

The Uncertainty of what is to come, is such a dark Cloud, that neither Reason nor Religion can quite break through it ; and the Condition of Mankind is to be weary of what we do know, and afraid of what we do not.

The World is beholden to *generous Mistakes* for the greatest Part of the Good that is done in it.

Our *Vices* and *Virtues* couple with one another, and get Children that resemble both their Parents.

If a Man can hardly inquire into a Thing he undervalueth, how can a Man of good Sense take pains to understand the World ?

To understand the World, and to like it, are two things not easily to be reconciled.

That which is called an Able Man is a great Over-Valuer of the World, and all that belongeth to it.

All that can be said of him is, that he maketh the best of the General Mistake.

It is the Fools and Knaves that make the Wheels of the World turn. *They* are *the World* ; those few who have Sense or Honesty sneak up and down single, but never go in Herds.

To be too much *troubled* is a worse way of over-valuing the World than the being too much *pleased*.

A Man that steps aside from the World, and hath leisure to observe it without Interest or Design, thinks all Mankind as mad as they think him, for not agreeing with them in their Mistakes.

Moral Thoughts and Reflections. 1750.

MEDITATION ON A BROOMSTICK

Jonathan Swift

This single stick, which you now behold ingloriously
lying in that neglected corner, I once knew in a flourishing
state in a forest ; it was full of sap, full of leaves, and full
of boughs ; but now in vain does the busy art of man
pretend to vie with nature, by tying that withered bundle
of twigs to its sapless trunk ; it is now at best but the
reverse of what it was, a tree turned upside down, the
branches on the earth, and the root in the air ; it is now
handled by every dirty wench, condemned to do her
drudgery, and, by a capricious kind of fate, destined to
make her things clean, and be nasty itself ; at length, worn
out to the stumps in the service of the maids, it is either
thrown out of doors, or condemned to the last use of
kindling a fire.   When I beheld this, I sighed, and said
within myself : Surely mortal man is a broomstick !
nature sent him into the world strong and lusty, in a
thriving condition, wearing his own hair on his head, the
proper branches of this reasoning vegetable, until the axe of
intemperance has lopped off his green boughs, and left
him a withered trunk ; he then flies to art, and puts on a
periwig, valuing himself upon an unnatural bundle of
hairs, all covered with powder, that never grew on his
head ; but now should this our broomstick pretend to
enter the scene, proud of those birchen spoils it never bore,
and all covered with dust, though the sweepings of the
finest lady's chamber, we should be apt to ridicule and

despise its vanity.   Partial judges that we are of our own excellences, and other men's defaults !

But a broomstick, perhaps you will say, is an emblem of a tree standing on its head : and pray, what is man but a topsy-turvy creature, his animal faculties perpetually mounted on his rational, his head where his heels should be—grovelling on the earth ! and yet, with all his faults, he sets up to be a universal reformer and corrector of abuses, a remover of grievances ; rakes into every slut's corner of nature, bringing hidden corruptions to the light, and raises a mighty dust where there was none before, sharing deeply all the while in the very same pollutions he pretends to sweep away.   His last days are spent in slavery to women, and generally the least deserving ; till, worn to the stumps, like his brother-besom, he is either kicked out of doors, or made use of to kindle flames for others to warm themselves by.

Miscellanies.   1704.

SIR ROGER AT HOME

Joseph Addison

HAVING often received an Invitation from my Friend Sir ROGER DE COVERLEY to pass away a Month with him in the Country, I last week accompanied him thither, and am settled with him for some Time at his Country-house, where I intend to form several of my ensuing Speculations. Sir ROGER, who is very well acquainted with my Humour, lets me rise and go to Bed when I please, dine at his own Table or in my Chamber as I think fit, sit still and say nothing without bidding me be merry. When the Gentlemen of the County come to see him, he only shows me at a distance : As I have been walking in his Fields I have observed them stealing a Sight of me over an Hedge, and have heard the Knight desiring them not to let me see them for that I hated to be stared at.

I am the more at Ease in Sir Roger's Family, because it consists of sober and staid Persons ; for as the Knight is the best Master in the World, he seldom changes his Servants ; and as he is beloved by all about him, his Servants never care for leaving him : By this Means his Domesticks are all in Years, and grown old with their Master. You would take his Valet de Chambre for his Brother, his Butler is grey-headed, his Groom is one of the gravest Men that I have ever seen, and his Coachman has the Looks of a Privy-Councillor. You see the Goodness of the Master even in the old House-dog, and in a grey Pad that is kept in the Stable with great Care and tenderness out of Regard to his past Services, tho' he has been useless for several Years.

I could not but observe with a great deal of Pleasure the Joy that appeared in the Countenances of these ancient Domesticks upon my Friend's Arrival at his Country-Seat. Some of them could not refrain from Tears at the Sight of their old Master ; every one of them press'd forward to do something for him, and seemed discouraged if they were not employed. At the same Time the good old Knight, with a Mixture of the Father and the Master of the Family, tempered the Enquiries after his own affairs with several kind Questions relating to themselves. This Humanity and Good nature engages every Body to him, so that when he is pleasant upon any of them, all his Family are in good Humour, and none so much as the Person whom He diverts himself with : On the Contrary, if he coughs, or betrays any Infirmity of old Age, it is easy for a Stander-by to observe a secret Concern in the Looks of all his Servants.

My worthy Friend has put me under the particular Care of his Butler, who is a very prudent Man, and, as well as the rest of his Fellow-Servants, wonderfully desirous of pleasing me, because they have often heard their Master talk of me as of his particular Friend.

My chief Companion, when Sir ROGER is diverting himself in the Woods or the Fields, is a very venerable Man who is ever with Sir ROGER, and has lived at his House in the Nature of a Chaplain above thirty Years. This Gentleman is a Person of good Sense and some Learning, of a very regular Life and obliging Conversation : He heartily loves Sir ROGER, and knows that he is very much in the old Knight's Esteem ; so that he lives in the Family rather as a Relation than a Dependant.

I have observed in several of my Papers that my Friend Sir ROGER, amidst all his good Qualities, is something of an Humourist ; and that his Virtues, as well as Imperfections, are as it were tinged by a certain Extravagance, which makes them particularly *his*, and distinguishes them from those of other Men. This Cast of Mind, as it is generally very innocent in itself, so it renders his Conversation highly agreeable, and more delightful than the same Degree of Sense and Virtue would appear in their common and ordinary Colours. As I was walking with him last Night, he ask'd me how I liked the good Man whom I have just now mentioned ? and without staying for my Answer, told me, That he was afraid of being insulted with Latin and Greek at his own Table ; for which Reason, he desired a particular Friend of his at the University to find him out a Clergyman rather of plain Sense than much Learning, of a good Aspect, a clear Voice, a sociable Temper, and, if possible, a Man that understood a little of Back-Gammon. " My friend," says Sir ROGER, " found me out this Gentleman, who, besides the Endowments required of him, is, they tell me, a good Scholar though he does not shew it. I have given him the Parsonage of the Parish ; and because I know his Value, have settled upon him a good Annuity for Life. If he out-lives me, he shall find that he was higher in my Esteem than perhaps he thinks he is. He has now been with me thirty Years ; and though he does not know I have taken Notice of it, has never in all that Time asked anything of me for himself, tho' he is every Day solliciting me for something in Behalf of one or other of my Tenants his Parishioners. There has not been a Law-Suit in the Parish since he has lived among them : If any Dispute arises, they apply themselves to him for the Decision ; if they do not acquiesce in his judgment, which I think never happened above once, or twice at most, they appeal to me. At his first settling with me, I made him a Present of all the good Sermons which have been printed in *English*, and only begged of him that every *Sunday* he would pronounce one of them in the Pulpit. Accordingly, he has digested them into such a Series, that they follow one another naturally, and make a continued System of practical Divinity."

As Sir ROGER was going on in his Story, the Gentleman we were talking of came up to us ; and upon the Knight's asking him who preached to Morrow (for it was *Saturday* Night) told us, the Bishop of St. *Asaph* in the Morning, and Doctor *South* in the Afternoon.   He then shewed us his List of Preachers for the whole Year, where I saw with a great deal of Pleasure Archbishop *Tillotson*, Bishop *Saunderson*, Doctor *Barrow*, Doctor *Calamy*, with several living Authors who have published Discourses of Practical Divinity.   I no sooner saw this venerable Man in the Pulpit, but I very much approved of my Friend's insisting upon the Qualifications of a good Aspect and a clear Voice ; for I was so charmed with the Gracefulness of his Figure and Delivery, as well as with the Discourses he pro- nounced, that I think I never passed any Time more to my Satisfaction.   A Sermon repeated after this Manner, is like the Composition of a Poet in the Mouth of a graceful Actor.

I could heartily wish that more of our Country-Clergy would follow this Example ; and instead of wasting their Spirits in laborious Compositions of their own, would endeavour after a handsome Elocution, and all those other Talents that are proper to enforce what has been penned by greater Masters.   This would not only be more easy to themselves, but more edifying to the People.

The Spectator.   1711.

SIR ROGER AT CHURCH

JOSEPH ADDISON

I AM always very well pleased with a Country *Sunday*; and think, if keeping holy the Seventh Day were only a human Institution, it would be the best Method that could have been thought of for the polishing and civilizing of Mankind. It is certain the Country-People would soon degenerate into a kind of Savages and Barbarians, were there not such frequent Returns of a stated Time, in which the whole Village meet together with their best Faces, and in their cleanliest Habits, to converse with one another upon indifferent Subjects, hear their Duties explained to them, and join together in Adoration of the Supreme Being. *Sunday* clears away the Rust of the whole Week, not only as it refreshes in their Minds the Notions of Religion, but as it puts both the Sexes upon appearing in their most agreeable Forms, and exerting all such Qualities as are apt to give them a Figure in the Eye of the Village. A Country-Fellow distinguishes himself as much in the *Churchyard*, as a Citizen does upon the *Change*; the whole Parish-Politicks being generally discuss'd in that Place either after Sermon or before the Bell rings.

My Friend Sir ROGER being a good Churchman, has beautified the Inside of his Church with several Texts of his own chusing: He has likewise given a handsome Pulpit-Cloth, and railed in the Communion-Table at his own Expense. He has often told me, that at his coming to his Estate he found his Parishioners very irregular ; and that in order to make them kneel and join in the Responses, he gave every one of them a Hassock and a Common-prayer Book : and at the same Time employed an itinerant Singing-Master, who goes about the Country for that Purpose, to instruct them rightly in the Tunes of the Psalms ; upon which they now very much value themselves, and indeed out-do most of the Country Churches that I have ever heard.

As Sir ROGER is Landlord to the whole Congregation, he keeps them in very good Order, and will suffer no Body to sleep in it besides himself ; for if by Chance he has been surprized into a short Nap at Sermon, upon recovering out of it he stands up and looks about him, and if he sees any Body else nodding, either wakes them himself, or sends his Servants to them.   Several other of the old Knight's Particularities break out upon these Occasions : Sometimes he will be lengthening out a Verse in the Singing-Psalms, half a Minute after the rest of the Congregation have done with it ; sometimes, when he is pleased with the Matter of his Devotion, he pronounces *Amen* three or four times to the same Prayer ; and some-times stands up when every Body else is upon their Knees, to count the Congregation, or see if any of his Tenants are missing.

I was yesterday very much surprized to hear my old Friend, in the Midst of the Service, calling out to one *John Matthews* to mind what he was about, and not dis-turb the Congregation.   This *John Matthews* it seems is remarkable for being an idle Fellow, and at that Time was kicking his Heels for his Diversion.   This Authority of the Knight, though exerted in that odd Manner which accompanies him in all Circumstances of Life, has a very good Effect upon the Parish, who are not polite enough to see anything ridiculous in his Behaviour ; besides that, the general good Sense and Worthiness of his Character, make his friends observe these little Singularities as Foils that rather set off than blemish his good Qualities.

As soon as the Sermon is finished, no Body presumes to stir till Sir ROGER is gone out of the Church. The Knight walks down from his Seat in the Chancel between a double Row of his Tenants, that stand bowing to him on each Side ; and every now and then enquires how such an one's Wife, or Mother, or Son, or Father do whom he does not see at Church ; which is understood as a secret Reprimand to the Person that is absent.

The Chaplain has often told me, that upon a Catechizing-day, when Sir ROGER has been pleased with a Boy that answers well, he has ordered a Bible to be given him next Day for his Encouragement ; and sometimes accompanies it with a Flitch of Bacon to his Mother. Sir ROGER has likewise added five Pounds a Year to the Clerk's Place ; and that he may encourage the young Fellows to make themselves perfect in the Church-Service, has promised upon the Death of the present Incumbent, who is very old, to bestow it according to Merit.

The fair Understanding between Sir ROGER and his Chaplain, and their mutual Concurrence in doing Good, is the more remarkable, because the very next Village is famous for the Differences and Contentions that rise between the Parson and the 'Squire, who live in a per-petual State of War. The Parson is always preaching at the 'Squire, and the 'Squire to be revenged on the Parson never comes to Church. The 'Squire has made all his Tenants Atheists and Tithe-Stealers ; while the Parson instructs them every *Sunday* in the Dignity of his Order, and insinuates to them in almost every Sermon, that he is a better Man than his Patron. In short, Matters are come to such an Extremity, that the 'Squire has not said his Prayers either in publick or private this half Year ; and that the Parson threatens him, if he does not mend his Manners, to pray for him in the Face of the whole Congregation.

Feuds of this Nature, though too frequent in the Country, are very fatal to the ordinary People ; who are so used to be dazled with Riches, that they pay as much Deference to the Understanding of a Man of an Estate, as of a Man of Learning ; and are very hardly brought to regard any Truth, how important soever it may be, that is preached to them, when they know there are several Men of five hundred a Year who do not believe it.

The Spectator.   1711.

SIR ROGER AT THE PLAY

JOSEPH ADDISON

MY Friend Sir ROGER DE COVERLEY, when we last met together at the Club, told me that he had a great mind to see the new Tragedy with me, assuring me at the same Time, that he had not been at a Play these twenty Years. The last I saw, says Sir ROGER, was the *Committee*, which I should not have gone to neither, had I not been told before-hand that it was a good Church of *England* Comedy. He then proceeded to enquire of me who this Distress'd Mother was, and upon hearing that she was *Hector's* Widow, he told me, that her Husband was a brave Man, and that when he was a School-Boy, he had read his Life at the end of the Dictionary. My Friend asked me, in the next Place, if there would not be some Danger in coming home late, in case the *Mohocks* should be abroad. I assure you, says he, I thought I had fallen into their hands last Night, for I observ'd two or three lusty black Men that followed me half way up *Fleet Street*, and mended their Pace behind me, in Proportion as I put on to get away from them. You must know, continued the Knight with a Smile, I fancied they had a mind to *hunt* me ; for I remember an honest Gentleman in my Neighbourhood, who was serv'd such a Trick in King *Charles* the Second's Time ; for which Reason he has not ventured himself in Town ever since. I might have shown them very good Sport, had this been their Design, for as I am an old Fox-hunter, I should have turned and dodged, and have play'd them a thousand Tricks they had never seen in their Lives before. Sir ROGER added, that if these Gentlemen had any such Intention, they did not succeed very well in it ; for I threw them out, says he, at the End of *Norfolk Street*, where I doubled the Corner, and got Shelter in my Lodgings before they could imagine what was become of me. However, says the Knight, if Captain SENTRY will make one with us to Morrow Night, and if you will both of you call upon me about Four a-Clock, that we may be at the House before it is full, I will have my own Coach in Readiness to attend you, for *John* tells me he has got the Fore-Wheels mended.

The Captain, who did not fail to meet me there at the appointed Hour, bid Sir ROGER fear nothing, for that he had put on the same Sword which he made use of at the Battel of *Steenkirk*. Sir ROGER's Servants, and among the rest my old Friend the Butler, had, I found, provided themselves with good oaken Plants, to attend their Master upon this Occasion. When we had plac'd him in his Coach, with my self at his Left hand, the Captain before him, and his Butler at the Head of his Footmen in the Rear, we convoy'd him in Safety to the Play-house ; where, after having march'd up the Entry in good Order, the Captain and I went in with him, and seated him betwixt us in the Pit. As soon as the House was full, and the Candles lighted, my old Friend stood up and looked about him with that Pleasure, which a Mind seasoned with Humanity naturally feels in it self, at the Sight of a Multitude of People who seem pleased with one another, and partake of the same common Entertainment. I could not but fancy to my self, as the old Man stood up in the Middle of the Pit, that he made a very proper Center to a Tragick Audience. Upon the Entring of *Pyrrhus*, the Knight told me, that he did not believe the King of *France* himself had a better Strut. I was indeed very attentive to my old Friend's Remarks, because I looked upon them as a Piece

of Natural Criticism, and was well pleased to hear him
at the Conclusion of almost every Scene, telling me that
he could not imagine how the Play would end. One while
he appear'd much concerned for *Andromache ;* and a little
while after as much for *Hermione ;* and was extremely
puzzled to think what would become of *Pyrrhus.*

When Sir ROGER saw *Andromache's* obstinate Refusal
to her Lover's Importunities, he whispered me in the Ear,
that he was sure she would never have him ; to which he
added, with a more than ordinary Vehemence, You can't
imagine, Sir, what 'tis to have to do with a Widow.
Upon *Pyrrhus* his threatening afterwards to leave her, the
Knight shook his Head, and muttered to himself, Ay, do
if you can. This Part dwelt so much upon my Friend's
Imagination, that at the Close of the Third Act, as I was
thinking of something else, he whispered in my Ear,
These Widows, Sir, are the most perverse Creatures in
the World. But pray, says he, you that are a Critick, is
the Play according to your Dramatick Rules, as you call
them ? Should your People in Tragedy always talk to be
understood ? Why, there is not a single Sentence in this
Play that I do not know the Meaning of.

The Fourth Act very luckily begun before I had Time
to give the old Gentleman an Answer ; Well, says the
Knight, sitting down with great Satisfaction, I suppose
we are now to see *Hector's* Ghost. He then renewed his
Attention, and, from Time to Time, fell a praising the
Widow. He made, indeed, a little Mistake as to one of
her Pages, whom at his first Entring, he took for *Astyanax* ;
but he quickly set himself right in that Particular, though,
at the same time, he owned he should have been very glad
to have seen the little Boy, who, says he, must needs be a
very fine Child by the Account that is given of him. Upon
Hermione's going off with a menace to *Pyrrhus,* the Audience
gave a loud Clap, to which Sir ROGER added, On my
Word, a notable Young Baggage.

As there was a very remarkable Silence and Stillness in the Audience during the whole Action, it was natural for them to take the Opportunity of these Intervals between the Acts, to express their Opinion of the Players, and of their respective Parts. Sir ROGER hearing a Cluster of them praise *Orestes*, struck in with them, and told them, that he thought his Friend *Pylades* was a very sensible Man. As they were afterwards applauding *Pyrrhus*, Sir ROGER put in a second time, And let me tell you, says he, though he speaks but little, I like the old Fellow in Whiskers as well as any of them. Captain SENTRY, seeing two or three Waggs who sat near us lean with an attentive Ear towards Sir ROGER, and fearing lest they should smoak the Knight, pluck'd him by the Elbow, and whispered something in his Ear, that lasted till the Opening of the Fifth Act. The Knight was wonderfully attentive to the Account which *Orestes* gives of *Pyrrhus* his Death, and at the Conclusion of it, told me it was such a bloody Piece of Work, that he was glad it was not done upon the Stage. Seeing afterwards *Orestes* in his raving Fit, he grew more than ordinary serious, and took Occasion to moralize (in his Way) upon an evil Conscience, adding that *Orestes, in his Madness, looked as if he saw something.*

As we were the first that came into the House, so we were the last that went out of it ; being resolved to have a clear Passage for our old Friend, whom we did not care to venture among the Justling of the Crowd. Sir ROGER went out fully satisfy'd with his Entertainment, and we guarded him to his Lodgings in the same manner that we brought him to the Play-house ; being highly pleased, for my own Part, not only with the Performance of the excellent Piece which had been presented, but with the Satisfaction which it had given to the good old Man.

The Spectator. 1711.

SIR ROGER AT THE ASSIZES

JOSEPH ADDISON

A MAN'S first Care should be to avoid the Reproaches
of his own Heart ; his next, to escape the Censures of the
World : If the last interferes with the former, it ought to
be entirely neglected ; but otherwise, there cannot be a
greater Satisfaction to an honest Mind, than to see those
Approbations which it gives itself seconded by the
Applauses of the Publick ; A Man is more sure of his
Conduct, when the Verdict which he passes upon his own
Behaviour is thus warranted, and confirmed by the
Opinion of all that know him.

My worthy Friend Sir ROGER is one of those who is not
only at Peace within himself, but beloved and esteemed
by all about him. He receives a suitable Tribute for his
universal Benevolence to mankind, in the Returns of Affection and Good-will, which are paid him by every one that
lives within his Neighbourhood. I lately met with two
or three odd Instances of that general Respect which is
shewn to the good old Knight. He would needs carry
Will. Wimble and myself with him to the County-Assizes :
As we were upon the Road *Will. Wimble* joined a couple
of plain Men who rid before us, and conversed with them
for some Time ; during which my Friend Sir ROGER
acquainted me with their Characters.

The first of them, says he, that has a spaniel by his
Side, is a Yeoman of about an hundred Pounds a Year,
an honest Man : He is just within the Game-Act, and
qualified to kill an Hare or a Pheasant : He knocks down

a Dinner with his Gun twice or thrice a Week ; and by that Means lives much cheaper than those who have not so good an Estate as himself. He would be a good Neighbour if he did not destroy so many Partridges : in short, he is a very sensible Man ; shoots flying ; and has been several Times Foreman of the Petty-Jury.

The other that rides along with him is *Tom Touchy*, a Fellow famous for *taking the Law* of every Body. There is not one in the Town where he lives that he has not sued at a Quarter-Sessions. The Rogue had once the Impudence to go to Law with the *Widow*. His head is full of Costs, Damages, and Ejectments : He plagued a couple of honest Gentlemen so long for a Trespass in breaking one of his Hedges, till he was forced to sell the Ground it enclosed to defray the Charges of the Prosecution : His Father left him fourscore Pounds a Year ; but he has *cast* and been cast so often, that he is not now worth thirty. I suppose he is going upon the old Business of the Willow-Tree.

As Sir ROGER was giving me this Account of *Tom Touchy*, *Will. Wimble* and his two Companions stopped short till we came up to them. After having paid their Respects to Sir ROGER, *Will.* told him that Mr. *Touchy* and he must appeal to him upon a Dispute that arose between them. *Will.* it seems had been giving his Fellow Traveller an Account of his Angling one Day in such a Hole ; when *Tom Touchy*, instead of hearing out his Story, told him, that Mr. such an One, if he pleased, might *take the law of him* for fishing in that Part of the River. My Friend Sir ROGER heard them both, upon a round Trot ; and after having paused some Time told them, with the Air of a Man who would not give his Judgment rashly, that *much might be said on both Sides.* They were neither of them dissatisfied with the Knight's Determination, because neither of them found himself in the Wrong by it : Upon which we made the best of our Way to the Assizes.

The Court was sat before Sir ROGER came, but notwithstanding all the Justices had taken their Places upon the Bench, they made Room for the old Knight at the Head of them ; who for his Reputation in the Country took Occasion to whisper in the Judge's Ear, That *he was glad his Lordship had met with so much good Weather in his Circuit.* I was listening to the Proceedings of the Court with much Attention, and infinitely pleased with that great Appearance and Solemnity which so properly accompanies such a publick Administration of our Laws ; when, after about an Hour's Sitting, I observed to my great Surprize, in the midst of a Trial, that my Friend Sir ROGER was getting up to speak. I was in some Pain for him, till I found he had acquitted himself of two or three Sentences, with a Look of much Business and great Intrepidity.

Upon his first Rising the Court was hushed, and a general Whisper ran among the Country-People that Sir ROGER *was up.* The Speech he made was so little to the Purpose, that I shall not trouble my Readers with an account of it ; and I believe was not so much designed by the Knight himself to inform the Court, as to give him a Figure in my Eye, and keep up his Credit in the Country.

I was highly delighted, when the Court rose, to see the Gentlemen of the Country gathering about my old Friend, and striving who should compliment him most ; at the same Time that the ordinary People gazed upon him at a Distance, not a little admiring his Courage, that was not afraid to speak to the Judge.

In our Return home we met with a very odd Accident ; which I cannot forbear relating, because it shews how desirous all who know Sir ROGER are of giving him Marks of their Esteem. When we were arrived upon the Verge of his Estate, we stopped at a little Inn to rest our selves and our Horses. The Man of the House had it seems been formerly a Servant in the Knight's Family ; and to do Honour to his old Master, had some Time since, un-known to Sir ROGER, put him up in a Sign-post before the

Door ; so that the *Knight's Head* had hung out upon the Road about a Week before he himself knew anything of the Matter. As soon as Sir ROGER was acquainted with it, finding that his Servant's Indiscretion proceeded wholly from Affection and Good-will, he only told him that he had made him too high a Compliment ; and when the Fellow seemed to think that could hardly be, added with a more decisive Look, That it was too great an Honour for any Man under a Duke ; but told him at the same time that it might be altered with a very few Touches, and that he himself would be at the Charge of it. Accordingly they got a Painter by the Knight's Directions to add a pair of Whiskers to the Face, and by a little Aggravation of the Features to change it into the *Saracen's Head.* I should not have known this Story, had not the Inn-keeper upon Sir ROGER's alighting told him in my Hearing, That his Honour's head was brought back last Night with the alterations that he had ordered to be made in it. Upon this my Friend with his usual Chearfulness related the Particulars above-mentioned, and ordered the Head to be brought into the Room. I could not forbear discovering greater Expressions of Mirth than ordinary upon the Appearance of this monstrous Face, under which, notwithstanding it was made to frown and stare in a most extraordinary Manner, I could still discover a distant Resemblance of my old Friend. Sir ROGER, upon seeing me laugh, desired me to tell him truly if I thought it possible for people to know him in that Disguise. I at first kept my usual Silence ; but upon the Knight's conjuring me to tell him whether it was not still more like himself than a *Saracen,* I composed my Countenance in the best Manner I could, and replied, *That much might be said on both Sides.*

These several Adventures, with the Knight's Behaviour in them, gave me as pleasant a Day as ever I met with in any of my Travels.

The Spectator.   1711.

THE DEATH OF SIR ROGER

JOSEPH ADDISON

WE last Night received a Piece of ill News at our Club, which very sensibly afflicted every one of us. I question not but my Readers themselves will be troubled at the hearing of it. To keep them no longer in Suspense, Sir ROGER DE COVERLEY *is dead*. He departed this Life at his House in the Country, after a few Weeks' Sickness. Sir ANDREW FREEPORT has a Letter from one of his Correspondents in those Parts, that informs him the old Man caught a Cold at the County Sessions, as he was very warmly promoting an Address of his own penning, in which he succeeded according to his Wishes. But this Particular comes from a Whig Justice of Peace, who was always Sir ROGER'S Enemy and Antagonist. I have Letters both from the Chaplain and Captain *Sentry* which mention Nothing of it, but are filled with many Particulars to the Honour of the good old Man. I have likewise a Letter from the Butler, who took so much Care of me last Summer when I was at the Knight's House. As my Friend the Butler mentions, in the Simplicity of his Heart, several circumstances the others have passed over in Silence, I shall give my Reader a Copy of his Letter without any Alteration or Diminution.

" *Honoured Sir*,
" Knowing that you was my old Master's good Friend, I could not forbear sending you the melancholy News of

his Death, which has afflicted the whole Country, as well
as his poor Servants, who loved him, I may say, better
than we did our Lives. I am afraid he caught his Death
the last County Sessions, where he would go to see
Justice done to a poor Widow Woman, and her Fatherless
Children that had been wronged by a Neighbouring
Gentleman ; for you know, Sir, my good Master was
always the poor Man's Friend. Upon his coming home,
the first Complaint he made was, that he had lost his
Roast-Beef Stomach, not being able to touch a Sirloin,
which was served up according to Custom ; and you know
he used to take a great Delight in it. From that Time forward he grew worse and worse, but still kept a good
Heart to the last. Indeed we were once in great Hope
of his Recovery, upon a kind Message that was sent him
from the Widow Lady whom he had made Love to the
forty last Years of his Life ; but this only proved a
Light'ning before Death. He has bequeathed to this
Lady, as a Token of his Love, a great Pearl Necklace, and
a Couple of Silver Bracelets set with Jewels, which
belonged to my good old Lady, his Mother ; He has
bequeathed the fine white Gelding, that he used to ride
a hunting upon, to his Chaplain, because he thought he
would be kind to him, and has left you all his Books. He
has, moreover, bequeathed to the Chaplain a very pretty
Tenement with good Lands about it. It being a very cold
Day when he made his Will, he left for Mourning, to
every Man in the Parish, a great Frize Coat, and to every
Woman a black Riding-hood. It was a most moving
Sight to see him take Leave of his poor Servants, com-
mending us all for our Fidelity, whilst we were not able
to speak a Word for weeping. As we most of us are
grown gray-headed in our Dear Master's Service, he has
left us Pensions and Legacies, which we may live very
comfortably upon, the remaining Part of our Days. He
has bequeathed a great Deal more in Charity, which is not

yet come to my Knowledge, and it is peremptorily said in the Parish, that he has left Money to build a Steeple to the Church ; for he was heard to say some Time ago, that if he lived two Years longer *Coverley* Church should have a Steeple to it. The Chaplain tells every Body that he made a very good End, and never speaks of him without Tears. He was buried, according to his own Directions, among the Family of the *Coverleys*, on the left Hand of his Father Sir *Arthur*. The Coffin was carried by Six of his Tenants, and the Pall held up by Six of the *Quorum :* The whole Parish followed the Corps with heavy Hearts, and in their Mourning-Suits, the Men in Frize, and the Women in Riding-hoods. Captain *Sentry*, my Master's Nephew, has taken Possession of the Hall-House, and the whole Estate. When my old Master saw him a little before his Death, he shook him by the Hand, and wished him Joy of the Estate which was falling to him, desiring him only to make a good Use of it, and to pay the several Legacies, and the Gifts of Charity which he told him he had left as Quit-rents upon the Estate. The Captain truly seems a courteous Man, though he says but little. He makes much of those whom my Master loved, and shews great Kindness to the old House-dog, that you know my poor Master was so fond of. It wou'd have gone to your Heart to have heard the Moans the dumb Creature made on the Day of my Master's Death. He has ne'er joyed himself since ; no more has any of us. 'Twas the melancholiest Day for the poor People that ever happened in *Worcestershire*. This being all from,

> *Honoured Sir,*
> *Your most sorrowful Servant,*
> Edward Biscuit.

P. S. My Master desired, some Weeks before he died, that a Book which comes up to you by the Carrier should be given to Sir *Andrew Freeport*, in his Name."

This Letter, notwithstanding the poor Butler's Manner of Writing it, gave us such an Idea of our good old Friend, that upon the Reading of it there was not a dry Eye in the Club. Sir *Andrew* opening the Book found it to be a Collection of Acts of Parliament. There was in Particular the Act of Uniformity, with some Passages in it marked by Sir *Roger's* own Hand. Sir *Andrew* found that they related to two or three Points, which he had disputed with Sir *Roger* the last Time he appeared at the Club. Sir *Andrew*, who would have been merry at such an Incident on another Occasion, at the Sight of the Old Man's Handwriting burst into Tears, and put the Book into his Pocket. Captain *Sentry* informs me, that the Knight has left Rings and Mourning for every one in the Club.

The Spectator. 1711.

SIR ROGER'S PORTRAIT GALLERY

Sir Richard Steele

I was this Morning walking in the Gallery, when Sir ROGER enter'd at the end opposite to me, and advancing towards me, said, he was glad to meet me among his Relations the DE COVERLEYS, and hoped I liked the Conversation of so much good Company, who were as silent as my self. I knew he alluded to the Pictures, and as he is a Gentleman who does not a little value himself upon his ancient Descent, I expected he would give me some Account of them. We were now arrived at the upper End of the Gallery, when the Knight faced towards one of the Pictures, and as we stood before it, he entered into the Matter, after his blunt way of saying things, as they occur to his Imagination, without regular Introduction, or Care to preserve the Appearance of Chain of Thought.

" It is," said he, " worth while to consider the Force of Dress ; and how the Persons of one Age differ from those of another, merely by that only. One may observe also that the General Fashion of one Age has been follow'd by one particular Set of People in another, and by them preserved from one Generation to another. Thus the vast Jetting Coat and small Bonnet, which was the Habit in *Harry* the Seventh's time, is kept on in the Yeoman of the Guard ; not without a good and Politick View, because they look a Foot taller, and a Foot and an half broader : Besides, that the Cap leaves the Face expanded, and consequently more Terrible, and fitter to stand at the Entrance of Palaces.

" This Predecessor of ours, you see, is dressed after this Manner, and his Cheeks would be no larger than mine were he in a Hat as I am. He was the last Man that won a Prize in the Tilt-Yard (which is now a Common Street before *Whitehall*). You see the broken Lance that lyes there by his right Foot : he shivered that Lance of his Adversary all to pieces ; and bearing himself, look you, Sir, in this manner, at the same time he came within the Target of the Gentleman who rode again him, and taking him with incredible Force before him on the Pummel of his Saddle, he in that manner rid the Turnament over, with an Air that shewed he did it rather to perform the Rule of the Lists, than Expose his Enemy ; however, it appeared he knew how to make use of a Victory, and with a gentle Trot he marched up to a Gallery where their Mistress sat (for they were Rivals) and let him down with laudable Courtesy and pardonable Insolence. I don't know but it might be exactly where the Coffee-house is now.

" You are to know this my Ancestor was not only of a military Genius but fit also for the Arts of Peace, for he play'd on the Base-viol as well as any Gentleman at Court ; you see where his Viol hangs by his Basket-hilt Sword. The Action at the Tilt-yard you may be sure won the Fair Lady, who was a Maid of Honour, and the greatest Beauty of her time ; here she stands, the next Picture. You see, Sir, my Great Great Great Grandmother has on the new-fashioned Petticoat, except that the Modern is gathered at the Waste ; my Grandmother appears as if she stood in a large Drum, whereas the Ladies now walk as if they were in a Go-Cart. For all this Lady was bred at Court, she became an Excellent Country-Wife, she brought ten Children, and when I shew you the Library, you shall see in her own hand (allowing for the Difference of the

Language) the best Receipt now in *England* both for an Hasty-Pudding and a Whitepot.

" If you please to fall back a little, because it is necessary to look at the three next Pictures at one View ; these are three Sisters. She on the right Hand, who is so very beautiful, dyed a Maid ; the next to her, still handsomer, had the same Fate, against her Will ; this homely thing in the middle had both their Portions added to her own, and was Stolen by a neighbouring Gentleman, a Man of Stratagem and Resolution, for he poisoned three Mastiffs to come at her, and knocked down two Dear-stealers in carrying her off. Misfortunes happen in all Families : The Theft of this Romp and so much Money, was no great matter to our Estate. But the next Heir that possessed it was this soft Gentleman whom you see there : Observe the small buttons, the little Boots, the Laces, the Slashes about his Cloaths, and above all the Posture he is drawn in (which to be sure was his own chusing) ; you see he sits with one Hand on a Desk writing, and looking as it were another way, like an easie Writer, or a Sonneteer : He was one of those that had too much Wit to know how to live in the World ; he was a man of no Justice, but great good Manners ; he ruined every body that had any thing to do with him, but never said a rude thing in his Life ; the most indolent Person in the World, he would sign a Deed that passed away half his Estate with his Gloves on, but would not put on his Hat before a Lady, if it were to save his Country. He is said to be the first that made Love by squeezing the Hand. He left the Estate with ten thousand Pounds Debt upon it, but however by all Hands I have been informed that he was every way the finest Gentleman in the World. That Debt lay heavy on our House for one Generation, but it was retrieved by a Gift from that Honest Man you see there, a Citizen of our Name, but nothing at all a-kin to us. I know Sir ANDREW FREEPORT has said behind my Back, that this Man was descended from one of the ten Children of the Maid of Honour I shewed you above. But it was never made out ; we winked at the thing indeed, because Money was wanting at that time."

Here I saw my Friend a little embarrassed, and turned my Face to the next Portraiture.

Sir ROGER went on with his Account of the Gallery in the following manner. " This man " (pointing to him I look'd at) " I take to be the Honour of our House. Sir HUMPHREY DE COVERLEY ; he was in his Dealings as punctual as a Tradesman, and as generous as a Gentleman. He would have thought himself as much undone by breaking his Word, as if it were to be followed by Bankruptcy. He served his Country as Knight of this Shire to his dying Day : He found it no easie matter to maintain an integrity in his Words and Actions, even in things that regarded the Offices which were incumbent upon him, in the care of his own Affairs and Relations of Life, and therefore dreaded (tho' he had great Talents) to go into Employments of State, where he must be exposed to the Snares of Ambition. Innocence of Life and great Ability were the distinguishing Parts of his Character ; the latter, he had often observed, had led to the Destruction of the former, and used frequently to lament that Great and Good had not the same Signification. He was an Excellent Husbandman, but had resolved not to exceed such a degree of Wealth ; all above it he bestowed in secret Bounties many Years after the Sum he aimed at for his own use was attained. Yet he did not slacken his Industry, but to a decent old Age spent the Life and Fortune which was superfluous to himself, in the Service of his Friends and Neighbours."

Here we were called to Dinner, and Sir ROGER ended the Discourse of this Gentleman, by telling me, as we followed the Servant, that this his Ancestor was a Brave Man, and narrowly escaped being killed in the Civil Wars ;

" for," said he, " he was sent out of the Field upon a private Message the Day before the Battle of *Worcester*." The Whim of narrowly escaping, by having been within a Day of Danger ; with other Matters above mentioned, mixed with good Sense, left me at a Loss whether I was more delighted with my Friend's Wisdom or Simplicity.

The Spectator.   1711.

THE TRUMPET CLUB

Sir Richard Steele

Habeo senectuti magnam gratiam, quæ mihi sermonis aviditatem auxit, potionis et cibi sustulit.—Tull. *de Senect.*

After having applied my mind with more than ordinary attention to my studies, it is my usual custom to relax and unbend it in the conversation of such as are rather easy than shining companions. This I find particularly necessary for me before I retire to rest, in order to draw my slumbers upon me by degrees, and fall asleep insensibly. This is the particular use I make of a set of heavy honest men, with whom I have passed many hours with much indolence, though not with great pleasure. Their conversation is a kind of preparative for sleep : it takes the mind down from its abstractions, leads it into the familiar traces of thought, and lulls it into that state of tranquillity, which is the condition of a thinking man when he is but half awake. After this, my reader will not be surprised to hear the account which I am about to give of a club of my own contemporaries, among whom I pass two or three hours every evening. This I look upon as taking my first nap before I go to bed. The truth of it is, I should think myself unjust to posterity, as well as to the society at the *Trumpet*, of which I am a member, did not I in some part of my writings give an account of the persons among whom I have passed almost a sixth part of my time for these last forty years. Our club consisted originally of fifteen ; but, partly by the severity of the law in arbitrary times, and partly by the natural effects of old age, we are at present reduced to a third part of that number ; in which, however, we have this consolation, that the best company is said to consist of five persons. I must confess, besides the aforementioned benefit which I meet with in the conversation of this select society, I am not the less pleased with the company, in that I find myself the greatest wit among them, and am heard as their oracle in all points of learning and difficulty.

Sir Jeoffery Notch, who is the oldest of the club, has been in possession of the right-hand chair time out of mind, and is the only man among us that has the liberty of stirring the fire. This, our foreman, is a gentleman of an ancient family, that came to a great estate some years before he had discretion, and run it out in hounds, horses, and cock-fighting ; for which reason he looks upon himself as an honest, worthy gentleman, who has had misfortunes in the world, and calls every thriving man a pitiful upstart.

Major Matchlock is the next senior, who served in the last civil wars, and has all the battles by heart. He does not think any action in Europe worth talking of since the fight of Marston Moor ; and every night tells us of his having been knocked off his horse at the rising of the London apprentices ; for which he is in great esteem among us.

Honest old Dick Reptile is the third of our society. He is a good-natured indolent man, who speaks little himself, but laughs at our jokes ; and brings his young nephew along with him, a youth of eighteen years old, to show him good company and give him a taste of the world. This young fellow sits generally silent ; but whenever he opens his mouth, or laughs at anything that passes, he is constantly told by his uncle, after a jocular manner, " Ay, ay, Jack, you young men think us fools ; but we old men know you are."

The greatest wit of our company, next to myself, is

a bencher of the neighbouring inn, who in his youth frequented the ordinaries about Charing Cross, and pretends to have been intimate with Jack Ogle. He has about ten distichs of Hudibras without book, and never leaves the club until he has applied them all. If any modern wit be mentioned, or any town-frolic spoken of, he shakes his head at the dullness of the present age, and tells us a story of Jack Ogle.

For my own part, I am esteemed among them, because they see I am something respected by others ; though at the same time I understand by their behaviour, that I am considered by them as a man of a great deal of learning, but no knowledge of the world ; insomuch that the major sometimes, in the height of his military pride, calls me the Philosopher ; and Sir Jeoffery, no longer ago than last night, upon a dispute what day of the month it was then in Holland, pulled his pipe out of his mouth, and cried, " What does the scholar say to it ? "

Our club meets precisely at six o'clock in the evening ; but I did not come last evening until half an hour after seven, by which means I escaped the battle of Naseby, which the major usually begins at about three-quarters after six : I found also, that my good friend the bencher had already spent three of his distichs ; and only waited an opportunity to hear a sermon spoken of, that he might introduce the couplet where " a stick " rhymes to " ecclesiastic." At my entrance into the room, they were naming a red petticoat and a cloak, by which I found that the bencher had been diverting them with a story of Jack Ogle.

I had no sooner taken my seat, but Sir Jeoffery, to show his good-will towards me, gave me a pipe of his own tobacco, and stirred up the fire. I look upon it as a point of morality, to be obliged by those who endeavour to oblige me ; and therefore, in requital for his kindness, and to set the conversation a-going, I took the best occasion

I could to put him upon telling us the story of old Gauntlett, which he always does with very particular concern. He traced up his descent on both sides for several generations, describing his diet and manner of life, with his several battles, and particularly that in which he fell. This Gauntlett was a game cock, upon whose head the knight, in his youth, had won five hundred pounds, and lost two thousand. This naturally set the major upon the account of Edge-hill fight, and ended in a duel of Jack Ogle's.

Old Reptile was extremely attentive to all that was said, though it was the same he had heard every night for these twenty years, and, upon all occasions, winked upon his nephew to mind what passed.

This may suffice to give the world a taste of our innocent conversation, which we spun out until about ten of the clock, when my maid came with a lantern to light me home. I could not but reflect with myself, as I was going out, upon the talkative humour of old men, and the little figure which that part of life makes in one who cannot employ his natural propensity in discourses which would make him venerable. I must own, it makes me very melancholy in company, when I hear a young man begin a story ; and have often observed, that one of a quarter of an hour long in a man of five-and-twenty, gathers circumstances every time he tells it, until it grows into a long Canterbury tale of two hours by that time he is threescore.

The only way of avoiding such a trifling and frivolous old age is, to lay up in our way to it such stores of knowledge and observation, as may make us useful and agreeable in our declining years. The mind of man in a long life will become a magazine of wisdom or folly, and will consequently discharge itself in something impertinent or improving. For which reason, as there is nothing more ridiculous than an old trifling story-teller, so there is nothing more venerable, than one who has turned his experience to the entertainment and advantage of mankind.

In short, we, who are in the last stage of life, and are apt to indulge ourselves in talk, ought to consider, if what we speak be worth being heard, and endeavour to make our discourse like that of Nestor, which Homer compares to the flowing of honey for its sweetness.

I am afraid I shall be thought guilty of this excess I am speaking of, when I cannot conclude without observing, that Milton certainly thought of this passage in Homer, when, in his description of an eloquent spirit, he says,

His tongue dropped manna.

The Spectator. 1710.

A JOURNEY FROM RICHMOND

Sir Richard Steele

It is an inexpressible Pleasure to know a little of the World, and be of no Character or Significancy in it. To be ever unconcerned, and ever looking on new Objects with an endless Curiosity, is a Delight known only to those who are turned for Speculation : Nay, they who enjoy it, must value things only as they are the Objects of Speculation, without drawing any worldly Advantage to themselves from them, but just as they are what contribute to their Amusement, or the Improvement of the Mind. I lay one Night last Week at *Richmond* ; and being restless, not out of Dissatisfaction, but a certain busie Inclination one sometimes has, I arose at Four in the Morning, and took Boat for *London*, with a Resolution to rove by Boat and Coach for the next Four and twenty Hours, till the many different Objects I must needs meet with should tire my Imagination, and give me an Inclination to a Repose more profound than I was at that time capable of. I beg People's Pardon for an odd Humour I am guilty of, and was often that Day, which is saluting any Person whom I like, whether I know him or not. This is a Particularity would be tolerated in me, if they considered that the greatest Pleasure I know I receive at my Eyes, and that I am obliged to an agreeable Person for coming abroad into my View, as another is for a Visit of Conversation at their own Houses.

The Hours of the Day and Night are taken up in the

Cities of *London* and *Westminster* by People as different from each other as those who are Born in different Centuries. Men of Six-a-Clock give way to those of Nine, they of Nine to the Generation of Twelve, and they of Twelve disappear, and make Room for the fashionable World, who have made Two-a-Clock the Noon of the Day.

When we first put off from Shoar, we soon fell in with a Fleet of Gardiners bound for the several Market-Ports of *London*; and it was the most pleasing Scene imaginable to see the Chearfulness with which those industrious People ply'd their Way to a certain Sale of their Goods. The Banks on each Side are as well Peopled, and beautified with as agreeable Plantations, as any Spot on the Earth; but the *Thames* it self, loaded with the Product of each Shoar, added very much to the Landskip. It was very easie to observe by their Sailing, and the Countenances of the ruddy Virgins, who were Supercargos, the Parts of the Town to which they were bound. There was an Air in the Purveyors for *Covent-Garden*, who frequently converse with Morning Rakes, very unlike the seemly Sobriety of those bound for *Stocks-Market*.

Nothing remarkable happened in our Voyage; but I landed with Ten Sail of Apricock Boats at *Strand-Bridge*, after having put in at *Nine-Elmes*, and taken in Melons, consigned by Mr. *Cuffe* of that Place, to *Sarah-Sewell* and Company, at their Stall in *Covent-Garden*. We arrived at *Strand-Bridge* at Six of the Clock, and were unloading; when the Hackney-Coachmen of the foregoing Night took their Leave of each other at the *Dark-House*, to go to Bed before the Day was too far spent. Chimney-Sweepers pass'd by us as we made up to the Market, and some Raillery happened between one of the Fruit-Wenches and those black Men, about the Devil and *Eve*, with Allusion to their several Professions. I could not believe any Place more entertaining than *Covent-Garden*; where I strolled from one Fruit-shop to another, with Crowds of agreeable young Women around me, who were purchasing Fruit for their respective Families. It was almost Eight of the Clock before I could leave that Variety of Objects. I took Coach and followed a young Lady, who tripped into another just before me, attended by her Maid. I saw immediately she was of the Family of the *Vainloves*. There are a Sett of these, who of all things affect the Play of *Blindman's-Buff*, and leading Men into Love for they know not whom, who are fled they know not where. This sort of Woman is usually a janty Slattern ; she hangs on her Cloaths, plays her Head, varies her Posture, and changes place incessantly, and all with an Appearance of striving at the same time to hide her self, and yet give you to understand she is in Humour to laugh at you. You must have often seen the Coachmen make Signs with their Fingers as they drive by each other, to intimate how much they have got that Day. They can carry on that Language to give Intelligence where they are driving. In an Instant my Coachman took the Wink to pursue, and the Lady's Driver gave the Hint that he was going through *Long-Acre* towards St. *James's* : While he whipp'd up *James-Street*, we drove for *King-Street*, to save the Pass at St. *Martin's-Lane*. The Coachmen took care to meet, justle, and threaten each other for Way, and be intangled at the End of *Newport-Street* and *Long-Acre*. The Fright, you must believe, brought down the Lady's Coach Door, and obliged her, with her Mask off, to enquire into the Bustle, when she sees the Man she would avoid. The Tackle of the Coach-Window is so bad she cannot draw it up again, and she drives on sometimes wholly discovered, and sometimes half-escaped, according to the Accident of Carriages in her Way. One of these Ladies keeps her Seat in a Hackney-Coach as well as the best Rider does on a managed Horse. The laced Shooe on her Left Foot, with a careless Gesture, just appearing on the opposite Cushion, held her both firm, and in a proper Attitude to receive the next Jolt.

As she was an excellent Coach-Woman, many were the Glances at each other which we had for an Hour and an Half in all Parts of the Town by the Skill of our Drivers; till at last my Lady was conveniently lost with Notice from her Coachman to ours to make off, and he should hear where she went. This Chace was now at an End, and the Fellow who drove her came to us, and discovered that he was ordered to come again in an Hour, for that she was a Silk-Worm. I was surprized with this Phrase, but found it was a Cant among the Hackney Fraternity for their best Customers, Women who ramble twice or thrice a Week from Shop to Shop, to turn over all the Goods in Town without buying any thing. The Silk-Worms are, it seems, indulged by the Tradesmen: for tho' they never buy, they are ever talking of new Silks, Laces and Ribbands, and serve the Owners in getting them Customers, as their common Dunners do in making them pay.

The Day of People of Fashion began now to break, and Carts and Hacks were mingled with Equipages of Show and Vanity; when I resolved to walk it out of Cheapness; but my unhappy Curiosity is such, that I find it always my Interest to take Coach, for some odd Adventure among Beggars, Ballad-Singers, or the like, detains and throws me into Expence. It happened so immediately; for at the Corner of *Warwick-Street*, as I was listening to a new Ballad, a ragged Rascal, a Beggar who knew me, came up to me, and began to turn the Eyes of the good Company upon me, by telling me he was extream Poor, and should die in the Streets for want of Drink, except I immediately would have the Charity to give him Six-pence to go into the next Ale-House and save his life. He urged, with a melancholy Face, that all his Family had died of Thirst. All the Mob have Humour, and two or three began to take the jest ; by which Mr. *Sturdy* carried his Point, and let me sneak off to a Coach. As I drove along it was a pleasing Reflection to see the World so prettily chequered since I left *Richmond*, and the Scene still filling with Children of a new Hour. This Satisfaction encreased as I moved towards the City ; and gay Signs, well disposed Streets, magnificent publick Structures, and Wealthy Shops, adorned with contented Faces, made the Joy still rising till we came into the Centre of the City, and Centre of the World of Trade, the *Exchange of London*. As other Men in the Crowds about me were pleased with their Hopes and Bargains, I found my Account in observing them, in Attention to their several Interests. I, indeed, looked upon my self as the richest Man that walked the *Exchange* that Day ; for my Benevolence made me share the Gains of every Bargain that was made. It was not the least of the Satisfactions in my Survey, to go up Stairs, and pass the Shops of agreeable Females ; to observe so many pretty Hands busie in the Foldings of Ribbands, and the utmost Eagerness of agreeable Faces in the Sale of Patches, Pins, and Wires, on each Side the Counters, was an Amusement, in which I should longer have indulged my self, had not the dear Creatures called to me to ask what I wanted, when I could not answer, only *To look at you*. I went to one of the Windows which opened to the Area below, where all the several Voices lost their Distinction, and rose up in a confused Humming ; which created in me a Reflection that could not come into the Mind of any but of one a little studious ; for I said to my self, with a kind of Punn in thought, *What Nonsense is all the Hurry of this World to those who are above it ?* In these, or not much wiser Thoughts, I had like to have lost my Place at the Chop-House ; where every Man, according to the natural Bashfulness or Sullenness of our Nation, eats in a publick Room a Mess of Broth, or Chop of Meat, in dumb Silence, as if they had no Pretence to speak to each other on the Foot of being Men, except they were of each other's Acquaintance.

I went afterwards to *Robin's* and saw People who had dined with me at the Five-Penny Ordinary just before, give Bills for the Value of large Estates ; and could not but behold with great Pleasure, Property lodged in, and transferred in a Moment from such as would never be Masters of half as much as is seemingly in them, and given from them every Day they live. But before Five in the Afternoon I left the City, came to my common Scene of *Covent-Garden*, and passed the Evening at *Will's* in attending the Discourses of several Sets of People, who relieved each other within my Hearing on the Subjects of Cards, Dice, Love, Learning and Politicks. The last Subject kept me till I heard the Streets in the Possession of the Bell-man, who had now the World to himself, and cryed, *Past Two of Clock*. This rous'd me from my Seat, and I went to my Lodging, led by a Light, whom I put into the Discourse of his private Oeconomy, and made him give me an Account of the Charge, Hazard, Profit and Loss of a Family that depended upon a Link, with a Design to end my trivial Day with the Generosity of Six-pence, instead of a third Part of that Sum. When I came to my Chambers I writ down these Minutes ; but was at a Loss what Instruction I should propose to my Reader from the Enumeration of so many Insignificant Matters and Occurrences ; and I thought it of great Use, if they could learn with me to keep their minds open to Gratification, and ready to receive it from any thing it meets with. This one Circumstance will make every Face you see give you the Satisfaction you now take in beholding that of a Friend ; will make every Object a pleasing one ; will make all the Good which arrives to any Man, an Encrease of Happiness to your self.

The Spectator. 1711.

GOOD TEMPER

Sir Richard Steele

IT is an unreasonable thing some Men expect of their Acquaintance. They are ever complaining that they are out of Order, or displeas'd, or they know not how ; and are so far from letting that be a Reason for retiring to their own Homes, that they make it their Argument for coming into Company. What has any Body to do with Accounts of a Man's being indispos'd but his Physician ? If a man laments in Company, where the rest are in Humour enough to enjoy themselves, he should not take it ill if a Servant is order'd to present him with a Porringer of Cawdle or Posset-drink, by way of Admonition that he go home to Bed. That Part of Life which we ordinarily understand by the Word Conversation, is an Indulgence to the sociable Part of our Make ; and should incline us to bring our Proportion of good Will or good Humour among the Friends we meet with, and not to trouble them with Relations which must of Necessity oblige them to a real or feign'd Affliction. Cares, Distresses, Diseases, Uneasinesses, and Dislikes of our own, are by no Means to be obtruded upon our Friends. If we would consider how little of this Vicissitude of Motion and Rest, which we call Life, is spent with Satisfaction ; we should be more tender of our Friends, than to bring them little Sorrows which do not belong to them. There is no real Life, but chearful Life ; therefore Valetudinarians should be sworn, before they enter into Company, not to say a Word of themselves till the Meeting breaks up. It is not here pretended, that we should be always sitting with Chaplets of Flowers round our Heads, or be crowned with Roses, in order to make our Entertainment agreeable to us ; but if (as it is usually observed) they who resolve to be merry, seldom are so ; it will be much more unlikely for us to be well pleased, if they are admitted who are always complaining they are sad. Whatever we do we should keep up the Chearfulness of our Spirits, and never let them sink below an Inclination at least to be well pleased : The Way to this, is to keep our Bodies in Exercise, our Minds at Ease. That insipid State wherein neither are in Vigour, is not to be accounted any Part of our Portion of Being. When we are in the Satisfaction of some innocent Pleasure, or Pursuit of some laudable Design, we are in the Possession of Life, of human Life. Fortune will give us Disappointments enough, and Nature is attended with Infirmities enough, without our adding to the unhappy Side of our Account by our Spleen or ill Humour. Poor *Cottilus*, among so many real Evils, a chronical Distemper and a narrow Fortune, is never heard to complain : That equal Spirit of his, which any Man may have that, like him, will conquer Pride, Vanity, and Affectation, and follow Nature, is not to be broken, because it has no Points to contend for. To be anxious for nothing but what Nature demands as necessary, if it is not the way to an Estate, is the way to what Men aim at by getting an Estate. This Temper will preserve Health in the Body, as well as Tranquillity in the Mind. *Cottilus* sees the World in an Hurry, with the same Scorn that a sober Person sees a Man drunk. Had he been contented with what he ought to have been, how could, says he, such a one have met with such a Disappointment ? If another had valued his Mistress for what he ought to have loved her, he had not been in her Power : If her Virtue had had a Part of his Passion, her Levity had been his Cure ; she could not then have been false and amiable at the same Time.

Since we cannot promise our selves constant Health, let us endeavour at such a Temper as may be our best Support in the Decay of it. *Uranius* has arrived at that Composure of Soul, and wrought himself up to such a Neglect of every thing with which the Generality of Mankind is enchanted, that nothing but acute Pains can give him Disturbance, and against those too he will tell his intimate Friends he has a Secret which gives him present Ease. *Uranius* is so thoroughly perswaded of another Life, and endeavours so sincerely to secure an Interest in it, that he looks upon Pain but as a quickening of his Pace to an Home, where he shall be better provided for than in his present Apartment. Instead of the melancholy Views which others are apt to give themselves, he will tell you that he has forgot he is mortal, nor will he think of himself as such. He thinks at the Time of his Birth he entered into an eternal Being ; and the short Article of Death he will not allow an Interruption of Life, since that Moment is not of half the Duration as is his ordinary Sleep. Thus is his Being one uniform and consistent Series of chearful Diversions and moderate Cares, without Fear or Hope of Futurity. Health to him is more than Pleasure to another Man, and Sickness less affecting to him than Indisposition is to others.

I must confess, if one does not regard Life after this Manner, none but Idiots can pass it away with any tolerable Patience. Take a fine Lady who is of a delicate Frame, and you may observe from the Hour she rises a certain Weariness of all that passes about her. I know more than one who is much too nice to be quite alive. They are sick of such strange frightful People that they meet ; one is so awkward and another so disagreeable, that it looks like a Penance to breathe the same Air with them. You see this is so very true, that a great Part of Ceremony and Good-breeding among the Ladies turns upon their Uneasiness ; and I'll undertake, if the How-d'ye Servants of our Women were to make a weekly Bill of Sickness, as the Parish Clerks do of Mortality, you would not find in an Account of Seven Days, one in thirty that was not down-right Sick or indisposed, or but a very little better than she was, and so forth.

It is certain, that to enjoy Life and Health as a constant Feast, we should not think Pleasure necessary ; but, if possible, to arrive at an Equality of Mind. It is as mean to be overjoy'd upon Occasions of good Fortune, as to be dejected in Circumstances of Distress. Laughter in one Condition, is as unmanly as weeping in the other. We should not form our Minds to expect Transport on every Occasion, but know how to make Enjoyment to be out of Pain. Ambition, Envy, vagrant Desire, or impertinent Mirth will take up our Minds, without we can possess our selves in that Sobriety of Heart which is above all Pleasures, and can be felt much better than described : But the ready Way, I believe, to the right Enjoyment of Life, is by a Prospect towards another, to have but a very mean Opinion of it. A great Author of our Time has set this in an excellent Light, when with a philosophick Pity of human Life he spoke of it in his Theory of the Earth in the following Manner.

For what is this Life but a Circulation of little mean Actions ? We lie down and rise again, dress and undress, feed and wax hungry, work or play, and are weary, and then we lie down again, and the Circle returns. We spend the Day in Trifles, and when the Night comes we throw our selves into the Bed of Folly, amongst Dreams and broken Thoughts and wild Imaginations. Our Reason lies asleep by us, and we are for the Time as arrant Brutes as those that sleep in the Stalls or in the Field. Are not the Capacities of Man higher than these ? and ought not his Ambition and Expectations to be greater ? Let us be Adventurers for another World : 'Tis at least a fair and noble Chance; and there is nothing in this worth our Thoughts or our Passions. If we should be disappointed, we are still no worse than the rest of our Fellow-Mortals; and if we succeed in our Expectations, we are eternally happy.

The Spectator. 1711.

ON DUELLING

Sir Richard Steele

Quicquid agunt homines . . .
nostri est farrago libelle.—Juv. *Sat.* i. 85, 86.

A LETTER from a young lady, written in the most passionate terms, wherein she laments the misfortune of a gentleman, her lover, who was lately wounded in a duel, has turned my thoughts to that subject, and inclined me to examine into the causes which precipitate men into so fatal a folly. And as it has been proposed to treat of subjects of gallantry in the article from hence, and no one point in nature is more proper to be considered by the company who frequent this place than that of duels, it is worth our consideration to examine into this chimerical groundless humour, and to lay every other thought aside, until we have stripped it of all its false pretences to credit and reputation amongst men.

But I must confess, when I consider what I am going about, and run over in my imagination all the endless crowd of men of honour who will be offended at such a discourse ; I am undertaking, methinks, a work worthy an invulnerable hero in romance, rather than a private gentleman with a single rapier : but as I am pretty well acquainted by great opportunities with the nature of man, and know of a truth that all men fight against their will, the danger vanishes, and resolution rises upon this subject. For this reason, I shall talk very freely on a custom which all men wish exploded, though no man has courage enough to resist it.

But there is one unintelligible word, which I fear will extremely perplex my dissertation, and I confess to you I find very hard to explain, which is the term "satisfaction." An honest country gentleman had the misfortune to fall into company with two or three modern men of honour where he happened to be very ill treated ; and one of the company, being conscious of his offence, sends a note to him in the morning, and tells him, he was ready to give him *satisfaction*. "This is a fine doing," says the plain fellow ; "last night he sent me away cursedly out of humour, and this morning he fancies it would be a *satisfaction* to be run through the body !"

As the matter at present stands, it is not to do handsome actions denominates a man of honour ; it is enough if he dares to defend ill ones. Thus you often see a common sharper in competition with a gentleman of the first rank ; though all mankind is convinced, that a fighting gamester is only a pickpocket with the courage of a highwayman. One cannot with any patience reflect on the unaccountable jumble of persons and things in this town and nation, which occasions very frequently, that a brave man falls by a hand below that of a common hangman, and yet his executioner escapes the clutches of the hangman for doing it. I shall therefore hereafter consider, how the bravest men in other ages and nations have behaved themselves upon such incidents as we decide by combat ; and show, from their practice, that this resentment neither has its foundation from true reason or solid fame ; but is an imposture, made of cowardice, falsehood, and want of understanding. For this work, a good history of quarrels would be very edifying to the public, and I apply myself to the town for particulars and circumstances within their knowledge, which may serve to embellish the dissertation with proper cuts. Most of the quarrels I have ever known have proceeded from some valiant coxcomb's persisting in the wrong, to defend some prevailing folly, and preserve himself from the ingenuousness of owning a mistake.

By this means it is called " giving a man satisfaction," to urge your offence against him with your sword. . . . If the contradiction in the very terms of one of our challenges were as well explained and turned into downright English, would it not turn after this manner ?

" Sir,—Your extraordinary behaviour last night, and the liberty you were pleased to take with me, makes me this morning give you this, to tell you, because you are an ill-bred puppy, I will meet you in Hyde Park an hour hence ; and because you want both breeding and humanity, I desire you would come with a pistol in your hand, on horseback, and endeavour to shoot me through the head, to teach you more manners. If you fail of doing me this pleasure, I shall say, you are a rascal, on every post in town : and so, sir, if you will not injure me more, I shall never forgive what you have done already. Pray, sir, do not fail of getting everything ready ; and you will infinitely oblige, sir, your most obedient humble servant, etc."

Tatler. 1709.

THE GRAND ELIXIR

Alexander Pope

There is an oblique way of Reproof, which takes off from the Sharpness of it ; and an Address in Flattery, which makes it agreeable though never so gross : But of all Flatterers, the most skilful is he who can do what you like, without saying any thing which argues you do it for his Sake ; the most winning Circumstance in the World being the Conformity of Manners. I speak of this as a Practice necessary in gaining People of Sense, who are not yet given up to Self-Conceit ; those who are far gone in admiration of themselves need not be treated with so much Delicacy. The following Letter puts this Matter in a pleasant and uncommon Light : The Author of it attacks this Vice with an Air of Compliance, and alarms us against it by exhorting us to it.

To the Guardian

" Sir,

" As you profess to encourage all those who any way contribute to the Publick Good, I flatter my self I may claim your Countenance and Protection. I am by profession a Mad Doctor, but of a peculiar Kind, not of those whose Aim it is to remove Phrenzies, but one who makes it my Business to confer an agreeable Madness on my Fellow-Creatures, for their mutual Delight and Benefit. Since it is agreed by the Philosophers, that Happiness and Misery consist chiefly in the Imagination, nothing is more necessary to Mankind in general than this pleasing Delirium, which renders every one satisfied with himself, and persuades him that all others are equally so.

"I have for several Years, both at home and abroad, made this Science my particular Study, which I may venture to say I have improved in almost all the Courts of *Europe* ; and have reduced it into so safe and easie a Method, as to practise it on both Sexes, of what Disposition, Age or Quality soever, with Success. What enables me to perform this great Work, is the Use of my *Obsequium Catholicon*, or the *Grand Elixir*, to support the Spirits of human Nature. This Remedy is of the most grateful Flavour in the World, and agrees with all Tastes whatever. 'Tis delicate to the Senses, delightful in the Operation, may be taken at all Hours without Confinement, and is as properly given at a Ball or Play-house as in a private Chamber. It restores and vivifies the most dejected Minds, corrects and extracts all that is painful in the Knowledge of a Man's self. One Dose of it will instantly disperse it self through the whole Animal System, dissipate the first Motions of Distrust so as never to return, and so exhilerate the Brain and rarifie the Gloom of Reflection, as to give the Patients a new flow of Spirits, a Vivacity of Behaviour, and a pleasing Dependence upon their own Capacities.

"LET a Person be never so far gone, I advise him not to despair ; even though he has been troubled many Years with restless Reflections, which by long Neglect have hardened into settled Consideration. Those that have been stung with Satyr may here find a certain Antidote, which infallibly disperses all the Remains of Poison that has been left in the Understanding by bad Cures. It fortifies the Heart against the Rancour of Pamphlets, the Inveteracy of Epigrams, and the Mortification of Lampoons ; as has been often experienced by several Persons of both Sexes, during the Seasons of *Tunbridge* and the *Bath*.

" I could, as further Instances of my Success, produce
Certificates and Testimonials from the Favourites and
Ghostly Fathers of the most eminent Princes of *Europe* ;
but shall content my self with the Mention of a few Cures,
which I have performed by this my *Grand Universal
Restorative*, during the Practice of one Month only since
I came to this City."

Cures in the Month of February, 1713

" *GEORGE SPONDEE*, Esq. ; Poet, and Inmate of the
Parish of St. *Paul's Covent-Garden*, fell into violent Fits
of the Spleen upon a thin Third Night. He had been
frighted into a Vertigo by the Sound of Cat-calls on the
First Day ; and the frequent Hissings on the Second made
him unable to endure the bare Pronunciation of the Letter
S. I searched into the Causes of his Distemper ; and by
the Prescription of a Dose of my *Obsequium*, prepared
Secundum Artem, recovered him to his Natural State of
Madness. I cast in at proper Intervals the Words, *Ill
Taste of the Town, Envy of Criticks, bad Performance of
the Actors*, and the like. He is so perfectly cured that
he has promised to bring another Play upon the Stage
next Winter.

" A Lady of professed Virtue, of the Parish of St.
James's Westminster, who hath desired her Name may
be concealed, having taken Offence at a Phrase of double
Meaning in Conversation, undiscovered by any other in
the Company, suddenly fell into a cold Fit of Modesty.
Upon a right Application of Praise of her Virtue, I threw
the Lady into an agreeable waking Dream, settled the Fer-
mentation of her Blood into a warm Charity, so as to make
her look with Patience on the very Gentleman that offended.

" *HILARIA*, of the Parish of St. *Giles's in the Fields*,
a Coquet of long Practice, was by the Reprimand of an
old Maiden reduced to look grave in Company, and deny

her self the Play of the Fan. In short, she was brought to such Melancholy Circumstances, that she would sometimes unawares fall into Devotion at Church. I advis'd her to take a few *innocent Freedoms with occasional Kisses*, prescribed her the *Exercise of the Eyes*, and immediately raised her to her former State of Life. She on a sudden recovered her Dimples, furled her Fan, threw round her Glances, and for these two *Sundays* last past has not once been seen in an attentive Posture. This the Church-Wardens are ready to attest upon Oath.

" *ANDREW TERROR*, of the *Middle-Temple, Mohock,* was almost induced by an aged Bencher of the same House to leave off bright Conversation, and pore over *Cook upon Littleton*. He was so ill that his Hat began to flap, and he was seen one Day in the last Term at *Westminster-Hall*. This Patient had quite lost his Spirit of Contradiction ; I, by the Distillation of a few of my vivifying Drops in his Ear, drew him from his Lethargy, and restored him to his usual vivacious Misunderstanding. He is at present very easie in his Condition.

" I will not dwell upon the Recital of the innumerable Cures I have performed within Twenty Days last past ; but rather proceed to exhort all Persons, of whatever Age, Complexion or Quality, to take as soon as possible of this my intellectual Oyl ; which applied at the Ear seizes all the Senses with a most agreeable Transport, and discovers its Effects, not only to the Satisfaction of the Patient, but all who converse with, attend upon, or any way relate to him or her that receives the kindly Infection. It is often administered by Chamber-Maids, Valets, or any the most ignorant Domestick ; it being one peculiar Excellence of this my Oyl, that 'tis most prevalent, the more unskilful the Person is or appears who applies it. It is absolutely necessary for Ladies to take a Dose of it just before they take Coach to go a visiting.

" BUT I offend the Publick, as *Horace* said, when I

trespass on any of your Time.   Give me leave then, Mr.
Ironside, to make you a Present of a Drachm or two of
my Oyl ; though I have Cause to fear my Prescriptions
will not have the Effect upon you I could wish : Therefore
I do not endeavour to bribe you in my Favour by the
Present of my Oyl, but wholly depend upon your Publick
Spirit and Generosity ; which, I hope, will recommend to
the World the useful Endeavours of,

> " *SIR*,

> " *Your most Obedient, most Faithful, most Devoted, most
> Humble Servant and Admirer,*

> > " GNATHO.

" ★★★Beware of Counterfeits, for such are abroad.

" *N.B.* I teach the *Arcana* of my Art at reasonable
Rates to Gentlemen of the Universities, who desire to be
qualified for writing Dedications ; and to young Lovers
and Fortune-hunters, to be paid at the Day of Marriage.
I instruct Persons of bright Capacities to flatter others, and
those of the meanest to flatter themselves.

" I was the first Inventor of Pocket Looking-Glasses."

The Guardian.   1712.

THE SHORT CLUB

Alexander Pope

Thursday, June 25, 1713.

—Inest sua gratia parvis.

It is the great rule of behaviour, " to follow nature." The author of the following letter is so much convinced of this truth, that he turns what would render a man of little soul exceptious, humoursome, and particular in all his actions, to a subject of raillery and mirth. He is, you must know, but half as tall as an ordinary man, but is contented to be still at his friend's elbow, and has set up a club, to which he hopes to bring those of his own size into a little reputation.

> ## "TO NESTOR IRONSIDE, ESQ.
> " Sir,
> " I remember a saying of yours concerning persons in low circumstances of stature, that their littleness would hardly be taken notice of, if they did not manifest a consciousness of it themselves in all their behaviour. Indeed, the observation that no man is ridiculous, for being what he is, but only in the affectation of being something more, is equally true in regard to the mind and the body.
> " I question not but it will be pleasing to you to hear that a set of us have formed a society, who are sworn to ' dare to be short,' and boldly bear out the dignity of littleness under the noses of those enormous engrossers

of manhood, those hyperbolical monsters of the species, the tall fellows that overlook us.

" The day of our institution was the tenth of December, being the shortest of the year, on which we are to hold an annual feast over a dish of shrimps.

" The place we have chosen for this meeting is in the Little Piazza, not without an eye to the neighbourhood of Mr. Powel's opera,[1] for the performers of which we have, as becomes us, a brotherly affection.

" At our first resort hither an old woman brought her son to the clubroom, desiring he might be educated in this school, because she saw here were finer boys than ordinary. However, this accident no way discouraged our designs. We began with sending invitations to those of a stature not exceeding five foot, to repair to our assembly ; but the greater part returned excuses, or pretended they were not qualified.

" One said he was indeed but five foot at present, but represented he should soon exceed that proportion, his periwig-maker and shoe-maker having lately promised him three inches more betwixt them.

" Another alleged, he was so unfortunate as to have one leg shorter than the other, and whoever had determined his stature to five foot, had taken him at a disadvantage ; for when he was mounted on the other leg, he was at least five foot two inches and a half.

" There were some who questioned the exactness of our measures ; and others, instead of complying, returned us informations of people yet shorter than themselves. In a word, almost every one recommended some neighbour or acquaintance, whom he was willing we should look upon to be less than he. We were not a little ashamed that those who are past the years of growth, and whose beards pronounce them men, should be guilty of as many unfair tricks in this point, as the most aspiring children when they are measured.

" We therefore proceeded to fit up the clubroom, and provide conveniences for our accommodation. In the first place we caused a total removal of all chairs, stools, and tables, which had served the gross of mankind for many years. The disadvantages we had undergone while we made use of these were unspeakable. The president's whole body was sunk in the elbow chair : and when his arms were spread over it, he appeared (to the great lessening of his dignity) like a child in a go-cart. It was also so wide in the seat, as to give a wag occasion of saying, that notwithstanding the president sat in it, there was a *sede vacante*.

" The table was so high, that one who came by chance to the door, seeing our chins just above the pewter dishes, took us for a circle of men that sat ready to be shaved, and sent in half a dozen barbers. Another time one of the club spoke contumeliously of the president, imagining he had been absent, when he was only eclipsed by a flask of Florence which stood on the table in a parallel line before his face. We therefore new-furnished the room in all respects proportionably to us, and had the door made lower, so as to admit no man above five foot high, without brushing his foretop, which whoever does, is utterly unqualified to sit among us.

" *Some of the statutes of the club are as follows :*

" I. If it be proved upon any member, though never so duly qualified, that he strives as much as possible to get above his size, by stretching, cocking, or the like ; or that he hath stood on tiptoe in a crowd, with design to be taken for as tall a man as the rest : or hath privily conveyed any large book, cricket, or other device under him, to exalt him on his seat ; every such offender shall be sentenced to walk in pumps for a whole month.

" II. If any member shall take advantage from the fullness or length of his wig, or any part of his dress, or the immoderate extent of his hat, or otherwise, to seem larger and higher than he is ; it is ordered, he shall wear red heels to his shoes, and a red feather in his hat, which may apparently mark and set bounds to the extremities of his small dimension, that all people may readily find out between his hat and his shoes.

" III. If any member shall purchase a horse for his own riding above fourteen hands and a half in height, that horse shall forthwith be sold, a Scotch galloway bought in its stead for him, and the overplus of the money shall treat the club.

" IV. If any member, in direct contradiction to the fundamental laws of the society, shall wear the heels of his shoes exceeding one inch and half, it shall be interpreted as an open renunciation of littleness, and the criminal shall be instantly expelled. Note, The form to be used in expelling a member shall be in these words, ' Go from among us, and be tall if you can ! '

" It is the unanimous opinion of our whole society, that since the race of mankind is granted to have decreased in stature from the beginning to this present, it is the intent of nature itself, that men should be little ; and we believe that all human kind shall at last grow down to perfection, that is to say be reduced to our own measure.

I am, very literally,
Your humble servant,
BOB SHORT."
The Guardian.   1713.

OF CRUELTY TO ANIMALS

ALEXANDER POPE

——Primoque a cade ferarum
Incaluisse Putem maculatum sanguine ferrum.
OVID.

I CANNOT think it extravagant to imagine, that mankind
are no less, in proportion, accountable for the ill use of
their dominion over creatures of the lower rank of
beings, than for the exercise of tyranny over their own
species. The more entirely the inferior creation is sub-
mitted to our power, the more answerable we should
seem for our mismanagement of it; and the rather, as
the very condition of nature renders these creatures
incapable of receiving any recompense in another life,
for their ill treatment in this.

'Tis observable of those noxious animals, which have
qualities most powerful to injure us, that they naturally
avoid mankind, and never hurt us unless provoked, or
necessitated by hunger. Man, on the other hand, seeks
out and pursues even the most inoffensive animals on
purpose to prosecute and destroy them.

Montaigne thinks it some reflection upon human
nature itself, that few people take delight in seeing beasts
caress or play together, but almost every one is pleased
to see them lacerate and worry one another. I am sorry
this temper is become almost a distinguishing character
of our own nation, from the observation which is made
by foreigners of our beloved pastimes, *bear-baiting, cock-*

fighting, and the like. We should find it hard to vindicate the destroying of any thing that has life, merely out of wantonness ; yet in this principle our children are bred up, and one of the first pleasures we allow them is the licence of afflicting pain upon poor animals ; almost as soon as we are sensible what life is ourselves, we make it our sport to take it from other creatures. I cannot but believe a very good use might be made of the fancy which children have for birds and insects. Mr. *Locke* takes notice of a mother who permitted them to her children, but rewarded or punished them as they treated them well or ill. This was no other than entering them betimes into a daily exercise of humanity, and improving their very diversion to a virtue.

I fancy, too, some advantage might be taken of the common notion, that 'tis ominous or unlucky to destroy some sorts of birds, as *swallows* or *martins* ; this opinion might possibly arise from the confidence these birds seem to put in us by building under our roofs, so that it is a kind of violation of the laws of hospitality to murder them. As for *robin-redbreasts* in particular, 'tis not improbable they owe their security to the old ballad of *The Children in the Wood*. However it be, I don't know, I say, why this prejudice, well improved and carried as far as it would go, might not be made to conduce to the preservation of many innocent creatures, which are now exposed to all the wantonness of an ignorant barbarity.

There are other animals that have the misfortune, for no manner of reason, to be treated as common enemies wherever found. The conceit that a *cat* has *nine lives*, has cost at least nine lives in ten of the whole race of 'em ; Scarce a boy in the streets but has in this point outdone Hercules himself, who was famous for killing a monster that had but *three lives*. Whether the unaccountable animosity against this useful domestic may be any cause of the general persecution of *owls* (who are a sort of feather'd cats) or whether it be only an unreasonable pique the moderns have taken to a serious countenance, I shall not determine. Tho' I am inclined to believe the former ; since I observe the sole reason alleged for the destruction of *frogs* is because they are like *toads*. Yet amidst all the misfortunes of these unfriended creatures, 'tis some happiness that we have not yet taken a fancy to eat them : For should our countrymen refine upon the *French* never so little, 'tis not to be conceived to what unheard-of torments owls, cats and *frogs* may be yet reserved.

When we grow up to men, we have another succession of sanguinary sports ; in particular *hunting*. I dare not attack a diversion which has such authority and custom to support it, but must have leave to be of opinion, that the agitation of that exercise, with the example and number of the chasers, not a little contribute to resist those *checks*, which compassion would naturally suggest in behalf of the animal pursued. Nor shall I say with Monsieur *Fleury*, that this sport is a *remain of the* Gothic *barbarity* ; but I must animadvert upon a certain custom yet in use with us, and barbarous enough to be derived from the *Goths*, or even the *Scythians* ; I mean that savage compliment our huntsmen pass upon ladies of quality, who are present at the death of a stag, when they put the knife in their hands to cut the throat of a helpless, trembling and weeping creature,

——Questuque cruentus,
Atque imploranti similis.——

But if our *sports* are destructive, our *gluttony* is more so, and in a more inhuman manner. *Lobsters roasted alive, pigs whipt to death, fowls sewed up,* are testimonies of our outrageous luxury. Those who (as *Seneca* expresses it) divide their lives betwixt an anxious conscience and a nauseated stomach, have a just reward of their gluttony in the diseases it brings with it : For human savages, like other wild beasts, find snares and poison in the provisions of life, and are allured by their appetite to their destruction. I know nothing more shocking or horrid, than the prospect of one of their kitchens cover'd with blood, and filled with the cries of creatures expiring in tortures. It gives one an image of a *giant's den* in a romance, bestrow'd with scattered heads and mangled limbs of those who were slain by his cruelty.

The excellent *Plutarch* (who has more strokes of good-nature in his writings than I remember in any author) cites a saying of *Cato* to this effect, *That 'tis no easie task to preach to the belly, which has no ears.* " Yet if (says he) we are ashamed to be so out of fashion as not to offend, let us at least offend with some discretion and measure. If we kill an animal for our provision, let us do it with the meltings of compassion, and without tormenting it. Let us consider, that 'tis in its own nature cruelty to put a living creature to death ; we at least destroy a soul that has sense and perception. . . ." In the life of Cato the Censor, he takes occasion from the severe disposition of that man to discourse in this manner : " It ought to be esteem'd a happiness to mankind, that our humanity has a wider sphere to exert itself in, than bare justice. It is no more than the obligation of our very birth to practise equity to our own kind, but humanity may be extended thro' the whole order of creatures, even to the meanest : Such actions of charity are the overflowing of a mild good-nature on all below us. It is certainly the part of a well-natured man to take care of his horses and dogs, not only while they are foals and whelps, but even when their old age has made them incapable of service."

History tells us of a wise and polite nation that rejected a person of the first quality, who stood for a judicatory office, only because he had been observed, in his youth, to take pleasure in tearing and murdering of birds. And of another that expelled a man out of the Senate, for dashing a bird against the ground which had taken shelter in his bosom. Every one knows how remarkable the Turks are for their humanity in this kind : I remember an *Arabian* author, who has written a treatise to show, how far a man, supposed to have subsisted in a desert island, without any instruction, or so much as the sight of any other man, may, by the pure light of nature, attain the knowledge of philosophy and virtue. One of the first things he makes him observe is, that universal bene-volence of nature in the protection and preservation of its creatures. In imitation of which, the first act of virtue he thinks his self-taught philosopher would of course fall into is, to relieve and assist all the animals about him in their wants and distresses.

Ovid has some very tender and pathetic lines applicable to this occasion.

Quid meruistis oves, placidum pecus, inque regendos
Natum homines, pleno qua fertis in Ubere nectar ?
Mollia qua nobis vestras velamina lanas
Prabetis ; vitaque magis quam morte juvatis.
Quid meruëre boves, animal sine fraude dobisque,
Innocuum, simplex, natum tolerare labores :
Qui potuit, curvi dempto modo pondere aratri,
Ruricolam mastare suum——
    Quam male consuevit, quam se parat ille cruori
Impius himano, Vituli qui guttura cultro
Rumpit, & immotas prabet mugitibus aures !
Aut qui vagitus similes puerilibus hoedum
Edentem jugulare potest !

Perhaps that voice or cry so nearly resembling the human, with which Providence has endued so many different animals, might purposely be given them to move our pity, and prevent those cruelties we are too apt to inflict on our fellow-creatures.

There is a passage in the book of *Jonas*, when God declares his unwillingness to destroy *Nineveh*, where methinks that compassion of the Creator, which extends to the meanest rank of his creatures, is expressed with wonderful tenderness—*Should I not spare Nineveh the great city, wherein are more than six-score thousand persons—and also much cattel ?* And we have in *Deuteronomy* a precept of great good-nature of this sort, with a blessing in form annexed to it, in those words : *If thou shalt find a bird's nest in the way, thou shalt not take the damm with the young ; But thou shalt in any wise let the damm go ; that it may be well with thee, and that thou may'st prolong thy days.*

To conclude, there is certainly a degree of gratitude owing to those animals that serve us ; as for such as are mortal or noxious, we have a right to destroy them ; and for those that are neither of advantage or prejudice to us, the common enjoyment of life is what I cannot think we ought to deprive them of.

This whole matter, with regard to each of these considerations, is set in a very agreeable light in one of the *Persian* fables of *Pilpay*, with which I shall end this paper.

A traveller passing thro' a thicket, and feeling a few sparks of a fire, which some passengers had kindled as they went that way before, made up to it. On a sudden the sparks caught hold of a bush, in the midst of which lay an adder, and set it in flames. The adder entreated the traveller's assistance, who tying a bag to the end of his staff, reached it, and drew him out : He then bid him go where he pleased, but never more be hurtful to men, since he owed his life to a man's compassion. The adder, however, prepared to sting him, and when he expostulated how unjust it was to retaliate good with evil, I shall do no more (said the adder) than what you men practise every day, whose custom it is to requite benefits with ingratitude. If you cannot deny this truth, let us refer it to the first we meet. The man consented, and seeing a tree, put the question to it in what manner a good turn was to be recompensed : If you mean according to the usage of men (replied the tree) by its contrary : I have been standing here these hundred years to protect them from the scorching sun, and in requital they have cut down my branches, and are going to saw my body into planks. Upon this the adder insulting the man, he appealed to a second evidence, which was granted, and immediately they met a cow. The same demand was made, and much the same answer given, that among men it was certainly so. I know it (said the cow) by woeful experience ; for I have served a man this long time with milk, butter and cheese, and brought him besides a calf every year : but now I am old, he turns me into this pasture, with design to sell me to a butcher, who will shortly make an end of me. The traveller upon this stood confounded, but desired of courtesy one trial more, to be finally judged by the next beast they should meet. This happened to be a fox, who upon hearing the story in all its circumstances, could not be persuaded it was possible for the adder to enter in so narrow a bag. The adder to convince him went in again ; when the fox told the man he had now his enemy in his power, and with that he fastened the bag, and crushed him to pieces.

The Guardian. 1713.

AN ESSAY ON NOTHING

Henry Fielding

The Introduction

It is surprising, that while such trifling matters employ the masterly pens of the present age, the great and noble subject of this Essay should have passed totally neglected; and the rather, as it is a subject to which the genius of many of those writers who have unsuccessfully applied themselves to politics, religion, etc., is most peculiarly adapted.

Perhaps their unwillingness to handle what is of such importance may not improperly be ascribed to their modesty; though they may not be remarkably addicted to this vice on every occasion. Indeed I have heard it predicated of some, whose assurance in treating other subjects hath been sufficiently notable, that they have blushed at this. For such is the awe with which this Nothing inspires mankind, that I believe it is generally apprehended of many persons of very high character among us, that were title, power, or riches to allure them, they would stick at it.

But whatever be the reason, certain it is, that except a hardy wit in the reign of Charles II. none ever hath dared to write on this subject : I mean openly and avowedly; for it must be confessed, that most of our modern authors, however foreign the matter which they endeavour to treat may seem at their first setting out, they generally bring the work to this in the end.

I hope, however, this attempt will not be imputed to me as an act of immodesty ; since I am convinced there are many persons in this kingdom who are persuaded of my fitness for what I have undertaken. But as talking of a man's self is generally suspected to arise from vanity, I shall, without any more excuse or preface, proceed to my Essay.

Sect. I

Of the Antiquity of Nothing

There is nothing falser than that old proverb which (like many other falsehoods) is in every one's mouth :

Ex nihilo nihil fit.

Thus translated by Shakespeare, in *Lear* :

Nothing can come of nothing.

Whereas in fact from Nothing proceeds every thing. And this is a truth confessed by the philosophers of all sects : the only point in controversy between them being, whether Something made the world out of Nothing, or Nothing out of Something. A matter not much worth debating at present, since either will equally serve our turn. Indeed the wits of all ages seem to have ranged themselves on each side of this question, as their genius tended more or less to the spiritual or material substance. For those of the more spiritual species have inclined to the former, and those whose genius hath partaken more of the chief properties of matter, such as solidity, thickness, etc., have embraced the latter.

But whether Nothing was the *artifex* or *materies* only, it is plain in either case, it will have a right to claim to itself the origination of all things.

And further, the great antiquity of Nothing is apparent

from its being so visible in the accounts we have of the beginning of every nation. This is very plainly to be discovered in the first pages, and sometimes books, of all general historians ; and indeed, the study of this important subject fills up the whole life of an antiquary, it being always at the bottom of his inquiry, and is commonly at last discovered by him with infinite labour and pains.

Sect. II

Of the Nature of Nothing

Another falsehood which we must detect in the pursuit of this Essay is an assertion, "That no one can have an idea of Nothing " : but men who thus confidently deny us this idea, either grossly deceive themselves, or would impose a downright cheat on the world : for, so far from having none, I believe there are few who have not many ideas of it ; though perhaps they may mistake them for the idea of Something.

For instance, is there any one who hath not an idea of immaterial [1] substance ? Now what is immaterial substance, more than nothing ? But here we are artfully deceived by the use of words : for were we to ask another what idea he had of immaterial matter, or unsubstantial substance, the absurdity of affirming it to be Something would shock him, and he would immediately reply it was Nothing.

Some persons perhaps will say, then we have no idea of it ; but, as I can support the contrary by such undoubted

[1] The author would not be here understood to speak against the doctrine of immateriality, to which he is a hearty well-wisher ; but to point at the stupidity of those, who instead of immaterial *essence*, which would convey a rational meaning, have substituted immaterial *substance*, which is a contradiction in terms.

authority, I shall, instead of trying to confute such idle opinions, proceed to show ; first, what Nothing is : secondly, I shall disclose the various kinds of Nothing ; and, lastly, shall prove its great dignity, and that it is the end of every thing.

It is extremely hard to define Nothing in positive terms, I shall therefore do it in negative. Nothing then is not Something. And here I must object to a third error concerning it, which is, that it is in no place ; which is an indirect way of depriving it of its existence ; whereas indeed it possesses the greatest and noblest place on this earth ; viz. the human brain. But indeed this mistake hath been sufficiently refuted by many very wise men ; who, having spent their whole lives in the contemplation and pursuit of Nothing, have at last gravely concluded— *That there is Nothing in this world.*

Further, as Nothing is not Something, so every thing which is not Something is Nothing ; and wherever Something is not Nothing is : a very large allowance in its favour, as must appear to persons well skilled in human affairs.

For instance, when a bladder is full of wind, it is full of Something ; but when that is let out, we aptly say, there is Nothing in it.

The same may be as justly asserted of a man as of a bladder. However well he may be bedaubed with lace, or with title, yet if he have not Something in him, we may predicate the same of him as of an empty bladder.

But if we cannot reach an adequate knowledge of the true essence of Nothing, no more than we can of matter, let us, in imitation of the experimental philosophers, examine some of its properties or accidents.

And here we shall see the infinite advantages which Nothing hath over Something ; for, while the latter is confined to one sense, or two perhaps at the most, Nothing is the object of them all.

For, first, Nothing may be seen, as is plain from the relation of persons who have recovered from high fevers ; and perhaps may be suspected from some (at least) of those who have seen apparitions, both on earth and in the clouds. Nay, I have often heard it confessed by men, when asked what they saw at such a place and time, that they saw Nothing. Admitting then that there are two sights, viz. a first and second sight, according to the firm belief of some, Nothing must be allowed to have a very large share of the first ; and as to the second, it hath it all entirely to itself.

Secondly, Nothing may be heard : of which the same proofs may be given as of .the foregoing. The Argive mentioned by Horace is a strong instance of this :

> —Fuit haud ignobilis Argis
> Qui se credebat miros acedire Tragædos
> In vacuo lætos sessor, Plausorque Theatro.

That Nothing may be tasted and smelt is not only known to persons of delicate palates and nostrils. How commonly do we hear, that such a thing smells or tastes of Nothing ? The latter I have heard asserted of a dish compounded of five or six savoury ingredients. And as to the former, I remember an elderly gentlewoman who had a great antipathy to the smell of apples ; who, upon discovering that an idle boy had fastened some mellow apple to her tail, contracted a habit of smelling them whenever that boy came within her sight, though there were then none within a mile of her.

Lastly, feeling ; and sure if any sense seems more particularly the object of matter only, which must be allowed to be Something, this doth. Nay, I have heard it asserted (and with a colour of truth) of several persons, that they can feel nothing but a cudgel. Notwithstanding which some have felt the motions of the spirit ; and others have felt very bitterly the misfortunes of their friends, without endeavouring to relieve them. Now these seem two plain instances, that Nothing is an object of this sense. Nay, I have heard a surgeon declare, while he was cutting off a patient's leg, that *he was sure he felt Nothing*.

Nothing is as well the object of our passions as our senses. Thus there are many who love Nothing, some who hate Nothing, and some who fear Nothing, etc.

We have already mentioned three of the properties of a noun to belong to Nothing ; we shall find the fourth likewise to be as justly claimed by it : and that Nothing is as often the object of the understanding as of the senses.

Indeed some have imagined that knowledge, with the adjective *human* placed before it, is another word for Nothing. And one of the wisest men in the world declared he knew Nothing.

But, without carrying it so far, this I believe may be allowed, that it is at least possible for a man to know Nothing. And whoever hath read over many works of our ingenious moderns, with proper attention and emolument, will, I believe, confess, that if he understands them right, he understands Nothing.

This is a secret not known to all readers ; and want of this knowledge hath occasioned much puzzling ; for where a book, or chapter, or paragraph, hath seemed to the reader to contain Nothing, his modesty hath sometimes persuaded him, that the true meaning of the author hath escaped him, instead of concluding, as in reality the fact was, that the author, in the said book, etc., did truly, and *bona fide*, mean Nothing. I remember once, at the table of a person of great eminence, and one no less distinguished by superiority of wit than fortune, when a very dark passage was read out of a poet famous for being so sublime that he is often out of the sight of his reader, some persons present declared they did not understand the meaning. The gentleman himself, casting his eye over the performance, testified a surprise at the dullness of his company ; seeing Nothing could, he said, possibly be plainer than the meaning of the passage which they stuck at. This set all of us to puzzling again ; but with like success ; we frankly owned we could not find it out, and desired he would explain it. Explain it ! said the gentle-man, why he means Nothing.

In fact, this mistake arises from a too vulgar error among persons unacquainted with the mystery of writing, who imagine it impossible that a man should sit down to write without any meaning at all ! whereas, in reality, nothing is more common : for, not to instance in myself, who have confessedly set down to write this Essay with Nothing in my head, or, which is much the same thing, to write about Nothing, it may be incontestably proved, *ab effectu*, that Nothing is commoner among the moderns. The inimitable author of a preface to the Posthumous Eclogues of a late ingenious young gentleman, says, " There are men who sit down to write what they think, and others to think what they shall write. But indeed there is a third, and much more numerous sort, who never think either before they sit down or afterwards ; and who, when they produce on paper what was before in their heads, are sure to produce Nothing."

Thus we have endeavoured to demonstrate the nature of Nothing, by showing first, definitively, *what it is not* ; and, secondly, by describing *what it is*. The next thing therefore proposed is to show its various kinds.

Now some imagine these several kinds differ in name only. But without endeavouring to confute so absurd an opinion, especially as these different kinds of Nothing occur frequently in the best authors, I shall content myself with setting them down, and leave it to the determination of the distinguished reader, whether it is probable, or indeed possible, that they should all convey one and the same meaning.

These are, Nothing *per se* Nothing ; Nothing at all ; Nothing in the least ; Nothing in nature ; Nothing in the world ; Nothing in the whole world ; Nothing in the whole universal world. And perhaps many others of which we say—Nothing.

Sect. III

Of the Dignity of Nothing ; and an Endeavour to prove, that it is the End as well as Beginning of all Things

Nothing contains so much dignity as Nothing. Ask an infamous nobleman (if any such be) in what his dignity consists ? It may not be perhaps consistent with his dignity to give you an answer ; but suppose he should be willing to condescend so far, what could he in effect say ? Should he say he had it from his ancestors, I apprehend a lawyer would oblige him to prove, that the virtues to which this dignity was annexed descended to him. If he claims it as inherent in the title, might he not be told, that a title originally implied dignity, as it implied the presence of those virtues to which dignity is inseparably annexed ; but that no implication will fly in the face of downright positive proof to the contrary. In short, to examine no further, since his endeavour to derive it from any other fountain would be equally impotent, his dignity arises from Nothing, and in reality is Nothing. Yet, that this dignity really exists ; that it glares in the eyes of men, and produces much good to the person who wears it, is, I believe, incontestable.

Perhaps this may appear in the following syllogism.

The respect paid to men on account of their titles is paid at least to the supposal of their superior virtues and abilities, or it is paid to Nothing.

But when a man is a notorious knave or fool it is impossible there should be any such supposal.

The conclusion is apparent.

Now that no man is ashamed of either paying or receiving this respect I wonder not, since the great importance of Nothing seems, I think, to be pretty apparent ; but that they should deny the Deity worshipped, and endeavour to represent Nothing as Something, is more worthy reprehension. This is a fallacy extremely common. I have seen a fellow, whom all the world knew to have Nothing in him, not only pretend to Something himself, but supported in that pretension by others who have been less liable to be deceived. Now whence can this proceed but from their being ashamed of Nothing ? A modesty very peculiar to this age.

But, notwithstanding all such disguises and deceit, a man must have very little discernment who can live long in courts, or populous cities, without being convinced of the great dignity of Nothing ; and though he should, through corruption or necessity, comply with the vulgar worship and adulation, he will know to what it is paid : namely, to Nothing.

The most astonishing instance of this respect, so frequently paid to Nothing, is when it is paid (if I may so express myself) to something less than Nothing ; when the person who receives it is not only void of the quality for which he is respected, but is in reality notoriously guilty of the vices directly opposite to the virtues whose applause he receives. This is, indeed, the highest degree of Nothing, or (if I may be allowed the word), the Nothingest of all Nothings.

Here it is to be known, that respect may be aimed at Something and really light on Nothing. For instance, when mistaking certain things called gravity, canting, blustering, ostentation, pomp, and such like, for wisdom, piety, magnanimity, charity, true greatness, etc., we give to the former the honour and reverence due to the latter. Not that I would be understood so far to discredit my subject as to insinuate that gravity, canting, etc., are really Nothing ; on the contrary, there is much more reason to suspect (if we judge from the practice of the world) that wisdom, piety, and other virtues, have a good title to that name. But we do not, in fact, pay our respect to the former, but to the latter : in other words, we pay it to that which is not, and consequently pay it to Nothing.

So far then for the dignity of the subject on which I am treating. I am now to show, that Nothing is the end as well as beginning of all things.

That every thing is resolvable, and will be resolved into its first principles, will be, I believe, readily acknowledged by all philosophers. As, therefore, we have sufficiently proved the world came from Nothing, it follows, that it will likewise end in the same : but as I am writing to a nation of Christians, I have no need to be prolix on this head ; since every one of my readers, by his faith, acknowledges that the world is to have an end, *i.e.* is to come to Nothing.

And, as Nothing is the end of the world, so is it of every thing in the world. Ambition, the greatest, highest, noblest, finest, most heroic and godlike of all passions, what doth it end in ?—Nothing. What did Alexander, Cæsar, and all the rest of that heroic band, who have plundered and massacred so many millions, obtain by all their care, labour, pain, fatigue, and danger ?—Could they speak for themselves, must they not own, that the end of all their pursuit was Nothing ? Nor is this the end of private ambition only. What is become of that proud mistress of the world, the *Caput triumphati orbis* ? that Rome, of which her own flatterers so liberally prophesied the immortality. In what hath all her glory ended ? Surely in Nothing.

Again, what is the end of avarice ? Not power, or pleasure, as some think, for the miser will part with a shilling for neither : not ease or happiness ; for the more he attains of what he desires, the more uneasy and miserable he is. If every good in this world was put to him, he could not say he pursued one. Shall we say then he pursues misery only ? That surely would be contradictory to the first principles of human nature. May we not therefore, nay, must we not confess, that he aims at Nothing ? especially if he be himself unable to tell us what is the end of all this bustle and hurry, this watching and toiling, this self-denial and self-constraint ?

It will not, I apprehend, be sufficient for him to plead that his design is to amass a large fortune, which he never can nor will use himself, nor would willingly quit to any other person ; unless he can show us some substantial good which this fortune is to produce, we shall certainly be justified in concluding, that his end is the same with that of ambition.

The great Mr. Hobbes so plainly saw this, that as he was an enemy to that notable immaterial substance which we have here handled, and therefore unwilling to allow it the large province we have contended for, he advanced a very strange doctrine, and asserted truly, That in all these grand pursuits the means themselves were the end proposed, viz. to ambition, plotting, fighting, danger, difficulty, and such like :—to avarice, cheating, starving, watching, and the numberless painful arts by which this passion proceeds.

However easy it may be to demonstrate the absurdity of this opinion it will be needless to my purpose, since, if we are driven to confess that the means are the only end attained, I think we must likewise confess, that the end proposed is absolutely Nothing.

As I have shown the end of our two greatest and noblest pursuits, one or other of which engages almost every individual of the busy part of mankind, I shall not tire the reader with carrying him through all the rest, since

I believe the same conclusion may be easily drawn from them all.

I shall therefore finish this Essay with an inference, which aptly enough suggests itself from what hath been said : seeing that such is its dignity and importance, and that it is really the end of all those things which are supported with so much pomp and solemnity, and looked on with such respect and esteem, surely it becomes a wise man to regard Nothing with the utmost awe and adoration ; to pursue it with all his parts and pains ; and to sacrifice to it his ease, his innocence, and his present happiness. To which noble pursuit we have this great incitement, that we may assure ourselves of never being cheated or deceived in the end proposed. The virtuous, wise, and learned, may then be unconcerned at all the changes of ministries and of government ; since they may be well satisfied, that while ministers of state are rogues themselves, and have inferior knavish tools to bribe and reward ; true virtue, wisdom, learning, wit, and integrity, will most certainly bring their possessors—Nothing.

Miscellanies, Vol. I. 1743.

ON THE ADVANTAGES OF LIVING IN A GARRET

Samuel Johnson

Sir,

Nothing has more retarded the advancement of learning than the disposition of vulgar minds to ridicule and vilify what they cannot comprehend. All industry must be excited by hope ; and as the student often proposes no other reward to himself than praise, he is easily discouraged by contempt and insult. He who brings with him into a clamorous multitude the timidity of recluse speculation, and has never hardened his front in public life, or accustomed his passions to the vicissitudes and accidents, the triumphs and defeats of mixed conversation, will blush at the stare of petulant incredulity, and suffer himself to be driven by a burst of laughter from the fortresses of demonstration. The mechanist will be afraid to assert before hardy contradiction, the possibility of tearing down bulwarks with a silkworm's thread ; and the astronomer of relating the rapidity of light, the distance of the fixed stars, and the height of the lunar mountains.

If I could by any efforts have shaken off this cowardice, I had not sheltered myself under a borrowed name, nor applied to you for the means of communicating to the public the theory of a garret ; a subject which, except some slight and transient structures, has been hitherto neglected by those who were best qualified to adorn it, either for want of leisure to prosecute the various researches in which a nice discussion must engage them, or because it requires such diversity of knowledge, and such extent of curiosity, as is scarcely to be found in any single intellect : or perhaps others foresaw the tumults which would be raised against them, and confined their knowledge to their own breasts, and abandoned prejudice and folly to the direction of chance.

That the professors of literature generally reside in the highest storeys has been immemorially observed. The wisdom of the ancients was well acquainted with the intellectual advantages of an elevated situation ; why else were the Muses stationed on Olympus or Parnassus by those who could with equal right have raised them bowers in the vale of Tempe, or erected their altars among the flexures of Meander ? Why was Jove himself nursed upon a mountain ? or why did the goddesses, when the prize of beauty was contested, try the cause upon the top of Ida ? Such were the fictions by which the great masters of the earlier ages endeavoured to inculcate to posterity the importance of a garret, which, though they had been long obscured by the negligence and ignorance of succeeding times, were well enforced by the celebrated symbol of Pythagoras, ἀνεμων πνεοντων την ἠχω προσκυνει ; " when the wind blows, worship its echo." This could not but be understood by his disciples as an inviolable injunction to live in a garret, which I have found frequently visited by the echo and the wind. Nor was the tradition wholly obliterated in the age of Augustus, for Tibullus evidently congratulates himself upon his garret, not without some allusion to his Pythagorean precept.

> Quàm juvat immites ventos audire cubantem—
> Aut, gelidas hybernus aquas cûm fuderit auster,
>   Securum somnos, imbre juvante, sequi !

> How sweet in sleep to pass the careless hours,
> Lull'd by the beating winds and dashing showers !

And it is impossible not to discover the fondness of *Lucretius*, an earlier writer, for a garret, in his description of the lofty towers of serene learning, and of the pleasure with which a wise man looks down upon the confused and erratic state of the world moving below him.

> Sed nil dulcius est, bene quàm munita tenere
> Editâ doctrinâ sapientum templa serena ;
> Despicere unde queas alios, passimque videre
> Errare, atque viam palanteis quærere vitæ.

> 'Tis sweet thy lab'ring steps to guide
> To virtue's heights, with wisdom well supplied,
> And all the magazines of learning fortified :
> From thence to look below on human kind,
> Bewilder'd in the maze of life, and blind.
>
> DRYDEN.

The institution has, indeed, continued to our own time ; the garret is still the usual receptacle of the philosopher and poet ; but this, like many ancient customs, is perpetuated only by an accidental imitation, without knowledge of the original reason for which it was established.

> Causa latet ; res est notissima.

> The cause is secret, but the effect is known.
>
> ADDISON.

Conjectures have, indeed, been advanced concerning these habitations of literature, but without much satisfaction to the judicious inquirer. Some have imagined, that the garret is generally chosen by the wits, as most easily rented ; and concluded that no man rejoices in his aerial abode, but on the days of payment. Others suspect, that a garret is chiefly convenient, as it is remoter than any other part of the house from the outer door, which

is often observed to be infested by visitants, who talk
incessantly of beer, or linen, or a coat, and repeat the same
sounds every morning, and sometimes again in the afternoon, without any variation, except that they grow daily
more importunate and clamorous, and raise their voices
in time from mournful murmurs to raging vociferations.
This eternal monotony is always detestable to a man
whose chief pleasure is to enlarge his knowledge and vary
his ideas.   Others talk of freedom from noise, and abstraction from common business or amusements ; and some,
yet more visionary, tell us that the faculties are enlarged
by open prospects, and that the fancy is more at liberty
when the eye ranges without confinement.

These conveniences may perhaps all be found in a well-
chosen garret ; but surely they cannot be supposed sufficiently important to have operated unvariably upon
different climates, distant ages, and separate nations.   Of
a universal practice, there must still be presumed a
universal cause, which, however recondite and abstruse,
may be perhaps reserved to make me illustrious by its
discovery, and you by its promulgation.

It is universally known that the faculties of the mind are
invigorated or weakened by the state of the body, and that
the body is in a great measure regulated by the various
compressions of the ambient element.   The effects of the
air in the production or cure of corporeal maladies have
been acknowledged from the time of *Hippocrates* ; but no
man has yet sufficiently considered how far it may influence the operations of the genius, though every day
affords instances of local understanding, of wits and
reasoners, whose faculties are adapted to some single spot,
and who, when they are removed to any other place, sink
at once into silence and stupidity.   I have discovered, by
a long series of observations, that invention and elocution
suffer great impediments from dense and impure vapours,
and that the tenuity of a defecated air at a proper distance

from the surface of the earth, accelerates the fancy, and sets at liberty those intellectual powers which were before shackled by too strong attraction, and unable to expand themselves under the pressure of a gross atmosphere. I have found dullness to quicken into sentiment in a thin ether, as water, though not very hot, boils in a receiver partly exhausted ; and heads, in appearance empty, have teemed with notions upon rising ground, as the flaccid sides of a football would have swelled out into stiffness and extension.

For this reason I never think myself qualified to judge decisively of any man's faculties, whom I have only known in one degree of elevation ; but take some opportunity of attending him from the cellar to the garret, and try upon him all the various degrees of rarefaction and condensation, tension and laxity. If he is neither vivacious aloft, nor serious below, I then consider him as hopeless ; but as it seldom happens that I do not find the temper to which the texture of his brain is fitted, I accommodate him in time with a tube of mercury, first marking the point most favourable to his intellects, according to rules which I have long studied, and which I may, perhaps, reveal to mankind in a complete treatise of barometrical pneumatology.

Another cause of the gaiety and sprightliness of the dwellers in garrets is probably the increase of that vertiginous motion, with which we are carried round by the diurnal revolution of the earth. The power of agitation upon the spirits is well known ; every man has felt his heart lightened in a rapid vehicle, or on a galloping horse ; and nothing is plainer than that he who towers to the fifth storey is whirled through more space by every circumrotation, than another that grovels upon the ground-floor. The nations between the tropics are known to be fiery, inconstant, inventive, and fanciful ; because, living at the utmost length of the earth's diameter, they are carried about with more swiftness than those whom nature has placed nearer to the poles ; and therefore, as it becomes a wise man to struggle with the inconveniences of his country, whenever celerity and acuteness are requisite, we must actuate our languor by taking a few turns round the centre in a garret.

If you imagine that I ascribe to air and motion effects which they cannot produce, I desire you to consult your own memory, and consider whether you have never known a man acquire reputation in his garret, which, when fortune or a patron had placed him upon the first floor, he was unable to maintain ; and who never recovered his former vigour of understanding till he was restored to his original situation.   That a garret will make every man a wit, I am very far from supposing ; I know there are some who would continue blockheads, even on the summit of the Andes, or on the peak of Teneriffe. But let not any man be considered as unimprovable till this potent remedy has been tried ; for perhaps he was formed to be great only in a garret, as the joiner of Aretæus was rational in no other place but his own shop.

I think a frequent removal to various distances from the centre so necessary to a just estimate of intellectual abilities, and consequently of so great use in education, that if I hoped that the public could be persuaded to so expensive an experiment, I would propose, that there should be a cavern dug, and a tower erected, like those which Bacon describes in Solomon's house, for the expansion and concentration of understanding, according to the exigence of different employments or constitutions.   Perhaps some that fume away in meditations upon time and space in the tower, might compose tables of interest at a certain depth ; and he that upon level ground stagnates in silence, or creeps in narrative, might, at the height of half a mile, ferment into merriment, sparkle with repartee, and froth with declamation.

Addison observes, that we may find the heat of Virgil's climate in some lines of his Georgic : so, when I read a composition, I immediately determine the height of the author's habitation.   As an elaborate performance is commonly said to smell of the lamp, my commendation of a noble thought, a sprightly sally, or a bold figure, is to pronounce it fresh from the garret ; an expression which would break from me upon the perusal of most of your papers, did I not believe, that you sometimes quit the garret, and ascend into the cock-loft.

The Rambler.   1751.

CHARACTERISTICS OF GREATNESS

Oliver Goldsmith

In every duty, in every science in which we would wish to arrive at perfection, we should propose for the object of our pursuit some certain station even beyond our abilities ; some imaginary excellence, which may amuse and serve to animate our inquiry. In deviating from others, in following an unbeaten road, though we, perhaps, may never arrive at the wished-for object, yet it is possible we may meet several discoveries by the way ; and the certainty of small advantages, even while we travel with security, is not so amusing as the hopes of great rewards, which inspire the adventurer. *Evenit nonnunquam*, says Quintilian, *ut aliquid grande inveniat qui semper quaerit quod nimium est.*

This enterprising spirit is, however, by no means the character of the present age ; every person who should now leave received opinions, who should attempt to be more than a commentator upon philosophy, or an imitator in polite learning, might be regarded as a chimerical projector. Hundreds would be ready not only to point out his errors, but to load him with reproach. Our probable opinions are now regarded as certainties ; the difficulties hitherto undiscovered, as utterly inscrutable ; and the writers of the last age inimitable, and therefore the properest models of imitation.

One might be almost induced to deplore the philosophic spirit of the age, which in proportion as it enlightens the mind, increases its timidity, and represses the vigour of every undertaking. Men are now content with being prudently in the right ; which, though not the way to make new acquisitions, it must be owned, is the best method of securing what we have. Yet this is certain, that the writer who never deviates, who never hazards a new thought, or a new expression, though his friends may compliment him upon his sagacity, though criticism lifts her feeble voice in his praise, will seldom arrive at any degree of perfection. The way to acquire lasting esteem, is not by the fewness of a writer's faults, but the greatness of his beauties ; and our noblest works are generally most replete with both.

An author, who would be sublime, often runs his thought into burlesque ; yet I can readily pardon his mistaking ten times for once succeeding. True Genius walks along a line ; and, perhaps, our greatest pleasure is in seeing it so often near falling, without being ever actually down.

Every science has its hitherto undiscovered mysteries, after which men should travel undiscouraged by the failure of former adventurers. Every new attempt serves, perhaps, to facilitate its future invention. We may not find the Philosopher's stone, but we shall probably hit upon new inventions in pursuing it. We shall, perhaps, never be able to discover the longitude, yet, perhaps, we may arrive at new truths in the investigation.

Were any of these sagacious minds among us (and surely no nation, or no period, could ever compare with us in this particular), were any of those minds, I say, who now sit down contented with exploring the intricacies of another's system, bravely to shake off admiration, and, undazzled with the splendour of another's reputation, to chalk out a path to fame for themselves, and boldly cultivate untried experiment, what might not be the result of their inquiries, should the same study that has made them wise, make them enterprising also ? What could not such qualities, united, produce ? But such is not the character of the English, while our neighbours of the Continent launch out into the ocean of science, without proper stores for the voyage, we fear shipwreck in every breeze, and consume in port those powers which might probably have weathered every storm.

Projectors in a state are generally rewarded above their deserts ; projectors in the republic of letters, never. If wrong, every inferior dunce thinks himself entitled to laugh at their disappointment ; if right, men of superior talents think their honour engaged to oppose, since every new discovery is a tacit diminution of their own pre-eminence.

To aim at excellence, our reputation, our friends, and our all, must be ventured ; by aiming only at mediocrity, we run no risk, and we do little service. Prudence and greatness are ever persuading us to contrary pursuits. The one instructs us to be content with our station, and to find happiness in bounding every wish. The other impels us to superiority, and calls nothing happiness but rapture. The one directs to follow mankind, and to act and think with the rest of the world. The other drives us from the crowd, and exposes us as a mark to all the shafts of envy, or ignorance.

Nec minus periculum ex magna fama quam ex mala.
TACIT.

The rewards of mediocrity are immediately paid, those attending excellence generally paid in reversion. In a word, the little mind who loves itself, will write and think with the vulgar, but the great mind will be bravely eccentric, and scorn the beaten road, from universal benevolence.

The Bee. 1759.

A CITY NIGHT-PIECE

Oliver Goldsmith

THE clock just struck two, the expiring taper rises and sinks in the socket, the watchman forgets the hour in slumber, the laborious and the happy are at rest, and nothing wakes but meditation, guilt, revelry, and despair. The drunkard once more fills the destroying bowl, the robber walks his midnight round, and the suicide lifts his guilty arm against his own sacred person.

Let me no longer waste the night over the page of antiquity, or the sallies of contemporary genius, but pursue the solitary walk, where vanity, ever changing, but a few hours past walked before me ; where she kept up the pageant, and now, like a froward child, seems hushed with her own importunities.

What a gloom hangs all around ! The dying lamp feebly emits a yellow gleam ; no sound is heard but of the chiming clock, or the distant watch-dog. All the bustle of human pride is forgotten ; an hour like this may well display the emptiness of human vanity.

There will come a time, when this temporary solitude may be made continual, and the city itself, like its inhabitants, fade away, and leave a desert in its room.

What cities as great as this have once triumphed in existence, had their victories as great, joy as just, and as unbounded ; and, with short-sighted presumption, promised themselves immortality ! Posterity can hardly trace the situation of some ; the sorrowful traveller wanders over the awful ruins of others ; and, as he beholds, he learns wisdom, and feels the transience of every sublunary possession.

"Here," he cries, "stood their citadel, now grown over with weeds ; there their senate house, but now the haunt of every noxious reptile ; temples and theatres stood here, now only an undistinguished heap of ruin. They are fallen, for luxury and avarice first made them feeble. The rewards of the state were conferred on amusing and not on useful members of society. Their riches and opulence invited the invaders, who, though at first repulsed, returned again, conquered by perseverance, and at last swept the defendants into undistinguished destruction."

How few appear in those streets which but some few hours ago were crowded ! and those who appear now no longer wear their daily mask, nor attempt to hide their lewdness or their misery.

But who are those who make the streets their couch, and find a short repose from wretchedness at the doors of the opulent ? These are strangers, wanderers, and orphans, whose circumstances are too humble to expect redress, and whose distresses are too great even for pity. Their wretchedness excites rather horror than pity. Some are without the covering even of rags, and others emaciated with disease ; the world has disclaimed them ; society turns its back upon their distress, and has given them up to nakedness and hunger. These poor shivering females have once seen happier days, and been flattered into beauty. They have been prostituted to the gay luxurious villain, and are now turned out to meet the severity of winter. Perhaps, now lying at the doors of their betrayers, they sue to wretches whose hearts are insensible, or debauchees who may curse, but will not relieve them.

Why, why was I born a man, and yet see the sufferings of wretches I cannot relieve ? Poor houseless creatures ! the world will give you reproaches, but will not give you relief. The slightest misfortunes of the great, the most imaginary uneasiness of the rich, are aggravated with all the power of eloquence, and held up to engage our attention and sympathetic sorrow. The poor weep unheeded, persecuted by every subordinate species of tyranny ; and every law which gives others security, becomes an enemy to them.

Why was this heart of mine formed with so much sensibility ? or why was not my fortune adapted to its impulse ? Tenderness, without a capacity of relieving, only makes the man who feels it more wretched than the object which sues for assistance.

Citizen of the World. 1762.

BEAU TIBBS

Oliver Goldsmith

I

THOUGH naturally pensive, yet I am fond of gay company,
and take every opportunity of thus dismissing the mind
from duty. From this motive I am often found in the
centre of a crowd ; and wherever pleasure is to be sold,
am always a purchaser. In those places, without being
remarked by any, I join in whatever goes forward, work
my passions into a similitude of frivolous earnestness, shout
as they shout, and condemn as they happen to disapprove.
A mind thus sunk for a while below its natural standard,
is qualified for stronger flights ; as those first retire who
would spring forward with greater vigour.

Attracted by the serenity of the evening, a friend and
I lately went to gaze upon the company in one of the
public walks near the city. Here we sauntered together
for some time, either praising the beauty of such as were
handsome, or the dresses of such as had nothing else to
recommend them. We had gone thus deliberately forward
for some time, when my friend stopping on a sudden,
caught me by the elbow, and led me out of the public
walk ; I could perceive, by the quickness of his pace, and
by his frequently looking behind, that he was attempting
to avoid somebody who followed ; we now turned to the
right, then to the left ; as we went forward, he still went

faster, but in vain ; the person whom he attempted to escape, hunted us through every doubling, and gained upon us each moment ; so that, at last, we fairly stood still, resolving to face what we could not avoid.

Our pursuer soon came up, and joined us with all the familiarity of an old acquaintance. " My dear Charles," cries he, shaking my friend's hand, " where have you been hiding this half a century ? Positively I had fancied you were gone down to cultivate matrimony and your estate in the country." During the reply, I had an opportunity of surveying the appearance of our new companion. His hat was pinched up with peculiar smartness ; his looks were pale, thin, and sharp ; round his neck he wore a broad black ribbon, and in his bosom a buckle studded with glass ; his coat was trimmed with tarnished twist ; he wore by his side a sword with a black hilt ; and his stockings of silk, though newly washed, were grown yellow by long service. I was so much engaged with the peculiarity of his dress, that I attended only to the latter part of my friend's reply, in which he complimented Mr. Tibbs on the taste of his clothes, and the bloom in his countenance. " Psha, psha, Charles," cried the figure, " no more of that if you love me ; you know I hate flattery, on my soul I do ; and yet to be sure an intimacy with the great will improve one's appearance, and a course of venison will fatten ; and yet, faith, I despise the great as much as you do ; but there are a great many damned honest fellows among them ; and we must not quarrel with one half because the other wants breeding. If they were all such as my Lord Mudler, one of the most good-natured creatures that ever squeezed a lemon, I should myself be among the number of their admirers. I was yesterday to dine at the Duchess of Picca-dilly's. My lord was there. ' Ned,' says he to me, ' Ned,' says he, ' I'll hold gold to silver I can tell where you were poaching last night.' ' Poaching, my lord,' says I ; ' faith, you have missed already ; for I stayed at home and let the girls poach for me.' That's my way ; I take a fine woman as some animals do their prey ; stand still, and swoop, they fall into my mouth."

"Ah, Tibbs, thou art a happy fellow," cried my companion with looks of infinite pity, "I hope your fortune is as much improved as your understanding in such company ?" "Improved !" replied the other ; "you shall know,—but let it go no further,—a great secret—five hundred a year to begin with—My lord's word of honour for it—His lordship took me down in his own chariot yesterday, and we had a *tête-à-tête* dinner in the country, where we talked of nothing else." "I fancy you forgot, sir," cried I, "you told us but this moment of your dining yesterday in town !" "Did I say so ?" replied he coolly. "To be sure, if I said so it was so.—Dined in town : egad, now I do remember I did dine in town ; but I dined in the country too : for you must know, my boys, I eat two dinners. By-the-bye, I am grown as nice as the devil in my eating. I'll tell you a pleasant affair about that : we were a select party of us to dine at Lady Grogram's : an affected piece, but let it go no further ; a secret : 'Well, says I, I'll hold a thousand guineas, and say done first, that'—But dear Charles, you are an honest creature, lend me half a crown for a minute or two, or so, just till—But hark'e, ask me for it the next time we meet, or it may be twenty to one but I forgot to pay you."

When he left us, our conversation naturally turned upon so extraordinary a character. "His very dress," cries my friend, "is not less extraordinary than his conduct. If you meet him this day, you find him in rags ; if the next, in embroidery. With those persons of distinction, of whom he talks so familiarly, he has scarce a coffee-house acquaintance. However, both for the interest of society, and perhaps for his own, Heaven has made him poor ; and, while all the world perceives his wants, he fancies them concealed from every eye. An agreeable companion, because he understands flattery ; and all must be pleased with the first part of his conversation, though all are sure of its ending with a demand on their purse. While his youth countenances the levity of his conduct, he may thus earn a precarious subsistence ; but, when age comes on, the gravity of which is incomparable with buffoonery, then will he find himself forsaken by all. Condemned in the decline of life to hang upon some rich family whom he once despised, there to undergo all the ingenuity of studied contempt ; to be employed only as a spy upon the servants, or a bugbear to fright children into duty."

II

There are some acquaintances whom it is no easy matter to shake off. My little beau yesterday overtook me again in one of the public walks, and, slapping me on the shoulder, saluted me with an air of the most perfect familiarity. His dress was the same as usual, except that he had more powder in his hair, wore a dirtier shirt, and had on a pair of temple spectacles, with his hat under his arm.

As I knew him to be a harmless amusing little thing, I could not return his smiles with any degree of severity ; so we walked forward on terms of the utmost intimacy, and in a few minutes discussed all the usual topics of a general conversation.

The oddities that marked his character, however, soon began to appear ; he bowed to several well-dressed persons, who, by their manner of returning the compliment, appeared perfect strangers. At intervals he drew out a pocket-book, seeming to take memorandums before all the company, with much importance and assiduity. In this manner he led me through the length of the whole Mall, fretting at his absurdities, and fancying myself laughed at as well as he by every spectator.

When we were got to the end of our procession,
"Blast me," cries he, with an air of vivacity, "I never saw
the Park so thin in my life before ; there's no company at
all to-day. Not a single face to be seen." "No company !" interrupted I peevishly ; "no company where
there is such a crowd ! Why, man, there is too much.
What are the thousands that have been laughing at us
but company ?" "Lord, my dear," returned he, with
the utmost good humour, "you seem immensely cha-
grined ; but, blast me, when the world laughs at me, I
laugh at the world, and so we are even. My Lord Trip,
Bill Squash the Creolian, and I, sometimes make a party
at being ridiculous ; but I see you are grave ; so if you are
for a fine grave sentimental companion, you shall dine
with my wife ; I must insist on't. I'll introduce you to
Mrs. Tibbs, a lady of as elegant qualifications as any in
nature ; she was bred, but that's between ourselves, under
the inspection of the Countess of Shoreditch. A charming
body of voice ! But no more of that, she shall give us a
song. You shall see my little girl too, Carolina Wilhelmina Amelia Tibbs, a sweet pretty creature ; I design her
for my Lord Drumstick's eldest son ; but that's in friendship, let it go no further ; she's but six years old, and yet
she walks a minuet, and plays on the guitar immensely
already. I intend she shall be as perfect as possible in every
accomplishment. In the first place, I'll make her a scholar ;
I'll teach her Greek myself, and I intend to learn that language purposely to instruct her ; but let that be a secret."

Thus saying, without waiting for a reply, he took me
by the arm, and hauled me along. We passed through
many dark alleys and winding ways. From some motives
to me unknown, he seemed to have a particular aversion
to every frequented street ; but, at last, we got to the
door of a dismal-looking house in the outlets of the town,
where he informed me he chose to reside for the benefit
of the air.

We entered the lower door, which seemed ever to lie most hospitably open ; and began to ascend an old and creaking staircase ; when, as he mounted to show me the way, he demanded whether I delighted in prospects ; to which answering in the affirmative, " Then," says he, " I shall show you one of the most charming out of my windows, for I live at the top of the house ; we shall see the ships sailing, and the whole country for twenty miles round, tip-top, quite high. My Lord Swamp would give ten thousand guineas for such a one ; but, as I sometimes pleasantly tell him, I always love to keep my prospects at home, that my friends may come to see me the oftener."

By this time we were arrived as high as the stairs would permit us to ascend, till we came to what he was facetiously pleased to call the first floor down the chimney ; and knocking at the door, a voice, with a Scotch accent, from within, demanded, "Wha's there ? " My conductor answered, that it was him. But this not satisfying the querist, the voice again repeated the demand ; to which he answered louder than before ; and now the door was opened by an old maid-servant, with cautious reluctance.

When we were got in, he welcomed me to his house with great ceremony, and turning to the old woman, asked where her lady was. " Good troth," replied she in the northern dialect, " she's washing your twa shirts at the next door, because they have taken an oath against lending out the tub any longer." " My two shirts ! " cries he, in a tone that faltered with confusion, " what does the idiot mean ? " " I ken what I mean well enough," replied the other ; " she's washing your twa shirts at the next door, because—" " Fire and fury, no more of thy stupid explanations," cried he ; " go and inform her we have got company. Were that Scotch hag," continued he, turning to me, " to be for ever in my family, she would never learn politeness, nor forget that absurd poisonous accent of hers, or testify the smallest specimen of breeding or high life ; and yet it is very surprising too, as I had her from a Parliament-man, a friend of mine, from the Highlands, one of the politest men in the world ; but that's a secret."

We waited some time for Mrs. Tibbs's arrival, during which interval I had a full opportunity of surveying the chamber and all its furniture ; which consisted of four chairs with old wrought bottoms, that he assured me were his wife's embroidery ; a square table that had been once japanned, a cradle in one corner, a lumbering cabinet in the other ; a broken shepherdess, and a Mandarin without a head, were stuck over the chimney ; and round the walls several paltry, unframed pictures, which he observed were all of his own drawing : " What do you think, sir, of that head in the corner, done in the manner of Grisoni ? There's the true keeping in it ; it's my own face , and, though there happens to be no likeness, a countess offered me a hundred for its fellow : I refused her, for, hang it, that would be mechanical, you know."

The wife, at last, made her appearance, at once a slattern and a coquette ; much emaciated, but still carrying the remains of beauty. She made twenty apologies for being seen in such an odious dishabille but hoped to be excused, as she had stayed out all night at Vauxhall Gardens with the countess, who was excessively fond of the horns. " And, indeed, my dear," added she, turning to her husband, " his lordship drank your health in a bumper." " Poor Jack," cries he, " a dear good-natured creature, I know he loves me. But I hope, my dear, you have given orders for dinner ; you need make no great preparations neither, there are but three of us ; something elegant and little will do ; a turbot, an ortolan, or a—." " Or what do you think, my dear," interrupts the wife, " of a nice pretty bit of ox-cheek, piping hot, and dressed with a little of my own sauce ? " " The very thing," replies he ; " it will eat best with some smart bottled beer ; but be sure to let's have the sauce his grace was so fond of. I hate

your immense loads of meat ; that is country all over ;
extreme disgusting to those who are in the least acquainted
with high life."

By this time my curiosity began to abate, and my
appetite to increase ; the company of fools may at first
make us smile, but at last never fails of rendering us melancholy. I therefore pretended to recollect a prior engagement, and, after having shown my respect to the house,
by giving the old servant a piece of money at the door, I
took my leave ; Mr. Tibbs assuring me, that dinner, if I
stayed, would be ready at least in less than two hours.

Citizen of the World.   1762.

A COMMON COUNCILMAN GOES TO
SEE THE CORONATION

OLIVER GOLDSMITH

SIR,

I am the same Common Councilman who troubled
you some days ago. To whom can I complain but to
you ? for you have many a dismal correspondent ; in this
time of joy my wife does not choose to hear me, because
she says I'm always melancholy when she's in spirits.
I have been to see the Coronation, and a fine sight it was,
as I am told. To those who had the pleasure of being near
spectators, the diamonds, I am told, were as thick as Bristol
stones in a show-glass ; the ladies and gentlemen walked
all along, one foot before another, and threw their eyes
about them, on this side and that, perfectly like clock-work.
Oh ! Mr. Printer, it had been a fine sight indeed, if there
was but a little more eating.

Instead of that, there we sat, penned up in our scaffold-
ings, like sheep upon a market-day in Smithfield ; but
the devil a thing could I get to eat (God pardon me for
swearing) except the fragments of a plum-cake, that was all
squeezed into crumbs in my wife's pocket, as she came
through the crowd.

You must know, sir, that in order to do the thing gen-
teelly, and that all my family might be amused at the same
time, my wife, my daughter, and I, took two guinea places
for the Coronation, and I gave my two eldest boys (who,
by-the-bye, are twins, fine children) eighteenpence apiece
to go to Sudrick Fair, to see the court of the Black King

of Morocco, which will serve to please children well enough.

That we might have good places on the scaffolding, my wife insisted upon going at seven o'clock the evening before the Coronation, for she said she would not lose a full prospect for the world. This resolution I own shocked me. " Grizzle," said I to her, " Grizzle, my dear, consider that you are but weakly, always ailing, and will never bear sitting out all night upon the scaffold. You remember what a cold you caught the last fast-day, by rising but half an hour before your time to go to church, and how I was scolded as the cause of it. Beside, my dear, our daughter Anna Amelia Wilhelmina Carolina will look like a perfect fright, if she sits up, and you know the girl's face is something at her time of life, considering her fortune is but small." " Mr. Grogan," replied my wife, " Mr. Grogan, this is always the case, when you find me in spirits ; I don't want to go, not I ; nor I don't care whether I go at all, it is seldom that I am in spirits, but this is always the case." In short, Mr. Printer, what will you have on't ? to the Coronation we went.

What difficulties we had in getting a coach, how we were shoved about in the mob, how I had my pocket picked of the last new almanac, and my steel tobacco-box ; how my daughter lost half an eyebrow and her laced shoe in a gutter ; my wife's lamentation upon this, with the adventures of the crumbled plum cake, and broken brandy-bottle, what need I relate all these ; we suffered this and ten times more before we got to our places.

At last, however, we were seated. My wife is certainly a heart of oak ; I thought sitting up in the damp night air would have killed her ; I have known her for two months take possession of our easy-chair, mobbed up in flannel nightcaps, and trembling at a breath of air ; but she now bore the night as merrily as if she had sat up at a christening. My daughter and she did not seem to value it of a farthing. She told me two or three stories that she knows will always make me laugh, and my daughter sung me the Noontide air, towards one o'clock in the morning. However, with all their endeavours I was as cold and as dismal as ever I remember. If this be the pleasures of a Coronation, cried I to myself, I had rather see the court of King Solomon in all his glory at my ease in Bartholomew Fair.

Towards morning sleep began to come fast upon me ; and the sun rising and warming the air, still inclined me to rest a little. You must know, sir, that I am naturally of a sleepy constitution ; I have often sat up at table with my eyes open, and have been asleep all the while. What will you have on't ? just about eight o'clock in the morning I fell fast asleep. I fell into the most pleasing dream in the world. I shall never forget it ; I dreamed that I was at my Lord Mayor's feast, and had scaled the crust of a venison pasty. I kept eating and eating, in my sleep, and thought I could never have enough. After some time, the pasty methought was taken away, and the dessert was brought in its room. Thought I to myself, if I have not got enough of the venison, I am resolved to make it up by the largest snap at the sweetmeats. Accordingly, I grasped a whole pyramid ; the rest of the guests seeing me with so much, one gave me a snap, and the other gave me a snap, I was pulled this way by my neighbour on the right hand, and that by my neighbour on the left, but still kept my ground without flinching, and continued eating and pocketing as fast as I could. I never was so pulled and hauled in my whole life. At length, however, going to smell to a lobster that lay before me, methought it caught me with its claws fast by the nose. The pain I felt upon this occasion is inexpressible ; in fact it broke my dream ; when, awaking, I found my wife and daughter applying a smelling-bottle to my nose ; and telling me it was time to go home, they assured me every means had been tried to awake me, while the procession was going forward, but that I still continued to sleep till the whole ceremony was over.   Mr. Printer, this is a hard case, and as I read your most ingenious work, it will be some comfort, when I see this inserted, to find that——I write for it too.

I am,

Sir,

Your distressed,

Humble Servant,

L. GROGAN.

Essays.   1766

THE DISTRESSES OF A COMMON
SOLDIER

Oliver Goldsmith

THE misfortunes of the great, my friend, are held up to
engage our attention, are enlarged upon in tones of declamation, and the world is called upon to gaze at the noble
sufferers : they have at once the comfort of admiration and
pity.

Yet, where is the magnanimity of bearing misfortunes
when the whole world is looking on ? Men in such circumstances can act bravely even from motives of vanity.
He only who in the vale of obscurity can brave adversity—
who, without friends to encourage, acquaintances to pity,
or even without hope to alleviate his distresses, can behave
with tranquillity and indifference, is truly great ; whether
peasant or courtier, he deserves admiration, and should be
held up for our imitation and respect.

The miseries of the poor are, however, entirely dis-
regarded ; though some undergo more real hardships in
one day, than the great in their whole lives. It is indeed
inconceivable what difficulties the meanest English sailor
or soldier endures without murmuring or regret. Every
day to him is a day of misery, and yet he bears his hard fate
without repining.

With what indignation do I hear the heroes of tragedy
complain of misfortunes and hardships, whose greatest
calamity is founded in arrogance and pride ! Their
severest distresses are pleasures compared to what many of

the adventuring poor every day sustain, without murmuring. These may eat, drink, and sleep ; have slaves to attend them, and are sure of subsistence for life ; while many of their fellow-creatures are obliged to wander, without a friend to comfort or to assist them, find enmity in every law, and are too poor to obtain even justice.

I have been led into these reflections from accidentally meeting, some days ago, a poor fellow begging at one of the outlets of this town, with a wooden leg. I was curious to learn what had reduced him to his present situation ; and, after giving him what I thought proper, desired to know the history of his life and misfortunes, and the manner in which he was reduced to his present distress. The disabled soldier, for such he was, with an intrepidity truly British, leaning on his crutch, put himself into an attitude to comply with my request, and gave me his history as follows :

" As for misfortunes, sir, I cannot pretend to have gone through more than others. Except the loss of my limb, and my being obliged to beg, I don't know any reason, thank Heaven, that I have to complain : there are some who have lost both legs and an eye ; but, thank Heaven, it is not quite so bad with me.

" My father was a labourer in the country, and died when I was five years old ; so I was put upon the parish. As he had been a wandering sort of a man, the parishioners were not able to tell to what parish I belonged, or where I was born ; so they sent me to another parish, and that parish sent me to a third : till at last it was thought I belonged to no parish at all. At length, however, they fixed me. I had some disposition to be a scholar, and had actually learned my letters ; but the master of the workhouse put me to business as soon as I was able to handle a mallet.

" Here I lived an easy kind of a life for five years. I only wrought ten hours in the day, and had my meat and drink provided for my labour. It is true, I was not suffered to stir far from the house, for fear I should run away : but what of that ? I had the liberty of the whole house, and the yard before the door, and that was enough for me.

"I was next bound out to a farmer, where I was up both early and late ; but I ate and drank well, and liked my business well enough, till he died. Being then obliged to provide for myself, I was resolved to go and seek my fortune. Thus I lived, and went from town to town, working when I could get employment, and starving when I could get none, and might have lived so still ; but happening one day to go through a field belonging to a magistrate, I spied a hare crossing the path just before me. I believe the devil put it in my head to fling my stick at it : well, what will you have on't ? I killed the hare, and was bringing it away in triumph, when the Justice himself met me : he called me a villain, and collaring me, desired I would give an account of myself. I began immediately to give a full account of all that I knew of my breed, seed, and generation ; but though I gave a very long account, the Justice said I could give no account of myself ; so I was indicted, and found guilty of being poor, and sent to Newgate, in order to be transported to the plantations.

"People may say this and that of being in gaol ; but, for my part, I found Newgate as agreeable a place as ever I was in in all my life. I had my bellyful to eat and drink, and did no work ; but, alas ! this kind of life was too good to last for ever. I was taken out of prison, after five months, put on board of a ship, and sent off with two hundred more. Our passage was but indifferent, for we were all confined in the hold, and died very fast, for want of sweet air and provisions : but, for my part, I did not want meat, because I had a fever all the way : Providence was kind ; when provisions grew short, it took away my desire of eating. When we came ashore, we were sold to the planters. I was bound for seven years, and as I was no scholar—for I had forgot my letters—I was obliged to work among the negroes ; and served out my time, as in duty bound to do.

"When my time was expired, I worked my passage home, and glad I was to see old England again, because I loved my country. O liberty ! liberty ! liberty ! that is the property of every Englishman, and I will die in its defence. I was afraid, however, that I should be indicted for a vagabond once more ; so I did not much care to go into the country, but kept about town ; and did little jobs when I could get them. I was very happy in this manner for some time ; till one evening, coming home from work, two men knocked me down, and then desired me to stand still. They belonged to a pressgang ; I was carried before the Justice, and as I could give no account of myself (that was the thing that always hobbled me), I had my choice left, whether to go on board a man-of-war, or list for a soldier. I chose to be a soldier ; and in this post of a gentleman I served two campaigns in Flanders, was at the battles of Val and Fontenoy, and received but one wound through the breast, which is troublesome to this day.

"When the peace came on, I was discharged ; and as I could not work, because my wound was sometimes painful, I listed for a landman in the East India Company's service. I here fought the French in six pitched battles ; and verily believe, that if I could read and write, our captain would have given me promotion, and made me a corporal. But that was not my good fortune ; I soon fell sick, and when I became good for nothing, got leave to return home again with forty pounds in my pocket, which I saved in the service. This was at the beginning of the present war, so I hoped to be set on shore, and to have the pleasure of spending my money, but the government wanted men, and I was pressed again, before ever I could set foot on shore.

"The boatswain found me, as he said, an obstinate

fellow : he swore that I understood my business perfectly well, but that I shammed Abraham merely to be idle. God knows, I knew nothing of sea business : he beat me without considering what he was about. But still my forty pounds was some comfort to me under every beating : the money was my comfort, and the money I might have had to this day, but that our ship was taken by the French, and so I lost it all.

" Our crew was carried into a French prison, and many of them died, because they were not used to live in a gaol ; but, for my part, it was nothing to me, for I was seasoned. One night, however, as I was sleeping on a bed of boards, with a warm blanket about me (for I always loved to lie well), I was awakened by the boatswain, who had a dark lantern in his hand. ' Jack,' says he to me, ' will you knock out the French sentry's brains ? '—' I don't care,' says I, striving to keep myself awake, ' if I lend a hand.' —' Then follow me,' says he, ' and I hope we shall do business.' So up I got, and tied my blanket, which was all the clothes I had, about my middle, and went with him to fight the Frenchmen. We had no arms ; but one Englishman is able to beat five Frenchmen at any time ; so we went down to the door, where both the sentries were posted, and, rushing upon them, seized their arms in a moment, and knocked them down. From thence nine of us ran together to the quay, and seizing the first boat we met, got out of the harbour, and put to sea. We had not been here three days before we were taken up by an English privateer, who was glad of so many good hands ; and we consented to run our chance. However, we had not so much luck as we expected. In three days we fell in with a French man-of-war, of forty guns, while we had but twenty-three ; so to it we went. The fight lasted for three hours, and I verily believe we should have taken the Frenchman, but unfortunately we lost almost all our men, just as we were going to get the victory. I was once more in the power of the French, and I believe it would have gone hard with me, had I been brought back to my old gaol in Brest ; but, by good fortune, we were retaken, and carried to England once more.

"I had almost forgot to tell you, that in this last engagement I was wounded in two places,—I lost four fingers of the left hand, and my leg was shot off. Had I had the good fortune to have lost my leg and use of my hand on board a king's ship, and not a privateer, I should have been entitled to clothing and maintenance during the rest of my life ; but that was not my chance : one man is born with a silver spoon in his mouth, and another with a wooden ladle. However, blessed be God, I enjoy good health, and have no enemy in this world that I know of, but the French and the Justice of Peace."

Thus saying, he limped off, leaving my friend and me in admiration of his intrepidity and content ; nor could we avoid acknowledging, that an habitual acquaintance with misery is the truest school of fortitude and philosophy.

Citizen of the World. 1762.

NATIONAL PREJUDICES

Oliver Goldsmith

As I am one of that sauntering tribe of mortals who spend
the greatest part of their time in taverns, coffee-houses, and
other places of public resort, I have thereby an opportunity
of observing an infinite variety of characters, which to a
person of a contemplative turn is a much higher entertainment than a view of all the curiosities of art or nature. In
one of these my late rambles I accidentally fell into a company of half a dozen gentlemen, who were engaged in a
warm dispute about some political affair, the decision of
which, as they were equally divided in their sentiments,
they thought proper to refer to me, which naturally drew
me in for a share of the conversation.

Amongst a multiplicity of other topics, we took occasion
to talk of the different characters of the several nations of
Europe ; when one of the gentlemen, cocking his hat,
and assuming such an air of importance as if he had possessed all the merit of the English nation in his own person,
declared, that the Dutch were a parcel of avaricious
wretches ; the French a set of flattering sycophants ; that
the Germans were drunken sots, and beastly gluttons ; and
the Spaniards proud, haughty, and surly tyrants ; but that
in bravery, generosity, clemency, and in every other virtue,
the English excelled all the world.

This very learned and judicious remark was received
with a general smile of approbation by all the company—
all, I mean, but your humble servant, who, endeavouring

to keep my gravity as well as I could, and reclining my head upon my arm, continued for some time in a posture of affected thoughtfulness, as if I had been musing on something else, and did not seem to attend to the subject of conversation ; hoping by this means to avoid the disagreeable necessity of explaining myself, and thereby depriving the gentleman of his imaginary happiness.

But my pseudo-patriot had no mind to let me escape so easily. Not satisfied that his opinion should pass without contradiction, he was determined to have it ratified by the suffrage of every one in the company ; for which purpose, addressing himself to me with an air of inexpressible confidence, he asked me if I was not of the same way of thinking. As I am never forward in giving my opinion, especially when I have reason to believe that it will not be agreeable ; so, when I am obliged to give it, I always hold it for a maxim to speak my real sentiments. I therefore told him that, for my own part, I should not have ventured to talk in such a peremptory strain unless I had made the tour of Europe, and examined the manners of these several nations with great care and accuracy : that perhaps a more impartial judge would not scruple to affirm, that the Dutch were more frugal and industrious, the French more temperate and polite, the Germans more hardy and patient of labour and fatigue, and the Spaniards more staid and sedate, than the English ; who, though undoubtedly brave and generous, were at the same time rash, headstrong, and impetuous ; too apt to be elated with prosperity, and to despond in adversity.

I could easily perceive, that all the company began to regard me with a jealous eye before I had finished my answer, which I had no sooner done, than the patriotic gentleman observed, with a contemptuous sneer, that he was greatly surprised how some people could have the conscience to live in a country which they did not love, and to enjoy the protection of a government to which in their hearts they were inveterate enemies. Finding that by this modest declaration of my sentiments I had forfeited the good opinion of my companions, and given them occasion to call my political principles in question, and well knowing that it was in vain to argue with men who were so very full of themselves, I threw down my reckoning and retired to my own lodgings, reflecting on the absurd and ridiculous nature of national prejudice and pre-possession.

Among all the famous sayings of antiquity, there is none that does greater honour to the author, or affords greater pleasure to the reader (at least if he be a person of a gener-ous and benevolent heart), than that of the philosopher who, being asked what countryman he was, replied, that he was " a citizen of the world." How few are there to be found in modern times who can say the same, or whose conduct is consistent with such a profession ! We are now become so much Englishmen, Frenchmen, Dutchmen, Spaniards, or Germans, that we are no longer citizens of the world ; so much the natives of one particular spot, or members of one petty society, that we no longer consider ourselves as the general inhabitants of the globe, or members of that grand society which comprehends the whole human kind.

Did these prejudices prevail only among the meanest and lowest of the people, perhaps they might be excused, as they have few, if any, opportunities of correcting them by reading, travelling, or conversing with foreigners : but the misfortune is, that they infect the minds, and influence the conduct, even of our gentlemen ; of those, I mean, who have every title to this appellation but an exemption from prejudice, which, however, in my opinion, ought to be regarded as the characteristical mark of a gentleman ; for let a man's birth be ever so high, his station ever so exalted, or his fortune ever so large, yet if he is not free from national and other prejudices, I should make bold to

tell him, that he had a low and vulgar mind, and had no
just claim to the character of a gentleman. And, in fact,
you will always find that those are most apt to boast of
national merit, who have little or no merit of their own to
depend on ; than which, to be sure, nothing is more
natural : the slender vine twists around the sturdy oak,
for no other reason in the world but because it has not
strength sufficient to support itself.

Should it be alleged in defence of national prejudice,
that it is the natural and necessary growth of love to our
country, and that therefore the former cannot be destroyed
without hurting the latter, I answer that this is a gross
fallacy and delusion. That it is the growth of love to our
country, I will allow ; but that it is the natural and necessary growth of it, I absolutely deny. Superstition and enthusiasm, too, are the growth of religion ; but who ever
took it in his head to affirm, that they are the necessary
growth of this noble principle ? They are, if you will,
the bastard sprouts of this heavenly plant, but not its
natural and genuine branches, and may safely enough be
lopped off, without doing any harm to the parent stock :
nay, perhaps, till once they are lopped off, this goodly tree
can never flourish in perfect health and vigour.

Is it not very possible that I may love my own country,
without hating the natives of other countries ? that I may
exert the most heroic bravery, the most undaunted resolution, in defending its laws and liberty, without despising
all the rest of the world as cowards and poltroons ? Most
certainly it is ; and if it were not—But why need I suppose
what is absolutely impossible ?—But if it were not, I must
own I should prefer the title of the ancient philosopher, viz.
a citizen of the world, to that of an Englishman, a Frenchman, an European, or to any other appellation whatever.

Essays. 1798.

THE CHRISTMAS DINNER

WASHINGTON IRVING

> Lo ! now is come our joyful'st feast !
>   Let every man be jolly ;
> Eache roome with yvie leaves is drest,
>   And every post with holly.
> Now all our neighbours' chimneys smoke,
>   And Christmas blocks are burning ;
> Their ovens they with bak't meats choke,
>   And all their spits are turning.
>   Without the door let sorrow lie,
>   And if, for cold, it hap to die,
>   We'll bury 't in a Christmas pye,
>   And evermore be merry.
>   WITHERS' "JUVENILLA."

I HAD finished my toilet, and was loitering with Frank Bracebridge in the library, when we heard a distinct thwacking sound, which he informed me was a signal for the serving up of the dinner. The squire kept up old customs in kitchen as well as hall ; and the rolling-pin, struck upon the dresser by the cook, summoned the servants to carry in the meats.

> Just in this nick the cook knock'd thrice,
> And all the waiters in a trice
>   His summons did obey ;
> Each serving-man, with dish in hand,
> March'd boldly up, like our train band,
>   Presented and away.[1]

[1] Sir John Suckling.

The dinner was served up in the great hall, where the squire always held his Christmas banquet. A blazing crackling fire of logs had been heaped on to warm the spacious apartment, and the flame went sparkling and wreathing up the wide-mouthed chimney. The great picture of the crusader and his white horse had been profusely decorated with greens for the occasion ; and holly and ivy had likewise been wreathed round the helmet and weapons on the opposite wall, which I understood were the arms of the same warrior. I must own, by-the-bye, I had strong doubts about the authenticity of the painting and armour as having belonged to the crusader, they certainly having the stamp of more recent days ; but I was told that the painting had been so considered time out of mind ; and that, as to the armour, it had been found in a lumber-room, and elevated to its present situation by the squire, who at once determined it to be the armour of the family hero ; and as he was absolute authority on all such subjects in his own household, the matter had passed into current acceptation. A sideboard was set out just under this chivalric trophy, on which was a display of plate that might have vied (at least in variety) with Belshazzar's parade of the vessels of the temple ; " flagons, cans, cups, beakers, goblets, basins, and ewers " ; the gorgeous utensils of good companionship that had gradually accumulated through many generations of jovial housekeepers. Before these stood the two Yule candles, beaming like two stars of the first magnitude ; other lights were distributed in branches, and the whole array glittered like a firmament of silver.

We were ushered into this banqueting scene with the sound of minstrelsy, the old harper being seated on a stool beside the fireplace, and twanging his instrument with a vast deal more power than melody. Never did Christmas board display a more goodly and gracious assemblage of countenances ; those who were not hand-some were, at least, happy ; and happiness is a rare im-prover of your hard-favoured visage. I always consider an old English family as well worth studying as a collec-tion of Holbein's portraits or Albert Dürer's prints. There is much antiquarian lore to be acquired ; much knowledge of the physiognomies of former times. Per-haps it may be from having continually before their eyes those rows of old family portraits with which the man-sions of this country are stocked ; certain it is, that the quaint features of antiquity are often most faithfully perpetuated in these ancient lines ; and I have traced an old family nose through a whole picture-gallery, legiti-mately handed down from generation to generation, almost from the time of the Conquest. Something of the kind was to be observed in the worthy company around me. Many of their faces had evidently originated in a gothic age, and been merely copied by succeeding genera-tions ; and there was one little girl in particular, of staid demeanour, with a high Roman nose, and an antique vinegar aspect, who was a great favourite of the squire's, being, as he said, a Bracebridge all over, and the very counterpart of one of his ancestors who figured in the court of Henry VIII.

The parson said grace, which was not a short familiar one, such as is commonly addressed to the Deity in these unceremonious days ; but a long, courtly, well-worded one of the ancient school. There was now a pause, as if something was expected ; when suddenly the butler entered the hall with some degree of bustle : he was attended by a servant on each side with a large wax-light, and bore a silver dish, on which was an enormous pig's head, decorated with rosemary, with a lemon in its mouth, which was placed with great formality at the head of the table. The moment this pageant made its appearance, the harper struck up a flourish ; at the con-

clusion of which the young Oxonian, on receiving a hint
from the squire, gave, with an air of the most comic
gravity, an old carol, the first verse of which was as
follows :

> Caput apri defero,
> Reddens laudes Domino.
> The boar's head in hand bring I,
> With garlands gay and rosemary.
> I pray you all synge merily.
> Qui estis in convivio.

Though prepared to witness many of these little eccentricities, from being apprised of the peculiar hobby of
mine host ; yet, I confess, the parade with which so odd
a dish was introduced somewhat perplexed me, until I
gathered from the conversation of the squire and the
parson, that it was meant to represent the bringing in of
the boar's head ; a dish formerly served up with much
ceremony and the sound of minstrelsy and song, at great
tables, on Christmas day. " I like the old custom," said
the squire, " not merely because it is stately and pleasing
in itself, but because it was observed at the college at
Oxford at which I was educated. When I hear the old
song chanted, it brings to mind the time when I was
young and gamesome—and the noble old college hall—
and my fellow-students loitering about in their black
gowns ; many of whom, poor lads, are now in their
graves ! "

The parson, however, whose mind was not haunted by
such associations, and who was always more taken up
with the text than the sentiment, objected to the Oxonian's version of the carol, which, he affirmed, was different
from that sung at college. He went on, with the dry
perseverance of a commentator, to give the college reading, accompanied by sundry annotations ; addressing
himself at first to the company at large ; but finding

their attention gradually diverted to other talk and other objects, he lowered his tone as his number of auditors diminished, until he concluded his remarks in an under voice to a fat-headed old gentleman next him, who was silently engaged in the discussion of a huge plateful of turkey.[1]

The table was literally loaded with good cheer, and presented an epitome of country abundance, in this season of overflowing larders. A distinguished post was allotted to " ancient sirloin," as mine host termed it ; being, as he added, " the standard of old English hospitality, and a joint of goodly presence, and full of expectation." There were several dishes quaintly decorated, and which had evidently something traditional in their embellishments ; but about which, as I did not like to appear over-curious, I asked no questions.

[1] The old ceremony of serving up the boar's head on Christmas day is still observed in the hall of Queen's College, Oxford. I was favoured by the parson with a copy of the carol as now sung ; and as it may be acceptable to such of my readers as are curious in these grave and learned matters, I give it entire :

> The boar's head in hand bear I,
> Bedeck'd with bays and rosemary ;
> And I pray you, my masters, be merry,
>> Quot estis in convivio,
>>> Caput apri defero,
>>> Reddens laudes Domino.

> The boar's head, as I understand,
> Is the rarest dish in all this land,
> Which thus bedeck'd with a gay garland
>> Let us servire cantico.
>>> Caput apri defero, etc.

> Our steward hath provided this
> In honour of the King of Bliss,
> Which on this day to be served is
>> In Reginensi Atrio.
>>> Caput apri defero, etc., etc., etc.

I could not, however, but notice a pie, magnificently decorated with peacock's feathers, in imitation of the tail of that bird, which overshadowed a considerable tract of the table. This, the squire confessed, with some little hesitation, was a pheasant pie, though a peacock pie was certainly the most authentical ; but there had been such a mortality among the peacocks this season, that he could not prevail upon himself to have one killed.[1]

It would be tedious, perhaps, to my wiser readers, who may not have that foolish fondness for odd and obsolete things, to which I am a little given, were I to mention the other makeshifts of this worthy old humorist, by which he was endeavouring to follow up, though at humble distance, the quaint customs of antiquity. I was pleased, however, to see the respect shown to his whims by his children and relatives ; who, indeed, entered readily into the full spirit of them, and seemed all well versed in their parts ; having doubtless been present at many a rehearsal. I was amused, too, at the air of profound gravity, with which the butler and other servants executed the duties assigned them, however eccentric. They had

---

[1] The peacock was anciently in great demand for stately entertainments. Sometimes it was made into a pie, at one end of which the head appeared above the crust, in all its plumage, with the beak richly gilt ; at the other end the tail was displayed. Such pies were served up at the solemn banquets of chivalry, when knights-errant pledged themselves to undertake any perilous enterprise ; whence came the ancient oath, used by Justice Shallow, " by cock and pie."

The peacock was also an important dish for the Christmas feast ; and Massinger, in his " City Madam," gives some idea of the extravagance with which this, as well as other dishes, was prepared for the gorgeous revels of the olden times :

" Men may talk of country Christmasses :
  Their thirty pound butter'd eggs—their pies of carps' tongues :
  Their pheasants drench'd with ambergris ; *the carcasses of three fat
    wethers bruised for gravy to make sauce for a single peacock !* "

an old-fashioned look ; having, for the most part, been brought up in the household, and grown into keeping with the antiquated mansion, and the humours of its lord ; and most probably looked upon all his whimsical regulations as the established laws of honourable house-keeping.

When the cloth was removed, the butler brought in a huge silver vessel of rare and curious workmanship, which he placed before the squire. Its appearance was hailed with acclamation ; being the Wassail Bowl, so renowned in Christmas festivity. The contents had been prepared by the squire himself ; for it was a beverage in the skilful mixture of which he particularly prided himself ; alleging that it was too abstruse and complex for the comprehension of an ordinary servant. It was a potation, indeed, that might well make the heart of a toper leap within him ; being composed of the richest and raciest wines, highly spiced and sweetened, with roasted apples bobbing about the surface.[1]

The old gentleman's whole countenance beamed with a serene look of indwelling delight, as he stirred this mighty bowl. Having raised it to his lips, with a hearty wish of a merry Christmas to all present, he sent it brimming round the board, for every one to follow his example, according to the primitive style ; pronouncing it "the

[1] The Wassail Bowl was sometimes composed of ale instead of wine ; with nutmeg, sugar, toast, ginger, and roasted crabs ; in this way the nut-brown beverage is still prepared in some old families, and round the hearths of substantial farmers at Christmas. It is also called Lamb's Wool, and is celebrated by Herrick in his "Twelfth Night" :

> Next crowne the bowle full
>   With gentle Lamb's Wool ;
> Add sugar, nutmeg, and ginger,
>   With store of ale too ;
>   And thus ye must doe
> To make the Wassaile a swinger.

ancient fountain of good-feeling, where all hearts met together." [1]

There was much laughing and rallying as the honest emblem of Christmas joviality circulated, and was kissed rather coyly by the ladies. When it reached Master Simon, he raised it in both hands, and with the air of a boon companion struck up an old Wassail chanson :

> The brown bowle,
> The merry brown bowle,
> As it goes round-about-a,
>   Fill
>   Still,
> Let the world say what it will,
> And drink your fill all out-a.
>
> The deep canne,
> The merry deep canne,
> As thou dost freely quaff-a,
>   Sing
>   Fling,
> Be as merry as a king,
> And sound a lusty laugh-a. [2]

Much of the conversation during dinner turned upon family topics, to which I was a stranger. There was, however, a great deal of rallying of Master Simon about some gay widow, with whom he was accused of having a flirtation. This attack was commenced by the ladies ; but it was continued throughout the dinner by the fat-headed old gentleman next the parson, with the persever-

[1] The custom of drinking out of the same cup gave place to each having his cup. When the steward came to the doore with the Wassel, he was to cry three times, *Wassel, Wassel, Wassel*, and then the chappell (chaplein) was to answer with a song.—*Archæologia.*

[2] From Poor Robin's *Almanac.*

ing assiduity of a slow hound ; being one of those long-
winded jokers, who, though rather dull at starting game,
are unrivalled for their talent in hunting it down. At
every pause in the general conversation, he renewed his
bantering in pretty much the same terms ; winking hard
at me with both eyes, whenever he gave Master Simon
what he considered a home thrust. The latter, indeed,
seemed fond of being teased on the subject, as old bachelors
are apt to be ; and he took occasion to inform me, in an
undertone, that the lady in question was a prodigiously
fine woman, and drove her own curricle.

The dinner-time passed away in this flow of innocent
hilarity ; and, though the old hall may have resounded
in its time with many a scene of broader rout and revel,
yet I doubt whether it ever witnessed more honest and
genuine enjoyment. How easy it is for one benevolent
being to diffuse pleasure around him ; and how truly is
a kind heart a fountain of gladness, making everything
in its vicinity to freshen into smiles ! the joyous disposition of the worthy squire was perfectly contagious ; he
was happy himself, and disposed to make all the world
happy ; and the little eccentricities of his humour did
but season, in a manner, the sweetness of his philanthropy.

When the ladies had retired, the conversation, as usual,
became still more animated ; many good things were
broached which had been thought of during dinner, but
which would not exactly do for a lady's ear ; and though
I cannot positively affirm that there was much wit uttered,
yet I have certainly heard many contests of rare wit produce much less laughter. Wit, after all, is a mighty, tart,
pungent ingredient, and much too acid for some stomachs ;
but honest good humour is the oil and wine of a merry
meeting, and there is no jovial companionship equal to that
where the jokes are rather small, and the laughter abundant.

The squire told several long stories of early college
pranks and adventures, in some of which the parson had

been a sharer ; though in looking at the latter, it required some effort of imagination to figure such a little dark anatomy of a man into the perpetrator of a madcap gambol. Indeed, the two college chums presented pictures of what men may be made by their different lots in life. The squire had left the university to live lustily on his paternal domains, in the vigorous enjoyment of prosperity and sunshine, and had flourished on to a hearty and florid old age ; whilst the poor parson, on the contrary, had dried and withered away, among dusty tomes, in the silence and shadows of his study. Still there seemed to be a spark of almost extinguished fire, feebly glimmering in the bottom of his soul ; and as the squire hinted at a sly story of the parson and a pretty milkmaid, whom they once met on the banks of the Isis, the old gentleman made an " alphabet of faces," which, as far as I could decipher his physiognomy, I verily believe was indicative of laughter ; indeed, I have rarely met with an old gentleman that took absolute offence at the imputed gallantries of his youth.

I found the tide of wine and wassail fast gaining on the dry land of sober judgment. The company grew merrier and louder as their jokes grew duller. Master Simon was in as chirping a humour as a grasshopper filled with dew, his old songs grew of a warmer complexion, and he began to talk maudlin about the widow. He even gave a long song about the wooing of a widow, which he informed me he had gathered from an excellent black-letter work, entitled *Cupid's Solicitor for Love*, containing store of good advice for bachelors, and which he promised to lend me ; the first verse was to this effect :

> He that will woo a widow must not dally,
>   He must make hay while the sun doth shine ;
> He must not stand with her—shall I, shall I ?
>   But boldly say, Widow, thou must be mine.

This song inspired the fat-headed old gentleman, who made several attempts to tell a rather broad story out of Joe Miller, that was pat to the purpose ; but he always stuck in the middle, everybody recollecting the latter part excepting himself. The parson, too, began to show the effects of good cheer, having gradually settled down into a doze, and his wig sitting most suspiciously on one side. Just at this juncture we were summoned to the drawing-room, and I suspect, at the private instigation of mine host, whose joviality seemed always tempered with a proper love of decorum.

After the dinner-table was removed, the hall was given up to the younger members of the family who, prompted to all kind of noisy mirth by the Oxonian and Master Simon, made its old walls ring with their merriment, as they played at romping games. I delight in witnessing the gambols of children, and particularly at this happy holiday season, and could not help stealing out of the drawing-room on hearing one of their peals of laughter. I found them at the game of blind-man's-buff. Master Simon, who was the leader of their revels, and seemed on all occasions to fulfil the office of that ancient potentate, the Lord of Misrule,[1] was blinded in the midst of the hall. The little beings were as busy about him as the mock fairies about Falstaff ; pinching him, plucking at the skirts of his coat, and tickling him with straws. One fine blue-eyed girl of about thirteen, with her flaxen hair all in beautiful confusion, her frolic face in a glow, her frock half torn off her shoulders, a complete picture of a romp, was the chief tormentor ; and, from the slyness with which Master Simon avoided the smaller game, and hemmed this wild little nymph in corners, and obliged

[1] At Christmasse there was in the Kinge's house, wheresoever hee was lodged, a lorde of misrule, or mayster of merie disportes, and the like had ye in the house of every nobleman of honour, or good worshippe, were he spirituall or temporall.—STOWE.

her to jump shrieking over chairs, I suspected the rogue of being not a whit more blinded than was convenient.

When I returned to the drawing-room, I found the company seated round the fire listening to the parson, who was deeply ensconced in a high-backed oaken chair, the work of some cunning artificer of yore, which had been brought from the library for his particular accommo-dation. From this venerable piece of furniture, with which his shadowy figure and dark weazen face so admir-ably accorded, he was dealing out strange accounts of the popular superstitions and legends of the surrounding country, with which he had become acquainted in the course of his antiquarian researches. I am half inclined to think that the old gentleman was himself somewhat tinctured with superstition, as men are very apt to be who live a recluse and studious life in a sequestered part of the country, and pore over black-letter tracts, so often filled with the marvellous and supernatural. He gave us several anecdotes of the fancies of the neighbouring peasantry, concerning the effigy of the crusader, which lay on the tomb by the church altar. As it was the only monument of the kind in that part of the country it had always been regarded with feelings of superstition by the good wives of the village. It was said to get up from the tomb and walk the rounds of the churchyard in stormy nights, particularly when it thundered ; and one old woman, whose cottage bordered on the churchyard, had seen it through the windows of the church, when the moon shone, slowly pacing up and down the aisles. It was the belief that some wrong had been left unredressed by the deceased, or some treasure hidden, which kept the spirit in a state of trouble and restlessness. Some talked of gold and jewels buried in the tomb, over which the spectre kept watch ; and there was a story current of a sexton in old times who endeavoured to break his way to the coffin at night, but, just as he reached it, received a violent blow from the marble hand of the effigy, which stretched him senseless on the pavement. These tales were often laughed at by some of the sturdier among the rustics, yet when night came on, there were many of the stoutest unbelievers that were shy of venturing alone in the footpath that led across the churchyard.

From these and other anecdotes that followed, the crusader appeared to be the favourite hero of ghost stories throughout the vicinity. His picture, which hung up in the hall, was thought by the servants to have something supernatural about it ; for they remarked that, in whatever part of the hall you went, the eyes of the warrior were still fixed on you. The old porter's wife too, at the lodge, who had been born and brought up in the family, and was a great gossip among the maid-servants, affirmed, that in her young days she had often heard say, that on Midsummer eve, when it was well known all kinds of ghosts, goblins, and fairies become visible and walk abroad, the crusader used to mount his horse, come down from his picture, ride about the house, down the avenue, and so to the church to visit the tomb ; on which occasion the church door most civilly swung open of itself ; not that he needed it ; for he rode through closed gates and even stone walls, and had been seen by one of the dairymaids to pass between two bars of the great park gate, making himself as thin as a sheet of paper.

All these superstitions I found had been very much countenanced by the squire, who, though not superstitious himself, was very fond of seeing others so. He listened to every goblin tale of the neighbouring gossips with infinite gravity, and held the porter's wife in high favour on account of her talent for the marvellous. He was himself a great reader of old legends and romances, and often lamented that he could not believe in them ; for a superstitious person, he thought, must live in a kind of fairy land.

Whilst we were all attention to the parson's stories, our ears were suddenly assailed by a burst of heterogeneous sounds from the hall, in which were mingled something like the clang of rude minstrelsy, with the uproar of many small voices and girlish laughter. The door suddenly flew open, and a train came trooping into the room, that might almost have been mistaken for the breaking-up of the court of Fairy. That indefatigable spirit, Master Simon, in the faithful discharge of his duties as Lord of Misrule, had conceived the idea of a Christmas mummery or mask-ing; and having called in to his assistance the Oxonian and the young officer, who were equally ripe for anything that should occasion romping and merriment, they had carried it into instant effect. The old housekeeper had been consulted; the antique clothes-presses and ward-robes rummaged, and made to yield up the relics of finery that had not seen the light for several generations; the younger part of the company had been privately convened from the parlour and hall, and the whole had been be-dizened out, into a burlesque imitation of an antique mask.[1]

Master Simon led the van, as " Ancient Christmas," quaintly apparelled in a ruff, a short cloak, which had very much the aspect of one of the old housekeeper's petti-coats, and a hat that might have served for a village steeple, and must indubitably have figured in the days of the Covenanters. From under this his nose curved boldly forth, flushed with a frost-bitten bloom, that seemed the very trophy of a December blast. He was accompanied by the blue-eyed romp, dished up as " Dame Mince Pie," in the venerable magnificence of a faded

[1] Maskings or mummeries were favourite sports at Christmas in old times; and the wardrobes at halls and manor-houses were often laid under contribution to furnish dresses and fantastic disguisings. I strongly suspect Master Simon to have taken the idea of his from Ben Jonson's " Masque of Christmas."

brocade, long stomacher, peaked hat, and high-heeled shoes. The young officer appeared as Robin Hood, in a sporting dress of Kendal green, and a foraging cap with a gold tassel.

The costume, to be sure, did not bear testimony to deep research, and there was an evident eye to the picturesque, natural to a young gallant in the presence of his mistress. The fair Julia hung on his arm in a pretty rustic dress, as " Maid Marian." The rest of the train had been metamorphosed in various ways ; the girls trussed up in the finery of the ancient belles of the Bracebridge line, and the striplings bewhiskered with burnt cork, and gravely clad in broad skirts, hanging sleeves, and full-bottomed wigs, to represent the character of Roast Beef, Plum Pudding, and other worthies celebrated in ancient maskings. The whole was under the control of the Oxonian, in the appropriate character of Misrule ; and I observed that he exercised rather a mischievous sway with his wand over the smaller personages of the pageant.

The irruption of this motley crew, with beat of drum, according to ancient custom, was the consummation of uproar and merriment. Master Simon covered himself with glory by the stateliness with which, as Ancient Christmas, he walked a minuet with the peerless, though giggling, Dame Mince Pie. It was followed by a dance of all the characters, which, from its medley of costumes, seemed as though the old family portraits had skipped down from their frames to join in the sport. Different centuries were figuring at cross hands and right and left ; the dark ages were cutting pirouettes and rigadoons ; and the days of Queen Bess jiggling merrily down the middle, through a line of succeeding generations.

The worthy squire contemplated these fantastic sports, and this resurrection of his old wardrobe, with the simple relish of childish delight. He stood chuckling and rubbing his hands, and scarcely hearing a word the parson said, notwithstanding that the latter was discoursing most authentically on the ancient and stately dance at the Paon, or peacock, from which he conceived the minuet to be derived.[1] For my part I was in a continual excitement, from the varied scenes of whim and innocent gaiety passing before me. It was inspiring to me to see wild-eyed frolic and warm-hearted hospitality breaking out from among the chills and glooms of winter, and old age throwing off his apathy, and catching once more the freshness of youthful enjoyment. I felt also an interest in the scene, from the consideration that these fleeting customs were posting fast into oblivion, and that this was, perhaps, the only family in England in which the whole of them were still punctiliously observed. There was a quaintness, too, mingled with all this revelry, that gave it a peculiar zest : it was suited to the time and place ; and as the old manor-house almost reeled with mirth and wassail, it seemed echoing back the joviality of long-departed years.[2]

But enough of Christmas and its gambols ; it is time for me to pause in this garrulity. Methinks I hear the questions asked by my grave readers, " To what purpose is all this—how is the world to be made wiser by this talk ? " Alas ! is there not wisdom enough extant for

[1] Sir John Hawkins, speaking of the dance called the Pavon, from pavo, a peacock, says, " It is a grave and majestic dance ; the method of dancing it anciently was by gentlemen dressed with caps and swords, by those of the long robe in their gowns, by the peers in their mantles, and by the ladies in gowns with long trains, the motion whereof, in dancing, resembled that of a peacock."— *History of Music.*

[2] At the time of the first publication of this paper, the picture of an old-fashioned Christmas in the country was pronounced by some as out of date. The author had afterwards an opportunity of witnessing almost all the customs above described, existing in unexpected vigour in the skirts of Derbyshire and Yorkshire, where he passed the Christmas holidays. The reader will find some notice of them in the author's account of his sojourn at Newstead Abbey.

the instruction of the world ? And if not, are there not thousands of abler pens labouring for its improvement !— It is so much pleasanter to please than to instruct—to play the companion rather than the preceptor.

What, after all, is the mite of wisdom that I could throw into the mass of knowledge ; or how am I sure that my sagest deductions may be safe guides for the opinion of others ? But in writing to amuse, if I fail, the only evil is in my own disappointment. If, however, I can by any lucky chance, in these days of evil, rub out one wrinkle from the brow of care, or beguile the heavy heart of one moment of sorrow ; if I can now and then penetrate through the gathering film of misanthropy, prompt a benevolent view of human nature, and make my reader more in good humour with his fellow-beings and himself, surely, surely, I shall not then have written entirely in vain.

The Sketch-Book of Geoffrey Crayon. 1820.

ALL FOOLS' DAY

Charles Lamb

The compliments of the season to my worthy masters, and a merry first of April to us all !

Many happy returns of this day to you—and you—and *you*, Sir—nay, never frown, man, nor put a long face upon the matter. Do not we know one another ? what need of ceremony among friends ? we have all a touch of *that same*—you understand me—a speck of the motley. Beshrew the man who on such a day as this, the *general festival*, should affect to stand aloof. I am none of those sneakers. I am free of the corporation, and care not who knows it. He that meets me in the forest to-day, shall meet with no wise-acre, I can tell him. *Staltus sum.* Translate me that, and take the meaning of it to yourself for your pains. What, man, we have four quarters of the globe on our side, at the least computation.

Fill us a cup of that sparkling gooseberry—we will drink no wise, melancholy, politic port on this day—and let us troll the catch of Amiens—*duc ad me—duc ad me*—how goes it ?

> Here shall he see
> Gross fools as he.

Now would I give a trifle to know historically and authentically, who was the greatest fool that ever lived. I would certainly give him in a bumper. Marry, of the

present breed, I think I could without much difficulty
name you the party.

Remove your cap a little further, if you please ; it
hides my bauble. And now each man bestride his hobby,
and dust away his bells to what tune he pleases. I will
give you, for my part,

>——The crazy old church clock,
>And the bewildered chimes.

Good master Empedocles, you are welcome. It is long
since you went a salamander-gathering down Ætna.
Worse than samphire-picking by some odds. 'Tis a
mercy your worship did not singe your mustachios.

Ha ! Cleombrotus ! and what salads in faith did you
light upon at the bottom of the Mediterranean ? You
were founder, I take it, of the disinterested sect of the
Calenturists.

Gebir, my old free-mason, and prince of plasterers at
Babel, bring in your trowel, most Ancient Grand ! You
have claim to a seat here at my right hand, as patron of
the stammerers. You left your work, if I remember
Heredotus correctly, at eight hundred million toises, or
thereabout, above the level of the sea. Bless us, what
a long bell you must have pulled, to call your top workmen to their nuncheon on the low grounds of Sennaar.
Or did you send up your garlick and onions by a rocket ?
I am a rogue if I am not ashamed to show you our Monument on Fish Street Hill, after your altitudes. Yet we think
it somewhat.

What, the magnanimous Alexander in tears ?—cry,
baby, put its finger in its eye, it shall have another globe,
round as an orange, pretty moppet !

Mister Adams——'odso, I honour your coat—pray do
us the favour to read to us that sermon, which you lent
to Mistress Slipslop—the twenty and second in your

portmanteau there—on Female Incontinence—the same—
it will come in most irrelevantly and impertinently seasonable to the time of the day.

Good Master Raymund Lully, you look wise. Pray
correct that error.——

Duns, spare your definitions. I must fine you a bumper,
or a paradox. We will have nothing said or done syllogis-
tically this day. Remove those logical forms, waiter, that
no gentleman break the tender shins of his apprehension
stumbling across them.

Master Stephen, you are late.—Ha ! Cokes, is it you ?
—Aguecheek, my dear knight, let me pay my devoir to
you.—Master Shallow, your worship's poor servant to
command.—Master Silence, I will use few words with
you.—Slender, it shall go hard if I edge not you in somewhere.—You six will engross all the poor wit of the
company to-day.—I know it, I know it.

Ha ! honest R——, my fine old Librarian of Ludgate,
time out of mind, art thou here again ? Bless thy doublet,
it is not over-new, threadbare as thy stories :—what dost
thou flitting about the world at this rate ? Thy customers
are extinct, defunct, bed-rid, have ceased to read long ago.
—Thou goest still among them, seeing if, peradventure,
thou canst hawk a volume or two.—Good Granville
S——, thy last patron, is flown.

> King Pandion, he is dead,
> All thy friends are lapt in lead.—

Nevertheless, noble R——, come in, and take your
seat here, between Armado and Quisada ; for in true
courtesy, in gravity, in fantastic smiling to thyself, in
courteous smiling upon others, in the goodly ornature of
well-apparelled speech, and the commendation of wise
sentences, thou art nothing inferior to those accomplished Dons of Spain. The spirit of chivalry forsake

me for ever, when I forget thy singing the song of Mac-
heath, which declares that he might be *happy with either*,
situated between those two ancient spinsters—when I
forget the inimitable formal love which thou didst make,
turning now to the one, and now to the other, with that
Malvolian smile—as if Cervantes, not Gay, had written
it for his hero ; and as if thousands of periods must revolve,
before the mirror of courtesy could have given his invidious
preference between a pair of so goodly-propertied and
meritorious-equal damsels.

To descend from these altitudes, and not to protract
our Fools' Banquet beyond its appropriate day,—for I
fear the second of April is not many hours distant—in
sober verity I will confess a truth to thee, reader. I
love a *Fool*—as naturally, as if I were of kith and kin to
him. When a child, with child-like apprehensions, that
dived not below the surface of the matter, I read those
Parables—not guessing at their involved wisdom—I had
more yearnings towards that simple architect, that built
his house upon the sand, than I entertained for his more
cautious neighbour ; I grudged at the hard censure pronounced upon the quiet soul that kept his talent ; and—
prizing their simplicity beyond the more provident, and,
to my apprehension, somewhat *unfeminine* wariness of
their competitors—I felt a kindliness, that almost amounted
to a *tendre*, for those five thoughtless virgins—I have never
made an acquaintance since, that lasted ; or a friendship,
that answered ; with any that had not some tincture of
the absurd in their characters. I venerate an honest ob-
liquity of understanding. The more laughable blunders
a man shall commit in your company, the more tests he
giveth you, that he will not betray or overreach you. I
love the safety which a palpable hallucination warrants ;
the security, which a word out of season ratifies. And take
my word for this, reader, and say a fool told it you, if you
please, that he who hath not a dram of folly in his mixture,

had pounds of much worse matter in his composition. It is observed, that " the foolisher the fowl or fish—woodcocks,—dotterels,—cod's-heads, etc., the finer the flesh thereof," and what are commonly the world's received fools, but such whereof the world is not worthy ? and what have been some of the kindliest patterns of our species, but so many darlings of absurdity, minions of the goddess, and her white boys ?—Reader, if you wrest my words beyond their fair construction, it is you, and not I, that are the *April Fool.*

The Essays of Elia. 1823.

DREAM-CHILDREN

A Reverie

CHARLES LAMB

CHILDREN love to listen to stories about their elders, when *they* were children ; to stretch their imagination to the conception of a traditionary great-uncle or grandame, whom they never saw. It was in this spirit that my little ones crept about me the other evening to hear about their great-grandmother Field, who lived in a great house in Norfolk (a hundred times bigger than that in which they and papa lived) which had been the scene—so at least it was generally believed in that part of the country —of the tragic incidents which they had lately become familiar with from the ballad of the Children in the Wood. Certain it is that the whole story of the children and their cruel uncle was to be seen fairly carved out in wood upon the chimney-piece of the great hall, the whole story down to the Robin Redbreasts, till a foolish rich person pulled it down to set up a marble one of modern invention in its stead, with no story upon it. Here Alice put out one of her dear mother's looks, too tender to be called upbraiding. Then I went on to say, how religious and how good their great-grandmother Field was, how beloved and respected by everybody, though she was not indeed the mistress of this great house, but had only the charge of it (and yet in some respects she might be said to be the mistress of it too)

committed to her by the owner, who preferred living
in a newer and more fashionable mansion which he had
purchased somewhere in the adjoining county ; but still
she lived in it in a manner as if it had been her own, and
kept up the dignity of the great house in a sort while she
lived, which afterwards came to decay, and was nearly
pulled down, and all its old ornaments stripped and
carried away to the owner's other house, where they were
set up, and looked as awkward as if some one were to
carry away the old tombs they had seen lately at the
Abbey, and stick them up in Lady C.'s tawdry gilt
drawing-room. Here John smiled, as much as to say,
"that would be foolish indeed." And then I told how,
when she came to die, her funeral was attended by a
concourse of all the poor, and some of the gentry too,
of the neighbourhood for many miles round, to show their
respect for her memory, because she had been such a good
and religious woman ; so good indeed that she knew all
the Psaltery by heart, ay, and a great part of the Testament besides. Here little Alice spread her hands. Then
I told what a tall, upright, graceful person their great-
grandmother Field once was ; and how in her youth she
was esteemed the best dancer—here Alice's little right foot
played an involuntary movement, till upon my looking
grave, it desisted—the best dancer, I was saying, in the
county, till a cruel disease, called a cancer, came, and
bowed her down with pain ; but it could never bend her
good spirits, or make them stoop, but they were still
upright, because she was so good and religious. Then I
told how she was used to sleep by herself in a lone chamber
of the great lone house ; and how she believed that an
apparition of two infants was to be seen at midnight gliding
up and down the great staircase near where she slept, but
she said "those innocents would do her no harm" ; and
how frightened I used to be, though in those days I had
my maid to sleep with me, because I was never half so

good or religious as she—and yet I never saw the infants. Here John expanded all his eyebrows and tried to look courageous. Then I told how good she was to all her grand-children, having us to the great house in the holy-days, where I in particular used to spend many hours by myself, in gazing upon the old busts of the Twelve Cæsars, that had been Emperors of Rome, till the old marble heads would seem to live again, or I to be turned into marble with them ; how I never could be tired with roaming about that huge mansion, with its vast empty rooms, with their worn-out hangings, fluttering tapestry, and carved oaken panels, with the gilding almost rubbed out—some-times in the spacious old-fashioned gardens, which I had almost to myself, unless when now and then a solitary gardening man would cross me—and how the nectarines and peaches hung upon the walls, without my ever offering to pluck them, because they were forbidden fruit, unless now and then,—and because I had more pleasure in strolling about among the old melancholy-looking yew trees, or the firs, and picking up the red berries, and the fir apples, which were good for nothing but to look at—or in lying about upon the fresh grass, with all the fine garden smells around me—or basking in the orangery, till I could almost fancy myself ripening too along with the oranges and the limes in that grateful warmth—or in watching the dace that darted to and fro in the fish-pond, at the bottom of the garden, with here and there a great sulky pike hanging midway down the water in silent state, as if it mocked at their impertinent friskings, —I had more pleasure in these busy-idle diversions than in all the sweet flavours of peaches, nectarines, oranges, and such like common baits of children. Here John slyly deposited back upon the plate a bunch of grapes, which, not unobserved by Alice, he had meditated dividing with her, and both seemed willing to relinquish them for the present as irrelevant. Then in somewhat a more heightened tone, I told how, though their great-grandmother Field loved all her grand-children, yet in an especial manner she might be said to love their uncle, John L——, because he was so handsome and spirited a youth, and a king to the rest of us ; and, instead of moping about in solitary corners, like some of us, he would mount the most mettlesome horse he could get, when but an imp no bigger than themselves, and make it carry him half over the county in a morning, and join the hunters when there were any out— and yet he loved the old great house and gardens too, but had too much spirit to be always pent up within their boundaries—and how their uncle grew up to man's estate as brave as he was handsome, to the admiration of every body, but of their great-grandmother Field most especially ; and how he used to carry me upon his back when I was a lame-footed boy—for he was a good bit older than me— many a mile when I could not walk for pain ;—and how in after life he became lame-footed too, and I did not always (I fear) make allowances enough for him when he was impatient, and in pain, nor remember sufficiently how considerate he had been to me when I was lame-footed ; and how, when he died, though he had not been dead an hour, it seemed as if he had died a great while ago, such a distance there is betwixt life and death ; and how I bore his death as I thought pretty well at first, but afterwards it haunted and haunted me ; and though I did not cry or take it to heart as some do, and as I think he would have done if I had died, yet I missed him all day long, and knew not till then how much I had loved him. I missed his kindness, and I missed his crossness, and wished him to be alive again, to be quarrelling with him (for we quarrelled sometimes), rather than not have him again, and was as uneasy without him, as he their poor uncle must have been when the doctor took off his limb. Here the children fell a crying, and asked if their little mourning which they had on was not for uncle John, and they looked

up, and prayed me not to go on about their uncle, but to
tell them some stories about their pretty dead mother.
Then I told how for seven long years, in hope sometimes,
sometimes in despair, yet persisting ever, I courted the fair
Alice W——n ; and, as much as children could understand,
I explained to them what coyness, and difficulty, and denial
meant in maidens—when suddenly, turning to Alice, the
soul of the first Alice looked out at her eyes with such a
reality of re-presentment, that I became in doubt which of
them stood there before me, or whose that bright hair was ;
and while I stood gazing, both the children gradually grew
fainter to my view, receding, and still receding, till nothing
at last but two mournful features were seen in the uttermost distance, which, without speech, strangely impressed
upon me the effects of speech ; " We are not of Alice, nor
of thee, nor are we children at all. The children of Alice
call Bartrum father. We are nothing ; less than nothing,
and dreams. We are only what might have been, and
must wait upon the tedious shores of Lethe millions of ages
before we have existence, and a name "—and immediately
awaking, I found myself quietly seated in my bachelor
armchair, where I had fallen asleep, with the faithful
Bridget unchanged by my side—but John L. (or James
Elia) was gone for ever.

The Essays of Elia.   1823.

MY FIRST PLAY

Charles Lamb

At the north end of Cross Court there yet stands a portal, of some architectural pretensions, though reduced to humble use, serving at present for an entrance to a printing-office. This old door-way, if you are young, reader, you may not know was the identical pit entrance to Old Drury —Garrick's Drury—all of it that is left. I never pass it without shaking some forty years from off my shoulders, recurring to the evening when I passed through it to see *my first play*. The afternoon had been wet, and the condition of our going (the elder folks and myself) was, that the rain should cease. With what a beating heart did I watch from the window the puddles, from the stillness of which I was taught to prognosticate the desired cessation ! I seem to remember the last spurt, and the glee with which I ran to announce it.

We went with orders, which my godfather F. had sent us. He kept the oil shop (now Davies's) at the corner of Featherstone Building, in Holborn. F. was a tall grave person, lofty in speech, and had pretensions above his rank. He associated in those days with John Palmer the comedian, whose gait and bearing he seemed to copy ; if John (which is quite as likely) did not rather borrow somewhat of his manner from my godfather. He was also known to, and visited by, Sheridan. It was to his house in Holborn that young Brinsley brought his first wife on her elopement with him from a boarding-school at Bath—the beautiful Maria Linley. My parents were present (over a quadrille table) when he arrived in the evening with his harmonious charge. From either of these connexions it may be inferred that my godfather could command an order for the then Drury Lane theatre at pleasure—and, indeed, a pretty liberal issue of those cheap billets, in Brinsley's easy autograph, I have heard him say was the sole remuneration which he had received for many years' nightly illumination of the orchestra and various avenues of that theatre—and he was content it should be so. The honour of Sheridan's familiarity—or supposed familiarity—was better to my godfather than money.

F. was the most gentlemanly of oilmen : grandiloquent, yet courteous. His delivery of the commonest matters of fact was Ciceronian. He had two Latin words almost constantly in his mouth (how odd sounds Latin from an oilman's lips !), which my better knowledge since has enabled me to correct. In strict pronunciation they should have been sounded *vice versâ*—but in those young years they impressed me with more awe than they would now do, read aright from Seneca or Varro—in his own peculiar pronunciation monosyllabically elaborated, or Anglicized, into something like *verse verse*. By an imposing manner, and the help of those distorted syllables, he climbed (but that was little) to the highest parochial honours which St. Andrew's has to bestow.

He is dead—and thus much I thought due to his memory, both for my first orders (little wondrous talismans !— slight keys, and insignificant to outward sight, but opening to me more than Arabian paradises !) and moreover, that by his testamentary beneficence I came into possession of the only landed property which I could ever call my own —situate near the road-way village of pleasant Puckeridge, in Hertfordshire. When I journeyed down to take possession, and planted foot on my own ground, the stately habits of the donor descended upon me, and I strode (shall I confess the vanity ?) with larger paces over my allotment of three-quarters of an acre, with its commodious mansion in the midst, with the feeling of an English freeholder that all betwixt sky and centre was my own. The estate has passed into more prudent hands, and nothing but an agrarian can restore it.

In those days were pit orders. Beshrew the uncomfortable manager who abolished them !—with one of these we went. I remember the waiting at the door—not that which is left—but between that and an inner door in shelter—O when shall I be such an expectant again !—with the cry of nonpareils, an indispensable play-house accompaniment in those days. As near as I can recollect, the fashionable pronunciation of the theatrical fruiteresses then was, " Chase some oranges, chase some numparels, chase a bill of the play ; "—chase *pro* chuse. But when we got in, and I beheld the green curtain that veiled a heaven to my imagination, which was soon to be disclosed——the breathless anticipations I endured ! I had seen something like it in the plate prefixed to Troilus and Cressida, in Rowe's Shakespeare—the tent scene with Diomede—and a sight of that plate can always bring back in a measure the feeling of that evening.—The boxes at that time, full of well-dressed women of quality, projected over the pit ; and the pilasters reaching down were adorned with a glistering substance (I know not what) under glass (as it seemed), resembling—a homely fancy—but I judged it to be sugar-candy—yet, to my raised imagination, divested of its homelier qualities, it appeared a glorified candy !—The orchestra lights at length arose, those " fair Auroras ! " Once the bell sounded. It was to ring out yet once again —and, incapable of the anticipation, I reposed my shut eyes in a sort of resignation upon the maternal lap. It rang the second time. The curtain drew up—I was not past six years old—and the play was Artaxerxes !

I had dabbled a little in the Universal History—the ancient part of it—and here was the court of Persia. It was being admitted to a sight of the past. I took no proper interest in the action going on, for I understood not its import—but I heard the word Darius, and I was in the midst of Daniel. All feeling was absorbed in vision. Gorgeous vests, gardens, palaces, princesses, passed before me. I knew not players. I was in Persepolis for the time ; and the burning idol of their devotion almost converted me into a worshipper. I was awe-struck, and believed those significations to be something more than elemental fires. It was all enchantment and a dream. No such pleasure has since visited me but in dreams.—Harlequin's Invasion followed ; where, I remember, the transformation of the magistrates into reverend beldams seemed to me a piece of grave historic justice, and the tailor carrying his own head to be as sober a verity as the legend of St. Denys.

  The next play to which I was taken was the Lady of the Manor, of which, with the exception of some scenery, very faint traces are left in my memory. It was followed by a pantomime, called Lun's Ghost—a satiric touch, I apprehend, upon Rich, not long since dead—but to my apprehension (too sincere for satire), Lun was as remote a piece of antiquity as Lud—the father of a line of Harlequins—transmitting his dagger of lath (the wooden sceptre) through countless ages. I saw the primeval Motley come from his silent tomb in a ghastly vest of white patch-work, like the apparition of a dead rainbow. So Harlequins (thought I) look when they are dead.

  My third play followed in quick succession. It was the Way of the World. I think I must have sat at it as grave as a judge ; for, I remember, the hysteric affectations of good Lady Wishfort affected me like some solemn tragic passion. Robinson Crusoe followed ; in which Crusoe, man Friday, and the parrot, were as good and authentic as in the story.—The clownery and pantaloonery of these pantomimes have clean passed out of my head. I believe, I no more laughed at them, than at the same age I should have been disposed to laugh at the grotesque Gothic heads (seeming to me then replete with devout meaning) that gape, and grin, in stone around the inside of the old Round Church (my church) of the Templars.

I saw these plays in the season 1781-2, when I was from six to seven years old. After the intervention of six or seven other years (for at school all play-going was inhibited) I again entered the doors of a theatre. That old Artaxerxes evening had never done ringing in my fancy. I expected the same feelings to come again with the same occasion. But we differ from ourselves less at sixty and sixteen, than the latter does from six. In that interval what had I not lost ! At the first period I knew nothing, understood nothing, discriminated nothing. I felt all, loved all, wondered all—

Was nourished, I could not tell how—

I had left the temple a devotee, and was returned a rationalist. The same things were there materially ; but the emblem, the reference, was gone !—The green curtain was no longer a veil, drawn between two worlds, the unfolding of which was to bring back past ages, to present "a royal ghost,"—but a certain quantity of green baize, which was to separate the audience for a given time from certain of their fellow-men who were to come forward and pretend those parts. The lights—the orchestra lights —came up a clumsy machinery. The first ring, and the second ring, was now but a trick of the prompter's bell— which had been, like the note of the cuckoo, a phantom of a voice, no hand seen or guessed at which ministered to its warning. The actors were men and women painted. I thought the fault was in them ; but it was in myself, and the alteration which those many centuries—of six short twelvemonths—had wrought in me.—Perhaps it was fortunate for me that the play of the evening was but an indifferent comedy as it gave me time to crop some un-reasonable expectations, which might have interfered with the genuine emotions with which I was soon after enabled to enter upon the first appearance to me of Mrs. Siddons in Isabella.   Comparison and retrospection soon yielded to the present attraction of the scene ; and the theatre became to me, upon a new stock, the most delightful of recreations.

The Essays of Elia.   1823.

A DISSERTATION UPON ROAST PIG

Charles Lamb

MANKIND, says a Chinese manuscript, which my friend M. was obliging enough to read and explain to me, for the first seventy thousand ages ate their meat raw, clawing or biting it from the living animal, just as they do in Abyssinia to this day. This period is not obscurely hinted at by their great Confucius in the second chapter of his Mundane Mutations, where he designates a kind of golden age by the term Cho-fang, literally the Cook's holiday. The manuscript goes on to say, that the art of roasting, or rather broiling (which I take to be the elder brother), was accidentally discovered in the manner following. The swine-herd, Ho-ti, having gone out into the woods one morning, as his manner was, to collect mast for his hogs, left his cottage in the care of his eldest son Bo-bo, a great lubberly boy, who being fond of playing with fire, as youngsters of his age commonly are, let some sparks escape into a bundle of straw, which kindling quickly, spread the conflagration over every part of their poor mansion, till it was reduced to ashes. Together with the cottage (a sorry antediluvian make-shift of a building, you may think it), what was of much more importance, a fine litter of new-farrowed pigs, no less than nine in number, perished. China pigs have been esteemed a luxury all over the East from the remotest periods that we read of. Bo-bo was in utmost consternation, as you may think, not so much for the sake of the tenement, which his father and he could easily build up again with a few dry branches, and the labour of an hour or two, at any time, as for the loss of the pigs. While he was thinking what he should say to his father, and wringing his hands over the smoking remnants of one of those untimely sufferers, an odour assailed his nostrils, unlike any scent which he had before experienced. What could it proceed from ?—not from the burnt cottage—he had smelt that smell before—indeed, this was by no means the first accident of the kind which had occurred through the negligence of this unlucky young fire-brand. Much less did it resemble that of any known herb, weed, or flower. A premonitory moistening at the same time over-flowed his nether lip. He knew not what to think. He next stooped down to feel the pig, if there were any signs of life in it. He burnt his fingers, and to cool them he applied them in his booby fashion to his mouth. Some of the crums of the scorched skin had come away with his fingers, and for the first time in his life (in the world's life indeed, for before him no man had known it) he tasted—*crackling* ! Again he felt and fumbled at the pig. It did not burn him so much now, still he licked his fingers from a sort of habit. The truth at length broke into his slow understanding, that it was the pig that smelt so, and the pig that tasted so delicious ; and, surrendering himself up to the newborn pleasure, he fell to tearing up whole handfuls of the scorched skin with the flesh next it, and was cramming it down his throat in his beastly fashion, when his sire entered amid the smoking rafters, armed with retributory cudgel, and finding how affairs stood, began to rain blows upon the young rogue's shoulders, as thick as hailstones, which Bo-bo heeded not any more than if they had been flies. The tickling pleasure, which he ex-perienced in his lower regions, had rendered him quite callous to any inconveniences he might feel in those remote quarters. His father might lay on, but he could not beat him from his pig, till he had fairly made an end of it, when, becoming a little more sensible of his situation, something like the following dialogue ensued.

"You graceless whelp, what have you got there devouring? Is it not enough that you have burnt me down three houses with your dog's tricks, and be hanged to you, but you must be eating fire, and I know not what—what have you got there, I say?"

"O, father, the pig, the pig, do come and taste how nice the burnt pig eats."

The ears of Ho-ti tingled with horror. He cursed his son, and he cursed himself that ever he should beget a son that should eat burnt pig.

Bo-bo, whose scent was wonderfully sharpened since morning, soon raked out another pig, and fairly rending it asunder, thrust the lesser half by main force into the fists of Ho-ti, still shouting out "Eat, eat, eat the burnt pig, father, only taste—O Lord,"—with such-like barbarous ejaculations, cramming all the while as if he would choke.

Ho-ti trembled every joint while he grasped the abominable thing, wavering whether he should not put his son to death for an unnatural young monster, when the crackling scorching his fingers, as it had done his son's, and applying the same remedy to them, he in his turn tasted some of its flavour, which, make what sour mouths he would for a pretence, proved not altogether displeasing to him. In conclusion (for the manuscript here is a little tedious) both father and son fairly sat down to the mess, and never left off till they had despatched all that remained of the litter.

Bo-bo was strictly enjoined not to let the secret escape, for the neighbours would certainly have stoned them for a couple of abominable wretches, who could think of improving upon the good meat which God had sent them. Nevertheless, strange stories got about. It was observed that Ho-ti's cottage was burnt down now more frequently than ever. Nothing but fires from this time forward. Some would break out in broad day, others in the night-time. As often as the sow farrowed, so sure was the house of Ho-ti to be in a blaze ; and Ho-ti himself, which was the more remarkable, instead of chastising his son, seemed to grow more indulgent to him than ever. At length they were watched, the terrible mystery discovered, and father and son summoned to take their trial at Pekin, then an inconsiderable assize town. Evidence was given, the obnoxious food itself produced in court, and verdict about to be pronounced, when the foreman of the jury begged that some of the burnt pig, of which the culprits stood accused, might be handed into the box. He handled it, and they all handled it, and burning their fingers, as Bo-bo and his father had done before them, and nature prompting to each of them the same remedy, against the face of all the facts, and the clearest charge which judge had ever given,— to the surprise of the whole court, townsfolk, strangers, reporters, and all present—without leaving the box, or any manner of consultation whatever, they brought in a simul- taneous verdict of Not Guilty.

The judge, who was a shrewd fellow, winked at the manifest iniquity of the decision ; and, when the court was dismissed, went privily, and bought up all the pigs that could be had for love or money. In a few days his Lordship's town house was observed to be on fire. The thing took wing, and now there was nothing to be seen but fires in every direction. Fuel and pigs grew enor- mously dear all over the district. The insurance offices one and all shut up shop. People built slighter and slighter every day, until it was feared that the very science of architecture would in no long time be lost to the world. Thus this custom of firing houses continued, till in process of time, says my manuscript, a sage arose, like our Locke, who made a discovery, that the flesh of swine, or indeed of any other animal, might be cooked (*burnt*, as they called it) without the necessity of consuming a whole house to dress it. Then first began the rude form of a gridiron. Roasting by the string, or spit, came in a century or two later, I forget in whose dynasty. By such slow degrees, concludes the manuscript, do the most useful, and seemingly the most obvious arts, make their way among mankind.——

Without placing too implicit faith in the account above given, it must be agreed, that if a worthy pretext for so dangerous an experiment as setting houses on fire (especially in these days) could be assigned in favour of any culinary object, that pretext and excuse might be found in ROAST PIG.

Of all the delicacies in the whole *mundus edibilis*, I will maintain it to be the most delicate—*princeps obsoniorum*.

I speak not of your grown porkers—things between pig and pork—those hobbydehoys—but a young and tender suckling—under a moon old—guiltless as yet of the sty—with no original speck of the *amor immunditiæ*, the hereditary failing of the first parent, yet manifest— his voice as yet not broken, but something between a childish treble, and a grumble—the mild forerunner, or *præludium*, of a grunt.

He must be roasted. I am not ignorant that our ancestors ate them seethed, or boiled—but what a sacrifice of the exterior tegument !

There is no flavour comparable, I will contend, to that of the crisp, tawny, well-watched, not over-roasted, *crackling*, as it is well called—the very teeth are invited to their share of the pleasure at this banquet in overcoming the coy, brittle resistance—with the adhesive oleaginous —O call it not fat—but an indefinable sweetness growing up to it—the tender blossoming of fat—fat cropped in the bud—taken in the shoot—in the first innocence—the cream and quintessence of the child-pig's yet pure food——

the lean, no lean, but a kind of animal manna—or, rather, fat and lean (if it must be so), so blended and running into each other, that both together make but one ambrosian result, or common substance.

Behold him, while he is doing—it seemeth rather a refreshing warmth, than a scorching heat, that he is so passive to. How equably he twirleth round the string !— Now he is just done. To see the extreme sensibility of that tender age, he hath wept out his pretty eyes—radiant jellies—shooting stars—

See him in the dish, his second cradle, how meek he lieth !—wouldst thou have had this innocent grow up to the grossness and indocility which too often accompany maturer swinehood ? Ten to one he would have proved a glutton, a sloven, an obstinate, disagreeable animal— wallowing in all manner of filthy conversation—from these sins he is happily snatched away—

> Ere sin could blight, or sorrow fade,
> Death came with timely care—

his memory is odoriferous—no clown curseth, while his stomach half rejecteth, the rank bacon—no coalheaver bolteth him in reeking sausages—he hath a fair sepulchre in the grateful stomach of the judicious epicure—and for such a tomb might be content to die.

He is the best of Sapors. Pine-apple is great. She is indeed almost too transcendent—a delight, if not sinful, yet so like to sinning, that really a tender-conscienced person would do well to pause—too ravishing for mortal taste, she woundeth and excoriateth the lips that approach her—like lovers' kisses, she biteth—she is a pleasure bordering on pain from the fierceness and insanity of her relish—but she stoppeth at the palate—she meddleth not with the appetite—and the coarsest hunger might barter her consistently for a mutton chop.

Pig—let me speak his praise—is no less provocative of the appetite, than he is satisfactory to the criticalness of the censorious palate. The strong man may batten on him, and weakling refuseth not his mild juices.

Unlike to mankind's mixed characters, a bundle of virtues and vices, inexplicably intertwisted, and not to be unravelled without hazard, he is—good throughout. No part of him is better or worse than another. He helpeth, as far as his little means extend, all around. He is the least envious of banquets. He is all neighbours' fare.

I am one of those, who freely and ungrudgingly impart a share of the good things of this life which fall to their lot (few as mine are in this kind) to a friend. I protest I take as great an interest in my friend's pleasures, his relishes, and proper satisfactions, as in mine own. " Presents," I often say, " endear Absents." Hares, pheasants, partridges, snipes, barn-door chickens (those " tame villatic fowl "), capons, plovers, brawn, barrels of oysters. I dispense as freely as I receive them. I love to taste them, as it were, upon the tongue of my friend. But a stop must be put somewhere. One would not, like Lear, " give everything." I make my stand upon pig. Methinks it is an ingratitude to the Giver of all good flavours, to extra-domiciliate, or send out of the house, slightingly (under pretext of friendship, or I know not what) a blessing so particularly adapted, predestined, I may say, to my individual palate—It argues an insensibility.

I remember a touch of conscience in this kind at school. My good old aunt, who never parted from me at the end of a holiday without stuffing a sweetmeat, or some nice thing, into my pocket, had dismissed me one evening with a smoking plum-cake, fresh from the oven. In my way to school (it was over London Bridge) a grey-headed old beggar saluted me (I have no doubt at this time of day that he was a counterfeit). I had no pence to console him with, and in the vanity of self-denial, and the very coxcombry of charity, school-boy-like, I made him a present of—the whole cake ! I walked on a little, buoyed up, as one is on such occasions, with a sweet soothing of self-satisfaction ; but before I had got to the end of the bridge, my better feelings returned, and I burst into tears, thinking how ungrateful I had been to my good aunt, to go and give her good gift away to a stranger, that I had never seen before, and who might be a bad man for aught I knew ; and then I thought of the pleasure my aunt would be taking in thinking that I—I myself, and not another—would eat her nice cake—and what should I say to her the next time I saw her—how naughty I was to part with her pretty present—and the odour of that spicy cake came back upon my recollection, and the pleasure and the curiosity I had taken in seeing her make it, and her joy when she sent it to the oven, and how disappointed she would feel that I had never had a bit of it in my mouth at last—and I blamed my impertinent spirit of alms-giving, and out-of-place hypocrisy of goodness, and above all I wished never to see the face again of that insidious, good-for-nothing, old grey impostor.

Our ancestors were nice in their method of sacrificing these tender victims. We read of pigs whipt to death with something of a shock, as we hear of any other obsolete custom. The age of discipline is gone by, or it would be curious to inquire (in a philosophical light merely) what effect this process might have towards intenerating and dulcifying a substance, naturally so mild and dulcet as the flesh of young pigs. It looks like refining a violet. Yet we should be cautious, while we condemn the inhumanity, how we censure the wisdom of the practice. It might impart a gusto—

I remember an hypothesis, argued upon by the young students, when I was at St. Omer's, and maintained with much learning and pleasantry on both sides, " Whether, supposing that the flavour of a pig who obtained his death by whipping (*per flagellationem extremam*) superadded a pleasure upon the palate of a man more intense than any possible suffering we can conceive in the animal, is man justified in using that method of putting the animal to death ? " I forget the decision.

His sauce should be considered. Decidedly, a few bread crumbs, done up with his liver and brains, and a dash of mild sage. But, banish, dear Mrs. Cook, I beseech you, the whole onion tribe. Barbecue your whole hogs to your palate, steep them in shalots, stuff them out with plantations of the rank and guilty garlic ; you cannot poison them, or make them stronger than they are—but consider, he is a weakling—a flower.

The Essays of Elia. 1823.

IMPERFECT SYMPATHIES

Charles Lamb

> I am of a constitution so general, that it consorts and sympathiseth with all things ; I have no antipathy, or rather idiosyncrasy in anything. Those national repugnances do not touch me, nor do I behold with prejudice the French, Italian, Spaniard, or Dutch.—*Religio Medici*.

THAT the author of the Religio Medici, mounted upon the airy stilts of abstraction, conversant about notional and conjectural essences ; in whose categories of Being the possible took the upper hand of the actual ; should have overlooked the impertinent individualities of such poor concretions as mankind, is not much to be admired. It is rather to be wondered at, that in the genus of animals he should have condescended to distinguish that species at all. For myself—earth-bound and fettered to the scene of my activities,—

Standing on earth, not rapt above the sky,

I confess that I do feel the differences of mankind, national or individual, to an unhealthy excess. I can look with no indifferent eye upon things or persons. Whatever is, is to me a matter of taste or distaste ; or when once it becomes indifferent, it begins to be disrelishing. I am, in plainer words, a bundle of prejudices—made up of likings and dislikings—the veriest thrall to sympathies, apathies, antipathies. In a certain sense, I hope it may be said of me that

I am a lover of my species. I can feel for all indifferently, but I cannot feel towards all equally. The more purely-English word that expresses sympathy will better explain my meaning. I can be a friend to a worthy man, who upon another account cannot be my mate or *fellow*. I cannot *like* all people alike.[1]

I have been trying all my life to like Scotchmen, and am obliged to desist from the experiment in despair. They cannot like me—and in truth, I never knew one of that nation who attempted to do it. There is something more plain and ingenuous in their mode of proceeding. We know one another at first sight. There is an order of imperfect intellects (under which mine must be content to rank) which in its constitution is essentially anti-Caledonian. The owners of the sort of faculties I allude to,

[1] I would be understood as confining myself to the subject of *imperfect sympathies*. To nations or classes of men there can be no direct *antipathy*. There may be individuals born and constellated so opposite to another individual nature, that the same sphere cannot hold them. I have met with my moral antipodes, and can believe the story of two persons meeting (who never saw one another before in their lives) and instantly fighting.

> ——We by proof find there should be
> 'Twixt man and man such an antipathy,
> That though he can show no just reason why
> For any former wrong or injury,
> Can neither find a blemish in his fame,
> Nor aught in face or feature justly blame,
> Can challenge or accuse him of no evil,
> Yet notwithstanding hates him as a devil.

The lines are from old Heywood's " Hierarchie of Angels," and he subjoins a curious story in confirmation, of a Spaniard who attempted to assassinate a King Ferdinand of Spain, and being put to the rack could give no other reason for the deed but an inveterate antipathy which he had taken to the first sight of the King

> ——The cause which to that act compell'd him
> Was, he ne'er loved him since he first beheld him.

have minds rather suggestive than comprehensive. They have no pretences to much clearness or precision in their ideas, or in their manner of expressing them. Their intellectual wardrobe (to confess fairly) has few whole pieces in it. They are content with fragments and scattered pieces of Truth. She presents no full front to them—a feature or side-face at the most. Hints and glimpses, germs and crude essays at a system, is the utmost they pretend to. They beat up a little game peradventure—and leave it to knottier heads, more robust constitutions, to run it down. The light that lights them is not steady and polar, but mutable and shifting ; waxing, and again waning. Their conversation is accordingly. They will throw out a random word in or out of season, and be content to let it pass for what it is worth. They cannot speak always as if they were upon their oath—but must be understood, speaking or writing, with some abatement. They seldom wait to mature a proposition, but e'en bring it to market in the green ear. They delight to impart their defective discoveries as they arise, without waiting for their full development. They are no systematisers, and would but err more by attempting it. Their minds, as I said before, are suggestive merely. The brain of a true Caledonian (if I am not mistaken) is constituted upon quite a different plan. His Minerva is born in panoply. You are never admitted to see his ideas in their growth—if, indeed, they do grow, and are not rather put together upon principles of clockwork. You never catch his mind in an undress. He never hints or suggests anything, but unlades his stock of ideas in perfect order and completeness. He brings his total wealth into company, and gravely unpacks it. His riches are always about him. He never stoops to catch a glittering something in your presence, to share it with you, before he quite knows whether it be true touch or not. You cannot cry *halves* to anything that he finds. He does not find, but bring.

You never witness his first apprehension of a thing. His understanding is always at its meridian—you never see the first dawn, the early streaks.—He has no falterings of self-suspicion. Surmises, guesses, misgivings, half-intuitions, semi-consciousnesses, partial illuminations, dim instincts, embryo conceptions, have no place in his brain, or vocabulary. The twilight of dubiety never falls upon him. Is he orthodox—he has no doubts. Is he an infidel—he has none either. Between the affirmative and the negative there is no border-land with him. You cannot hover with him upon the confines of truth, or wander in the maze of a probable argument. He always keeps the path. You cannot make excursions with him—for he sets you right. His taste never fluctuates. His morality never abates. He cannot compromise, or understand middle actions. There can be but a right and a wrong. His conversation is as a book. His affirmations have the sanctity of an oath. You must speak upon the square with him. He stops a metaphor like a suspected person in an enemy's country. " A healthy book ! "—said one of his countrymen to me, who had ventured to give that appellation to John Buncle,—" did I catch rightly what you said ? I have heard of a man in health, and of a healthy state of body, but I do not see how that epithet can be properly applied to a book." Above all, you must beware of indirect expressions before a Caledonian. Clap an extinguisher upon your irony, if you are unhappily blest with a vein of it. Remember you are upon your oath. I have a print of a graceful female after Leonardo da Vinci, which I was showing off to Mr. * * * *. After he had examined it minutely, I ventured to ask him how he liked MY BEAUTY (a foolish name it goes by among my friends)—when he very gravely assured me, that " he had considerable respect for my character and talents " (so he was pleased to say), " but had not given himself much thought about the degree of my personal pretensions." The misconception staggered me, but did not seem much to disconcert him.—Persons of this nation are particularly fond of affirming a truth—which nobody doubts. They do not so properly affirm, as annunciate. They do indeed appear to have such a love of truth (as if, like virtue, it were valuable for itself) that all truth becomes equally valuable, whether the proposition that contains it be new or old, disputed, or such as is impossible to become a subject of disputation. I was present not long since at a party of North Britons, where a son of Burns was expected ; and happened to drop a silly expression (in my South British way) that I wished it were the father instead of the son— when four of them started up at once to inform me, that " that was impossible, because he was dead." An impracticable wish, it seems, was more than they could conceive. Swift has hit off this part of their character, namely their love of truth, in his biting way, but with an illiberality that necessarily confines the passages to the margin.[1] The tediousness of these people is certainly provoking. I wonder if they ever tire one another !— In my early life I had a passionate fondness for the poetry of Burns. I have sometimes foolishly hoped to ingratiate myself with his countrymen by expressing it. But I have always found that a true Scot resents your admiration of his compatriot, even more than he would your contempt of him. The latter he imputes to your " imperfect acquaintance with many of the words which he uses ; " and the same objection makes it a presumption in you to

---

[1] There are some people who think they sufficiently acquit themselves and entertain their company, with relating facts of no consequence, not at all out of the road of such common incidents as happen every day ; and this I have observed more frequently among the Scots than any other nation, who are very careful not to omit the minutest circumstances of time or place ; which kind of discourse, if it were not a little relieved by the uncouth terms and phrases, as well as accent and gesture peculiar to that country, would be hardly tolerable.—*Hints towards an Essay on Conversation.*

suppose that you can admire him.—Thomson they seem to have forgotten. Smollett they have neither forgotten nor forgiven for his delineation of Rory and his companion, upon their first introduction to our metropolis.— Speak of Smollett as a great genius, and they will retort upon you Hume's History compared with *his* Continuation of it. What if the historian had continued "Humphry Clinker"?

I have, in the abstract, no disrespect for Jews. They are a piece of stubborn antiquity, compared with which Stonehenge is in its nonage. They date beyond the pyramids. But I should not care to be in habits of familiar intercourse with any of that nation. I confess that I have not the nerves to enter their synagogues. Old prejudices cling about me. I cannot shake off the story of Hugh of Lincoln. Centuries of injury, contempt, and hate, on the one side,—of cloaked revenge, dissimulation, and hate on the other, between our and their fathers, must, and ought to affect the blood of the children. I cannot believe it can run clear and kindly yet ; or that a few fine words, such as candour, liberality, the light of a nineteenth century, can close up the breaches of so deadly a disunion. A Hebrew is nowhere congenial to me. He is least distasteful on 'Change—for the mercantile spirit levels all distinctions, as all are beauties in the dark. I boldly confess that I do not relish the approximation of Jew and Christian, which has become so fashionable. The reciprocal endearments have, to me, something hypocritical and unnatural in them. I do not like to see the Church and Synagogue kissing and congeeing in awkward postures of an affected civility. If *they* are converted, why do they not come over to us altogether? Why keep up a form of separation, when the life of it is fled? If they can sit with us at table, why do they keck at our cookery? I do not understand these half convertites. Jews christianising—Christians judaising —puzzle me. I like fish or flesh. A moderate Jew is a

more confounding piece of anomaly than a wet Quaker.
The spirit of the synagogue is essentially *separative*. B——
would have been more in keeping if he had abided by the
faith of his forefathers. There is a fine scorn in his face,
which nature meant to be of——Christians. The Hebrew
spirit is strong in him, in spite of his proselytism. He cannot conquer the Shibboleth. How it breaks out, when he
sings, "The Children of Israel passed through the Red
Sea !" The auditors, for the moment, are as Egyptians
to him, and he rides over our necks in triumph. There is
no mistaking him.—B—— has a strong expression of sense
in his countenance, and it is confirmed by his singing. The
foundation of his vocal excellence is sense. He sings with
understanding, as Kemble delivered dialogue. He would
sing the Commandments, and give an appropriate character to each prohibition. His nation, in general, have not
over-sensible countenances. How should they ?—but you
seldom see a silly expression among them. Gain, and the
pursuit of gain, sharpen a man's visage. I never heard of
an idiot being born among them.—Some admire the
Jewish female physiognomy. I admire it—but with
trembling. Jael had those full dark inscrutable eyes.

In the Negro countenance you will often meet with
strong traits of benignity. I have felt yearnings of tenderness towards some of these faces—or rather masks—that
have looked out kindly upon one in casual encounters in
the streets and highways. I love what Fuller beautifully
calls—these "images of God cut in ebony." But I should
not like to associate with them, to share my meals and my
good-nights with them—because they are black.

I love Quaker ways, and Quaker worship. I venerate
the Quaker principles. It does me good for the rest of
the day when I meet any of their people in my path.
When I am ruffled or disturbed by any occurrence, the
sight, or quiet voice of a Quaker, acts upon me as a
ventilator, lightening the air, and taking off a load from

the bosom.   But I cannot like the Quakers (as Desde-
mona would say) " to live with them."   I am all over
sophisticated—with humours, fancies, craving hourly
sympathy.   I must have books, pictures, theatres, chit-chat,
scandal, jokes, ambiguities, and a thousand whim-whams,
which their simpler taste can do without.   I should starve
at their primitive banquet.   My appetites are too high for
the salads which (according to Evelyn) Eve dressed for the
angel, my gusto too excited

   To sit a guest with Daniel at his pulse.

   The indirect answers which Quakers are often found to
return to a question put to them may be explained, I
think, without the vulgar assumption, that they are more
given to evasion and equivocating than other people.   They
naturally look to their words more carefully, and are more
cautious of committing themselves.   They have a peculiar
character to keep up on this head.   They stand in a manner
upon their veracity.   A Quaker is by law exempted from
taking an oath.   The custom of resorting to an oath in
extreme cases, sanctified as it is by all religious antiquity,
is apt (it must be confessed) to introduce into the laxer sort
of minds the notion of two kinds of truth—the one applicable to the solemn affairs of justice, and the other to the
common proceedings of daily intercourse.   As truth bound
upon the conscience by an oath can be but truth, so in
the common affirmations of the shop and the market-place
a latitude is expected, and conceded upon questions
wanting this solemn covenant.   Something less than truth
satisfies.   It is common to hear a person say, " You do not
expect me to speak as if I were upon my oath."   Hence a
great deal of incorrectness and inadvertency, short of
falsehood, creeps into ordinary conversation ; and a kind
of secondary or laic-truth is tolerated, where clergy-truth
—oath-truth, by the nature of the circumstances, is not

required. A Quaker knows none of this distinction.
His simple affirmation being received, upon the most
sacred occasions, without any further test, stamps a value
upon the words which he is to use upon the most indifferent topics of life. He looks to them, naturally, with more
severity. You can have of him no more than his word.
He knows, if he is caught tripping in a casual expression,
he forfeits, for himself, at least, his claim to the invidious
exemption. He knows that his syllables are weighed—and
how far a consciousness of this particular watchfulness, exerted against a person, has a tendency to produce indirect
answers, and a diverting of the question by honest means
might be illustrated, and the practice justified, by a more
sacred example than is proper to be adduced upon this
occasion. The admirable presence of mind, which is notorious in Quakers upon all contingencies, might be traced
to this imposed self-watchfulness—if it did not seem rather
an humble and secular scion of that old stock of religious
constancy, which never bent or faltered in the Primitive
Friends, or gave way to the winds of persecution, to the
violence of judge or accuser under trials and racking
examinations. "You will never be the wiser, if I sit here
answering your questions till midnight," said one of those
upright Justices to Penn, who had been putting law-cases
with a puzzling subtlety. "Thereafter as the answers may
be," retorted the Quaker. The astonishing composure of
this people is sometimes ludicrously displayed in lighter
instances.—I was travelling in a stage coach with three male
Quakers, buttoned up in the straitest non-conformity of
their sect. We stopped to bait at Andover, where a meal,
partly tea apparatus, partly supper, was set before us. My
friends confined themselves to the tea-table. I in my way
took supper. When the landlady brought in the bill, the
eldest of my companions discovered that she had charged
for both meals. This was resisted. Mine hostess was very
clamorous and positive. Some mild arguments were used

on the part of the Quakers, for which the heated mind of the good lady seemed by no means a fit recipient. The guard came in with his usual peremptory notice. The Quakers pulled out their money, and formally tendered it —so much for tea—I, in humble imitation, tendering mine—for the supper which I had taken. She would not relax in her demand. So they all three quietly put up their silver, as did myself, and marched out of the room, the eldest and gravest going first, with myself closing up the rear, who thought I could not do better than follow the example of such grave and warrantable personages. We got in. The steps went up. The coach drove off. The murmurs of mine hostess, not very indistinctly or ambiguously pronounced, became after a time inaudible —and now my conscience, which the whimsical scene had for a time suspended, beginning to give some twitches, I waited, in the hope that some justification would be offered by these serious persons for the seeming injustice of their conduct. To my great surprise, not a syllable was dropped on the subject. They sat as mute as at a meeting. At length the eldest of them broke the silence, by inquiring of his next neighbour, " Hast thee heard how indigos go at the India House ? " and the question operated as a soporific on my moral feeling as far as Exeter.

The Essays of Elia. 1823.

THE SUPERANNUATED MAN

CHARLES LAMB

Sera tamen respexit
Libertas.   VIRGIL.

A Clerk I was in London gay.
            O'KEEFE.

IF peradventure, Reader, it has been thy lot to waste the
golden years of thy life—thy shining youth—in the irksome
confinement of an office ; to have thy prison days prolonged through middle age down to decrepitude and silver
hairs, without hope of release or respite ; to have lived
to forget that there are such things as holy-days, or to
remember them but as the prerogatives of childhood ;
then, and then only, will you be able to appreciate my
deliverance.

It is now six and thirty years since I took my seat at
the desk in Mincing Lane. Melancholy was the transition
at fourteen from the abundant playtime, and the frequently intervening vacations of school days, to the eight,
nine, and sometimes ten hours' a-day attendance at a
counting-house. But time partially reconciles us to
anything. I gradually became content—doggedly content, as wild animals in cages.

It is true I had my Sundays to myself ; but Sundays,
admirable as the institution of them is for purposes of
worship, are for that very reason the very worst adapted
for days of unbending and recreation. In particular, there
is a gloom for me attendant upon a city Sunday, a weight

in the air. I miss the cheerful cries of London, the music, and the ballad-singers—the buzz and stirring murmur of the streets. Those eternal bells depress me. The closed shops repel me. Prints, pictures, all the glittering and endless succession of knacks and gewgaws, and ostentatiously displayed wares of tradesmen, which make a week-day saunter through the less busy parts of the metropolis so delightful—are shut out. No book-stalls deliciously to idle over—No busy faces to recreate the idle man who contemplates them ever passing by—the very face of business a charm by contrast to his temporary relaxation from it. Nothing to be seen but unhappy countenances—or half-happy at best—of emancipated 'prentices and little trades-folks, with here and there a servant maid that has got leave to go out, who, slaving all the week, with the habit has lost almost the capacity of enjoying a free hour ; and, livelily expressing the hollowness of a day's pleasuring. The very strollers in the fields on that day looked anything but comfortable.

But besides Sundays I had a day at Easter, and a day at Christmas, with a full week in the summer to go and air myself in my native fields of Hertfordshire. This last was a great indulgence ; and the prospect of its recurrence, I believe, alone kept me up through the year, and made my durance tolerable. But when the week came round, did the glittering phantom of the distance keep touch with me ? or rather was it not a series of seven uneasy days, spent in restless pursuit of pleasure, and a wearisome anxiety to find out how to make the most of them ? Where was the quiet, where the promised rest ? Before I had a taste of it, it was vanished. I was at the desk again, counting upon fifty-one tedious weeks that must intervene before such another snatch would come. Still the prospect of its coming threw something of an illumination upon the darker side of my captivity. Without it, as I have said, I could scarcely have sustained my thraldom.

Independently of the rigours of attendance, I have ever been haunted with a sense (perhaps a mere caprice) of incapacity for business. This, during my latter years, had increased to such a degree, that it was visible in all the lines of my countenance. My health and my good spirits flagged. I had perpetually a dread of some crisis, to which I should be found unequal. Besides my daylight servitude, I served over again all night in my sleep, and would awake with terrors of imaginary false entries, errors in my accounts, and the like. I was fifty years of age, and no prospect of emancipation presented itself. I had grown to my desk, as it were ; and the wood had entered into my soul.

My fellows in the office would sometimes rally me upon the trouble legible in my countenance ; but I did not know that it had raised the suspicions of any of my employers, when on the 5th of last month, a day ever to be remembered by me, L——, the junior partner in the firm, calling me on one side, directly taxed me with my bad looks, and frankly inquired the cause of them. So taxed, I honestly made confession of my infirmity, and added that I was afraid I should eventually be obliged to resign his service. He spoke some words of course to hearten me, and there the matter rested. A whole week I remained labouring under the impression that I had acted imprudently in my disclosure ; that I had foolishly given a handle against myself, and had been anticipating my own dismissal. A week passed in this manner, the most anxious one, I verily believe, in my whole life, when on the evening of the 12th of April, just as I was about quitting my desk to go home (it might be about eight o'clock) I received an awful summons to attend the presence of the whole assembled firm in the formidable back parlour. I thought now my time is surely come, I have done for myself, I am going to be told that they have no longer occasion for me. L——, I could see, smiled at the terror I was in, which was a little relief to me,—when, to my utter astonishment, B——, the eldest partner, began a formal harangue to me on the length of my services, my very meritorious conduct during the whole of the time (the deuce, thought I, how did he find out that ? I protest I never had the confidence to think as much). He went on to descant on the expediency of retiring at a certain time of life (how my heart panted !), and asking me a few questions as to the amount of my own property, of which I have a little, ended with a proposal, to which his three partners nodded a grave assent, that I should accept from the house, which I had served so well, a pension for life to the amount of two-thirds of my accustomed salary—a magnificent offer ! I do not know what I answered between surprise and gratitude, but it was understood that I accepted their proposal, and I was told that I was free from that hour to leave their service. I stammered out a bow, and at just ten minutes after eight I went home—for ever. This noble benefit—gratitude forbids me to conceal their names— I owe to the kindness of the most munificent firm in the world, the house of Boldero, Merryweather, Bosanquet, and Lacy.

Esto perpetua !

For the first day or two I felt stunned, overwhelmed. I could only apprehend my felicity ; I was too confused to taste it sincerely. I wandered about, thinking I was happy, and knowing that I was not. I was in the condition of a prisoner of the Old Bastile, suddenly let loose after a forty years' confinement. I could scarce trust myself with myself. It was like passing out of Time into Eternity—for it is a sort of Eternity for a man to have his Time all to himself. It seemed to me that I had more time on my hands than I could ever manage. From a poor man, poor in Time, I was suddenly lifted up into a vast revenue ; I could see no end of my possessions ; I wanted some

steward, or judicious bailiff, to manage my estates in Time
for me. And here let me caution persons grown old in
active business, not lightly, nor without weighing their
own resources, to forego their customary employment all
at once, for there may be danger in it. I feel it by myself,
but I know that my resources are sufficient ; and now that
those first giddy raptures have subsided, I have a quiet
home-feeling of the blessedness of my condition. I am
in no hurry. Having all holidays, I am as though I had
none. If Time hung heavy upon me, I could walk it
away ; but I do *not* walk all day long, as I used to do in
these old transient holidays, thirty miles a day, to make the
most of them. If Time were troublesome, I could read
it away, but I do *not* read in that violent measure, with
which, having no Time my own but candlelight Time,
I used to weary out my head and eyesight in bygone
winters. I walk, read, or scribble (as now) just when the
fit seizes me. I no longer hunt after pleasure ; I let it come
to me. I am like the man

———that's born, and has his years come to him,
In some green desert.

" Years," you will say ; " what is this superannuated
simpleton calculating upon ? He has already told us he
is past fifty."
I have indeed lived nominally fifty years, but deduct out
of them the hours which I have lived to other people, and
not to myself, and you will find me still a young fellow.
For *that* is the only true Time, which a man can properly
call his own, that which he has all to himself : the rest,
though in some sense he may be said to live it, is other
people's time, not his. The remnant of my poor days, long
or short, is at least multiplied for me threefold. My ten
next years, if I stretch so far, will be as long as any preceding thirty. 'Tis a fair rule-of-three sum.

Among the strange fantasies which beset me at the commencement of my freedom, and of which all traces are not yet gone, one was, that a vast tract of time had intervened since I quitted the Counting House. I could not conceive of it as an affair of yesterday. The partners, and the clerks with whom I had for so many years, and for so many hours in each day of the year, been so closely associated—being suddenly removed from them—they seemed as dead to me. There is a fine passage, which may serve to illustrate this fancy, in a Tragedy, by Sir Robert Howard, speaking of a friend's death.—

> ——'Twas but just now he went away ;
> I have not since had time to shed a tear ;
> And yet the distance does the same appear
> As if he had been a thousand years from me.
> Time takes no measure in Eternity.

To dissipate this awkward feeling, I have been fain to go among them once or twice since ; to visit my old desk-fellows—my co-brethren of the quill—that I had left below in the state militant. Not all the kindness with which they received me could quite restore to me that pleasant familiarity, which I had heretofore enjoyed among them. We cracked some of our old jokes, but methought they went off but faintly. My old desk ; the peg where I hung my hat, were appropriated to another. I knew it must be, but I could not take it kindly. D——l take me if I did not feel some remorse—beast, if I had not,—at quitting my old compeers, the faithful partners of my toils for six and thirty years, that smoothed for me with their jokes and conundrums the ruggedness of my professional road. Had it been so rugged then after all ? or was I a coward simply ? Well, it is too late to repent ; and I also know, that these suggestions are a common fallacy of the mind on such occasions. But my heart

smote me. I had violently broken the bands betwixt us.
It was at least not courteous. I shall be some time before
I get quite reconciled to the separation. Farewell, old
cronies, yet not for long, for again and again I will come
among ye, if I shall have your leave. Farewell, Ch——,
dry, sarcastic, and friendly ! Do——, mild, slow to move,
and gentlemanly ! Pl——, officious to do, and to volunteer, good services !—and thou, thou dreary pile, fit mansion for a Gresham or a Whittington of old stately House
of Merchants ; with thy labyrinthine passages, and light-
excluding, pent-up offices, where candles for one half the
year supplied the place of the sun's light ; unhealthy
contributor to my weal, stern fosterer of my living,
farewell ! In thee remain, and not in the obscure collection of some wandering bookseller, my " works ! " There
let them rest, as I do from my labours, piled on thy
massy shelves, more MSS. in folio than ever Aquinas left,
and full as useful ! My mantle, I bequeath among ye.

A fortnight has passed since the date of my first communication. At that period I was approaching to tranquillity, but had not reached it. I boasted of a calm
indeed, but it was comparative only. Something of the
first flutter was left ; an unsettling sense of novelty ; the
dazzle to weak eyes of unaccustomed light. I missed my
old chains, forsooth, as if they had been some necessary
part of my apparel. I was a poor Carthusian, from strict
cellular discipline suddenly by some revolution returned
upon the world. I am now as if I had never been other
than my own master. It is natural to me to go where I
please, to do what I please. I find myself at eleven o'clock
in the day in Bond Street, and it seems to me that I have
been sauntering there at that very hour for years past. I
digress into Soho, to explore a book-stall. Methinks I
have been thirty years a collector. There is nothing
strange nor new in it. I find myself before a fine picture
in the morning. Was it ever otherwise ? What is become

of Fish Street Hill ?   Where is Fenchurch Street ?   Stones
of old Mincing Lane which I have worn with my daily
pilgrimage for six-and-thirty years, to the footsteps of
what toil-worn clerk are your everlasting flints now vocal ?
I indent the gayer flags of Pall Mall.   It is 'Change time,
and I am strangely among the Elgin marbles.   It was no
hyperbole when I ventured to compare the change in my
condition to a passing into another world.   Time stands
still in a manner to me.   I have lost all distinction of season.
I do not know the day of the week, or of the month.
Each day used to be individually felt by me in its reference
to the foreign post days ;   in its distance from, or propinquity to the next Sunday.   I had my Wednesday feelings,
my Saturday nights' sensations.   The genius of each day
was upon me distinctly during the whole of it, affecting
my appetite, spirits, etc.   The phantom of the next day,
with the dreary five to follow, sate as a load upon my poor
Sabbath recreations.   What charm has washed the Ethiop
white ?   What is gone of Black Monday ?   All days are
the same.   Sunday itself—that unfortunate failure of a
holiday as it too often proved, what with my sense of its
fugitiveness, and over-care to get the greatest quantity of
pleasure out of it—is melted down into a week-day.   I
can spare to go to church now, without grudging the
huge cantle which it used to seem to cut out of the holiday.
I have Time for everything.   I can visit a sick friend.   I
can interrupt the man of much occupation when he is
busiest.   I can insult over him with an invitation to take
a day's pleasure with me to Windsor this fine May morning.   It is Lucretian pleasure to behold the poor drudges,
whom I have left behind in the world, carking and caring ;
like horses in a mill, drudging on in the same eternal round
—and what is it all for ?   A man can never have too much
Time to himself, nor too little to do.   Had I a little son
I would christen him NOTHING-TO-DO ;   he should do
nothing.   Man, I verily believe, is out of his element as

long as he is operative. I am altogether for the life contemplative. Will no kindly earthquake come and swallow
up those accursed cotton-mills ? Take me that lumber of
a desk there, and bowl it down

As low as to the fiends.

I am no longer * * * * * *, clerk to the firm of, etc.
I am Retired Leisure. I am to be met with in trim
gardens. I am already come to be known by my vacant
face and careless gesture, perambulating at no fixed pace
nor with any settled purpose. I walk about ; not to and
from. They tell me, a certain *cum dignitate* air, that has
been buried so long with my other good parts, has begun
to shoot forth in my person. I grow into gentility per-
ceptibly. When I take up a newspaper it is to read the
state of the opera. *Opus operatum est.* I have done all
that I came into this world to do. I have worked task-
work, and have the rest of the day to myself.

Last Essays of Elia. 1833.

OLD CHINA

CHARLES LAMB

I HAVE an almost feminine partiality for old china. When I go to see any great house, I enquire for the china-closet, and next for the picture gallery. I cannot defend the order of preference, but by saying, that we have all some taste or other, of too ancient a date to admit of our remembering distinctly that it was an acquired one. I can call to mind the first play, and the first exhibition, that I was taken to ; but I am not conscious of a time when china jars and saucers were introduced into my imagination.

I had no repugnance then—why should I now have ?— to those little, lawless, azure-tinctured grotesques, that under the notion of men and women, float about, un-circumscribed by any element, in that world before perspective—a china tea-cup.

I like to see my old friends—whom distance cannot diminish—figuring up in the air (so they appear to our optics), yet on *terra firma* still—for so we must in courtesy interpret that speck of deeper blue,—which the decorous artist, to prevent absurdity, had made to spring up beneath their sandals.

I love the men with women's faces, and the women, if possible, with still more womanish expressions.

Here is a young and courtly Mandarin, handing tea to a lady from a salver—two miles off. See how distance seems to set off respect ! And here the same lady, or another—for likeness is identity on tea-cups—is stepping into a little fairy boat, moored on the hither side of this calm garden river, with a dainty mincing foot, which in a right angle of incidence (as angles go in our world) must infallibly land her in the midst of a flowery mead—a furlong off on the other side of the same strange stream !

Farther on—if far or near can be predicated of their world—see horses, trees, pagodas, dancing the hays.

Here—a cow and rabbit couchant, and co-extensive— so objects show, seen through the lucid atmosphere of fine Cathay.

I was pointing out to my cousin last evening, over our Hyson (which we are old fashioned enough to drink unmixed still of an afternoon), some of these *speciosa miracula* upon a set of extraordinary old blue china (a recent purchase) which we were now for the first time using ; and could not help remarking, how favourable circumstances had been to us of late years, that we could afford to please the eye sometimes with trifles of this sort—when a passing sentiment seemed to overshade the brows of my companion. I am quick at detecting these summer clouds in Bridget.

"I wish the good old times would come again," she said, "when we were not quite so rich. I do not mean, that I want to be poor ; but there was a middle state "— so she was pleased to ramble on,—" in which I am sure we were a great deal happier. A purchase is but a purchase, now that you have money enough and to spare. Formerly it used to be a triumph. When we coveted a cheap luxury (and, O ! how much ado I had to get you to consent in those times !)—we were used to have a debate two or three days before, and to weigh the *for* and *against*, and think what we might spare it out of, and what saving we could hit upon, that should be an equivalent. A thing was worth buying then, when we felt the money that we paid for it."

"Do you remember the brown suit, which you made to hang upon you, till all your friends cried shame upon you, it grew so thread-bare—and all because of that folio Beaumont and Fletcher, which you dragged home late at night from Barker's in Covent Garden? Do you remember how we eyed it for weeks before we could make up our minds to the purchase, and had not come to a determination till it was near ten o'clock of the Saturday night, when you set off from Islington, fearing you should be too late—and when the old bookseller with some grumbling opened his shop, and by the twinkling taper (for he was setting bedwards) lighted out the relic from his dusty treasures—and when you lugged it home, wishing it were twice as cumbersome—and when you presented it to me—and when we were exploring the perfectness of it (*collating* you called it)—and while I was repairing some of the loose leaves with paste, which your impatience would not suffer to be left till daybreak—was there no pleasure in being a poor man? or can those neat black clothes, which you wear now, and are so careful to keep brushed, since we have become rich and finical, give you half the honest vanity, with which you flaunted it about in that overworn suit—your old corbeau —for four or five weeks longer than you should have done, to pacify your conscience for the mighty sum of fifteen—or sixteen shillings was it?—a great affair we thought it then—which you had lavished on the old folio. Now you can afford to buy any book that pleases you, but I do not see that you ever bring me home any nice old purchases now."

"When you came home with twenty apologies for laying out a less number of shillings upon that print after Lionardo, which we christened the 'Lady Blanch'; when you looked at the purchase, and thought of the money—and thought of the money, and looked again at the picture—was there no pleasure in being a poor man?

Now, you have nothing to do but to walk into Colnaghi's, and buy a wilderness of Lionardos. Yet do you ? "

" Then, do you remember our pleasant walks to Enfield, and Potter's Bar, and Waltham, when we had a holyday— holydays, and all other fun, are gone, now we are rich— and the little hand-basket in which I used to deposit our day's fare of savoury cold lamb and salad—and how you would pry about at noon-tide for some decent house, where we might go in, and produce our store—only paying for the ale that you must call for—and speculate upon the looks of the landlady, and whether she was likely to allow us a table-cloth—and wish for such another honest hostess, as Izaak Walton has described many a one on the pleasant banks of the Lea, when he went a fishing—and sometimes they would prove obliging enough, and sometimes they would look grudgingly upon us—but we had cheerful looks still for one another, and would eat our plain food savorily, scarcely grudging Piscator his Trout Hall ? Now, —when we go out a day's pleasuring, which is seldom moreover, we *ride* part of the way—and go into a fine inn, and order the best of dinners, never debating the expense —which, after all, never has half the relish of those chance country snaps, when we were at the mercy of uncertain usage, and a precarious welcome."

" You are too proud to see a play anywhere now but in the pit. Do you remember where it was we used to sit, when we saw the Battle of Hexham, and the Surrender of Calais, and Bannister and Mrs. Bland in the Children in the Wood—when we squeezed out our shillings a-piece to sit three or four times in a season in the one-shilling gallery—where you felt all the time that you ought not to have brought me—and more strongly I felt obligation to you for having brought me—and the pleasure was the better for a little shame—and when the curtain drew up, what cared we for our place in the house, or what mattered it where we were sitting, when our thoughts were with

Rosalind in Arden, or with Viola at the Court of Illyria ?
You used to say, that the Gallery was the best place of all
for enjoying a play socially—that the relish of such exhibi-
tions must be in proportion to the infrequency of going—
that the company we met there, not being in general
readers of plays, were obliged to attend the more, and did
attend, to what was going on, on the stage—because a
word lost would have been a chasm, which it was impossible for them to fill up. With such reflections we
consoled our pride then—and I appeal to you, whether,
as a woman, I met generally with less attention and accommodation, than I have done since in more expensive
situations in the house ? The getting in indeed, and the
crowding up those inconvenient staircases, was bad
enough,—but there was still a law of civility to woman
recognized to quite as great an extent as we ever found in
the other passages—and how a little difficulty overcome
heightened the snug seat, and the play, afterwards ! Now
we can only pay our money and walk in. You cannot see,
you say, in the galleries now. I am sure we saw, and heard
too, well enough then—but sight, and all, I think, is gone
with our poverty."

" There was pleasure in eating strawberries, before they
became quite common—in the first dish of peas, while
they were yet dear—to have them for a nice supper, a
treat. What treat can we have now ? If we were to
treat ourselves now—that is, to have dainties a little above
our means, it would be selfish and wicked. It is very little
more that we allow ourselves beyond what the actual poor
can get at, that makes what I call a treat—when two people
living together, as we have done, now and then indulge
themselves in a cheap luxury, which both like ; while each
apologizes, and is willing to take both halves of the blame
to his single share. I see no harm in people making much
of themselves in that sense of the word. It may give them
a hint how to make much of others. But now—what I

mean by the word—we never do make much of ourselves.
None but the poor can do it. I do not mean the veriest
poor of all, but persons as we were, just above poverty.

"I know what you were going to say, that it is mighty
pleasant at the end of the year to make all meet,—and
much ado we used to have every Thirty-first Night of
December to account for our exceedings—many a long
face did you make over your puzzled accounts, and in
contriving to make it out how we had spent so much—
or that we had not spent so much—or that it was impossible
we should spend so much next year—and still we found
our slender capital decreasing—but then, betwixt ways,
and projects, and compromises of one sort or another,
and talk of curtailing this charge, and doing without that
for the future—and the hope that youth brings, and
laughing spirits (in which you were never poor till now)
we pocketed up our loss, and in conclusion, with 'lusty
brimmers' (as you used to quote it out of *hearty cheerful
Mr. Cotton*, as you called him), we used to welcome in the
'coming guest.' Now we have no reckoning at all at
the end of the old year—no flattering promises about the
new year doing better for us."

Bridget is so sparing of her speech on most occasions,
that when she gets into a rhetorical vein, I am careful
how I interrupt it. I could not help, however, smiling
at the phantom of wealth which her dear imagination
had conjured up out of a clear income of a poor—hundred
pounds a year. "It is true we were happier when we
were poorer, but we were also younger, my cousin. I
am afraid we must put up with the excess, for if we were
to shake the superflux into the sea, we should not much
mend ourselves. That we had much to struggle with, as
we grew up together, we have reason to be most thank-
ful. It strengthened, and knit our compact closer. We
could never have been what we have been to each other,
if we had always had the sufficiency which you now

complain of. The resisting power—those natural dilations of the youthful spirit, which circumstances cannot straighten—with us are long since passed away. Competence to age is supplementary youth, a sorry supplement indeed, but I fear the best that is to be had. We must ride, where we formerly walked : live better, and lie softer—and shall be wise to do so—than we had means to do in those good old days you speak of. Yet could those days return—could Bannister and Mrs. Bland again be young, and you and I be young to see them—could the good old one-shilling gallery days return—they are dreams, my cousin, now—but could you and I at this moment, instead of this quiet argument, by our well-carpeted fire-side, sitting on this luxurious sofa—be once more struggling up those inconvenient stair cases, pushed about, and squeezed, and elbowed by the poorest rabble of poor gallery scramblers—could I once more hear those anxious shrieks of yours—and the delicious *Thank God, we are safe*, which always followed when the topmost stair, conquered, let in the first light of the whole cheerful theatre down beneath us—I know not the fathom line that ever touched a descent so deep as I would be willing to bury more wealth in than Crœsus had, or the great Jew R—— is supposed to have, to purchase it. And now do just look at that merry little Chinese waiter holding an umbrella, big enough for a bed-tester, over the head of that pretty insipid half-Madonaish chit of a lady in that very blue summer house."

Last Essays of Elia. 1833.

THE CHILD ANGEL

A Dream

CHARLES LAMB

I CHANCED upon the prettiest, oddest, fantastical thing of a dream the other night, that you shall hear of. I had been reading the " Loves of the Angels," and went to bed with my head full of speculations, suggested by that extraordinary legend. It had given birth to innumerable conjectures ; and, I remember, the last waking thought, which I gave expression to on my pillow, was a sort of wonder "what could come of it."

I was suddenly transported, how or whither I could scarcely make out—but to some celestial region. It was not the real heavens either—not the downright Bible heaven—but a kind of fairyland heaven, about which a poor human fancy may have leave to sport and air itself, I will hope, without presumption.

Methought—what wild things dreams are !—I was present—at what would you imagine ?—at an angel's gossiping.

Whence it came, or how it came, or who bid it come, or whether it came purely of its own head, neither you nor I know—but there lay, sure enough, wrapt in its little cloudy swaddling-bands—a Child Angel.

Sun-threads—filmy beams—ran through the celestial napery of what seemed its princely cradle. All the winged orders hovered around, watching when the new-born should open its yet closed eyes ; which, when it did, first one, and then the other—with a solicitude and apprehension, yet not such as, stained with fear, dim the expanding eye-lids of mortal infants, but as if to explore its path in those its unhereditary palaces—what an inextinguishable titter that time spared not celestial visages ! Nor wanted there to my seeming—O the inexplicable simpleness of dreams !—bowls of that cheering nectar,

—which mortals *caudle* call below.

Nor were wanting faces of female ministrants,—stricken in years, as it might seem,—so dexterous were those heavenly attendants to counterfeit kindly similitudes of earth, to greet, with terrestrial child-rites the young *present*, which earth had made to heaven.

Then were celestial harpings heard, not in full symphony as those by which the spheres are tutored ; but, as loudest instruments on earth speak oftentimes, muffled ; so to accommodate their sound the better to the weak ears of the imperfect-born. And, with the noise of those subdued soundings, the Angelet sprang forth, fluttering its rudiments of pinions—but forthwith flagged and was recovered into the arms of those full-winged angels. And a wonder it was to see how, as years went round in heaven— a year in dreams is as a day—continually its white shoulders put forth buds of wings, but, wanting the perfect angelic nutriment, anon was shorn of its aspiring, and fell fluttering —still caught by angel hands—for ever to put forth shoots, and to fall fluttering, because its birth was not of the unmixed vigour of heaven.

And a name was given to the Babe Angel, and it was to be called *Ge-Urania,* because its production was of earth and heaven.

And it could not taste of death, by reason of its adoption into immortal palaces : but it was to know weakness, and reliance, and the shadow of human imbecility ; and it went with a lame gait ; but in its goings it exceeded all mortal children in grace and swiftness. Then pity first sprang up in angelic bosoms ; and yearnings (like the human) touched them at the sight of the immortal lame one.

And with pain did then first those Intuitive Essences, with pain and strife to their natures (not grief), put back their bright intelligences, and reduce their ethereal minds, schooling them to degrees and slower processes, so to adapt their lessons to the gradual illumination (as must needs be) of the half-earth-born ; and what intuitive notices they could not repel (by reason that their nature is, to know all things at once), the half-heavenly novice, by the better part of its nature, aspired to receive into its understanding ; so that Humility and Aspiration went on even-paced in the instruction of the glorious Amphibium.

But, by reason that Mature Humanity is too gross to breathe the air of that super-subtile region, its portion was, and is, to be a child for ever.

And because the human part of it might not press into the heart and inwards of the palace of its adoption, those full-natured angels tended it by turns in the purlieus of the palace, where were shady groves and rivulets, like this green earth from which it came : so Love, with Voluntary Humility, waited upon the entertainment of the new-adopted.

And myriads of years rolled round (in dreams Time is nothing), and still it kept, and is to keep, perpetual childhood, and is the Tutelar Genius of Childhood upon earth, and still goes lame and lovely.

By the banks of the river Pison is seen, lone-sitting by the grave of the terrestrial Adah, whom the angel Nadir loved, a Child ; but not the same which I saw in heaven. A mournful hue overcasts its lineaments ; nevertheless, a correspondency is between the child by the grave, and that celestial orphan, whom I saw above ; and the dimness of the grief upon the heavenly, is a shadow or emblem of that which stains the beauty of the terrestrial. And this correspondency is not to be understood but by dreams.

And in the archives of heaven I had grace to read, how that once the angel Nadir, being exiled from his place for mortal passion, upspringing on the wings of parental love (such power had parental love for a moment to suspend the else-irrevocable law) appeared for a brief instant in his station ; and, depositing a wondrous Birth, straightway disappeared, and the palaces knew him no more. And this charge was the self-same Babe, who goeth lame and lovely—but Adah sleepeth by the river Pison.

Last Essays of Elia.   1833.

THE COWSLIP-BALL

Mary Russell Mitford

MAY 16TH.—There are moments in life when, without any visible or immediate cause, the spirits sink and fail, as it were, under the mere pressure of existence ; moments of unaccountable depression, when one is weary of one's very thoughts, haunted by images that will not depart— images many and various, but all painful ; friends lost, or changed, or dead ; hopes disappointed even in their accomplishment ; fruitless regrets, powerless wishes, doubt and fear, and self-distrust and self-disapprobation. They who have known these feelings (and who is there so happy as not to have known some of them ?) will understand why Alfieri became powerless and Froissart dull ; and why even needlework, the most effectual sedative, that grand soother and composer of woman's distress, fails to comfort me to-day. I will go out into the air this cool pleasant afternoon, and try what that will do. I fancy that exercise, or exertion of any kind, is the true specific for nervousness. " Fling but a stone, the giant dies." I will go to the meadows, the beautiful meadows ! and I will have my materials of happiness, Lizzy and May, and a basket for flowers, and we will make a cowslip-ball. " Did you ever see a cowslip-ball, my Lizzy ? " " No." " Come away, then ; make haste ! run, Lizzy ! "

And on we go, fast, fast ! down the road, across the lea, past the workhouse, along by the great pond, till we slide into the deep, narrow lane, whose hedges seem to meet over the water, and win our way to the little farm-house at the end. " Through the farm-yard, Lizzy ; over the gate ; never mind the cows ; they are quiet enough."—" I don't mind 'em," said Miss Lizzy, boldly and truly, and with a proud, affronted air, displeased at being thought to mind anything, and showing by her attitude and manner some design of proving her courage by an attack on the largest of the herd, in the shape of a pull by the tail. " I don't mind 'em."—" I know you don't, Lizzy ; but let them alone, and don't chase the turkey-cock. Come to me, my dear ! " and, for a wonder, Lizzy came.

In the meantime, my other pet, Mayflower, had also gotten into a scrape. She had driven about a huge un-wieldy sow, till the animal's grunting had disturbed the repose of a still more enormous Newfoundland dog, the guardian of the yard. Out he sailed, growling, from the depth of his kennel, erecting his tail, and shaking his long chain. May's attention was instantly diverted from the sow to this new playmate, friend or foe, she cared not which ; and he of the kennel, seeing his charge unhurt, and out of danger, was at leisure to observe the charms of his fair enemy, as she frolicked around him, always beyond the reach of his chain, yet always, with the natural instinc-tive coquetry of her sex, alluring him to the pursuit which she knew to be vain. I never saw a prettier flirtation. At last the noble animal, wearied out, retired to the inmost recesses of his habitation, and would not even approach her when she stood right before the entrance. " You are properly served, May. Come along, Lizzy. Across this wheat-field, and now over the gate. Stop ! let me lift you down. No jumping, no breaking of necks, Lizzy ! " And here we are in the meadows, and out of the world. Robinson Crusoe in his lonely island had scarcely a more complete or a more beautiful solitude.

These meadows consist of a double row of small en-

closures of rich grass-land, a mile or two in length, sloping
down from high arable grounds on either side, to a little
nameless brook that winds between them with a course
which, in its infinite variety, clearness, and rapidity, seems
to emulate the bold rivers of the north, of whom, far more
than of our lazy southern streams, our rivulet presents a
miniature likeness.   Never was water more exquisitely
tricksy,—now darting over the bright pebbles, sparkling
and flashing in the light with a bubbling music, as sweet
and wild as the song of the woodlark ; now stretching
quietly along, giving back the rich tufts of the golden
marsh-marigolds which grow on its margin ; now sweeping round a fine reach of green grass, rising steeply into
a high mount, a mimic promontory, whilst the other side
sinks softly away, like some tiny bay, and the water flows
between, so clear, so wide, so shallow, that Lizzy, longing
for adventure, is sure she could cross unwetted ; now
dashing through two sand-banks, a torrent deep and
narrow, which May clears at a bound ; now sleeping,
half hidden, beneath the alders, hawthorns, and wild
roses, with which the banks are so profusely and variously
fringed, whilst flags, lilies, and other aquatic plants, almost
cover the surface of the stream.   In good truth, it is a
beautiful brook, and one that Walton himself might have
sitten by and loved, for trout are there ; we see them as
they dart up the stream, and hear and start at the sudden
plunge when they spring to the surface for the summer
flies.   Izaak Walton would have loved our brook and our
quiet meadows ; they breathe the very spirit of his own
peacefulness, a soothing quietude that sinks into the soul.
There is no path through them, not one ; we might
wander a whole spring day and not see a trace of human
habitation.   They belong to a number of small proprietors,
who allow each other access through their respective
grounds from pure kindness and neighbourly feeling ;
a privilege never abused ; and the fields on the other side

of the water are reached by a rough plank, or a tree thrown across, or some such homely bridge. We ourselves possess one of the most beautiful ; so that the strange pleasure of property, that instinct which makes Lizzy delight in her broken doll, and May in the bare bone which she has pilfered from the kennel of her recreant admirer of Newfoundland, is added to the other charms of this enchanting scenery ; a strange pleasure it is, when one so poor as I can feel it ! Perhaps it is felt most by the poor, with the rich it may be less intense—too much diffused and spread out, becoming thin by expansion, like leaf-gold ; the little of the poor may be not only more precious, but more pleasant to them ; certain that bit of grassy and blossomy earth, with its green knolls and tufted bushes, its old pollards wreathed with ivy, and its bright and babbling waters, is very dear to me. But I must always have loved these meadows, so fresh, and cool, and delicious to the eye and to the tread, full of cowslips, and of all vernal flowers ; Shakespeare's song of spring bursts irrepressibly from our lips as we step on them :

> " When daisies pied, and violets blue,
>   And lady-smocks all silver white,
> And cuckoo-buds of yellow hue,
>   Do paint the meadows with delight,
> The cuckoo then on every tree——"

" Cuckoo ! cuckoo ! " cried Lizzy, breaking in with her clear, childish voice ; and immediately, as if at her call, the real bird, from a neighbouring tree (for these meadows are dotted with timber like a park), began to echo my lovely little girl, " Cuckoo ! cuckoo ! " I have a prejudice very unpastoral and unpoetical (but I cannot help it, I have many such) against this " harbinger of spring." His note is so monotonous, so melancholy ; and then the boys mimic him ; one hears " Cuckoo ! cuckoo ! " in dirty streets, amongst smoky houses, and the bird is hated for faults not his own. But prejudices of taste, likings, and dislikings, are not always vanquishable by reason ; so, to escape the serenade from the tree, which promised to be of considerable duration (when once that eternal song begins, on it goes ticking like a clock)—to escape that noise, I determined to excite another, and challenged Lizzy to a cowslip-gathering ; a trial of skill and speed, to see which should soonest fill her basket. My stratagem succeeded completely. What scrambling, what shouting, what glee from Lizzy ! twenty cuckoos might have sung unheard whilst she was pulling her own flowers, and stealing mine, and laughing, screaming, and talking through all.

At last the baskets were filled, and Lizzy declared victor ; and down we sat, on the brink of the stream, under a spreading hawthorn, just disclosing its own pearly buds, and surrounded with the rich and enamelled flowers of the wild hyacinth, blue and white, to make our cowslip-ball. Every one knows the process : to nip off the tuft of flowerets just below the top of the stalk, and hang each cluster nicely balanced across a riband, till you have a long string like a garland ; then to press them closely together, and tie them tightly up. We went on very prosperously, *considering*—as people say of a young lady's drawing, or a Frenchman's English, or a woman's tragedy, or of the poor little dwarf who works without fingers, or the ingenious sailor who writes with his toes, or generally of any performance which is accomplished by means seemingly inadequate to its production. To be sure we met with a few accidents. First, Lizzy spoiled nearly all her cowslips by snapping them off too short ; so there was a fresh gathering ; in the next place, May overset my full basket, and sent the blossoms floating, like so many fairy flowers, down the brook : then, when we were going on pretty steadily, just as we had made a superb wreath, and were thinking of tying it together, Lizzy, who held the riband, caught a glimpse of a gorgeous butterfly, all brown and red and purple, and skipping off to pursue the new object, let go her hold ; so all our treasures were abroad again. At last, however, by dint of taking a branch of alder as a substitute for Lizzy, and hanging the basket in a pollard-ash, out of sight of May, the cowslip-ball was finished. What a concentration of fragrance and beauty it was ! golden and sweet to satiety ! rich to sight, and touch, and smell ! Lizzy was enchanted, and ran off with her prize, hiding amongst the trees in the very coyness of ecstasy, as if any human eye, even mine, would be a restraint on her innocent raptures.

In the meanwhile I sat listening, not to my enemy the cuckoo, but to a whole concert of nightingales, scarcely interrupted by any meaner bird, answering and vying with each other in those short, delicious strains which are to the ear as roses to the eye ; those snatches of lovely sound which come across us as airs from heaven. Pleasant thoughts, delightful associations, awoke as I listened ; and almost unconsciously I repeated to myself the beautiful story of the Lutist and the Nightingale, from Ford's *Lover's Melancholy*. Here it is. Is there in English poetry anything finer ?

> " Passing from Italy to Greece, the tales
>   Which poets of an elder time have feign'd
>   To glorify their Tempe, bred in me
>   Desire of visiting Paradise,
>   To Thessaly I came, and living private,
>   Without acquaintance of more sweet companions
>   Than the old inmates to my love, my thoughts,
>   I day by day frequented silent groves
>   And solitary walks. One morning early
>   This accident encounter'd me : I heard
>   The sweetest and most ravishing contention

That art and nature ever were at strife in.
A sound of music touch'd mine ears, or rather,
Indeed, entranced my soul ; as I stole nearer,
Invited by the melody, I saw
This youth, this fair-faced youth, upon his lute
With strains of strange variety and harmony
Proclaiming, as it seem'd, so bold a challenge
To the clear choristers of the woods, the birds,
That as they flock'd about him, all stood silent,
Wondering at what they heard. I wonder'd too.
A nightingale,
Nature's best skill'd musician, undertakes
The challenge ; and for every several strain
The well-shaped youth could touch, she sang him down.
He could not run divisions with more art
Upon his quaking instrument than she.
The Nightingale, did with her various notes
Reply to.
Some time thus spent, the young man grew at last
Into a pretty anger, that a bird,
Whom art had never taught cleffs, moods, or notes,
Should vie with him for mastery, whose study
Had busied many hours to perfect practice.
To end the controversy, in a rapture
Upon his instrument he plays so swiftly,
So many voluntaries, and so quick,
That there was curiosity and cunning,
Concord in discord, lines of different method
Meeting in one full centre of delight.
The bird (ordain'd to be
Music's first martyr) strove to imitate
These several sounds ; which, when her warbling throat
Fail'd in, for grief down dropt she on his lute,
And brake her heart. It was the quaintest sadness
To see the conqueror upon her hearse
To weep a funeral elegy of tears.

He look'd upon the trophies of his art,
Then sigh'd, then wiped his eyes ; then sigh'd and cry'd,
' Alas ! poor creature, I will soon revenge
This cruelty upon the author of it.
Henceforth this lute, guilty of innocent blood,
Shall never more betray a harmless peace
To an untimely end ; ' and in that sorrow,
As he was pashing it against a tree,
I suddenly stept in."

When I had finished the recitation of this exquisite
passage, the sky, which had been all the afternoon dull
and heavy, began to look more and more threatening ;
darker clouds, like wreaths of black smoke, flew across
the dead leaden tint ; a cooler, damper air blew over
the meadows, and a few large, heavy drops splashed in
the water. " We shall have a storm. Lizzy ! May !
where are ye ? Quick, quick, my Lizzy ! run, run !
faster, faster ! "

And off we ran ; Lizzy not at all displeased at the
thoughts of a wetting, to which, indeed, she is almost as
familiar as a duck ; May, on the other hand, peering
up at the weather, and shaking her pretty ears with
manifest dismay. Of all animals, next to a cat, a grey-
hound dreads rain. She might have escaped it ; her
light feet would have borne her home long before the
shower ; but May is too faithful for that, too true a
comrade, understands too well the laws of good-fellow-
ship ; so she waited for us. She did, to be sure, gallop
on before, and then stop and look back, and beckon
as it were, with some scorn in her black eyes at the slow-
ness of our progress. We in the meanwhile got on as fast
as we could, encouraging and reproaching each other.
" Faster, my Lizzy ! Oh, what a bad runner ! "—" Faster,
faster ! Oh, what a bad runner ! " echoed my sauce-box.
" You are so fat, Lizzy, you make no way ! "—" Ah, who

else is fat ? " retorted the darling. Certainly her mother is right ; I do spoil that child.

By this time we were thoroughly soaked, all three. It was a pelting shower, that drove through our thin summer clothing, and poor May's short glossy coat, in a moment. And then, when we were wet to the skin, the sun came out, actually the sun, as if to laugh at our plight ; and then, more provoking still, when the sun was shining, and the shower over, came a maid and a boy to look after us, loaded with cloaks and umbrellas enough to fence us against a whole day's rain. Never mind ! on we go, faster and faster ; Lizzy obliged to be most ignobly carried, having had the misfortune to lose a shoe in the mud, which we left the boy to look after.

Here we are at home—dripping ; but glowing and laughing, and bearing our calamity most manfully. May, a dog of excellent sense, went instantly to bed in the stable, and is at this moment over head and ears in straw ; Lizzy is gone to bed too, coaxed into that wise measure by a promise of tea and toast, and of not going home till to-morrow, and the story of Little Red Riding Hood ; and I am enjoying the luxury of dry clothing by a good fire. Really, getting wet through now and then is no bad thing, finery apart ; for one should not like spoiling a new pelisse, or a handsome plume ; but when there is nothing in question but a white gown and a straw bonnet, as was the case to-day, it is rather pleasant than not. The little chill refreshes, and our enjoyment of the subsequent warmth and dryness is positive and absolute. Besides, the stimulus and exertion do good to the mind as well as body. How melancholy I was all the morning ! how cheerful I am now ! Nothing like a shower-bath—a real shower-bath, such as Lizzy and May and I have undergone, to cure low spirits. Try it, my dear readers, if ever ye be nervous—I will answer for its success.

Our Village. 1832.

THE FIGHT

WILLIAM HAZLITT

———" The *fight*, the *fight's* the thing,
Wherein I'll catch the conscience of the king."

Where there's a will, there's a way.—I said so to myself,
as I walked down Chancery lane, about half-past six
o'clock on Monday the 10th of December, to inquire at
Jack Randall's where the fight the next day was to be ;
and I found " the proverb " nothing " musty " in the
present instance. I was determined to see this fight, come
what would, and see it I did, in great style. It was my
first fight, yet it more than answered my expectations.
Ladies ! it is to you I dedicate this description ; nor let
it seem out of character for the fair to notice the exploits
of the brave. Courage and modesty are the old English
virtues ; and may they never look cold and askance on
one another ! Think, ye fairest of the fair, loveliest of the
lovely kind, ye practisers of soft enchantment, how many
more ye kill with poisoned baits than ever fell in the ring ;
and listen with subdued air and without shuddering, to a
tale tragic only in appearance, and sacred to the FANCY !

I was going down Chancery lane, thinking to ask at
Jack Randall's where the fight was to be, when looking
through the glass-door of the *Hole in the Wall*, I heard a
gentleman asking the same question *at* Mrs. Randall, as
the author of *Waverley* would express it. Now Mrs.
Randall stood answering the gentleman's question, with

the authenticity of the lady of the Champion of the Light
Weights. Thinks I, I'll wait till this person comes out,
and learn from him how it is. For to say a truth, I was
not fond of going into this house of call for heroes and
philosophers, ever since the owner of it (for Jack is no
gentleman) threatened once upon a time to kick me out
of doors for wanting a mutton-chop at his hospitable
board, when the conqueror in thirteen battles was more
full of *blue ruin* than of good manners. I was the more
mortified at this repulse, inasmuch as I had heard Mr. James
Simpkins, hosier in the Strand, one day when the character
of the *Hole in the Wall* was brought in question, observe—
" The house is a very good house, and the company quite
genteel : I have been there myself ! " Remembering
this unkind treatment of mine host, to which mine hostess
was also a party, and not wishing to put her in unquiet
thoughts at a time jubilant like the present, I waited at the
door, when, who should issue forth but my friend Joe
Toms, and turning suddenly up Chancery lane with that
quick jerk and impatient stride which distinguishes a lover
of the FANCY, I said, " I'll be hanged if that fellow is not
going to the fight, and is on his way to get me to go with
him." So it proved in effect, and we agreed to adjourn
to my lodgings to discuss measures with that cordiality
which makes old friends like new, and new friends like
old, on great occasions. We are cold to others only when
we are dull in ourselves, and have neither thoughts nor
feelings to impart to them. Give a man a topic in his head,
a throb of pleasure in his heart, and he will be glad to
share it with the first person he meets. Toms and I,
though we seldom meet, were an *alter idem* on this memorable occasion, and had not an idea that we did not candidly
impart ; and " so carelessly did we fleet the time," that I
wish no better, when there is another fight, than to have
him for a companion on my journey down, and to return
with my friend Jack Pigott, talking of what was to happen

or of what did happen, with a noble subject always at hand, and liberty to digress to others whenever they offered. Indeed, on my repeating the lines from Spenser in an involuntary fit of enthusiasm,

> " What more felicity can fall to creature,
>   Than to enjoy delight with liberty ? "

my last-named ingenious friend stopped me by saying that this, translated into the vulgate, meant " *Going to see a fight.*"

   Joe Toms and I could not settle about the method of going down. He said there was a caravan, he understood, to start from Tom Belcher's at two, which would go there *right out* and back again the next day. Now I never travel all night, and said I should get a cast to Newbury by one of the mails. Joe swore the thing was impossible, and I could only answer that I had made up my mind to it. In short, he seemed to me to waver, said he only came to see if I was going, had letters to write, a cause coming on the day after, and faintly said at parting (for I was bent on setting out that moment)—" Well, we meet at Philippi ! " I made the best of my way to Piccadilly. The mail coach stand was bare. " They are all gone," said I—" this is always the way with me—in the instant I lose the future— if I had not stayed to pour out that last cup of tea, I should have been just in time ; "—and cursing my folly and ill- luck together, without inquiring at the coach-office whether the mails were gone or not, I walked on in despite, and to punish my own dilatoriness and want of deter- mination. At any rate, I would not turn back : I might get to Hounslow, or perhaps farther, to be on my road the next morning. I passed Hyde park corner (my Rubicon), and trusted to fortune. Suddenly I heard the clattering of a Brentford stage, and the fight rushed full upon my fancy. I argued (not unwisely) that even a Brentford

coachman was better company than my own thoughts
(such as they were just then), and at his invitation mounted
the box with him. I immediately stated my case to him—
namely, my quarrel with myself for missing the Bath or
Bristol mail, and my determination to get on in consequence as well as I could, without any disparagement or
insulting comparison between longer or shorter stages.
It is a maxim with me that stage-coaches, and consequently stage-coachmen, are respectable in proportion
to the distance they have to travel : so I said nothing on
that subject to my Brentford friend.   Any incipient
tendency to an abstract proposition, or (as he might have
construed it) to a personal reflection of this kind, was however nipped in the bud ; for I had no sooner declared
indignantly that I had missed the mails, than he flatly
denied that they were gone along, and lo ! at the instant
three of them drove by in rapid, provoking, orderly
succession, as if they would devour the ground before
them.   Here again I seemed in the contradictory situation
of the man in Dryden who exclaims,

"I follow Fate, which does too hard pursue ! "

If I had stopped to inquire at the White Horse Cellar,
which would not have taken me a minute, I should now
have been driving down the road in all the dignified
unconcern and *ideal* perfection of mechanical conveyance.
The Bath mail I had set my mind upon, and I had missed
it, as I miss every thing else, by my own absurdity, in
putting the will for the deed, and aiming at ends without
employing means.   " Sir," said he of the Brentford,
" the Bath mail will be up presently, my brother-in-law
drives it, and I will engage to stop him if there is a place
empty." I almost doubted my good genius ; but, sure
enough, up it drove like lightning, and stopped directly
at the call of the Brentford Jehu.   I would not have

believed this possible, but the brother-in-law of a mail-coach driver is himself no mean man. I was transferred without loss of time from the top of one coach to that of the other, desired the guard to pay my fare to the Brentford coachman for me as I had no change, was accommodated with a great coat, put up my umbrella to keep off a drizzling mist, and we began to cut through the air like an arrow. The mile-stones disappeared one after another, the rain kept off; Tom Turtle,[1] the trainer, sat before me on the coach-box, with whom I exchanged civilities as a gentleman going to the fight; the passion that had transported me an hour before was subdued to pensive regret and conjectural musing on the next day's battle; I was promised a place inside at Reading, and upon the whole, I thought myself a lucky fellow. Such is the force of imagination ! On the outside of any other coach on the 10th of December, with a Scotch mist drizzling through the cloudy moonlight air, I should have been cold, comfortless, impatient, and, no doubt, wet through; but seated on the Royal mail, I felt warm and comfortable, the air did me good, the ride did me good, I was pleased with the progress we had made, and confident that all would go well through the journey. When I got inside at Reading, I found Turtle and a stout valetudinarian, whose costume bespoke him one of the FANCY, and who had risen from a three months' sickbed to get into the mail to see the fight. They were intimate, and we fell into a lively discourse. My friend the trainer was confined in his topics to fighting dogs and men, to bears and badgers; beyond this he was " quite chap-fallen," had not a word to throw at a dog, or indeed very wisely fell asleep, when any other game was started. The whole art of training (I, however, learnt from him) consists in two things, exercise and abstinence, abstinence and exercise, repeated

[1] John Thurtell, to wit.

alternately and without end. A yolk of an egg with a spoonful of rum in it is the first thing in a morning, and then a walk of six miles till breakfast. This meal consists of a plentiful supply of tea and toast and beef-steaks. Then another six or seven miles till dinner-time, and another supply of solid beef or mutton with a pint of porter, and perhaps, at the utmost, a couple of glasses of sherry. Martin trains on water, but this increases his infirmity on another very dangerous side. The Gas-man takes now and then a chirping glass (under the rose) to console him, during a six weeks' probation, for the absence of Mrs. Hickman—an agreeable woman, with (I understand) a pretty fortune of two hundred pounds. How matter presses on me ! What stubborn things are facts ! How inexhaustible is nature and art ! " It is well," as I once heard Mr. Richmond observe, " to see a variety." He was speaking of cock-fighting as an edifying spectacle. I cannot deny but that one learns more of what *is* (I do not say of what *ought to be*) in this desultory mode of practical study, than from reading the same book twice over, even though it should be a moral treatise. Where was I ? I was sitting at dinner with the candidate for the honours of the ring, " where good digestion waits on appetite, and health on both." Then follows an hour of social chat and native glee ; and afterwards, to another breathing over heathy hill or dale. Back to supper, and then to bed, and up by six again—Our hero

> " Follows so the ever-running sun,
>   With profitable *ardour*——"

to the day that brings him victory or defeat in the green fairy circle. Is not this life more sweet than mine ? I was going to say ; but I will not libel any life by comparing it to mine, which is (at the date of these presents) bitter as coloquintida and the dregs of aconitum !

The invalid in the Bath mail soared a pitch above the trainer, and did not sleep so sound, because he had " more figures and more fantasies." We talked the hours away merrily. He had faith in surgery, for he had had three ribs set right, that had been broken in a *turn-up* at Belcher's, but thought physicians old women, for they had no antidote in their catalogue for brandy. An indigestion is an excellent common-place for two people that never met before. By way of ingratiating myself, I told him the story of my doctor, who, on my earnestly representing to him that I thought his regimen had done me harm, assured me that the whole pharmacopeia contained nothing comparable to the prescription he had given me ; and, as a proof of its undoubted efficacy, said, that " he had had one gentleman with my complaint under his hands for the last fifteen years." This anecdote made my companion shake the rough sides of his three great coats with boisterous laughter ; and Turtle, starting out of his sleep, swore he knew how the fight would go, for he had had a dream about it. Sure enough the rascal told us how the three first rounds went off, but " his dream," like others, " denoted a foregone conclusion." He knew his men. The moon now rose in silver state, and I ventured, with some hesitation, to point out this object of placid beauty, with the blue serene beyond, to the man of science, to which his ear he " seriously inclined," the more as it gave promise *d'un beau jour* for the morrow, and showed the ring undrenched by envious showers, arrayed in sunny smiles. Just then, all going on well, I thought on my friend Toms, whom I had left behind, and said innocently, " There was a blockhead of a fellow I left in town, who said there was no possibility of getting down by the mail, and talked of going by a caravan from Belcher's at two in the morning, after he had written some letters." " Why," said he of the lapells, " I should not wonder if that was the very person we saw running about like mad from one coach-door to another, and asking if any one had seen a friend of his, a gentleman going to the fight, whom he had missed stupidly enough by staying to write a note." " Pray, Sir," said my fellow-traveller, " had he a plaid-cloak on ? "—" Why, no," said I, " not at the time I left him, but he very well might afterwards, for he offered to lend me one." The plaid-cloak and the letter decided the thing. Joe, sure enough, was in the Bristol mail, which preceded us by about fifty yards. This was droll enough. We had now but a few miles to our place of destination, and the first thing I did on alighting at Newbury, both coaches stopping at the same time, was to call out, " Pray, is there a gentleman in that mail of the name of Toms ? " " No," said Joe, borrowing something of the vein of Gilpin, " for I have just got out." " Well ! " says he, " this is lucky ; but you don't know how vexed I was to miss you ; for," added he, lowering his voice, " do you know when I left you I went to Belcher's to ask about the caravan, and Mrs. Belcher said very obligingly, she couldn't tell about that, but there were two gentlemen who had taken places by the mail, and were gone on in a landau, and she could frank us. It's a pity I didn't meet with you ; we could then have got down for nothing. But *mum's the word*." It's the devil for any one to tell me a secret, for it is sure to come out in print. I do not care so much to gratify a friend, but the public ear is too great a temptation to me.

Our present business was to get beds and a supper at an inn ; but this was no easy task. The public-houses were full, and where you saw a light at a private house, and people poking their heads out of the casement to see what was going on, they instantly put them in and shut the window, the moment you seemed advancing with a suspicious overture for accommodation. Our guard and coachman thundered away at the outer gate of the Crown for some time without effect—such was the greater noise within ;—and when the doors were unbarred, and we got admittance, we found a party assembled in the kitchen round a good hospitable fire, some sleeping, others drinking, others talking on politics and on the fight. A tall English yeoman (something like Matthews in the face, and quite as great a wag)—

"A lusty man to ben an abbot able,"—

was making such a prodigious noise about rent and taxes, and the price of corn now and formerly, that he had prevented us from being heard at the gate. The first thing I heard him say was to a shuffling fellow who wanted to be off a bet for a shilling glass of brandy and water— "Confound it, man, don't be *insipid* !" Thinks I, that is a good phrase. It was a good omen. He kept it up so all night, nor flinched with the approach of morning. He was a fine fellow, with sense, wit, and spirit, frank, convivial—one of that true English breed that went with Harry the Fifth to the siege of Harfleur—" standing like greyhounds in the slips," etc. We ordered tea and eggs (beds were soon found to be out of the question) and this fellow's conversation was *sauce piquante*. It did one's heart good to see him brandish his oaken towel and to hear him talk. He made mince-meat of a drunken, stupid, red-faced, quarrelsome, *frowsy* farmer, whose nose "he moralized into a thousand similes," making it out a fire-brand like Bardolph's. "I'll tell you what, my friend," says he, "the landlady has only to keep you here to save fire and candle. If one was to touch your nose, it would go off like a piece of charcoal." At this the other only grinned like an idiot, the sole variety in his purple face being his little peering grey eyes and yellow teeth ; called for another glass, swore he would not stand it ; and after many attempts to provoke his humorous antagonist to single combat, which the other turned off (after working

him up to a ludicrous pitch of choler) with great adroitness,
he fell quietly asleep with a glass of liquor in his hand,
which he could not lift to his head. His laughing perse-
cutor made a speech over him, and turning to the opposite
side of the room, where they were all sleeping in the midst
of this " loud and furious fun," said, " There's a scene,
by G–d, for Hogarth to paint. I think he and Shakspeare
were our two best men at copying life." This confirmed
me in my good opinion of him. Hogarth, Shakspeare,
and Nature, were just enough for him (indeed for any man)
to know. I said, " You read Cobbett, don't you ? At
least," says I, " you talk just as well as he writes." He
seemed to doubt this. But I said, " We have an hour to
spare : if you'll get pen, ink, and paper, and keep on
talking, I'll write down what you say ; and if it doesn't
make a capital ' Political Register,' I'll forfeit my head.
You have kept me alive to-night, however, I don't know
what I should have done without you." He did not dislike
this view of the thing, nor my asking if he was not about
the size of Jem Belcher ; and told me soon afterwards,
in the confidence of friendship, that " the circumstance
which had given him nearly the greatest concern in his
life, was Cribb's beating Jem after he had lost his eye by
racket playing." The morning dawns ; that dim but yet
clear light appears, which weighs like solid bars of metal
on the sleepless eyelids ; the guests drop down from their
chambers one by one—but it was too late to think of
going to bed now (the clock was on the stroke of seven),
we had nothing for it but to find a barber's (the pole that
glittered in the morning sun lighted us to his shop), and
then a nine miles' march to Hungerford. The day was
fine, the sky was blue, the mists were retiring from the
marshy ground, the path was tolerably dry, the sitting-
up all night had not done us much harm—at least the cause
was good ; we talked of this and that with amicable
difference, roving and sipping of many subjects, but still

invariably we returned to the fight. At length, a mile to the left of Hungerford, on a gentle eminence, we saw the ring surrounded by covered carts, gigs, and carriages, of which hundreds had passed us on the road ; Toms gave a youthful shout, and we hastened down a narrow lane to the scene of action.

Reader, have you ever seen a fight ? If not, you have a pleasure to come, at least if it is a fight like that between the Gas-man and Bill Neate. The crowd was very great when we arrived on the spot ; open carriages were coming up, with streamers flying and music playing, and the country-people were pouring in over hedge and ditch in all directions, to see their hero beat or be beaten. The odds were still on Gas, but only about five to four. Gully had been down to try Neate, and had backed him considerably, which was a damper to the sanguine confidence of the adverse party. About two hundred thousand pounds were pending. The Gas says, he has lost 3000*l.* which were promised him by different gentlemen if he had won. He had presumed too much on himself, which had made others presume on him. This spirited and formidable young fellow seems to have taken for his motto the old maxim, that " there are three things necessary to success in life—*Impudence* ; *Impudence* ; *Impudence* ; " It is so in matters of opinion, but not in the *Fancy*, which is the most practical of all things, though even here confidence is half the battle, but only half. Our friend had vapoured and swaggered too much, as if he wanted to grin and bully his adversary out of the fight. " Alas ! the Bristol man was not so tamed ! " " This is *the grave-digger* " (would Tom Hickman exclaim in the moments of intoxication from gin and success, showing his tremendous right hand), " this will send many of them to their long homes ; I haven't done with them yet ! " Why should he—though he had licked four of the best men within the hour, yet why should he threaten to inflict dishonourable chastisement on my old master Richmond, a veteran going off the stage, and who has borne his sable honours meekly ? Magnanimity, my dear Tom, and bravery, should be inseparable. Or why should he go up to his antagonist, the first time he ever saw him at the Fives Court, and measuring him from head to foot with a glance of contempt, as Achilles surveyed Hector, say to him, " What, are you Bill Neate ? I'll knock more blood out of that great carcass of thine, this day fortnight, than you ever knock'd out of a bullock's ! " It was not manly, 'twas not fighter-like. If he was sure of the victory (as he was not), the less said about it the better. Modesty should accompany the *Fancy* as its shadow. The best men were always the best behaved. Jem Belcher, the Game Chicken (before whom the Gas-man could not have lived) were civil, silent men. So is Cribb, so is Tom Belcher, the most elegant of sparrers, and not a man for every one to take by the nose. I enlarged on this topic in the mail (while Turtle was asleep), and said very wisely (as I thought) that impertinence was a part of no profession. A boxer was bound to beat his man, but not to thrust his fist, either actually or by implication, in every one's face. Even a highwayman, in the way of trade, may blow out your brains, but if he uses foul language at the same time, I should say he was no gentleman. A boxer, I would infer, need not be a blackguard or a coxcomb, more than another. Perhaps I press this point too much on a fallen man—Mr. Thomas Hickman has by this time learnt that first of all lessons, " That man was made to mourn." He has lost nothing by the late fight but his presumption ; and that every man may do as well without ! By an over-display of this quality, however, the public had been prejudiced against him, and the *knowing-ones* were taken in. Few but those who had bet on him wished Gas to win. With my own prepossessions on the subject, the result of the 11th of December appeared to me as fine a piece of poetical

justice as I had ever witnessed. The difference of weight
between the two combatants (14 stone to 12) was nothing
to the sporting men. Great, heavy, clumsy, long-armed
Bill Neate kicked the beam in the scale of the Gas-man's
vanity. The amateurs were frightened at his big words,
and thought they would make up for the difference of six
feet and five feet nine. Truly, the *Fancy* are not men of
imagination. They judge of what has been, and cannot
conceive of anything that is to be. The Gas-man had
won hitherto ; therefore he must beat a man half as big
again as himself—and that to a certainty. Besides, there are
as many feuds, factions, prejudices, pedantic notions in the
Fancy as in the state or in the schools. Mr. Gully is almost
the only cool, sensible man among them, who exercises
an unbiassed discretion, and is not a slave to his passions
in these matters. But enough of reflections, and to our
tale. The day, as I have said, was fine for a December
morning. The grass was wet, and the ground miry, and
ploughed up with multitudinous feet, except that, within
the ring itself, there was a spot of virgin-green closed in
and unprofaned by vulgar tread, that shone with dazzling
brightness in the mid-day sun. For it was now noon, and
we had an hour to wait. This is the trying time. It is
then the heart sickens, as you think what the two champions are about, and how short a time will determine their
fate. After the first blow is struck, there is no opportunity
for nervous apprehensions ; you are swallowed up in the
immediate interest of the scene—but

> " Between the acting of a dreadful thing
> And the first motion, all the interim is
> Like a phantasma, or a hideous dream."

I found it so as I felt the sun's rays clinging to my back,
and saw the white wintry clouds sink below the verge of
the horizon. " So, I thought, my fairest hopes have faded

from my sight !—so will the Gas-man's glory, or that of his adversary, vanish in an hour." The *swells* were parading in their white box-coats, the outer ring was cleared with some bruises on the heads and shins of the rustic assembly (for the *cockneys* had been distanced by the sixty-six miles) ; the time drew near ; I had got a good stand ; a bustle, a buzz, ran through the crowd ; and from the opposite side entered Neate, between his second and bottle-holder. He rolled along, swathed in his loose great coat, his knock-knees bending under his huge bulk ; and, with a modest cheerful air, threw his hat into the ring. He then just looked round, and began quietly to undress ; when from the other side there was a similar rush and an opening made, and the Gas-man came forward with a conscious air of anticipated triumph, too much like the cock-of-the-walk. He strutted about more than became a hero, sucked oranges with a supercilious air, and threw away the skin with a toss of his head, and went up and looked at Neate, which was an act of supererogation. The only sensible thing he did was, as he strode away from the modern Ajax, to fling out his arms, as if he wanted to try whether they would do their work that day. By this time they had stripped, and presented a strong contrast in appearance. If Neate was like Ajax, "with Atlantean shoulders, fit to bear" the pugilistic reputation of all Bristol, Hickman might be compared to Diomed, light, vigorous, elastic, and his back glistened in the sun, as he moved about, like a panther's hide. There was now a dead pause—attention was awe-struck. Who at that moment, big with a great event, did not draw his breath short—did not feel his heart throb ? All was ready. They tossed up for the sun, and the Gas-man won. They were led up to the *scratch*—shook hands, and went at it.

In the first round every one thought it was all over. After making play a short time, the Gas-man flew at his adversary like a tiger, struck five blows in as many seconds, three first, and then following him as he staggered back, two more, right and left, and down he fell, a mighty ruin. There was a shout, and I said, " There is no standing this." Neate seemed like a lifeless lump of flesh and bone, round which the Gas-man's blows played with the rapidity of electricity or lightning, and you imagined he would only be lifted up to be knocked down again. It was as if Hickman held a sword or a fire in that right hand of his, and directed it against an unarmed body. They met again, and Neate seemed, not cowed, but particularly cautious. I saw his teeth clenched together and his brows knit close against the sun. He held out both his arms at full length straight before him, like two sledge-hammers, and raised his left an inch or two higher. The Gas-man could not get over this guard—they struck mutually and fell, but without advantage on either side. It was the same in the next round ; but the balance of power was thus restored—the fate of the battle was suspended. No one could tell how it would end. This was the only moment in which opinion was divided ; for, in the next, the Gas-man, aiming a mortal blow at his adversary's neck, with his right hand, and failing from the length he had to reach, the other returned it with his left at full swing, planted a tremendous blow on his cheek-bone and eye-brow, and made a red ruin of that side of his face. The Gas-man went down, and there was another shout—a roar of triumph as the waves of fortune rolled tumultuously from side to side. This was a settler. Hickman got up, and " grinned horrible a ghastly smile," yet he was evidently dashed in his opinion of himself ; it was the first time he had ever been so punished ; all one side of his face was perfect scarlet, and his right eye was closed in dingy blackness, as he advanced to the fight, less confident, but still determined. After one or two rounds, not receiving another such remembrancer, he rallied and went at it with his former impetuosity. But in vain. His strength had been weakened—his blows could not tell at such a distance—he was obliged to fling himself at his adversary, and could not strike from his feet ; and almost as regularly as he flew at him with his right hand, Neate warded the blow, or drew back out of its reach, and felled him with the return of his left. There was little cautious sparring—no half-hits—no tapping and trifling, none of the *petit-maîtreship* of the art—they were almost all knock-down blows :—the fight was a good stand-up fight. The wonder was the half-minute time. If there had been a minute or more allowed between each round, it would have been intelligible how they should by degrees recover strength and resolution ; but to see two men smashed to the ground, smeared with gore, stunned, senseless, the breath beaten out of their bodies ; and then, before you recover from the shock, to see them rise up with new strength and courage, stand ready to inflict or receive mortal offence, and rush upon each other " like two clouds over the Caspian "—this is the most astonishing thing of all :—this is the high and heroic state of man ! From this time forward the event became more certain every round ; and about the twelfth it seemed as if it must have been over. Hickman generally stood with his back to me ; but in the scuffle, he had changed positions, and Neate just then made a tremendous lunge at him, and hit him full in the face. It was doubtful whether he would fall backwards or forwards ; he hung suspended for a second or two, and then fell back, throwing his hands in the air, and with his face lifted up to the sky. I never saw anything more terrific than his aspect just before he fell. All traces of life, of natural expression, were gone from him. His face was like a human skull, a death's head, spouting blood. The eyes were filled with blood, the nose streamed with blood, the mouth gaped blood. He was not like an actual man, but like a preter-natural, spectral appearance, or like one of the figures in Dante's *Inferno*. Yet he fought on after this for several rounds, still striking the first desperate blow, and Neate standing on the defensive, and using the same cautious guard to the last, as if he had still all his work to do ; and it was not till the Gas-man was so stunned in the seventeenth or eighteenth round, that his senses forsook him, and he could not come to time, that the battle was declared over.[1] Ye who despise the Fancy, do something to show as much *pluck*, or as much self-possession as this, before you assume a superiority which you have never given a single proof of by any one action in the whole course of your lives !—When the Gas-man came to himself, the first words he uttered were, " Where am I ?   What is the matter ? "   " Nothing is the matter, Tom ; you have lost the battle, but you are the bravest man alive."   And Jackson whispered to him, " I am collecting a purse for you, Tom."   Vain sounds, and unheard at that moment ! Neate instantly went up and shook him cordially by the hand, and seeing some old acquaintance, began to flourish with his fists, calling out, " Ah ! you always said I couldn't fight. What do you think now ? " But all in good humour, and without any appearance of arrogance ; only it was evident Bill Neate was pleased that he had won the fight. When it was over, I asked Cribb if he did not think it was a good one ? He said, " *Pretty well !* "   The carrier-pigeons now mounted into the air, and one of them flew with the news of her husband's victory to the bosom of Mrs. Neate. Alas, for Mrs. Hickman !

Mais au revoir, as Sir Fopling Flutter says. I went down with Toms ; I returned with Jack Pigott, whom I met on

---

[1] Scroggins said of the Gas-man, that he thought he was a man of that courage, that if his hands were cut off, he would still fight on with the stumps—like that of Wildrington,—

——" In doleful dumps,
Who, when his legs were smitten off,
Still fought upon his stumps."

the ground. Toms is a rattle-brain ; Pigott is a sentimentalist. Now, under favour, I am a sentimentalist too—therefore I say nothing, but that the interest of the excursion did not flag as I came back. Pigott and I marched along the causeway leading from Hungerford to Newbury, now observing the effect of a brilliant sun on the tawny meads or moss-coloured cottages, now exulting in the fight, now digressing to some topic of general and elegant literature. My friend was dressed in character for the occasion, or like one of the Fancy ; that is, with a double portion of great coats, clogs, and overhauls : and just as we had agreed with a couple of country-lads to carry his superfluous wearing-apparel to the next town, we were overtaken by a return post-chaise, into which I got, Pigott preferring a seat on the bar. There were two strangers already in the chaise, and on their observing they supposed I had been to the fight, I said I had, and concluded they had done the same. They appeared, however, a little shy and sore on the subject ; and it was not till after several hints dropped, and questions put, that it turned out that they had missed it. One of these friends had undertaken to drive the other there in his gig : they had set out, to make sure work, the day before at three in the afternoon. The owner of the one-horse vehicle scorned to ask his way, and drove right on to Bagshot, instead of turning off at Hounslow ; there they stopped all night, and set off the next day across the country to Reading, from whence they took coach, and got down within a mile or two of Hungerford, just half an hour after the fight was over. This might be safely set down as one of the miseries of human life. We parted with these two gentlemen who had been to see the fight, but had returned as they went, at Wolhampton, where we were promised beds (an irresistible temptation, for Pigott had passed the preceding night at Hungerford as we had done at Newbury), and we turned into an old bow-windowed parlour with a carpet and a snug fire ; and after devouring a quantity of tea, toast, and eggs, sat down to consider, during an hour of philosophic leisure, what we should have for supper. In the midst of an Epicurean deliberation between a roasted fowl and mutton chops with mashed potatoes, we were interrupted by an inroad of Goths and Vandals— *O procul este profani*—not real flash-men, but interlopers, noisy pretenders, butchers from Tothill-fields, brokers from Whitechapel, who called immediately for pipes and tobacco, hoping it would not be disagreeable to the gentlemen, and began to insist that it was *a cross*. Pigott withdrew from the smoke and noise into another room, and left me to dispute the point with them for a couple of hours *sans intermission* by the dial. The next morning we rose refreshed ; and on observing that Jack had a pocket volume in his hand, in which he read in the intervals of our discourse, I inquired what it was, and learned to my particular satisfaction that it was a volume of the *New Eloise*. Ladies, after this, will you contend that a love for the Fancy is incompatible with the cultivation of sentiment ? —We jogged on as before, my friend setting me up in a genteel drab great coat and green silk handkerchief (which I must say became me exceedingly), and after stretching our legs for a few miles, and seeing Jack Randall, Ned Turner, and Scroggins, pass on the top of one of the Bath coaches, we engaged with the driver of the second to take us to London for the usual fee. I got inside, and found three other passengers. One of them was an old gentleman with an aquiline nose, powdered hair, and a pigtail, and who looked as if he had played many a rubber at the Bath rooms. I said to myself, he is very like Mr. Windham ; I wish he would enter into conversation, that I might hear what fine observations would come from those finely-turned features. However, nothing passed, till, stopping to dine at Reading, some inquiry was made by the company about the fight, and I gave (as the reader may believe) an eloquent and animated description of it. When we got into the coach again, the old gentleman, after a graceful exordium, said, he had, when a boy, been to a fight between the famous Broughton and George Stevenson, who was called the *Fighting Coachman*, in the year 1770, with the late Mr. Windham. This beginning flattered the spirit of prophecy within me, and riveted my attention. He went on—" George Stevenson was coachman to a friend of my father's. He was an old man when I saw him some years afterwards. He took hold of his own arm and said, ' there was muscle here once, but now it is no more than this young gentleman's.' He added, ' well, no matter ; I have been here long, I am willing to go hence, and I hope I have done no more harm than another man.' Once," said my unknown companion, " I asked him if he had ever beat Broughton ? He said Yes ; that he had fought with him three times, and the last time he fairly beat him, though the world did not allow it. ' I'll tell you how it was, master. When the seconds lifted us up in the last round, we were so exhausted that neither of us could stand, and we fell upon one another, and as Master Broughton fell uppermost, the mob gave it in his favour, and he was said to have won the battle. But the fact was, that as his second (John Cuthbert) lifted him up, he said to him, " I'll fight no more, I've had enough ; " which,' says Stevenson, ' you know gave me the victory. And to prove to you that this was the case, when John Cuthbert was on his death-bed, and they asked him if there was any thing on his mind which he wished to confess, he answered, " Yes, that there was one thing he wished to set right, for that certainly Master Stevenson won that last fight with Master Broughton ; for he whispered him as he lifted him up in the last round of all, that he had had enough." ' " This," said the Bath gentleman, " was a bit of human nature ; " and I have written this account of the fight on purpose that it might not be lost to the world. He also stated as a proof of the candour of mind in this class of men, that Stevenson acknowledged that Broughton could have beat him in his best day ; but that he (Broughton) was getting old in their last encounter. When we stopped in Piccadilly, I wanted to ask the gentleman some questions about the late Mr. Windham, but had not courage. I got out, resigned my coat and green silk handkerchief to Pigott (loth to part with these ornaments of life), and walked home in high spirits.

P.S.—Toms called upon me the next day, to ask me if I did not think the fight was a complete thing ? I said I thought it was. I hope he will relish my account of it.

Literary Remains. February 1822.

ON THE FEELING OF IMMORTALITY
IN YOUTH

William Hazlitt

No young man believes he shall ever die. It was a saying of my brother's, and a fine one. There is a feeling of Eternity in youth, which makes us amends for everything. To be young is to be as one of the Immortal Gods. One half of time indeed is flown—the other half remains in store for us with all its countless treasures ; for there is no line drawn, and we see no limit to our hopes and wishes. We make the coming age our own.——

" The vast, the unbounded prospect lies before us."

Death, old age, are words without a meaning, that pass by us like the idle air which we regard not. Others may have undergone, or may still be liable to them—we " bear a charmed life," which laughs to scorn all such sickly fancies. As in setting out on a delightful journey, we strain our eager gaze forward—

" Bidding the lovely scenes at distance hail,"—

and see no end to the landscape, new objects presenting themselves as we advance ; so, in the commencement of life, we set no bounds to our inclinations, nor to the unrestricted opportunities of gratifying them. We have as yet found no obstacle, no disposition to flag ; and it seems that we can go on so for ever. We look round in a new world, full of life, and motion, and ceaseless progress ; and feel in ourselves all the vigour and spirit to keep pace with it, and do not foresee from any present symptoms how we shall be left behind in the natural course of things, decline into old age, and drop into the grave. It is the simplicity, and as it were *abstractedness* of our feelings in youth, that (so to speak) identifies us with nature, and (our experience being slight and our passions strong) deludes us into a belief of being immortal like it. Our short-lived connection with existence, we fondly flatter ourselves, is an indissoluble and lasting union—a honeymoon that knows neither coldness, jar, nor separation. As infants smile and sleep, we are rocked in the cradle of our wayward fancies, and lulled into security by the roar of the universe around us—we quaff the cup of life with eager haste without draining it, instead of which it only overflows the more—objects press around us, filling the mind with their magnitude and with the throng of desires that wait upon them, so that we have no room for the thoughts of death. From that plenitude of our being, we cannot change all at once to dust and ashes, we cannot imagine " this sensible, warm motion, to become a kneaded clod "—we are too much dazzled by the brightness of the waking dream around us to look into the darkness of the tomb. We no more see our end than our beginning : the one is lost in oblivion and vacancy, as the other is hid from us by the crowd and hurry of approaching events. Or the grim shadow is seen lingering in the horizon, which we are doomed never to overtake, or whose last, faint, glimmering outline touches upon Heaven and translates us to the skies ! Nor would the hold that life has taken of us permit us to detach our thoughts from present objects and pursuits, even if we would. What is there more opposed to health, than sickness ; to strength and beauty, than decay and dissolution ; to the active search of knowl-

edge than mere oblivion ?   Or is there none of the usual
advantage to bar the approach of Death, and mock his
idle threats ; Hope supplies their place, and draws a veil
over the abrupt termination of all our cherished schemes.
While the spirit of youth remains unimpaired, ere the
" wine of life is drank up," we are like people intoxicated
or in a fever, who are hurried away by the violence of
their own sensations : it is only as present objects begin
to pall upon the sense, as we have been disappointed in
our favourite pursuits, cut off from our closest ties, that
passion loosens its hold upon the breast, that we by
degrees become weaned from the world, and allow ourselves to contemplate, " as in a glass, darkly," the possibility of parting with it for good. The example of others,
the voice of experience, has no effect upon us whatever.
Casualties we must avoid : the slow and deliberate ad-
vances of age we can play at *hide-and-seek* with.   We
think ourselves too lusty and too nimble for that blear-
eyed decrepid old gentleman to catch us. Like the foolish
fat scullion, in Sterne, when she hears that Master Bobby
is dead, our only reflection is—" So am not I ! " The idea
of death, instead of staggering our confidence, rather
seems to strengthen and enhance our possession and our
enjoyment of life. Others may fall around us like leaves,
or be mowed down like flowers by the scythe of Time :
these are but tropes and figures to the unreflecting ears
and overweening presumption of youth. It is not till we
see the flowers of Love, Hope, and Joy, withering around
us, and our own pleasures cut up by the roots, that we
bring the moral home to ourselves, that we abate something of the wanton extravagance of our pretensions, or
that the emptiness and dreariness of the prospect before
us reconciles us to the stillness of the grave !

> " Life ! thou strange thing, that hast a power to feel
>   Thou art, and to perceive that others are."

Well might the poet begin his indignant invective against an art, whose professed object is its destruction, with this animated apostrophe to life. Life is indeed a strange gift, and its privileges are most miraculous. Nor is it singular that when the splendid boon is first granted us, our gratitude, our admiration, and our delight should prevent us from reflecting on our own nothingness, or from thinking it will ever be recalled. Our first and strongest impressions are taken from the mighty scene that is opened to us, and we very innocently transfer its durability as well as magnificence to ourselves. So newly found, we cannot make up our minds to parting with it yet and at least put off that consideration to an indefinite term. Like a clown at a fair, we are full of amazement and rapture, and have no thoughts of going home, or that it will soon be night. We know our existence only for external objects, and we measure it by them. We can never be satisfied with gazing ; and nature will still want us to look on and applaud. Otherwise, the sumptuous entertainment, " the feast of reason and the flow of soul," to which they were invited, seems little better than a mockery and a cruel insult. We do not go from a play till the scene is ended, and the lights are ready to be extinguished. But the fair face of things still shines on ; shall we be called away, before the curtain falls, or ere we have scarce had a glimpse of what is going on ? Like children, our step-mother Nature holds us up to see the raree-show of the universe ; and then, as if life were a burthen to support, lets us instantly down again. Yet in that short interval, what " brave sublunary things" does not the spectacle unfold ; like a bubble, at one minute reflecting the universe, and the next, shook to air !—To see the golden sun and the azure sky, the outstretched ocean, to walk upon the green earth, and to be lord of a thousand creatures, to look down giddy precipices or over distant flowery vales, to see the world spread out under one's finger in a map, to

bring the stars near, to view the smallest insects in a
microscope, to read history, and witness the revolutions of
empires and the succession of generations, to hear of the
glory of Sidon and Tyre, of Babylon and Susa, as of a
faded pageant, and to say all these were, and are now
nothing, to think that we exist in such a point of time,
and in such a corner of space, to be at once spectators
and a part of the moving scene, to watch the return of the
seasons, of spring and autumn, to hear

> ——" The stockdove plain amid the forest deep,
> That drowsy rustles to the sighing gale "——

to traverse desert wildernesses, to listen to the midnight
choir, to visit lighted halls, or plunge into the dungeon's
gloom, or sit in crowded theatres and see life itself mocked,
to feel heat and cold, pleasure and pain, right and wrong,
truth and falsehood, to study the works of art and refine
the sense of beauty to agony, to worship fame and to
dream of immortality, to have read Shakspeare and belong
to the same species as Sir Isaac Newton ; [1] to be and to do

---

[1] Lady Wortley Montagu says, in one of her letters, that " she
would much rather be a rich *effendi*, with all his ignorance, than Sir
Isaac Newton, with all his knowledge."   This was not perhaps an
impolitic choice, as she had a better chance of becoming one than
the other, there being many rich effendis to one Sir Isaac Newton.
The wish was not a very intellectual one.   The same petulance of
rank and sex breaks out everywhere in these " *Letters.*"   She is
constantly reducing the poets or philosophers who have the misfortune of her acquaintance, to the figure they might make at her
Ladyship's levee or toilette, not considering that the public mind
does not sympathize with this process of a fastidious imagination.
In the same spirit, she declares of Pope and Swift, that " had it not
been for the *good-nature* of mankind, these two superior beings were
entitled, by their birth and hereditary fortune, to be only a couple
of link-boys."   Gulliver's Travels, and the Rape of the Lock, go
for nothing in this critical estimate, and the world raised the authors
to the rank of superior beings, in spite of their disadvantages of birth
and fortune, *out of pure good-nature* !   So, again, she says of Richardson, that he had never got beyond the servants' hall, and was utterly

all this, and then in a moment to be nothing, to have it
all snatched from one like a juggler's ball or a phantasma-
goria ; there is something revolting and incredible to sense
in the transition, and no wonder that, aided by youth and
warm blood, and the flush of enthusiasm, the mind contrives for a long time to reject it with disdain and loathing

unfit to describe the manners of people of quality ; till, in the
capricious workings of her vanity, she persuades herself that Clarissa
is very like what she was at her age, and that Sir Thomas and Lady
Grandison strongly resembled what she had heard of her mother
and remembered of her father. It is one of the beauties and advantages of literature, that it is the means of abstracting the mind from
the narrowness of local and personal prejudices, and of enabling us
to judge of truth and excellence by their inherent merits alone.
Woe be to the pen that would undo this fine illusion (the only
reality), and teach us to regulate our notions of genius and virtue by
the circumstances in which they happen to be placed ! You would
not expect a person whom you saw in a servants' hall, or behind a
counter, to write Clarissa ; but after he had written the work,
to *pre-judge* it from the situation of the writer, is an unpardonable
piece of injustice and folly. His merit could only be the greater
from the contrast. If literature is an elegant accomplishment,
which none but persons of birth and fashion should be allowed to
excel in, or to exercise with advantage to the public, let them by all
means take upon them the task of enlightening and refining mankind : if they decline this responsibility as too heavy for their
shoulders, let those who do the drudgery in their stead, however
inadequately, for want of their polite example, receive the meed
that is their due, and not to be treated as low pretenders who have
encroached on the province of their betters. Suppose Richardson
to have been acquainted with the great man's steward, or valet,
instead of the great man himself, I will venture to say that there was
more difference between him who lived in an *ideal world*, and had
the genius and felicity to open that world to others, and his friend
the steward, than between the lacquey and the mere lord, or between those who lived in different rooms of the same house, who
dined on the same luxuries at different tables, who rode outside
or inside of the same coach, and were proud of wearing or of
bestowing the same tawdry livery. If the lord is distinguished from
his valet by any thing else, it is by education and talent, which he has
in common with our author. But if the latter shows these in the
highest degree, it is asked what are his pretensions ? Not birth or

as a monstrous and improbable fiction, like a monkey on
a house-top, that is loath, amidst its fine discoveries and
specious antics, to be tumbled head-long into the street,
and crushed to atoms, the sport and laughter of the
multitude !

fortune, for neither of these would enable him to write a Clarissa.
One man is born with a title and estate, another with genius.
That is sufficient ; and we have no right to question the genius for
want of *gentility*, unless the former ran in families, or could be
bequeathed with a fortune, which is not the case.   Were it so, the
flowers of literature, like jewels and embroidery, would be confined
to the fashionable circles ; and there would be no pretenders to
taste or elegance but those whose names were found in the court
list.   No one objects to Claude's Landscapes as the work of a pastry-
cook, or withholds from Raphael the epithet of *divine*, because his
parents were not rich.   This impertinence is confined to men of
letters ; the evidence of the senses baffles the envy and foppery of
mankind.   No quarter ought to be given to this *aristocratic* tone of
criticism whenever it appears.   People of quality are not contented
with carrying all the external advantages for their own share, but
would persuade you that all the intellectual ones are packed up
in the same bundle.   Lord Byron was a later instance of this double
and unwarrantable style of pretension—*monstrum ingens, biforme*.
He could not endure a lord who was not a wit, nor a poet who was
not a lord.   Nobody but himself answered to his own standard
of perfection.   Mr. Moore carries a proxy in his pocket from some
noble persons to estimate literary merit by the same rule.   Lady
Mary calls Fielding names, but she afterwards makes atonement by
doing justice to his frank, free, hearty nature, where she says " his
spirits gave him raptures with his cook-maid, and cheerfulness when
he was starving in a garret, and his happy constitution made him
forget every thing when he was placed before a venison-pasty or
over a flask of champagne."   She does not want shrewdness and
spirit when her petulance and conceit do not get the better of her,
and she has done ample and merited execution on Lord Boling-
broke.   She is, however, very angry at the freedoms taken with the
Great ; *smells a rat* in this indiscriminate scribbling, and the familiarity
of writers with the reading public ; and inspired by her Turkish
costume, foretells a French or English revolution as the consequence
of transferring the patronage of letters from the *quality* to the mob,
and of supposing that ordinary writers or readers can have any
notions in common with their superiors.

The change, from the commencement to the close of
life, appears like a fable, after it has taken place ; how
should we treat it otherwise than as a chimera before it
has come to pass ?   There are some things that happened
so long ago, places or persons we have formerly seen, of
which such dim traces remain, we hardly know whether it
was sleeping or waking they occurred ; they are like dreams
within the dream of life, a mist, a film before the eye of
memory, which, as we try to recall them more distinctly,
elude our notice altogether.   It is but natural that the lone
interval that we thus look back upon, should have appeared
long and endless in prospect.   There are others so distinct
and fresh, they seem but of yesterday—their very vividness might be deemed a pledge of their permanence.
Then, however far back our impressions may go, we
find others still older (for our years are multiplied in
youth) ;   descriptions of scenes that we had read, and
people before our time, Priam and the Trojan war ;   and
even then, Nestor was old and dwelt delighted on his
youth, and spoke of the race, of heroes that were no more ;
—what wonder that, seeing this long line of being
pictured in our minds, and reviving as it were in us, we
should give ourselves involuntary credit for an indeterminate period of existence ?   In the Cathedral at Peter-
borough there is a monument to Mary, Queen of Scots, at
which I used to gaze when a boy, while the events of the
period, all that had happened since, passed in review before
me.   If all this mass of feeling and imagination could be
crowded into a moment's compass, what might not the
whole of life be supposed to contain ?   We are heirs of
the past ;   we count upon the future as our natural reversion.   Besides, there are some of our early impressions so
exquisitely tempered, it appears that they must always
last—nothing can add to or take away from their sweetness and purity—the first breath of spring, the hyacinth
dipped in the dew, the mild lustre of the evening-star, the

rainbow after a storm—while we have the full enjoyment
of these, we must be young ; and what can ever alter us
in this respect ? Truth, friendship, love, books, are also
proof against the canker of time ; and while we live, but
for them we can never grow old. We take out a new
lease of existence from the objects on which we set our
affections, and become abstracted, impassive, immortal in
them. We cannot conceive how certain sentiments should
ever decay or grow cold in our breasts ; and, consequently,
to maintain them in their first youthful glow and vigour,
the flame of life must continue to burn as bright as ever,
or rather, they are the fuel that feed the sacred lamp, that
kindle " the purple light of love," and spread a golden
cloud around our heads ! Again, we not only flourish and
survive in our affections (in which we will not listen to the
possibility of a change, any more than we foresee the
wrinkles on the brow of a mistress), but we have a farther
guarantee against the thoughts of death in our favourite
studies and pursuits, and in their continual advance. Art
we know is long ; life, we feel, should be so too. We see
no end of the difficulties we have to encounter : perfection
is slow of attainment, and we must have time to accom-
plish it in. Rubens complained that when he had just
learnt his art, he was snatched away from it : we trust
we shall be more fortunate ! A wrinkle in an old head
takes whole days to finish it properly : but to catch " the
Raphael grace, the Guido air," no limit should be put to
our endeavours. What a prospect for the future ! What
a task we have entered upon ! and shall we be arrested in
the middle of it ? We do not reckon our time thus employed lost, or our pains thrown away, or our progress
slow—we do not droop or grow tired, but " gain new
vigour at our endless task ; "—and shall Time grudge us
the opportunity to finish what we have auspiciously begun,
and have formed a sort of compact with nature to achieve ?
The fame of the great names we look up to is also im-

perishable ; and shall not we, who contemplate it with such intense yearnings, imbibe a portion of ethereal fire, the *divinæ particula auræ*, which nothing can extinguish ? I remember to have looked at a print of Rembrandt for hours together, without being conscious of the flight of time, trying to resolve it into its component parts, to connect its strong and sharp gradations, to learn the secret of its reflected lights, and found neither satiety nor pause in the prosecution of my studies. The print over which I was poring would last long enough ; why should the idea in my mind, which was finer, more impalpable, perish before it ? At this, I redoubled the ardour of my pursuit, and by the very subtlety and refinement of my inquiries, seemed to bespeak for them an exemption from corruption and the rude grasp of Death.[1]

Objects, on our first acquaintance with them, have that singleness and integrity of impression that it seems as if nothing could destroy or obliterate them, so firmly are they stamped and rivetted on the brain. We repose on them with a sort of voluptuous indolence, in full faith and boundless confidence. We are absorbed in the present moment, or return to the same point—idling away a great deal of time in youth, thinking we have enough and to spare. There is often a local feeling in the air, which is as fixed as if it were of marble ; we loiter in dim cloisters, losing ourselves in thought and in their glimmering arches ; a winding road before us seems as long as the journey of life, and as full of events. Time and experience dissipate this illusion ; and by reducing them to detail, circumscribe the limits of our expectations. It is only as the pageant of life passes by and the masques turn their backs upon us, that we see through the deception, or believe that the

[1] Is it not this that frequently keeps artists alive so long, *viz.* the constant occupation of their minds with vivid images, with little of the *wear-and-tear* of the body ?

train will have an end. In many cases, the slow progress
and monotonous texture of our lives, before we mingle
with the world and are embroiled in its affairs, has a
tendency to aid the same feeling. We have a difficulty,
when left to ourselves, and without the resource of books
or some more lively pursuit, to " beguile the slow and
creeping hours of time," and argue that if it moves on
always at this tedious snail's-pace, it can never come to
an end. We are willing to skip over certain portions of
it that separate us from favourite objects, that irritate ourselves at the unnecessary delay. The young are prodigal
of life from a superabundance of it ; the old are tenacious
on the same score, because they have little left, and cannot
enjoy even what remains of it.

For my part, I set out in life with the French Revolution, and that event had considerable influence on my early
feelings, as on those of others. Youth was then doubly
such. It was the dawn of a new era, a new impulse had
been given to men's minds, and the sun of Liberty rose
upon the sun of Life in the same day, and both were proud
to run their race together. Little did I dream, while my
first hopes and wishes went hand in hand with those of
the human race, that long before my eyes should close,
that dawn would be overcast, and set once more in the
night of despotism—" total eclipse ! " Happy that I did
not. I felt for years, and during the best part of my
existence, *heart-whole* in that cause, and triumphed in the
triumphs over the enemies of man ! At that time, while
the fairest aspirations of the human mind seemed about
to be realized, ere the image of man was defaced and his
breast mangled in scorn, philosophy took a higher, poetry
could afford a deeper range. At that time, to read the
" ROBBERS," was indeed delicious, and to hear

" From the dungeon of the tower time-rent,
   That fearful voice, a famish'd father's cry "

could be borne only amidst the fullness of hope, the crash of the fall of the strongholds of power, and the exulting sounds of the march of human freedom. What feelings the death-scene in Don Carlos sent into the soul ! In that headlong career of lofty enthusiasm, and the joyous opening of the prospects of the world and our own, the thought of death crossing it, smote doubly cold upon the mind ; there was a stifling sense of oppression and confinement, an impatience of our present knowledge, a desire to grasp the whole of our existence in one strong embrace, to sound the mystery of life and death, and in order to put an end to the agony of doubt and dread, to burst through our prison-house, and confront the King of Terrors in his grisly palace ! . . . As I was writing out this passage, my miniature-picture when a child lay on the mantel-piece, and I took it out of the case to look at it. I could perceive few traces of myself in it ; but there was the same placid brow, the dimpled mouth, the same timid, inquisitive glance as ever. But its careless smile did not seem to reproach me with having become a recreant to the sentiments that were then sown in my mind, or with having written a sentence that could call up a blush in this image of ingenuous youth !

" That time is past with all its giddy raptures." Since the future was barred to my progress, I have turned for consolation to the past, gathering up the fragments of my early recollections, and putting them into a form that might live. It is thus, that when we find our personal and substantial identity vanishing from us, we strive to gain a reflected and substituted one in our thoughts : we do not like to perish wholly, and wish to bequeath our names at least to posterity. As long as we can keep alive our cherished thoughts and nearest interests in the minds of others, we do not appear to have retired altogether from the stage, we still occupy a place in the estimation of mankind, exercise a powerful influence over them, and it is only our bodies that are trampled into dust or dispersed to air. Our darling speculations still find favour and encouragement, and we make as good a figure in the eyes of our descendants, nay, perhaps, a better than we did in our life-time. This is one point gained ; the demands of our self-love are so far satisfied. Besides, if by the proofs of intellectual superiority we survive ourselves in this world, by exemplary virtue or unblemished faith, we are taught to ensure an interest in another and a higher state of being, and to anticipate at the same time the applauses of men and angels.

> " Even from the tomb the voice of nature cries ;
> Even in our ashes live their wonted fires."

As we advance in life, we acquire a keener sense of the value of time. Nothing else, indeed, seems of any consequence ; and we become misers in this respect. We try to arrest its few last tottering steps, and to make it linger on the brink of the grave. We can never leave off wondering how that which has ever been should cease to be, and would still live on, that we may wonder at our own shadow, and when " all the life of life is flown," dwell on the retrospect of the past. This is accompanied by a mechanical tenaciousness of whatever we possess, by a distrust and a sense of fallacious hollowness in all we see. Instead of the full, pulpy feeling of youth, everything is flat and insipid. The world is a painted witch, that puts us off with false shows and tempting appearances. The ease, the jocund gaiety, the unsuspecting security of youth are fled ; nor can we, without flying in the face of common sense,

> " From the last dregs of life, hope to receive
> What its first sprightly runnings could not give."

If we can slip out of the world without notice or mischance, can tamper with bodily infirmity, and frame our minds to the becoming composure of *still-life*, before we sink into total insensibility, it is as much as we ought to expect. We do not in the regular course of nature die all at once ; we have mouldered away gradually long before ; faculty after faculty, attachment after attachment, we are torn from ourselves piece-meal while living ; year after year takes something from us ; and death only consigns the last remnant of what we were to the grave. The revulsion is not so great, and a quiet *euthanasia* is a winding-up of the plot, that is not out of reason or nature.

That we should thus in a manner outlive ourselves, and dwindle imperceptibly into nothing, is not surprising, when even in our prime the strongest impressions leave so little traces of themselves behind, and the last object is driven out by the succeeding one. How little effect is produced on us at any time by the books we have read, the scenes we have witnessed, the sufferings we have gone through ! Think only of the variety of feelings we experience in reading an interesting romance, or being present at a fine play —what beauty, what sublimity, what soothing, what heart-rending emotions ! You would suppose these would last for ever, or at least subdue the mind to a correspondent tone and harmony—while we turn over the page, while the scene is passing before us, it seems as if nothing could ever after shake our resolution, that " treason domestic, foreign levy, nothing could touch us farther ! " The first splash of mud we get, on entering the street, the first pettifogging shop-keeper that cheats us out of twopence, and the whole vanishes clean out of our remembrance, and we become the idle prey of the most petty and annoying circumstances. The mind soars by an effort to the grand and lofty : it is at home, in the grovelling, the disagreeable, and the little. This happens in the height and hey-day of our existence, when novelty gives a stronger impulse to the blood and takes a faster hold of the brain, (I have known the impression on coming out of a gallery of pictures then last half a day)—as we grow old, we become more feeble and querulous, every object " reverbs its own hollowness," and both worlds are not enough to satisfy the peevish importunity and extravagant presumption of our desires ! There are a few superior, happy beings, who are born with a temper exempt from every trifling annoyance. This spirit sits serene and smiling as in its native skies, and a divine harmony (whether heard or not) plays around them. This is to be at peace. Without this, it is in vain to fly into deserts, or to build a hermitage on the top of rocks, if regret and ill-humour follow us there : and with this, it is needless to make the experiment. The only true retirement is that of the heart ; the only true leisure is the repose of the passions. To such persons it makes little difference whether they are young or old ; and they die as they have lived, with graceful resignation.

Literary Remains.   1827.

MY FIRST ACQUAINTANCE WITH POETS

WILLIAM HAZLITT

MY father was a Dissenting Minister, at Wem, in Shrop-
shire ; and in the year 1798 (the figures that compose the
date are to me like the "dreadful name of Demogorgon ")
Mr. Coleridge came to Shrewsbury, to succeed Mr. Rowe
in the spiritual charge of a Unitarian Congregation there.
He did not come till late on the Saturday afternoon before
he was to preach ; and Mr. Rowe, who himself went down
to the coach, in a state of anxiety and expectation, to look
for the arrival of his successor, could find no one at all
answering the description but a round-faced man, in a
short black coat (like a shooting-jacket) which hardly
seemed to have been made for him, but who seemed
to be talking at a great rate to his fellow passengers.
Mr. Rowe had scarce returned to give an account of his
disappointment when the round-faced man in black entered,
and dissipated all doubts on the subject by beginning to talk.
He did not cease while he stayed ; nor has he since, that I
know of. He held the good town of Shrewsbury in delightful suspense for three weeks that he remained there,
"fluttering the *proud Salopians*, like an eagle in a dovecote" ; and the Welsh mountains that skirt the horizon
with their tempestuous confusion, agree to have heard no
such mystic sounds since the days of

> " High-born Hoel's harp or soft Llewellyn's lay."

As we passed along between Wem and Shrewsbury,
and I eyed their blue tops seen through the wintry branches,

or the red rustling leaves of the sturdy oak-trees by the road-side, a sound was in my ears as of a Syren's song ; I was stunned, startled with it, as from deep sleep ; but I had no notion then that I should ever be able to express my admiration to others in motley imagery or quaint allusion, till the light of his genius shone into my soul, like the sun's rays glittering in the puddles of the road. I was at that time dumb, inarticulate, helpless, like a worm by the way-side, crushed, bleeding, lifeless ; but now, bursting the deadly bands that bound them,

" With Styx nine times round them "

my ideas float on winged words, and as they expand their plumes, catch the golden light of other years. My soul has indeed remained in its original bondage, dark, obscure, with longings infinite and unsatisfied ; my heart, shut up in the prison-house of this rude clay, has never found, nor will it ever find, a heart to speak to ; but that my under-standing also did not remain dumb and brutish, or at length found a language to express itself, I owe to Coleridge. But this is not to my purpose.

My father lived ten miles from Shrewsbury, and was in the habit of exchanging visits with Mr. Rowe, and with Mr. Jenkins of Whitchurch (nine miles farther on), according to the custom of Dissenting Ministers in each other's neighbourhood. A line of communication is thus established, by which the flame of civil and religious liberty is kept alive, and nourishes its smouldering fire unquenchable, like the fires in the *Agamemnon* of Æschylus, placed at different stations, that waited for ten long years to announce with their blazing pyramids the destruction of Troy. Coleridge had agreed to come over and see my father, according to the courtesy of the country, as Mr. Rowe's probable successor ; but in the meantime, I had gone to hear him preach the Sunday after his arrival. A poet and a philosopher getting up into a Unitarian pulpit to preach the gospel, was a romance in these degenerate days, a sort of revival of the primitive spirit of Christianity, which was not to be resisted.

It was in January of 1798, that I rose one morning before daylight, to walk ten miles in the mud, to hear this celebrated person preach. Never, the longest day I have to live, shall I have such another walk as this cold, raw, comfortless one, in the winter of the year 1798. *Il y a des impressions que ni le tems ni les circonstances peuvent effacer. Dussé-je vivre des siècles entiers, le doux tems de ma jeunesse ne peut renaître pour moi, ni s'effacer jamais dans ma mémoire.* When I got there, the organ was playing the 100th Psalm, and when it was done, Mr. Coleridge rose and gave out his text, " And he went up into the mountain to pray, HIMSELF, ALONE." As he gave out this text, his voice " rose like a steam of rich distilled perfumes," and when he came to the two last words, which he pronounced loud, deep, and distinct, it seemed to me, who was then young, as if the sounds had echoed from the bottom of the human heart, and as if that prayer might have floated in solemn silence through the universe. The idea of St. John came into my mind, " of one crying in the wilderness, who had his loins girt about, and whose food was locusts and wild honey." The preacher then launched into his subject, like an eagle dallying with the wind. The sermon was upon peace and war ; upon church and state—not their alliance but their separation—on the spirit of the world and the spirit of Christianity, not as the same, but as opposed to one another. He talked of those who had " inscribed the cross of Christ on banners dripping with human gore." He made a poetical and pastoral excursion—and to show the fatal effects of war, drew a striking contrast between the simple shepherd-boy, driving his team afield, or sitting under the hawthorn, piping to his flock, " as though he should never be old," and the same poor country lad, crimped, kidnapped, brought into town, made drunk at an alehouse,

turned into a wretched drummer-boy, with his hair sticking on end with powder and pomatum, a long cue at his
back, and tricked out in the loathsome finery of the profession of blood :

" Such were the notes our once-loved poet sung."

And for myself, I could not have been more delighted
if I had heard the music of the spheres.   Poetry and
Philosophy had met together.   Truth and Genius had
embraced, under the eye and with the sanction of Religion.
This was even beyond my hopes.   I returned home well
satisfied.   The sun that was still labouring pale and wan
through the sky, obscured by thick mists, seemed an
emblem of the *good cause* ; and the cold dank drops of dew,
that hung half melted on the beard of the thistle, had
something genial and refreshing in them ; for there was a
spirit of hope and youth in all nature, that turned everything into good.   The face of nature had not then the
brand of Jus DIVINUM on it :

" Like to that sanguine flower inscrib'd with woe."

On the Tuesday following, the half-inspired speaker
came.   I was called down into the room where he was,
and went half-hoping, half-afraid.   He received me very
graciously, and I listened for a long time without uttering
a word.   I did not suffer in his opinion by my silence.
" For those two hours," he afterwards was pleased to say,
" he was conversing with William Hazlitt's forehead ! "
His appearance was different from what I had anticipated
from seeing him before.   At a distance, and in the dim
light of the chapel, there was to me a strange wildness in
his aspect, a dusky obscurity, and I thought him pitted
with the small-pox.   His complexion was at that time
clear, and even bright—

" As are the children of yon azure sheen."

His forehead was broad and high, light as if built of ivory, with large projecting eyebrows, and his eyes rolling beneath them, like a sea with darkened lustre. " A certain tender bloom his face o'erspread," a purple tinge as we see it in the pale thoughtful complexions of the Spanish portrait-painters, Murillo and Valasquez. His mouth was gross, voluptuous, open, eloquent ; his chin good-humoured and round ; but his nose, the rudder of the face, the index of the will, was small, feeble, nothing —like what he has done. It might seem that the genius of his face as from a height surveyed and projected him (with sufficient capacity and huge aspiration) into the world unknown of thought and imagination, with nothing to support or guide his veering purpose, as if Columbus had launched his adventurous course for the New World in a scallop, without oars or compass. So, at least, I comment on it after the event. Coleridge, in his person, was rather above the common size, inclining to the corpulent, or like Lord Hamlet, " somewhat fat and pursy." His hair (now, alas ! grey) was then black and glossy as the raven's, and fell in smooth masses over his forehead. This long pendulous hair is peculiar to enthusiasts, to those whose minds tend heavenward ; and is traditionally inseparable (though of a different colour) from the pictures of Christ. It ought to belong, as a character, to all who preach *Christ crucified*, and Coleridge was at that time one of those !

It was curious to observe the contrast between him and my father, who was a veteran in the cause, and then declining into the vale of years. He had been a poor Irish lad, carefully brought up by his parents, and sent to the University of Glasgow (where he studied under Adam Smith) to prepare him for his future destination. It was his mother's proudest wish to see her son a Dissenting Minister. So, if we look back to past generations (as far as eye can reach), we see the same hopes, fears, wishes, followed by the same disappointments, throbbing in the human heart ; and so we may see them (if we look forward) rising up for ever, and disappearing, like vapourish bubbles, in the human breast ! After being tossed about from congregation to congregation in the heats of the Unitarian controversy, and squabbles about the American war, he had been relegated to an obscure village, where he was to spend the last thirty years of his life, far from the only converse that he loved, the talk about disputed texts of Scripture, and the cause of civil and religious liberty. Here he passed his days, repining, but resigned, in the study of the Bible, and the perusal of the Commentators—huge folios, not easily got through, one of which would outlast a winter ! Why did he pore on these from morn to night (with the exception of a walk in the fields or a turn in the garden to gather broccoli-plants or kidney beans of his own rearing, with no small degree of pride and pleasure) ? Here were " no figures nor no fantasies "—neither poetry nor philosophy—nothing to dazzle, nothing to excite modern curiosity ; but to his lack-lustre eyes there appeared within the pages of the ponderous, unwieldy, neglected tomes, the sacred name of JEHOVAH in Hebrew capitals : pressed down by the weight of the style, worn to the last fading thinness of the understanding, there were glimpses, glimmering notions of the patriarchal wanderings, with palm-trees hovering in the horizon, and processions of camels at the distance of three thousand years ; there was Moses with the Burning Bush, the number of the Twelve Tribes, types, shadows, glosses on the law and the prophets ; there were discussions (dull enough) on the age of Methuselah, a mighty speculation ! there were outlines, rude guesses at the shape of Noah's Ark and of the riches of Solomon's Temple ; questions as to the date of the creation, predictions of the end of all things ; the great lapses of time, the strange mutations of the globe were unfolded with the voluminous leaf, as it turned over ; and though the soul might slumber with an hieroglyphic veil of inscrutable mysteries drawn over it, yet it was in a slumber ill-exchanged for all the sharpened realities of sense, wit, fancy, or reason. My father's life was comparatively a dream ; but it was a dream of infinity and eternity, of death, the resurrection, and a judgment to come !

No two individuals were ever more unlike than were the host and his guest. A poet was to my father a sort of nondescript ; yet whatever added grace to the Unitarian cause was to him welcome. He could hardly have been more surprised or pleased, if our visitor had worn wings. Indeed, his thoughts had wings : and as the silken sounds rustled round our little wainscoted parlour, my father threw back his spectacles over his forehead, his white hairs mixing with its sanguine hue ; and a smile of delight beamed across his rugged, cordial face, to think that Truth had found a new ally in Fancy ! [1] Besides, Coleridge seemed to take considerable notice of me, and that of itself was enough. He talked very familiarly, but agreeably, and glanced over a variety of subjects. At dinnertime he grew more animated, and dilated in a very edifying manner on Mary Wolstonecraft and Mackintosh. The last, he said, he considered (on my father's speaking of his *Vindiciæ Gallicæ* as a capital performance) as a clever, scholastic man—a master of the topics—or, as the ready warehouseman of letters, who knew exactly where to lay his hand on what he wanted, though the goods were not his own. He thought him no match for Burke, either in style or matter. Burke was a metaphysician, Mackintosh a mere logician. Burke was an orator (almost a poet) who

[1] My father was one of those who mistook his talent, after all. He used to be very much dissatisfied that I preferred his *Letters* to his *Sermons.* The last were forced and dry ; the first came naturally from him. For ease, half-plays on words, and a supine, monkish, indolent pleasantry, I have never seen them equalled.

reasoned in figures, because he had an eye for nature : Mackintosh, on the other hand, was a rhetorician, who had only an eye to commonplaces. On this I ventured to say that I had always entertained a great opinion of Burke, and that (as far as I could find) the speaking of him with contempt might be made the test of a vulgar, democratical mind. This was the first observation I ever made to Coleridge, and he said it was a very just and striking one. I remember the leg of Welsh mutton and the turnips on the table that day had the finest flavour imaginable. Coleridge added that Mackintosh and Tom Wedgwood (of whom, however, he spoke highly) had expressed a very indifferent opinion of his friend Mr. Wordsworth, on which he remarked to them—" He strides on so far before you, that he dwindles in the distance ! " Godwin had once boasted to him of having carried on an argument with Mackintosh for three hours with dubious success ; Coleridge told him—" If there had been a man of genius in the room he would have settled the question in five minutes." He asked me if I had ever seen Mary Wolstonecraft, and I said, I had once for a few moments, and that she seemed to me to turn off Godwin's objections to something she advanced with quite a playful, easy air. He replied, that " this was only one instance of the ascendency which people of imagination exercised over those of mere intellect." He did not rate Godwin very high [1] (this was caprice or prejudice, real or affected), but he had a great idea of Mrs. Wolstonecraft's powers of conversation ; none at all of her talent for book-making. We talked a little about Holcroft. He had been asked if he was not much struck *with* him, and he said, he thought himself in

[1] He complained in particular of the presumption of his attempting to establish the future immortality of man, " without " (as he said) " knowing what Death was or what Life was "—and the tone in which he pronounced these two words seemed to convey a complete image of both.

more danger of being struck *by* him. I complained that he would not let me get on at all, for he required a definition of even the commonest word, exclaiming, "What do you mean by *sensation*, Sir? What do you mean by an *idea*?" This, Coleridge said, was barricadoing the road to truth; it was setting up a turnpike-gate at every step we took. I forget a great number of things, many more than I remember; but the day passed off pleasantly, and the next morning Mr. Coleridge was to return to Shrewsbury. When I came down to breakfast, I found that he had just received a letter from his friend, T. Wedgwood, making him an offer of 150*l.* a year if he chose to waive his present pursuit, and devote himself entirely to the study of poetry and philosophy. Coleridge seemed to make up his mind to close with this proposal in the act of tying on one of his shoes. It threw an additional damp on his departure. It took the wayward enthusiast quite from us to cast him into Deva's winding vales, or by the shores of old romance. Instead of living at ten miles' distance, of being the pastor of a Dissenting congregation at Shrewsbury, he was henceforth to inhabit the Hill of Parnassus, to be a Shepherd on the Delectable Mountains. Alas! I knew not the way thither, and felt very little gratitude for Mr. Wedgwood's bounty. I was presently relieved from this dilemma; for Mr. Coleridge, asking for a pen and ink, and going to a table to write something on a bit of card, advanced towards me with undulating step, and giving me the precious document, said that that was his address, *Mr. Coleridge, Nether-Stowey, Somersetshire*; and that he should be glad to see me there in a few weeks' time, and, if I chose, would come half-way to meet me. I was not less surprised than the shepherd-boy (this simile is to be found in *Cassandra*), when he sees a thunderbolt fall close at his feet. I stammered out my acknowledgments and acceptance of this offer (I thought Mr. Wedgwood's annuity a trifle to it) as well as I could ; and this mighty business being settled, the poet preacher took leave, and I accompanied him six miles on the road. It was a fine morning in the middle of winter, and he talked the whole way. The scholar in Chaucer is described as going

——" Sounding on his way."

So Coleridge went on his. In digressing, in dilating, in passing from subject to subject, he appeared to me to float in air, to slide on ice. He told me in confidence (going along) that he should have preached two sermons before he accepted the situation at Shrewsbury, one on Infant Baptism, the other on the Lord's Supper, showing that he could not administer either, which would have effectually disqualified him for the object in view. I observed that he continually crossed me on the way by shifting from one side of the footpath to the other. This struck me as an odd movement ; but I did not at that time connect it with any instability of purpose or involuntary change of principle, as I have done since. He seemed unable to keep on in a straight line. He spoke slightingly of Hume (whose *Essay on Miracles* he said was stolen from an objection started in one of South's sermons—*Credat Judæus Appella !*). I was not very much pleased at this account of Hume, for I had just been reading, with infinite relish, that completest of all metaphysical *chokepears*, his *Treatise on Human Nature*, to which the *Essays* in point of scholastic subtility and close reasoning, are mere elegant, trifling, light summer reading. Coleridge even denied the excellence of Hume's general style, which I think betrayed a want of taste or candour. He however made me amends by the manner in which he spoke of Berkeley. He dwelt particularly on his *Essay on Vision* as a masterpiece of analytical reasoning. So it undoubtedly is. He was exceedingly angry with Dr. Johnson for striking the stone with his foot, in allusion to this author's *Theory of Matter and Spirit*, and saying, " Thus I confute him, Sir." Coleridge drew a parallel (I don't know how he brought about the connection) between Bishop Berkeley and Tom Paine. He said the one was an instance of a subtle, the other of an acute mind, than which no two things could be more distinct. The one was a shop-boy's quality, the other the characteristic of a philosopher. He considered Bishop Butler as a true philosopher, a profound and conscientious thinker, a genuine reader of nature and his own mind. He did not speak of his *Analogy*, but of his *Sermons at the Rolls' Chapel*, of which I had never heard. Coleridge somehow always contrived to prefer the *unknown* to the *known*. In this instance he was right. The *Analogy* is a tissue of sophistry, of wire-drawn, theological special-pleading ; the *Sermons* (with the preface to them) are in a fine vein of deep, matured reflection, a candid appeal to our observation of human nature, without pedantry and without bias. I told Coleridge I had written a few remarks, and was sometimes foolish enough to believe that I had made a discovery on the same subject (the *Natural disinterestedness of the Human Mind*)—and I tried to explain my view of it to Coleridge, who listened with great willingness, but I did not succeed in making myself understood. I sat down to the task shortly afterwards for the twentieth time, got new pens and paper, determined to make clear work of it, wrote a few meagre sentences in the skeleton style of a mathematical demonstration, stopped half-way down the second page ; and, after trying in vain to pump up any words, images, notions, apprehensions, facts, or observations, from that gulf of abstraction in which I had plunged myself for four or five years preceding, gave up the attempt as labour in vain, and shed tears of helpless despondency on the blank, unfinished paper. I can write fast enough now. Am I better than I was then ? Oh no ! One truth discovered, one pang of regret at not being able to express it, is better than all the fluency

and flippancy in the world. Would that I could go back
to what I then was ! Why can we not revive past times
as we can revisit old places ? If I had the quaint Muse
of Sir Philip Sidney to assist me, I would write a *Sonnet
to the Road between Wem and Shrewsbury*, and immortalize
every step of it by some fond enigmatical conceit. I would
swear that the very milestones had ears, and that Harmer
hill stooped with all its pines, to listen to a poet, as he
passed ! I remember but one other topic of discourse in
this walk. He mentioned Paley, praised the naturalness
and clearness of his style, but condemned his sentiments,
thought him a mere time-serving casuist, and said that " the
fact of his work on Moral and Political Philosophy being
made a text-book in our Universities was a disgrace to
the national character." We parted at the six-mile stone ;
and I returned homeward, pensive, but much pleased.
I had met with unexpected notice from a person whom I
believed to have been prejudiced against me. " Kind and
affable to me had been his condescension, and should be
honoured ever with suitable regard." He was the first
poet I had known, and he certainly answered to that
inspired name. I had heard a great deal of his powers of
conversation and was not disappointed. In fact, I never
met with anything at all like them, either before or since.
I could easily credit the accounts which were circulated
of his holding forth to a large party of ladies and gentlemen, an evening or two before, on the Berkeleian Theory,
when he made the whole material universe look like a
transparency of fine words ; and another story (which
I believe he has somewhere told himself) of his being asked
to a party at Birmingham, of his smoking tobacco and
going to sleep after dinner on a sofa, where the company
found him, to their no small surprise, which was increased
to wonder when he started up of a sudden, and rubbing his
eyes, looked about him, and launched into a three hours'
description of the third heaven, of which he had had a

dream, very different from Mr. Southey's *Vision of Judgment*, and also from that other *Vision of Judgment*, which Mr. Murray, the Secretary of the Bridge-street Junta, took into his especial keeping.

On my way back I had a sound in my ears—it was the voice of Fancy ; I had a light before me—it was the face of Poetry. The one still lingers there, the other has not quitted my side ! Coleridge, in truth, met me half-way on the ground of philosophy, or I should not have been won over to his imaginative creed. I had an uneasy, pleasurable sensation all the time, till I was to visit him. During those months the chill breath of winter gave me a welcoming ; the vernal air was balm and inspiration to me. The golden sunsets, the silver star of evening, lighted me on my way to new hopes and prospects. *I was to visit Coleridge in the spring.* This circumstance was never absent from my thoughts, and mingled with all my feelings. I wrote to him at the time proposed, and received an answer postponing my intended visit for a week or two, but very cordially urging me to complete my promise then. This delay did not damp, but rather increased my ardour. In the meantime, I went to Llangollen Vale, by way of initiating myself in the mysteries of natural scenery ; and I must say I was enchanted with it. I had been reading Coleridge's description of England in his fine *Ode on the Departing Year*, and I applied it, *con amore*, to the objects before me. That valley was to me (in a manner) the cradle of a new existence : in the river that winds through it, my spirit was baptized in the waters of Helicon !

I returned home, and soon after set out on my journey with unworn heart, and untired feet. My way lay through Worcester and Gloucester, and by Upton, where I thought of Tom Jones and the adventure of the muff. I remember getting completely wet through one day, and stopping at an inn (I think it was at Tewkesbury) where I sat up all night to read *Paul and Virginia*. Sweet were the showers in early youth that drenched my body, and sweet the drops of pity that fell upon the books I read ! I recollect a remark of Coleridge's upon this very book that nothing could show the gross indelicacy of French manners and the entire corruption of their imagination more strongly than the behaviour of the heroine in the last fatal scene, who turns away from a person on board the sinking vessel, that offers to save her life, because he has thrown off his clothes to assist him in swimming. Was this a time to think of such a circumstance ? I once hinted to Wordsworth, as we were sailing in his boat on Grasmere lake, that I thought he had borrowed the idea of his *Poems on the Naming of Places* from the local inscriptions of the same kind in *Paul and Virginia*. He did not own the obligation, and stated some distinction without a difference in defence of his claim to originality. Any, the slightest variation, would be sufficient for this purpose in his mind ; for whatever *he* added or altered would inevitably be worth all that any one else had done, and contain the marrow of the sentiment. I was still two days before the time fixed for my arrival, for I had taken care to set out early enough. I stopped these two days at Bridgewater ; and when I was tired of sauntering on the banks of its muddy river, returned to the inn and read *Camilla*. So have I loitered my life away, reading books, looking at pictures, going to plays, hearing, thinking, writing on what pleased me best. I have wanted only one thing to make me happy ; but wanting that have wanted everything !

I arrived, and was well received. The country about Nether Stowey is beautiful, green and hilly, and near the sea-shore. I saw it but the other day, after an interval of twenty years, from a hill near Taunton. How was the map of my life spread out before me, as the map of the country lay at my feet ! In the afternoon, Coleridge took me over to All-Foxden, a romantic old family mansion of the St. Aubins, where Wordsworth lived. It was then in the possession of a friend of the poet's, who gave him the free use of it. Somehow, that period (the time just after the French Revolution) was not a time when *nothing was given for nothing*. The mind opened and a softness might be perceived coming over the heart of individuals, beneath "the scales that fence" our self-interest. Wordsworth himself was from home, but his sister kept house, and set before us a frugal repast ; and we had free access to her brother's poems, the *Lyrical Ballads*, which were still in manuscript, or in the form of *Sybilline Leaves*. I dipped into a few of these with great satisfaction, and with the faith of a novice. I slept that night in an old room with blue hangings, and covered with the round-faced family portraits of the age of George I. and II., and from the wooded declivity of the adjoining park that overlooked my window, at the dawn of day, could

——" hear the loud stag speak."

In the outset of life (and particularly at this time I felt it so) our imagination has a body to it. We are in a state between sleeping and waking, and have indistinct but glorious glimpses of strange shapes, and there is always something to come better than what we see. As in our dreams the fulness of the blood gives warmth and reality to the coinage of the brain, so in youth our ideas are clothed, and fed, and pampered with our good spirits ; we breathe thick with thoughtless happiness, the weight of future years presses on the strong pulses of the heart, and we repose with undisturbed faith in truth and good. As we advance, we exhaust our fund of enjoyment and of hope. We are no longer wrapped in *lamb's-wool*, lulled in Elysium. As we taste the pleasures of life, their spirit evaporates, the sense palls ; and nothing is left but the phantoms, the lifeless shadows of what *has been !*

That morning, as soon as breakfast was over, we strolled out into the park, and seating ourselves on the trunk of an old ash-tree that stretched along the ground, Coleridge read aloud with a sonorous and musical voice, the ballad of *Betty Foy*. I was not critically or sceptically inclined. I saw touches of truth and nature, and took the rest for granted. But in the *Thorn*, the *Mad Mother*, and the *Complaint of a Poor Indian Woman*, I felt that deeper power and pathos which have been since acknowledged,

" In spite of pride, in erring reason's spite,"

as the characteristics of this author ; and the sense of a new style and a new spirit in poetry came over me. It had to me something of the effect that arises from the turning up of the fresh soil, or of the first welcome breath of Spring :

" While yet the trembling year is unconfirmed."

Coleridge and myself walked back to Stowey that evening, and his voice sounded high

" Of Providence, foreknowledge, will, and fate,
    Fix'd fate, free-will, foreknowledge absolute,"

as we passed through echoing grove, by fairy stream or waterfall, gleaming in the summer moonlight ! He lamented that Wordsworth was not prone enough to believe in the traditional superstitions of the place, and that there was a something corporeal, a *matter-of-fact-ness*, a clinging to the palpable, or often to the petty, in his poetry, in consequence. His genius was not a spirit that descended to him through the air ; it sprung out of the ground like a flower, or unfolded itself from a green spray, on which the goldfinch sang. He said, however (if I remember right), that this objection must be confined to his descriptive pieces, that his philosophic poetry had a grand and comprehensive spirit in it, so that his soul seemed to inhabit the universe like a palace, and to discover truth by intuition, rather than by deduction. The next day Wordsworth arrived from Bristol at Coleridge's cottage. I think I see him now. He answered in some degree to his friend's description of him, but was more gaunt and Don Quixote-like. He was quaintly dressed (according to the *costume* of that unconstrained period) in a brown fustian jacket and striped pantaloons. There was something of a roll, a lounge in his gait, not unlike his own *Peter Bell*. There was a severe, worn pressure of thought about his temples, a fire in his eye (as if he saw something in objects more than the outward appearance), an intense, high, narrow forehead, a Roman nose, cheeks furrowed by strong purpose and feeling, and a convulsive inclination to laughter about the mouth, a good deal at variance with the solemn, stately expression of the rest of his face. Chantrey's bust wants the marking traits ; but he was teased into making it regular and heavy : Haydon's head of him, introduced into the *Entrance of Christ into Jerusalem*, is the most like his drooping weight of thought and expression. He sat down and talked very naturally and freely, with a mixture of clear, gushing accents in his voice, a deep guttural intonation, and a strong tincture of the northern *burr*, like the crust on wine. He instantly began to make havoc of the half of a Cheshire cheese on the table, and said, triumphantly, that " his marriage with experience had not been so productive as Mr. Southey's in teaching him a knowledge of the good things of this life." He had been to see the *Castle Spectre* by Monk Lewis, while at Bristol, and described it very well. He said " it fitted the taste of the audience like a glove." This *ad captandum* merit was however by no means a recommendation of it, according to the severe principles of the new school, which reject rather than court popular effect. Wordsworth, looking out of the low, latticed window, said, " How beautifully the sun sets on that yellow bank ! " I thought within myself, " With what eyes these poets see nature ! " and ever after, when I saw the sunset stream upon the objects facing it, conceived I had made a discovery, or thanked Mr. Wordsworth for having made one for me ! We went over to All-Foxden again the day following, and Wordsworth read us the story of *Peter Bell* in the open air ; and the comment upon it by his face and voice was very different from that of some later critics ! Whatever might be thought of the poem, " his face was as a book where men might read strange matters," and he announced the fate of his hero in prophetic tones. There is a *chaunt* in the recitation both of Coleridge and Wordsworth, which acts as a spell upon the hearer, and disarms the judgment. Perhaps they have deceived themselves by making habitual use of this ambiguous accompaniment. Coleridge's manner is more full, animated, and varied ; Wordsworth's more equable, sustained, and internal. The one might be termed more *dramatic*, the other more *lyrical.* Coleridge has told me that he himself liked to compose in walking over uneven ground, or breaking through the straggling branches of a copse-wood ; whereas Wordsworth always wrote (if he could) walking up and down a straight gravel walk, or in some spot where the continuity of his verse met with no collateral interruption. Returning that same evening, I got into a metaphysical argument with Wordsworth, while Coleridge was explaining the different notes of the nightingale to his sister, in which we neither of us succeeded in making ourselves perfectly clear and intelligible. Thus I passed three weeks at Nether Stowey and in the neighbourhood, generally devoting the afternoons to a delightful chat in an arbour made of bark by the poet's friend Tom Poole, sitting under two fine elm-trees, and listening to the bees humming round us, while we quaffed our *flip*. It was agreed, among other things, that we should make a jaunt down the Bristol Channel, as far as Linton. We set off together on foot, Coleridge, John Chester, and I. This Chester was a native of Nether Stowey, one of those who were attracted to Coleridge's discourse as flies are to honey, or bees in swarming-time to the sound of a brass pan. He " followed in the chase like a dog who hunts, not like one that made up the cry." He had on a brown cloth coat, boots, and corduroy breeches, was low in stature, bow-legged, had a drag in his walk like a drover, which he assisted by a hazel switch, and kept on a sort of trot by the side of Coleridge, like a running footman by a state coach, that he might not lose a syllable or sound that fell from Coleridge's lips. He told me his private opinion, that Coleridge was a wonderful man. He scarcely opened his lips, much less offered an opinion the whole way : yet of the three, had I to choose during that journey, I would be John Chester. He afterwards followed Coleridge into Germany, where the Kantean philosophers were puzzled how to bring him under any of their categories. When he sat down at table with his idol, John's felicity was complete ; Sir Walter Scott's, or Mr. Blackwood's, when they sat down at the same table with the King, was not more so. We passed Dunster on our right, a small town between the brow of a hill and the sea. I remember eyeing it wistfully as it lay below us : contrasted with the woody scene around, it looked as clear, as pure, as *embrowned* and ideal as any landscape I have seen since, of Gaspar Poussin's or Domenichino's. We had a long day's march (our feet kept time to the echoes of Coleridge's tongue) through Minehead and by the Blue Anchor, and on to Linton, which we did not reach till near midnight, and where we had some difficulty in making a lodgment. We, however, knocked the people of the house up at last, and we were repaid for our apprehensions and fatigue by some excellent rashers of fried bacon and eggs. The view in coming along had been splendid. We walked for miles and miles on dark brown heaths overlooking the Channel, with the Welsh hills beyond, and at times descended into little sheltered valleys close by the sea-side, with a smuggler's face scowling by us, and then had to ascend conical hills with a path winding up through a coppice to a barren top, like a monk's shaven crown, from one of which I pointed out to Coleridge's notice the bare masts of a vessel on the very edge of the horizon, and within the red, orbed disk of the setting sun, like his own spectre-ship in the *Ancient Mariner*. At Linton the character of the sea-coast becomes more marked and rugged. There is a place called the *Valley of Rocks* (I suspect this was only the poetical name for it), bedded among precipices overhanging the sea, with rocky caverns beneath, into which the waves dash, and where the sea-gull for ever wheels its screaming flight. On the tops of these are huge stones thrown transverse, as if an earthquake had tossed them there, and behind these is a fretwork of perpendicular rocks, something like the *Giant's Causeway*. A thunder-storm came on while we were at the inn, and Coleridge was running out bare-headed to enjoy the commotion of the elements in the *Valley of Rocks*, but as if in spite, the clouds only muttered a few angry sounds, and let fall a few refreshing drops. Coleridge told me that he and Wordsworth were to have made this place the scene of a prose-tale, which was to have been in the manner of, but far superior to, the *Death of Abel*, but they had relinquished the design. In the morning of the second day, we breakfasted luxuriously in an old-fashioned parlour on tea, toast, eggs, and honey, in the very sight of the bee-hives from which it had been taken, and a garden full of thyme and wild flowers that had produced it. On this occasion Coleridge spoke of Virgil's *Georgics*, but not well. I do not think he had much feeling for the classical or elegant.[1] It was in this room that we found a little worn-

---

[1] He had no idea of pictures, of Claude or Raphael, and at this time I had as little as he. He sometimes gives a striking account at present of the Cartoons at Pisa by Buffamalco and others ; of one in particular, where Death is seen in the air brandishing his scythe,

out copy of the *Seasons*, lying in a window-seat, on which Coleridge exclaimed, " *That* is true fame ! " He said Thomson was a great poet, rather than a good one ; his style was as meretricious as his thoughts were natural. He spoke of Cowper as the best modern poet. He said the *Lyrical Ballads* were an experiment about to be tried by him and Wordsworth, to see how far the public taste would endure poetry written in a more natural and simple style than had hitherto been attempted ; totally discarding the artifices of poetical diction, and making use only of such words as had probably been common in the most ordinary language since the days of Henry II. Some comparison was introduced between Shakspeare and Milton. He said " he hardly knew which to prefer. Shakspeare appeared to him a mere stripling in the art ; he was as tall and as strong, with infinitely more activity than Milton, but he never appeared to have come to man's estate ; or if he had, he would not have been a man, but a monster." He spoke with contempt of Gray, and with intolerance of Pope. He did not like the versification of the latter. He observed that " the ears of these couplet-writers might be charged with having short memories, that could not retain the harmony of whole passages." He thought little of Junius as a writer ; he had a dislike of Dr. Johnson ; and a much higher opinion of Burke as an orator and politician, than of Fox or Pitt. He, however, thought him very inferior in richness of style and imagery to some of our elder prose-writers, particularly Jeremy Taylor. He liked Richardson, but not Fielding ; nor could I get him to enter into the merits of *Caleb Williams*. In short, he was profound and discriminating with respect to those authors whom he liked, and where he gave his judgment fair play ; capri-

and the great and mighty of the earth shudder at his approach, while the beggars and the wretched kneel to him as their deliverer. He would, of course, understand so broad and fine a moral as this at any time.

cious, perverse, and prejudiced in his antipathies and distastes. We loitered on the " ribbed sea-sands," in such
talk as this a whole morning, and, I recollect, met with
a curious seaweed, of which John Chester told us the
country name ! A fisherman gave Coleridge an account
of a boy that had been drowned the day before, and that
they had tried to save him at the risk of their own lives.
He said " he did not know how it was that they ventured,
but, Sir, we have a *nature* towards one another." This expression, Coleridge remarked to me, was a fine illustration
of that theory of disinterestedness which I (in common with
Butler) had adopted. I broached to him an argument of
mine to prove that *likeness* was not mere association of
ideas. I said that the mark in the sand put one in mind
of a man's foot, not because it was part of a former impression of a man's foot (for it was quite new), but because
it was like the shape of a man's foot. He assented to the
justness of this distinction (which I have explained at
length elsewhere, for the benefit of the curious) and John
Chester listened ; not from any interest in the subject, but
because he was astonished that I should be able to suggest
anything to Coleridge that he did not already know. We
returned on the third morning, and Coleridge remarked
the silent cottage-smoke curling up the valleys where, a
few evenings before, we had seen the lights gleaming
through the dark.

In a day or two after we arrived at Stowey, we set
out, I on my return home, and he for Germany. It was
a Sunday morning, and he was to preach that day for Dr.
Toulmin of Taunton. I asked him if he had prepared anything for the occasion ? He said he had not even thought
of the text, but should as soon as we parted. I did not go
to hear him—this was a fault—but we met in the evening
at Bridgewater. The next day we had a long day's walk
to Bristol, and sat down, I recollect, by a well-side on the
road, to cool ourselves and satisfy our thirst, when Cole-

ridge repeated to me some descriptive lines of his tragedy of *Remorse* ; which I must say became his mouth and that occasion better than they, some years after, did Mr. Elliston's and the Drury-lane boards—

" Oh memory ! shield me from the world's poor strife,
    And give those scenes thine everlasting life."

I saw no more of him for a year or two, during which period he had been wandering in the Hartz Forest, in Germany ; and his return was cometary, meteorous, unlike his setting out. It was not till some time after that I knew his friends Lamb and Southey. The last always appears to me (as I first saw him) with a commonplace book under his arm, and the first with a *bon-mot* in his mouth. It was at Godwin's that I met him with Holcroft and Coleridge, where they were disputing fiercely which was the best—*Man as he was, or man as he is to be*. " Give me," says Lamb, " man as he is *not* to be." This saying was the beginning of a friendship between us, which I believe still continues. Enough of this for the present.

" But there is matter for another rhyme,
    And I to this may add a second tale."

The Liberal.   April 1823.

THE LETTER-BELL

William Hazlitt

COMPLAINTS are frequently made of the vanity and shortness of human life, when, if we examine its smallest details,
they present a world by themselves. The most trifling
objects, retraced with the eye of memory, assume the
vividness, the delicacy, and importance of insects seen
through a magnifying glass. There is no end of the
brilliancy or the variety. The habitual feeling of the love
of life may be compared to " one entire and perfect chrysolite," which, if analysed, breaks into a thousand shining
fragments. Ask the sum-total of the value of human life,
and we are puzzled with the length of the account, and the
multiplicity of items in it : take any one of them apart,
and it is wonderful what matter for reflection will be found
in it ! As I write this, the *Letter-Bell* passes ; it has a lively,
pleasant sound with it, and not only fills the street with its
importunate clamour, but rings clear through the length
of many half-forgotten years. It strikes upon the ear, it
vibrates to the brain, it wakes me from the dream of time,
it flings me back upon my first entrance into life, the period
of my first coming up to town, when all around was
strange, uncertain, adverse—a hubbub of confused noises,
a chaos of shifting objects—and when this sound alone,
startling me with the recollection of a letter I had to send
to the friends I had lately left, brought me as it were to
myself, made me feel that I had links still connecting me

with the universe, and gave me hope and patience to persevere. At that loud-tinkling, interrupted sound, the long line of blue hills near the place where I was brought up waves in the horizon, a golden sunset hovers over them, the dwarf oaks rustle their red leaves in the evening breeze, and the road from Wem to Shrewsbury, by which I first set out on my journey through life, stares me in the face as plain, but, from time and change, not less visionary and mysterious than the pictures in the *Pilgrim's Prigress*. Or if the Letter-Bell does not lead me a dance into the country, it fixes me in the thick of my town recollections, I know not how long ago. It was a kind of alarm to break off from my work when there happened to be company to dinner or when I was going to the play. *That* was going to the play, indeed, when I went twice a year, and had not been more than half a dozen times in my life. Even the idea that any one else in the house was going, was a sort of reflected enjoyment, and conjured up a lively anticipation of the scene. I remember a Miss D——, a maiden lady from Wales (who in her youth was to have been married to an earl), tantalized me greatly in this way, by talking all day of going to see Mrs. Siddons' " airs and graces " at night in some favourite part ; and when the Letter-Bell announced that the time was approaching, and its last receding sound lingered on the ear, or was lost in silence, how anxious and uneasy I became, lest she and her companion should not be in time to get good places —lest the curtain should draw up before they arrived— and lest I should lose one line or look in the intelligent report which I should hear the next morning ! The punctuating of time at that early period—everything that gives it an articulate voice—seems of the utmost consequence ; for we do not know what scenes in the *ideal* world may run out of them : a world of interest may hang upon every instant, and we can hardly sustain the weight of future years which are contained in embryo in the most minute and inconsiderable passing events. How often have I put off writing a letter till it was too late ! How often have I had to run after the postman with it—now missing, now recovering the sound of his bell—breathless, angry with myself—then hearing the welcome sound come full round a corner—and seeing the scarlet costume which set all my fears and self-reproaches at rest ! I do not recollect having ever repented giving a letter to the postman or wishing to retrieve it after he had once deposited it in his bag. What I have once set my hand to, I take the consequences of, and have been always pretty much of the same humour in this respect. I am not like the person who, having sent off a letter to his mistress, who resided a hundred and twenty miles in the country, and disapproving, on second thoughts, of some expressions contained in it, took a post-chaise and four to follow and intercept it the next morning. At other times, I have sat and watched the decaying embers in a little back painting-room (just as the wintry day declined), and brooded over the half-finished copy of a Rembrandt, or a landscape by Vangoyen, placing it where it might catch a dim gleam of light from the fire ; while the Letter-Bell was the only sound that drew my thoughts to the world without, and reminded me that I had a task to perform in it. As to that landscape, methinks I see it now—

> The slow canal, the yellow-blossomed vale,
> The willow-tufted bank, the gliding sail.

There was a windmill, too, with a poor low clay-built cottage beside it : how delighted I was when I had made the tremulous, undulating reflection in the water, and saw the dull canvas become a lucid mirror of the commonest features of nature ! Certainly, painting gives one a strong interest in nature and humanity (it is not the *dandy-school* of morals or sentiment)—

> While with an eye made quiet by the power
> Of harmony and the deep power of joy,
> We see into the life of things.

Perhaps there is no part of a painter's life (if we must tell " the secrets of the prison-house ") in which he has more enjoyment of himself and his art, than that in which, after his work is over, and with furtive, sidelong glances at what he has done, he is employed in washing his brushes and cleaning his pallet for the day. Afterwards, when he gets a servant in livery to do this for him, he may have other and more ostensible sources of satisfaction—greater splendour, wealth, or fame ; but he will not be so wholly in his art, nor will his art have such a hold on him as when he was too poor to transfer its meanest drudgery to others —too humble to despise aught that had to do with the object of his glory and his pride, with that on which all his projects of ambition of pleasure were founded. " Entire affection scorneth nicer hands." When the professor is above this mechanical part of his business, it may have become a *stalking-horse* to other worldly schemes, but is no longer his *hobby-horse* and the delight of his inmost thoughts.

I used sometimes to hurry through this part of my occupation, while the Letter-Bell (which was my dinner-bell) summoned me to the fraternal board, where youth and hope

> Made good digestion wait on appetite
> And health on both ;

or oftener I put it off till after dinner, that I might loiter longer and with more luxurious indolence over it, and connect it with the thoughts of my next day's labours.

The dustman's bell, with its heavy monotonous noise, and the brisk, lively tinkle of the muffin-bell, have something in them, but not much. They will bear dilating upon with the utmost licence of inventive prose. All things are not alike *conductors* to the imagination. A learned Scotch professor found fault with an ingenious friend and arch-critic for cultivating a rookery on his grounds : the professor declared " he would as soon think of encouraging a *froggery.*" This was barbarous as it was senseless. Strange, that a country that has produced the *Scotch Novels* and *Gertrude of Wyoming* should want sentiment !

The postman's double knock at the door the next morning is " more germain to the matter." How that knock often goes to the heart ! We distinguish to a nicety the arrival of the Twopenny or the General Post. The summons of the latter is louder and heavier, as bringing news from a greater distance, and as, the longer it has been delayed, fraught with a deeper interest. We catch the sound of what is to be paid—eightpence, ninepence, a shilling—and our hopes generally rise with the postage. How we are provoked at the delay in getting change—at the servant who does not hear the door ! Then if the postman passes, and we do not hear the expected knock, what a pang is there ! It is like the silence of death—of hope ! We think he does it on purpose, and enjoys all the misery of our suspense. I have sometimes walked out to see the Mail-Coach pass, by which I had sent a letter, or to meet it when I expected one. I never see a Mail-Coach, for this reason, but I look at it as the bearer of glad tidings—the messenger of fate. I have reason to say so. The finest sight in the metropolis is that of the Mail-Coaches setting off from Piccadilly. The horses paw the ground, and are impatient to be gone, as if conscious of the precious burden they convey. There is a peculiar secrecy and despatch, significant and full of meaning, in all the proceedings concerning them. Even the outside passengers have an erect and supercilious air, as if proof against the accidents of the journey. In fact, it seems indifferent whether they are to encounter the summer's heat or winter's cold, since they are borne on through the air in a winged chariot. The Mail-Carts drive up ; the transfer of packages is made ; and, at a signal given, they start off, bearing the irrevocable scrolls that give wings to thought, and that bind or sever hearts for ever. How we hate the Putney and Brentford stages that draw up in a line after they are gone ! Some persons think the sublimest object in nature is a ship launched on the bosom of the ocean ; but give me, for my private satisfaction, the Mail-Coaches that pour down Piccadilly of an evening, tear up the pavement, and devour the way before them to the Land's-End !

In Cowper's time, Mail-Coaches were hardly set up ; but he has beautifully described the coming-in of the Post-Boy :

> Hark ! 'tis the twanging horn o'er yonder bridge,
> That with its wearisome but needful length
> Bestrides the wintry flood, in which the moon
> Sees her unwrinkled face reflected bright :
> He comes, the herald of a noisy world,
> With spattered boots, strapped waist, and frozen locks ;
> News from all nations lumbering at his back.
> True to his charge, the close-packed load behind.
> Yet careless what he brings, his one concern
> Is to conduct it to the destined inn ;
> And having dropped the expected bag, pass on.
> He whistles as he goes, light-hearted wretch !
> Cold and yet cheerful ; messenger of grief
> Perhaps to thousands, and of joy to some ;
> To him indifferent whether grief or joy.
> Houses in ashes and the fall of stocks,
> Births, deaths, and marriages, epistles wet
> With tears that trickled down the writer's cheeks
> Fast as the periods from his fluent quill,
> Or charged with amorous sighs of absent swains
> Or nymphs responsive, equally affect
> His horse and him, unconscious of them all.

And yet, notwithstanding this, and so many other passages that seem like the very marrow of our being, Lord Byron denies that Cowper was a poet !—The Mail-Coach is an improvement on the Post-Boy ; but I fear it will hardly bear so poetical a description. The picturesque and dramatic do not keep pace with the useful and mechanical. The telegraphs that lately communicated the intelligence of the new revolution to all France within a few hours, are a wonderful contrivance ; but they are less striking and appalling than the beacon-fires (mentioned by Æschylus), which, lighted from hilltop to hilltop, announced the taking of Troy, and the return of Agamemnon.

Sketches and Essays.   1831.

A " NOW "

LEIGH HUNT

DESCRIPTIVE OF A HOT DAY

Now the rosy- (and lazy-) fingered Aurora, issuing from
her saffron house, calls up the moist vapours to surround
her, and goes veiled with them as long as she can ; till
Phœbus, coming forth in his power, looks everything out
of the sky, and holds sharp, uninterrupted empire from his
throne of beams. Now the mower begins to make his
sweeping cuts more slowly, and resorts oftener to the beer.
Now the carter sleeps a-top of his load of hay, or plods with
double slouch of shoulder, looking out with eyes winking
under his shading hat, and with a hitch upward of one side
of his mouth. Now the little girl at her grandmother's
cottage-door watches the coaches that go by, with her
hand held up over her sunny forehead. Now labourers
look well resting in their white shirts at the doors of rural
ale-houses. Now an elm is fine there, with a seat under it ;
and horses drink out of the trough, stretching their yearning
necks with loosened collars ; and the traveller calls for his
glass of ale, having been without one for more than ten
minutes ; and his horse stands wincing at the flies, giving
sharp shivers of his skin, and moving to and fro his ineffectual docked tail ; and now Miss Betty Wilson, the
host's daughter, comes streaming forth in a flowered
gown and ear-rings, carrying with four of her beautiful
fingers the foaming glass, for which, after the traveller

has drank it, she receives with an indifferent eye, looking another way, the lawful twopence. Now grasshoppers " fry," as Dryden says. Now cattle stand in water, and ducks are envied. Now boots, and shoes, and trees by the roadside, are thick with dust ; and dogs, rolling in it, after issuing out of the water, into which they have been thrown to fetch sticks, come scattering horror among the legs of the spectators. Now a fellow who finds he has three miles further to go in a pair of tight shoes is in a pretty situation. Now rooms with the sun upon them become intolerable ; and the apothecary's apprentice, with a bitterness beyond aloes, thinks of the pond he used to bathe in at school. Now men with powdered heads (especially if thick) envy those that are unpowdered, and stop to wipe them up hill, with countenances that seem to expostulate with destiny. Now boys assemble round the village pump with a ladle to it, and delight to make a forbidden splash and get wet through the shoes. Now also they make suckers of leather, and bathe all day long in rivers and ponds, and make mighty fishings for " tittle-bats." Now the bee, as he hums along, seems to be talking heavily of the heat. Now doors and brick-walls are burning to the hand ; and a walled lane, with dust and broken bottles in it, near a brick-field, is a thing not to be thought of. Now a green lane, on the contrary, thick-set with hedgerow elms, and having the noise of a brook " rumbling in pebble-stone," is one of the pleasantest things in the world.

Now, in town, gossips talk more than ever to one another, in rooms, in doorways, and out of window, always beginning the conversation with saying that the heat is overpowering. Now blinds are let down, and doors thrown open, and flannel waistcoats left off, and cold meat preferred to hot, and wonder expressed why tea continues so refreshing, and people delight to sliver lettuces into bowls, and apprentices water doorways with tin canisters that lay several atoms of dust. Now the water-cart, jumbling along the middle of the street, and jolting the showers out of its box of water, really does something. Now fruiterers' shops and dairies look pleasant, and ices are the only things to those who can get them. Now ladies loiter in baths ; and people make presents of flowers ; and wine is put into ice ; and the after-dinner lounger recreates his head with applications of perfumed water out of long-necked bottles. Now the lounger, who cannot resist riding his new horse, feels his boots burn him. Now buckskins are not the lawn of Cos. Now jockeys, walking in greatcoats to lose flesh, curse inwardly. Now five fat people in a stage-coach hate the sixth fat one who is coming in, and think he has no right to be so large. Now clerks in office do nothing but drink soda-water and spruce-beer, and read the newspaper. Now the old-clothesman drops his solitary cry more deeply into the areas on the hot and forsaken side of the street ; and bakers look vicious ; and cooks are aggravated ; and the steam of a tavern-kitchen catches hold of us like the breath of Tartarus. Now delicate skins are beset with gnats ; and boys make their sleeping companion start up, with playing a burning-glass on his hand ; and blacksmiths are super-carbonated ; and cobblers in their stalls almost feel a wish to be transplanted ; and butter is too easy to spread ; and the dragoons wonder whether the Romans liked their helmets ; and old ladies, with their lappets unpinned, walk along in a state of dilapidation ; and the servant maids are afraid they look vulgarly hot ; and the author, who has a plate of strawberries brought him, finds that he has come to the end of his writing.

Indicator. 1820.

DEATHS OF LITTLE CHILDREN

Leigh Hunt

A Grecian philosopher being asked why he wept for the death of his son, since the sorrow was in vain, replied, " I weep on that account." And his answer became his wisdom. It is only for sophists to contend that we, whose eyes contain the fountains of tears, need never give way to them. It would be unwise not to do so on some occasions. Sorrow unlocks them in her balmy moods. The first bursts may be bitter and overwhelming ; but the soil on which they pour would be worse without them. They refresh the fever of the soul—the dry misery which parches the countenance into furrows, and renders us liable to our most terrible " flesh-quakes."

There are sorrows, it is true, so great, that to give them some of the ordinary vents is to run a hazard of being overthrown. These we must rather strengthen ourselves to resist, or bow quietly and drily down, in order to let them pass over us, as the traveller does the wind of the desert. But where we feel that tears would relieve us, it is false philosophy to deny ourselves at least that first refreshment ; and it is always false consolation to tell people that because they cannot help a thing, they are not to mind it. The true way is, to let them grapple with the unavoidable sorrow, and try to win it into gentleness by a reasonable yielding. There are griefs so gentle in their very nature that it would be worse than false heroism to refuse them a tear. Of this kind are the deaths of infants. Particular circumstances may render it more or less advisable to indulge in grief for the loss of a little child ; but, in general, parents should be no more advised to repress their first tears on such an occasion, than to repress their smiles towards a child surviving, or to indulge in any other sympathy. It is an appeal to the same gentle tenderness ; and such appeals are never made in vain. The end of them is an acquittal from the harsher bonds of affliction—from the tying down of the spirit to one melancholy idea.

It is the nature of tears of this kind, however strongly they may gush forth, to run into quiet waters at last. We cannot easily, for the whole course of our lives, think with pain of any good and kind person whom we have lost. It is the divine nature of their qualities to conquer pain and death itself ; to turn the memory of them into pleasure ; to survive with a placid aspect in our imaginations. We are writing at this moment just opposite a spot which contains the grave of one inexpressibly dear to us. We see from our window the trees about it, and the church spire. The green fields lie around. The clouds are travelling overhead, alternately taking away the sunshine and restoring it. The vernal winds, piping of the flowery summer-time, are nevertheless calling to mind the far distant and dangerous ocean, which the heart that lies in that grave had many reasons to think of. And yet the sight of this spot does not give us pain. So far from it, it is the existence of that grave which doubles every charm of the spot ; which links the pleasures of our childhood and manhood together ; which puts a hushing tenderness in the winds, and a patient joy upon the landscape ; which seems to unite heaven and earth, mortality and immortality, the grass of the tomb and the grass of the green field ; and gives a more maternal aspect to the whole kindness of nature. It does not hinder gaiety itself. Happiness was what its tenant, through all her troubles, would have diffused. To diffuse happiness, and to enjoy it, is not only carrying on her wishes, but realizing her hopes; and gaiety, freed from its only pollutions, malignity and want of sympathy, is but a child playing about the knees of its mother.

The remembered innocence and endearments of a child stand us instead of virtues that have died older. Children have not exercised the voluntary offices of friendship ; they have not chosen to be kind and good to us ; nor stood by us, from conscious will, in the hour of adversity. But they have shared their pleasures and pains with us as well as they could ; the interchange of good offices between us has, of necessity, been less mingled with the troubles of the world ; the sorrow arising from their death is the only one which we can associate with their memories. These are happy thoughts that cannot die. Our loss may always render them pensive ; but they will not always be painful. It is a part of the benignity of Nature that pain does not survive like pleasure, at any time, much less where the cause of it is an innocent one. The smile will remain reflected by memory, as the moon reflects the light upon us when the sun has gone into heaven.

When writers like ourselves quarrel with earthly pain (we mean writers of the same intentions, without implying, of course, anything about abilities or otherwise), they are misunderstood if they are supposed to quarrel with pains of every sort. This would be idle and effeminate. They do not pretend, indeed, that humanity might not wish, if it could, to be entirely free from pain ; for it endeavours, at all times, to turn pain into pleasure : or at least to set off the one with the other, to make the former a zest and the latter a refreshment. The most unaffected dignity of suffering does this, and, if wise, acknowledges it. The greatest benevolence towards others, the most unselfish relish of their pleasures, even at its own expense, does not look to increasing the general stock of happiness, though content, if it could, to have its identity swallowed up in that splendid contemplation. We are far from meaning that this is to be called selfishness. We are far, indeed, from thinking so, or of so confounding words. But neither is it to be called pain when most unselfish, if disinterestedness be truly understood. The pain that is in it softens into pleasure, as the darker hue of the rainbow melts into the brighter. Yet even if a harsher line is to be drawn between the pain and pleasure of the most unselfish mind (and ill-health, for instance, may draw it), we should not quarrel with it if it contributed to the general mass of comfort, and were of a nature which general kindliness could not avoid. Made as we are, there are certain pains without which it would be difficult to conceive certain great and overbalancing pleasures. We may conceive it possible for beings to be made entirely happy ; but in our composition something of pain seems to be a necessary ingredient, in order that the materials may turn to as fine account as possible, though our clay, in the course of ages and experience, may be refined more and more. We may get rid of the worst earth, though not of earth itself.

Now the liability of the loss of children—or rather what renders us sensible of it, the occasional loss itself—seems to be one of these necessary bitters thrown into the cup of humanity. We do not mean that every one must lose one of his children in order to enjoy the rest ; or that every individual loss afflicts us in the same proportion. We allude to the deaths of infants in general. These might be as few as we could render them. But if none at all ever took place, we should regard every little child as a man or woman secured ; and it will easily be conceived what a world of endearing cares and hopes this security would endanger. The very idea of infancy would lose its continuity with us. Girls and boys would be future men and women, not present children. They would have attained their full growth in our imaginations, and might as well have been men and women at once. On the other hand, those who have lost an infant, are never, as it were, without an infant child. They are the only persons who, in one sense, retain it always, and they furnish their neighbours with the same idea. The other children grow up to manhood and womanhood, and suffer all the changes of mortality. This one alone is rendered an immortal child. Death has arrested it with his kindly harshness, and blessed it into an eternal image of youth and innocence.

Of such as these are the pleasantest shapes that visit our fancy and our hopes. They are the ever-smiling emblems of joy ; the prettiest pages that wait upon imagination. Lastly, " Of these are the kingdom of heaven." Wherever there is a province of that benevolent and all-accessible empire, whether on earth or elsewhere, such are the gentle spirits that must inhabit it. To such simplicity, or the resemblance of it, must they come. Such must be the ready confidence of their hearts and creativeness of their fancy. And so ignorant must they be of the " knowledge of good and evil," losing their discernment of that self-created trouble, by enjoying the garden before them, and not being ashamed of what is kindly and innocent.

Indicator. 1820.

GETTING UP ON COLD MORNINGS

Leigh Hunt

An Italian author—Giulio Cordara, a Jesuit—has written a poem upon insects, which he begins by insisting, that those troublesome and abominable little animals were created for our annoyance, and that they were certainly not inhabitants of Paradise. We of the north may dispute this piece of theology ; but on the other hand, it is clear as the snow on the house-tops, that Adam was not under the necessity of shaving ; and that when Eve walked out of her delicious bower, she did not step upon ice three inches thick.

Some people say it is a very easy thing to get up of a cold morning. You have only, they tell you, to take the resolution ; and the thing is done. This may be very true ; just as a boy at school has only to take a flogging, and the thing is over. But we have not at all made up our minds upon it ; and we find it a very pleasant exercise to discuss the matter, candidly, before we get up. This at least is not idling, though it may be lying. It affords an excellent answer to those, who ask how lying in bed can be indulged in by a reasoning being,—a rational creature. How ? Why with the argument calmly at work in one's head, and the clothes over one's shoulder. Oh— it is a fine way of spending a sensible, impartial half-hour.

If these people would be more charitable, they would get on with their argument better. But they are apt to reason so ill, and to assert so dogmatically, that one could wish to have them stand round one's bed of a bitter morning, and lie before their faces. They ought to hear both sides of the bed, the inside and out. If they cannot entertain themselves with their own thoughts for half an hour or so, it is not the fault of those who can. If their will is never pulled aside by the enticing arms of imagination, so much the luckier for the stage-coachman.

Candid inquiries into one's decumbency, besides the greater or less privileges to be allowed a man in proportion to his ability of keeping early hours, the work given his faculties, etc., will at least concede their due merits to such representations as the following. In the first place, says the injured but calm appealer, I have been warm all night, and find my system in a state perfectly suitable to a warm-blooded animal. To get out of this state into the cold, besides the inharmonious and uncritical abruptness of the transition, is so unnatural to such a creature, that the poets, refining upon the tortures of the damned, make one of their greatest agonies consist in being suddenly transported from heat to cold,—from fire to ice. They are "haled" out of their "beds," says Milton, by "harpy-footed furies,"—fellows who come to call them. On my first movement towards the anticipation of getting up, I find that such parts of the sheets and bolster, as are exposed to the air of the room, are stone-cold. On opening my eyes, the first thing that meets them is my own breath rolling forth, as if in the open air, like smoke out of a cottage chimney. Think of this symptom. Then I turn my eyes sideways and see the window all frozen over. Think of that. Then the servant comes in. "It is very cold this morning, is it not?"—"Very cold, Sir."—"Very cold indeed, isn't it?"—"Very cold indeed, Sir."—"More than usually so, isn't it, even for this weather?" (Here the servant's wit and good-nature are put to a considerable test, and the inquirer lies on thorns for the

answer.) "Why, Sir . . . I think it *is*." (Good creature ! There is not a better, or more truth-telling servant
going.) "I must rise, however—get me some warm
water."—Here comes a fine interval between the departure
of the servant and the arrival of the hot water ; during
which, of course, it is of "no use" to get up. The hot
water comes. "Is it quite hot ? "—"Yes, Sir."—"Perhaps too hot for shaving : I must wait a little ? "—"No,
Sir ; it will just do." (There is an over-nice propriety
sometimes, an officious zeal of virtue, a little troublesome.)
"Oh—the shirt—you must air my clean shirt ;—linen
gets very damp this weather."—"Yes, Sir." Here
another delicious five minutes. A knock at the door.
"Oh, the shirt—very well. My stockings—I think the
stockings had better be aired too."—"Very well, Sir."—
Here another interval. At length everything is ready,
except myself. I now, continues our incumbent (a happy
word, by-the-bye, for a country vicar)—I now cannot
help thinking a good deal—who can ?—upon the unnecessary and villainous custom of shaving : it is a thing so
unmanly (here I nestle closer)—so effeminate (here I recoil
from an unlucky step into the colder part of the bed.)—
No wonder that the Queen of France took part with the
rebels against the degenerate King, her husband, who
first affronted her smooth visage with a face like her own.
The Emperor Julian never showed the luxuriancy of his
genius to better advantage than in reviving the flowing
beard. Look at Cardinal Bembo's picture—at Michael
Angelo's—at Titian's—at Shakespeare's—at Fletcher's—
at Spenser's—at Chaucer's—at Alfred's—at Plato's—I
could name a great man for every tick of my watch.—
Look at the Turks, a grave and otiose people.—Think of
Haroun Al Raschid and Bed-ridden Hassan.—Think of
Wortley Montagu, the worthy son of his mother, a man
above the prejudice of his time.—Look at the Persian
gentlemen, whom one is ashamed of meeting about the

suburbs, their dress and appearance are so much finer than
our own.—Lastly, think of the razor itself—how totally
opposed to every sensation of bed—how cold, how edgy,
how hard ! how utterly different from anything like the
warm and circling amplitude, which

> Sweetly recommends itself
> Unto our gentle senses.

Add to this, benumbed fingers, which may help you to cut
yourself, a quivering body, a frozen towel, and a ewer full
of ice ; and he that says there is nothing to oppose in
all this, only shows, at any rate, that he has no merit in
opposing it.

Thomson the poet, who exclaims in his Seasons—

> Falsely luxurious !   Will not man awake ?

used to lie in bed till noon, because he said he had no
motive in getting up. He could imagine the good of
rising ; but then he could also imagine the good of lying
still ; and his exclamation, it must be allowed, was made
upon summer-time, not winter. We must proportion the
argument to the individual character. A money-getter
may be drawn out of his bed by three and four pence ;
but this will not suffice for a student. A proud man may
say, " What shall I think of myself, if I don't get up ? "
but the more humble one will be content to waive this
prodigious notion of himself, out of respect to his kindly
bed. The mechanical man shall get up without any ado
at all ; and so shall the barometer. An ingenious lier in
bed will find hard matter of discussion even on the score
of health and longevity. He will ask us for our proofs
and precedents of the ill effects of lying later in cold
weather ; and sophisticate much on the advantages of an
even temperature of body ; of the natural propensity

(pretty universal) to have one's way ; and of the animals that roll themselves up, and sleep all the winter. As to longevity, he will ask whether the longest life is of necessity the best ; and whether Holborn is the handsomest street in London.

We only know of one confounding, not to say confounded argument, fit to overturn the huge luxury, the " enormous bliss "—of the vice in question. A lier in bed may be allowed to profess a disinterested indifference for his health or longevity ; but while he is showing the reasonableness of consulting his own or one person's comfort, he must admit the proportionate claim of more than one ; and the best way to deal with him is this, especially for a lady ; for we earnestly recommend the use of that sex on such occasions, if not somewhat *over*-persuasive ; since extremes have an awkward knack of meeting. First then, admit all the ingeniousness of what he says, telling him that the bar has been deprived of an excellent lawyer. Then look at him in the most good-natured manner in the world, with a mixture of assent and appeal in your countenance, and tell him that you are waiting breakfast for him ; that you never like to breakfast without him ; that you really want it too ; that the servants want theirs ; that you shall not know how to get the house into order, unless he rises ; and that you are sure he would do things twenty times worse, even than getting out of his warm bed, to put them all into good humour and a state of comfort. Then, after having said this, throw in the comparatively indifferent matter, to *him*, about his health ; but tell him that it is no indifferent matter to you ; that the sight of his illness makes more people suffer than one ; but that if, nevertheless, he really does feel so very sleepy and so very much refreshed by—— Yet stay ; we hardly know whether the frailty of a—— Yes, yes ; say that too, especially if you say it with sincerity ; for if the weakness of human nature on the one hand and the *vis inertiæ* on the other, should lead him to take advantage of it once or twice, good-humour and sincerity form an irresistible junction at last ; and are still better and warmer things than pillows and blankets.

Other little helps of appeal may be thrown in, as occasion requires. You may tell a lover, for instance, that lying in bed makes people corpulent ; a father, that you wish him to complete the fine manly example he sets his children ; a lady, that she will injure her bloom or her shape, which M. or W. admires so much ; and a student or artist, that he is always so glad to have done a good day's work, in his best manner.

Reader. And pray, Mr. Indicator, how do *you* behave yourself in this respect ?

Indic. Oh, Madam, perfectly, of course ; like all advisers.

Reader. Nay, I allow that your mode of argument does not look quite so suspicious as the old way of sermonizing and severity, but I have my doubts, especially from that laugh of yours. If I should look in to-morrow morning—

Indic. Ah, Madam, the look in of a face like yours does anything with me. It shall fetch me up at nine, if you please—*six*, I meant to say.

Indicator. 1820.

FINE DAYS IN JANUARY AND FEBRUARY

Leigh Hunt

WE speak of those days, unexpected, sunshiny, cheerful, even vernal, which come towards the end of January, and are too apt to come alone. They are often set in the midst of a series of rainy ones, like a patch of blue in the sky. Fine weather is much at any time, after or before the end of the year ; but, in the latter case, the days are still winter days ; whereas, in the former, the year being turned, and March and April before us, we seem to feel the coming of spring. In the streets and squares, the ladies are abroad, with their colours and glowing cheeks. If you can hear anything but noise, you hear the sparrows. People anticipate at breakfast the pleasure they shall have in " getting out." The solitary poplar in a corner looks green against the sky : and the brick wall has a warmth in it. Then in the noisier streets, what a multitude and a new life ! What horseback ! What promenading ! What shopping, and giving good day ! Bonnets encounter bonnets :—all the Miss Williamses meet all the Miss Joneses ; and everybody wonders, particularly at nothing. The shop windows, putting forward their best, may be said to be in blossom. The yellow carriages flash in the sunshine ; footmen rejoice in their white calves, not dabbed upon, as usual, with rain ; the gossips look out of their three pair-of-stairs windows ; other windows are thrown open ; fruiterers' shops look well, swelling with full baskets ; pavements are found to be dry ; lap-dogs frisk under their asthmas ; and old gentlemen issue forth, peering up at the region of the north-east.

Then in the country, how emerald the green, how open-looking the prospect ! Honeysuckles (a name alone with a garden in it) are detected in blossom ; the hazel follows ; the snowdrop hangs its white perfection, exquisite with green ; we fancy the trees are already thicker ; voices of winter birds are taken for new ones ; and in February new ones come—the thrush, the chaffinch, and the wood-lark. Then rooks begin to pair ; and the wagtail dances in the lane. As we write this article, the sun is on our paper, and chanticleer (the same, we trust, that we heard the other day) seems to crow in a very different style, lord of the ascendant, and as willing to be with his wives abroad as at home. We think we see him, as in Chaucer's homestead :

> He looketh, as it were a grim leoùn ;
> And on his toes he roameth up and down ;
> Him deigneth not to set his foot to ground ;
> He clucketh when he hath a corn yfound,
> And to him runnen then his wives all.

Will the reader have the rest of the picture, as Chaucer gave it ? It is as bright and strong as the day itself, and as suited to it as a falcon to a knight's fist. Hear how the old poet throws forth his strenuous music ; as fine, considered as mere music and versification, as the description is pleasant and noble.

> His comb was redder than the fine coràll,
> Embatteled, as it were a castle wall.
> His bill was black, and as the jet it shone ;
> Like azure were his leggès and his tone ;
> His nailès, whiter than the lilly flower,
> And like the burnèd gold was his coloùr.

Hardly one pause like the other throughout, and yet all winged and sweet. The pause on the third syllable in the last line but one, and that on the sixth in the last, together with the deep variety of vowels, make a beautiful concluding couplet ; and indeed the whole is a study for versification. So little were those old poets unaware of their task, as some are apt to suppose them : and so little have others dreamt, that they surpassed them in their own pretensions. The accent, it is to be observed, in those concluding words, as *coral* and *colour*, is to be thrown on the last syllable, as it is in Italian. *Colòr, colòre*, and Chaucer's old Anglo-Gallican word, is a much nobler one than our modern *còlour*. We have injured many such words by throwing back the accent.

We should beg pardon for this digression, if it had not been part of our understood agreement with the reader to be as desultory as we please, and as befits Companions. Our very enjoyment of the day we are describing would not let us do otherwise. It is also an old fancy of ours to associate the ideas of Chaucer with that of any early and vigorous manifestation of light and pleasure. He is not only the " morning-star " of our poetry, as Denham called him, but the morning itself, and a good bit of the noon ; and we could as soon help quoting him at the beginning of the year, as we could help wishing to hear the cry of primroses, and thinking of the sweet faces that buy them.

Indicator. 1820.

THE MAID-SERVANT

Leigh Hunt

Must be considered as young, or else she has married the butcher, the butler, or *her cousin*, or has otherwise settled into a character distinct from her original one, so as to become what is properly called the domestic. The Maid-servant,[1] in her apparel, is either slovenly and fine by turns, and dirty always ; or she is at all times snug and neat, and dressed according to her station. In the latter case, her ordinary dress is black stockings, a stuff gown, a cap, and a neck-handkerchief pinned cornerwise behind. If you want a pin, she just feels about her, and has always one to give you. On Sundays and holidays, and perhaps of afternoons, she changes her black stockings for white, puts on a gown of better texture and fine pattern, sets her cap and her curls jauntily, and lays aside the neck-handkerchief for a high-body, which, by the way, is not half so pretty. There is something very warm and latent in the handkerchief—something easy, vital, and genial. A woman in a high-bodied gown, made to fit her like a case, is by no means more modest, and is much less tempting. She looks like a figure at the head of a ship. We could almost see her chucked out of doors into a cart, with as little remorse as a couple of sugar-loaves. The tucker is much better, as well as the handkerchief, and is to the other what the young lady is to the servant.

[1] In some respects, particularly of costume, this portrait must be understood of originals existing twenty or thirty years ago.

The one always reminds us of the Sparkler in Sir Richard Steele ; the other of Fanny in " Joseph Andrews."

But to return. The general furniture of her ordinary room, the kitchen, is not so much her own as her Master's and Mistress's, and need not be described : but in a drawer of the dresser or the table, in company with a duster and a pair of snuffers, may be found some of her property, such as a brass thimble, a pair of scissors, a thread-case, a piece of wax much wrinkled with the thread, an odd volume of " Pamela," and perhaps a sixpenny play, such as " George Barnwell," or Mrs. Behn's " Oroonoko." There is a piece of looking-glass in the window. The rest of her furniture is in the garret, where you may find a good looking-glass on the table, and in the window a Bible, a comb, and a piece of soap. Here stands also, under stout lock and key, the mighty mystery,—the box,—containing, among other things, her clothes, two or three song-books, consisting of nineteen for the penny ; sundry Tragedies at a halfpenny the sheet ; the " Whole Nature of Dreams Laid Open," together with the " Fortune-teller " and the " Account of the Ghost of Mrs. Veal " ; the " Story of the Beautiful Zoa " " who was cast away on a desart island, showing how," etc. ; some half-crowns in a purse, including pieces of country-money, with the good Countess of Coventry on one of them, riding naked on the horse ; a silver penny wrapped up in cotton by itself ; a crooked sixpence, given her before she came to town, and the giver of which has either forgotten or been forgotten by her, she is not sure which ;—two little enamel boxes, with looking-glass in the lids, one of them a fairing, the other " a Trifle from Margate " ; and lastly, various letters, square and ragged, and directed in all sorts of spellings, chiefly with little letters for capitals. One of them, written by a girl who went to a day-school, is directed " Miss."

In her manners, the Maid-servant sometimes imitates her young mistress ; she puts her hair in papers, cultivates

a shape, and occasionally contrives to be out of spirits.
But her own character and condition overcome all sophis-
tications of this sort : her shape, fortified by the mop and
scrubbing-brush, will make its way ; and exercise keeps
her healthy and cheerful. From the same cause her temper
is good ; though she gets into little heats when a stranger
is over-saucy, or when she is told not to go so heavily
down stairs, or when some unthinking person goes up
her wet stairs with dirty shoes,—or when she is called
away often from dinner ; neither does she much like to be
seen scrubbing the street-door steps of a morning ; and
sometimes she catches herself saying, " Drat that butcher,"
but immediately adds, " God forgive me." The tradesmen indeed, with their compliments and arch looks, seldom
give her cause to complain. The milkman bespeaks her
good-humour for the day with " Come, pretty maids " :
—then follow the butcher, the baker, the oilman, etc., all
with their several smirks and little loiterings ; and when
she goes to the shops herself, it is for her the grocer pulls
down his string from its roller with more than the ordinary
whirl, and tosses his parcel into a tie.

Thus pass the mornings between working, and singing,
and giggling, and grumbling, and being flattered. If she
takes any pleasure unconnected with her office before the
afternoon, it is when she runs up the area-steps or to the
door to hear and purchase a new song, or to see a troop
of soldiers go by ; or when she happens to thrust her head
out of a chamber window at the same time with a servant
at the next house, when a dialogue infallibly ensues,
stimulated by the imaginary obstacles between. If the
Maid-servant is wise, the best part of her work is done
by dinner-time ; and nothing else is necessary to give
perfect zest to the meal. She tells us what she thinks of
it, when she calls it " a bit o' dinner." There is the same
sort of eloquence in her other phrase, " a cup o' tea " ;
but the old ones, and the washerwomen, beat her at that.

After tea in great houses, she goes with the other servants
to hot cockles, or What-are-my-thoughts-like, and tells
Mr. John to " have done then " ; or if there is a ball given
that night, they throw open the doors, and make use of
the music up stairs to dance by. In smaller houses, she
receives the visits of her aforesaid cousin ; and sits down
alone, or with a fellow maid-servant, to work ; talks of
her young master or mistress and Mr. Ivins (Evans) ; or
else she calls to mind her own friends in the country ;
where she thinks the cows and " all that " beautiful, now
she is away. Meanwhile, if she is lazy, she snuffs the candle
with her scissors ; or if she has eaten more heartily than
usual, she sighs double the usual number of times, and
thinks that tender hearts were born to be unhappy.

Such being the Maid-servant's life in-doors, she scorns,
when abroad, to be anything but a creature of sheer
enjoyment. The Maid-servant, the sailor, and the school-
boy, are the three beings that enjoy a holiday beyond all
the rest of the world ;—and all for the same reason,—
because their inexperience, peculiarity of life, and habit of
being with persons of circumstances or thoughts above
them, give them all, in their way, a cast of the romantic.
The most active of the money-getters is a vegetable compared with them. The Maid-servant when she first goes
to Vauxhall, thinks she is in heaven. A theatre is all
pleasure to her, whatever is going forward, whether the
play or the music, or the waiting which makes others
impatient, or the munching of apples and gingerbread,
which she and her party commence almost as soon as they
have seated themselves. She prefers tragedy to comedy,
because it is grander, and less like what she meets with
in general ; and because she thinks it more in earnest
also, especially in the love-scenes. Her favourite play is
" Alexander the Great, or the Rival Queens." Another
great delight is in going a shopping. She loves to look
at the pictures in the windows, and the fine things labelled

with those corpulent numerals of " only 7s."—" only
6s. 6d." She has also, unless born and bred in London,
been to see my Lord Mayor, the fine people coming out
of Court, and the " beasties " in the Tower ; and at all
events she has been to Astley's and the Circus, from which
she comes away, equally smitten with the rider, and sore
with laughing at the clown. But it is difficult to say what
pleasure she enjoys most. One of the completest of all
is the fair, where she walks through an endless round of
noise, and toys, and gallant apprentices, and wonders.
Here she is invited in by courteous and well-dressed
people, as if she were a mistress. Here also is the con-
jurer's booth, where the operator himself, a most stately
and genteel person all in white, calls her Ma'am ; and says
to John by her side, in spite of his laced hat, " Be good
enough, sir, to hand the card to the lady."

Ah ! may her " cousin " turn out as true as he says he
is ; or may she get home soon enough and smiling enough
to be as happy again next time.

Indicator. 1820.

THE INSIDE OF AN OMNIBUS

Leigh Hunt

Enough has been said, in this quick and graphic age, respecting coachmen and cabmen, and conductors, and horses, and all the exterior phenomena of things vehicular ; but we are not aware that an "article" has yet been devoted to the subject before us.

Come, then, our old friend Truth ! do what thou canst for us. If thou dost not, we know, that with all our trying, we can do nothing for ourselves. Men will have nothing to do with our representations, though we paint for them the prettiest girl in the world—unlike !

By the invention of the Omnibus, all the world keeps its coach !—And with what cheapness ! And to how much social advantage ! No "plague with servants ; "—no expense for liveries ;—no coach-makers' and horse-doctors' bills ;—no keeping one's fellow-creatures waiting for us in the cold night-time and rain, while the dance is going down the room, or another hour is spent in bidding good-bye, and lingering over the comfortable fire. We have no occasion to think of it at all till we want it ; and then it either comes to one's door, or you go forth, and in a few minutes see it *hulling* up the street,—the man-of-war among coaches,—the whale's back in the metropolitan flood,—while the driver is beheld sitting, super-eminent, like the guide of the elephant on his neck.

We cannot say much for the beauty of the omnibus ; but there is a certain might of utility in its very bulk, which supersedes the necessity of beauty, as in the case of the whale itself, or in the idea that we entertain of Dr. Johnson, who shouldered porters as he went, and "laughed like a rhinoceros." Virgil metamorphosed ships into sea-nymphs. The Doctor, by a process not more violent, might be supposed transformed into a vehicle for his favourite London streets ; and, if so, he would un-doubtedly have anticipated the date of the present inven-tion, and become an omnibus. His mouth seems to utter the word.

BOSWELL (*in Elysium*).—" Sir, if you were living now, and were to be turned into a coach, what sort of coach would you become ? "

JOHNSON (*rolling about, and laughing with bland contempt*). —" Sir, in parliamentary language, you are ' frivolous and vexatious ; ' but the frivolity surmounts the vexatious-ness."

BOSWELL (*tenderly*).—" Nay, sir, but to oblige an humble, and, I hope, not altogether undeserving friend."

JOHNSON.—" Sir, where reply is obvious, interrogation is disgusting. Nay, sir (*seeing the tears in Boswell's eyes*), I would not be harsh or uncomplying : but do you not see the case at once ? I should formerly have chosen to be a bishop's carriage perhaps, or a chancellor's, or any respectable lord's."

BOSWELL (*smiling*).—" Except a lord mayor's."

JOHNSON (*angrily*).—" And why, sir, should I not have been a lord mayor's ? What have I done, that it should be doubted whether I would countenance the dignity of integrity and the universality of commerce ? "

BOSWELL (*in confusion*).—" Sir, I beg pardon ; but, to confess the truth, I was thinking of Mr. Wilkes."

JOHNSON.—" And why, sir, think of Mr. Wilkes, when the smaller idea should be merged into the greater ? when the great office itself is concerned, and not the pettiness of an exception ? Besides, sir, Wilkes, though a rascal and a Whig, was a gentleman in *manners*, as well as birth (*looking sternly at Boswell*). He would not have made such a remark.—To be sure (*relenting a little, and looking arch*) he got drunk sometimes."

BOSWELL (*interrupting*).—" Dear sir !——"

JOHNSON.—" Neither was he scrupulous in his admiration of beauty."

BOSWELL.—" Dearest sir ! "

JOHNSON.—" Though whatsoever the frenzy of his inebriation, or the vagrancy of his nocturnal revels, he would hardly have mistaken an oyster-woman for a Hebe. Well, well, sir, let us be mutually considerate. Let us be decent. To cut this matter short, sir, I should be an *omnibus*."

BOSWELL (*with grateful earnestness*).—" May I presume, dear sir, to inquire the reason ? "

JOHNSON.—" Sir, I should not be a cart. That would be low. Neither should I aspire to be the triumphant chariot of an Alexander, or the funeral car of a Napoleon. Posthumous knowledge has corrected those sympathies with ambition. A gig is pert ; a curricle coxcombical ; and the steam-carriage is too violent, perturbed, and migratory. Sir, the omnibus for me. It suits with my past state and my present ; with the humanities I have retained, and with those which I have acquired. Sir, it even makes me beg pardon for what I have said of Wilkes. *Mors omnibus communis.* Like death, it is common to all, and gathers them into its friendly bosom. It is decent, deliberate, and unpretending ; no respecter of persons ; a king has been known to ride in it ; [1] and opposite the king may have sat a republican weaver."

BOSWELL.—" But you would choose, sir, to be a London omnibus, rather than a Parisian one, or even a Litchfield ? "

JOHNSON (*with bland indulgence*).—" Surely, sir ; and to

[1] So it has been said of Louis Philippe, during his " citizen-king " days.

go up the Strand and Fleet-street, and occasionally to stop at the Mitre. And, sir, I would not be driven by everybody, though I can now tolerate everybody. I would have a humane and respectable driver ; an elderly man, sir ;—and my windows should be taken care of, that the people might not catch cold."

Here Boswell, begging a thousand pardons, with shrugged shoulders, lifted eyebrows, and hands spread out in deprecation of offence, bursts, nevertheless, into an incontrollable fit of laughter, at the idea of the solemn and illustrious Johnson converted into an omnibus. And the Doctor, though a little angry at first, recollects his Elysian experiences, and at length contributes to a roar worthy of the inextinguishable laughter of the gods in Homer.

JOHNSON (*subsiding into a human measure of joviality*).— " Sir, it was ludicrous enough, if you consider it as a man ; but if you consider it as a child, or as a divine person (to speak in the language of our new friend, Plato), the subject will be invested with the mild gravity of an impartial universality. I see, however, that it will take many more draughts of Lethe, before you, Boswell, can get the fumes of the old tavern wine out of your head ; so let us consult your capabilities, and return to human measures of discourse ; let us have *reason* once more, sir ;—sir (for I see you wish me to say it), let us be good mortal jolly dogs, and have t'other bottle."

Vanish the ever-pleasant shades of Johnson and Boswell, and enter the omnibus in its own proper person. If a morning omnibus, it is full of clerks and merchants ; if a noon, of chance fares ; if a night, of returning citizens and fathers of families ; if a midnight, of playgoers, and gentlemen lax with stiff glasses of brandy-and-water.

Being one of the chance fares, we enter an omnibus which has yet no other inside passenger : and having no book with us, we make intense acquaintance with two objects : the one being the heel of an outside passenger's boot, who is sitting on the coach-top ; and the other, that universally studied bit of literature, which is inscribed at the further end of every such vehicle, and which purports, that it is under the charming jurisdiction of the royal lady now reigning over us,

V. R.

by whom it is permitted to carry " *twelve inside passengers,* AND NO MORE ; " thus showing extreme consideration on her Majesty's part, and that she will not have the sides of her loving subjects squeezed together like figs.

Enter a precise personage, probably a Methodist, certainly " well off," who seats himself right in the midway of his side of the omnibus ; that is to say, at equal distances between the two extremities ; because it is the spot in which you least feel the inconvenience of the motion. He is a man who seldom makes a remark, or takes notice of what is going forward, unless a payment is to be resisted, or the entrance of a passenger beyond the lawful number. Now and then he hems, and adjusts a glove ; or wipes a little dust off one of the cuffs of his coat.

In leaps a youngster, and seats himself close at the door, in order to be ready to leap out again.

Item, a maid-servant, flustered with the fear of being too late, and reddening furthermore betwixt awkwardness, and the resentment of it, at not being quite sure where to seat herself. A jerk of the omnibus pitches her against the precisian, and makes both her and the youngster laugh.

Enter a young lady, in colours and big earrings, and excessively flounced and ringleted, and seats herself opposite the maid-servant, who beholds her with admiration, but secretly thinks herself handsomer, and what a pity it is she was not a lady herself, to become the ringlets and flounces better.

Enter two more young ladies, in white, who pass to the

other end in order to be out of the way of the knees and boots of those who quit. They whisper and giggle much, and are quizzing the young lady in the reds and ringlets ; who, for her part (though she knows it, and could squeeze all their bonnets together for rage), looks as firm and unconcerned as a statue.

Enter a dandy, too handsome to be quizzed ; and then a man with a bundle, who is agreeably surprised with the gentlemanly toleration of the dandy, and unaware of the secret disgust of the Methodist.

Item, an old gentleman ; then, a very fat man ; then, two fat elderly women, one of whom is very angry at the incommodious presence of her counterparts, while the other, full of good humour, is comforted by it. The youngster has in the meantime gone to sit on the coach-top, in order to make room ; and we set off to the place of our destination.

What an intense intimacy we get with the face, neck-cloth, waistcoat, and watch-chain of the man who sits opposite us ! Who is he ? What is his name ? Is his care a great care,—an affliction ? Is his look of cheerfulness real ? At length he looks at ourselves, asking himself, no doubt, similar questions ; and, as it is less pleasant to be scrutinized than to scrutinize, we now set him the example of turning the eyes another way. How unpleasant it must be to the very fat man to be so gazed at ! Think, if he sat as close to us in a private room, in a chair ! How he would get up, and walk away ! But here, sit he must, and have his portrait taken by our memories. We sigh for his plethora, with a breath almost as piteous as his wheezing. And he has a sensible face withal, and has, perhaps, acquired a painful amount of intellectual as well as physical knowledge, from the melancholy that has succeeded to his joviality. Fat men always appear to be " good fellows," unless there is some manifest proof to the contrary ; so we wish, for his sake, that everybody in this world could do just as he pleased, and die of a very dropsy of delight.

Exeunt our fat friend, and the more ill-humoured of the two fat women ; and enter, in their places, two young mothers,—one with a good-humoured child, a female ; the other with a great, handsome, red-cheeked wilful boy, all flounce and hat and feathers, and red legs, who is eating a bun, and who seems resolved that the other child, who does nothing but look at it, shall not partake a morsel. His mother, who "snubs" him one instant, and lets him have his way the next, has been a spoiled child herself, and is doing her best to learn to repent the sorrow she caused her own mother, by the time she is a dozen years older. The elderly gentleman compliments the boy on his likeness to his mamma, who laughs and says he is "very polite." As to the young gentleman, he fancies he is asked for a piece of his bun, and falls a-kicking ; and the young lady in the ringlets tosses her head.

Exit the Methodist, and enter an affable man ; who, having protested it is very cold, and lamented a stoppage, and vented the original remark that you gain nothing by an omnibus in point of time, subsides into an elegant silence ; but he is fastened upon by the man with the bundle, who, encouraged by his apparent good-nature, tells him, in an under-tone, some anecdotes relative to his own experience of omnibuses ; which the affable gentleman endures with a variety of assenting exclamations, intended quite as much to stop as to encourage, not one of which succeeds ; such as " Ah ! "—" Oh ! "— " Indeed ! "—" Precisely "—" I daresay "—" I see "— " Really ? "—" Very likely ; "—jerking the top of his stick occasionally against his mouth as he speaks, and nobody pitying him.

Meantime the good-humoured fat woman having expressed a wish to have a window closed which the ill-humoured one had taken upon her to open, and the two young ladies in the corner giving their assent, but none of the three being able to pull it up, the elderly gentleman, in an ardour of gallantry, anxious to show his pleasing combination of strength and tenderness, exclaims, " Permit *me* ; " and jumping up, cannot do it at all. The window cruelly sticks fast. It only brings up all the blood into his face with the mingled shame and incompetence of the endeavour. He is a conscientious kind of incapable, however, is the elderly gentleman ; so he calls in the conductor, who does it in an instant. " He knows the trick," says the elderly gentleman. " It's only a little bit new," says the conductor, who hates to be called in.

Exeunt elderly and the maid-servant, and enter an unreflecting young gentleman who has bought an orange and must eat it immediately. He accordingly begins by peeling it, and is first made aware of the delicacy of his position by the gigglement of the two young ladies, and his doubt where he shall throw the peel. " He is in for it," however, and must proceed ; so being unable to divide the orange into its segments, he ventures upon a great liquid bite, which resounds through the omnibus, and covers the whole of the lower part of his face with pip and drip. The young lady with the ringlets is right before him. The two other young ladies stuff their handkerchiefs into their mouths, and he into his own mouth the whole of the rest of the fruit, " sloshy " and too big, with desperation in his heart, and the tears in his eyes. Never will he eat an orange again in an omnibus. He doubts whether he shall even venture upon one at all in the presence of his friends, the Miss Wilkinsons.

Enter, at various times, an irascible gentleman, who is constantly threatening to go out ; a long-legged dragoon, at whose advent the young ladies are smit with sudden gravity and apparent objection ; a young sailor, with a face innocent of everything but a pride in his slops, who says his mother does not like his going to sea ; a gentleman with a book, which we long to ask him to let us look at; a man with a dog, which embitters the feet and ankles of a sharp-visaged old lady, and completes her horror by getting on the empty seat next her, and looking out of the window; divers bankers' clerks and tradesmen, who think of nothing but the bills in their pockets; two estranged friends, *ignoring* each other; a pompous fellow who suddenly looks modest and bewitched, having detected a baronet in the corner; a botanist with his tin *herbarium*; a young married couple, assuming a right to be fond in public; another from the country, who exalt all the rest of the passengers in self-opinion by betraying the amazing fact, that they have never before seen Piccadilly; a footman, intensely clean in his habiliments, and very respectful, for his hat subdues him, as well as the strange feeling of sitting inside; four boys going to school, very pudding-faced, and not knowing how to behave (one pulls a string and top half-way out of his pocket, and all reply to questions in mono-syllables); a person with a constant smile on his face, having just cheated another in a bargain; close to him a very melancholy person, going to see a daughter on her deathbed, and not hearing a single one of the cheater's happy remarks; a French lady looking at once amiable and worldly,—hard, as it were, in the midst of her softness, or soft in the midst of her hardness,—which you will,—probably an actress, or a teacher; two immense-whiskered Italians, uttering their delicious language with a precision which shows that they are singers; a man in a smock-frock, who, by his sitting on the edge of the seat, and perpetually watching his time to go out, seems to make a constant apology for his presence; ditto, a man with some huge mysterious accompaniment of mechanism, or implement of trade, too big to be lawfully carried inside; a pedant or a fop, ostentatious of some ancient or foreign language, or talking of a lord; all sorts of people talking of the weather, and the harvest, and the

Queen, and the last bit of news ; in short, every description of age, rank, temper, occupation, appearance, life,
character, and behaviour, from the thorough gentleman
who quietly gives himself a lift out of the rain, secure in
his easy unaffected manner and his accommodating good-
breeding, down to the blackguard who attempts to thrust
his opinion down the throat of his neighbour, or keeps his
legs thrust out across the door-way, or lets his umbrella
drip against a sick child.

Tempers are exhibited most at night, because people
by that time have dined and drunk, and finished their
labours, and because the act of going home serves to bring
out the domestic habit. You do not then, indeed, so often
see the happy fatigue, delighted with the sudden opportunity of rest ; nor the anxious look, as if it feared its
journey's end ; nor the bustling one, eager to get there.
The seats are most commonly reckoned upon, and more
allowance is made for delays ; though some passengers
make a point of always being in a state of indignation and
ill-treatment, and express an impatience to get home, as if
their house were a paradise (which is assuredly what it is
not, to those who expect them there). But at night,
tongues are loosened, wills and pleasures more freely
expressed, and faces rendered less bashful by the comparative darkness. It is then that the jovial " old boy "
lets out the secret of his having dined somewhere, perhaps
at some Company's feast in Goldsmiths' or Stationers'
Hall ; and it is with difficulty he hinders himself from
singing. Then the arbitrary or the purse-proud are wrath-
ful if they are not driven up to the identical inch of curb-
stone fronting their door. Then the incontinent nature,
heedless of anything but its own satisfaction, snores in its
corner ; then politicians are loud ; and gay fellows gallant,
especially if they are old and ugly ; and lovers, who seem
unconscious of one another's presence, are intensely the
reverse. Then also the pickpocket is luckiest at his circum-

ventions ; and the lady, about to pay her fare, suddenly
misses her reticule. Chiefly now also, sixpences, nay,
purses, are missed in the straw, and lights are brought to
look for them, and the conductor is in an agonizing perplexity whether to pronounce the loser an impudent cheat,
or to love him for being an innocent and a ninny. Finally,
now is the time when selfishness and generosity are most
exhibited, It rains, and the coach is full ; a lady applies
for admittance ; a gentleman offers to go outside ; and,
according to the natures of the various passengers, he is
despised or respected accordingly. It rains *horribly* ; a
" young woman " applies for admittance ; the coach is
overstocked already ; a crapulous fellow who has been
allowed to come in by special favour, protests against the
exercise of the like charity to a female (*we have seen it!*)
and is secretly detested by the least generous ; a similar
gentleman to the above, offers to take the applicant on
his knee, if she has no objection ; and she enters accordingly, and sits.—Is she pretty ?—Is she ugly ?—Above all,
is she good-humoured ? A question of some concern,
even to the least interested of knee-givers. On the other
hand, is the gentleman young or old, pleasant or disagreeable, a real gentleman, or only a formal " old frump,"
who has hardly a right to be civil ? At length the parties
get a look at one another, the gentleman first, the young
woman suddenly from under her bonnet.—Ought she to
have looked at all ?—And what is the particular retrospec-
tive expression which she instinctively chooses out of many,
when she has looked ? It is a nice question, varying
according to circumstances.—" Making room " for a fair
interloper is no such dilemma as that; though we may be
allowed to think that the pleasure is greatly enhanced by
the pleasantness of the countenance. It is astonishing how
much grace is put, even into the tip of an elbow, by the
turn of an eye.

There is a reflection which all omnibus passengers are

agreed upon, and which every one of them perhaps has
made, without exception, in the course of their intellectual
reciprocities ;   which is, that omnibuses are " very convenient ; " —" an astonishing accommodation to the
public ; "—not quick,—save little time (as aforesaid),—and
the conductors are very tiresome ;   but a most useful
invention, and wonderfully cheap.   There are also certain
things which almost all omnibus passengers *do* ;   such as
help ladies to and fro ;   gradually get nearer to the door
whenever a vacant seat occurs, so as to force the new
comer farther up than he likes ;   and all people stumble,
forward or sideways, when they first come in, and the
coach sets off before they are seated.   Among the pleasures,
are seeing the highly satisfied faces of persons suddenly
relieved from a long walk ;   being able to read a book ;
and, occasionally, observing one of a congenial sort in the
hands of a fellow-passenger.   Among the evils, are dirty
boots and wetting umbrellas ;   broken panes of glass in
bad weather, afflicting the napes of the necks of invalids ;
and fellows who endeavour to convenience themselves
at everybody's expense, by taking up as much room as
possible, and who pretend to alter their oblique position
when remonstrated with, without really doing it.   Item,
cramps in the leg, when thrusting it excessively backwards
underneath the seat, in making way for a new comer,
—the patient thrusting it forth again with an agonized
vivacity that sets the man opposite him laughing.   Item,
cruel treadings upon corns, the whole being of the old
lady or gentleman seeming to be mashed into the burning
foot, and the sufferer looking in an ecstasy of tormented
doubt whether to be decently quiet or murderously voci-
ferous,—the inflictor, meanwhile, thinking it sufficient to
say, " Very sorry," in an indifferent tone of voice, and
taking his seat with an air of luxurious complacency.
Among the pleasures also, particularly in going home at
night, must not be forgotten the having the omnibus

finally to yourself, re-adjusting yourself in a corner betwixt slumbering and waking, and throwing up your feet
on the seat opposite ; though, as the will becomes piqued
in proportion to its luxuries, you always regret that the
seats are not wider, and that you cannot treat your hat,
on cold nights, as freely as if it were a nightcap.

The last lingerers on these occasions (with the exception
of playgoers) are apt to be staid suburb-dwelling citizens,
—sitters with hands crossed upon their walking-sticks,—
men of parcels and eatables, breakers of last baskets of
oranges, chuckling over their bargains. There's one in the
corner, sleeping,—the last of the dwellers in Paddington.
To deposit him at his door is the sole remaining task of
the conductor. He wakes up ; hands forth a bag of apples,
—a tongue,—a bonnet, and four pairs of ladies' shoes. A
most considerate spouse and "papa" is he, and a most
worthy and flourishing hosier. Venerable is his lax throat
in his bit of white neckcloth (he has never taken to black) ;
but jovially also he shakes his wrinkles, if you talk of the
stationer's widow, or the last city feast.

"Don't drop them ladies' shoes, Tom," says he, chuckling ; "they'll be worn out before their time."

"Wery expensive, I believe, sir, them 'ere kind o' shoes,"
says Tom.

"Very ;—oh, sadly. And no better than paper. But
men well-to-do in the world can't live as cheap as poor
ones."

Tom thinks this a very odd proposition ; but it does not
disconcert him. Nothing disconcerts a conductor, except
a passenger without a sixpence.

"True, sir," says Tom ; "it's a hard case to be forced to
spend one's money ; but then you know—I beg pardon "
(with a tone of modest deference and secret contempt),
"it's much harder, as they say, where there's none to
spend."

"Hah ! Ha, ha ! Why, yes, eh ? " returns the old

gentleman, again chuckling ; "so there's your sixpence, Tom, and good-night."

"Good-night, sir." And up jumps Tom on the coach-box, where he amuses the driver with an account of the dirt which the hosier has got from the coach-wheel without his knowing it ; and off they go to a far less good supper, but it must be added, a much better sleep, than the rich old citizen.

Men, Women and Books. 1847.

BRIEF OBSERVATIONS UPON BREVITY

HARTLEY COLERIDGE

" BREVITY " says Polonius, " is the soul of wit," and twenty men as wise as he have said so after him. " Truth," says Mr. Stephen Jones, the worthy compiler of various Biographical, Geographical, and Lexicographical Duo-decimos, " is the soul of my work, and brevity is its body." Strange quality, that can at once be body and soul ! Rare coincidence, that the soul of wit should be the body of a pocket dictionary.

Many excellent things, good reader of six feet high, partake of the property which thou dost look down upon, or else overlook, so scornfully. To take a few casual instances, such as life, pleasure, a good style, and good resolutions, all which are notoriously, nay, proverbially *brief*, would scantly raise the matter to the altitude of the apprehension. Go then, and learn by experience ; read lawyers' briefs without a fee ; study the Statutes at Large ; regale thyself with Viner's Abridgement ; if thou beest a tradesman, give long credit ; if thou dost set a value on the moments, bind thine ears to seven hours' apprenticeship to the British Senate, or the British Forum : or, if thou canst, recal the days of Auld Lang Syne, of long sermons, and the long Parliament ; when the long-winded preachers were accustomed to hold forth over their glasses, to the long-eared and long-suffering multitude : over their glasses, I say, but not such glasses as were wont to inspire the tragic sublimity of Æschylus, the blistering humour of Aristophanes, and the blustering humour of Old Ben ; not such glasses as whetted the legal acumen of Blackstone, and assisted the incomparable Brinsley to weep for the calamities of India. No, my jovial friends, the Gospel trumpeters were as dry as they were lengthy. Their glasses were such as that which old Time is represented as running away with, though in sober truth they run, or rather creep, away with him ; such glasses as we naturally associate with a death's head, a college fag, or a lawyer's office. Should a modern pulpit orator undertake to preach by the hour-glass, I am inclined to think he would be building his hopes of preferment on a sandy foundation, and would most probably see his congregation run out before his sand. At all events, he would make the world (meaning thereby the parish clerk, and charity children, who were compelled to a final perseverance) as much in love with brevity, as if they had each inherited a chancery suit, or had their several properties charged with long annuities.

I am brief myself ; brief in stature, brief in discourse, short of memory and money, and far short of my wishes. In most things, too, I am an admirer of brevity ; I cannot endure long dinners. All the delicate viands that sea and land, with all the points " on the shipman's card," produce, are not so irresistible a temptation to gluttony, as the ennui of a needless half-hour at table : certain motions of the jaws are undoubtedly infectious ; such are laughing, yawning, and eating. Should the nightmare, " and her nine fold," descend visibly upon the dishes ; should indigestion, after the old fashion, assume the shape of Abernethy to admonish me, and gout appear in the yet more formidable likeness of a racking toe, the mere dead weight of time would turn the balance of my resolves. I am partial to short ladies. Here I shall be told, perhaps, that the Greeks include size in their ideal of beauty ; that all Homer's fair ones are " large and comely," and that Lord Byron has expressed his detestation of "dumpy women." All this is very true, but what is it all to me? Women are not ideals, nor do we love or admire them as such; Homer makes his heroes tall as well as his heroines; there cannot, as Falstaff says, be better sympathy. And as for his Lordship, when I am the Grand Turk, he shall choose for me. I revere the sex as much as any man, but I do not like to look up to them. I had rather be consorted "with the youngest wren of nine," than with any daughter of Eve whose morning stature was taller than my evening shadow. Whatever such an Amazon might condescend to say to me, it would sound of "nothing but low and little." Those pretty diminutives, which in all languages are the terms of affection, from her lips would seem like personalities; she could have but one set of phrases for fondness and for scorn. If I would "whisper soft nonsense in her ear," I must get on my legs, as if I were going to move a resolution; if in walking I would keep step with her, I must stride as if I were measuring the ground for two duellists, one of whom was my very good friend, and the other a very good shot. Should I dance with her, (alas, I am past my dancing days,) I should seem like a cock-boat tossing in a storm, at the stern of a three-decker. And should I wed her: (proh dolor; I am declared by signs infallible an old bachelor elect; cats, the coyest of the breed, leap on my knees; that saucy knave,[1] called the old bachelor, falls eternally to my share, and no soft look of contradiction averts the omen; candles shrink self-extinguished when I would snuff them, and no sweet voice will chide my awkwardness): but *should* I wed her, I must "stand the push of every beardless vain comparative." The young Etonian jackanapes would call us Elegiacs (carmen lugubre!); the Cantab pedants would

---

[1] It is needless to mention that this alludes to a Christmas gambol, wherein a particular knave in the pack is called the old bachelor, and the person drawing it is set down as a confirmed Cœlebs.

talk of their duplicate ratios ; yea, unbreeched urchins, old ale-wives, and coblers in their stalls, would cry out after us, There goes eighteen pence ; and prudential punsters would wish the match might prove happy, but it was certainly very *unequal.*

But of all *long* things, there are three which I hold in special abhorrence : a long bill, a long coach, and a long debate. Bills, it must be observed, are apt to grow long in proportion as the means of paying them are short ; and tradesmen do not, like " honourable gentlemen," move for leave to bring them in. But it is not the appalling sum total that I regard. It is the mizzling insignificant items, the heart-breaking fractions, the endless subdivisions of misery, that provoke me. It is as if one were condemned to be blown up with a mass of gunpowder, and at the same time to feel the separate explosion of every grain.

Few of those pestilential vehicles called long coaches infest our roads at present ; but when I was a young traveller, they were frequent, especially on the northern stages. Their external semblance was that of a hearse, and their inward accommodations might vie with those of a slave ship. An incontinent vestal might have rehearsed her living inhumation in one of them. They carried ten inside ! Authors, children, and dandies, were only counted as fractions ; and Daniel Lambert himself would only have been considered as an unit. Their pace was intolerably slow ; their stages long ; their drivers thirsty ; and ale-houses innumerable. It is difficult to conceive what a variety of distress they sometimes contained. I remember a journey in one of them,—I think it was between Lancaster and Manchester, perhaps the dullest road in England, —which beat the miseries of human life hollow. It was during the high fever of trade, and just after the summer holidays. I was then a minim, and counted as nobody. Three youths, returning " unwillingly to school," with all their consolatory store of half-eaten apples and gingerbread, and with looks that indicated a woeful neglect of regimen during the vacation, composed one passenger. The landlady of the Swan inn, in bulk a Falstaff, and clothed like the Grave-digger, ditto ; (bearing a brandy-bottle, which, with most importunate civility, she proffered to the company, in spite of repeated and sincere refusals ;) a consumptive gentleman, who supplied his lack of natural dimension by a huge box-coat ; a sick lady, with her son, (who, by the way, was very disagreeably affected by the motion of the carriage,) her sister, and a lap-dog ; a strong ministerialist of eighteen stone ; and an equally violent, and almost equally bulky, partizan of opposition ; (neither of these worthies was perfectly sober, and their vociferation was such as to drown every other sound, except the complaints of the sick lady, and the occasional yelping of the lap-dog ;) a very smart, yet innocent-looking young woman, who was sadly pestered with the coarse gallantry of a middle-aged manufacturer of cotton ; there was also a very prim and self-complacent young gentleman, who seemed to value himself much on his acute sense of the disagreeable, and not less on a peculiar delicate mode of swearing, mincing and clipping his oaths till they were almost softened into nonsense——

Such were the intestines : the roof and box were proportionably loaded. There was some little danger of breaking down, and no little fear of it. Every jolt produced a scream from the sick lady, a yelp from the lap-dog, an oath from the young gentleman, and a nauseous jest, or a vulgar proffer of service to the females, from the cotton-manufacturer. Against this chaos of discords we had to balance the momentary interruption of the political jangle, and a shriek in exchange for the customary groans of the landlady.

Scenes of this kind are particularly distressing to children ; confinement and the want of fresh air are themselves sufficiently painful to them, and they seldom possess the faculty of deriving amusement from inconveniences. But all the troubles of our progress were nothing to the intolerable stopping. All conversation, even that of the politicians, ceased instantly. Sigh answered sigh, and groans were heard in all the notes of the gamut. The very horses seemed to sympathise with the feelings of the passengers, by various inarticulate sounds expressing, not, indeed, impatience to be gone, but uneasiness at staying. It was a hopeless condition. Every face was a glass, in which one might perceive the lengthening of one's own. For the last stage, a dozing silence prevailed, which made me almost wish for noise again. Anything to drown the rumble of the wheels, and the perpetual and unavailing crack of the whip, which was applied unmercifully, and, as it were, mechanically, without the smallest acceleration.

I am not sure whether these machines have not been put down by the legislature. Would that the same august body would exercise their authority upon long speeches as well as on long coaches, and be as careful of the national time as of the bones of His Majesty's locomotive subjects. Oh ! that the value of brevity were understood within the walls of St. Stephen's ! I never cast an eye on the close-printed columns of a paper, without being transported by imagination into the Speaker's chair. (I had rather be transported to Botany Bay.) How anxiously must that model of enforced patience keep watch for some irregularity ! and with what joy must he seize the opportunity of crying Order ! How sweet to his ears must be the sound of his own voice, thus coupled with the sense of authority !

A long debate, is to me, like a long story, of which I know the conclusion before it is begun. To read or listen to it is as tedious as to play a game which you are sure of losing, or to fight for your life when you know that, in case of defeat or victory, it is alike forfeited. The catastrophe of every discussion may be so clearly foreseen, and the very arguments, and almost the very metaphors of each member, so easily anticipated, that it is a cruel oppression to force a man to thread the intricate mazes of eloquence, in order to arrive at a point to which a hop, step, and jump, may carry him. I proposed to speak briefly of brevity, and, lo ! I have produced a long discourse upon length. I intended to show that lovely things are brief, and I have digressed into an exposition of the unloveliness of lengthiness. Lest I should utterly belie my title, I will even conclude here.

TOM THUMB THE GREAT.

Miscellanies. 1851.

GONE ASTRAY

Charles Dickens

When I was a very small boy indeed, both in years and stature, I got lost one day in the City of London. I was taken out by Somebody (shade of Somebody forgive me for remembering no more of thy identity !), as an immense treat, to be shown the outside of Saint Giles's Church. I had romantic ideas in connection with that religious edifice ; firmly believing that all the beggars who pretended through the week to be blind, lame, one-armed, deaf and dumb, and otherwise physically afflicted, laid aside their pretences every Sunday, dressed themselves in holiday clothes, and attended divine service in the temple of their patron saint. I had a general idea that the reigning successor of Bamfylde Moore Carew acted as a sort of churchwarden on these occasions, and sat in a high pew with red curtains.

It was in the spring-time when these tender notions of mine, bursting forth into new shoots under the influence of the season, became sufficiently troublesome to my parents and guardians to occasion Somebody to volunteer to take me to see the outside of Saint Giles's Church, which was considered likely (I suppose) to quench my romantic fire, and bring me to a practical state. We set off after breakfast. I have an impression that Somebody was got up in a striking manner—in cord breeches of fine texture and milky hue, in long jean gaiters, in a green coat with bright buttons, in a blue neckerchief, and a monstrous shirt-collar. I think he must have newly come (as I had myself) out of the hop-grounds of Kent. I considered him the glass of fashion and the mould of form : a very Hamlet without the burden of his difficult family affairs.

We were conversational together, and saw the outside of Saint Giles's Church with sentiments of satisfaction, much enhanced by a flag flying from the steeple. I infer that we then went down to Northumberland House in the Strand to view the celebrated lion over the gateway. At all events, I know that in the act of looking up with mingled awe and admiration at that famous animal I lost Somebody.

The child's unreasoning terror of being lost, comes as freshly on me now as it did then. I verily believe that if I had found myself astray at the North Pole instead of in the narrow, crowded, inconvenient street over which the lion in those days presided, I could not have been more horrified. But, this first fright expended itself in a little crying and tearing up and down ; and then I walked, with a feeling of dismal dignity upon me, into a court, and sat down on a step to consider how to get through life.

To the best of my belief, the idea of asking my way home never came into my head. It is possible that I may, for the time, have preferred the dismal dignity of being lost ; but I have a serious conviction that in the wide scope of my arrangements for the future, I had no eyes for the nearest and most obvious course. I was but very juvenile ; from eight to nine years old, I fancy.

I had one and fourpence in my pocket, and a pewter ring with a bit of red glass in it on my little finger. This jewel had been presented to me by the object of my affections, on my birthday, when we had sworn to marry, but had foreseen family obstacles to our union, in her being (she was six years old) of the Wesleyan persuasion, while I was devotedly attached to the Church of England. The one and fourpence were the remains of half-a-crown

presented on the same anniversary by my godfather—a
man who knew his duty and did it.

Armed with these amulets, I made up my little mind to
seek my fortune. When I had found it, I thought I would
drive home in a coach and six, and claim my bride. I
cried a little more at the idea of such a triumph, but soon
dried my eyes and came out of the court to pursue my
plans. These were, first to go (as a species of investment)
and see the Giants in Guildhall, out of whom I felt it not
improbable that some prosperous adventure would arise ;
failing that contingency, to try about the City for any
opening of a Whittington nature ; baffled in that too, to go
into the army as a drummer.

So, I began to ask my way to Guildhall : which I
thought meant, somehow, Gold or Golden Hall ; I was
too knowing to ask my way to the Giants, for I felt it
would make people laugh. I remember how immensely
broad the streets seemed now I was alone, how high the
houses, how grand and mysterious everything. When I
came to Temple Bar, it took me half an hour to stare at it,
and I left it unfinished even then. I had read about heads
being exposed on the top of Temple Bar, and it seemed a
wicked old place, albeit a noble monument of architecture
and a paragon of utility. When at last I got away from
it, behold I came, the next minute, on the figures at Saint
Dunstan's ! Who could see those obliging monsters
strike upon the bells and go ? Between the quarters there
was the toyshop to look at—still there, at this present
writing, in a new form—and even when that enchanted
spot was escaped from, after an hour and more, then Saint
Paul's arose, and how was I to get beyond its dome, or to
take my eyes from its cross of gold ? I found it a long
journey to the Giants, and a slow one.

I came into their presence at last, and gazed up at them
with dread and veneration. They looked better-tempered,
and were altogether more shiny-faced, than I had expected ;

but they were very big, and, as I judged their pedestals to be about forty feet high, I considered that they would be very big indeed if they were walking on the stone pavement. I was in a state of mind as to these and all such figures, which I suppose holds equally with most children. While I knew them to be images made of something that was not flesh and blood, I still invested them with attributes of life—with consciousness of my being there, for example, and the power of keeping a sly eye upon me. Being very tired I got into the corner under Magog, to be out of the way of his eye, and fell asleep.

When I started up after a long nap, I thought the giants were roaring, but it was only the City. The place was just the same as when I fell asleep : no beanstalk, no fairy, no princess, no dragon, no opening in life of any kind. So, being hungry, I thought I would buy something to eat, and bring it in there and eat it, before going forth to seek my fortune on the Whittington plan.

I was not ashamed of buying a penny roll in a baker's shop, but I looked into a number of cooks' shops before I could muster courage to go into one. At last I saw a pile of cooked sausages in a window with the label, " Small Germans, A Penny." Emboldened by knowing what to ask for, I went in and said, " If you please will you sell me a small German ? " which they did, and I took it, wrapped in paper in my pocket, to Guildhall.

The giants were still lying by, in their sly way, pretending to take no notice, so I sat down in another corner, when what should I see before me but a dog with his ears cocked. He was a black dog, with a bit of white over one eye, and bits of white and tan in his paws, and he wanted to play— frisking about me, rubbing his nose against me, dodging at me sideways, shaking his head and pretending to run away backwards, and making himself good-naturedly ridiculous, as if he had no consideration for himself, but wanted to raise my spirits. Now, when I saw this dog I thought of Whittington, and felt that things were coming right ; I encouraged him by saying, " Hi, boy ! " " Poor fellow ! " " Good dog ! " and was satisfied that he was to be my dog for ever afterwards, and that he would help me to seek my fortune.

Very much comforted by this (I had cried a little at odd times ever since I was lost), I took the small German out of my pocket, and began my dinner by biting off a bit and throwing it to the dog, who immediately swallowed it with a one-sided jerk, like a pill. While I took a bit myself, and he looked me in the face for a second piece, I considered by what name I should call him. I thought Merrychance would be an expressive name, under the circumstances ; and I was elated, I recollect, by inventing such a good one, when Merrychance began to growl at me in a most ferocious manner.

I wondered he was not ashamed of himself, but he didn't care for that ; on the contrary he growled a good deal more. With his mouth watering, and his eyes glistening, and his nose in a very damp state, and his head very much on one side, he sidled about on the pavement in a threatening manner and growled at me, until he suddenly made a snap at the small German, tore it out of my hand, and went off with it. He never came back to help me seek my fortune. From that hour to the present, when I am forty years of age, I have never seen my faithful Merrychance again.

I felt very lonely. Not so much for the loss of the small German, though it was delicious (I knew nothing about highly-peppered horse at that time), as on account of Merrychance's disappointing me so cruelly ; for I had hoped he would do every friendly thing but speak, and perhaps even come to that. I cried a little more, and began to wish that the object of my affections had been lost with me, for company's sake. But, then I remembered that *she* could not go into the army as a drummer ; and I dried my eyes and ate my loaf. Coming out, I met a milkwoman of whom I bought a pennyworth of milk ; quite set up again by my repast, I began to roam about the City, and to seek my fortune in the Whittington direction.

When I go into the City, now, it makes me sorrowful to think that I am quite an artful wretch. Strolling about it as a lost child, I thought of the British Merchant and the Lord Mayor, and was full of reverence. Strolling about it now, I laugh at the sacred liveries of state, and get indignant with the corporation as one of the strongest practical jokes of the present day. What did I know, then, about the multitude who are always being disappointed in the City ; who are always expecting to meet a party there, and to receive money there, and whose expectations are never fulfilled ? What did I know, then, about that wonderful person, the friend in the City, who is to do so many things for so many people ; who is to get this one into a post at home, and that one into a post abroad ; who is to settle with this man's creditors, provide for that man's son, and see that other man paid ; who is to " throw himself " into this grand Joint-Stock certainty, and is to put his name down on that Life Assurance Directory, and never does anything predicted of him ? What did I know, then, about him as the friend of gentlemen, Mosaic Arabs and others, usually to be seen at races, and chiefly residing in the neighbourhood of Red Lion Square ; and as being unable to discount the whole amount of that paper in money, but as happening to have by him a cask of remarkable fine sherry, a dressing-case, and a Venus by Titian, with which he would be willing to make up the balance ? Had I ever heard of him, in those innocent days, as confiding information (which never by any chance turned out to be in the remotest degree correct) to solemn bald men, who mysteriously imparted it to breathless dinner tables ? No. Had I ever learned to dread him as a shark, disregard him as a humbug, and know him for a

myth ? Not I. Had I ever heard of him as associated
with tightness in the money market, gloom in consols,
the exportation of gold, or that rock ahead in everybody's
course, the bushel of wheat ? Never. Had I the least idea
what was meant by such terms as jobbery, rigging the
market, cooking accounts, getting up a dividend, making
things pleasant, and the like ? Not the slightest. Should
I have detected in Mr. Hudson himself, a staring carcass
of golden veal ? By no manner of means. The City was
to me a vast emporium of precious stones and metals,
casks and bales, honour and generosity, foreign fruits and
spices. Every merchant and banker was a compound of
Mr. Fitz-Warren and Sinbad the Sailor. Smith, Payne,
and Smith, when the wind was fair for Barbary and the
captain present, were in the habit of calling their servants
together (the cross cook included) and asking them to
produce their little shipments. Glyn and Halifax had
personally undergone great hardships in the valley of
diamonds. Baring Brothers had seen Rocs' eggs and
travelled with caravans. Rothschild had sat in the Bazaar
at Bagdad with rich stuffs for sale ; and a veiled lady from
the Sultan's harem, riding on a donkey, had fallen in love
with him.

Thus I wandered about the City, like a child in a dream,
staring at the British merchants, and inspired by a mighty
faith in the marvellousness of everything. Up courts
and down courts—in and out of yards and little squares—
peeping into counting-house passages and running away
—poorly feeding the echoes in the court of the South Sea
House with my timid steps—roaming down into Austin
Friars, and wondering how the Friars used to like it—ever
staring at the British merchants, and never tired of the
shops—I rambled on, all through the day. In such stories
as I made, to account for the different places, I believed
as devoutly as in the City itself. I particularly remember
that when I found myself on 'Change, and saw the shabby

people sitting under the placards about ships, I settled that they were Misers, who had embarked all their wealth to go and buy gold-dust or something of that sort, and were waiting for their respective captains to come and tell them that they were ready to set sail. I observed that they all munched dry biscuits, and I thought it was to keep off sea-sickness.

This was very delightful ; but it still produced no result according to the Whittington precedent. There was a dinner preparing at the Mansion House, and when I peeped in at a grated kitchen window, and saw the men cooks at work in their white caps, my heart began to beat with hope that the Lord Mayor, or the Lady Mayoress, or one of the young Princesses their daughters, would look out of an upper apartment and direct me to be taken in. But, nothing of the kind occurred. It was not until I had been peeping in some time that one of the cooks called to me (the window was open), " Cut away, you sir ! " which frightened me so, on account of his black whiskers, that I instantly obeyed.

After that, I came to the India House, and asked a boy what it was, who made faces and pulled my hair before he told me, and behaved altogether in an ungenteel and discourteous manner. Sir James Hogg himself might have been satisfied with the veneration in which I held the India House. I had no doubt of its being the most wonderful, the most magnanimous, the most incorruptible, the most practically disinterested, the most in all respects astonishing, establishment on the face of the earth. I understood the nature of an oath, and would have sworn it to be one entire and perfect chrysolite.

Thinking much about boys who went to India, and who immediately, without being sick, smoked pipes like curled-up bell-ropes, terminating in a large cut-glass sugar basin upside down, I got among the outfitting shops. There, I read the lists of things that were necessary for an India-

going boy, and when I came to " one brace of pistols,"
thought what happiness to be reserved for such a fate !
Still no British merchant seemed at all disposed to take
me into his house. The only exception was a chimney-
sweep—he looked at me as if he thought me suitable to
his business ; but I ran away from him.

I suffered very much, all day, from boys ; they chased
me down turnings, brought me to bay in doorways, and
treated me quite savagely, though I am sure I gave them
no offence. One boy, who had a stump of black-lead
pencil in his pocket, wrote his mother's name and address
(as he said) on my white hat, outside the crown. MRS.
BLORES, WOODEN LEG WALK, TOBACCO-STOPPER ROW,
WAPPING. And I couldn't rub it out.

I recollect resting in a little churchyard after this persecution, disposed to think upon the whole, that if I and the
object of my affections could be buried there together, at
once, it would be comfortable. But, another nap, and a
pump, and a bun, and above all a picture that I saw,
brought me round again.

I must have strayed by that time, as I recall my course,
into Goodman's Fields, or somewhere thereabouts. The
picture represented a scene in a play then performing at a
theatre in that neighbourhood which is no longer in
existence. It stimulated me to go to that theatre and see
that play. I resolved, as there seemed to be nothing doing
in the Whittington way, that on the conclusion of the
entertainments I would ask my way to the barracks,
knock at the gate, and tell them that I understood they
were in want of drummers, and there I was. I think I
must have been told, but I know I believed, that a soldier
was always on duty, day and night, behind every barrack-
gate, with a shilling ; and that a boy who could by any
means be prevailed on to accept it, instantly became a
drummer, unless his father paid four hundred pounds.

I found out the theatre—of its external appearance I only

remember the loyal initials G.R. untidily painted in yellow ochre on the front—and waited, with a pretty large crowd, for the opening of the gallery doors. The greater part of the sailors and others composing the crowd, were of the lowest description, and their conversation was not improving ; but I understood little or nothing of what was bad in it then, and it had no depraving influence on me. I have wondered since, how long it would take, by means of such association, to corrupt a child nurtured as I had been, and innocent as I was.

Whenever I saw that my appearance attracted attention, either outside the doors or afterwards within the theatre, I pretended to look out for somebody who was taking care of me, and from whom I was separated, and to exchange nods and smiles with that creature of my imagination. This answered very well. I had my sixpence clutched in my hand ready to pay ; and when the doors opened, with a clattering of bolts, and some screaming from women in the crowd, I went on with the current like a straw. My sixpence was rapidly swallowed up in the money-taker's pigeon-hole, which looked to me like a sort of mouth, and I got into the freer staircase above and ran on (as everybody else did) to get a good place. When I came to the back of the gallery, there were very few people in it, and the seats looked so horribly steep, and so like a diving arrangement to send me, headforemost, into the pit, that I held by one of them in a terrible fright. However, there was a good-natured baker with a young woman, who gave me his hand, and we all three scrambled over the seats together down into the corner of the first row. The baker was very fond of the young woman, and kissed her a good deal in the course of the evening.

I was no sooner comfortably settled, than a weight fell upon my mind, which tormented it most dreadfully, and which I must explain. It was a benefit night—the benefit of the comic actor—a little fat man with a very large face and, as I thought then, the smallest and most diverting hat that ever was seen. This comedian, for the gratification of his friends and patrons, had undertaken to sing a comic song on a donkey's back, and afterwards to give away the donkey so distinguished, by lottery. In this lottery, every person admitted to the pit and gallery had a chance. On paying my sixpence, I had received the number, forty-seven ; and I now thought, in a perspiration of terror, what should I ever do if that number was to come up the prize, and I was to win the donkey !

It made me tremble all over to think of the possibility of my good fortune. I knew I never could conceal the fact of my holding forty-seven, in case that number came up, because, not to speak of my confusion, which would immediately condemn me, I had shown my number to the baker. Then, I pictured to myself the being called upon to come down on the stage and receive the donkey. I thought how all the people would shriek when they saw it had fallen to a little fellow like me. How should I lead him out—for of course he wouldn't go ? If he began to bray, what should I do ? If he kicked, what would become of me ? Suppose he backed into the stage-door, and stuck there, with me upon him ? For I felt that if I won him, the comic actor would have me on his back, the moment he could touch me. Then if I got him out of the theatre, what was I to do with him ? How was I to feed him ? Where was I to stable him ? It was bad enough to have gone astray by myself, but to go astray with a donkey, too, was a calamity more tremendous than I could bear to contemplate.

These apprehensions took away all my pleasure in the first piece. When the ship came on—a real man-of-war she was called in the bills—and rolled prodigiously in a very heavy sea, I couldn't, even in the terrors of the storm, forget the donkey. It was awful to see the sailors pitching about, with telescopes and speaking trumpets (they looked very tall indeed aboard the man-of-war), and it was awful to suspect the pilot of treachery, though impossible to avoid it, for when he cried—" We are lost ! To the raft, to the raft ! A thunderbolt has struck the main-mast ! " —I myself saw him take the main-mast out of its socket and drop it overboard ; but even these impressive circumstances paled before my dread of the donkey. Even, when the good sailor (and he was very good) came to good fortune, and the bad sailor (and he was very bad) threw himself into the ocean from the summit of a curious rock, presenting something of the appearance of a pair of steps, I saw the dreadful donkey through my tears.

At last the time came when the fiddlers struck up the comic song, and the dreaded animal, with new shoes on, as I inferred from the noise they made, came clattering in with the comic actor on his back. He was dressed out with ribbons (I mean the donkey was), and as he persisted in turning his tail to the audience, the comedian got off him, turned about, and sitting with his face that way, sang the song three times, amid thunders of applause. All this time, I was fearfully agitated ; and when two pale people, a good deal splashed with the mud of the streets, were invited out of the pit to superintend the drawing of the lottery, and were received with a round of laughter from everybody else, I could have begged and prayed them to have mercy on me, and not draw number forty-seven.

But, I was soon put out of my pain now, for a gentleman behind me, in a flannel jacket and a yellow neck-kerchief, who had eaten two fried soles and all his pockets-full of nuts before the storm began to rage, answered to the winning number, and went down to take possession of the prize. This gentleman had appeared to know the donkey, rather, from the moment of his entrance, and had taken a great interest in his proceedings ; driving him to himself, if I use an intelligible phrase, and saying, almost in my ear, when he made any mistake, " Kum up, you precious Moke.

Kum up !" He was thrown by the donkey on first mounting him, to the great delight of the audience (including myself), but rode him off with great skill afterwards, and soon returned to his seat quite calm. Calmed myself by the immense relief I had sustained, I enjoyed the rest of the performance very much indeed. I remember there were a good many dances, some in fetters and some in roses, and one by a most divine little creature, who made the object of my affections look but common-place. In the concluding drama, she reappeared as a boy (in arms, mostly), and was fought for, several times. I rather think a Baron wanted to drown her, and was on various occasions prevented by the comedian, a ghost, a Newfoundland dog, and a church bell. I only remember beyond this, that I wondered where the Baron expected to go to, and that he went there in a shower of sparks. The lights were turned out while the sparks died out, and it appeared to me as if the whole play—ship, donkey, men and women, divine little creature, and all—were a wonderful firework that had gone off, and left nothing but dust and darkness behind it.

It was late when I got out into the streets, and there was no moon, and there were no stars, and the rain fell heavily. When I emerged from the dispersing crowd, the ghost and the baron had an ugly look in my remembrance ; I felt unspeakably forlorn ; and now, for the first time, my little bed and the dear familiar faces came before me, and touched my heart. By daylight, I had never thought of the grief at home. I had never thought of my mother. I had never thought of anything but adapting myself to the circumstances in which I found myself, and going to seek my fortune.

For a boy who could do nothing but cry, and run about, saying, " O I am lost ! " to think of going into the army was, I felt sensible, out of the question. I abandoned the idea of asking my way to the barracks—or rather the idea abandoned me—and ran about, until I found a watchman in his box. It is amazing to me, now, that he should have been sober ; but I am inclined to think he was too feeble to get drunk.

This venerable man took me to the nearest watch-house ; —I say he took me, but in fact I took him, for when I think of us in the rain, I recollect that we must have made a composition, like a vignette of Infancy leading Age. He had a dreadful cough, and was obliged to lean against a wall, whenever it came on. We got at last to the watch-house, a warm and drowsy sort of place embellished with great-coats and rattles hanging up. When a paralytic messenger had been sent to make inquiries about me, I fell asleep by the fire, and awoke no more until my eyes opened on my father's face. This is literally and exactly how I went astray. They used to say I was an odd child, and I suppose I was. I am an odd man perhaps.

Shade of Somebody, forgive me for the disquiet I must have caused thee ! When I stand beneath the Lion, even now, I see thee rushing up and down, refusing to be comforted. I have gone astray since, many times, and farther afield. May I therein have given less disquiet to others, than herein I gave to thee !

Household Words. 1853.

GONE TO THE DOGS

Charles Dickens

We all know what treasures Posterity will inherit, in the fullness of time. We all know what handsome legacies are bequeathed to it every day, what long luggage-trains of Sonnets it will be the better for, what patriots and statesmen it will discover to have existed in this age whom we have no idea of, how very wide awake it will be, and how stone blind the Time is. We know what multitudes of disinterested persons are always going down to it, laden, like processions of genii, with inexhaustible and incalculable wealth. We have frequent experience of the generosity with which the profoundest wits, the subtlest politicians, unerring inventors, and lavish benefactors of mankind, take beneficent aim at it with a longer range than Captain Warner's, and blow it up to the very heaven of heavens, one hundred years after date. We all defer to it as the great capitalist in expectation, the world's residuary legatee in respect of all the fortunes that are not just now convertible, the heir of a long and fruitful minority, the fortunate creature on whom all the true riches of the earth are firmly entailed. When Posterity does come into its own at last, what a coming of age there will be !

It seems to me that Posterity, as the subject of so many handsome settlements, has only one competitor. I find the Dogs to be every day enriched with a vast amount of valuable property.

What has become—to begin like Charity at home—what has become, I demand, of the inheritance I myself entered on, at nineteen years of age ! A shining castle (in the air) with young Love looking out of window, perfect content-ment and repose of spirit standing with ethereal aspect in the porch, visions surrounding it by night and day with an atmosphere of pure gold. This was my only inheritance, and I never squandered it. I hoarded it like a miser. Say, bright-eyed Araminta (with the obdurate parents), thou who wast sole lady of the castle, did I not ? Down the flowing river by the walls, called Time, how blest we sailed together, treasuring our happiness unto death, and never knowing change, or weariness, or separation ! Where is that castle now, with all its magic furniture ? Gone to the Dogs. Canine possession was taken of the whole of that estate, my youthful Araminta, about a quarter of a century ago.

Come back, friend of my youth. Come back from the glooms and shadows that have gathered round thee, and let us sit down once more, side by side, upon the rough, notched form at school ! Idle is Bob Tample, given to shirking his work and getting me to do it for him, inkier than a well-regulated mind in connection with a well-regulated body is usually observed to be, always com-pounding with his creditors on pocket-money days, fre-quently selling off pen-knives by auction, and disposing of his sister's birthday presents at an enormous sacrifice. Yet, a rosy, cheerful, thoughtless fellow is Bob Tample, borrowing with an easy mind, sixpences of Dick Sage the prudent, to pay eighteenpences after the holidays, and freely standing treat to all comers. Musical is Bob Tample. Able to sing and whistle anything. Learns the piano (in the parlour), and once plays a duet with the musical pro-fessor, Mr. Goavus of the Royal Italian Opera (occasional-deputy-assistant-copyist in that establishment, I have since seen reason to believe), whom Bob's friends and supporters,

I foremost in the throng, consider tripped up in the first half-dozen bars. Not without bright expectations is Bob Tample, being an orphan with a guardian near the Bank, and destined for the army. I boast of Bob at home that his name is "down at the Horse Guards," and that his father left it in his will that "a pair of colours" (I like the expression without particularly knowing what it means) should be purchased for him. I go with Bob on one occasion to look at the building where his name is down. We wonder in which of the rooms it is down, and whether the two horse soldiers on duty know it. I also accompany Bob to see his sister at Miss Maggiggs's boarding establishment at Hammersmith, and it is unnecessary to add that I think his sister beautiful and love her. She will be independent, Bob says. I relate at home that Mr. Tample left it in his will that his daughter was to be independent. I put Mr. Tample, entirely of my own accord and invention, into the army ; and I perplex my family circle by relating feats of valour achieved by that lamented officer at the Battle of Waterloo, where I leave him dead, with the British flag (which he wouldn't give up to the last) wound tightly round his left arm. So we go on, until Bob leaves for Sandhurst. *I* leave in course of time—everybody leaves. Years have gone by, when I twice or thrice meet a gentleman with a moustache, driving a lady in a very gay bonnet, whose face recalls the boarding establishment of Miss Maggiggs at Hammersmith, though it does not look so happy as it did under Miss Maggiggs, iron-handed despot as I believed that accomplished woman to be. This leads me to the discovery that the gentleman with the moustache is Bob ; and one day Bob pulls up, and talks, and asks me to dinner ; but, on subsequently ascertaining that I don't play billiards, hardly seems to care as much about me as I had expected. I ask Bob at this period, if he is in the service still ? Bob answers no my boy, he got bored and sold out ; which induces me to think (for I am

growing worldly), either that Bob must be very independent indeed, or must be going to the Dogs. More years
elapse, and having quite lost sight and sound of Bob
meanwhile, I say on an average twice a week during three
entire twelvemonths, that I really will call at the guardian's
near the Bank, and ask about Bob. At length I do so.
Clerks, on being apprised of my errand, became disrespect-
ful. Guardian, with bald head highly flushed, bursts out
of inner office, remarks that he hasn't the honour of my
acquaintance, and bursts in again, without exhibiting the
least desire to improve the opportunity of knowing me.
I now begin sincerely to believe that Bob is going to the
Dogs. More years go by, and as they pass Bob sometimes
goes by me too, but never twice in the same aspect—
always tending lower and lower. No redeeming trace of
better things would hang about him now, were he not
always accompanied by the sister. Gay bonnet gone ;
exchanged for something limp and veiled, that might be
a mere porter's knot of the feminine gender, to carry a load
of misery on—shabby, even slipshod. I, by some vague
means or other, come to the knowledge of the fact that she
entrusted that independence to Bob, and that Bob—in
short, that it has all gone to the Dogs. One summer day,
I descry Bob idling in the sun, outside a public-house near
Drury Lane ; she, in a shawl that clings to her, as only
the robes of poverty do cling to their wearers when all
things else have fallen away, waiting for him at the street
corner ; he, with a stale, accustomed air, picking his teeth
and pondering ; two boys watchful of him, not unadmir-
ingly. Curious to know more of this, I go round that way
another day, look at a concert-bill in the public-house
window, and have not a doubt that Bob is Mr. Berkeley,
the celebrated bacchanalian vocalist, who presides at
the piano. From time to time, rumours float by me afterwards, I can't say how, or where they come from—from
the expectant and insatiate Dogs for anything I know—

touching hushed-up pawnings of sheets from poor furnished lodgings, begging letters to old Miss Maggiggs at Hammersmith, and the clearing away of all Miss Maggiggs's umbrellas and clogs, by the gentleman who called for an answer on a certain foggy evening after dark. Thus downward, until the faithful sister begins to beg of *me*, whereupon I moralize as to the use of giving her any money (for I have grown quite worldly now), and look furtively out of my window as she goes away by night with that half-sovereign of mine, and think, contemptuous of myself, can I ever have admired the crouching figure plashing through the rain, in a long round crop of curls at Miss Maggiggs's ! Oftentimes she comes back with bedridden lines from the brother, who is always nearly dead and never quite, until he does tardily make an end of it, and at last this Actæon reversed has rung the Dogs wholly down and betaken himself to them finally. More years have passed, when I dine at Withers's at Brighton on a day, to drink 'Forty-one claret ; and there, Spithers, the new Attorney-General, says to me across the table, " Weren't you a Mithers's boy ? " To which I say, " To be sure I was ! " To which he retorts, " And don't you remember me ? " To which I retort, " To be sure I do " —which I never did until that instant—and then he says how the fellows have all dispersed, and he has never seen one of them since, and have I ? To which I, finding that my learned friend has a pleasant remembrance of Bob from having given him a black eye on his fifteenth birthday in assertion of his right to " smug " a pen-wiper forwarded to said Bob by his sister on said occasion, make response by generalizing the story I have now completed, and adding that I have heard that, after Bob's death, Miss Maggiggs, though deuced poor through the decay of her school, took the sister home to live with her. My learned friend says, upon his word it does Miss Whatshername credit, and all old Mitherses ought to subscribe a trifle for her. Not seeing the necessity of that, I praise the wine, and we send it round, the way of the world (which world I am told is getting nearer to the Sun every year of its existence), and we bury Bob's memory with the epitaph that he went to the Dogs.

Sometimes, whole streets, inanimate streets of brick and mortar houses, go to the Dogs. Why, it is impossible to say, otherwise than that the Dogs bewitch them, fascinate them, magnetize them, summon them and they must go. I know of such a street at the present writing. It was a stately street in its own grim way, and the houses held together like the last surviving members of an aristocratic family, and, as a general rule, were—still not unlike them—very tall and very dull. How long the Dogs may have had their eyes of temptation upon this street is unknown to me, but they called to it, and it went. The biggest house—it was a corner one—went first. An ancient gentleman died in it ; and the undertaker put up a gaudy hatchment that looked like a very bad transparency, not intended to be seen by day, and only meant to be illuminated at night ; and the attorney put up a bill about the lease, and put in an old woman (apparently with nothing to live upon but a cough), who crept away into a corner like a scared old dormouse, and rolled herself up in a blanket. The mysterious influence of the Dogs was on the house, and it immediately began to tumble down. Why the infection should pass over fourteen houses to seize upon the fifteenth, I don't know ; but, fifteen doors off next began to be fatally dim in the windows ; and after a short decay, its eyes were closed by brokers, and its end was desolation. The best house opposite, unable to bear these sights of woe, got out a black board with all despatch, respecting un-expired remainder of term, and cards to view ; and the family fled, and a bricklayer's wife and children came in to " mind " the place, and dried their little weekly wash on lines hung across the dining-room. Black boards, like the doors of so many hearses taken off the hinges, now became abundant. Only one speculator, without suspicion of the Dogs upon his soul, responded. He repaired and stuccoed number twenty-four, got up an ornamented parapet and balconies, took away the knockers, and put in plate glass, found too late that all the steam power on earth could never have kept the street from the Dogs when it was once influenced to go, and drowned himself in a water butt. Within a year, the house he had renewed became the worst of all ; the stucco decomposing like a Stilton cheese, and the ornamented parapet coming down in fragments like the sugar of a broken twelfth cake. Expiring efforts were then made by a few of the black boards to hint at the eligibility of these commodious mansions for public institutions, and suites of chambers. It was useless. The thing was done. The whole street may now be bought for a mere song. But, nobody will hear of it, for who dares dispute possession of it with the Dogs !

Sometimes, it would seem as if the least yelp of these dreadful animals, did the business at once. Which of us does not remember that eminent person—with indefinite resources in the City, tantamount to a gold mine—who had the delightful house near town, the famous gardens and gardener, the beautiful plantations, the smooth green lawns, the pineries, the stabling for five-and-twenty horses, and the standing for half a dozen carriages, the billiard-room, the music-room, the picture gallery, the accomplished daughters and aspiring sons, all the pride, pomp and circumstance of riches ? Which of us does not recall how we knew him through the good offices of our esteemed friend Swallowfly, who was ambassador on the occasion ? Which of us cannot still hear the gloating roundness of tone with which Swallowfly informed us that our new friend was worth five hun-dred thou-sand pounds, sir, if he was worth a penny ? How we dined there with all the Arts and Graces ministering to us, and how we came away reflecting that wealth after all was a desirable delight, I need not say. Neither need I tell, how we every one of us met Swallowfly within six little months of that same day, when Swallowfly observed, with such surprise, "You haven't heard ? Lord bless me ! Ruined—Channel Islands—gone to the Dogs ! "

Sometimes again, it would seem as though in exceptional cases here and there, the Dogs relented, or lost their power over the imperilled man in an inscrutable way. There was my own cousin—he is dead now, therefore I have no objection to mention his name—Tom Flowers. He was a bachelor (fortunately), and, among other ways he had of increasing his income and improving his prospects, betted pretty high. He did all sorts of things that he ought not to have done, and he did everything at a great pace, so it was clearly seen by all who knew him that nothing would keep him from the Dogs ; that he was running them down hard, and was bent on getting into the very midst of the pack with all possible speed. Well ! He was as near them, I suppose, as ever man was, when he suddenly stopped short, looked them full in their jowls, and never stirred another inch onward, to the day of his death. He walked about for seventeen years, a very neat little figure, with a capital umbrella, an excellent neckcloth, and a pure white shirt, and he had not got a hair's-breadth nearer to the horrible animals at the end of that time than he had when he stopped. How he lived, our family could never make out—whether the Dogs can have allowed him anything will always be a mystery to me—but, he disappointed all of us in the matter of the canine epitaph with which we had expected to dismiss him, and merely enabled us to remark that poor Tom Flowers was gone at sixty-seven.

It is overwhelming to think of the Treasury of the Dogs. There are no such fortunes embarked in all the enterprises of life, as have gone their way. They have a capital

Drama, for their amusement and instruction. They have got hold of all the People's holidays for the refreshment of weary frames, and the renewal of weary spirits. They have left the People little else in that way but a Fast now and then for the ignorances and imbecilities of their rulers. Perhaps those days will go next. To say the plain truth very seriously, I shouldn't be surprised.

Consider the last possessions that have gone to the Dogs. Consider, friends and countrymen, how the Dogs have been enriched, by your despoilment at the hands of your own blessed governors—to whom be honour and renown, stars and garters, for ever and ever !—on the shores of a certain obscure spot called Balaklava, where Britannia rules the waves in such an admirable manner, that she slays her children (who never never never will be slaves, but very very very often will be dupes), by the thousand, with every movement of her glorious trident ! When shall there be added to the possessions of the Dogs, those columns of talk, which, let the columns of British soldiers vanish as they may, still defile before us wearily, wearily, leading to nothing, doing nothing, for the most part even saying nothing, only enshrouding us in a mist of idle breath that obscures the events which are forming themselves—not into playful shapes, believe me—beyond. If the Dogs, lately so gorged, still so voracious and strong, could and would deliver a most gracious bark, I have a strong impression that their warning would run thus :

" My Lords and Gentlemen. We are open-mouthed and eager. Either you must send suitable provender to us without delay, or you must come to us yourselves. There is no avoidance of the alternative. Talk never softened the three-headed dog that kept the passage to the Shades ; less will it appease us. No jocular old gentleman throwing somersaults on stilts because his great-grandmother is not worshipped in Nineveh, is a sop to us for a moment ; no hearing, cheering, sealing-waxing, tapeing, fire-eating, vote-eating, or other popular Club-performance, at all imports us. We are the Dogs. We are known to you just now, as the Dogs of War. We crouched at your feet for employment, as William Shakespeare, plebeian, saw us crouching at the feet of the Fifth Harry—and you gave it us ; crying Havoc ! in good English, and letting us slip (quite by accident), on good Englishmen. With our appetites so whetted, we are hungry. We are sharp of scent and quick of sight, and we see and smell a great deal coming to us rather rapidly. Will you give us such old rubbish as must be ours in any case ? My Lords and Gentlemen, make haste ! Something must go to the Dogs in earnest. Shall it be you, or something else ? ''

Household Words. 1855.

THE GLORY OF MOTION

Thomas De Quincey

Some twenty or more years before I matriculated at Oxford, Mr. Palmer, at that time M.P. for Bath, had accomplished two things, very hard to do on our little planet, the Earth, however cheap they may be held by eccentric people in comets—he had invented mail-coaches, and he had married the daughter of a duke. He was, therefore, just twice as great a man as Galileo, who did certainly invent (or, which is the same thing, discover) the satellites of Jupiter, those very next things extant to mail-coaches in the two capital pretensions of speed and keeping time, but, on the other hand, who did *not* marry the daughter of a duke.

These mail-coaches, as organized by Mr. Palmer, are entitled to a circumstantial notice from myself, having had so large a share in developing the anarchies of my subsequent dreams ; an agency which they accomplished, 1st, through velocity, at that time unprecedented—for they first revealed the glory of motion ; 2ndly, through grand effects for the eye between lamp-light and the darkness upon solitary roads ; 3rdly, through animal beauty and power so often displayed in the class of horses selected for this mail service ; 4thly, through the conscious presence of a central intellect, that, in the midst of vast distances—of storms, of darkness, of danger—overruled all obstacles into one steady co-operation to a national result. For my own feeling, this post-office service spoke as by some mighty orchestra, where a thousand instruments, all disregarding each other, and so far in danger of discord, yet all obedient as slaves to the supreme *baton* of some great leader, terminate in a perfection of harmony like that of heart, brain, and lungs, in a healthy animal organization. But, finally, that particular element in this whole combination which most impressed myself, and through which it is that to this hour Mr. Palmer's mail-coach system tyrannizes over my dreams by terror and terrific beauty, lay in the awful *political* mission which at that time it fulfilled. The mail-coach it was that distributed over the face of the land, like the opening of apocalyptic vials, the heart-shaking news of Trafalgar, of Salamanca, of Vittoria, of Waterloo. These were the harvests that, in the grandeur of their reaping, redeemed the tears and blood in which they had been sown. Neither was the meanest peasant so much below the grandeur and the sorrow of the times as to confound battles such as these, which were gradually moulding the destinies of Christendom, with the vulgar conflicts of ordinary warfare, so often no more than gladiatorial trials of national prowess. The victories of England in this stupendous contest rose of themselves as natural *Te Deums* to heaven ; and it was felt by the thoughtful that such victories, at such a crisis of general prostration, were not more beneficial to ourselves than finally to France, our enemy, and to the nations of all western or central Europe, through whose pusillanimity it was that the French domination had prospered.

The mail-coach, as the national organ for publishing these mighty events thus diffusively influential, became itself a spiritualized and glorified object to an impassioned heart ; and naturally, in the Oxford of that day, *all* hearts were impassioned, as being all (or nearly all) in *early* manhood. In most universities there is one single college ; in Oxford there were five-and-twenty, all of which were peopled by young men, the *élite* of their own generation ; not boys, but men ; none under eighteen. In some of

these many colleges, the custom permitted the student
to keep what are called " short terms " ; that is, the four
terms of Michaelmas, Lent, Easter, and Act, were kept
by a residence, in the aggregate, of ninety-one days, or
thirteen weeks. Under this interrupted residence, it was
possible that a student might have a reason for going down
to his home four times in the year. This made eight
journeys to and fro. But, as these homes lay dispersed
through all the shires of the island, and most of us disdained
all coaches except his majesty's mail, no city out of London
could pretend to so extensive a connection with Mr.
Palmer's establishment at Oxford. Three mails, at the
least, I remember as passing every day through Oxford,
and benefiting by my personal patronage—viz., the
Worcester, the Gloucester, and the Holyhead mail.
Naturally, therefore, it became a point of some interest
with us, whose journeys revolved every six weeks on an
average, to look a little into the executive details of the
system. With some of these Mr. Palmer had no concern ;
they rested upon bye-laws enacted by posting-houses for
their own benefit, and upon other bye-laws, equally stern,
enacted by the inside passengers, for the illustration of their
own haughty exclusiveness. These last were of a nature
to rouse our scorn, from which the transition was not very
long to systematic mutiny. Up to this time, say 1804, or
1805 (the year of Trafalgar), it had been the fixed assumption of the four inside people (as an old tradition of all
public carriages derived from the reign of Charles II.),
that they, the illustrious quaternion, constituted a porcelain
variety of the human race, whose dignity would have been
compromised by exchanging one word of civility with the
three miserable delf-ware outsides. Even to have kicked
an outsider, might have been held to attaint the foot concerned in that operation ; so that, perhaps, it would have
required an act of parliament to restore its purity of blood.
What words, then, could express the horror, and the sense

of treason, in that case, which *had* happened, where all three outsides (the trinity of Pariahs) made a vain attempt to sit down at the same breakfast-table or dinner-table with the consecrated four ? I myself witnessed such an attempt ; and on that occasion a benevolent old gentleman endeavoured to soothe his three holy associates, by suggesting that, if the outsides were indicted for this criminal attempt at the next assizes, the court would regard it as a case of lunacy, or *delirium tremens*, rather than of treason. England owes much of her grandeur to the depth of the aristocratic element in her social composition, when pulling against her strong democracy. I am not the man to laugh at it. But sometimes, undoubtedly, it expressed itself in comic shapes. The course taken with the infatuated outsiders, in the particular attempt which I have noticed, was, that the waiter, beckoning them away from the privileged *salle-à-manger*, sang out, " This way, my good men," and then enticed these good men away to the kitchen. But that plan had not always answered. Sometimes, though rarely, cases occurred where the intruders, being stronger than usual, or more vicious than usual, resolutely refused to budge, and so far carried their point, as to have a separate table arranged for themselves in a corner of the general room. Yet, if an Indian screen could be found ample enough to plant them out from the very eyes of the high table, or *dais*, it then became possible to assume as a fiction of law—that the three delf fellows, after all, were not present. They could be ignored by the porcelain men, under the maxim, that objects not appearing, and not existing, are governed by the same logical construction.

Such being, at that time, the usages of mail-coaches, what was to be done by us of young Oxford ? We, the most aristocratic of people, who were addicted to the practice of looking down superciliously even upon the insides themselves as often very questionable characters —were we, by voluntarily going outside, to court indignities ? If our dress and bearing sheltered us, generally, from the suspicion of being " raff " (the name at that period for " snobs "), we really *were* such constructively, by the place we assumed. If we did not submit to the deep shadow of eclipse, we entered at least the skirts of its penumbra. And the analogy of theatres was valid against us, where no man can complain of the annoyances incident to the pit or gallery, having his instant remedy in paying the higher price of the boxes. But the soundness of this analogy we disputed. In the case of the theatre, it cannot be pretended that the inferior situations have any separate attractions, unless the pit may be supposed to have an advantage for the purposes of the critic or the dramatic reporter. But the critic or reporter is a rarity. For most people, the sole benefit is in the price. Now, on the contrary, the outside of the mail had its own incommunicable advantages. These we could not forego. The higher price we would willingly have paid, but not the price connected with the condition of riding inside ; which condition we pronounced insufferable. The air, the freedom of prospect, the proximity to the horses, the elevation of seat—these were what we required ; but, above all, the certain anticipation of purchasing occasional opportunities of driving.

Such was the difficulty which pressed us ; and under the coercion of this difficulty, we instituted a searching inquiry into the true quality and valuation of the different apartments about the mail. We conducted this inquiry on metaphysical principles ; and it was ascertained satisfactorily, that the roof of the coach, which by some weak men had been called the attics, and by some the garrets, was in reality the drawing-room ; in which drawing-room the box was the chief ottoman or sofa ; whilst it appeared that the *inside*, which had been traditionally regarded as the only room tenantable by gentlemen, was, in fact, the coal-cellar in disguise.

Great wits jump. The very same idea had not long before struck the celestial intellect of China. Amongst the presents carried out by our first embassy to that country was a state-coach. It had been specially selected as a personal gift by George III. ; but the exact mode of using it was an intense mystery to Pekin. The ambassador, indeed (Lord Macartney), had made some imperfect explanations upon this point ; but, as his excellency communicated these in a diplomatic whisper, at the very moment of his departure, the celestial intellect was very feebly illuminated, and it became necessary to call a cabinet council on the grand state question, " Where was the emperor to sit ? " The hammer-cloth happened to be unusually gorgeous ; and partly on that consideration, but partly also because the box offered the most elevated seat, was nearest to the moon, and undeniably went foremost, it was resolved by acclamation that the box was the imperial throne, and for the scoundrel who drove, he might sit where he could find a perch. The horses, therefore, being harnessed, solemnly his imperial majesty ascended his new English throne under a flourish of trumpets, having the first lord of the treasury on his right hand, and the chief jester on his left. Pekin gloried in the spectacle ; and in the whole flowery people, constructively present by representation, there was but one discontented person, and *that* was the coachman. This mutinous individual audaciously shouted, " Where am *I* to sit ? " But the privy council, incensed by his disloyalty, unanimously opened the door, and kicked him into the inside. He had all the inside places to himself, but such is the rapacity of ambition, that he was still dissatisfied. " I say," he cried out in an extempore petition, addressed to the emperor through the window— " I say, how am I to catch hold of the reins ? "—" Anyhow," was the imperial answer ; " don't trouble *me*, man, in my glory. How catch the reins ? Why, through the windows, through the keyholes—*any*how." Finally this contumacious coachman lengthened the check-strings into a sort of jury-reins, communicating with the horses ; with these he drove as steadily as Pekin had any right to expect. The emperor returned after the briefest of circuits ; he descended in great pomp from his throne, with the severest resolution never to remount it. A public thanksgiving was ordered for his majesty's happy escape from the disease of broken neck ; and the state-coach was dedicated thenceforward as a votive offering to the god Fo, Fo—whom the learned more accurately called Fi, Fi.

A revolution of this same Chinese character did young Oxford of that era effect in the constitution of mail-coach society. It was a perfect French revolution ; and we had good reason to say, *Ça ira*. In fact, it soon became *too* popular. The " public "—a well-known character, particularly disagreeable, though slightly respectable, and notorious for affecting the chief seats in synagogues—had at first loudly opposed this revolution ; but when the opposition showed itself to be ineffectual, our disagreeable friend went into it with headlong zeal. At first it was a sort of race between us ; and, as the public is usually from thirty to fifty years old, naturally we of young Oxford, that averaged about twenty, had the advantage. Then the public took to bribing, giving fees to horse-keepers, etc., who hired out their persons as warming-pans on the box-seat. *That*, you know, was shocking to all moral sensibilities. Come to bribery, said we, and there is an end to all morality, Aristotle's, Zeno's, Cicero's, or anybody's. And, besides, of what use was it ? For *we* bribed also. And as our bribes to those of the public were as five shillings to sixpence, here again young Oxford had the advantage. But the contest was ruinous to the principles of the stables connected with the mails. This whole corporation was constantly bribed, rebribed, and often sur-rebribed ; a mail-coach yard was like the hustings in a contested election ; and a horse-keeper, ostler, **or** helper, was held by the philosophical at that time to be the most corrupt character in the nation.

There was an impression upon the public mind, natural enough from the continually augmenting velocity of the mail, but quite erroneous, that an outside seat on this class of carriages was a post of danger. On the contrary, I maintained that, if a man had become nervous from some gipsy prediction in his childhood, allocating to a particular moon now approaching some unknown danger, and he should inquire earnestly, " Whither can I fly for shelter ? Is a prison the safest retreat ? or a lunatic hospital ? or the British Museum ? " I should have replied, " Oh, no ; I'll tell you what to do. Take lodgings for the next forty days on the box of his majesty's mail. Nobody can touch you there. If it is by bills at ninety days after date that you are made unhappy—if noters and protesters are the sort of wretches whose astrological shadows darken the house of life—then note you what I vehemently protest—viz., that no matter though the sheriff and under-sheriff in every county should be running after you with his *posse*, touch a hair of your head he cannot whilst you keep house, and have your legal domicile on the box of the mail. It is felony to stop the mail ; even the sheriff cannot do that. And an *extra* touch of the whip to the leaders (no great matter if it grazes the sheriff) at any time guarantees your safety." In fact, a bedroom in a quiet house seems a safe enough retreat, yet it is liable to its own notorious nuisances —to robbers by night, to rats, to fire. But the mail laughs at these terrors. To robbers, the answer is packed up and ready for delivery in the barrel of the guard's blunderbuss. Rats again !—there *are* none about mail-coaches, any more than snakes in Von Troil's Iceland ; except, indeed, now and then a parliamentary rat, who always hides his shame in what I have shown to be the " coal-cellar." And as to fire, I never knew but one in a mail-coach, which was in the Exeter mail, and caused by an obstinate sailor bound to

Devonport. Jack, making light of the law and the law-giver that had set their faces against his offence, insisted on taking up a forbidden seat in the rear of the roof, from which he could exchange his own yarns with those of the guard. No greater offence was then known to mail-coaches ; it was treason, it was *læsa majestas*, it was by tendency arson ; and the ashes of Jack's pipe, falling amongst the straw of the hinder boot containing the mail-bags, raised a flame which (aided by the wind of our motion) threatened a revolution in the republic of letters. Yet even this left the sanctity of the box unviolated. In dignified repose, the coachman and myself sat on, resting with benign composure upon our knowledge that the fire would have to burn its way through four inside passengers before it could reach ourselves. I remarked to the coachman, with a quotation from Virgil's "Æneid" really too hackneyed—

> "Jam proximus ardet
> Ucalegon."

But, recollecting that the Virgilian part of the coachman's education might have been neglected, I interpreted so far as to say, that perhaps at that moment the flames were catching hold of our worthy brother and inside passenger, Ucalegon. The coachman made no answer, which is my own way when a stranger addresses me either in Syriac or in Coptic, but by his faint sceptical smile he seemed to in-sinuate that he knew better ; for that Ucalegon, as it happened, was not in the way-bill, and therefore could not have been booked.

No dignity is perfect which does not at some point ally itself with the mysterious. The connexion of the mail with the state and the executive government—a connexion obvious, but yet not strictly defined—gave to the whole mail establishment an official grandeur which did us service on the roads, and invested us with seasonable terrors. Not the less impressive were those terrors, because their legal limits were imperfectly ascertained. Look at those turnpike gates ; with what deferential hurry, with what an obedient start, they fly open at our approach ! Look at that long line of carts and carters ahead, audaciously usurping the very crest of the road. Ah ! traitors, they do not hear us as yet ; but, as soon as the dreadful blast of our horn reaches them with proclamation of our approach, see with what frenzy of trepidation they fly to their horses' heads, and deprecate our wrath by the precipitation of their crane-neck quarterings. Treason they feel to be their crime ; each individual carter feels himself under the ban of confiscation and attainder ; his blood is attainted through six generations ; and nothing is wanting but the headsman and his axe, the block and the saw-dust, to close up the vista of his horrors. What ! shall it be within benefit of clergy to delay the king's message on the high road ?—to interrupt the great respirations, ebb and flood, *systole* and *diastole*, of the national intercourse ?— to endanger the safety of tidings, running day and night between all nations and languages ? Or can it be fancied, amongst the weakest of men, that the bodies of the criminals will be given up to their widows for Christian burial ? Now the doubts which were raised as to our powers did more to wrap them in terror, by wrapping them in uncertainty, than could have been effected by the sharpest definitions of the law from the Quarter Sessions. We, on our parts (we, the collective mail, I mean), did our utmost to exalt the idea of our privileges by the insolence with which we wielded them. Whether this insolence rested upon law that gave it a sanction, or upon conscious power that haughtily dispensed with that sanction, equally it spoke from a potential station ; and the agent, in each particular insolence of the moment, was viewed reverentially, as one having authority.

Sometimes after breakfast his majesty's mail would become frisky ; and in its difficult wheelings amongst the intricacies of early markets, it would upset an apple-cart, a cart loaded with eggs, etc. Huge was the affliction and dismay, awful was the smash. I, as far as possible, endeavoured in such a case to represent the conscience and moral sensibilities of the mail ; and, when wildernesses of eggs were lying poached under our horses' hoofs, then would I stretch forth my hands in sorrow, saying (in words too celebrated at that time, from the false echoes of Marengo), " Ah ! wherefore have we not time to weep over you ? " which was evidently impossible, since, in fact, we had not time to laugh over them. Tied to post-office allowance, in some cases of fifty minutes for eleven miles, could the royal mail pretend to undertake the offices of sympathy and condolence ? Could it be expected to provide tears for the accidents of the road ? If even it seemed to trample on humanity, it did so, I felt, in discharge of its own more peremptory duties.

Upholding the morality of the mail, *à fortiori* I upheld its rights ; as a matter of duty, I stretched to the uttermost its privilege of imperial precedency, and astonished weak minds by the feudal powers which I hinted to be lurking constructively in the charters of this proud establishment. Once I remember being on the box of the Holyhead mail, between Shrewsbury and Oswestry, when a tawdry thing from Birmingham, some " Tallyho " or " Highflyer," all flaunting with green and gold, came up alongside of us. What a contrast to our royal simplicity of form and colour in this plebeian wretch ! The single ornament on our dark ground of chocolate colour was the mighty shield of the imperial arms, but emblazoned in proportions as modest as a signet-ring bears to a seal of office. Even this was displayed only on a single panel, whispering, rather than proclaiming, our relations to the mighty state ; whilst the beast from Birmingham, our green-and-gold friend from false, fleeting, perjured Brummagem, had as much writing and painting on its sprawling flanks as would have puzzled a decipherer from the tombs of Luxor. For some time this Birmingham machine ran along by our side—a piece of familiarity that already of itself seemed to me sufficiently jacobinical. But all at once a movement of the horses announced a desperate intention of leaving us behind. " Do you see *that* ? " I said to the coachman.— " I see," was his short answer. He was wide awake, yet he waited longer than seemed prudent ; for the horses of our audacious opponent had a disagreeable air of freshness and power. But his motive was loyal ; his wish was, that the Birmingham conceit should be full-blown before he froze it. When *that* seemed right, he unloosed, or, to speak by a stronger word, he *sprang*, his known resources : he slipped our royal horses like cheetahs, or hunting-leopards, after the affrighted game. How they could retain such a reserve of fiery power after the work they had accomplished, seemed hard to explain. But on our side, besides the physical superiority, was a tower of moral strength, namely, the king's name, " which they upon the adverse faction wanted." Passing them without an effort, as it seemed, we threw them into the rear with so lengthening an interval between us, as proved in itself the bitterest mockery of their presumption ; whilst our guard blew back a shattering blast of triumph, that was really too painfully full of derision.

I mention this little incident for its connection with what followed. A Welsh rustic, sitting behind me, asked if I had not felt my heart burn within me during the progress of the race ? I said, with philosophic calmness, *No* ; because we were not racing with a mail, so that no glory could be gained. In fact, it was sufficiently mortifying that such a Birmingham thing should dare to challenge us. The Welshman replied, that he didn't see *that* ; for that a cat might look at a king, and a Brummagem coach might lawfully race the Holyhead mail. " *Race* us, if you like," I replied, " though even *that* has an air of sedition, but not *beat* us. This would have been treason ; and for its own sake I am glad that the ' Tallyho ' was disappointed." So dissatisfied did the Welshman seem with this opinion, that at last I was obliged to tell him a very fine story from one of our elder dramatists—viz., that once, in some far oriental kingdom, when the sultan of all the land, with his princes, ladies, and chief omrahs, were flying their falcons, a hawk suddenly flew at a majestic eagle ; and in defiance of the eagle's natural advantages, in contempt also of the eagle's traditional royalty, and before the whole assembled field of astonished spectators from Agra and Lahore, killed the eagle on the spot. Amazement seized the sultan at the unequal contest, and burning admiration for its unparalleled result. He commanded that the hawk should be brought before him ; he caressed the bird with enthusiasm ; and he ordered that, for the commemoration of his matchless courage, a diadem of gold and rubies should be solemnly placed on the hawk's head ; but then that, immediately after this solemn coronation, the bird should be led off to execution, as the most valiant indeed of traitors, but not the less a traitor, as having dared to rise rebelliously against his liege lord and anointed sovereign, the eagle. "Now," said I to the Welshman, " to you and me, as men of refined sensibilities, how painful it would have been that this poor Brummagem brute, the ' Tallyho,' in the impossible case of a victory over us, should have been crowned with Birmingham tinsel, with paste diamonds, and Roman pearls, and then led off to instant execution." The Welshman doubted if that could be warranted by law. And when I hinted at the 6th of Edward Longshanks, chap. 18, for regulating the precedency of coaches, as being probably the statute relied on for the capital punishment of such offences, he replied drily, that if the attempt to pass a mail really were treasonable, it was a pity that the "Tallyho" appeared to have so imperfect an acquaintance with law.

The modern modes of travelling cannot compare with the old mail-coach system in grandeur and power. They boast of more velocity, not, however, as a consciousness, but as a fact of our lifeless knowledge, resting upon *alien* evidence ; as, for instance, because somebody *says* that we have gone fifty miles in the hour, though we are far from feeling it as a personal experience, or upon the evidence of a result, as that actually we find ourselves in York four hours after leaving London. Apart from such an assertion, or such a result, I myself am little aware of the pace. But, seated on the old mail-coach, we needed no evidence out of ourselves to indicate the velocity. On this system the word was, *Non magna loquimur*, as upon railways, but *vivimus*. Yes, "magna *vivimus*" ; we do not make verbal ostentation of our grandeurs, we realize our grandeurs in act, and in the very experience of life. The vital experience of the glad animal sensibilities made doubts impossible on the question of our speed ; we heard our speed, we saw it, we felt it as a thrilling ; and this speed was not the product of blind insensate agencies, that had no sympathy to give, but was incarnated in the fiery eyeballs of the noblest amongst brutes, in his dilated nostril, spasmodic muscles, and thunder-beating hoofs. The sensibility of the horse, uttering itself in the maniac light of his eye, might be the last vibration of such a movement ; the glory of Salamanca might be the first. But the intervening links that connected them, that spread the earthquake of battle into the eyeball of the horse, were the heart of man and its electric thrillings—kindling in the rapture of the fiery strife, and then propagating its own tumults by contagious shouts and gestures to the heart of his servant the horse.

But now, on the new system of travelling, iron tubes and boilers have disconnected man's heart from the ministers of his locomotion. Nile nor Trafalgar has power to raise an extra bubble in a steam-kettle. The galvanic cycle is broken up for ever ; man's imperial nature no longer sends itself forward through the electric sensibility of the horse ; the inter-agencies are gone in the mode of communication between the horse and his master, out of which grew so many aspects of sublimity under accidents of mists that hid, or sudden blazes that revealed, of mobs that agitated, or midnight solitudes that awed. Tidings, fitted to convulse all nations, must henceforwards travel by culinary process ; and the trumpet that once announced from afar the laurelled mail, heart-shaking, when heard screaming on the wind, and proclaiming itself through the darkness to every village or solitary house on it route, has now given way for ever to the pot-wallopings of the boiler.

Thus have perished multiform openings for public expressions of interest, scenical yet natural, in great national tidings ; for revelations of faces and groups that could not offer themselves amongst the fluctuating mobs of a railway station. The gatherings of gazers about a laurelled mail had one centre, and acknowledged one sole interest. But the crowds attending at a railway station have as little unity as running water, and own as many centres as there are separate carriages in the train.

How else, for example, than as a constant watcher for the dawn, and for the London mail that in summer months entered about daybreak amongst the lawny thickets of Marlborough forest, couldst thou, sweet Fanny of the Bath road, have become the glorified inmate of my dreams ? Yet Fanny, as the loveliest young woman for face and person that perhaps in my whole life I have beheld, merited the station which even now, from a distance of forty years, she holds in my dreams ; yes, though by links of natural association she brings along with her a troop of dreadful creatures, fabulous and not fabulous, that are more

abominable to the heart, than Fanny and the dawn are
delightful.

Miss Fanny of the Bath road, strictly speaking, lived
at a mile's distance from that road ; but came so continually
to meet the mail, that I on my frequent transits rarely
missed her, and naturally connected her image with the
great thoroughfare where only I had ever seen her. Why
she came so punctually, I do not exactly know ; but I
believe with some burden of commissions to be executed
in Bath, which had gathered to her own residence as a
central rendezvous for converging them. The mail-
coachman who drove the Bath mail, and wore the royal
livery, happened to be Fanny's grandfather. A good man
he was, that loved his beautiful granddaughter ; and, loving
her wisely, was vigilant over her deportment in any case
where young Oxford might happen to be concerned. Did
my vanity then suggest that I myself, individually, could
fall within the line of his terrors ? Certainly not, as regarded any physical pretensions that I could plead ; for
Fanny (as a chance passenger from her own neighbourhood
once told me) counted in her train a hundred and ninety-
nine professed admirers, if not open aspirants to her
favour ; and probably not one of the whole brigade but
excelled myself in personal advantages. Ulysses even,
with the unfair advantage of his accursed bow, could hardly
have undertaken that amount of suitors. So the danger
might have seemed slight—only that woman is universally
aristocratic ; it is amongst her nobilities of heart that she
is so. Now, the aristocratic distinctions in my favour
might easily with Miss Fanny have compensated my
physical deficiencies. Did I then make love to Fanny ?
Why, yes ; about as much love as one *could* make whilst
the mail was changing horses—a process which, ten years
later, did not occupy above eighty seconds ; but *then*—
viz., about Waterloo—it occupied five times eighty. Now,
four hundred seconds offer a field quite ample enough for

whispering into a young woman's ear a great deal of truth, and (by way of parenthesis) some trifle of falsehood. Grandpapa did right, therefore, to watch me. And yet, as happens too often to the grandpapas of earth, in a contest with the admirers of granddaughters, how vainly would he have watched me had I meditated any evil whispers to Fanny ! She, it is my belief, would have protected herself against any man's evil suggestions. But he, as the result showed, could not have intercepted the opportunities for such suggestions. Yet, why not ? Was he not active ? Was he not blooming ? Blooming he was as Fanny herself.

" Say, all our praises why should lords——"

Stop, that's not the line.

" Say, all our roses why should girls engross ? "

The coachman showed rosy blossoms on his face deeper even than his granddaughter's—*his* being drawn from the ale-cask, Fanny's from the fountains of the dawn. But, in spite of his blooming face, some infirmities he had ; and one particularly in which he too much resembled a croco-dile. This lay in a monstrous inaptitude for turning round. The crocodile, I presume, owes that inaptitude to the absurd *length* of his back ; but in our grandpapa it arose rather from the absurd *breadth* of his back, combined, possibly, with some growing stiffness in his legs. Now, upon this crocodile infirmity of his I planted a human advantage for tendering my homage to Miss Fanny. In defiance of all his honourable vigilance, no sooner had he presented to us his mighty Jovian back (what a field for displaying to mankind his royal scarlet !), whilst inspecting professionally the buckles, the straps, and the silvery turrets of his harness, than I raised Miss Fanny's hand to my lips, and, by the mixed tenderness and respectfulness of my manner, caused her easily to understand how happy it would make me to rank upon her list as No. 10 or 12, in which case a few casualties amongst her lovers (and observe, they *hanged* liberally in those days) might have promoted me speedily to the top of the tree ; as, on the other hand, with how much loyalty of submission I acquiesced by anticipation in her award, supposing that she should plant me in the very rearward of her favour, as No. 199+1. Most truly I loved this beautiful and ingenuous girl ; and had it not been for the Bath mail, timing all courtships by post-office allowance, heaven only knows what might have come of it. People talk of being over head and ears in love ; now, the mail was the cause that I sank only over ears in love, which, you know, still left a trifle of brain to overlook the whole conduct of the affair.

Ah, reader ! when I look back upon those days, it seems to me that all things change—all things perish. " Perish the roses and the palms of kings " : perish even the crowns and trophies of Waterloo : thunder and lightning are not the thunder and lightning which I remember. Roses are degenerating. The Fannies of our island—though this I say with reluctance—are not visibly improving ; and the Bath road is notoriously superannuated. Crocodiles, you will say, are stationary. Mr. Waterton tells me that the crocodile does *not* change ; that a cayman, in fact, or an alligator, is just as good for riding upon as he was in the time of the Pharaohs. *That* may be ; but the reason is, that the crocodile does not live fast—he is a slow coach. I believe it is generally understood among naturalists, that the crocodile is a blockhead. It is my own impression that the Pharaohs were also blockheads. Now, as the Pharaohs and the crocodile domineered over Egyptian society, this accounts for a singular mistake that prevailed through innumerable generations on the Nile. The crocodile made the ridiculous blunder of supposing man to be meant chiefly for his own eating. Man, taking a different view of the subject, naturally met that mistake by another : he viewed the crocodile as a thing sometimes to worship, but always to run away from. And this continued until Mr. Waterton changed the relations between the animals. The mode of escaping from the reptile he showed to be, not by running away, but by leaping on its back, booted and spurred. The two animals had misunderstood each other. The use of the crocodile has now been cleared up—viz., to be ridden ; and the final cause of man is, that he may improve the health of the crocodile by riding him afoxhunting before breakfast. And it is pretty certain that any crocodile, who has been regularly hunted through the season, and is master of the weight he carries, will take a six-barred gate now as well as ever he would have done in the infancy of the pyramids.

If, therefore, the crocodile does *not* change, all things else undeniably *do* : even the shadow of the pyramids grows less. And often the restoration in vision of Fanny and the Bath road, makes me too pathetically sensible of that truth. Out of the darkness, if I happen to call back the image of Fanny, up rises suddenly from a gulf of forty years a rose in June ; or, if I think for an instant of the rose in June, up rises the heavenly face of Fanny. One after the other, like the antiphonies in the choral service, rise Fanny and the rose in June, then back again the rose in June and Fanny. Then come both together, as in a chorus—roses and Fannies, Fannies and roses, without end, thick as blossoms in paradise. Then comes a venerable crocodile, in a royal livery of scarlet and gold, with sixteen capes ; and the crocodile is driving four-in-hand from the box of the Bath mail. And suddenly we upon the mail are pulled up by a mighty dial, sculptured with the hours, that mingle with the heavens and the heavenly host. Then all at once we are arrived at Marlborough forest, amongst the lovely households of the roe-deer ; the deer and their fawns retire into the dewy thickets ; the thickets are rich with roses ; once again the roses call up the sweet countenance of Fanny ; and she, being the granddaughter of a crocodile, awakens a dreadful host of semi-legendary animals—griffins, dragons, basilisks, sphinxes—till at length the whole vision of fighting images crowds into one towering armorial shield, a vast emblazonry of human charities and human loveliness that have perished, but quartered heraldically with unutterable and demoniac natures, whilst over all rises, as a surmounting crest, one fair female hand, with the forefinger pointing, in sweet, sorrowful admonition, upwards to heaven, where is sculptured the eternal writing which proclaims the frailty of earth and her children.

The English Mail-Coach. 1849.

ON THE KNOCKING AT THE GATE IN
" MACBETH "

Thomas De Quincey

From my boyish days I had always felt a great perplexity on one point in *Macbeth* : it was this : the knocking at the gate, which succeeds to the murder of Duncan, produced to my feelings an effect for which I never could account : the effect was—that it reflected back upon the murder a peculiar awfulness and a depth of solemnity : yet, however obstinately I endeavoured with my understanding to comprehend this, for many years I never could see *why* it should produce such an effect.——

Here I pause for one moment to exhort the reader never to pay any attention to his understanding when it stands in opposition to any other faculty of his mind. The mere understanding, however useful and indispensable, is the meanest faculty in the human mind and the most to be distrusted : and yet the great majority of people trust to nothing else ; which may do for ordinary life, but not for philosophic purposes. Of this, out of ten thousand instances that I might produce, I will cite one. Ask of any person whatsoever, who is not previously prepared for the demand by a knowledge of perspective, to draw in the rudest way the commonest appearance which depends upon the laws of that science—as for instance, to represent the effect of two walls standing at right angles to each other, or the appearance of the houses on each side of a street, as seen by a person looking down the street from one extremity. Now in all cases, unless the person has happened to observe in pictures how it is that artists produce these effects, he will be utterly unable to make the smallest approximation to it. Yet why ?—For he has actually seen the effect every day of his life. The reason is—that he allows his understanding to overrule his eyes. His understanding, which includes no intuitive knowledge of the laws of vision, can furnish him with no reason why a line which is known and can be proved to be a horizontal line, should not *appear* a horizontal line : a line, that made any angle with the perpendicular less than a right angle, would seem to him to indicate that his houses were all tumbling down together. Accordingly he makes the line of his houses a horizontal line, and fails of course to produce the effect demanded. Here then is one instance out of many, in which not only the understanding is allowed to overrule the eyes, but where the understanding is positively allowed to obliterate the eyes as it were : for not only does the man believe the evidence of his understanding in opposition to that of his eyes, but (which is monstrous !) the idiot is not aware that his eyes ever gave such evidence. He does not know that he has seen (and therefore *quoad* his consciousness has *not* seen) that which he *has* seen every day of his life. But to return from this digression,—my understanding could furnish no reason why the knocking at the gate in *Macbeth* should produce any effect direct or reflected : in fact, my understanding said positively that it could *not* produce any effect. But I knew better : I felt that it did : and I waited and clung to the problem until further knowledge should enable me to solve it.—At length, in 1812, Mr. Williams made his *debut* on the stage of Ratcliffe Highway, and executed those unparalleled murders which have procured for him such a brilliant and undying reputation. On which murders, by the way, I must observe, that in one

respect they have had an ill effect, by making the con-
noisseur in murder very fastidious in his taste, and dissatisfied with any thing that has been since done in that
line. All other murders look pale by the deep crimson
of his : and, as an amateur once said to me in a querulous
tone, " There has been absolutely nothing *doing* since his
time, or nothing that's worth speaking of." But this is
wrong : for it is unreasonable to expect all men to be great
artists, and born with the genius of Mr. Williams.—Now
it will be remembered that in the first of these murders
(that of the Marrs) the same incident (of a knocking at
the door soon after the work of extermination was complete) did actually occur which the genius of Shakspeare
had invented : and all good judges and the most eminent
dilettanti acknowledged the felicity of Shakspeare's suggestion as soon as it was actually realized. Here then
was a fresh proof that I had been right in relying on my
own feeling in opposition to my understanding ; and again
I set myself to study the problem : at length I solved it
to my own satisfaction ; and my solution is this. Murder
in ordinary cases, where the sympathy is wholly directed
to the case of the murdered person, is an incident of coarse
and vulgar horror ; and for this reason—that it flings the
interest exclusively upon the natural but ignoble instinct
by which we cleave to life ; an instinct which, as being
indispensable to the primal law of self-preservation, is the
same in kind (though different in degree) amongst all
living creatures ; this instinct therefore, because it annihi-
lates all distinctions, and degrades the greatest of men to
the level of " the poor beetle that we tread on," exhibits
human nature in its most abject and humiliating attitude.
Such an attitude would little suit the purposes of the
poet. What then must he do ? He must throw the interest on the murderer : our sympathy must be with *him* ;
(of course I mean a sympathy of comprehension, a sympathy by which we enter into his feelings, and are made

to understand them,—not a sympathy [1] of pity or approbation :) in the murdered person all strife of thought, all
flux and reflux of passion and of purpose, are crushed by
one overwhelming panic : the fear of instant death smites
him " with its petrific mace." But in the murderer, such
a murderer as a poet will condescend to, there must be
raging some great storm of passion,—jealousy, ambition,
vengeance, hatred,—which will create a hell within him ;
and into this hell we are to look. In *Macbeth*, for the
sake of gratifying his own enormous and teeming faculty
of creation, Shakspeare has introduced two murderers :
and, as usual in his hands, they are remarkably discriminated : but though in Macbeth the strife of mind is greater
than in his wife, the tiger spirit not so awake, and his
feelings caught chiefly by contagion from her,—yet, as
both were finally involved in the guilt of murder, the
murderous mind of necessity is finally to be presumed in
both. This was to be expressed ; and on its own account,
as well as to make it a more proportionable antagonist
to the unoffending nature of their victim, " the gracious
Duncan," and adequately to expound " the deep damnation
of his taking off," this was to be expressed with peculiar
energy. We were to be made to feel that the human
nature, *i.e.* the divine nature of love and mercy, spread
through the hearts of all creatures, and seldom utterly
withdrawn from man,—was gone, vanished, extinct ; and
that the fiendish nature had taken its place. And, as this
effect is marvellously accomplished in the dialogues and

---

[1] It seems almost ludicrous to guard and explain my use of a word
in a situation where it should naturally explain itself. But it has
become necessary to do so, in consequence of the unscholarlike
use of the word sympathy, at present so general, by which, instead
of taking it in its proper use, as the act of reproducing in our minds
the feelings of another, whether for hatred, indignation, love, pity,
or approbation, it is made a mere synonym of the word *pity* ; and
hence, instead of saying, " sympathy *with* another," many writers
adopt the monstrous barbarism of " sympathy *for* another."

soliloquies themselves, so it is finally consummated by the expedient under consideration ; and it is to this that I now solicit the reader's attention. If the reader has ever witnessed a wife, daughter, or sister, in a fainting fit, he may chance to have observed that the most affecting moment in such a spectacle, is *that* in which a sigh and a stirring announce the recommencement of suspended life. Or, if the reader has ever been present in a vast metropolis on the day when some great national idol was carried in funeral pomp to his grave, and chancing to walk near to the course through which it passed, has felt powerfully in the silence and desertion of the streets and in the stagnation of ordinary business, the deep interest which at that moment was possessing the heart of man, —if all at once he should hear the death-like stillness broken up by the sound of wheels rattling away from the scene, and making known that the transitory vision was dissolved, he will be aware that at no moment was his sense of the complete suspension and pause in ordinary human concerns so full and affecting as at that moment when the suspension ceases, and the goings-on of human life are suddenly resumed. All action in any direction is best expounded, measured, and made apprehensible, by reaction. Now apply this to the case in *Macbeth*. Here, as I have said, the retiring of the human heart and the entrance of the fiendish heart was to be expressed and made sensible. Another world has stepped in ; and the murderers are taken out of the region of human things, human purposes, human desires. They are transfigured : Lady Macbeth is " unsexed " ; Macbeth has forgot that he was born of woman ; both are conformed to the image of devils ; and the world of devils is suddenly revealed. But how shall this be conveyed and made palpable ? In order that a new world may step in, this world must for a time disappear. The murderers, and the murder, must be insulated—cut off by an immeasurable gulf from the ordinary tide and succession of human affairs—locked up and sequestered in some deep recess : we must be made sensible that the world of ordinary life is suddenly arrested —laid asleep—tranced—racked into a dread armistice : time must be annihilated ; relation to things without abolished ; and all must pass self-withdrawn into a deep syncope and suspension of earthly passion. Hence it is that when the deed is done—when the work of darkness is perfect, then the world of darkness passes away like a pageantry in the clouds : the knocking at the gate is heard ; and it makes known audibly that the reaction has commenced : the human has made its reflux upon the fiendish : the pulses of life are beginning to beat again : and the re-establishment of the goings-on of the world in which we live, first makes us profoundly sensible of the awful parenthesis that had suspended them.

Oh ! mighty poet !—Thy works are not as those of other men, simply and merely great works of art ; but are also like the phenomena of nature, like the sun and the sea, the stars and the flowers,—like frost and snow, rain and dew, hail-storm and thunder, which are to be studied with entire submission of our own faculties, and in the perfect faith that in them there can be no too much or too little, nothing useless or inert—but that, the further we press in our discoveries, the more we shall see proofs of design and self-supporting arrangement where the care-less eye had seen nothing but accident !

N.B. In the above specimen of psychological criticism, I have purposely omitted to notice another use of the knocking at the gate, viz. the opposition and contrast which it produces in the porter's comments to the scenes immediately preceding ; because this use is tolerably obvious to all who are accustomed to reflect on what they read.

Collected Essays. 1853.

SAVANNAH-LA-MAR

Thomas De Quincey

GOD smote Savannah-la-mar, and in one night, by earth-quake, removed her, with all her towers standing and population sleeping, from the steadfast foundations of the shore to the coral floors of ocean. And God said,—
"Pompeii did I bury and conceal from men through seventeen centuries : this city I will bury, but not conceal. She shall be a monument to men of my mysterious anger, set in azure light through generations to come ; for I will enshrine her in a crystal dome of my tropic seas." This city, therefore, like a mighty galleon with all her apparel mounted, streamers flying, and tackling perfect, seems floating along the noiseless depths of ocean ; and often-times in glassy calms, through the translucid atmosphere of water that now stretches like an air-woven awning above the silent encampment, mariners from every clime look down into her courts, and terraces, count her gates, and number the spires of her churches. She is one ample cemetery, and *has* been for many a year ; but, in the mighty calms that brood for weeks over tropic latitudes, she fascinates the eye with a *Fata-Morgana* revelation, as of human life still subsisting in submarine asylums sacred from the storms that torment our upper air.

Thither, lured by the loveliness of cerulean depths, by the peace of human dwellings privileged from molestation, by the gleam of marble altars sleeping in everlasting sanctity, oftentimes in dreams did I and the Dark Interpreter cleave

the watery veil that divided us from her streets.   We looked
into the belfries, where the pendulous bells were waiting
in vain for the summons which should.awaken their marriage peals ; together we touched the mighty organ-keys,
that sang no *jubilates* for the ear of heaven, that sang no
requiems for the ear of human sorrow ; together we
searched the silent nurseries, where the children were all
asleep, and *had* been asleep through five generations.
" They are waiting for the heavenly dawn," whispered
the Interpreter to himself : " and, when *that* comes, the
bells and the organs will utter a *jubilate* repeated by the
echoes of Paradise."   Then, turning to me, he said,—
" This is sad, this is piteous ; but less would not have
sufficed for the purpose of God.   Look here.   Put into a
Roman clepsydra one hundred drops of water ; let these
run out as the sands in an hour-glass, every drop measuring
the hundredth part of a second, so that each shall represent
but the three-hundred-and-sixty-thousandth part of an
hour.   Now, count the drops as they race along ; and,
when the fiftieth of the hundred is passing, behold !
forty-nine are not, because already they have perished,
and fifty are not, because they are yet to come.   You see,
therefore, how narrow, how incalculably narrow, is the
true and actual present.   Of that time which we call the
present, hardly a hundredth part but belongs either to a
past which has fled, or to a future which is still on the wing.
It has perished, or it is not born.   It was, or it is not.   Yet
even this approximation to the truth, is *infinitely* false.
For again subdivide that solitary drop, which only was
found to represent the present, into a lower series of similar
fractions, and the actual present which you arrest measures
now but the thirty-six-millionth of an hour ; and so by
infinite declensions the true and very present, in which
only we live and enjoy, will vanish into a mote of a mote,
distinguishable only by a heavenly vision.   Therefore the
present, which only man possesses, offers less capacity

for his footing than the slenderest film that ever spider twisted from her womb. Therefore, also, even this incalculable shadow from the narrowest pencil of moonlight is more transitory than geometry can measure, or thought of angel can overtake. The time which *is* contracts into a mathematic point ; and even that point perishes a thousand times before we can utter its birth. All is finite in the present ; and even that finite is infinite in its velocity of flight towards death. But in God there is nothing finite ; but in God there is nothing transitory ; but in God there *can* be nothing that tends to death. Therefore it follows that for God there can be no present. The future is the present of God, and to the future it is that He sacrifices the human present. Therefore it is that He works by earthquake. Therefore it is that He works by grief. O, deep is the ploughing of earthquake ! O, deep ”—(and His voice swelled like a *sanctus* rising from the choir of a cathedral)— “ O, deep is the ploughing of grief ! But oftentimes less would not suffice for the agriculture of God. Upon a night of earthquake He builds a thousand years of pleasant habitations for man. Upon the sorrow of an infant He raises oftentimes from human intellect glorious vintages that could not else have been. Less than these fierce ploughshares would not have stirred the stubborn soil. The one is needed for Earth, our planet,—for Earth itself as the dwelling-place of man ; but the other is needed yet oftener for God’s mightiest instrument,—yes ” (and He looked solemnly at myself), “ is needed for the mysterious children of the Earth ! ”

Suspiria de Profundis. 1845.

ON THE WRITING OF ESSAYS

Alexander Smith

. . . Love in a cottage, with a broken window to let in
the rain, is not my idea of comfort ; no more is Dignity,
walking forth richly clad, to whom every head uncovers,
every knee grows supple. Bruin in winter-time fondly
sucking his own paws, loses flesh ; and love, feeding upon
itself, dies of inanition. Take the candle of death in your
hand, and walk through the stately galleries of the world,
and their splendid furniture and array are as the tinsel
armour and pasteboard goblets of a penny theatre ; fame
is but an inscription on a grave, and glory the melancholy
blazon on a coffin lid. We argue fiercely about happiness.
One insists that she is found in the cottage which the
hawthorn shades. Another that she is a lady of fashion,
and treads on cloth of gold. Wisdom, listening to both,
shakes a white head, and considers that " a good deal
may be said on both sides."

There is a wise saying to the effect that " a man can eat
no more than he can hold." Every man gets about the
same satisfaction out of life. Mr. Suddlechops, the barber
of Seven Dials, is as happy as Alexander at the head of his
legions. The business of the one is to depopulate kingdoms,
the business of the other to reap beards seven days old ;
but their relative positions do not affect the question.
The one works with razors and soap-lather, the other with
battle-cries and well-greaved Greeks. The one of a Saturday night counts up his shabby gains and grumbles ; the

other on *his* Saturday night sits down and weeps for other worlds to conquer. The pence to Mr. Suddlechops are as important as are the worlds to Alexander. Every condition of life has its peculiar advantages, and wisdom points these out and is contented with them. The varlet who sang—

> A king cannot swagger
> Or get drunk like a beggar,
> Nor be half so happy as I—

had the soul of a philosopher in him. The harshness of the parlour is revenged at night in the servants' hall. The coarse rich man rates his domestic, but there is a thought in the domestic's brain, docile and respectful as he looks, which makes the matter equal, which would madden the rich man if he knew it—make him wince as with a shrewdest twinge of hereditary gout. For insult and degradation are not without their peculiar solaces. You may spit upon Shylock's gaberdine, but the day comes when he demands his pound of flesh ; every blow, every insult, not without a certain satisfaction, he adds to the account running up against you in the day-book and ledger of his hate—which at the proper time he will ask you to discharge. Every way we look we see even-handed nature administering her laws of compensation. Grandeur has a heavy tax to pay. The usurper rolls along like a god, surrounded by his guards. He dazzles the crowd—all very fine ; but look beneath his splendid trappings and you see a shirt of mail, and beneath *that* a heart cowering in terror of an air-drawn dagger. Whom did the memory of Austerlitz most keenly sting ? The beaten emperors ? or the mighty Napoleon, dying like an untended watch-fire on St. Helena ?

Giddy people may think the life I lead here staid and humdrum, but they are mistaken. It is true, I hear no concerts, save those in which the thrushes are performers in the spring mornings. I see no pictures, save those painted on the wide sky-canvas with the colours of sunrise and sunset. I attend neither rout nor ball ; I have no deeper dissipation than the tea-table ; I hear no more exciting scandal than quiet village gossip. Yet I enjoy my concerts more than I would the great London ones. I like the pictures I see, and think them better painted, too, than those which adorn the walls of the Royal Academy ; and the village gossip is more after my turn of mind than the scandals that convulse the clubs. It is wonderful how the whole world reflects itself in the simple village life. The people around me are full of their own affairs and interests ; were they of imperial magnitude, they could not be excited more strongly. Farmer Worthy is anxious about the next market ; the likelihood of a fall in the price of butter and eggs hardly allows him to sleep o' nights. The village doctor—happily we have only one—skirrs hither and thither in his gig, as if man could neither die nor be born without his assistance. He is continually standing on the confines of existence, welcoming the new-comer, bidding farewell to the goer-away. And the robustious fellow who sits at the head of the table when the Jolly Swillers meet at the Blue Lion on Wednesday evenings is a great politician, sound of lung metal, and wields the village in the taproom, as my Lord Palmerston wields the nation in the House. His listeners think him a wiser personage than the Premier, and he is inclined to lean to that opinion himself. I find everything here that other men find in the big world. London is but a magnified Dreamthorp.

And just as the Rev. Mr. White took note of the on-goings of the seasons in and around Hampshire Selborne, watched the colonies of the rooks in the tall elms, looked after the swallows in the cottage and rectory eaves, played the affectionate spy on the private lives of chaffinch and hedge-sparrow, was eavesdropper to the solitary cuckoo ;

so here I keep eye and ear open ; take note of man, woman, and child ; find many a pregnant text imbedded in the commonplace of village life ; and, out of what I see and hear, weave in my own room my essays as solitarily as the spider weaves his web in the darkened corner. The essay, as a literary form, resembles the lyric, in so far as it is moulded by some central mood—whimsical, serious, or satirical. Give the mood, and the essay, from the first sentence to the last, grows around it as the cocoon grows around the silkworm. The essay-writer is a chartered libertine, and a law unto himself. A quick ear and eye, an ability to discern the infinite suggestiveness of common things, a brooding meditative spirit, are all that the essayist requires to start business with. Jacques, in *As You Like It,* had the makings of a charming essayist. It is not the essayist's duty to inform, to build pathways through metaphysical morasses, to conceal abuses, any more than it is the duty of the poet to do these things. Incidentally he may do something in that way, just as the poet may, but it is not his duty, and should not be expected of him. Skylarks are primarily created to sing, although a whole choir of them may be baked in pies and brought to table ; they were born to make music, although they may incidentally stay the pangs of vulgar hunger. The essayist is a kind of poet in prose, and if questioned harshly as to his uses, he might be unable to render a better apology for his existence than a flower might. The essay should be pure literature as the poem is pure literature. The essayist wears a lance, but he cares more for the sharpness of its point than for the pennon that flutters on it, than for the banner of the captain under whom he serves. He plays with death as Hamlet plays with Yorick's skull, and he reads the morals—strangely stern, often, for such fragrant lodging—which are folded up in the bosoms of roses. He has no pride, and is deficient in a sense of the congruity and fitness of things. He lifts a pebble from the ground, and puts it aside more carefully than any gem ; and on a nail in a cottage-door he will hang the mantle of his thought, heavily brocaded with the gold of rhetoric. He finds his way into the Elysian fields through portals the most shabby and commonplace.

The essayist plays with his subject, now in whimsical, now in grave, now in melancholy mood. He lies upon the idle grassy bank, like Jacques, letting the world flow past him, and from this thing and the other he extracts his mirth and his moralities. His main gift is an eye to discover the suggestiveness of common things ; to find a sermon in the most unpromising texts. Beyond the vital hint, the first step, his discourses are not beholden to their titles. Let him take up the most trivial subject, and it will lead him away to the great questions over which the serious imagination loves to brood,—fortune, mutability, death,— just as inevitably as the runnel, trickling among the summer hills, on which sheep are bleating, leads you to the sea ; or as, turning down the first street you come to in the city, you are led finally, albeit by many an intricacy, out into the open country, with its waste places and its woods, where you are lost in a sense of strangeness and solitariness. The world is to the meditative man what the mulberry plant is to the silkworm. The essay-writer has no lack of subject-matter. He has the day that is passing over his head ; and, if unsatisfied with that, he has the world's six thousand years to depasture his gay or serious humour upon. I idle away my time here, and I am finding new subjects every hour. Everything I see or hear is an essay in bud. The world is everywhere whispering essays, and one need only be the world's amanuensis. The proverbial expression which last evening the clown dropped as he trudged homeward to supper, the light of the setting sun on his face, expands before me to a dozen pages. The coffin of the pauper, which to-day I saw carried carelessly along, is as good a subject as the funeral procession of an emperor. Craped drum and banner add nothing to death ; penury and disrespect take nothing away. Incontinently my thought moves like a slow-paced hearse with sable nodding plumes. Two rustic lovers, whispering between the darkening hedges, are as potent to project my mind into the tender passion as if I had seen Romeo touch the cheek of Juliet in the moonlight garden. Seeing a curly-headed child asleep in the sunshine before a cottage-door is sufficient excuse for a discourse on childhood ; quite as good as if I had seen infant Cain asleep in the lap of Eve with Adam looking on. A lark cannot rise to heaven without raising as many thoughts as there are notes in its song. Dawn cannot pour its white light on my village without starting from their dim lair a hundred reminiscences ; nor can sunset burn above yonder trees in the west without attracting to itself the melancholy of a lifetime. When spring unfolds her green leaves I would be provoked to indite an essay on hope and youth, were it not that it is already written in the carols of the birds ; and I might be tempted in autumn to improve the occasion, were it not for the rustle of the withered leaves as I walk through the woods. Compared with that simple music, the saddest-cadenced words have but a shallow meaning.

The essayist who feeds his thoughts upon the segment of the world which surrounds him cannot avoid being an egotist ; but then his egotism is not unpleasing. If he be without taint of boastfulness, of self-sufficiency, of hungry vanity, the world will not press the charge home. If a man discourses continually of his wines, his plate, his titled acquaintances, the number and quality of his horses, his men-servants and maid-servants, he must discourse very skilfully indeed if he escapes being called a coxcomb. If a man speaks of death—tells you that the idea of it continually haunts him, that he has the most insatiable curiosity as to death and dying, that his thought mines in church-yards like a " demon-mole "—no one is specially offended, and that this is a dull fellow is the hardest thing likely to be said of him. Only, the egotism that overcrows you is offensive, that exalts trifles and takes pleasure in them, that suggests superiority in matters of equipage and furniture ; and the egotism is offensive, because it runs counter to and jostles your self-complacency. The egotism which rises no higher than the grave is of a solitary and a hermit kind—it crosses no man's path, it disturbs no man's *amour-propre.* You may offend a man if you say you are as rich as he, as wise as he, as handsome as he. You offend no man if you tell him that, like him, you have to die. The king, in his crown and coronation robes, will allow the beggar to claim that relationship with him. To have to die is a dis-tinction of which no man is proud. The speaking about one's self is not necessarily offensive. A modest, truthful man speaks better about himself than about anything else, and on that subject his speech is likely to be most profitable to his hearers. Certainly, there is no subject with which he is better acquainted, and on which he has a better title to be heard. And it is this egotism, this perpetual refer-ence to self, in which the charm of the essayist resides. If a man is worth knowing at all, he is worth knowing well. The essayist gives you his thoughts, and lets you know, in addition, how he came by them. He has nothing to conceal ; he throws open his doors and windows, and lets him enter who will. You like to walk round peculiar or important men as you like to walk round a building, to view it from different points, and in different lights. Of the essayist, when his mood is communicative, you obtain a full picture. You are made his contemporary and familiar friend. You enter into his humours and his seriousness. You are made heir of his whims, prejudices, and playful-ness. You walk through the whole nature of him, as you walk through the streets of Pompeii, looking into the interior of stately mansions, reading the satirical scribblings on the walls. And the essayist's habit of not only giving you his thoughts, but telling you how he came by them, is interesting, because it shows you by what alchemy the ruder world becomes transmuted into the finer. We like to know the lineage of ideas, just as we like to know the lineage of great earls and swift race-horses. We like to know that the discovery of the law of gravitation was born of the fall of an apple in an English garden on a summer afternoon. Essays written after this fashion are racy of the soil in which they grow, as you taste the lava in the vines grown on the slopes of Etna, they say. There is a healthy Gascon flavour in Montaigne's Essays ; and Charles Lamb's are scented with the primroses of Covent Garden.

The essayist does not usually appear early in the literary history of a country : he comes naturally after the poet and the chronicler. His habit of mind is leisurely ; he does not write from any special stress of passionate impulse ; he does not create material so much as he comments upon material already existing. It is essential for him that books should have been written, and that they should, at least to some extent, have been read and digested. He is usually full of allusions and references, and these his reader must be able to follow and understand. And in this literary walk, as in most others, the giants came first : Montaigne and Lord Bacon were our earliest essayists, and, as yet, they are our best. In point of style, these essays are different from anything that could now be produced. Not only is the thinking different—the manner of setting forth the thinking is different also. We despair of reaching the thought, we despair equally of reaching the language. We can no more bring back their turns of sentence than we can bring back their tournaments. Montaigne, in his serious moods, has a curiously rich and intricate eloquence ; and Bacon's sentence bends beneath the weight of his thought, like a branch beneath the weight of its fruit. Bacon seems to have written his essays with Shakespeare's pen. There is a certain want of ease about the old writers

(4,316)

which has an irresistible charm. The language flows like
a stream over a pebbled bed, with propulsion, eddy, and
sweet recoil—the pebbles, if retarding movement, giving
ring and dimple to the surface, and breaking the whole
into babbling music. There is a ceremoniousness in the
mental habits of these ancients. Their intellectual garniture is picturesque, like the garniture of their bodies.
Their thoughts are courtly and high mannered. A singular
analogy exists between the personal attire of a period and
its written style. The peaked beard, the starched collar,
the quilted doublet, have their correspondences in the high
sentence and elaborate ornament (worked upon the thought
like figures upon tapestry) of Sidney and Spencer. In
Pope's day men wore rapiers, and their weapons they
carried with them into literature, and frequently un-
sheathed them too. They knew how to stab to the heart
with an epigram. Style went out with the men who wore
knee-breeches and buckles in their shoes. We write more
easily now ; but in our easy writing there is ever a taint
of flippancy : our writing is to theirs what shooting-coat
and wide-awake are to doublet and plumed hat.

Montaigne and Bacon are our earliest and greatest
essayists, and likeness and unlikeness exist between the
men. Bacon was constitutionally the graver nature. He
writes like one on whom presses the weight of affairs, and
he approaches a subject always on its serious side. He
does not play with it fantastically. He lives amongst great
ideas, as with great nobles, with whom he dare not be too
familiar. In the tone of his mind there is ever something
imperial. When he writes on building, he speaks of a
palace with spacious entrances, and courts, and banqueting-
halls ; when he writes on gardens, he speaks of alleys and
mounts, waste places and fountains, of a garden " which is
indeed prince-like." To read over his table of contents,
is like reading over a roll of peers' names. We have, taking
them as they stand, essays treating *Of Great Place, Of Bald-*

ness, Of Goodness, and Goodness of Nature, Of Nobility, Of Seditions and Troubles, Of Atheism, Of Superstition, Of Travel, Of Empire, Of Counsel,—a book plainly to lie in the closets of statesmen and princes, and designed to nurture the noblest natures. Bacon always seems to write with his ermine on. Montaigne was different from all this. His table of contents reads in comparison like a medley, or a catalogue of an auction. He was quite as wise as Bacon ; he could look through men quite as clearly, and search them quite as narrowly ; certain of his moods were quite as serious, and in one corner of his heart he kept a yet profounder melancholy ; but he was volatile, a humorist, and a gossip. He could be dignified enough on great occasions, but dignity and great occasions bored him. . . .

Bacon is the greatest of the serious and stately essayists,—Montaigne the greatest of the garrulous and communicative. The one gives you his thoughts on Death, Travel, Government, and the like, and lets you make the best of them ; the other gives you his on the same subjects, but he wraps them up in personal gossip and reminiscence. With the last it is never Death or Travel alone ; it is always Death one-fourth, and Montaigne three-fourths ; or Travel one-fourth, and Montaigne three-fourths. He pours his thought into the water of gossip, and gives you to drink. He gilds his pill always, and he always gilds it with himself. . . .

The Essays contain a philosophy of life, which is not specially high, yet which is certain to find acceptance more or less with men who have passed out beyond the glow of youth, and who have made trial of the actual world. The essence of his philosophy is a kind of cynical common sense. He will risk nothing in life ; he will keep to the beaten track ; he will not let passion blind or enslave him ; he will gather around him what good he can, and will therewith endeavour to be content. He will be, as far as possible, self-sustained ; he will not risk his happiness in the hands of man, or of woman either. He is shy of friendship, he fears love, for he knows that both are dangerous. He knows that life is full of bitters, and he holds it wisdom that a man should console himself, as far as possible, with its sweets, the principal of which are peace, travel, leisure, and the writing of essays. He values obtainable Gascon bread and cheese more than the unobtainable stars. He thinks crying for the moon the foolishest thing in the world. He will remain where he is. He will not deny that a new world may exist beyond the sunset, but he knows that to reach the new world there is a troublesome Atlantic to cross ; and he is not in the least certain that, putting aside the chance of being drowned on the way, he will be one whit happier in the new world than he is in the old. For his part he will embark with no Columbus. He feels that life is but a sad thing at best ; but as he has little hope of making it better, he accepts it, and will not make it worse by murmuring. When the chain galls him, he can at least revenge himself by making jests on it. He will temper the despotism of nature by epigrams. He has read Æsop's fable, and is the last man in the world to relinquish the shabbiest substance to grasp at the finest shadow.

Of nothing under the sun was Montaigne quite certain, except that every man—whatever his station—might travel farther and fare worse ; and that the playing with his own thoughts, in the shape of essay-writing, was the most harmless of amusements. . . .

And on style depends the success of the essayist. Montaigne said the most familiar things in the finest way. Goldsmith could not be termed a thinker ; but everything he touched he brightened, as after a month of dry weather, the shower brightens the dusty shrubbery of the suburban villa. The world is not so much in need of new thoughts as that when thought grows old and worn with usage it should, like current coin, be called in, and, from the mint of genius, reissued fresh and new. Love is an old story enough, but in every generation it is re-born, in the downcast eyes and blushes of young maidens. And so, although he fluttered in Eden, Cupid is young to-day. If Montaigne had lived in Dreamthorp, as I am now living, had he written essays as I am now writing them, his English Essays would have been as good as his Gascon ones. Looking on, the country cart would not for nothing have passed him on the road to market, the setting sun would be arrested in its splendid colours, the idle chimes of the church would be translated into a thoughtful music. As it is, the village life goes on, and there is no result. My sentences are not much more brilliant than the speeches of the clowns ; in my book there is little more life than there is in the market-place on the days when there is no market.

Dreamthorp. 1863.

A LARK'S FLIGHT

Alexander Smith

RIGHTLY or wrongly, during the last twenty or thirty years a strong feeling has grown up in the public mind against the principle, and a still stronger feeling against the practice, of capital punishments. Many people who will admit that the execution of the murderer may be, abstractly considered, just enough, sincerely doubt whether such execution be expedient, and are in their own minds perfectly certain that it cannot fail to demoralize the spectators. In consequence of this, executions have become rare ; and it is quite clear that many scoundrels, well worthy of the noose, contrive to escape it. When, on the occasion of a wretch being turned off, the spectators are few, it is remarked by the newspapers that the mob is beginning to lose its proverbial cruelty, and to be stirred by humane pulses ; when they are numerous, and especially when girls and women form a majority, the circumstance is noticed and deplored. It is plain enough that, if the newspaper considered such an exhibition beneficial, it would not lament over a few thousand eager witnesses : if the sermon be edifying, you cannot have too large a congregation ; if you teach a moral lesson in a grand, impressive way, it is difficult to see how you can have too many pupils. Of course, neither the justice nor the expediency of capital punishments falls to be discussed here. This, however, may be said, that the popular feeling against them may not be so admirable a proof of enlightenment as many believe. It is true that the spectacle is painful, horrible ; but in pain and horror there is often hidden a certain salutariness, and the repulsion of which we are conscious is as likely to arise from debilitation of public nerve, as from a higher reach of public feeling. To my own thinking, it is out of this pain and hatefulness that an execution becomes invested with an ideal grandeur. It is sheer horror to all concerned—sheriffs, halbertmen, chaplain, spectators, Jack Ketch, and culprit ; but out of all this, and towering behind the vulgar and hideous accessories of the scaffold, gleams the majesty of implacable law. When every other fine morning a dozen cut-purses were hanged at Tyburn, and when such sights did not run very strongly against the popular current, the spectacle *was* vulgar, and could be of use only to the possible cut-purses congregated around the foot of the scaffold. Now, when the law has become so far merciful ; when the punishment of death is reserved for the murderer ; when he can be condemned only on the clearest evidence ; when, as the days draw slowly on to doom, the frightful event impending over one stricken wretch throws its shadow over the heart of every man, woman, and child in the great city ; and when the official persons whose duty it is to see the letter of the law carried out perform that duty at the expense of personal pain, a public execution is not vulgar, it becomes positively sublime. It is dreadful, of course ; but its dreadfulness melts into pure awfulness. The attention is taken off the criminal, and is lost in a sense of the grandeur of justice ; and the spectator who beholds an execution, solely as it appears to the eye, without recognition of the idea which towers behind it, must be a very unspiritual and unimaginative spectator indeed.

It is taken for granted that the spectators of public executions—the artisans and country people who take up their stations over-night as close to the barriers as possible, and the wealthier classes who occupy hired windows and employ opera-glasses—are merely drawn together by a morbid relish for horrible sights. He is a bold man who will stand forward as the advocate of such persons—so completely is the popular mind made up as to their tastes and motives. It is not disputed that the large body of the mob, and of the occupants of windows, have been drawn together by an appetite for excitement ; but it is quite possible that many come there from an impulse altogether different. Just consider the nature of the expected sight— a man in tolerable health probably, in possession of all his faculties, perfectly able to realize his position, conscious that for him this world and the next are so near that only a few seconds divide them—such a man stands in the seeing of several thousand eyes. He is so peculiarly circumstanced, so utterly lonely—hearing the tolling of his own death-bell, yet living, wearing the mourning clothes for his own funeral—that he holds the multitude together by a shuddering fascination. The sight is a peculiar one, you must admit, and every peculiarity has its attractions. Your volcano is more attractive than your ordinary mountain. Then consider the unappeasable curiosity as to death which haunts every human being, and how pathetic that curiosity is, in so far as it suggests our own ignorance and helplessness, and we see at once that people *may* flock to public executions for other purposes than the gratification of morbid tastes : that they would pluck if they could some little knowledge of what death is ; that imaginatively they attempt to reach to it, to touch and handle it through an experience which is not their own. It is some obscure desire of this kind, a movement of curiosity not altogether ignoble, but in some degree pathetic ; some rude attempt of the imagination to wrest from the death of the criminal information as to the great secret in which each is profoundly interested, which draws around the scaffold people from the country harvest-fields, and from the streets and alleys of the town. Nothing interests men so much as death.

Age cannot wither it, nor custom stale it. " A greater crowd would come to see me hanged," Cromwell is reported to have said when the populace came forth on a public occasion. The Lord Protector was right in a sense of which, perhaps, at the moment he was not aware. Death is greater than official position. When a man has to die, he may safely dispense with stars and ribbands. He is invested with a greater dignity than is held in the gift of kings. A greater crowd *would* have gathered to see Cromwell hanged, but the compliment would have been paid to death rather than to Cromwell. Never were the motions of Charles I. so scrutinized as when he stood for a few moments on the scaffold that winter morning at Whitehall. King Louis was no great orator usually, but when on January 2, 1793, he attempted to speak a few words in the Place de la Révolution, it was found necessary to drown his voice in a harsh roll of soldiers' drums. Not without a meaning do people come forth to see men die. We stand in the valley, they on the hill-top, and on their faces strikes the light of the other world, and from some sign or signal of theirs we attempt to discover or extract a hint of what it is all like.

To be publicly put to death, for whatever reason, must ever be a serious matter. It is always bitter, but there are degrees in its bitterness. It is easy to die like Stephen with an opened heaven above you, crowded with angel faces. It is easy to die like Balmerino with a chivalrous sigh for the White Rose, and an audible " God bless King James." Such men die for a cause in which they glory, and are supported thereby ; they are conducted to the portals of the next world by the angels, Faith, Pity, Admiration. But it is not easy to die in expiation of a crime like murder, which engirdles you with trembling and horror even in the loneliest places, which cuts you off from the sympathies of your kind, which reduces the universe to two elements —a sense of personal identity, and a memory of guilt.

In so dying, there must be inconceivable bitterness ; a man can have no other support than what strength he may pluck from despair, or from the iron with which nature may have originally braced heart and nerve. Yet, taken as a whole, criminals on the scaffold comport themselves creditably. They look Death in the face when he wears his cruellest aspect, and if they flinch somewhat, they can at least bear to look. I believe that, for the criminal, execution within the prison walls, with no witnesses save some half-dozen official persons, would be infinitely more terrible than execution in the presence of a curious, glaring mob. The daylight and the publicity are alien elements, which wean the man a little from himself. He steadies his dizzy brain on the crowd beneath and around him. He has his last part to play, and his manhood rallies to play it well. Nay, so subtly is vanity intertwined with our motives, the noblest and the most ignoble, that I can fancy a poor wretch with the noose dangling at his ear, and with barely five minutes to live, soothed somewhat with the idea that his firmness and composure will earn him the approbation, perhaps the pity, of the spectators. He would take with him, if he could, the good opinion of his fellows. This composure of criminals puzzles one. Have they looked at death so long and closely, that familiarity has robbed it of terror ? Has life treated them so harshly, that they are tolerably well pleased to be quit of it on any terms ? Or is the whole thing mere blind stupor and delirium, in which thought is paralysed, and the man an automaton ? Speculation is useless. The fact remains that criminals for the most part die well and bravely. It is said that the championship of England was to be decided at some little distance from London on the morning of the day on which Thurtell was executed, and that, when he came out on the scaffold, he inquired privily of the executioner if the result had yet become known. Jack Ketch was not aware, and Thurtell expressed his regret that the ceremony in which he was chief actor should take place so inconveniently early in the day. Think of a poor Thurtell forced to take his long journey an hour, perhaps, before the arrival of intelligence so important !

More than twenty years ago I saw two men executed, and the impression then made remains fresh to this day. For this there were many reasons. The deed for which the men suffered created an immense sensation. They were hanged on the spot where the murder was committed— on a rising ground, some four miles north-east of the city ; and as an attempt at rescue was apprehended, there was a considerable display of military force on the occasion. And when, in the dead silence of thousands, the criminals stood beneath the halters, an incident occurred, quite natural and slight in itself, but when taken in connection with the business then proceeding, so unutterably tragic, so overwhelming in its pathetic suggestion of contrast, that the feeling of it has never departed, and never will. At the time, too, I speak of, I was very young ; the world was like a die newly cut, whose every impression is fresh and vivid.

While the railway which connects two northern capitals was being built, two brothers from Ireland, named Doolan, were engaged upon it in the capacity of navvies. For some fault of negligence, one of the brothers was dismissed by the overseer—a Mr. Green—of that particular portion of the line on which they were employed. The dismissed brother went off in search of work, and the brother who remained—Dennis was the Christian name of him— brooded over this supposed wrong, and in his dull, twilighted brain revolved projects of vengeance. He did not absolutely mean to take Green's life, but he meant to thrash him to within an inch of it. Dennis, anxious to thrash Green, but not quite seeing his way to it, opened his mind one afternoon, when work was over, to his friends—fellow-Irishmen and navvies—Messrs. Redding and Hickie. These took up Doolan's wrong as their own, and that evening, by the dull light of a bothy fire, they held a rude parliament, discussing ways and means of revenge. It was arranged that Green should be thrashed—the amount of thrashing left an open question, to be decided, unhappily, when the blood was up and the cinder of rage blown into a flame. Hickie's spirit was found not to be a mounting one, and it was arranged that the active partners in the game should be Doolan and Redding. Doolan, as the aggrieved party, was to strike the first blow, and Redding, as the aggrieved party's particular friend, asked and obtained permission to strike the second. The main conspirators, with a fine regard for the feelings of the weaker Hickie, allowed him to provide the weapons of assault—so that by some slight filament of aid he might connect himself with the good cause. The unambitious Hickie at once applied himself to his duty. He went out, and in due time returned with two sufficient iron pokers. The weapons were examined, approved of, and carefully laid aside. Doolan, Redding, and Hickie ate their suppers, and retired to their several couches to sleep, peacefully enough no doubt. About the same time, too, Green, the English overseer, threw down his weary limbs, and entered on his last sleep—little dreaming what the morning had in store for him.

Uprose the sun, and uprose Doolan and Redding, and dressed, and thrust each his sufficient iron poker up the sleeve of his blouse, and went forth. They took up their station on a temporary wooden bridge which spanned the line, and waited there. Across the bridge, as was expected, did Green ultimately come. He gave them good morning ; asked " why they were loafing about " ; received no very pertinent answer, perhaps did not care to receive one ; whistled—the unsuspecting man !—thrust his hands into his breeches pockets, turned his back on them, and leaned over the railing of the bridge, inspecting the progress of

the works beneath. The temptation was really too great.
What could wild Irish flesh and blood do ? In a moment
out from the sleeve of Doolan's blouse came the hidden
poker, and the first blow was struck, bringing Green to the
ground. The friendly Redding, who had bargained for the
second, and who, naturally enough, was in fear of being
cut out altogether, jumped on the prostrate man, and fulfilled his share of the bargain with a will. It was Redding
it was supposed who sped the unhappy Green. They
overdid their work—like young authors—giving many
more blows than were sufficient, and then fled. The
works, of course, were that morning in consternation.
Redding and Hickie were, if I remember rightly, apprehended in the course of the day. Doolan got off, leaving
no trace of his whereabouts.

These particulars were all learned subsequently. The
first intimation which we schoolboys received of anything unusual having occurred, was the sight of a detach-
ment of soldiers with fixed bayonets, trousers rolled up
over muddy boots, marching past the front of the Cathedral
hurriedly home to barracks. This was a circumstance
somewhat unusual. We had, of course, frequently seen
a couple of soldiers trudging along with sloped muskets,
and that cruel glitter of steel which no one of us could look
upon quite unmoved ; but in such cases, the deserter
walking between them in his shirt-sleeves, his pinioned
hands covered from public gaze by the loose folds of his
greatcoat, explained everything. But from the hurried
march of these mud-splashed men nothing could be
gathered, and we were left to speculate upon its meaning.
Gradually, however, before the evening fell, the rumour
of a murder having been committed spread through the
city, and with that I instinctively connected the apparition
of the file of muddy soldiers. Next day, murder was in
every mouth. My schoolfellows talked of it to the detri-
ment of their lessons ; it flavoured the tobacco of the fustian

artisan as he smoked to work after breakfast ; it walked on
'Change amongst the merchants. It was known that two
of the persons implicated had been captured, but that the
other, and guiltiest, was still at large ; and in a few days
out on every piece of boarding and blank wall came the
" Hue and cry "—describing Doolan like a photograph,
to the colour and cut of his whiskers, and offering £100
as reward for his apprehension, or for such information
as would lead to his apprehension—like a silent, implacable
bloodhound following close on the track of the murderer.
This terrible broadsheet I read, was certain that *he* had read
it also, and fancy ran riot over the ghastly fact. For him
no hope, no rest, no peace, no touch of hands gentler than
the hangman's ; all the world is after him like a roaring
prairie of flame ! I thought of Doolan, weary, foot-sore,
heart-sore entering some quiet village of an evening ; and
to quench his thirst, going up to the public well, around
which the gossips are talking, and hearing that they were
talking of *him* ; and seeing from the well itself, IT glaring
upon him, as if conscious of his presence, with a hundred
eyes of vengeance. I thought of him asleep in out-houses,
and starting up in wild dreams of the policeman's hand
upon his shoulder fifty times ere morning. He had committed the crime of Cain, and the weird of Cain he had to
endure. But yesterday innocent, how unimportant ; to-
day bloody-handed, the whole world is talking of him, and
everything he touches, the very bed he sleeps on, steals from
him his secret, and is eager to betray !

Doolan was finally captured in Liverpool, and in the
Spring Assize the three men were brought to trial. The
jury found them guilty, but recommended Hickie to
mercy on account of some supposed weakness of mind on
his part. Sentence was, of course, pronounced with the
usual solemnities. They were set apart to die ; and when
snug abed o' nights—for imagination is most mightily
moved by contrast—I crept into their desolate hearts, and

tasted a misery which was not my own. As already said, Hickie was recommended to mercy, and the recommendation was ultimately in the proper quarter given effect to.

The evening before the execution has arrived, and the reader has now to imagine the early May sunset falling pleasantly on the outskirts of the city. The houses looking out upon an open square or space have little plots of garden-ground in their fronts, in which mahogany-coloured wallflowers and mealy auriculas are growing. The side of this square, along which the City Road stretches northward, is occupied by a blind asylum, a brick building, the bricks painted red and picked out with white, after the tidy English fashion, and a high white cemetery wall, over which peers the spire of the Gothic Cathedral ; and beyond that, on the other side of the ravine, rising out of a populous city of the dead, a stone John Knox looks down on the Cathedral, a Bible clutched in his outstretched and menacing hand. On all this the May sunset is striking, dressing everything in its warm, pleasant pink, lingering in the tufts of foliage that nestle around the asylum, and dipping the building itself one half in light, one half in tender shade. This open space or square is an excellent place for the games of us boys, and " Prisoners' Base " is being carried out with as much earnestness as the business of life now by those of us who are left. The girls, too, have their games of a quiet kind, which we hold in huge scorn and contempt. In two files, linked arm-in-arm, they alternately dance towards each other and then retire, singing the while, in their clear, girlish treble, verses, the meaning and pertinence of which time has worn away—

The Campsie Duke's a-riding, a-riding, a-riding,

being the oft-recurring " owercome " or refrain. All this is going on in the pleasant sunset light, when by the apparition of certain wagons coming up from the city, piled high with blocks and beams, and guarded by a dozen dragoons, on whose brazen helmets the sunset danced, every game is dismembered, and we are in a moment a mere mixed mob of boys and girls, flocking around to stare and wonder. Just at this place something went wrong with one of the wagon wheels, and the procession came to a stop. A crowd collected, and we heard some of the grown-up people say that the scaffold was being carried out for the ceremony of to-morrow. Then, more intensely than ever, one realized the condition of the doomed men. *We* were at our happy games in the sunset, *they* were entering on their last night on earth. After hammering and delay the wheel was put to rights, the sunset died out, wagons and dragoons got into motion and disappeared ; and all the night through, whether awake or asleep, I saw the torches burning, and heard the hammers clinking, and witnessed as clearly as if I had been an onlooker, the horrid structure rising, till it stood complete, with a huge cross-beam from which two empty halters hung, in the early morning light.

Next morning the whole city was in commotion. Whether the authorities were apprehensive that a rescue would be attempted, or were anxious merely to strike terror into the hundreds of wild Irishry engaged on the railway, I cannot say ; in any case, there was a display of military force quite unusual. The carriage in which the criminals —Catholics both—and their attendant priests were seated, was guarded by soldiers with fixed bayonets ; indeed, the whole regiment then lying in the city was massed in front and behind, with a cold, frightful glitter of steel. Besides the foot soldiers, there were dragoons, and two pieces of cannon ; a whole little army, in fact. With a slenderer force battles have been won which have made a mark in history. What did the prisoners think of their strange importance, and of the tramp and hurly-burly all around ? When the procession moved out of the city, it seemed to draw with it almost the entire population ; and when once the country roads were reached, the crowd spread over the fields on either side, ruthlessly treading down the tender wheat braird, I got a glimpse of the doomed, blanched faces which had haunted me so long, at the turn of the road, where, for the first time, the black crossbeam with its empty halters first became visible to them. Both turned and regarded it with a long, steady look ; that done, they again bent their heads attentively to the words of the clergyman. I suppose in that long, eager, fascinated gaze they practically *died*—that for them death had no additional bitterness. When the mound was reached on which the scaffold stood, there was immense confusion. Around it a wide space was kept clear by the military ; the cannon were placed in position ; out flashed the swords of the dragoons ; beneath and around on every side was the crowd. Between two brass helmets I could see the scaffold clearly enough, and when in a little while the men, bare-headed and with their attendants, appeared upon it, the surging crowd became stiffened with fear and awe. And now it was that the incident so simple, so natural, so much in the ordinary course of things, and yet so frightful in its tragic suggestions, took place. Be it remembered that the season was early May, that the day was fine, that the wheat-fields were clothing themselves in the green of the young crop, and that around the scaffold, standing on a sunny mound, a wide space was kept clear. When the men appeared beneath the beam, each under his proper halter, there was a dead silence—every one was gazing too intently to whisper to his neighbour even. Just then, out of the grassy space at the foot of the scaffold, in the dead silence audible to all, a lark rose from the side of its nest, and went singing upward in its happy flight. O heaven ! how did that song translate itself into dying ears ? Did it bring in one wild burning moment father, and mother, and poor Irish cabin, and prayers said at bedtime, and the smell of turf fires, and innocent sweethearting, and rising and setting suns ?   Did it—but the dragoon's horse has become restive, and his brass helmet bobs up and down and blots everything ; and there is a sharp sound, and I feel the great crowd heave and swing, and hear it torn by a sharp shiver of pity, and the men whom I saw so near but a moment ago are at immeasurable distance, and have solved the great enigma—and the lark has not yet finished his flight : you can see and hear him yonder in the fringe of a white May cloud.

This ghastly lark's flight, when the circumstances are taken into consideration, is, I am inclined to think, more terrible than anything of the same kind which I have encountered in books.   The artistic uses of contrast as background and accompaniment are well known to nature and the poets.   Joy is continually worked on sorrow, sorrow on joy ;   riot is framed in peace, peace in riot.   Lear and the Fool always go together.   Trafalgar is being fought while Napoleon is sitting on horseback watching the Austrian army laying down its arms at Ulm. In Hood's poem, it is when looking on the released school-boys at their games that Eugene Aram remembers he is a murderer.   And these two poor Irish labourers could not die without hearing a lark singing in their ears.   It is Nature's fashion.   She never quite goes along with us.   She is sombre at weddings, sunny at funerals, and she frowns on ninety-nine out of a hundred picnics.

There is a stronger element of terror in this incident of the lark than in any story of a similar kind I can re-member.

A good story is told of an Irish gentleman—still known in London society—who inherited the family estates and the family banshee.   The estates he lost—no uncommon circumstance in the history of Irish gentlemen,—but the banshee, who expected no favours, stuck to him in his adversity, and crossed the channel with him, making her-

self known only on occasions of deathbeds and sharp
family misfortunes. This gentleman had an ear, and,
seated one night at the opera, the *keen*—heard once or
twice before on memorable occasions—thrilled through
the din of the orchestra and the passion of the singers. He
hurried home of course, found his immediate family well,
but on the morrow a telegram arrived with the announcement of a brother's death. Surely of all superstitions that
is the most imposing which makes the other world interested in the events which befall our mortal lot. For the
mere pomp and pride of it, your ghost is worth a dozen
retainers, and it is entirely inexpensive. The peculiarity
and supernatural worth of this story lies in the idea of the
old wail piercing through the sweet entanglement of
stringed instruments and extinguishing Grisi. Modern
circumstances and luxury crack, as it were, and reveal for
a moment misty and aboriginal time big with portent.
There is a ridiculous Scotch story in which one gruesome
touch lives. A clergyman's female servant was seated in
the kitchen one Saturday night reading the Scriptures,
when she was somewhat startled by hearing at the door
the tap and voice of her sweetheart. Not expecting him,
and the hour being somewhat late, she opened it in astonishment, and was still more astonished to hear him on entering
abuse Scripture-reading. He behaved altogether in an
unprecedented manner, and in many ways terrified the
poor girl. Ultimately he knelt before her, and laid his head
on her lap. You can fancy her consternation when glanc-
ing down she discovered that, *instead of hair, the head was
covered with the moss of the moorland.* By a sacred name she
adjured him to tell who he was, and in a moment the figure
was gone. It was the Fiend, of course—diminished sadly
since Milton saw him bridge chaos—fallen from worlds
to kitchen-wenches. But just think how in the story, in
half-pity, in half-terror, the popular feeling of homelessness,
of being outcast, of being unsheltered as waste and desert

places, has incarnated itself in that strange covering of the head. It is a true supernatural touch. One other story I have heard in the misty Hebrides. A Skye gentleman was riding along an empty moorland road. All at once, as if it had sprung from the ground, the empty road was crowded by a funeral procession. Instinctively he drew his horse to a side to let it pass, which it did without sound of voice, without tread of foot. Then he knew it was an apparition. Staring on it, he knew every person who either bore the corpse or who walked behind as mourners. There were the neighbouring proprietors at whose houses he dined, there were the members of his own kirk-session, there were the men to whom he was wont to give good-morning when he met them on the road or at market. Unable to discover his own image in the throng, he was inwardly marvelling whose funeral it *could* be, when the troop of spectres vanished, and the road was empty as before. Then, remembering that the coffin had an invisible occupant, he cried out, " It is my funeral ! " and, with all his strength taken out of him, rode home to die. All these stories have their own touches of terror ; yet I am inclined to think that my lark rising from the scaffold foot, and singing to two such auditors, is more terrible than any one of them.

Dreamthorp. 1863.

ON A CHALK-MARK ON THE DOOR

W. M. THACKERAY

ON the door-post of the house of a friend of mine, a few inches above the lock, is a little chalk-mark, which some sportive boy in passing has probably scratched on the pillar. The doorsteps, the lock, handle, and so forth, are kept decently enough ; but this chalk-mark, I suppose some three inches out of the housemaid's beat, has already been on the door for more than a fortnight, and I wonder whether it will be there whilst this paper is being written, whilst it is at the printer's, and, in fine, until the month passes over ? I wonder whether the servants in that house will read these remarks about the chalk-mark ? That the *Cornhill Magazine* is taken in in that house I know.   In fact I have seen it there.   In fact I have read it there.   In fact I have written it there.   In a word, the house to which I allude is mine—the " editor's private residence," to which, in spite of prayers, entreaties, commands, and threats, authors, and ladies especially, *will* send their communications, although they won't understand that they injure their own interests by so doing ; for how is a man who has his own work to do, his own exquisite inventions to form and perfect—Maria to rescue from the unprincipled Earl—the atrocious general to confound in his own machinations—the angelic Dean to promote to a bishopric, and so forth—how is a man to do all this, under a hundred interruptions, and keep his nerves and temper in that just and equable state in which they ought to be when he comes to assume the critical office ? As you will send here, ladies, I must tell you you have a much worse chance than if you forward your valuable articles to Cornhill. Here your papers arrive, at dinner-time, we will say. Do you suppose that is a pleasant period, and that we are to criticize you between the *ovum* and *malum*, between the soup and the dessert ? I have touched, I think, on this subject before. I say again, if you want real justice shown you, don't send your papers to the private residence. At home, for instance, yesterday, having given strict orders that I was to receive nobody, " except on business," do you suppose a smiling young Scottish gentleman, who forced himself into my study, and there announced himself as agent of a Cattle-food Company, was received with pleasure ? There, as I sat in my armchair, suppose he had proposed to draw a couple of my teeth, would I have been pleased ? I could have throttled that agent. I dare say the whole of that day's work will be found tinged with a ferocious misanthropy, occasioned by my clever young friend's intrusion. Cattle-food indeed ! As if beans, oats, warm mashes, and a ball, are to be pushed down a man's throat just as he is meditating on the great social problem, or (for I think it was my epic I was going to touch up) just as he was about to soar to the height of the empyrean !

Having got my cattle-agent out of the door, I resume my consideration of that little mark on the door-post, which is scored up as the text of the present little sermon ; and which I hope will relate, not to chalk, nor to any of its special uses or abuses (such as milk, neck-powder, and the like), but to servants. Surely ours might remove that unseemly little mark. Suppose it were on my coat, might I not request its removal ? I remember, when I was at school, a little careless boy, upon whose forehead an ink-mark remained, and was perfectly recognizable for three weeks after its first appearance. May I take any notice of this chalk-stain on the forehead of my house ? Whose

business is it to wash that forehead ? and ought I to fetch
a brush and a little hot water, and wash it off myself ?

Yes. But that spot removed, why not come down at
six, and wash the doorsteps ? I dare say the early rising
and exercise would do me a great deal of good. The
housemaid, in that case, might lie in bed a little later, and
have her tea and the morning paper brought to her in
bed : then, of course, Thomas would expect to be helped
about the boots and knives ; cook about the saucepans,
dishes, and what not ; the lady's-maid would want
somebody to take the curl-papers out of her hair, and get
her bath ready. You should have a set of servants for
the servants, and these under-servants should have slaves
to wait on them. The king commands the first lord in
waiting to desire the second lord to intimate to the gentleman usher to request the page of the ante-chamber to
entreat the groom of the stairs to implore John to ask the
captain of the buttons to desire the maid of the still-room
to beg the housekeeper to give out a few more lumps of
sugar, as His Majesty has none for his coffee, which probably
is getting cold during the negotiation. In our little Brent-
fords we are all kings, more or less. There are orders,
gradations, hierarchies, everywhere. In your house and
mine there are mysteries unknown to us. I am not going
into the horrid old question of " followers." I don't mean
cousins from the country, love-stricken policemen, or
gentlemen in mufti from Knightsbridge Barracks ; but
people who have an occult right on the premises ; the un-
covenanted servants of the house ; grey women who are
seen at evening with baskets flitting about area-railings ;
dingy shawls which drop you furtive curtseys in your
neighbourhood ; demure little Jacks, who start up from
behind boxes in the pantry. Those outsiders wear
Thomas's crest and livery, and call him " Sir " ; those
silent women address the female servants as " Mum," and
curtsey before them, squaring their arms over their

wretched lean aprons. Then, again, those *servi servorum* have dependants in the vast, silent, poverty-stricken world outside your comfortable kitchen fire, in the world of darkness, and hunger, and miserable cold, and dank flagged cellars, and huddled straw, and rags, in which pale children are swarming. It may be your beer (which runs with great volubility) has a pipe or two which communicates with those dark caverns where hopeless anguish pours the groan, and would scarce see light but for a scrap or two of candle which has been whipped away from your worship's kitchen. Not many years ago—I don't know whether before or since that white mark was drawn on the door— a lady occupied the confidential place of housemaid in this " private residence," who brought a good character, who seemed to have a cheerful temper, whom I used to hear clattering and bumping overhead or on the stairs long be- fore daylight—there, I say, was poor Camilla, scouring the plain, trundling, and brushing, and clattering with her pans and brooms, and humming at her work. Well, she had established a smuggling communication of beer over the area frontier. This neat-handed Phyllis used to pack up the nicest baskets of my provender, and convey them to somebody outside—I believe, on my conscience, to some poor friend in distress. Camilla was consigned to her doom. She was sent back to her friends in the country : and when she was gone we heard of many of her faults. She expressed herself, when displeased, in language that I shall not repeat. As for the beer and meat, there was no mistake about them. But *après ?* Can I have the heart to be very angry with that poor jade for helping another poorer jade out of my larder ? On your honour and conscience, when you were a boy, and the apples looked temptingly over Farmer Quarringdon's hedge, did you never—— ? When there was a grand dinner at home, and you were sliding, with Master Bacon, up and down the stairs, and the dishes came out, did you ever do such

a thing as just to—— ?   Well, in many and many a respect
servants are like children.   They are under domination.
They are subject to reproof, to ill-temper, to petty exactions and stupid tyrannies not seldom.   They scheme,
conspire, fawn, and are hypocrites.   "Little boys should
not loll on chairs."   " Little girls should be seen, and not
heard ; " and so forth.   Have we not almost all learnt
these expressions of old foozles : and uttered them ourselves when in the square-toed state ?   The Eton master
who was breaking a lance with our Paterfamilias of late,
turned on Paterfamilias, saying, He knows not the nature
and exquisite candour of well-bred English boys.   Exquisite fiddlestick's end, Mr. Master ! Do you mean for
to go for to tell us that the relations between young gentlemen and their schoolmasters are entirely frank and cordial ;
that the lad is familiar with the man who can have him
flogged ; never shirks his exercises ; never gets other boys
to do his verses ; never does other boys' verses ; never
breaks bounds ; never tells fibs—I mean the fibs permitted
by scholastic honour ?   Did I know of a boy who pretended to such a character, I would forbid my scapegraces
to keep company with him.   Did I know a schoolmaster
who pretended to believe in the existence of many hundred
such boys in one school at one time, I would set that man
down as a baby in knowledge of the world.   " Who was
making that noise ? "   " I don't know, sir."—And he
knows it was the boy next him in school.   " Who was
climbing over that wall ? "   " I don't know, sir."—And
it is in the speaker's own trousers, very likely, the glass
bottle-tops have left their cruel scars.   And so with
servants.   " Who ate up the three pigeons which went
down in the pigeon-pie at breakfast this morning ? "   " Oh
dear me ! sir, it was John, who went away last month ! "—
or, " I think it was Miss Mary's canary-bird, which got out
of the cage, and is so fond of pigeons, it never can have
enough of them."   Yes, it *was* the canary-bird ; and Eliza

saw it ; and Eliza is ready to vow she did. These statements are not true ; but please don't call them lies. This is
not lying ; this is voting with your party. You *must* back
your own side. The servants'-hall stands by the servants'-
hall against the dining-room. The schoolboys don't tell
tales of each other. They agree not to choose to know
who has made the noise, who has broken the window,
who has eaten up the pigeons, who has picked all the
plovers' eggs out of the aspic, how it is that liqueur brandy
of Gledstane's is in such porous glass bottles—and so forth.
Suppose Brutus had a footman, who came and told him
that the butler drank the curaçoa : which of these servants
would you dismiss ?—the butler, perhaps, but the footman
certainly.

No. If your plate and glass are beautifully bright, your
bell quickly answered, and Thomas ready, neat, and good-
humoured, you are not to expect absolute truth from him.
The very obsequiousness and perfection of his service
prevents truth. He may be ever so unwell in mind or
body, and he must go through his service—hand the shining
plate, replenish the spotless glass, lay the glittering fork—
never laugh when you yourself or your guests joke—be
profoundly attentive, and yet look utterly impassive—
exchange a few hurried curses at the door with that unseen
slavey who ministers without, and with you be perfectly
calm and polite. If you are ill, he will come twenty times
in an hour to your bell ; or leave the girl of his heart—his
mother, who is going to America—his dearest friend, who
has come to say farewell—his lunch, and his glass of beer
just freshly poured out—any or all of these, if the door-
bell rings, or the master calls out " THOMAS " from the hall.
Do you suppose you can expect absolute candour from a
man whom you may order to powder his hair ? As between the Reverend Henry Holyshade and his pupil, the
idea of entire unreserve is utter bosh : so the truth as
between you and Jeames or Thomas, or Mary the house-

maid, or Betty the cook, is relative and not to be demanded
on one side or the other. Why, respectful civility is itself
a lie, which poor Jeames often has to utter or perform to
many a swaggering vulgarian, who should black Jeames's
boots, did Jeames wear them and not shoes. There is your
little Tom, just ten, ordering the great, large, quiet, orderly
young man about—shrieking calls for hot water—bullying
Jeames because the boots are not varnished enough, or
ordering him to go to the stables, and ask Jenkins why the
deuce Tomkins hasn't brought his pony round—or what
you will. There is mamma rapping the knuckles of Pincot
the ladysmaid, and little Miss scolding Martha, who waits
up five pair of stairs in the nursery. Little Miss, Tommy,
papa, mamma, you all expect from Martha, from Pincot,
from Jenkins, from Jeames, obsequious civility and willing
service. My dear good people, you can't have truth too.
Suppose you ask for your newspaper, and Jeames says,
" I'm reading it, and jest beg not to be disturbed " : or
suppose you ask for a can of water, and he remarks, " You
great big 'ulking fellar, ain't you big enough to bring it
hup yoursulf ? " what would your feelings be ? Now, if
you made similar proposals or requests to Mr. Jones next
door, this is the kind of answer Jones would give you.
You get truth habitually from equals only ; so my good
Mr. Holyshade, don't talk to me about the habitual
candour of the young Etonian of high birth, or I have my
own opinion of *your* candour or discernment when you do.
No. Tom Bowling is the soul of honour and has been true
to Black-eyed Syousan since the last time they parted at
Wapping Old Stairs ; but do you suppose Tom is perfectly frank, familiar, and above-board in his conversation with Admiral Nelson, K.C.B. ? There are secrets,
prevarications, fibs, if you will, between Tom and the
Admiral—between your crew and *their* captain. I know
I hire a worthy, clean, agreeable, and conscientious male
or female hypocrite, at so many guineas a year, to do so

and so for me. Were he other than hypocrite I would send him about his business. Don't let my displeasure be too fierce with him for a fib or two on his own account.

Some dozen years ago, my family being absent in a distant part of the country, and my business detaining me in London, I remained in my own house with three servants on board wages. I used only to breakfast at home ; and future ages will be interested to know that this meal used to consist, at that period, of tea, a penny roll, a pat of butter, and, perhaps, an egg. My weekly bill used invariably to be about fifty shillings ; so that as I never dined in the house, you see, my breakfast, consisting of the delicacies before mentioned, cost about seven shillings and threepence per diem. I must, therefore, have consumed daily—

		s.	d.
A quarter of a pound of tea (say)	. .	1	3
A penny roll (say)	. . . .	1	0
One pound of butter (say) .	. .	1	3
One pound of lump sugar .	. .	1	0
A new-laid egg	. .	2	9

Which is the only possible way in which I can make out the sum.

Well, I fell ill while under this regimen, and had an illness which, but for a certain doctor, who was brought to me by a certain kind friend I had in those days, would, I think, have prevented the possibility of my telling this interesting anecdote now a dozen years after. Don't be frightened, my dear madam ; it is not a horrid sentimental account of a malady you are coming to—only a question of grocery. This illness, I say, lasted some seventeen days, during which the servants were admirably attentive and kind ; and poor John, especially, was up at all hours, watching night after night—amiable, cheerful, untiring, respectful, the very best of the Johns and nurses.

Twice or thrice in the seventeen days I may have had a glass of *eau sucrée*—say half a dozen glasses of *eau sucrée* —certainly not more. Well, this admirable, watchful, cheerful, tender, affectionate John brought me in a little bill for seventeen pounds of sugar consumed during the illness—"Often 'ad sugar-and-water ; always was a-callin' for it," says John, wagging his head quite gravely. You are dead, years and years ago, poor John—so patient, so friendly, so kind, so cheerful to the invalid in the fever. But confess, now, wherever you are, that seventeen pounds of sugar to make six glasses of *eau sucrée* was a *little* too strong, wasn't it, John ? Ah, how frankly, how trustily, how bravely he lied, poor John ! One evening, being at Brighton in the convalescence, I remember John's step was unsteady, his voice thick, his laugh queer—and having some quinine to give me, John brought the glass to me—not to my mouth, but struck me with it pretty smartly in the eye, which was not the way in which Doctor Elliotson had intended his prescription should be taken. Turning that eye upon him, I ventured to hint that my attendant had been drinking. Drinking ! I never was more humiliated at the thought of my own injustice than at John's reply. "Drinking ! Sulp me ! I have had ony an 'alf-pint of beer with my dinner at one o'clock ! " and he retreats, holding on by a chair. These are fibs, you see, appertaining to the situation. John is drunk. *Sulp* him, he has only had an 'alf-pint of beer with his dinner six hours ago ! and none of his fellow-servants will say otherwise. Polly is smuggled on board ship. Who tells the lieutenant when he comes his rounds ? Boys are playing cards in the bedroom. The outlying fag announces master coming—out go candles— cards popped into bed—boys sound asleep. Who had that light in the dormitory ? Law bless you ! the poor dear innocents are every one snoring. Every one snoring, and every snore is a lie told through the nose ! Suppose one of your boys or mine is engaged in that awful crime, are we going to break our hearts about it ?　Come, come. We pull a long face, waggle a grave head, and chuckle within our waistcoats.

Between me and those fellow-creatures of mine who are sitting in the room below, how strange and wonderful is the partition !　We meet at every hour of the daylight, and are indebted to each other for a hundred offices of duty and comfort of life ;　and we live together for years, and don't know each other.　John's voice to me is quite different from John's voice when it addresses his mates below.　If I met Hannah in the street with a bonnet on, I doubt whether I should know her.　And all these good people with whom I may live for years and years, have cares, interests, dear friends and relatives, mayhap schemes, passions, longing hopes, tragedies of their own, from which a carpet and a few planks and beams utterly separate me. When we were at the seaside, and poor Ellen used to look so pale, and run after the postman's bell, and seize a letter in a great scrawling hand, and read it, and cry in a corner, how should we know that the poor little thing's heart was breaking ?　She fetched the water, and she smoothed the ribbons, and she laid out the dresses, and brought the early cup of tea in the morning just as if she had had no cares to keep her awake.　Henry (who lived out of the house) was a servant of a friend of mine, who lived in chambers.　There was a dinner one day, and Henry waited all through the dinner.　The champagne was properly iced, the dinner was excellently served ;　every guest was attended to ;　the dinner disappeared ;　the dessert was set ;　the claret was in perfect order, carefully decanted, and more ready.　And then Henry said, "If you please, sir, may I go home ? "　He had received word that his house was on fire ;　and having seen through his dinner, he wished to go and look after his children, and little sticks of furniture.　Why, such a man's livery is a uniform of honour. The crest on his button is a badge of bravery.

Do you see—I imagine I do myself—in these little instances, a tinge of humour? Ellen's heart is breaking for handsome Jeames of Buckley Square, whose great legs are kneeling, and who has given a lock of his precious powdered head to some other than Ellen. Henry is preparing the sauce for his master's wild-ducks while the engines are squirting over his own little nest and brood. Lift these figures up but a storey from the basement to the ground-floor, and the fun is gone. We may be *en pleine tragédie*. Ellen may breathe her last sigh in blank verse, calling down blessings upon James the profligate who deserts her. Henry is a hero, and epaulettes are on his shoulders. *Atqui sciebat*, etc. : whatever tortures are in store for him, he will be at his post of duty.

You concede, however, that there is a touch of humour in the two tragedies here mentioned. Why is it that the idea of persons in service is somehow ludicrous? Perhaps it is made more so in this country by the splendid appearance of the liveried domestics of great people. When you think that we dress in black ourselves, and put our fellow-creatures in green, pink or canary-coloured breeches ; that we order them to plaster their hair with flour, having brushed that nonsense out of our own heads fifty years ago ; that some of the most genteel and stately among us cause the men who drive their carriages to put on little albino wigs, and sit behind great nosegays—I say I suppose it is this heaping of gold lace, gaudy colours, blooming plushes, on honest John Trot, which makes the man absurd in our eyes, who need be nothing but a simple reputable citizen and indoor labourer. Suppose, my dear sir, that you yourself were suddenly desired to put on a full dress, or even undress, domestic uniform with our friend Jones's crest repeated in varied combinations of button on your front and back? Suppose, madam, your

son were told, that he could not get out except in lower
garments of carnation or amber-coloured plush—would
you let him ? . . . But, as you justly say, this is not the
question, and besides it is a question fraught with danger,
sir ; and radicalism, sir ; and subversion of the very
foundations of the social fabric, sir. . . . Well, John, we
won't enter on your great domestic question. Don't let
us disport with Jeames's dangerous strength, and the edge-
tools about his knife-board : but with Betty and Susan
who wield the playful mop, and set on the simmering
kettle. Surely you have heard Mrs. Toddles talking to
Mrs. Doddles about their mutual maids. Miss Susan
must have a silk gown and Miss Betty must wear flowers
under her bonnet when she goes to church if you please,
and did you ever hear such impudence ? The servant in
many small establishments is a constant and endless theme
of talk. What small wage, sleep, meal, what endless
scouring, scolding, tramping on messages fall to that poor
Susan's lot ; what indignation at the little kindly passing
word with the grocer's young man, the pot-boy, the
chubby butcher ! Where such things will end, my dear
Mrs. Toddles, I don't know. What wages they will want
next, my dear Mrs. Doddles, etc.

Here, dear ladies, is an advertisement which I cut out
of the *Times* a few days since, expressly for you :—

"A LADY is desirous of obtaining a SITUATION for
a very respectable young woman as HEAD
KITCHEN-MAID under a man-cook. She has lived
four years under a very good cook and housekeeper. Can
make ice, and is an excellent baker. She will only take
a place in a very good family, where she can have the
opportunity of improving herself, and, if possible, staying
for two years. Apply by letter to," etc. etc.

There, Mrs. Toddles, what do you think of that, and
did you ever ? Well, no, Mrs. Doddles. Upon my

word now, Mrs. T., I don't think I ever did.   A respectable young woman—as head kitchen-maid—under
a man-cook, will only take a place in a very good family,
where she can improve, and stay two years.   Just note
up the conditions, Mrs. Toddles, mum, if you please,
mum, and *then* let us see :—

1. This young woman is to be HEAD kitchen-maid, that
   is to say, there is to be a chorus of kitchen-maids,
   of which Y. W. is to be chief.

2. She will only be situated under a man-cook.   (A)
   Ought he to be a French cook ; and (B), if so,
   would the lady desire him to be a Protestant ?

3. She will only take a place in a *very good family*.   How
   old ought the family to be, and what do you call
   good ?   that is the question.   How long after the
   Conquest will do ?   Would a banker's family do,
   or is a baronet's good enough ?   Best say what
   rank in the peerage would be sufficiently high.
   But the lady does not say whether she would like
   a High Church or a Low Church family.   Ought
   there to be unmarried sons, and may they follow
   a profession ? and please say how many daughters ;
   and would the lady like them to be musical ?   And
   how many company dinners a week ?   Not too
   many, for fear of fatiguing the upper kitchen-
   maid ; but sufficient, so as to keep the upper
   kitchen-maid's hand in.   [*N.B.*—I think I can see
   a rather bewildered expression on the countenances
   of Mesdames Doddles and Toddles as I am prattling
   on in this easy bantering way.]

4. The head kitchen-maid wishes to stay for two years,
   and improve herself under the man-cook, and
   having of course sucked the brains (as the phrase is)

from under the chef's nightcap, then the head kitchen-maid wishes to go.

And upon my word, Mrs. Toddles, mum, I will go and fetch the cab for her. The cab ? Why not her Lady-ship's own carriage and pair, and the head coachman to drive away the head kitchen-maid ? You see she stipu-lates for everything—the time to come ; the time to stay ; the family she will be with ; and as soon as she has im-proved herself enough, of course the upper kitchen-maid will step into the carriage and drive off.

Well, upon my word and conscience, if things are coming to *this* pass, Mrs Toddles and Mrs. Doddles, mum, I think I will go upstairs and get a basin and a sponge, and then downstairs and get some hot water ; and then I will go and scrub that chalk-mark off my own door with my own hands.

It is wiped off, I declare ! After ever so many weeks ! Who has done it ? It was just a little roundabout mark, you know, and it was there for days and weeks, before I ever thought it would be the text of a Roundabout Paper.

Roundabout Papers. 1863.

ON OGRES

W. M. Thackeray

I dare say the reader has remarked that the upright and independent vowel, which stands in the vowel-list between E and O, has formed the subject of the main part of these essays. How does that vowel feel this morning ?—fresh, good-humoured, and lively ? The Roundabout lines, which fall from this pen, are correspondingly brisk and cheerful. Has anything, on the contrary, disagreed with the vowel ? Has its rest been disturbed, or was yesterday's dinner too good, or yesterday's wine not good enough ? Under such circumstances, a darkling misanthropic tinge, no doubt, is cast upon the paper. The jokes, if attempted, are elaborate and dreary. The bitter temper breaks out. That sneering manner is adopted, which you know, and which exhibits itself so especially when the writer is speaking about women. A moody carelessness comes over him. He sees no good in anybody or thing : and treats gentlemen, ladies, history, and things in general, with a like gloomy flippancy. Agreed, when the vowel in question is in that mood, if you like airy gaiety and tender gushing benevolence—if you want to be satisfied with yourself and the rest of your fellow-beings ; I recommend you, my dear creature, to go to some other shop in Cornhill, or turn to some other article. There are moods in the mind of the vowel of which we are speaking when it is ill-conditioned and captious. Who always keeps good health and good humour ? Do not philosophers grumble ? Are not sages sometimes out of temper ? And do not angel-women go off in tantrums ? To-day my mood is dark. I scowl as I dip my pen in the inkstand.

Here is the day come round—for everything here is done with the utmost regularity :—intellectual labour, sixteen hours ; meals, thirty-two minutes ; exercise, a hundred and forty-eight minutes ; conversation with the family, chiefly literary, and about the housekeeping, one hour and four minutes ; sleep, three hours and fifteen minutes (at the end of the month, when the Magazine is complete, I own I take eight minutes more) ; and the rest for the toilette and the world. Well, I say, the *Roundabout Paper Day* being come, and the subject long since settled in my mind, an excellent subject—a most telling, lively, and popular subject—I go to breakfast determined to finish the meal in $9\frac{3}{4}$ minutes, as usual, and then retire to my desk and work, when oh,—provoking ! —here in the paper is the very subject treated on which I was going to write ! Yesterday another paper which I saw treated it—and of course, as I need not tell you, spoiled it. Last Saturday, another paper had an article on the subject ; perhaps you may guess what it was—but I won't tell you. Only this is true, my favourite subject, which was about to make the best paper we have had for a long time ; my bird, my game that I was going to shoot and serve up with such a delicate sauce, has been found by other sportsmen ; and pop, pop, pop, a half-dozen of guns have banged at it, mangled it, and brought it down.

" And can't you take some other text ? " say you. All this is mighty well. But if you have set your heart on a certain dish for dinner, be it cold boiled veal, or what you will, and they bring you turtle and venison, don't you feel disappointed ! During your walk you have been making up your mind that that cold meat, with modera-tion and a pickle, will be a very sufficient dinner : you have accustomed your thoughts to it ; and here, in place of it, is a turkey, surrounded by coarse sausages, or a reeking pigeon-pie, or a fulsome roast pig. I have known many a good and kind man made furiously angry by such a *contretemps*. I have known him lose his temper, call his wife and servants names, and a whole household made miserable. If, then, as is notoriously the case, it is too dangerous to balk a man about his dinner, how much more about his article ! I came to my meal with an ogre-like appetite and gusto. Fee, faw, fum ! Wife, where is that tender little princekin ? Have you trussed him, and did you stuff him nicely, and have you taken care to baste him, and do him, not too brown, as I told you ? Quick ! I am hungry ! I begin to whet my knife, to roll my eyes about, and roar and clap my huge chest like a gorilla ; and then my poor Ogrina has to tell me that the little princes have all run away, whilst she was in the kitchen, making the paste to bake them in ? I pause in the description. I won't condescend to report the bad language, which you know must ensue, when an ogre, whose mind is ill-regulated, and whose habits of self-indulgence are notorious, finds himself disappointed of his greedy hopes. What treatment of his wife, what abuse and brutal behaviour to his children, who, though ogrillons, are children ! My dears, you may fancy, and need not ask my delicate pen to describe, the language and behaviour of a vulgar, coarse, greedy, large man with an immense mouth and teeth, which are too frequently employed in the gobbling and crunching of raw man's meat.

And in this circuitous way you see I have reached my present subject, which is, Ogres. You fancy they are dead or only fictitious characters—mythical representatives of strength, cruelty, stupidity, and lust for blood ? Though they had seven-leagued boots, you remember all sorts of little whipping-snapping Tom Thumbs used to elude and outrun them. They were so stupid that they gave in to the most shallow ambuscades and artifices : witness that well-known ogre, who, because Jack cut open the hasty pudding, instantly ripped open his own stupid waistcoat and interior. They were cruel, brutal, disgusting, with their sharpened teeth, immense knives, and roaring voices ! but they always ended by being overcome by little Tom Thumbkins, or some other smart little champion.

Yes ; they were conquered in the end there is no doubt. They plunged headlong (and uttering the most frightful bad language) into some pit where Jack came with his smart *couteau de chasse*, and whipped their brutal heads off. They would be going to devour maidens,

> ' But ever when it seemed
> Their need was at the sorest,
> A knight, in armour bright,
> Came riding through the forest.'

And down, after a combat, would go the brutal perse-cutor, with a lance through his midriff. Yes, I say, this is very true and well. But you remember that round the ogre's cave the ground was covered, for hundreds and hundreds of yards, *with the bones of the victims* whom he had lured into the castle. Many knights and maids came to him and perished under his knife and teeth. Were dragons the same as ogres ? monsters dwelling in caverns, whence they rushed, attired in plate armour, wielding pikes and torches, and destroying stray passengers who passed by their lair ? Monsters, brutes, rapacious tyrants, ruffians, as they were, doubtless they ended by being over-come. But, before they were destroyed, they did a deal of mischief. The bones round their caves were countless. They had sent many brave souls to Hades, before their own fled, howling out of their rascal carcasses, to the same place of gloom.

There is no greater mistake than to suppose that fairies, champions, distressed damsels, and by consequence ogres, have ceased to exist. It may not be *ogreable* to them (pardon the horrible pleasantry, but as I am writing in the solitude of my chamber, I am grinding my teeth—yelling, roaring, and cursing—brandishing my scissors and paper-cutter and as it were have become an ogre). I say there is no greater mistake than to suppose that ogres have ceased to exist. We all *know* ogres. Their caverns are round us, and about us. There are the castles of several ogres within a mile of the spot where I write. I think some of them suspect I am an ogre myself. I am not, but I know they are. I visit them. I don't mean to say that they take a cold roast prince out of the cupboard, and have a cannibal feast before *me*. But I see the bones lying about the roads to their houses, and in the areas and gardens. Politeness, of course, prevents me from making any remarks : but I know them well enough. One of the ways to know 'em is to watch the scared looks of the ogres' wives and children. They lead an awful life. They are present at dreadful cruelties. In their excesses those ogres will stab about and kill not only strangers who happen to call in and ask a night's lodging, but they will outrage, murder, and chop up their own kin. We all know ogres, I say, and have been in their dens often. It is not necessary that ogres who ask you to dine should offer their guests the *peculiar dish* which they like. They cannot always get a Tom Thumb family. They eat mutton and beef too ; and I dare say even go out to tea, and invite you to drink it. But I tell you there are numbers of them going about in the world. And now you have my word for it, and this little hint, it is quite curious what an interest society may be made to have for you by your determining to find out the ogres you meet there.

What does the man mean ? says Mrs. Downright, to whom a joke is a very grave thing. I mean, madam,

that in the company assembled in your genteel drawing-
room, who bow here and there, and smirk in white
neckcloths, you receive men who elbow through life
successfully enough, but who are ogres in private : men
wicked, false, rapacious, flattering ; cruel hectors at home,
smiling courtiers abroad ; causing wives, children, servants, parents, to tremble before them, and smiling and
bowing, as they bid strangers welcome into their castles.
I say, there are men who have crunched the bones of
victim after victim ; in whose closets lie skeletons picked
frightfully clean. When these ogres come out into the
world, you don't suppose they show their knives, and
their great teeth ? A neat simple white neckcloth, a
merry rather obsequious manner, a cadaverous look,
perhaps, now and again, and a rather dreadful grin ; but I
know ogres very considerably respected : and when you
hint to such and such a man, "My dear sir, Mr. Sharpus,
whom you appear to like, is, I assure you, a most dreadful
cannibal;" the gentleman cries, "Oh, psha, nonsense !
Dare say not so black as he is painted. Dare say not worse
than his neighbours." We condone everything in this
country—private treason, falsehood, flattery, cruelty at
home, roguery, and double-dealing. What ! Do you
mean to say in your acquaintance you don't know ogres
guilty of countless crimes of fraud and force, and that
knowing them you don't shake hands with them ; dine
with them at your table ; and meet them at their own ?
Depend upon it in the time when there were real live
ogres, in real caverns or castles, gobbling up real knights
and virgins, when they went into the world—the neighbouring market-town, let us say, or earl's castle—though
their nature and reputation were pretty well known, their
notorious foibles were never alluded to. You would say,
"What, Blunderbore, my boy ! How do you do ?
How well and fresh you look ! What's the receipt you
have for keeping so young and rosy ?" And your wife

would softly ask after Mrs. Blunderbore and the dear children. Or it would be, "My dear Humguffin! try that pork. It is home-bred, home-fed, and, I promise you, tender. Tell me if you think it is as good as yours? John, a glass of Burgundy to Colonel Humguffin!" You don't suppose there would be any unpleasant allusions to disagreeable home-reports regarding Humguffin's manner of furnishing his larder? I say we all of us know ogres. We shake hands and dine with ogres. And if inconvenient moralists tell us we are cowards for our pains, we turn round with a *tu quoque*, or say that we don't meddle with other folk's affairs; that people are much less black than they are painted, and so on. What! Won't half the county go to Ogreham Castle? Won't some of the clergy say grace at dinner? Won't the mothers bring their daughters to dance with the young Rawheads? And if Lady Ogreham happens to die—I won't say to go the way of all flesh, that is too revolting—I say if Ogreham is a widower, do you aver, on your conscience and honour, that mothers will not be found to offer their young girls to supply the lamented lady's place? How stale this misanthropy is! Something must have disagreed with this cynic. Yes, my good woman. I dare say you would like to call another subject. Yes, my fine fellow; ogre at home, supple as a dancing-master abroad, and shaking in thy pumps, and wearing a horrible grin of sham gaiety to conceal thy terror, lest I should point thee out:—thou art prosperous and honoured, art thou? I say thou hast been a tyrant and a robber. Thou hast plundered the poor. Thou hast bullied the weak. Thou hast laid violent hands on the goods of the innocent and confiding. Thou hast made a prey of the meek and gentle who asked for thy protection. Thou hast been hard to thy kinsfolk, and cruel to thy family. Go, monster! Ah, when shall little Jack come and drill daylight through thy wicked cannibal carcass? I see the ogre pass on, bowing right and left to the company ; and he gives a dreadful sidelong glance of suspicion as he is talking to my Lord Bishop in the corner there.

Ogres in our days need not be giants at all. In former times, and in children's books, where it is necessary to paint your moral in such large letters that there can be no mistake about it, ogres are made with that enormous mouth and *râtelier* which you know of, and with which they can swallow down a baby, almost without using that great knife which they always carry. They are too cunning nowadays. They go about in society, slim, small, quietly dressed, and showing no especially great appetite. In my own young days there used to be play ogres—men who would devour a young fellow in one sitting, and leave him without a bit of flesh on his bones. They were quiet gentlemanlike-looking people. They got the young fellow into their cave. Champagne, pâté-de-foie-gras, and numberless good things, were handed about ; and then, having eaten, the young man was devoured in his turn. I believe these card and dice ogres have died away almost as entirely as the hasty-pudding giants whom Tom Thumb overcame. Now, there are ogres in city courts who lure you into their dens. About our Cornish mines I am told there are many most plausible ogres, who tempt you into their caverns and pick your bones there. In a certain newspaper there used to be lately a whole column of advertisements from ogres who would put on the most plausible, nay, piteous appearance, in order to inveigle their victims. You would read, " A tradesman, established for seventy years in the City, and known and much respected by Messrs. N. M. Rothschild and Baring Brothers, has pressing need for three pounds until next Saturday. He can give security for half a million, and forty thousand pounds will be given for the use of the loan," and so on ; or, " An influential body of capitalists are about to establish a company, of which the business will be enormous and the profits proportionately prodigious. They will require a SECRETARY, of good address and appearance, at a salary of two thousand per annum. He need not be able to write, but address and manners are absolutely necessary. As a mark of confidence in the company, he will have to deposit," etc.; or, "A young widow (of pleasing manners and appearance) who has a pressing necessity for four pounds ten for three weeks, offers her Erard's grand piano valued at three hundred guineas ; a diamond cross of eight hundred pounds ; and board and lodging in her elegant villa near Banbury Cross, with the best references and society, in return for the loan." I suspect these people are ogres. There are ogres and ogres. Polyphemus was a great, tall, one-eyed, notorious ogre, fetching his victims out of a hole, and gobbling them one after another. There could be no mistake about him. But so were the Sirens ogres —pretty blue-eyed things, peeping at you coaxingly from out of the water, and singing their melodious wheedles. And the bones round their caves were more numerous than the ribs, skulls, and thigh-bones round the cavern of hulking Polypheme.

To the castle-gates of some of these monsters up rides the dapper champion of the pen ; puffs boldly upon the horn which hangs by the chain ; enters the hall resolutely, and challenges the big tyrant sulking within. We defy him to combat, the enormous roaring ruffian ! We give him a meeting on the green plain before his castle. Green ? No wonder it should be green : it is manured with human bones. After a few graceful wheels and curvets, we take our ground. We stoop over our saddle. 'Tis but to kiss the locket of our lady-love's hair. And now the vizor is up : the lance is in rest (Gillott's iron is the point for me). A touch of the spur in the gallant sides of Pegasus, and we gallop at the great brute.

"Cut off his ugly head, Flibbertigibbet, my squire !"

And who are those who pour out of the castle ? the imprisoned maidens, the maltreated widows, the poor old hoary grandfathers, who have been locked up in the dungeons these scores and scores of years, writhing under the tyranny of that ruffian ! Ah, ye knights of the pen ! May honour be your shield, and truth tip your lances ! Be gentle to all gentle people. Be modest to women. Be tender to children. And as for the Ogre Humbug, out sword and have at him.

Roundabout Papers.   1863.

ON FRIENDSHIP

R. W. EMERSON

A ruddy drop of manly blood
The surging sea outweighs ;
The world uncertain comes and goes,
The lover rooted stays.
I fancied he was fled,
And, after many a year,
Glowed unexhausted kindliness
Like daily sunrise there.
My careful heart was free again,—
O friend, my bosom said,
Through thee alone the sky is arched,
Through thee the rose is red,
All things through thee take nobler form
And look beyond the earth,
The mill-round of our fate appears
A sun-path in thy worth.
Me too thy nobleness has taught
To master my despair ;
The fountains of my hidden life
Are through thy friendship fair.

WE have a great deal more kindness than is ever spoken. Maugre all the selfishness that chills like east winds the world, the whole human family is bathed with an element of love like a fine ether. How many persons we meet in houses, whom we scarcely speak to, whom yet we honour, and who honour us ! How many we see in the street, or sit with in church, whom, though silently, we warmly rejoice to be with ! Read the language of these wandering eye-beams. The heart knoweth.

The effect of the indulgence of this human affection is a certain cordial exhilaration. In poetry and in common speech the emotions of benevolence and complacency which are felt towards others are likened to the material effects of fire ; so swift, or much more swift, more active, more cheering, are these fine inward irradiations. From the highest degree of passionate love to the lowest degree of good-will, they make the sweetness of life.

Our intellectual and active powers increase with our affection. The scholar sits down to write, and all his years of meditation do not furnish him with one good thought or happy expression ; but it is necessary to write a letter to a friend,—and forthwith troops of gentle thoughts invest themselves, on every hand, with chosen words. See, in any house where virtue and self-respect abide, the palpitation which the approach of a stranger causes. A commended stranger is expected and an-nounced, and an uneasiness betwixt pleasure and pain invades all the hearts of a household. His arrival almost brings fear to the good hearts that would welcome him. The house is dusted, all things fly into their places, the old coat is exchanged for the new, and they must get up a dinner if they can. Of a commended stranger, only the good report is told by others, only the good and new is heard by us. He stands to us for humanity. He is what we wish. Having imagined and invested him, we ask how we should stand related in conversation and action with such a man, and are uneasy with fear. The same idea exalts conversation with him. We talk better than we are wont. We have the nimblest fancy, a richer memory, and our dumb devil has taken leave for the time. For long hours we can continue a series of sincere, graceful, rich communications, drawn from the oldest, secretest experience, so that they who sit by, of our own kinsfolk and acquaintance, shall feel a lively surprise at our unusual powers. But as soon as the stranger begins to intrude his partialities, his definitions, his defects into the conversation, it is all over. He has heard the first, the last and best he will ever hear from us. He is no stranger now. Vulgarity, ignorance, misapprehension are old acquaintances. Now, when he comes, he may get the order, the dress and the dinner,—but the throbbing of the heart and the communications of the soul, no more.

What is so pleasant as these jets of affection which make a young world for me again ? What so delicious as a just and firm encounter of two, in a thought, in a feeling ? How beautiful, on their approach to this beating heart, the steps and forms of the gifted and the true ! The moment we indulge our affections, the earth is metamorphosed ; there is no winter and no night ; all tragedies, all ennuis vanish—all duties even ; nothing fills the proceeding eternity but the forms all radiant of beloved persons. Let the soul be assured that somewhere in the universe it should rejoin its friend, and it would be content and cheerful alone for a thousand years.

I awoke this morning with devout thanksgiving for my friends, the old and the new. Shall I not call God the Beautiful, who daily showeth himself so to me in his gifts ? I chide society, I embrace solitude, and yet I am not so ungrateful as not to see the wise, the lovely and the noble-minded, as from time to time they pass my gate. Who hears me, who understands me, becomes mine—a possession for all time. Nor is Nature so poor but she gives me this joy several times, and thus we weave social threads of our own, a new web of relations ; and, as many thoughts in succession substantiate themselves, we shall by and by stand in a new world of our own creation, and no longer strangers and pilgrims in a traditionary globe. My friends have come to me unsought. The great God gave them to me. By oldest right, by the divine affinity of virtue with itself, I find them, or rather not I but the Deity in me and in them

derides and cancels the thick walls of individual character, relation, age, sex, circumstance, at which he usually
connives, and now makes many one.   High thanks I
owe you, excellent lovers, who carry out the world for
me to new and noble depths, and enlarge the meaning
of all my thoughts.   These are new poetry of the first
Bard—poetry without stop—hymn, ode and epic, poetry
still flowing, Apollo and the Muses chanting still.   Will
these two separate themselves from me again, or some of
them ?   I know not, but I fear it not ; for my relation to
them is so pure that we hold by simple affinity, and the
Genius of my life being thus social, the same affinity will
exert its energy on whomsoever is as noble as these men
and women, wherever I may be.

  I confess to an extreme tenderness of nature on this
point.   It is almost dangerous to me to " crush the
sweet poison of misused wine " of the affections.   A new
person is to me a great event and hinders me from sleep.
I have often had fine fancies about persons which have
given me delicious hours ; but the joy ends in the day ;
it yields no fruit.   Thought is not born of it ; my action
is very little modified.   I must feel pride in my friend's
accomplishments as if they were mine, and a property in
his virtues.   I feel as warmly when he is praised, as the
lover when he hears applause of his engaged maiden.   We
over-estimate the conscience of our friend.   His goodness
seems better than our goodness, his nature finer, his
temptations less.   Everything that is his—his name, his
form, his dress, books and instruments—fancy enhances.
Our own thought sounds new and larger from his mouth.

  Yet the systole and diastole of the heart are not without
their analogy in the ebb and flow of love.   Friendship,
like the immortality of the soul, is too good to be believed.
The lover, beholding his maiden, half knows that she is
not verily that which he worships ; and in the golden
hour of friendship we are surprised with shades of suspicion

and unbelief. We doubt that we bestow on our hero the virtues in which he shines, and afterwards worship the form to which we have ascribed this divine inhabitation. In strictness, the soul does not respect men as it respects itself. In strict science all persons underlie the same condition of an infinite remoteness. Shall we fear to cool our love by mining for the metaphysical foundation of this Elysian temple ? Shall I not be as real as the things I see ? If I am, I shall not fear to know them for what they are. Their essence is not less beautiful than their appearance, though it needs finer organs for its apprehension. The root of the plant is not unsightly to science, though for chaplets and festoons we cut the stem short. And I must hazard the production of the bald fact amidst these pleasing reveries, though it should prove an Egyptian skull at our banquet. A man who stands united with his thought conceives magnificently of himself. He is conscious of a universal success, even though bought by uniform particular failures. No advantages, no powers, no gold or force, can be any match for him. I cannot choose but rely on my own poverty more than on your wealth. I cannot make your consciousness tantamount to mine. Only the star dazzles ; the planet has a faint, moon-like ray. I hear what you say of the admirable parts and tried temper of the party you praise, but I see well that, for all his purple cloaks, I shall not like him, unless he is at last a poor Greek like me. I cannot deny it, O friend, that the vast shadow of the Phenomenal includes thee also in its pied and painted immensity,— thee also, compared with whom all else is shadow. Thou art not Being, as Truth is, as Justice is,—thou art not my soul, but a picture and effigy of that. Thou hast come to me lately, and already thou art seizing thy hat and cloak. Is it not that the soul puts forth friends as the tree puts forth leaves, and presently, by the germination of new buds, extrudes the old leaf ? The law of nature is alterna-

tion for evermore.   Each electrical state superinduces the
opposite.   The soul environs itself with friends that it
may enter into a grander self-acquaintance or solitude ;
and it goes alone for a season that it may exalt its conversation or society.   This method betrays itself along the
whole history of our personal relations.   The instinct of
affection revives the hope of union with our mates, and
the returning sense of insulation recalls us from the chase.
Thus every man passes his life in the search after friendship, and if he should record his true sentiment, he might
write a letter like this to each new candidate for his love :

DEAR FRIEND,
    If I was sure of thee, sure of thy capacity, sure
to match my mood with thine, I should never think
again of trifles in relation to thy comings and goings.
I am not very wise ; my moods are quite attain-
able, and I respect thy genius ; it is to me as yet
unfathomed ; yet dare I not presume in thee a
perfect intelligence of me, and so thou art to me
a delicious torment.   Thine ever, or never.

Yet these uneasy pleasures and fine pains are for curiosity
and not for life.   They are not to be indulged.   This is
to weave cobweb, and not cloth.   Our friendships hurry
to short and poor conclusions, because we have made
them a texture of wine and dreams, instead of the tough
fibre of the human heart.   The laws of friendship are
austere and eternal, of one web with the laws of nature
and of morals.   But we have aimed at a swift and petty
benefit, to suck a sudden sweetness.   We snatch at the
slowest fruit in the whole garden of God, which many
summers and many winters must ripen.   We seek our
friend not sacredly, but with an adulterate passion which
would appropriate him to ourselves.   In vain.   We are
armed all over with subtle antagonisms, which, as soon

as we meet, begin to play, and translate all poetry into stale prose. Almost all people descend to meet. All association must be a compromise, and, what is worst, the very flower and aroma of the flower of each of the beautiful natures disappears as they approach each other. What a perpetual disappointment is actual society, even of the virtuous and gifted ! After interviews have been compassed with long foresight we must be tormented presently by baffled blows, by sudden, unseasonable apathies, by epilepsies of wit and of animal spirits, in the heyday of friendship and thought. Our faculties do not play us true, and both parties are relieved by solitude.

I ought to be equal to every relation. It makes no difference how many friends I have and what content I can find in conversing with each, if there be one to whom I am not equal. If I have shrunk unequal from one contest, the joy I find in all the rest becomes mean and cowardly. I should hate myself, if then I made my other friends my asylum.

> The valiant warrior famoused for fight,
> After a hundred victories, once foiled,
> Is from the book of honour razed quite
> And all the rest forgot for which he toiled.

Our impatience is thus sharply rebuked. Bashfulness and apathy are a tough husk in which a delicate organization is protected from premature ripening. It would be lost if it knew itself before any of the best souls were yet ripe enough to know and own it. Respect the *Naturlangsamkeit* which hardens the ruby in a million years, and works in duration in which Alps and Andes come and go as rainbows. The good spirit of our life has no heaven which is the price of rashness. Love, which is the essence of God, is not for levity, but for the total worth of man. Let us not have this childish luxury in our regards, but the austerest worth ; let us approach our friend with an audacious trust in the truth of his heart, in the breadth, impossible to be overturned, of his foundations.

The attractions of this subject are not to be resisted, and I leave, for the time, all account of subordinate social benefit, to speak of that select and sacred relation which is a kind of absolute, and which even leaves the language of love suspicious and common, so much is this purer, and nothing is so much divine.

I do not wish to treat friendships daintily, but with roughest courage. When they are real, they are not glass threads or frostwork, but the solidest thing we know. For now, after so many ages of experience, what do we know of nature or of ourselves ? Not one step has man taken toward the solution of this problem of his destiny. In one condemnation of folly stand the whole universe of men. But the sweet sincerity of joy and peace which I draw from this alliance with my brother's soul is the nut itself whereof all nature and all thought is but the husk and shell. Happy is the house that shelters a friend ! It might well be built, like a festal bower or arch, to entertain him a single day. Happier, if he knew the solemnity of that relation and honour its law ! He who offers himself a candidate for that covenant comes up, like an Olympian, to the great games where the first-born of the world are the competitors. He proposes himself for contests where Time, Want, Danger, are in the lists, and he alone is victor who has truth enough in his con-stitution to preserve the delicacy of his beauty from the wear and tear of all these. The gifts of fortune may be present or absent, but all the speed in that contest depends on intrinsic nobleness and the contempt of trifles. There are two elements that go to the composition of friendship, each so sovereign that I can detect no superiority in either, no reason why either should be first named. One is truth. A friend is a person with whom I may be sincere. Before him I may think aloud. I am arrived at last in the presence of a man so real and equal that I may drop even those undermost garments of dissimulation, courtesy, and second thought, which men never put off, and may deal with him with the simplicity and wholeness with which one chemical atom meets another. Sincerity is the luxury allowed, like diadems and authority, only to the highest rank ; *that* being permitted to speak truth, as having none above it to court or conform unto. Every man alone is sincere. At the entrance of a second person, hypocrisy begins. We parry and fend the approach of our fellow-man by compliments, by gossip, by amusements, by affairs. We cover up our thoughts from him under a hundred folds. I knew a man who under a certain religious frenzy cast off this drapery, and omitting all compliment and commonplace, spoke to the conscience of every person he encountered, and that with great insight and beauty. At first he was resisted, and all men agreed he was mad. But persisting—as indeed he could not help doing—for some time in this course, he attained to the advantage of bringing every man of his acquaintance into true relations with him. No man would think of speaking falsely with him, or of putting him off with any chat of markets or reading-rooms. But every man was constrained by so much sincerity to the like plain-dealing, and what love of nature, what poetry, what symbol of truth he had, he did certainly show him. But to most of us society shows not its face and eye, but its side and its back. To stand in true relations with men in a false age is worth a bit of insanity, is it not ? We can seldom go erect. Almost every man we meet requires some civility —requires to be humoured ; he has some fame, some talent, some whim of religion or philanthropy in his head that is not to be questioned, and which spoils all conversa-

tion with him.   But a friend is a sane man who exercises
not my ingenuity, but me.   My friend gives me entertainment without requiring any stipulation on my part.
A friend therefore is a sort of paradox in nature.   I who
alone am, I who see nothing in nature whose existence I
can affirm with equal evidence to my own, behold how
the semblance of my being, in all its height, variety and
curiosity, reiterated in a foreign form ;   so that a friend
may well be reckoned the masterpiece of nature.

The other element of friendship is tenderness.   We
are holden to men by every sort of tie, by blood, by pride,
by fear, by hope, by lucre, by lust, by hate, by admiration,
by every circumstance and badge and trifle,—but we can
scarce believe that so much character can subsist in another as to draw us by love.   Can another be so blessed
and we so pure that we can offer him tenderness ?   When
a man becomes dear to me I have touched the goal of
fortune.   I find very little written directly to the heart
of this matter in books.   And yet I have one text which I
cannot choose but remember.   My author says " I offer
myself faintly and bluntly to those whose I effectually am,
and tender myself least to him to whom I am the most
devoted."   I wish that friendship should have feet, as well
as eyes and eloquence.   It must plant itself on the ground,
before it vaults over the moon.   I wish it to be a little of
a citizen, before it is quite a cherub.   We chide the citizen
because he makes love a commodity.   It is an exchange of
gifts, of useful loans ;   it is good neighbourhood ;   it
watches with the sick ;   it holds the pall at the funeral ;
and quite loses sight of the delicacies and nobility of the
relation.   But though we cannot find the god under this
disguise of a sutler, yet on the other hand we cannot
forgive the poet if he spins his thread too fine and does
not substantiate his romance by the municipal virtues of
justice, punctuality, fidelity, and pity.   I hate the prosti-
tution of the name of friendship to signify modish and

worldly alliances.   I much prefer the company of plough-
boys and tin-pedlars to the silken and perfumed amity
which celebrates its days of encounter by a frivolous
display, by rides in a curricle and dinners at the best
taverns.   The end of friendship is a commerce the most
strict and homely that can be joined ; more strict than
any of which we have experience.   It is for aid and
comfort through all the relations and passages of life and
death.   It is fit for serene days and graceful gifts and
country rambles, but also for rough roads and hard fare,
shipwreck, poverty and persecution.   It keeps company
with the sallies of the wit and the trances of religion.   We
are to dignify to each other the daily needs and offices of
man's life, and embellish it by courage, wisdom and
unity.   It should never fall into something usual and
settled, but should be alert and inventive and add rhyme
and reason to what was drudgery.

Friendship may be said to require natures so rare and
costly, each so well tempered and so happily adapted, and
withal so circumstanced (for even in that particular, a
poet says, love demands that the parties be altogether
paired), that its satisfaction can very seldom be assured.
It cannot subsist in its perfection, say some of those who
are learned in this warm lore of the heart, betwixt more
than two.   I am not quite so strict in my terms, perhaps
because I have never known so high a fellowship as others.
I please my imagination more with a circle of godlike
men and women variously related to each other and
between whom subsists a lofty intelligence.   But I find
this law of *one to one* peremptory for conversation, which
is the practice and consummation of friendship.   Do not
mix waters too much.   The best mix as ill as good and
bad.   You shall have very useful and cheering discourse
at several times with two several men, but let all three ot
you come together and you shall not have one new and
hearty word.   Two may talk and one may hear, but

three cannot take part in a conversation of the most sincere and searching sort. In good company there is never such discourse between two, across the table, as takes place when you leave them alone. In good company the individuals merge their egotism into a social soul exactly co-extensive with the several consciousnesses there present. No partialities of friend to friend, no fondnesses of brother to sister, of wife to husband, are there pertinent, but quite otherwise. Only he may then speak who can sail on the common thought of the party, and not poorly limited to his own. Now this convention, which good sense demands, destroys the high freedom of great conversation, which requires an absolute running of two souls into one.

No two men but being left alone with each other enter into simpler relations. Yet it is affinity that determines *which* two shall converse. Unrelated men give little joy to each other, will never suspect the latent powers of each. We talk sometimes of a great talent for conversation, as if it were a permanent property in some individuals. Conversation is an evanescent relation—no more. A man is reputed to have thought and eloquence ; he cannot, for all that, say a word to his cousin or his uncle. They accuse his silence with as much reason as they would blame the insignificance of a dial in the shade. In the sun it will mark the hour. Among those who enjoy his thought he will regain his tongue.

Friendship requires that rare mean betwixt likeness and unlikeness that piques each with the presence of power and of consent in the other party. Let me be alone to the end of the world, rather than that my friend should overstep, by a word or a look, his real sympathy. I am equally baulked by antagonism and by compliance. Let him not cease an instant to be himself. The only joy I have in his being mine, is that the *not mine* is *mine*. I hate, when I looked for a manly furtherance or at least a manly resistance, to find a mush of concession. Better be a nettle in the side of your friend than his echo. The condition which high friendship demands is ability to do without it. That high office requires great and sublime parts. There must be very two, before there can be very one. Let it be an alliance of two large formidable natures, mutually beheld, mutually feared, before yet they recognize the deep identity which, beneath these disparities, unites them.

He only is fit for this society who is magnanimous ; who is sure that greatness and goodness are always economy ; who is not swift to intermeddle with his fortunes. Let him not intermeddle with this. Leave to the diamond its ages to grow, nor expect to accelerate the births of the eternal. Friendship demands a religious treatment. We talk of choosing our friends, but friends are self-elected. Reverence is a great part of it. Treat your friend as a spectacle. Of course he has merits that are not yours, and that you cannot honour if you must needs hold him close to your person. Stand aside ; give those merits room ; let them mount and expand. Are you the friend of your friend's buttons, or of his thought ? To a great heart he will still be a stranger in a thousand particulars, that he may come near in the holiest ground. Leave it to girls and boys to regard a friend as property, and to suck a short and all-confounding pleasure, instead of the noblest benefit.

Let us buy our entrance to this guild by a long probation. Why should we desecrate noble and beautiful souls by intruding on them ? Why insist on rash personal relations with your friend ? Why go to his house, or know his mother and brother and sisters ? Why be visited by him at your own ? Are these things material to our covenant ? Leave this touching and clawing. Let him be to me a spirit. A message, a thought, a sincerity, a glance from him, I want, but not news, nor

pottage. I can get politics and chat and neighbourly
conveniences from cheaper companions. Should not the
society of my friend be to me poetic, pure, universal, and
great as nature itself? Ought I to feel that our tie is
profane in comparison with yonder bar of cloud that
sleeps on the horizon, or that clump of waving grass that
divides the brook? Let us not vilify, but raise it to that
standard. That great defying eye, that scornful beauty
of his mien and action, do not pique yourself on reducing,
but rather fortify and enhance. Worship his superiorities ;
wish him not less by a thought, but hoard and tell them all.
Guard him as thy counterpart. Let him be to thee for
ever a sort of beautiful enemy, untamable, devoutly
revered, and not a trivial conveniency to be soon outgrown
and cast aside. The hues of the opal, the light of the
diamond, are not to be seen if the eye is too near. To
my friend I write a letter and from him I receive a letter.
That seems to you a little. It suffices me. It is a spiritual
gift, worthy of him to give and of me to receive. It
profanes nobody. In these warm lines the heart will
trust itself, as it will not to the tongue, and pour out the
prophecy of a godlier existence than all the annals of
heroism have yet made good.

Respect so far the holy laws of this fellowship as not
to prejudice its perfect flower by your impatience for
its opening. We must be our own before we can be
another's. There is at least this satisfaction in crime,
according to the Latin proverb ; you can speak to your
accomplice on even terms. *Crimen quos inquinat, æquat.*
To those whom we admire and love, at first we cannot.
Yet the least defect of self-possession vitiates, in my
judgment, the entire relation. There can never be deep
peace between two spirits, never mutual respect, until
in their dialogue each stands for the whole world.

What is so great as friendship, let us carry with what
grandeur of spirit we can. Let us be silent—so we may

hear the whisper of the gods. Let us not interfere. Who set you to cast about what you should say to the select souls, or how to say anything to such ? No matter how ingenious, no matter how graceful and bland. There are innumerable degrees of folly and wisdom, and for you to say aught is to be frivolous. Wait, and thy heart shall speak. Wait until the necessary and everlasting over-powers you, until day and night avail themselves of your lips. The only reward of virtue is virtue ; the only way to have a friend is to be one. You shall not come nearer a man by getting into his house. If unlike, his soul only flees the faster from you, and you shall never catch a true glance of his eye. We see the whole afar off and they repel us ; why should we intrude ? Late—very late— we perceive that no arrangements, no introductions, no consuetudes or habits of society would be of any avail to establish us in such relations with them as we desire, but solely the uprise of nature in us to the same degree it is in them ; then shall we meet as water with water ; and if we should not meet them then, we shall not want them, for we are already they. In the last analysis, love is only the reflection of a man's own worthiness from other men. Men have sometimes exchanged names with their friends, as if they would signify that in their friend each loved his own soul.

The higher the style we demand of friendship, of course the less easy to establish it with flesh and blood. We walk alone in the world. Friends such as we desire are dreams and fables. But a sublime hope cheers ever the faithful heart, that elsewhere, in other regions of the universal power, souls are now acting, enduring and daring, which can love us and which we can love. We may congratulate ourselves that the period of nonage, of follies, of blunders, and of shame, is passed in solitude, and when we are finished men we shall grasp heroic hands in heroic hands. Only be admonished by what you already see, not to strike leagues of friendship with cheap persons, where no friendship can be. Our impatience betrays us into rash and foolish alliances which no god attends. By persisting in your path, though you forfeit the little you gain the great. You demonstrate yourself, so as to put yourself out of the reach of false relations, and you draw to you the first-born of the world, —those rare pilgrims whereof only one or two wander in nature at once, and before whom the vulgar great show as spectres and shadows merely.

It is foolish to be afraid of making our ties too spiritual, as if so we could lose any genuine love. Whatever correction of our popular views we make from insight, nature will be sure to bear us out in, and though it seem to rob us of some joy, will repay us with a greater. Let us feel if we will the absolute insulation of man. We are sure that we have all in us. We go to Europe, or we pursue persons, or we read books, in the instinctive faith that these will call it out and reveal us to ourselves. Beggars all. The persons are such as we ; the Europe, an old faded garment of dead persons ; the books, their ghosts. Let us drop this idolatry. Let us give over this mendicancy. Let us even bid our dearest friends farewell, and defy them, saying " Who are you ? Unhand me : I will be dependent no more." Ah ! seest thou not, O brother, that thus we part only to meet again on a higher platform, and only be more each other's because we are more our own ? A friend is Janus-faced ; he looks to the past and the future. He is the child of all my foregoing hours, the prophet of those to come, and the harbinger of a greater friend.

I do then with my friends as I do with my books. I would have them where I can find them, but I seldom use them. We must have society on our own terms, and admit or exclude it on the slightest cause. I cannot afford to speak much with my friend. If he is great he makes me so great that I cannot descend to converse. In the great days, presentiments hover before me in the firmament. I ought then to dedicate myself to them. I go in that I may seize them, I go out that I may seize them. I fear only that I may lose them receding into the sky in which now they are only a patch of brighter light. Then, though I prize my friends, I cannot afford to talk with them and study their visions, lest I lose my own. It would indeed give me a certain household joy to quit this lofty seeking, this spiritual astronomy or search of stars, and come down to warm sympathies with you ; but then I know well I shall mourn always the vanishing of my mighty gods. It is true, next week I shall have languid moods, when I can well afford to occupy myself with foreign objects ; then I shall regret the lost literature of your mind, and wish you were by my side again. But if you come, perhaps you will fill my mind only with new visions ; not with yourself but with your lustres, and I shall not be able any more than now to converse with you. So I will owe to my friends this evanescent intercourse. I will receive from them not what they have but what they are. They shall give me that which properly they cannot give, but which emanates from them. But they shall not hold me by any relations less subtile and pure. We will meet as though we met not, and part as though we parted not.

It has seemed to me lately more possible than I knew, to carry a friendship greatly, on one side, without due correspondence on the other. Why should I cumber myself with regrets that the receiver is not capacious ? It never troubles the sun that some of his rays fall wide and vain into ungrateful space, and only a small part on the reflecting planet. Let your greatness educate the crude and cold companion. If he is unequal he will presently pass away ; but thou art enlarged by thy own shining, and no longer a mate for frogs and worms, dost soar and burn with the gods of the empyrean. It is thought a disgrace to love unrequited. But the great will see that true love cannot be unrequited. True love transcends the unworthy object and dwells and broods on the eternal, and when the poor interposed mask crumbles, it is not sad, but feels rid of so much earth and feels its independency the surer. Yet these things may hardly be said without a sort of treachery to the relation. The essence of friendship is entireness, a total magnanimity and trust. It must not surmise or provide for infirmity. It treats its object as a god, that it may deify both.

Essays. 1841.

THE CHILD IN THE HOUSE

WALTER PATER

As Florian Deleal walked, one hot afternoon, he overtook
by the wayside a poor aged man, and, as he seemed weary
with the road, helped him on with the burden which he
carried, a certain distance.   And as the man told his story,
it chanced that he named the place, a little place in the
neighbourhood of a great city, where Florian had passed
his earliest years, but which he had never since seen, and,
the story told, went forward on his journey comforted.
And that night, like a reward for his pity, a dream of that
place came to Florian, a dream which did for him the
office of the finer sort of memory, bringing its object to
mind with a great clearness, yet, as sometimes happens in
dreams, raised a little above itself, and above ordinary
retrospect.   The true aspect of the place, especially of the
house there in which he had lived as a child, the fashion
of its doors, its hearths, its windows, the very scent upon
the air of it, was with him in sleep for a season ;   only,
with tints more musically blent on wall and floor, and
some finer light and shadow running in and out along
its curves and angles, and with all its little carvings
daintier.   He awoke with a sigh at the thought of almost
thirty years which lay between him and that place, yet
with a flutter of pleasure still within him at the fair light,
as if it were a smile, upon it.   And it happened that this
accident of his dream was just the thing needed for the
beginning of a certain design he then had in view, the

noting, namely, of some things in the story of his spirit—
in that process of brain-building by which we are, each
one of us, what we are. With the image of the place so
clear and favourable upon him, he fell to thinking of
himself therein, and how his thoughts had grown up to
him. In that half-spiritualized house he could watch the
better, over again, the gradual expansion of the soul which
had come to be there—of which indeed, through the law
which makes the material objects about them so large an
element in children's lives, it had actually become a part ;
inward and outward being woven through and through
each other into one inextricable texture—half, tint and
trace and accident of homely colour and form, from the
wood and the bricks ; half, mere soul-stuff, floated thither
from who knows how far. In the house and garden of
his dream he saw a child moving, and could divide the
main streams at least of the winds that had played on him,
and study so the first stage in that mental journey.

The *old house*, as when Florian talked of it afterwards
he always called it (as all children do, who can recollect
a change of home, soon enough but not too soon to mark
a period in their lives), really was an old house ; and an
element of French descent in its inmates—descent from
Watteau, the old court-painter, one of whose gallant
pieces still hung in one of the rooms—might explain,
together with some other things, a noticeable trimness
and comely whiteness about everything there—the curtains, the couches, the paint on the walls with which the
light and shadow played so delicately ; might explain
also the tolerance of the great poplar in the garden, a tree
most often despised by English people, but which French
people love, having observed a certain fresh way its leaves
have of dealing with the wind, making it sound, in never
so slight a stirring of the air, like running water.

The old-fashioned, low wainscoting went round the
rooms, and up the staircase with carved balusters and

shadowy angles, landing half-way up at a broad
window, with a swallow's nest below the sill, and the
blossom of an old pear-tree showing across it in late
April, against the blue, below which the perfumed juice
of the rind of fallen fruit in autumn was so fresh. At the
next turning came the closet which held on its deep
shelves the best china. Little angel faces and reedy flut-
ings stood out round the fireplace of the children's room.
And on the top of the house, above the large attic, where
the white mice ran in the twilight—an infinite, unexplored
wonderland of childish treasures, glass beads, empty
scent-bottles, still sweet, thrum of coloured silks, among
its lumber—a flat space of roof, railed round, gave a view
of the neighbouring steeples ; for the house, as I said,
stood near a great city, which sent up heavenwards, over
the twisting weather-vanes, not seldom, its beds of
rolling cloud and smoke, touched with storm or sunshine.
But the child of whom I am writing did not hate the fog
because of the crimson lights which fell from it sometimes
upon the chimneys, and the whites which gleamed
through its openings, on summer mornings, on turret or
pavement. For it is false to suppose that a child's sense
of beauty is dependent on any choiceness or special fineness
in the objects which present themselves to it, though this
indeed comes to be the rule with most of us in later life ;
earlier, in some degree, we see inwardly ; and the child
finds for itself, and with unstinted delight, a difference
for the sense, in those whites and reds through the smoke
on very homely buildings, and in the gold of the dande-
lions at the roadside, just beyond the houses, where not
a handful of earth is virgin and untouched, in the lack
of better ministries to its desire of beauty.

This house then stood not far beyond the gloom and
rumours of the town, among high garden-walls bright
all summer-time with Golden-rod, and brown-and-golden
Wallflower—*Flos Parietis*, as the children's Latin-reading

(4,316) 18

father taught them to call it, while he was with them. Tracing back the threads of his complex spiritual habit, as he was used in after years to do, Florian found that he owed to the place many tones of sentiment afterwards customary with him, certain inward lights under which things most naturally presented themselves to him. The coming and going of travellers to the town along the way, the shadow of the streets, the sudden breath of the neighbouring gardens, the singular brightness of bright weather there, its singular darkness which linked themselves in his mind to certain engraved illustrations in the old big Bible at home, the coolness of the dark, cavernous shops round the great church, with its giddy winding stair up to the pigeons and the bells—a citadel of peace in the heart of the trouble—all this acted on his childish fancy, so that ever afterwards the like aspects and incidents never failed to throw him into a well-recognized imaginative mood, seeming actually to have become a part of the texture of his mind. Also, Florian could trace home to this point a pervading preference in himself for a kind of comeliness and dignity, an *urbanity* literally, in modes of life, which he connected with the pale people of towns, and which made him susceptible to a kind of exquisite satisfaction in the trimness and well-considered grace of certain things and persons he afterwards met with, here and there, in his way through the world.

So the child of whom I am writing lived on there quietly ; things without thus ministering to him, as he sat daily at the window with the birdcage hanging below it, and his mother taught him to read, wondering at the ease with which he learned, and at the quickness of his memory. The perfume of the little flowers of the lime-tree fell through the air upon them like rain ; while time seemed to move ever more slowly to the murmur of the bees in it, till it almost stood still on June afternoons. How insignificant, at the moment, seem the influences of the sensible things which are tossed and fall and lie about us, so, or so, in the environment of early childhood. How indelibly, as we afterwards discover, they affect us ; with what capricious attractions and associations they figure themselves on the white paper, the smooth wax, of our ingenuous souls, as " with lead in the rock for ever," giving form and feature, and as it were assigned house-room in our memory, to early experiences of feeling and thought, which abide with us ever afterwards, thus, and not otherwise.   The realities and passions, the rumours of the greater world without, steal in upon us, each by its own special little passage-way, through the wall of custom about us ;   and never afterwards quite detach themselves from this or that accident, or trick, in the mode of their first entrance to us.   Our susceptibilities, the discovery of our powers, manifold experiences—our various experiences of the coming and going of bodily pain, for instance—belong to this or the other well-remembered place in the material habitation—that little white room with the window across which the heavy blossoms could beat so peevishly in the wind, with just that particular catch or throb, such a sense of teasing in it, on gusty mornings ;   and the early habitation thus gradually becomes a sort of material shrine or sanctuary of sentiment ; a system of visible symbolism interweaves itself through all our thoughts and passions ; and irresistibly, little shapes, voices, accidents—the angle at which the sun in the morning fell on the pillow—become parts of the great chain wherewith we are bound.

Thus far, for Florian, what all this had determined was a peculiarly strong sense of home—so forcible a motive with all of us—prompting to us our customary love of the earth, and the larger part of our fear of death, that revulsion we have from it, as from something strange, untried, unfriendly ;   though life-long imprisonment, they tell you, and final banishment from home is a thing

bitterer still ; the looking forward to but a short space, a
mere childish *goûter* and dessert of it, before the end, being
so great a resource of effort to pilgrims and wayfarers,
and the soldier in distant quarters, and lending, in lack of
that, some power of solace to the thought of sleep in the
home churchyard, at least—dead cheek by dead cheek,
and with the rain soaking in upon one from above.

So powerful is this instinct, and yet accidents like those
I have been speaking of so mechanically determine it ; its
essence being indeed the early familiar, as constituting
our ideal, or typical conception, of rest and security.　Out
of so many possible conditions, just this for you and that
for me, brings ever the unmistakable realization of the
delightful *chez soi* ; this for the Englishman, for me and
you, with the closely drawn white curtain and the shaded
lamp ; that, quite other, for the wandering Arab, who
folds his tent every morning, and makes his sleeping-place
among haunted ruins, or in old tombs.

With Florian then the sense of home became singularly
intense, his good fortune being that the special character
of his home was in itself so essentially home-like.　As
after many wanderings I have come to fancy that some
parts of Surrey and Kent are, for Englishmen, the true
landscape, true home-counties, by right, partly, of a certain
earthy warmth in the yellow of the sand below their
gorse-bushes, and of a certain grey-blue mist after rain, in
the hollows of the hills there, welcome to fatigued eyes,
and never seen farther south ; so I think that the sort of
house I have described, with precisely those proportions
of red-brick and green, and with a just perceptible monotony in the subdued order of it, for its distinguishing
note, is for Englishmen at least typically home-life.　And
so for Florian that general human instinct was reinforced
by this special home-likeness in the place his wandering
soul had happened to light on, as, in the second degree,
its body and earthly tabernacle ; the sense of harmony

between his soul and its physical environment became, for a time at least, like perfectly played music, and the life led there singularly tranquil and filled with a curious sense of self-possession. The love of security, of an habitually undisputed standing-ground or sleeping-place, came to count for much in the generation and correcting of his thoughts, and afterwards as a salutary principle of restraint in all his wanderings of spirit. The wistful yearning towards home, in absence from it, as the shadows of evening deepened, and he followed in thought what was doing there from hour to hour, interpreted to him much of a yearning and regret he experienced afterwards, towards he knew not what, out of strange ways of feeling and thought in which, from time to time, his spirit found itself alone ; and in the tears shed in such absences there seemed always to be some soul-subduing foretaste of what his last tears might be.

And the sense of security could hardly have been deeper, the quiet of the child's soul being one with the quiet of its home, a place " inclosed " and " sealed." But upon this assured place, upon the child's assured soul which resembled it, there came floating in from the larger world without, as at windows left ajar unknowingly, or over the high garden walls, two streams of impressions, the sentiments of beauty and pain—recognitions of the visible, tangible, audible loveliness of things, as a very real and somewhat tyrannous element in them—and of the sorrow of the world, of grown people and children and animals, as a thing not to be put by in them. From this point he could trace two predominant processes of mental change in him—the growth of an almost diseased sensibility to the spectacle of suffering, and, parallel with this, the rapid growth of a certain capacity of fascination by bright colour and choice form—the sweet curvings, for instance, of the lips of those who seemed to him comely persons, modulated in such delicate unison to the things they said or sang,

—marking early the activity in him of a more than customary sensuousness, " the lust of the eye," as the Preacher says, which might lead him, one day, how far ! Could he have foreseen the weariness of the way ! In music sometimes the two sorts of impressions came together, and he would weep, to the surprise of older people. Tears of joy too the child knew, also to older people's surprise ; real tears, once, of relief from long-strung, childish expectation, when he found returned at evening, with new roses in her cheeks, the little sister who had been to a place where there was a wood, and brought back for him a treasure of fallen acorns, and black crow's feathers, and his peace at finding her again near him mingled all night with some intimate sense of the distant forest, the rumour of its breezes, with the glossy blackbirds aslant and the branches lifted in them, and of the perfect nicety of the little cups that fell. So those two elementary apprehensions of the tenderness and of the colour in things grew apace in him, and were seen by him afterwards to send their roots back into the beginnings of life.

Let me note first some of the occasions of his recognition of the element of pain in things—incidents, now and again, which seemed suddenly to awake in him the whole force of that sentiment which Goethe has called the *Weltschmerz*, and in which the concentrated sorrow of the world seemed suddenly to lie heavy upon him. A book lay in an old bookcase, of which he cared to remember one picture—a woman sitting, with hands bound behind her, the dress, the cap, the hair, folded with a simplicity which touched him strangely, as if not by her own hands, but with some ambiguous care at the hands of others—Queen Marie Antoinette, on her way to execution—we all remember David's drawing, meant merely to make her ridiculous. The face that had been so high had learned to be mute and resistless ; but out of its very resistlessness, seemed now to call on men to have pity, and forbear ; and he took note of that, as he closed the book, as a thing to look at again, if he should at any time find himself tempted to be cruel. Again, he would never quite forget the appeal in the small sister's face, in the garden under the lilacs, terrified at a spider lighted on her sleeve. He could trace back to the look then noted a certain mercy he conceived always for people in fear, even of little things, which seemed to make him, though but for a moment, capable of almost any sacrifice of himself. Impressible, susceptible persons, indeed, who had had their sorrows, lived about him ; and this sensibility was due in part to the tacit influence of their presence, enforcing upon him habitually the fact that there are those who pass their days, as a matter of course, in a sort of " going quietly." Most poignantly of all he could recall, in unfading minutest circumstance, the cry on the stair, sounding bitterly through the house, and struck into his soul for ever, of an aged woman, his father's sister, come now to announce his death in distant India ; how it seemed to make the aged woman like a child again ; and, he knew not why, but this fancy was full of pity to him. There were the little sorrows of the dumb animals too—of the white angora, with a dark tail like an ermine's, and a face like a flower, who fell into a lingering sickness, and became quite delicately human in its valetudinarianism, and came to have a hundred different expressions of voice —how it grew worse and worse, till it began to feel the light too much for it, and at last, after one wild morning of pain, the little soul flickered away from the body, quite worn to death already, and now but feebly retaining it.

So he wanted another pet ; and as there were starlings about the place, which could be taught to speak, one of them was caught, and he meant to treat it kindly ; but in the night its young ones could be heard crying after it, and the responsive cry of the mother-bird towards them ; and at last, with the first light, though not till after some debate with himself, he went down and opened the cage, and saw a sharp bound of the prisoner up to her nestlings ; and therewith came the sense of remorse,—that he too was become an accomplice in moving, to the limit of his small power, the springs and handles of that great machine in things, constructed so ingeniously to play pain-fugues on the delicate nerve-work of living creatures.

I have remarked how, in the process of our brain-building, as the house of thought in which we live gets itself together, like some airy bird's nest of floating thistle-down, and chance straws, compact at last, little accidents have their consequence ; and thus it happened that, as he walked one evening, a garden gate, usually closed, stood open ; and lo ! within, a great red hawthorn in full flower, embossing heavily the bleached and twisted trunk and branches, so aged that there were but few green leaves thereon—a plumage of tender, crimson fire out of the heart of the dry wood. The perfume of the tree had now and again reached him, in the currents of the wind, over the wall, and he had wondered what might be behind it, and was now allowed to fill his arms with the flowers—flowers enough for all the old blue-china pots along the chimney-piece, making *fête* in the children's room. Was it some periodic moment in the expansion of soul within him, or mere trick of heat in the heavily laden summer air ? But the beauty of the thing struck home to him feverishly ; and in dreams all night he loitered along a magic roadway of crimson flowers, which seemed to open ruddily in thick, fresh masses about his feet, and fill softly all the little hollows in the banks on either side. Always afterwards, summer by summer, as the flowers came on, the blossom of the red hawthorn still seemed to him absolutely the reddest of all things ; and the goodly crimson, still alive in the works of old Venetian masters or old Flemish tapestries, called out always from afar the recollection of the flame in those perishing little petals, as it pulsed gradually out of them, kept long in the drawers of an old cabinet. Also then, for the first time, he seemed to experience a passionateness in his relation to fair outward objects, an inexplicable excitement in their presence, which disturbed him, and from which he half longed to be free. A touch of regret or desire mingled all night with the remembered presence of the red flowers, and their perfume in the darkness about him ; and the longing for some undivined, entire possession of them was the beginning of a revelation to him, growing ever clearer, with the coming of the gracious summer guise of fields and trees and persons in each succeeding year, of a certain, at times seemingly exclusive, predominance in his interests, of beautiful physical things, a kind of tyranny of the senses over him.

In later years he came upon philosophies which occupied him much in the estimate of the proportion of the sensuous and the ideal elements in human knowledge, the relative parts they bear in it ; and, in his intellectual scheme, was led to assign very little to the abstract thought, and much to its sensible vehicle or occasion. Such metaphysical speculation did but reinforce what was instinctive in his way of receiving the world, and for him, everywhere, that sensible vehicle or occasion became, perhaps only too surely, the necessary concomitant of any perception of things, real enough to be of any weight or reckoning, in his house of thought. There were times when he could think of the necessity he was under of associating all thoughts to touch and sight, as a sympathetic link between himself and actual, feeling, living objects ; a protest in favour of real men and women against mere grey, unreal abstractions ; and he remembered gratefully how the Christian religion, hardly less than the religion of the ancient Greeks, translating so much of its spiritual verity into things that may be seen, condescends in part to sanction this infirmity, if so it be, of our human existence,

wherein the world of sense is so much with us, and welcomed this thought as a kind of keeper and sentinel over
his soul therein. But certainly, he came more and more
to be unable to care for, or think of soul but as in an
actual body, or of any world but that wherein are water
and trees, and where men and women look, so or so, and
press actual hands. It was the trick even his pity learned,
fastening those who suffered in anywise to his affections
by a kind of sensible attachments. He would think of
Julian, fallen into incurable sickness, as spoiled in the sweet
blossom of his skin like pale amber, and his honey like
hair ; of Cecil, early dead, as cut off from the lilies, from
golden summer days, from women's voices ; and then
what comforted him a little was the thought of the turning
of the child's flesh to violets in the turf above him. And
thinking of the very poor, it was not the things which
most men care most for that he yearned to give them ;
but fairer roses, perhaps, and power to taste quite as they
will, at their ease and not task-burdened, a certain desirable,
clear light in the new morning, through which sometimes
he had noticed them, quite unconscious of it, on their way
to their early toil.

So he yielded himself to these things, to be played
upon by them like a musical instrument, and began to
note with deepening watchfulness, but always with some
puzzled, unutterable longing in his enjoyment, the phases
of the seasons and of the growing or waning day, down
even to the shadowy changes wrought on bare wall or ceiling—the light cast up from the snow, bringing out their
darkest angles ; the brown light in the cloud, which
meant rain ; that almost too austere clearness, in the pro-
tracted light of the lengthening day, before warm weather
began, as if it lingered but to make a severer workday, with
the schoolbooks opened earlier and later ; that beam of
June sunshine, at last, as he lay awake before the time, a
way of gold-dust across the darkness ; all the humming,

the freshness, the perfume of the garden seemed to lie upon it—and coming in one afternoon in September, along the red gravel walk, to look for a basket of yellow crab-apples left in the cool old parlour, he remembered it the more, and how the colours struck upon him, because a wasp on one bitten apple stung him, and he felt the passion of sudden, severe pain. For this too brought its curious reflections ; and, in relief from it, he would wonder over it—how it had then been with him— puzzled at the depth of the charm or spell over him, which lay, for a little while at least, in the mere absence of pain ; once, especially, when an older boy taught him to make flowers of sealing-wax, and he had burnt his hand badly at the lighted taper, and been unable to sleep. He remembered that also afterwards, as a sort of typical thing—a white vision of heat about him, clinging closely, through the languid scent of the ointments put upon the place to make it well.

Also, as he felt this pressure upon him of the sensible world, then, as often afterwards, there would come another sort of curious questioning how the last impressions of eye and ear might happen to him, how they would find him—the scent of the last flower, the soft yellowness of the last morning, the last recognition of some object of affection, hand or voice ; it could not be but that the latest look of the eyes, before their final closing, would be strangely vivid ; one would go with the hot tears, the cry, the touch of the wistful bystander, impressed how deeply on one ! or would it be, perhaps, a mere frail retiring of all things, great or little, away from one, into a level distance ?

For with this desire of physical beauty mingled itself early the fear of death—the fear of death intensified by the desire of beauty. Hitherto he had never gazed upon dead faces, as sometimes, afterwards, at the *Morgue* in Paris, or in that fair cemetery at Munich, where all the dead must go and lie in state before burial, behind glass windows, among the flowers and incense and holy candles —the aged clergy with their sacred ornaments, the young men in their dancing-shoes and spotless white linen—after which visits, those waxen, resistless faces would always live with him for many days, making the broadest sunshine sickly. The child had heard indeed of the death of his father, and how, in the Indian station, a fever had taken him, so that though not in action he had yet died as a soldier ; and hearing of the " resurrection of the just," he could think of him as still abroad in the world, some-how, for his protection—a grand, though perhaps rather terrible figure, in beautiful soldier's things, like the figure in the picture of Joshua's Vision in the Bible—and of that, round which the mourners moved so softly, and after-wards with such solemn singing, as but a worn-out garment left at a deserted lodging. So it was, until on a summer day he walked with his mother through a fair churchyard. In a bright dress he rambled among the graves, in the gay weather, and so came, in one corner, upon an open grave for a child—a dark space on the brilliant grass—the black mould lying heaped up round it, weighing down the little jewelled branches of the dwarf rose-bushes in flower. And therewith came, full-grown, never wholly to leave him, with the certainty that even children do sometimes die, the physical horror of death, with its wholly selfish recoil from the association of lower forms of life, and the suffocating weight above. No benign, grave figure in beautiful soldier's things any longer abroad in the world for his protection ! only a few poor, piteous bones ; and above them, pos-sibly, a certain sort of figure he hoped not to see. For sitting one day in the garden below an open window, he heard people talking, and could not but listen, how, in a sleepless hour, a sick woman had seen one of the dead sitting beside her, come to call her hence ; and from the broken talk evolved with much clearness the notion that not all those dead people had really departed to the churchyard, nor were quite so motionless as they looked, but led a secret, half-fugitive life in their old homes, quite free by night, though sometimes visible in the day, dodging from room to room, with no great goodwill towards those who shared the place with them. All night the figure sat beside him in the reveries of his broken sleep, and was not quite gone in the morning—an odd, irreconcilable new member of the household, making the sweet familiar chambers unfriendly and suspect by its uncertain presence. He could have hated the dead he had pitied so, for being thus. Afterwards he came to think of those poor, home-returning ghosts, which all men have fancied to themselves—the *revenants*—pathetically, as crying, or beating with vain hands at the doors, as the wind came, their cries distinguishable in it as a wilder inner note. But, always making death more unfamiliar still, that old experience would ever, from time to time, return to him ; even in the living he sometimes caught its likeness ; at any time or place, in a moment, the faint atmosphere of the chamber of death would be breathed around him, and the image with the bound chin, the quaint smile, the straight, stiff feet, shed itself across the air upon the bright carpet, amid the gayest company, or happiest communing with himself.

To most children the sombre questionings to which impressions like these attach themselves, if they come at all, are actually suggested by religious books, which therefore they often regard with much secret distaste, and dismiss, as far as possible, from their habitual thoughts as a too depressing element in life. To Florian such impressions, these misgivings as to the ultimate tendency of the years, of the relationship between life and death, had been suggested spontaneously in the natural course of his mental growth by a strong innate sense for the soberer

tones in things, further strengthened by actual circumstances ; and religious sentiment, that system of biblical
ideas in which he had been brought up, presented itself
to him as a thing that might soften and dignify, and light
up as with a " lively hope," a melancholy already deeply
settled in him. So he yielded himself easily to religious
impressions, and with a kind of mystical appetite for
sacred things ; the more as they came to him through a
saintly person who loved him tenderly, and believed that
this early pre-occupation with them already marked the
child out for a saint. He began to love, for their own
sakes, church lights, holy days, all that belonged to the
comely order of the sanctuary, the secrets of its white linen,
and holy vessels, and fonts of pure water ; and its hieratic
purity and simplicity became the type of something he
desired always to have about him in actual life. He pored
over the pictures in religious books, and knew by heart
the exact mode in which the wrestling angel grasped
Jacob, how Jacob looked in his mysterious sleep, how
the bells and pomegranates were attached to the hem of
Aaron's vestment, sounding sweetly as he glided over the
turf of the holy place. His way of conceiving religion
came then to be in effect what it ever afterwards remained
—a sacred history indeed, but still more a sacred ideal, a
transcendent version or representation, under intenser
and more expressive light and shade, of human life and
its familiar or exceptional incidents, birth, death, marriage,
youth, age, tears, joy, rest, sleep, waking—a mirror,
towards which men might turn away their eyes from
vanity and dullness, and see themselves therein as angels,
with their daily meat and drink, even, become a kind of
sacred transaction—a complementary strain or burden,
applied to our every-day existence, whereby the stray
snatches of music in it reset themselves, and fall into the
scheme of some higher and more consistent harmony.
A place adumbrated itself in his thoughts, wherein those

sacred personalities, which are at once the reflex and the pattern of our nobler phases of life, housed themselves ; and this region in his intellectual scheme all subsequent experience did but tend still further to realize and define. Some ideal, hieratic persons he would always need to occupy it and keep a warmth there. And he could hardly understand those who felt no such need at all, finding themselves quite happy without such heavenly companionship, and sacred double of their life, beside them.

Thus a constant substitution of the typical for the actual took place in his thoughts. Angels might be met by the way, under English elm or beech-tree ; mere messengers seemed like angels, bound on celestial errands ; a deep mysticity brooded over real meetings and partings ; marriages were made in heaven ; and deaths also, with hands of angels thereupon, to bear soul and body quietly asunder, each to its appointed rest. All the acts and accidents of daily life borrowed a sacred colour and significance ; the very colours of things became themselves weighty with meanings like the sacred stuffs of Moses' tabernacle, full of penitence, or peace. Sentiment, congruous in the first instance only with those divine transactions, the deep, effusive unction of the House of Bethany, was assumed as the due attitude for the reception of our every-day existence ; and for a time he walked through the world in a sustained, not unpleasurable awe, generated by the habitual recognition, beside every circumstance and event of life, or its celestial correspondent.

Sensibility—the desire of physical beauty—a strange biblical awe, which made any reference to the unseen act on him like solemn music—these qualities the child took away with him, when, at about the age of twelve years, he left the old house, and was taken to live in another place. He had never left home before, and, anticipating much from this change, had long dreamed over it, jealously counting the days till the time fixed for departure should come ; had been a little careless about others even, in his strong desire for it—when Lewis fell sick, for instance, and they must wait still two days longer. At last the morning came, very fine ; and all things—the very pavement with its dust, at the roadside—seemed to have a white pearl-like lustre in them. They were to travel by a favourite road on which he had often walked a certain distance, and on one of those two prisoner days, when Lewis was sick, had walked farther than ever before, in his great desire to reach the new place. They had started and gone a little way when a pet bird was found to have been left behind, and must even now—so it presented itself to him—have already all the appealing fierceness and wild self-pity at heart of one left by others to perish of hunger in a closed house ; and he returned to fetch it, himself in hardly less stormy distress. But as he passed in search of it from room to room, lying so pale, with a look of meekness in their denudation, and at last through that little, stripped white room, the aspect of the place touched him like the face of one dead ; and a clinging back towards it came over him, so intense that he knew it would last long, and spoiling all his pleasure in the realization of a thing so eagerly anticipated. And so, with the bird found, but himself in an agony of home-sickness, thus capriciously sprung up within him, he was driven quickly away, far into the rural distance, so fondly speculated on, of that favourite country road.

Miscellaneous Studies.   1894.

THE LANTERN-BEARERS

R. L. STEVENSON

I

THESE boys congregated every autumn about a certain easterly fisher-village, where they tasted in a high degree the glory of existence. The place was created seemingly on purpose for the diversion of young gentlemen. A street or two of houses, mostly red and many of them tiled ; a number of fine trees clustered about the manse and the kirkyard, and turning the chief street into a shady alley ; many little gardens more than usually bright with flowers ; nets a-drying, and fisher-wives scolding in the backward parts ; a smell of fish, a genial smell of seaweed ; whiffs of blowing sand at the street-corners ; shops with golf-balls and bottled lollipops ; another shop with penny pickwicks (that remarkable cigar) and the *London Journal*, dear to me for its startling pictures, and a few novels, dear for their suggestive names : such, as well as memory serves me, were the ingredients of the town. These, you are to conceive posted on a spit between two sandy bays, and sparsely flanked with villas—enough for the boys to lodge in with their subsidiary parents, not enough (not yet enough) to cocknify the scene : a haven in the rocks in front : in front of that, a file of grey islets : to the left, endless links and sand wreaths, a wilderness of hiding-holes, alive with popping rabbits and soaring gulls : to the right, a range of seaward crags, one rugged brow

beyond another ; the ruins of a mighty and ancient fortress
on the brink of one ; coves between—now charmed into
sunshine quiet, now whistling with wind and clamorous
with bursting surges ; the dens and sheltered hollows
redolent of thyme and southernwood, the air at the cliff's
edge brisk and clean and pungent of the sea—in front of
all, the Bass Rock, tilted seaward like a doubtful bather,
the surf ringing it with white, the solan-geese hanging
round its summit like a great and glittering smoke. This
choice piece of seaboard was sacred, besides, to the wrecker ;
and the Bass, in the eye of fancy, still flew the colours of
King James ; and in the ear of fancy the arches of Tantallon still rang with horse-shoe iron, and echoed to the
commands of Bell-the-Cat.

There was nothing to mar your days, if you were a boy
summering in that part, but the embarrassment of pleasure.
You might golf if you wanted ; but I seem to have been
better employed. You might secrete yourself in the
Lady's Walk, a certain sunless dingle of elders, all mossed
over by the damp as green as grass, and dotted here and
there by the stream-side with roofless walls, the cold homes
of anchorites. To fit themselves for life, and with a special
eye to acquire the art of smoking, it was even common for
the boys to harbour there ; and you might have seen a
single penny pickwick, honestly shared in lengths with
a blunt knife, bestrew the glen with these apprentices.
Again, you might join our fishing parties, where we sat
perched as thick as solan-geese, a covey of little anglers,
boy and girl, angling over each other's heads, to the much
entanglement of lines and loss of podleys and consequent
shrill recrimination—shrill as the geese themselves. Indeed, had that been all, you might have done this often ;
but though fishing be a fine pastime, the podley is scarce
to be regarded as a dainty for the table ; and it was a
point of honour that a boy should eat all that he had
taken. Or again, you might climb the Law, where the

whale's jaw-bone stood landmark in the buzzing wind, and behold the face of many counties, and the smoke and spires of many towns, and the sails of distant ships. You might bathe, now in the flaws of fine weather, that we pathetically call our summer, now in a gale of wind, with the sand scourging your bare hide, your clothes thrashing abroad from underneath their guardian stone, the froth of the great breakers casting you headlong ere it had drowned your knees. Or you might explore the tidal rocks, above all in the ebb of springs, when the very roots of the hills were for the nonce discovered; following my leader from one group to another, groping in slippery tangle for the wreck of ships, wading in pools after the abominable creatures of the sea, and ever with an eye cast backward on the march of the tide and the menaced line of your retreat. And then you might go Crusoeing, a word that covers all extempore eating in the open air : digging perhaps a house under the margin of the links, kindling a fire of the sea-ware, and cooking apples there— if they were truly apples, for I sometimes suppose the merchant must have played us off with some inferior and quite local fruit, capable of resolving, in the neighbour-hood of fire, into mere sand and smoke and iodine ; or perhaps pushing to Tantallon, you might lunch on sand-wiches and visions in the grassy court, while the wind hummed in the crumbling turrets ; or clambering along the coast, eat geans [1] (the worst, I must suppose, in Christendom) from an adventurous gean tree that had taken root under a cliff, where it was shaken with an ague of east wind, and silvered after gales with salt, and grew so foreign among its bleak surroundings that to eat of its produce was an adventure in itself.

There are mingled some dismal memories with so many that were joyous. Of the fisher-wife, for instance,

[1] Wild cherries.

who had cut her throat at Canty Bay ; and of how I ran
with the other children to the top of the Quadrant, and
beheld a posse of silent people escorting a cart, and on the
cart, bound in a chair, her throat bandaged, and the
bandage all bloody—horror !—the fisher-wife herself,
who continued thenceforth to hag-ride my thoughts, and
even to-day (as I recall the scene) darkens daylight. She
was lodged in the little old jail in the chief street ; but
whether or no she died there, with a wise terror of the
worst, I never inquired. She had been tippling ; it was
but a dingy tragedy ; and it seems strange and hard that,
after all these years, the poor crazy sinner should be still
pilloried on her cart in the scrap-book of my memory.
Nor shall I readily forget a certain house in the Quadrant
where a visitor died, and a dark old woman continued to
dwell alone with the dead body ; nor how this old woman
conceived a hatred to myself and one of my cousins, and
in the dread hour of the dusk, as we were clambering on
the garden-walls, opened a window in that house of
mortality and cursed us in a shrill voice and with a
marrowy choice of language. It was a pair of very
colourless urchins that fled down the lane from this
remarkable experience ! But I recall with a more doubtful sentiment, compounded out of fear and exultation, the
coil of equinoctial tempests ; trumpeting squalls, scouring
flaws of rain ; the boats with their reefed lugsails scudding
for the harbour mouth, where danger lay, for it was hard
to make when the wind had any east in it ; the wives
clustered with blowing shawls at the pier-head, where (if
fate was against them) they might see boat and husband
and sons—their whole wealth and their whole family—
engulfed under their eyes ; and (what I saw but once) a
troop of neighbours forcing such an unfortunate homeward, and she squalling and battling in their midst, a
figure scarcely human, a tragic Mænad.

These are things that I recall with interest ; but what

my memory dwells upon the most I have been all this while withholding. It was a sport peculiar to the place, and indeed to a week or so of our two months' holiday there. Maybe it still flourishes in its native spot ; for boys and their pastimes are swayed by periodic forces inscrutable to man ; so that tops and marbles reappear in their due season, regular like the sun and moon ; and the harmless art of knuckle-bones has seen the fall of the Roman Empire and the rise of the United States. It may still flourish in its native spot, but nowhere else, I am persuaded ; for I tried myself to introduce it on Tweedside, and was defeated lamentably ; its charm being quite local, like a country wine that cannot be exported.

The idle manner of it was this :—

Toward the end of September, when school-time was drawing near and the nights were already black, we would begin to sally from our respective villas, each equipped with a tin bull's-eye lantern. The thing was so well known that it had worn a rut in the commerce of Great Britain ; and the grocers, about the due time, began to garnish their windows with our particular brand of luminary. We wore them buckled to the waist upon a cricket belt, and over them, such was the rigour of the game, a buttoned top-coat. They smelled noisomely of blistered tin ; they never burned aright, though they would always burn our fingers ; their use was naught ; the pleasure of them merely fanciful ; and yet a boy with a bull's-eye under his top-coat asked for nothing more. The fishermen used lanterns about their boats, and it was from them, I suppose, that we had got the hint ; but theirs were not bulls'-eyes, nor did we ever play at being fishermen. The police carried them at their belts, and we had plainly copied them in that ; yet we did not pretend to be policemen. Burglars, indeed, we may have had some haunting thoughts of ; and we had certainly an eye to past ages when lanterns were more common, and to certain story-books in which we had found them to figure very largely. But take it for all in all, the pleasure of the thing was substantive ; and to be a boy with a bull's-eye under his top-coat was good enough for us.

When two of these asses met, there would be an anxious " Have you got your lantern ? " and a gratified " Yes ! " That was the shibboleth, and very needful too ; for, as it was the rule to keep our glory contained, none could recognize a lantern-bearer, unless (like the polecat) by the smell. Four or five would sometimes climb into the belly of a ten-man lugger, with nothing but the thwarts above them—for the cabin was usually locked, or choose out some hollow of the links where the wind might whistle overhead. There the coats would be un-buttoned and the bulls'-eyes discovered ; and in the chequering glimmer, under the huge windy hall of the night, and cheered by a rich steam of toasting tinware, these fortunate young gentlemen would crouch together in the cold sand of the links or on the scaly bilges of the fishing-boat, and delight themselves with inappropriate talk. Woe is me that I may not give some specimens—some of their foresights of life, or deep inquiries into the rudiments of man and nature, these were so fiery and so innocent, they were so richly silly, so romantically young. But the talk, at any rate, was but a condiment ; and these gatherings themselves only accidents in the career of the lantern-bearer. The essence of this bliss was to walk by yourself in the black night ; the slide shut, the top-coat buttoned ; not a ray escaping, whether to conduct your footsteps or to make your glory public : a mere pillar of darkness in the dark ; and all the while, deep down in the privacy of your fool's heart, to know you had a bull's-eye at your belt, and to exult and sing over the knowledge.

II

It is said that a poet has died young in the breast of the most stolid. It may be contended, rather, that this (somewhat minor) bard in almost every case survives, and is the spice of life to his possessor. Justice is not done to the versatility and the unplumbed childishness of man's imagination. His life from without may seem but a rude mound of mud ; there will be some golden chamber at the heart of it, in which he dwells delighted ; and for as dark as his pathway seems to the observer, he will have some kind of a bull's-eye at his belt.

It would be hard to pick out a career more cheerless than that of Dancer, the miser, as he figures in the " Old Bailey Reports," a prey to the most sordid persecutions, the butt of his neighbourhood, betrayed by his hired man, his house beleaguered by the impish schoolboy, and he himself grinding and fuming and impotently fleeing to the law against these pin-pricks. You marvel at first that any one should willingly prolong a life so destitute of charm and dignity ; and then you call to memory that had he chosen, had he ceased to be a miser, he could have been freed at once from these trials, and might have built himself a castle and gone escorted by a squadron. For the love of more recondite joys, which we cannot estimate, which, it may be, we should envy, the man had willingly foregone both comfort and consideration. " His mind to him a kingdom was ; "and sure enough, digging into that mind, which seems at first a dust-heap, we unearth some priceless jewels. For Dancer must have had the love of power and the disdain of using it, a noble character in itself ; disdain of many pleasures, a chief part of what is commonly called wisdom ; disdain of the inevitable end, that finest trait of mankind ; scorn of men's opinions, another element of virtue ; and at the back of all, a conscience just like yours and mine, whining like a cur, swindling like a thimble-rigger, but still pointing (there or thereabout) to some conventional standard. Here were a cabinet portrait to which Hawthorne perhaps had done justice ; and yet not Hawthorne either, for he was mildly minded, and it lay not in him to create for us that throb of the miser's pulse, his fretful energy of gusto, his vast arms of ambition clutching in he knows not what : insatiable, insane, a god with a muck-rake. Thus, at least, looking in the bosom of the miser, consideration detects the poet in the full tide of life, with more, indeed, of the poetic fire than usually goes to epics ; and tracing that mean man about his cold hearth, and to and fro in his discomfortable house, spies within him a blazing bonfire of delight. And so with others, who do not live by bread alone, but by some cherished and perhaps fantastic pleasure ; who are meat salesmen to the external eye, and possibly to themselves are Shakespeares, Napoleons, or Beethovens ; who have not one virtue to rub against another in the field of active life, and yet perhaps, in the life of contemplation, sit with the saints. We see them on the street, and we can count their buttons ; but heaven knows in what they pride themselves ! heaven knows where they have set their treasure !

There is one fable that touches very near the quick of life : the fable of the monk who passed into the woods, heard a bird break into song, hearkened for a trill or two, and found himself on his return a stranger at his convent gates ; for he had been absent fifty years, and of all his comrades there survived but one to recognize him. It is not only in the woods that this enchanter carols, though perhaps he is native there. He sings in the most doleful places. The miser hears him and chuckles, and the days are moments. With no more apparatus than an ill-smelling lantern I have evoked him on the naked links.

All life that is not merely mechanical is spun out of two strands : seeking for that bird and hearing him. And it is just this that makes life so hard to value, and the delight of each so incommunicable ; and just a knowledge of this, and a remembrance of those fortunate hours in which the bird has sung to us, that fills us with such wonder when we turn the pages of the realist. There, to be sure, we find a picture of life in so far as it consists of mud and of old iron, cheap desires and cheap fears, that which we are ashamed to remember and that which we are careless whether we forget ; but of the note of that time-devouring nightingale we hear no news.

The case of these writers of romance is most obscure. They have been boys and youths ; they have lingered outside the window of the beloved, who was then most probably writing to some one else ; they have sat before a sheet of paper, and felt themselves mere continents of congested poetry, not one line of which would flow ; they have walked alone in the woods, they have walked in cities under the countless lamps ; they have been to sea, they have hated, they have feared, they have longed to knife a man, and maybe done it ; the wild taste of life has stung their palate. Or, if you deny them all the rest, one pleasure at least they have tasted to the full—their books are there to prove it—the keen pleasure of successful literary composition. And yet they fill the globe with volumes, whose cleverness inspires me with despairing admiration, and whose consistent falsity to all I care to call existence, with despairing wrath. If I had no better hope than to continue to revolve among the dreary and petty businesses, and to be moved by the paltry hopes and fears with which they surround and animate their heroes, I declare I would die now. But there has never an hour of mine gone quite so dully yet ; if it were spent waiting at a railway junction, I would have some scattering thoughts, I could count some grains of memory, compared to which the whole of one of these romances seems but dross.

These writers would retort (if I take them properly) that this was very true ; that it was the same with themselves and other persons of (what they call) the artistic temperament ; that in this we were exceptional, and should apparently be ashamed of ourselves ; but that our works must deal exclusively with (what they call) the average man, who was a prodigious dull fellow, and quite dead to all but the paltriest considerations. I accept the issue. We can only know others by ourselves. The artistic temperament (a plague on the expression !) does not make us different from our fellow-men, or it would make us incapable of writing novels ; and the average man (a murrain on the word !) is just like you and me, or he would not be average. It was Whitman who stamped a kind of Birmingham sacredness upon the latter phrase ; but Whitman knew very well, and showed very nobly, that the average man was full of joys and full of a poetry of his own. And this harping on life's dullness and man's meanness is a loud profession of incompetence ; it is one of two things : the cry of the blind eye, *I cannot see*, or the complaint of the dumb tongue, *I cannot utter*. To draw a life without delights is to prove I have not realized it. To picture a man without some sort of poetry—well, it goes near to prove my case, for it shows an author may have little enough. To see Dancer only as a dirty, old, small-minded, impotently fuming man, in a dirty house, besieged by Harrow boys, and probably beset by small attorneys, is to show myself as keen an observer as . . . the Harrow boys. But these young gentlemen (with a more becoming modesty) were content to pluck Dancer by the coat-tails ; they did not suppose they had surprised his secret or could put him living in a book : and it is there my error would have lain. Or say that in the same romance—I continue to call these books romances, in the hope of giving pain—say that in the same romance, which now begins really to take shape, I should leave to speak of Dancer, and follow instead the Harrow boys ; and say that I came on some such business as that of my lantern-bearers on the links ; and described the boys as very cold, spat upon by flurries of rain, and drearily surrounded, all of which they were ; and their talk as silly and indecent, which it certainly was. I might upon these lines, and had I Zola's genius, turn out, in a page or so, a gem of literary art, render the lantern-light with the touches of a master, and lay on the indecency with the ungrudging hand of love ; and when all was done, what a triumph would my picture be of shallowness and dullness ! how it would have missed the point ! how it would have belied the boys ! To the ear of the stenographer, the talk is merely silly and indecent ; but ask the boys themselves, and they are discussing (as it is highly proper they should) the possibilities of existence. To the eye of the observer they are wet and cold and drearily surrounded ; but ask themselves, and they are in the heaven of a recondite pleasure, the ground of which is an ill-smelling lantern.

III

For, to repeat, the ground of a man's joy is often hard to hit. It may hinge at times upon a mere accessory, like the lantern ; it may reside, like Dancer's, in the mysterious inwards of psychology. It may consist with perpetual failure, and find exercise in the continued chase. It has so little bond with externals (such as the observer scribbles in his note-book) that it may even touch them not ; and the man's true life, for which he consents to live, lie altogether in the field of fancy. The clergyman, in his spare hours, may be winning battles, the farmer sailing ships, the banker reaping triumph in the arts : all leading

another life, plying another trade from that they chose ;
like the poet's housebuilder, who, after all, is cased in
stone,

> " By his fireside, as impotent fancy prompts,
> Rebuilds it to his liking."

In such a case the poetry runs underground. The observer (poor soul, with his documents !) is all abroad.
For to look at the man is but to court deception. We
shall see the trunk from which he draws his nourishment ;
but he himself is above and abroad in the green dome
of foliage, hummed through by winds and nested in by
nightingales. And the true realism were that of the
poets, to climb up after him like a squirrel, and catch
some glimpse of the heaven for which he lives. And
the true realism, always and everywhere, is that of the
poets : to find out where joy resides, and give it a voice
far beyond singing.

For to miss the joy is to miss all. In the joy of the
actors lies the sense of any action. That is the explanation,
that the excuse. To one who has not the secret of the
lanterns, the scene upon the links is meaningless. And
hence the haunting and truly spectral unreality of realistic
books. Hence, when we read the English realists, the
incredulous wonder with which we observe the hero's
constancy under the submerging tide of dullness, and
how he bears up with his jibbing sweetheart, and endures
the chatter of idiot girls, and stands by his whole un-
featured wilderness of an existence, instead of seeking
relief in drink or foreign travel. Hence in the French, in
that meat-market of middle-aged sensuality, the disgusted
surprise with which we see the hero drift sidelong, and
practically quite untempted, into every description of
misconduct and dishonour. In each, we miss the personal poetry, the enchanted atmosphere, that rainbow
work of fancy that clothes what is naked and seems to

ennoble what is base ; in each, life falls dead like dough, instead of soaring away like a balloon into the colours of the sunset ; each is true, each inconceivable ; for no man lives in the external truth, among salts and acids, but in the warm, phantasmagoric chamber of the brain, with the painted windows and the storied walls.

Of this falsity we have had a recent example from a man who knows far better—Tolstoi's *Powers of Darkness*. Here is a piece full of force and truth, yet quite untrue. For before Mikita was led into so dire a situation he was tempted, and temptations are beautiful at least in part ; and a work which dwells on the ugliness of crime and gives no hint of any loveliness in the temptation, sins against the modesty of life, and even when a Tolstoi writes it, sinks to melodrama. The peasants are not understood ; they saw their life in fairer colours ; even the deaf girl was clothed in poetry for Mikita, or he had never fallen. And so, once again, even an Old Bailey melodrama, without some brightness of poetry and lustre of existence, falls into the inconceivable and ranks with fairy tales.

IV

In nobler books we are moved with something like the emotions of life ; and this emotion is very variously provoked. We are so moved when Levine labours in the field, when André sinks beyond emotion, when Richard Feverel and Lucy Desborough meet beside the river, when Antony, " not cowardly, puts off his helmet," when Kent has infinite pity on the dying Lear, when, in Dostoieffky's *Despised and Rejected*, the uncomplaining hero drains his cup of suffering and virtue. These are notes that please the great heart of man. Not only love, and the fields, and the bright face of danger, but sacrifice and death and unmerited suffering humbly supported, touch in us the vein of the poetic. We love to think of them, we long to try them, we are humbly hopeful that we may prove heroes also.

We have heard, perhaps, too much of lesser matters. Here is the door, here is the open air. *Itur in antiquam silvam.*

Across the Plains. 1892.

A PLEA FOR GAS LAMPS

R. L. STEVENSON

CITIES given, the problem was to light them. How to conduct individual citizens about the burgess-warren, when once heaven had withdrawn its leading luminary or—since we live in a scientific age—when once our spinning planet has turned its back upon the sun ? The moon, from time to time, was doubtless very helpful ; the stars had a cheery look among the chimney-pots ; and a cresset here and there, on church or citadel, produced a fine pictorial effect, and, in places where the ground lay unevenly, held out the right hand of conduct to the benighted. But sun, moon, and stars abstracted or concealed, the night-faring inhabitant had to fall back—we speak on the authority of old prints—upon stable lanthorns, two storeys in height. Many holes, drilled in the conical turret-roof of this vagabond Pharos, let up spouts of dazzlement into the bearer's eyes ; and as he paced forth in the ghostly darkness, carrying his own sun by a ring about his finger, day and night swung to and fro and up and down about his footsteps. Blackness haunted his path ; he was beleaguered by goblins as he went ; and, curfew being struck, he found no light but that he travelled in throughout the township.

Closely following on this epoch of migratory lanthorns in a world of extinction, came the era of oil-lights, hard to kindle, easy to extinguish, pale and wavering in the hour of their endurance. Rudely puffed the winds of

heaven ; roguishly clomb up the all-destructive urchin ;
and, lo ! in a moment night re-established her void
empire, and the cit groped along the wall, suppered but
bedless, occult from guidance, and sorrily wading in the
kennels.   As if gamesome winds and gamesome youths
were not sufficient, it was the habit to sling these feeble
luminaries from house to house above the fairway.
There, on invisible cordage, let them swing !   And suppose some crane-necked general to go speeding by on a
tall charger, spurring the destiny of nations, red-hot in
expedition, there would indubitably be some effusion of
military blood, and oaths, and a certain crash of glass ;
and while the chieftain rode forward with a purple
coxcomb, the street would be left to original darkness,
unpiloted, unvoyageable, a province of the desert night.

The conservative, looking before and after, draws from
each contemplation the matter for content.   Out of the
age of gas lamps he glances back slightingly at the mirk
and glimmer in which his ancestors wandered ; his heart
waxes jocund at the contrast ; nor do his lips refrain from
a stave, in the highest style of poetry, lauding progress
and the golden mean.   When gas first spread along a
city, mapping it forth about evenfall for the eye of
observant birds, a new age had begun for sociality and
corporate pleasure-seeking, and begun with proper circumstance, becoming its own birthright.   The work of
Prometheus had advanced by another stride.   Mankind
and its supper parties were no longer at the mercy of a
few miles of sea-fog ; sundown no longer emptied the
promenade ; and the day was lengthened out to every
man's fancy.   The city-folk had stars of their own ;
biddable, domesticated stars.

It is true that these were not so steady, nor yet so clear,
as their originals ; nor indeed was their lustre so elegant
as that of the best wax candles.   But then the gas stars, being nearer at hand, were more practically efficacious than

Jupiter himself. It is true, again, that they did not unfold their rays with the appropriate spontaneity of the planets, coming out along the firmament one after another, as the need arises. But the lamplighters took to their heels every evening, and ran with a good heart. It was pretty to see man thus emulating the punctuality of heaven's orbs ; and though perfection was not absolutely reached, and now and then an individual may have been knocked on the head by the ladder of the flying functionary, yet people commended his zeal in a proverb, and taught their children to say, " God bless the lamplighter ! " And since his passage was a piece of the day's programme, the children were well pleased to repeat the benediction, not, of course, in so many words, which would have been improper, but in some chaster circumlocution, suitable for infant lips.

God bless him, indeed ! For the term of his twilight diligence is near at hand ; and for not much longer shall we watch him speeding up the street and, at measured intervals, knocking another luminous hole into the dusk. The Greeks would have made a noble myth of such an one ; how he distributed starlight, and, as soon as the need was over, re-collected it ; and the little bull's-eye, which was his instrument, and held enough fire to kindle a whole parish, would have been fitly commemorated in the legend. Now, like all heroic tasks, his labours draw towards apotheosis, and in the light of victory himself shall disappear. For another advance has been effected. Our tame stars are to come out in future, not one by one, but all in a body and at once. A sedate electrician somewhere in a back office touches a spring—and behold ! from one end to another of the city, from east to west, from the Alexandra to the Crystal Palace, there is light ! *Fiat Lux*, says the sedate electrician. What a spectacle, on some clear, dark nightfall, from the edge of Hampstead Hill, when in a moment, in the twinkling of an eye, the design of the monstrous city flashes into vision—a glittering hieroglyph many square miles in extent ; and when, to borrow and debase an image, all the evening street-lamps burst together into song ! Such is the spectacle of the future, preluded the other day by the experiment in Pall Mall. Star-rise by electricity, the most romantic flight of civilization ; the compensatory benefit for an innumerable array of factories and bankers' clerks. To the artistic spirit exercised about Thirlmere, here is a crumb of consolation ; consolatory, at least, to such of them that look out upon the world through seeing eyes, and contentedly accept beauty where it comes.

But the conservative, while lauding progress, is ever timid of innovation ; his is the hand upheld to counsel pause ; his is the signal advising slow advance. The word *electricity* now sounds the note of danger. In Paris, at the mouth of the Passage des Princes, in the place before the Opera portico, and in the Rue Drouot at the *Figaro* office, a new sort of urban star now shines out nightly, horrible, unearthly, obnoxious to the human eye ; a lamp for a nightmare ! Such a light as this should shine only on murders and public crime, or along the corridors of lunatic asylums, a horror to heighten horror. To look at it only once is to fall in love with gas, which gives a warm domestic radiance fit to eat by. Mankind, you would have thought, might have remained content with what Prometheus stole for them and not gone fishing the profound heaven with kites to catch and domesticate the wildfire of the storm. Yet here we have the levin brand at our doors, and it is proposed that we should henceforward take our walks abroad in the glare of permanent lightning. A man need not be very superstitious if he scruple to follow his pleasures by the light of the Terror that Flieth, nor very epicurean if he prefer to see the face of beauty more becomingly displayed. That ugly blinding glare may not improperly advertise the home of slanderous *Figaro*, which is a back-shop to the infernal regions ; but where soft joys prevail, where people are convoked to pleasure and the philosopher looks on smiling and silent, where love and laughter and deifying wine abound, there, at least, let the old mild lustre shine upon the ways of man.

Virginibus Puerisque.   1881.

THE SPIRIT OF PLACE

Alice Meynell

With mimicry, with praises, with echoes, or with answers, the poets have all but outsung the bells. The inarticulate bell has found too much interpretation, too many rhymes professing to close with her inaccessible utterance, and to agree with her remote tongue. The bell, like the bird, is a musician pestered with literature.

To the bell, moreover, men do actual violence. You cannot shake together a nightingale's notes, or strike or drive them into haste, nor can you make a lark toll for you with intervals to suit your turn, whereas wedding-bells are compelled to seem gay by mere movement and hustling. I have known some grim bells, with not a single joyous note in the whole peal, so forced to hurry for a human festival, with their harshness made light of, as though the Bishop of Hereford had again been forced to dance in his boots by a merry highwayman.

The clock is an inexorable but less arbitrary player than the bellringer, and the chimes await their appointed time to fly—wild prisoners—by twos or threes, or in greater companies. Fugitives—one or twelve taking wing— they are sudden, they are brief, they are gone ; they are delivered from the close hands of this actual present. Not in vain is the sudden upper door opened against the sky ; they are away, hours of the past.

Of all unfamiliar bells, those which seem to hold the memory most surely after but one hearing are bells of

an unseen cathedral of France when one has arrived by
night ; they are no more to be forgotten that the bells
in *Parsifal*. They mingle with the sound of feet in unknown streets, they are the voices of an unknown tower ;
they are loud in their language. The spirit of place,
which is to be seen in the shapes of the fields and the
manner of the crops, to be felt in a prevalent wind,
breathed in the breath of the earth, overheard in a far
street-cry or in the tinkle of some blacksmith, calls out
and peals in the cathedral bells. It speaks its local tongue
remotely, steadfastly, largely, clamorously, loudly, and
greatly by these voices ; you hear the sound in its dignity,
and you know how familiar, how childlike, how life-
long it is in the ears of the people. The bells are strange,
and you know how homely they must be. Their utter-
ances are, as it were, the classics of a dialect.

Spirit of place ! It is for this we travel, to surprise its
subtlety ; and where it is a strong and dominant angel,
that place, seen once, abides entire in the memory with
all its own accidents, its habits, its breath, its name. It is
recalled all a lifetime, having been perceived a week, and
is not scattered but abides, one living body of remembrance. The untravelled spirit of place—not to be pursued, for it never flies, but always to be discovered, never
absent, without variation—lurks in the by-ways and rules
over the towers, indestructible, and indescribable unity.
It awaits us always in its ancient and eager freshness. It
is sweet and vivacious within its immemorial boundaries,
but it never crosses them. Long white roads outside have
mere suggestions of it and prophecies ; they give promise
not of its coming, for it abides, but of a new and singular
and unforeseen goal for our present pilgrimage, and of
an intimacy to be made. Was ever journey too hard or
too long that had to pay such a visit ? And if by good
fortune it is a child who is the pilgrim, the spirit of place
gives him a peculiar welcome, for antiquity and the con-

ceiver of antiquity (who is only a child) know one another ; nor is there a more delicate perceiver of locality
than a child. He is well used to words and voices that
he does not understand, and this is a condition of his
simplicity ; and when those unknown words are bells,
loud in the night, they are to him as homely and as old
as lullabies.

If, especially in England, we make rough and reluctant
bells go in gay measures, when we whip them to run down
the scale to ring in a wedding—bells that would step to
quite another and a less agile march with a better grace—
there are belfries that hold far sweeter companies. If
there is no music within Italian churches, there is a most
curious local immemorial music in many a campanile on
the heights. Their way is for the ringers to play a tune
on the festivals, and the tunes are not hymn tunes or popular
melodies, but proper bell-tunes, made for bells. Doubtless they were made in times better versed than ours in
the subdivisions of the arts, and better able to understand
the strength that lies ready in the mere little submission
to the means of a little art, and to the limits—nay, the very
embarrassments—of those means. If it were but possible
to give here a real bell-tune—which cannot be, for those
melodies are rather long—the reader would understand
how some village musician of the past used his narrow
means as a composer for the bells, with what freshness,
completeness, significance, fancy, and what effect of
liberty.

These hamlet-bells are the sweetest, as to their own
voices, in the world. When I speak of their antiquity I
use the word relatively. The belfries are no older than
the fifteenth or sixteenth century, the time when Italy
seems to have been generally rebuilt. But, needless to
say, this is antiquity for music, especially in Italy. At
that time they must have had foundries for bells of tender
voices, and pure, warm, light, and golden throats, pre-

cisely tuned. The hounds of Theseus had not a more just scale, tuned in a peal, than a North Italian belfry holds in leash. But it does not send them out in a mere scale, it touches them in the order of the game of a charming melody. Of all cheerful sounds made by man this is by far the most light-hearted. You do not hear it from the great churches, Giotto's coloured tower in Florence, that carries the bells for Santa Maria del Fiore and Brunelleschie's dome, does not ring more than four contralto notes, tuned with sweetness, depth, and dignity, and swinging one musical phrase which softly fills the country.

The village belfry it is that grows so fantastic and has such delicate bells. Obviously it stands alone with its own village, and can therefore hear its own tune from beginning to end. There are no other bells in earshot. Other dovecote doors are suddenly set open to the cloud, on a *festa* morning, to let fly those soft-voiced flocks, but the nearest is behind one of many mountains, and our local tune is uninterrupted. Doubtless this is why the little, secluded, sequestered art of composing melodies for bells—charming division of an art, having its own ends and means, and keeping its own wings for unfolding by law—dwells in these solitary places. No tunes in a town would get this hearing, or would be made clear to the end of their frolic amid such a wide and lofty silence.

Nor does every inner village of Italy hold a bell-tune of its own; the custom is Liqurian. Nowhere so much as in Genoa does the nervous tourist complain of church bells in the morning, and in fact he is made to hear an honest rout of them betimes. But the nervous tourist has not, perhaps, the sense of place, and the genius of place does not signal to him to go and find it among innumerable hills, where one by one, one by one, the belfries stand and play their tunes. Variable are those lonely melodies, having a differing gaiety for the festivals; and a pitiful air is played for the burial of a villager.

As for the poets, there is but one among so many of their bells that seems to toll with a spiritual music so loud as to be unforgotten when the mind goes up a little higher than the earth, to listen in thought to earth's untethered sounds. This is Milton's curfew, that sways across one of the greatest of all the seashores of poetry—" the wide-watered."

Essays. 1896.

ORION

Kenneth Grahame

The moonless night has a touch of frost, and is steely-clear. High and dominant amidst the Populations of the Sky, the restless and the steadfast alike, hangs the great Plough, lit with a hard radiance as of the polished and shining share. And yonder, low on the horizon, but half resurgent as yet, crouches the magnificent Hunter : watchful, seemingly, and expectant : with some hint of menace in his port.

Yet should his game be up, you would think, by now. Many a century has passed since the plough first sped a conqueror east and west, clearing forest and draining fen ; policing the valleys with barbed-wires and Sunday schools, with the chains that are forged of peace, the irking fetters of plenty : driving also the whole lot of us, these to sweat at its tail, those to plod with the patient team, but all to march in a great chain-gang, the convicts of peace and order and law : while the happy nomad, with his woodlands, his wild cattle, his pleasing nuptialities, has long since disappeared, dropping only in his flight some store of flint-heads, a legacy of confusion. Truly, we Children of the Plough, but for yon tremendous Monitor in the sky, were in right case to forget that the Hunter is still a quantity to reckon withal. Where, then, does he hide, the Shaker of the Spear ? Why, here, my brother, and here ; deep in the breasts of each and all of us ! And for this drop of primal quicksilver in the blood what poppy or mandragora shall purge it hence away ?

Of pulpiteers and parents it is called Original Sin : a term wherewith they brand whatever frisks and butts with rude goatish horns against accepted maxims and trim theories of education. In the abstract, of course, this fitful stirring of the old yeast is no more sin than a natural craving for a seat on a high stool, for the inscription— now horizontal, and now vertical—of figures, is sin. But the deskmen command a temporary majority : for the short while they shall hold the cards they have the right to call the game. And so—since we must bow to the storm—let the one thing be labelled Sin, and the other Salvation—for a season : ourselves forgetting never that it is all a matter of nomenclature. What we have now first to note is that this original Waft from the Garden asserts itself most vigorously in the Child. This it is that thrusts the small boy out under the naked heavens, to enact a sorry and shivering Crusoe on an islet in the duck-pond. This it is that sends the little girl footing it after the gipsy's van, oblivious of lessons, puddings, the embrace maternal, the paternal smack ; hearing naught save the faint, far bugle-summons to the prehistoric little savage that thrills and answers in the tingling blood of her ; seeing only a troop of dusky, dull-eyed guides along that shining highway to the dim land east o' the sun and west o' the moon : where freedom is, and you can wander and breathe, and at night tame street lamps there are none— only the hunter's fires, and the eyes of lions, and the mysterious stars. In later years it is stifled and gagged— buried deep, a green turf at the head of it, and on its heart a stone ; but it lives, it breathes, it lurks, it will up and out when 'tis looked for least. That stockbroker, some brief summers gone, who was missed from his wonted place one settling-day ! a goodly portly man, i' faith : and had a villa and a steam launch at Surbiton : and was versed in the esoteric humours of the House. Who could have thought that the Hunter lay hid in him ? Yet, after many weeks, they found him in a wild nook of Hampshire. Ragged, sunburnt, the nocturnal haystack calling aloud from his frayed and weather-stained duds, his trousers tucked, he was tickling trout with godless native urchins ; and when they would have won him to himself with honied whispers of American Rails, he answered but with babble of green fields. He is back in his wonted corner now : quite cured, apparently, and tractable. And yet—let the sun shine too wantonly in Throgmorton Street, let an errant zephyr, quick with the warm south, fan but his cheek too wooingly on his way to the station ; and will he not once more snap his chain and away ? Ay, truly ; and next time he will not be caught.

Deans have danced to the same wild piping, though their chapters have hushed the matter up. Even Duchesses (they say) have " come tripping doon the stair," rapt by the climbing passion from their strawberry-leaved surroundings into starlit spaces. Nay, ourselves, too—the douce, respectable mediocrities that we are—which of us but might recall some fearful outbreak whose details are mercifully unknown to the household that calls us breadwinner and chief ? What marvel that up yonder the Hunter smiles ? When he knows that every one in his ken, the tinker with the statesman, has caught his bugle blast and gone forth on its irresistible appeal !

Not that they are so easily followed as of yore, those flying echoes of the horn ! Joints are stiffer, maybe ; certainly the desolate suburbs creep ever farther into the retreating fields ; and when you reach the windy moorland, lo ! it is all staked out into building-lots. Mud is muddier now than heretofore ; and ruts are ruttier. And what friendless old beast comes limping down the dreary lane ? He seems sorely shrunk and shoulder-shotten ; but by the something of divinity in his look, still more than by the wings despondent along his mighty sides, 'tis ever the old Pegasus—not yet the knacker's own. " Hard

times I've been having," he murmurs, as you rub his nose.
" These fellows have really no seat except for a park hack.
As for this laurel, we were wont to await it trembling :
and in taking it we were afraid. Your English way of
hunting it down with yelpings and hallooings—well, I
may be out of date, but we wouldn't have stood that sort
of thing on Helicon." So he hobbles down the road.
Good-night, old fellow ! Out of date ? Well, it may
be so. And alas ! the blame is ours.

But for the Hunter—there he rises—couchant no more.
Nay, flung full stretch on the blue, he blazes, he domi-
nates, he appals ! Will his turn, then, really come at last ?
After some Armageddon of cataclysmal ruin, all levelling,
whelming the County Councillor with the Music-hall
artiste, obliterating the very furrows of the Plough, shall
the skin-clad nomad string his bow once more, and once
more loose the whistling shaft ? Wildly incredible it
seems. And yet—look up ! Look up and behold him
confident, erect, majestic—there on the threshold of the
sky !

Pagan Papers. 1898.

ON WAR

George Santayana

To fight is a radical instinct ; if men have nothing else
to fight over they will fight over words, fancies, or women,
or they will fight because they dislike each other's looks,
or because they have met walking in opposite directions.
To knock a thing down, especially if it is cocked at an
arrogant angle, is a deep delight to the blood. To fight
for a reason and in a calculating spirit is something your
true warrior despises ; even a coward might screw his
courage up to such a reasonable conflict. The joy and
glory of fighting lie in its pure spontaneity and consequent
generosity ; you are not fighting for gain, but for sport
and for victory. Victory, no doubt, has its fruits for the
victor. If fighting were not a possible means of livelihood
the bellicose instinct could never have established itself in
any long-lived race. A few men can live on plunder, just
as there is room for some beasts of prey ; other men are
reduced to living on industry, just as there are diligent
bees, ants, and herbivorous kine. But victory need have
no good fruits for the people whose army is victorious.
That it sometimes does so is an ulterior and blessed circumstance hardly to be reckoned upon.

Since barbarism has its pleasures it naturally has its
apologists. There are panegyrists of war who say that
without a periodical bleeding a race decays and loses its
manhood. Experience is directly opposed to this shameless
assertion. It is war that wastes a nation's wealth, chokes its

industries, kills its flower, narrows its sympathies, condemns it to be governed by adventurers, and leaves the puny, deformed, and unmanly to breed the next generation. Internecine war, foreign and civil, brought about the greatest set-back which the life of reason has ever suffered ; it exterminated the Greek and Italian aristocracies. Instead of being descended from heroes, modern nations are descended from slaves ; and it is not their bodies only that show it. After a long peace, if the conditions of life are propitious, we observe a people's energies bursting their barriers ; they become aggressive on the strength they have stored up in their remote and unchecked development. It is the unmutilated race, fresh from the struggle with nature (in which the best survive, while in war it is often the best that perish), that descends victoriously into the arena of nations and conquers disciplined armies at the first blow, becomes the military aristocracy of the next epoch and is itself ultimately sapped and decimated by luxury and battle, and merged at last into the ignoble conglomerate beneath. Then, perhaps, in some other virgin country a genuine humanity is again found, capable of victory because unbled by war. To call war the soil of courage and virtue is like calling debauchery the soil of love.

Blind courage is an animal virtue indispensable in a world full of dangers and evils where a certain insensibility and dash are requisite to skirt the precipice without vertigo. Such animal courage seems therefore beautiful rather than desperate or cruel, and being the lowest and most instinctive of virtues it is the one most widely and sincerely admired. In the form of steadiness under risks rationally taken, and perseverance so long as there is a chance of success, courage is a true virtue ; but it ceases to be one when the love of danger, a useful passion when danger is unavoidable, begins to lead men into evils which it was unnecessary to face. Bravado, provocativeness,

and a gambler's instinct, with a love of hitting hard for
the sake of exercise, is a temper which ought already to be
counted among the vices rather than the virtues of man.
To delight in war is a merit in the soldier, a dangerous
quality in the captain, and a positive crime in the statesman.

The panegyrist of war places himself on the lowest
level on which a moralist or patriot can stand and shows
as great a want of refined feeling as of right reason. For
the glories of war are all blood-stained, delirious, and
infected with crime ; the combative instinct is a savage
prompting by which one man's good is found in another's
evil. The existence of such a contradiction in the moral
world is the original sin of nature, whence flows every
other wrong. He is a willing accomplice of that per-
versity in things who delights in another's discomfiture
or in his own, and craves the blind tension of plunging
into danger without reason, or the idiot's pleasure in facing
a pure chance. To find joy in another's trouble is, as man
is constituted, not unnatural, though it is wicked ; and to
find joy in one's own trouble, though it be madness, is
not yet impossible for man. These are the chaotic depths
of that dreaming nature out of which humanity has to
grow.

The Life of Reason. 1905.

ON THE RELATIVITY OF SCIENCE

George Santayana

Science is nothing but developed perception, interpreted intent, common sense rounded out and minutely articulated. It is therefore as much an instinctive product, as much a stepping forth of human courage in the dark, as is any inevitable dream or impulsive action. Like life itself, like any form of determinate existence, it is altogether autonomous and unjustifiable from the outside. It must lean on its own vitality ; to sanction reason there is only reason, and to corroborate sense there is nothing but sense. Inferential thought is a venture not to be approved of, save by a thought no less venturesome and inferential. This is once for all the fate of a living being— it is the very essence of spirit—to be ever on the wing, borne by inner forces toward goals of its own imagining, confined to a passing apprehension of a represented world. Mind, which calls itself the organ of truth, is a permanent possibility of error. The encouragement and corroboration which science is alleged to receive from moment to moment may, for aught it knows, be simply a more ingenious self-deception, a form of that cumulative illusion by which madness can confirm itself, creating a whole world, with an endless series of martyrs, to bear witness to its sanity.

To insist on this situation may seem idle, since no positive doctrine can gain thereby in plausibility, and no particular line of action in reasonableness. Yet this transcendental exercise, this reversion to the immediate, may be recommended by way of a cathartic, to free the mind from ancient obstructions and make it hungrier and more agile in its rational faith. Scepticism is harmless when it is honest and universal ; it clears the air and is a means of reorganizing belief on its natural foundations. Belief is an inevitable accompaniment of practice and intent, both of which it will cling to all the more closely after a thorough criticism. When all beliefs are challenged together, the just and necessary ones have a chance to step forward and to re-establish themselves alone. The doubt cast on science, when it is an ingenuous and impartial doubt, will accordingly serve to show what sort of thing science is, and to establish it on a sure foundation. Science will then be seen to be tentative, genial, practical, and humane, full of ideality and pathos, like every great human undertaking.

Reason is not indispensable to life, nor needful if living anyhow be the sole and indeterminate aim ; as the existence of animals and of most men sufficiently proves. In so far as man is not a rational being and does not live in and by the mind, in so far as his chance volitions and dreamful ideas roll by without mutual representation or adjustment, in so far as his instinct takes the lead and even his galvanized action is a form of passivity, he may eschew science and say that life is not intellectual. Yet reason has the indomitable persistence of all natural tendencies ; it returns to the attack as waves beat on the shore. To observe its defeat is already to give it a new embodiment.

The Life of Reason. 1905.

THE WEST WIND

JOSEPH CONRAD

THE West Wind reigns over the seas surrounding the
coasts of these kingdoms ; and from the gateways of
the channels, from promontories as if from watch-towers,
from estuaries of rivers as if from postern gates, from
passage-ways, inlets, straits, firths, the garrison of the Isle
and the crews of the ships going and returning look to
the westward to judge by the varied splendours of his
sunset mantle the mood of that arbitrary ruler. The end
of the day is the time to gaze at the kingly face of the
Westerly Weather, who is the arbiter of ships' destinies.
Benignant and splendid, or splendid and sinister, the
western sky reflects the hidden purposes of the royal mind.
Clothed in a mantle of dazzling gold or draped in rags of
black clouds like a beggar, the might of the Westerly
Wind sits enthroned upon the western horizon with the
whole North Atlantic as a footstool for his feet and the
first twinkling stars making a diadem for his brow. Then
the seamen, attentive courtiers of the weather, think of
regulating the conduct of their ships by the mood of the
master. The West Wind is too great a king to be a dis-
sembler : he is no calculator plotting deep schemes in a
sombre heart ; he is too strong for small artifices ; there is
passion in all his moods, even in the soft mood of his
serene days, in the grace of his blue sky whose immense
and unfathomable tenderness reflected in the mirror of
the sea embraces, possesses, lulls to sleep the ships with

white sails. He is all things to all oceans ; he is like a poet seated upon a throne—magnificent, simple, barbarous, pensive, generous, impulsive, changeable, unfathomable—but when you understand him, always the same. Some of his sunsets are like pageants devised for the delight of the multitude, when all the gems of the royal treasure-house are displayed above the sea. Others are like the opening of his royal confidence, tinged with thoughts of sadness and compassion in a melancholy splendour meditating upon the short-lived peace of the waters. And I have seen him put the pent-up anger of his heart into the aspect of the inaccessible sun, and cause it to glare fiercely like the eye of an implacable autocrat out of a pale and frightened sky.

He is the war-lord who sends his battalions of Atlantic rollers to the assault of our seaboard. The compelling voice of the West Wind musters up to his service all the might of the ocean. At the bidding of the West Wind there arises a great commotion in the sky above these Islands, and a great rush of waters falls upon our shores. The sky of the westerly weather is full of flying clouds, of great big white clouds coming thicker and thicker till they seem to stand welded into a solid canopy, upon whose grey face the lower wrack of the gale, thin, black, and angry-looking, flies past with vertiginous speed. Denser and denser grows this dome of vapours, descending lower and lower upon the sea, narrowing the horizon around the ship. And the characteristic aspect of westerly weather, the thick, grey, smoky, and sinister tone sets in, circumscribing the view of the men, drenching their bodies, oppressing their souls, taking their breath away with booming gusts, deafening, blinding, driving, rushing them onwards in a swaying ship towards our coasts lost in mists and rain.

The caprice of the winds, like the wilfulness of men, is fraught with the disastrous consequences of self-indulgence. Long anger, the sense of his uncontrolled power, spoils the frank and generous nature of the West Wind. It is as if his heart were corrupted by a malevolent and brooding rancour. He devastates his own kingdom in the wantonness of his force. South-west is the quarter of the heavens where he presents his darkened brow. He breathes his rage in terrific squalls, and overwhelms his realm with an inexhaustible welter of clouds. He strews the seeds of anxiety upon the decks of scudding ships, makes the foam-stripped ocean look old, and sprinkles with grey hairs the heads of shipmasters in the homeward-bound ships running for the Channel. The Westerly Wind asserting his sway from the south-west quarter is often like a monarch gone mad, driving forth with wild imprecations the most faithful of his courtiers to shipwreck, disaster, and death.

The south-westerly weather is the thick weather *par excellence*. It is not the thickness of the fog ; it is rather a contraction of the horizon, a mysterious veiling of the shores with clouds that seem to make a low vaulted dungeon around the running ship. It is not blindness ; it is a shortening of the sight. The West Wind does not say to the seaman, " You shall be blind " ; it restricts merely the range of his vision and raises the dread of land within his breast. It makes of him a man robbed of half his force, of half his efficiency. Many times in my life, standing in long sea-boots and streaming oilskins at the elbow of my commander on the poop of a homeward-bound ship making for the Channel, and gazing ahead into the grey and tormented waste, I have heard a weary sigh shape itself into a studiously casual comment :

" Can't see very far in this weather."

And have made answer in the same low, perfunctory tone :

" No, sir."

It would be merely the instinctive voicing of an ever-present thought associated closely with the consciousness of the land somewhere ahead and of the great speed of the ship. Fair wind, fair wind ! Who would dare to grumble at a fair wind ? It was a favour of the Western King, who rules masterfully the North Atlantic from the latitude of the Azores to the latitude of Cape Farewell. A famous shove this to end a good passage with ; and yet, somehow, one could not muster upon one's lips the smile of a courtier's gratitude. This favour was dispensed to you from under an overbearing scowl, which is the true expression of the great autocrat when he has made up his mind to give a battering to some ships and to hunt certain others home in one breath of cruelty and benevolence, equally distracting.

" No, sir. Can't see very far."

Thus would the mate's voice repeat the thought of the master, both gazing ahead, while under their feet the ship rushes at some twelve knots in the direction of the lee shore ; and only a couple of miles in front of her swinging and dripping jib-boom, carried naked with an upward slant like a spear, a grey horizon closes the view with a multitude of waves surging upwards violently as if to strike at the stooping clouds.

Awful and threatening scowls darken the face of the West Wind in his clouded, south-west mood ; and from the King's throne-hall in the western board stronger gusts reach you, like the fierce shouts of raving fury to which only the gloomy grandeur of the scene imparts a saving dignity. A shower pelts the deck and the sails of the ship as if flung with a scream by an angry hand ; and when the night closes in, the night of a south-westerly gale, it seems more hopeless than the shade of Hades. The south-westerly mood of the great West Wind is a lightless mood, without sun, moon, or stars, with no gleam of light but the phosphorescent flashes of the great sheets of foam that, boiling up on each side of the ship, fling bluish gleams upon her dark and narrow hull, rolling as she runs, chased by enormous seas, distracted in the tumult.

There are some bad nights in the kingdom of the West

Wind for homeward-bound ships making for the Channel ;
and the days of wrath dawn upon them colourless and
vague like the timid turning up of invisible lights upon the
scene of a tyrannical and passionate outbreak, awful in the
monotony of its method and the increasing strength of its
violence. It is the same wind, the same clouds, the same
wildly racing seas, the same thick horizon around the ship.
Only the wind is stronger, the clouds seem denser and
more overwhelming, the waves appear to have grown
bigger and more threatening during the night. The hours,
whose minutes are marked by the crash of the breaking
seas, slip by with the screaming, pelting squalls overtaking
the ship as she runs on and on with darkened canvas, with
streaming spars and dripping ropes. The downpours
thicken. Preceding each shower a mysterious gloom, like
the passage of a shadow above the firmament of grey
clouds, filters down upon the ship. Now and then the rain
pours upon your head in streams as if from spouts. It
seems as if your ship were going to be drowned before she
sank, as if all atmosphere had turned to water, You gasp,
you splutter, you are blinded and deafened, you are sub-
merged, obliterated, dissolved, annihilated, streaming all
over as if your limbs, too, had turned to water. And every
nerve on the alert you watch for the clearing-up mood
of the Western King, that shall come with a shift of wind
as likely as not to whip all the three masts out of your ship
in the twinkling of an eye.

Heralded by the increasing fierceness of the squalls,
sometimes by a faint flash of lightning like the signal of
a lighted torch waved far away behind the clouds, the shift
of wind comes at last, the crucial moment of the change
from the brooding and veiled violence of the south-west
gale to the sparkling, flashing, cutting, clear-eyed anger of
the King's north-westerly mood. You behold another
phase of his passion, a fury bejewelled with stars, mayhap
bearing the crescent of the moon on its brow, shaking the

last vestiges of its torn cloud-mantle in inky-black squalls with hail and sleet descending like showers of crystals and pearls, bounding off the spars, drumming on the sails, pattering on the oilskin coats, whitening the decks of homeward-bound ships. Faint, ruddy flashes of lightning flicker in the starlight upon her mast-heads. A chilly blast hums in the taut rigging, causing the ship to tremble to her very keel, and the soaked men on her decks to shiver in their wet clothes to the very marrow of their bones. Before one squall has flown over to sink in the eastern board, the edge of another peeps up already above the western horizon, racing up swift, shapeless, like a black bag full of frozen water ready to burst over your devoted head. The temper of the ruler of the ocean has changed. Each gust of the clouded mood that seemed warmed by the heat of a heart flaming with anger has its counterpart in the chilly blasts that seem blown from a breast turned to ice with a sudden revulsion of feeling. Instead of blinding your eyes and crushing your soul with a terrible apparatus of cloud and mists and seas and rain, the King of the West turns his power to contemptuous pelting of your back with icicles, to making your weary eyes water as if in grief and your worn-out carcass quake pitifully. But each mood of the great autocrat has its own greatness, and each is hard to bear. Only the north-west phase of that mighty display is not demoralizing to the same extent, because between the hail and sleet squalls of a north-westerly gale one can see a long way ahead.

To see ! to see !—this is the craving of the sailor, as of the rest of blind humanity. To have his path made clear for him is the aspiration of every human being in our beclouded and tempestuous existence. I have heard a reserved, silent man, with no nerves to speak of, after three days of hard running in thick south-westerly weather, burst out passionately : " I wish to God we could get sight of something ! "

We had just gone down below for a moment to com-
mune in a battened-down cabin, with a large white chart
lying limp and damp upon a cold and clammy table under
the light of a smoky lamp. Sprawling over that seaman's
silent and trusted adviser, with one elbow upon the coast
of Africa and the other planted in the neighbourhood of
Cape Hatteras (it was a general track-chart of the North
Atlantic), my skipper lifted his rugged, hairy face, and
glared at me in a half-exasperated, half-appealing way.
We have seen no sun, moon, or stars for something like
seven days. By the effect of the West Wind's wrath the
celestial bodies had gone into hiding for a week or more,
and the last three days had seen the force of a south-west
gale grow from fresh, through strong, to heavy, as the
entries in my log-book could testify. Then we separated,
he to go on deck again, in obedience to that mysterious call
that seems to sound for ever in a shipmaster's ears, I to
stagger into my cabin with some vague notion of putting
down the words " Very heavy weather " in a log-book
not quite written up to date. But I gave it up, and crawled
into my bunk instead, boots and hat on, all standing (it did
not matter ; everything was soaking wet, a heavy sea
having burst the poop skylights the night before), to
remain in a nightmarish state between waking and sleeping
for a couple of hours of so-called rest.

The south-westerly mood of the West Wind is an
enemy of sleep, and even of a recumbent position, in
the responsible officers of a ship. After two hours of
futile, light-headed, inconsequent thinking upon all
things under heaven in that dark, dank, wet, and devas-
tated cabin, I arose suddenly and staggered up on deck.
The autocrat of the North Atlantic was still oppressing
his kingdom and its outlying dependencies, even as far
as the Bay of Biscay, in the dismal secrecy of thick, very
thick, weather. The force of the wind, though we were
running before it at the rate of some ten knots an hour,

was so great that it drove me with a steady push to the front of the poop, where my commander was holding on.

"What do you think of it ? " he addressed me in an interrogative yell.

What I really thought was that we both had had just about enough of it. The manner in which the great West Wind chooses at times to administer his possessions does not commend itself to a person of peaceful and law-abiding disposition, inclined to draw distinctions between right and wrong in the face of natural forces, whose standard, naturally, is that of might alone. But, of course, I said nothing. For a man caught, as it were, between his skipper and the great West Wind silence is the safest sort of diplomacy. Moreover, I knew my skipper. He did not want to know what I thought. Shipmasters hanging on a breath before the thrones of the winds ruling the seas have their psychology, whose workings are as important to the ship and those on board of her as the changing moods of the weather. The man, as a matter of fact, under no circumstances, ever cared a brass farthing for what I or anybody else in his ship thought. He had had just about enough of it, I guessed, and what he was at really was a process of fishing for a suggestion. It was the pride of his life that he had never wasted a chance, no matter how boisterous, threatening, and dangerous, of a fair wind. Like men racing blindfold for a gap in a hedge, we were finishing a splendidly quick passage from the Antipodes, with a tremendous rush for the Channel in as thick a weather as any I can remember, but his psychology did not permit him to bring the ship to with a fair wind blowing—at least not on his own initiative. And yet he felt that very soon indeed something would have to be done. He wanted the suggestion to come from me, so that later on, when the trouble was over, he could argue this point with his own uncompromising spirit, laying the blame upon my shoulders. I must render him the justice that this sort of pride was his only weakness.

But he got no suggestion from me. I understood his psychology. Besides, I had my own stock of weaknesses at the time (it is a different one now), and amongst them was the conceit of being remarkably well up in the psychology of the Westerly weather. I believed—not to mince matters—that I had a genius for reading the mind of the great ruler of high latitudes. I fancied I could discern already the coming of a change in his royal mood. And all I said was :

" The weather's bound to clear up with the shift of wind."

" Anybody knows that much ! " he snapped at me, at the highest pitch of his voice.

" I mean before dark ! " I cried.

This was all the opening he ever got from me. The eagerness with which he seized upon it gave me the measure of the anxiety he had been labouring under.

" Very well," he shouted, with an affectation of impatience, as if giving way to long entreaties. " All right. If we don't get a shift by then we'll take that foresail off her and put her head under her wing for the night."

I was struck by the picturesque character of the phrase as applied to a ship brought-to in order to ride out a gale with wave after wave passing under her breast. I could see her resting in the tumult of the elements like a sea-bird sleeping in wild weather upon the raging waters with its head tucked under its wing. In imaginative precision, in true feeling, this is one of the most expressive sentences I have ever heard on human lips. But as to taking the foresail off that ship before we put her head under her wing, I had my grave doubts. They were justified. That long-enduring piece of canvas was confiscated by the arbitrary decree of the West Wind, to whom belong the lives of men and the contrivances of their hands within the limits of his kingdom. With the sound of a faint explosion it vanished into the thick weather bodily, leaving behind of its stout substance not so much as one solitary strip big enough to be picked into a handful of lint for, say, a wounded elephant. Torn out of its bolt-ropes, it faded like a whiff of smoke in the smoky drift of clouds shattered and torn by the shift of wind. For the shift of wind had come. The unveiled, low sun glared angrily from a chaotic sky upon a confused and tremendous sea dashing itself upon a coast. We recognized the headland, and looked at each other in the silence of dumb wonder. Without knowing it in the least, we had run up alongside the Isle of Wight, and that tower, tinged a faint evening red in the salt wind-haze, was the lighthouse of St. Catherine's Point.

My skipper recovered first from his astonishment. His bulging eyes sank back gradually into their orbits. His psychology, taking it all round, was really very creditable for an average sailor. He had been spared the humiliation of laying his ship to with a fair wind ; and at once that man, of an open and truthful nature, spoke up in perfect good faith, rubbing together his brown, hairy hands—the hands of a master-craftsman upon the sea :

" Humph ! that's just about where I reckoned we had got to."

The transparency and ingenuousness, in a way, of that delusion, the airy tone, the hint of already growing pride, were perfectly delicious. But, in truth, this was one of the greatest surprises ever sprung by the clearing up mood of the West Wind upon one of the most accomplished of his courtiers.

The Mirror of the Sea. 1906.

THE RAGGED REGIMENT

Max Beerbohm

——" commonly called ' Longshanks ' on account of
his great height he was the first king crowned in the
Abbey as it now appears and was interred with great pomp
on St. Simon's and St. Jude's Day October 28th 1307 in
1774 the tomb was opened when the king's body was
found almost entire in the right hand was a richly em-
bossed sceptre and in the left "——

So much I gather as I pass one of the tombs on my
way to the Chapel of Abbot Islip. Anon the verger will
have stepped briskly forward, drawing a deep breath,
with his flock well to heel, and will be telling the secrets
of the next tomb on his tragic beat.

To be a verger in Westminster Abbey—what life
could be more unutterably tragic ? We are, all of us,
more or less enslaved to sameness ; but not all of us are
saying, every day, hour after hour, exactly the same thing,
in exactly the same place, in exactly the same tone of
voice, to people who hear it for the first time and receive
it with a gasp of respectful interest. In the name of
humanity, I suggest to the Dean and Chapter that they
should relieve these sad-faced men of their intolerable
mission, and purchase parrots. On every tomb, by every
bust or statue, under every memorial window, let a parrot
be chained by the ankle to a comfortable perch, therefrom
to enlighten the rustic and the foreigner. There can be
no objection on the ground of expense ; for parrots live
long. Vergers do not, I am sure.

It is only the rustic and the foreigner who go to West-minster Abbey for general enlightenment. If you pause beside any one of the verger-led groups, and analyse the murmur emitted whenever the verger has said his say, you will find the constituent parts of the sound to be such phrases as " Lor' ! " " Ach so ! " " Deary me ! " " Tiens ! " and " My ! " " My ! " preponderates ; for antiquities appeal with greatest force to the one race that has none of them ; and it is ever the Americans who hang the most tenaciously, in the greatest numbers, on the vergers' tired lips. We of the elder races are capable of taking antiquities as a matter of course. Certainly such of us as reside in London take Westminster Abbey as a matter of course. A few of us will be buried in it, but meanwhile we don't go to it, even as we don't go to the Tower, or the Mint, or the Monument. Only for some special purpose do we go—as to hear a sensational bishop preach-ing, or to see a monarch anointed. And on these rare occasions we cast but a casual glance at the Abbey—that close-packed chaos of beautiful things and worthless vulgar things. That the Abbey should be thus chaotic does not seem strange to us ; for lack of orderliness and discrimina-tion is an essential characteristic of the English genius. But to the Frenchman, with his passion for symmetry and harmony, how very strange it must all seem ! How very whole-hearted a generalizing " Tiens ! " must he utter when he leaves the edifice !

My own special purpose in coming is to see certain old waxen effigies that are here.[1] A key grates in the lock of a little door in the wall of (what I am told is) the North Ambulatory ; and up a winding wooden staircase I am ushered into a tiny paven chamber. Not much light comes through the very narrow and deeply

[1] In its original form this essay had the good fortune to accom-pany two very romantic drawings by William Nicholson—one of Queen Elizabeth's effigy, the other of Charles II.'s.

embrased window, and the space is so obstructed that I must pick my way warily. All around are deep wooden cupboards, faced with glass ; and I become dimly aware that through each glass some one is watching me. Like sentinels in sentry-boxes, they fix me with their eyes, seeming as though they would challenge me. How shall I account to them for my presence ? I slip my note-book into my pocket, and try, in the dim light, to look as unlike a spy as possible. But I cannot, try as I will, acquit myself of impertinence. Who am I that I should review this " ragged regiment " ? Who am I that I should come peering in upon this secret conclave of the august dead ? Immobile and dark, very gaunt and withered, these personages peer out at me with a malign dignity, through the ages which separate me from them, through the twilight in which I am so near to them. Their eyes . . .

Come, sir, their eyes are made of glass. It is quite absurd to take wax-works seriously. Wax-works are not a serious form of art. The aim of art is so to imitate life as to produce in the spectator an illusion of life. Wax-works, at best, can produce no such illusion. Don't pretend to be illuded. For its power to illude, an art depends on its limitations. Art never can be life, but it may seem to be so if it do but keep far enough away from life. A statue may seem to live. A painting may seem to live. That is because each is so far away from life that you do not apply the test of life to it. A statue is of bronze or marble, than either of which nothing could be less flesh-like. A painting is a thing in two dimensions, whereas man is in three. If sculptor or painter tried to dodge these conventions, his labour would be undone. If a painter swelled his canvas out and in according to the convexities and concavities of his model, or if a sculptor overlaid his material with authentic flesh-tints, then you would demand that the painted or sculptured figure should blink, or stroke its chin, or kick its foot in the air. That it could do none of these things would rob it of all power to illude you. An art that challenges life at close quarters is defeated through the simple fact that it is not life. Wax-works, being so near to life, having the exact proportions of men and women, having the exact texture of skin and hair and habiliments, must either be made animate or continue to be grotesque and pitiful failures. Lifelike? They? Rather do they give you the illusion of death. They are akin to photographs seen through stereoscopic lenses—those photographs of persons who seem horribly to be corpses, or, at least, catalepts; and . . . You see, I have failed to cheer myself up. Having taken up a strong academic line, and set bravely out to prove to myself the absurdity of wax-works, I find myself at the point where I started, irrefutably arguing to myself that I have good reason to be frightened, here in the Chapel of Abbot Islip, in the midst of these, the Abbot's glowering and ghastly tenants. Catalepsy! death! that is the atmosphere I am breathing.

If I were writing in the past tense, I might pause here to consider whether this emotion were a genuine one or a mere figment for literary effect. As I am writing in the present tense, such a pause would be inartistic, and shall not be made. I must seem not to be writing, but to be actually on the spot, suffering. But then, you may well ask, why should I stay here, to suffer? why not beat a hasty retreat? The answer is that my essay would then seem skimpy; and that you, moreover, would know hardly anything about the wax-works. So I must ask you to imagine me fighting down my fears, and consoling myself with the reflection that here, after all, a sense of awe and oppression is just what one ought to feel—just what one comes for. At Madame Tussaud's exhibition, by which I was similarly afflicted some years ago, I had no such consolation. There my sense of fitness was outraged. The place was meant to be cheerful. It was brilliantly lit. A band was playing popular tunes. Downstairs there was even a restaurant. (Let fancy fondly dwell, for a moment, on the thought of a dinner at Madame Tussaud's : a few carefully selected guests, and a menu well thought out ; conversation becoming general ; corks popping ; quips flying ; a sense of *bien-être* ; " thank you for a *most* delightful evening.") Madame's figures were meant to be agreeable and lively presentments. Her visitors were meant to have a thoroughly good time. But the Islip Chapel has no cheerful intent. It is, indeed, a place set aside, with all reverence, to preserve certain relics of a grim, yet not unlovely, old custom. These fearful images are no stock-in-trade of a showman ; we are not invited to " walk up " to them. They were fashioned with a solemn and wistful purpose. The reason of them lies in a sentiment which is as old as the world—lies in man's vain revolt from the prospect of death. If the soul must perish from the body, may not at least the body itself be preserved, somewhat in the semblance of life, and, for at least a while, on the face of the earth ? By subtle art, with far-fetched spices, let the body survive its day and be (even though hidden beneath the earth) for ever. Nay more, since death cause it straightway to dwindle somewhat from the true semblance of life, let cunning artificers fashion it anew—fashion it as it was. Thus, in the earliest days of England, the kings, as they died, were embalmed, and their bodies were borne aloft upon their biers, to a sepulture long delayed after death. In later days, an image of every king that died was forthwith carved in wood, and painted according to his remembered aspect, and decked in his own robes ; and, when they had sealed his tomb, the mourners, humouring, to the best of their power, his hatred of extinction, laid this image upon the tomb's slab, and left it so. In yet later days, the pretence became more realistic. The hands and

the face were modelled in wax ; and the figure stood upright, in some commanding posture, on a valanced platform above the tomb. Nor were only the kings thus
honoured. Every one who was interred in the Abbey,
whether in virtue of lineage or of achievements, was
honoured thus. It was the fashion for every great lady to
write in her will minute instructions as to the posture in
which her image was to be modelled, and which of her
gowns it was to be clad in, and with what of her jewellery
it was to glitter. Men, too, used to indulge in such pre-
cautions. Of all the images thus erected in the Abbey,
there remain but a few. The images had to take their
chance, in days that were without benefit of police.
Thieves, we may suppose, stripped the finery from many
of them. Rebels, we know, broke in, less ignobly, and
tore many of them limb from limb, as a protest against
the governing classes. So only a poor remnant, a " ragged
regiment," has been rallied, at length, into the sanctuary
of Islip's Chapel. Perhaps, if they were not so few, these
images would not be so fascinating.

Yes, I am fascinated by them now. Terror has been
toned to wonder. I am filled with a kind of wondering
pity. My academic theory about wax-works has broken
down utterly. These figures of kings, princes, duchesses,
queens—all are real to me now, and all are pathetic, in the
dignity of their fallen and forgotten greatness. With what
majesty they wear their rusty velvets and faded silks,
flaunting sere ruffles of point-lace, which at a touch now
would be shivered like cobwebs ! My heart goes out to
them through the glass that divides us. I have an idea
that they take pleasure in my propinquity. Even Queen
Elizabeth, beholding whom, as she stands here, gaunt and
imperious and appalling, I echo the words spoken by
Philip's envoy, " This woman is possessed of a hundred
thousand devils "—even she herself, though she gazes
askance into the air, seems to be conscious of my presence,

and to be willing me to stay. It is a relief to meet the bourgeois eye of good Queen Anne. It has restored my common sense. " These figures really are most curious, most interesting . . ." and anon I am asking intelligent questions about the contents of a big press which, by special favour, has been unlocked for me.

Perhaps the most romantic thing in the Islip Chapel is this press. Herein, huddled one against another in dark recesses, lie the battered and disjected remains of the earlier effigies—the primitive wooden ones. Edward I. and Eleanor are known to be among them ; and Henry VII. and Elizabeth of York ; and others not less illustrious. Which is which ? By size and shape you can distinguish the men from the women ; but beyond that is mere guesswork, be you never so expert. Time has broken and shuffled these erst so significant effigies till they have become as unmeaning for us as the bones in one of the old plague-pits. I feel that I ought to be more deeply moved than I am by this sad state of things. But—well, I seem to have exhausted my capacity for sentiment, and cannot rise to the level of my opportunity. Would that I were Thackeray ! Dear gentleman, how promptly and copiously he would have wept and moralized here, in his grandest manner, with that perfect technical mastery which makes even now his tritest and shallowest sermons sound remarkable, his hollowest sentiment ring true ! What a pity he never came to beat the muffled drum, on which he was so supreme a performer, around the Islip Chapel !

As I make my way down the stairs, I am trying to imagine what would have been the cadence of the final sentence in that essay by Thackeray. And, as I pass along the North Ambulatory, lo ! there is the same verger with a new party ; and I catch the words " was interred with great pomp on St. Simon's and St. Jude's Day October 28th 1307 in 1774 the tomb was opened when——"

Yet Again. 1928.

FIRES

E. V. Lucas

A FRIEND of mine making a list of the things needed for the cottage that he had taken, put at the head " bellows." Then he thought for some minutes, and was found merely to have added " tongs " and " poker." Then he asked some one to finish it. A fire, indeed, furnishes. Nothing else, not even a chair, is absolutely necessary ; and it is difficult for a fire to be too large. Some of the grates put into modern houses by the jerry-builders would move an Elizabethan to tears, so petty and mean are they, and so incapable of radiation. We English people would suffer no loss in kindliness and tolerance were the ingle-nook restored to our homes. The ingle humanizes.

Although the father of the family no longer, as in ancient Greece, performs on the hearth religious rites, yet it is still a sacred spot. Lovers whisper there, and there friends exchange confidences. Husband and wife face the fire hand in hand. The table is for wit and good humour, the hearth is for something deeper and more personal. The wisest counsels are offered beside the fire, the most loving sympathy and comprehension are there made explicit. It is the scene of the best dual companionship. The fire itself is a friend, having the prime attribute—warmth. One of the most human passages of that most human poem, *The Deserted Village*, tells how the wanderer was now and again taken by the memory of the hearth of his distant home :

" I still had hopes my latest hours to crown,
   Amidst these humble bowers to lay me down. . . .
   Around my fire an evening group to draw,
   And tell of all I felt, and all I saw. . . ."

Only by the fireside could a man so unbosom himself. A good fire extracts one's best ; it will not be resisted. Fitz-Gerald's " Meadows in Spring " contains some of the best fireside stanzas :

> " Then with an old friend
>   I talk of our youth—
> How 'twas gladsome, but often
>   Foolish, forsooth :
>   But gladsome, gladsome !
>
> Or to get merry
>   We sing some old rhyme,
> That made the wood ring again
>   In summer time—
>   Sweet summer time !
>
> Then we go to drinking,
>   Silent and snug ;
> Nothing passes between us
>   Save a brown jug—
>   Sometimes !
>
> And sometimes a tear
>   Will rise in each eye,
> Seeing the two old friends
>   So merrily—
>   So merrily ! "

The hearth also is for ghost stories ; indeed, a ghost story demands a fire. If England were warmed wholly by hot-water pipes or gas stoves, the Society for Psychical Research would be dissolved. Gas stoves are poor comforters. They heat the room, it is true, but they do so after a manner of their own, and there they stop. For encouragement, for inspiration, you seek the gas stove in vain. Who could be witty, who could be humane, before a gas stove ? It does so little for the eye and nothing for the imagination ; its flame is so artificial and restricted a thing, its glowing heart so shallow and ungenerous. It has no voice, no personality, no surprises ; it submits to the control of a gas company, which, in its turn, is controlled by Parliament. Now, a fire proper has nothing to do with Parliament. A fire proper has whims, ambitions, and impulses unknown to gas-burners, undreamed of by asbestos. Yet even the gas stove has advantages and merits when compared with hot-water pipes. The gas stove at least offers a focus for the eye, unworthy though it be ; and you can make a semicircle of good people before it. But with hot-water pipes not even that is possible. From the security of ambush they merely heat, and heat whose source is invisible is hardly to be coveted at all. Moreover, the heat of hot-water pipes is but one remove from stuffiness.

Coals are a perpetual surprise, for no two consignments burn exactly alike. There is one variety that does not burn—it explodes. This kind comes mainly from the slate quarries, and, we must believe, reaches the coal merchant by accident. Few accidents, however, occur so frequently. Another variety, found in its greatest perfection in railway waiting-rooms, does everything but emit heat. A third variety jumps and burns the hearthrug. One can predicate nothing definite concerning a new load of coal at any time, least of all if the consignment was ordered to be " exactly like the last."

A true luxury is a fire in the bedroom. This is fire at its most fanciful and mysterious. One lies in bed watching drowsily the play of the flames, the flicker of the shadows. The light leaps up and hides again, the room gradually becomes peopled with fantasies. Now and then a coal drops and accentuates the silence. Movement with silence is one of the curious influences that come to us : hence, perhaps, part of the fascination of the cinematoscope, wherein trains rush into stations, and streets are seen filled with hurrying people and bustling vehicles, and yet there is no sound save the clicking of the mechanism. With a fire in one's bedroom sleep comes witchingly.

Another luxury is reading by firelight, but this is less to the credit of the fire than the book. An author must have us in no uncertain grip when he can induce us to read him by a light so impermanent as that of the elfish coal. Nearer and nearer to the page grows the bended head, and nearer and nearer to the fire moves the book. Boys and girls love to read lying full length on the hearthrug.

Some people maintain a fire from January to December ; and, indeed, the days on which a ruddy grate offends are very few. According to Mortimer Collins, out of the three hundred and sixty-five days that make up the year only on the odd five is a fire quite dispensable. A perennial fire is, perhaps, luxury writ large. The very fact that sunbeams falling on the coals dispirit them to greyness and ineffectual pallor seems to prove that when the sun rides high it is time to have done with fuel except in the kitchen or in the open air.

The fire in the open air is indeed joy perpetual, and there is no surer way of renewing one's youth than by kindling and tending it, whether it be a rubbish fire for potatoes, or an aromatic offering of pine spindles and fir cones, or the scientific structure of the gipsy to heat a tripod-swung kettle. The gipsy's fire is a work of art. " Two short sticks were stuck in the ground, and a third across to them like a triangle. Against this frame a

number of the smallest and driest stick were leaned, so
that they made a tiny hut. Outside these there was a
second layer of longer sticks, all standing, or rather leaning, against the first. If a stick is placed across, lying
horizontally, supposing it catches fire, it just burns through
the middle and that is all, the ends go out. If it is stood
nearly upright, the flame draws up to it ; it is certain to
catch, burns longer, and leaves a good ember." So wrote
one who knew—Richard Jefferies, in *Bevis*, that epic of
boyhood. Having built the fire, the next thing is to light
it. An old gipsy woman can light a fire in a gale, just as
a sailor can always light his pipe, even in the cave of
Æolus ; but the amateur is less dexterous. The smoke
of the open-air fire is charged with memory. One whiff of
it, and for a swift moment we are in sympathy with our
remotest ancestors, and all that is elemental and primitive
in us is awakened.

An American poet, R. H. Messinger, wrote—

" Old wood to burn !—
Ay, bring the hillside beech
From where the owlets meet and screech,
    And ravens croak ;
The crackling pine, the cedar sweet ;
Bring, too, a clump of fragrant peat,
    Dug 'neath the fern ;
    The knotted oak,
    A faggot, too, perhaps,
Whose bright flame, dancing, winking,
Shall light us at our drinking ;
    While the oozing sap
Shall make sweet music to our thinking."

There is no fire of coals, not even the blacksmith's, that
can compare with the blazing fire of wood. The wood
fire is primeval. Centuries before coals were dreamed of,

our rude forefathers were cooking their meat and gaining warmth from burning logs.

Coal is modern, decadent. Look at this passage concerning fuel from an old Irish poem : " O man," begins the lay, " that for Fergus of the feasts does kindle fire, whether afloat or ashore never burn the king of woods. . . . The pliant woodbine, if thou burn, wailings for misfortunes will abound ; dire extremity at weapons' points or drowning in great waves will come after thee. Burn not the precious apple tree." The minstrel goes on to name wood after wood that may or may not be burned. This is the crowning passage : " Fiercest heat-giver of all timber is green oak, from him none may escape unhurt ; by partiality for him the head is set on aching, and by his acrid embers the eye is made sore. Alder, very battle-witch of all woods, tree that is hottest in the fight—undoubtedly burn at thy discretion both the alder and the white thorn. Holly, burn it green ; holly, burn it dry ; of all trees whatsoever the critically best is holly." Could any one write with this enthusiasm and poetic feeling about Derby Brights and Silkstone—even the best Silkstone and the best Derby Brights ?

The care of a wood fire is, in itself, daily work for a man ; for far more so than with coal is progress continuous. Something is always taking place and demanding vigilance—hence the superiority of a wood fire as a beguiling influence. The bellows must always be near at hand, the tongs not out of reach ; both of them more sensible implements than those that usually appertain to coals. The tongs have no pretensions to brightness and gentility ; the bellows, quite apart from their function in life, are a thing of beauty ; the fire-dogs, on whose backs the logs repose, are fine upstanding fellows ; and the bricks on which the fire is laid have warmth and simplicity and a hospitable air to which decorative tiles can never attain. Again, there is about the logs something cleanly, in charming contrast to the dirt of coal. The wood hails from the neighbouring coppice. You have watched it grow ; your interest in it is personal, and its interest in you is personal. It is as keen to warm you as you are to be warmed. Now there is nothing so impersonal as a piece of coal. Moreover, this wood was cut down and brought to the door by some good-humoured countryman of your acquaintance, whereas coal is obtained by miners—bad-tempered, truculent fellows that strike. Who ever heard of a strike among coppicers ? And the smoke from a wood fire !—clean and sweet and pungent, and, against dark foliage, exquisite in colour as the breast of a dove. The delicacy of its grey-blue is not to be matched.

Whittier's " Snow Bound " is the epic of the wood-piled hearth. Throughout we hear the crackling of the brush, the hissing of the sap. The texture of the fire was " the oaken log, green, huge, and thick, and rugged brush " :

> " Hovering near,
> We watched the first red blaze appear,
> Heard the sharp crackle, caught the gleam
> On whitewashed wall and sagging beam,
> Until the old, rude-furnished room
> *Burst flower-like into rosy bloom.*"

That italicized line—my own italics—is good. For the best fire (as for the best celery)—the fire most hearty, most inspired, and inspiring—frost is needed. When old Jack is abroad and there is a breath from the east in the air, then the sparks fly and the coals glow. In moist and mild weather the fire only burns, it has no enthusiasm for combustion. Whittier gives us a snowstorm :

> " Shut in from all the world without,
> We sat the clean-winged hearth about,
> Content to let the north wind roar
> In baffled rage at pane and door,

> While the red logs before us beat
> The frost line back with tropic heat ;
> And ever, when a louder blast
> Shook beam and rafter as it passed,
> The merrier up its roaring draught
> *The great throat of the chimney laughed.*"

But the wood fire is not for all. In London it is impracticable ; the builder has set his canon against it. Let us, then—those of us who are able to—build our coal fires the higher, and flourish in their kindly light. Whether one is alone or in company, the fire is potent to cheer. Indeed, a fire *is* company. No one need fear to be alone if the grate but glows. Faces in the fire will smile at him, mock him, frown at him, call and repulse ; or, if there be no faces, the smoke will take a thousand shapes and lead his thoughts by delightful paths to the land of reverie ; or he may watch the innermost heart of the fire burn blue (especially if there is frost in the air) ; or, poker in hand, he may coax a coal into increased vivacity. This is an agreeable diversion, suggesting the mediæval idea of the Devil in his domain.

Fireside and Sunshine. 1906.

THE CAPE HORN CALM

John Masefield

Off Cape Horn there are but two kinds of weather, neither one of them a pleasant kind. If you get the fine kind it is dead calm, without enough wind to lift the wind vane. The sea lies oily and horrible, heaving in slow, solemn swells, the colour of soup. The sky closes down upon the sea all round you, the same colour as the water. The sun never shines over those seas, though sometimes there is a red flush, in the east or in the west, to hint that somewhere, very far away, there is daylight brightening the face of things.

If you are in a ship in the Cape Horn calm you forge ahead, under all sail, a quarter of a mile an hour. The swell heaves you up and drops you, in long, slow, gradual movements, in a rhythm beautiful to mark. You roll, too, in a sort of horrible crescendo, half a dozen rolls and a lull. You can never tell when she will begin to roll. She will begin quite suddenly, for no apparent reason. She will go over and over with a rattling clatter of blocks and chains. Then she will swing back, groaning along the length of her, to slat the great sails and set the reef-points flogging, to a hard clack and jangle of staysail sheets. Then over she will go again, and back, and again over, rolling farther each time. At the last of her rolls there comes a clattering of tins, as the galley gear and whack pots slither across to leeward, followed by cursing seamen. The iron swing-ports bang to and fro. The straining and groaning sounds along her length. Every block aloft clacks and whines. The sea splashes up the scuppers. The sleepers curse her from their bunks for a drunken drogher. Then she lets up and stands on her dignity, and rolls no more perhaps for another quarter of an hour.

It is cold, this fine variety, for little snow squalls are always blowing by, to cover the decks with soft dry snow, and to melt upon the sails. If you go aloft you must be careful what you touch. If you touch a wire shroud, or a chain sheet, the skin comes from your hand as though a hot iron had scarred it. If you but scratch your hand aloft, in that fierce cold, the scratch will suppurate. I broke the skin of my hand once with a jagged scrap of wire in the main-rigging. The scratch festered so that I could not move my hand for a week. It was a little scratch, the eighth of an inch long. It has left its mark. The sailors used to prophesy that it would cause the loss of my arm.

On the whole we had an easy time of it in the Cape Horn calm. No work was being done about decks. Our rigging was all set up, our blocks all greased and overhauled, our chafing gear in its place, and the heavy-weather sails bent. When we came on deck we had little to do but stand by ready for a call, while the flurries of snow blew past and the ship's planking creaked. The old man was fond of mat-making. I don't know how he made the mats, whether with a " sword," in the usual way, or by a needle upon canvas. He used the coarse thread of bunting for his material. He made the boys unravel some old signal flags into little balls of thread while we were rolling in the swell. That was nearly all the work we did while the calm lasted.

When we were down below in the half-deck, the little room twelve feet square, where the six boys lived and slept, we were almost happy. We had rigged up a bogey stove, with a chimney which kinked into elbows whenever the roll was very heavy. It did not burn very well, this bogey stove, but we contrived to cook by it. We were only allowed coke for fuel, but we always managed to steal coal enough either from the cook or from the coal-hole. It was our great delight to sit upon our chests in the dog watch, looking at the bogey, listening to the creaking chimney, watching the smoke pouring out from the chinks. In the night watches, when the sleepers lay quiet in their bunks behind the red baize curtains, one or two of us who kept the deck would creep below to put on coal. That was the golden time, the time of the night watch, to sit there in the darkness among the sleepers hearing the coals click.

One of us in each night watch made cocoa for the others. At about four bells, when the watch was half through, the cocoa-maker would slink below to put the kettle on to boil and to mix the brew in the pannikins. There is an old poet (I think it is Ben Jonson ; it may be Marlowe) who asks, " Where are there greater atheists than your cooks ? " I would ask, less rhythmically perhaps, " Where are there loftier thinkers than your cocoa-makers ? " Ah, what profound thoughts I thought ; what mute, but Miltonic, poetry I made in that dim half-deck, by the smoky bogey, in the night, in the stillness, amid the many waters. The kings were ashore in their palaces, tossing uneasily (as who would not) upon their purple pillows. Couriers were flogging spent horses along the roads of the world, bringing news of battle, of death, of pestilence. Soldiers were going into action. Prisoners were scraping shot in the chain gang. Women were weeping, and the huntsmen were up in America. Sitting there in the dim half-deck, watching the kettle boil, I saw it all. I was like Buddha under the holy branches. My mind filled with pictures like the magical water in the bowl of a wizard.

Then what a joy it was to take the cocoa tin, containing a greasy dark stuff of cocoa and condensed milk, already mixed. One put a spoonful into each pannikin and then a spoonful of soft, brown, lumpy ship's sugar. Then with a spoon, or with a sheath knife, one bruised the ingredients together. With what a luscious crunch they blended ! How perfect was the smell of the crushed mixture ! How it covered away, like the smell of incense at a Mass, the rude, worldly scents, such as tar, and stale Negro Head, and oilskins, and newly greased sea boots. Then, as one mixed, one would hear the bells struck. Ting, ting. Ting, ting. Ting. Five bells—an hour and a half before the watch would end. One would hear the old men of the sea, the old sailors, as they shambled along to and fro biting on the pipe-stems, yarning about ships that were long ago bilged on the coral. One would hear the scraps of songs, little stray verses, set to old beautiful tunes. There was one old man who had no better voice than a donkey. He was for ever walking the deck when I brewed the cocoa, singing " Rolling Home," the most popular of all sailor songs. I think I would rather have written " Rolling Home " than " Hydriotaphia." If I had written " Rolling Home " I would pass my days at sea or in West Coast nitrate ports hearkening to the roll and the roar of it as the yards go jolting up the mast or the anchor comes to the bows.

Pipe all hands to man the capstan, see your ca—bles run down clear,
Heave away, and with a will, boys, 'tis to old England's shores we steer ;
And we'll sing in joyous chorus in the watches of the night,
For we'll sight the shores of England when the grey dawn brings the light.

I used to think that stanza, as the old sailor sang it in the dark watches, the most beautiful thing the tongue of man ever spoke.

While he sang, I used to take little tentative nibbles at the compound in the pannikins. Have you ever been an exile, reader, at sea, in pr-s-n, or somewhere, where the simple needs of life cannot possibly be gratified ? If you have you will know how that sweet mush of cocoa tasted. It was like bubbling water in the desert, like fern fronds above cool springs, like the voice of the bird in the moonlight, in the green shadows, in some southern spice garden, drowsy with odours. It was like a night in June in the forest, by the babbling brook, when the moon rises, red and solemn, over the hills where the deer feed. Ah, the taste of it ! the scent of it ! the hidden meaning of it !

Then as I nibbled, the kettle would come to the boil and the brew would be made. My watch-mate would come below puffing his pipe, humming his favourite tune of " The Sailor's Wives." I would fill a pannikin and carry it aft to the boy on the poop, my watch-mate stationed there, keeping the time. Round us were the waters, dark and ghostly ; the crying sea-birds : the whales with their pants and spoutings. There were the masts and the great sails filling and slatting. There were the sailors lying on the deck, their pipe-bowls ruddy in the blackness. There was the murmuring and talking sea, full of mysterious menace. And the sailors' quiet talk, and the smell of tar from the sailroom, and the man at the wheel abaft all, and the lame mate limping to the binnacle—it was all beautiful, solemn, sacred, like a thing in a dream. And then the taste of the brew, when one settled down in the half-deck. The talk we had, my sleepy mate and I ; talk of work and of ships, of topsails and mermaids, the old beautiful talk of youth, that needs but a listener to be brilliant.

A Tarpaulin Muster. 1907.

ON LYING IN BED

G. K. Chesterton

LYING in bed would be an altogether perfect and supreme experience if only one had a coloured pencil long enough to draw on the ceiling. This, however, is not generally a part of the domestic apparatus on the premises. I think myself that the thing might be managed with several pails of Aspinall and a broom. Only if one worked in a really sweeping and masterly way, and laid on the colour in great washes, it might drip down again on one's face in floods of rich and mingled colour like some strange fairy rain ; and that would have its disadvantages. I am afraid it would be necessary to stick to black and white in this form of artistic composition. To that purpose, indeed, the white ceiling would be of the greatest possible use ; in fact it is the only use I think of a white ceiling being put to.

But for the beautiful experiment of lying in bed I might never have discovered it. For years I have been looking for some blank spaces in a modern house to draw on. Paper is much too small for any really allegorical design ; as Cyrano de Bergerac says : " Il me faut des géants." But when I tried to find these fine clear spaces in the modern rooms such as we all live in I was continually disappointed. I found an endless pattern and complication of small objects hung like a curtain of fine links between me and my desire. I examined the walls ; I found them to my surprise to be already covered with wall-paper, and I found the wall-paper to be already covered with very uninteresting images, all bearing a ridiculous resemblance to each other. I could not understand why one arbitrary symbol (a symbol apparently entirely devoid of any religious or philosophical significance) should thus be sprinkled all over my nice walls like a sort of smallpox. The Bible must be referring to wall-papers, I think, when it says, " Use not vain repetitions, as the Gentiles do." I found the Turkey carpet a mass of unmeaning colours, rather like the Turkish Empire, or like the sweetmeat called Turkish Delight. I do not exactly know what Turkish Delight really is ; but I suppose it is Macedonian Massacres. Everywhere that I went forlornly, with my pencil or my paint brush, I found that others had unaccountably been before me, spoiling the walls, the curtains, and the furniture with their childish and barbaric designs.

. . . . . .

Nowhere did I find a really clear space for sketching until this occasion when I prolonged beyond the proper limit the process of lying on my back in bed. Then the light of that white heaven broke upon my vision, that breadth of mere white which is indeed almost the definition of Paradise, since it means purity and also means freedom. But alas ! like all heavens, now that it is seen it is found to be unattainable ; it looks more austere and more distant than the blue sky outside the window. For my proposal to paint on it with the bristly end of a broom has been discouraged—never mind by whom ; by a person debarred from all political rights—and even my minor proposal to put the other end of the broom into the kitchen fire and turn it into charcoal has not been conceded. Yet I am certain that it was from persons in my position that all the original inspiration came for covering the ceilings of palaces and cathedrals with a riot of fallen angels or victorious gods. I am sure that it was only because Michael Angelo was engaged in the ancient and honourable occupation of lying in bed that he ever realized how the roof of the Sistine Chapel might be made into an awful imitation of a divine drama that could only be acted in the heavens.

The tone now commonly taken towards the practice of lying in bed is hypocritical and unhealthy. Of all the marks of modernity that seem to mean a kind of decadence, there is none more menacing and dangerous than the exaltation of very small and secondary matters of conduct at the expense of very great and primary ones, at the expense of eternal ties and tragic human morality. If there is one thing worse than the modern weakening of major morals it is the modern strengthening of minor morals. Thus it is considered more withering to accuse a man of bad taste than of bad ethics. Cleanliness is not next to godliness nowadays, for cleanliness is made an essential and godliness is regarded as an offence. A playwright can attack the institution of marriage so long as he does not misrepresent the manners of society, and I have met Ibsenite pessimists who thought it wrong to take beer but right to take prussic acid. Especially this is so in matters of hygiene ; notably such matters as lying in bed. Instead of being regarded, as it ought to be, as a matter of personal convenience and adjustment, it has come to be regarded by many as if it were a part of essential morals to get up early in the morning. It is upon the whole part of practical wisdom ; but there is nothing good about it or bad about its opposite.

.   .   .   .   .   .

Misers get up early in the morning ; and burglars, I am informed, get up the night before. It is the great peril of our society that all its mechanism may grow more fixed while its spirit grows more fickle. A man's minor actions and arrangements ought to be free, flexible, creative ; the things that should be unchangeable are his principles, his ideals. But with us the reverse is true ; our views change constantly ; but our lunch does not change. Now, I should like men to have strong and rooted conceptions, but as for their lunch, let them have it sometimes in the garden, sometimes in bed, sometimes on the roof, sometimes in the top of a tree. Let them argue from the same first principles, but let them do it in a bed, or a boat, or a balloon. This alarming growth of good habits really means a too great emphasis on those virtues which mere custom can ensure, it means too little emphasis on those virtues which custom can never quite ensure, sudden and splendid virtues of inspired pity or of inspired candour. If ever that abrupt appeal is made to us we may fail. A man can get used to getting up at five o'clock in the morning. A man cannot very well get used to being burnt for his opinions ; the first experiment is commonly fatal. Let us pay a little more attention to these possibilities of the heroic and the unexpected. I dare say that when I get out of this bed I shall do some deed of an almost terrible virtue.

For those who study the great art of lying in bed there is one emphatic caution to be added. Even for those who can do their work in bed (like journalists), still more for those whose work cannot be done in bed (as, for example, the professional harpooners of whales), it is obvious that the indulgence must be very occasional. But that is not the caution I mean. The caution is this : if you do lie in bed, be sure you do it without any reason or justification at all. I do not speak, of course, of the seriously sick. But if a healthy man lies in bed, let him do it without a rag of excuse ; then he will get up a healthy man. If he does it for some secondary hygienic reason, if he has some scientific explanation, he may get up a hypochondriac.

Tremendous Trifles. 1909.

THE FOURTH ORDER OF HUMANITY

FRANCIS THOMPSON

IN the beginning of things came man, sequent to him woman ; on woman followed the child, and on the child the doll. It is a climax of development ; and the crown of these is the doll.

To the doll's supremacy in beauty woman's self bears testimony, implicit, if unconscious. For ages has she tricked her face in pigment, and her brows in alien hair ; her *contours* she has filled to counterfeit roundness, her eyes and lashes tinged : and all in a frustrate essay to compass by Art what in the doll is right of Nature. Even the child exhibits distinct inferiorities. It is full of thwartness and eating and drinking, and selffulness (selfishness were a term too dully immitigate), and a plentiful lack of that repose wherein the doll is nearest to the quiet gods. For my own part, I profess that much acquaintance only increases my consideration for this fourth order of humanity ; always excepting the very light-blue-eyed doll, in whose regard there is a certain chill *hauteur* against which my diffidence is not proof.

Consider the life of dolls. At the whim of some *debonair* maternal tyranness, they veer on every wind of mutability ; are the sport of imputed moods, suffer qualities over which they have no election,—are sorry or glad, indocile or amiable, at their mistress's whim and mandate ; they are visited with stripes, or the soft aspersion of kisses ; with love delectably persecuted, or consigned to the clement quiet of neglect ; exalted to the dimple of their mistress's cheek, or dejected to the servile floor rent and mutilated, or rocked and murmured over ; blamed or petted, be-rated or loved. Nor why it is thus or thus with them, are they any wise witting ; wherefore these things should be, they know not at all.

Consider the life of us—
Oh, my cousins the dolls !

Some consciousness, I take it, there was ; some secret sense of this occult co-rivalry in fate, which withheld me even in childhood from the youthful male's contempt for these short-lived parasites of the nursery. I questioned, with wounded feelings, the straitened feminine intolerance which said to the boy : " Thou shalt not hold a baby ; thou shalt not possess a doll." In the matter of babies, I was hopeless to shake the illiberal prejudice ; in the matter of dolls, I essayed to confound it. By eloquence and fine diplomacy I wrung from my sisters a concession of dolls ; whence I date my knowledge of the kind.

But ineluctable sex declared itself. I dramatized them, I fell in love with them ; I did not father them ; intolerance was justified of its children. One in particular I selected, one with surpassing fairness crowned, and bowed before the fourteen inches of her skirt. She was beautiful. She was one of Shakespeare's heroines. She was an amity of inter-removed miracles ; all wrangling excellencies at pact in one sole doll ; the frontiers of jealous virtues marched in her, yet trespassed not against her peace. I desired for her some worthy name ; and asked of my mother : Who was the fairest among living women ? Laughingly was I answered that I was a hard questioner, but that perhaps the Empress of the French bore the bell for beauty. Hence, accordingly, my Princess of puppet-dom received her style ; and at this hour, though she has

long since vanished to some realm where all sawdust is
wiped for ever from dolls' wounds, I cannot hear that
name but the Past touches me with a rigid agglomeration
of small china fingers.

But why with childhood and with her should I close the
blushing recital of my puppet-loves ? Men are but
children of a larger growth ; and your statue, I warrant
me, is but your crescent doll. Wherefore, then, should I
leave unmemorized the statue which thralled my youth
in a passion such as feminine mortality was skilless to
instigate ? Nor at this let any boggle ; for *she* was a
goddess. Statue I have called her ; but indeed she was a
bust, a head, a face—and who that saw that face could
have thought to regard further ? She stood nameless in
the gallery of sculptural casts which she strangely deigned
to inhabit ; but I have since learned that men called her
the Vatican Melpomene. Rightly stood she nameless,
for Melpomene she never was : never went words of hers
from bronzèd lyre in tragic order ; never through *her*
enspelled lips moaned any syllables of woe. Rather, with
her leaf-twined locks, she seemed some strayed Bacchante,
indissolubly filmed in secular reverie. The expression
which gave her divinity resistless I have always suspected for an accident of the cast ; since in frequent en-
gravings of her prototype I never met any such aspect.
The secret of this indecipherable significance, I slowly
discerned, lurked in the singularly diverse set of the two
corners of the mouth ; so that her profile wholly shifted
its meaning according as it was viewed from the right or
left. In one corner of her mouth the little languorous
firstling of a smile had gone to sleep ; as if she had fallen
a-dream, and forgotten that it was there. The other had
drooped, as of its own listless weight, into a something
which guessed at sadness ; guessed, but so as indolent lids
are easily grieved by the pricks of the slate-blue dawn. And
on the full countenance those two expressions blended to a

single expression inexpressible ; as if pensiveness had played the Maenad, and now her arms grew heavy under the cymbals. Thither each evening, as twilight fell, I stole to meditate and worship the baffling mysteries of her meaning : as twilight fell, and the blank noon surceased arrest upon her life, and in the vaguening countenance the eyes broke out from their day-long ambuscade. Eyes of violet blue, drowsed-amorous, which surveyed me not, but looked ever beyond, where a spell enfixed them.

Waiting for something, not for me.

And I was content. Content ; for by such tenure of unnoticedness I knew that I held my privilege to worship : had she beheld me, she would have denied, have contemned my gaze. Between us, now, are years and tears : but the years waste her not, and the tears wet her not ; neither misses she me or any man. There, I think, she is standing yet ; there, I think, she will stand for ever : the divinity of an accident, awaiting a divine thing impossible, which can never come to her, and she knows this not.

For I reject the vain fable that the ambrosial creature is really an unspiritual compound of lime, which the gross ignorant call plaster of Paris. If Paris indeed had to do with her, it was he of Ida. And for him, perchance, she waits.

Prose Works. **1923.**

MY PIPES

J. M. Barrie

In a select company of scoffers my briar was known as the Mermaid. The mouthpiece was a cigarette-holder, and months of unwearied practice were required before you found the angle at which the bowl did not drop off.

This brings me to one of the many advantages that my briar had over all other pipes. It has given me a reputation for gallantry, to which without it I fear I could lay no claim. I used to have a passion for repartee, especially in the society of ladies. But it is with me as with many other men of parts whose wit has ever to be fired by a long fuse : my best things strike me as I wend my way home. This embittered my early days ; and not till the pride of youth had been tamed could I stop to lay in a stock of repartee on likely subjects the night before. Then my pipe helped me. It was the apparatus that carried me to my prettiest compliment. Having exposed my pipe in some prominent place where it could hardly escape notice, I took measures for ensuring a visit from a lady, young, graceful, accomplished. Or I might have it ready for a chance visitor. On her arrival, I conducted her to a seat near my pipe. It is not good to hurry on to the repartee at once ; so I talked for a time of the weather, the theatres, the new novel. I kept my eye on her ; and by and by she began to look about her. She observed the strange-looking pipe. Now is the critical moment. It is possible that she may pass it by without remark, in which case all is lost ; but experience has shown me that four times out of six she touches it in assumed horror, to pass some humorous remark. Off tumbles the bowl. "Oh," she exclaims, "see what I have done ! I am so sorry !" I pull myself together. "Madam," I reply calmly and bowing low, "what else was to be expected ? You came near my pipe—and it lost its head !" She blushes, but cannot help being pleased ; and I set my pipe for the next visitor. By the help of a notebook, of course, I guarded myself against paying this very neat compliment to any person more than once. However, after I smoked the Arcadia the desire to pay ladies compliments went from me.

Journeying back into the past, I come to a time when my pipe had a mouthpiece of fine amber. The bowl and the rest of the stem were of briar, but it was a gentlemanly pipe, without silver mountings. Such tobacco I revelled in as may have filled the pouch of Pan as he lay smoking on the mountain-sides. Once I saw a beautiful woman with brown hair, in and out of which the rays of a morning sun played hide-and-seek, that might not unworthily have been compared to it. Beguiled by the exquisite Arcadia, the days and the years passed from me in delicate rings of smoke, and I contentedly watched them sailing to the skies. How continuous was the line of those lovely circles, and how straight. One could have passed an iron rod through them from end to end. But one day I had a harsh awakening. I bit the amber mouthpiece of my pipe through, and life was never the same again.

It is strange how attached we become to old friends, though they be but inanimate objects. The old pipe put aside, I turned to a meerschaum, which had been presented to me years before, with the caution that I must not smoke it unless I wore kid gloves. There was no savour in that pipe for me. I tried another briar, and it made me unhappy. Clays would not keep in with me. It seemed as if they knew I was hankering after the old pipe, and went

out in disgust.   Then I got a new amber mouthpiece for
my first love.   In a week I had bitten that through too,
and in an over-anxious attempt to file off the ragged edges
I broke the screw.   Moralists have said that the smoker
who has no thought but for his pipe never breaks it ; that
it is he only who while smoking concentrates his mind on
some less worthy object, that sends his teeth through the
amber.   This may be so ; for I am a philosopher, and when
working out new theories I may have been careless even
of that which inspired them most.

After this second accident nothing went well with me,
or with my pipe.   I took the mouthpieces out of other
pipes and fixed them on to the Mermaid.   In a little while
one of them became too wide ; another broke as I was
screwing it more firmly in.   Then the bowl cracked at the
rim, and split at the bottom.   This was an annoyance until
I found out what was wrong and plugged up the fissures
with sealing-wax.   The wax melted and dropped upon
my clothes after a time ; but it was easily renewed.

It was now that I had the happy thought of bringing a
cigarette-holder to my assistance.   But of course one cannot
make a pipe-stem out of a cigarette-holder all at once.   The
thread you wind round the screw has a disappointing way
of coming undone ; when down falls the bowl, with an
escape of sparks.   Twisting a piece of paper round the screw
is an improvement ; but until you have acquired the knack
the operation has to be renewed every time you relight
your pipe.   This involves a sad loss of time, and in my case
it afforded a butt for the dull wit of visitors.   Otherwise,
I found it satisfactory, and I was soon astonishingly adept
at making paper screws.   Eventually my briar became as
serviceable as formerly, though not, perhaps, so handsome.
I fastened on the holder with sealing-wax ; and often a
week passed without my having to renew the joint.

It was no easy matter lighting a pipe like mine, especially
when I had no matches.   I always meant to buy a number

of boxes ; but somehow I put off doing it. Occasionally I found a box of vestas on my mantelpiece, which some caller had left there by mistake, or sympathizing, perhaps, with my ease ; but they were such a novelty that I never felt quite at home with them. Generally I remembered they were there just after my pipe was lit. When I kept them in mind and looked forward to using them, they were at the other side of the room, and it would have been a pity to get up for them. Besides, the most convenient medium for lighting one's pipe is paper, after all ; and if you have not an old envelope in your pocket, there is probably a photograph standing on the mantelpiece. It is convenient to have the magazines lying handy ; or a page from a book—hand-made paper burns beautifully—will do. To be sure, there is the lighting of your paper. For this your lamp is practically useless, standing in the middle of the table, while you are in an easy-chair by the fireside ; and as for the tape-and-spark contrivance, it is the introduction of machinery into the softest joys of life. The fire is best. It is near you, and you drop your burning spill into it with a minimum waste of energy. The proper fire for pipes is one in a cheerful blaze. If your spill is carelessly constructed, the flame runs up into your fingers before you know what you are doing ; so that it is as well to marry and get your wife to make spills for you. Before you begin to smoke, scatter these about the fireplace. Then you will be able to reach them without rising. The irritating fire is the one that has burned low—when the coals are more than half cinders, and cling to each other in fear of death. With such a fire it is no use attempting to light a pipe all at once. Your better course now is to drop little bits of paper into the likely places in the fire, and have a spill ready to apply to the one that lights first. It is an anxious moment, for they may merely shrivel up sullenly without catching fire, and in that case some men lose their tempers. Bad to lose your temper over your pipe——

No pipe ever really rivalled the briar in my affections, though I can recall a mad month when I fell in love with two little meerschaums, which I christened Romulus and Remus. They lay together in one case in Regent Street, and it was with difficulty that I could pass the shop without going in. Often I took side streets to escape their glances, but at last I asked the price. It startled me, and I hurried home to the briar.

I forget when it was that a sort of compromise struck me. This was that I should present the pipes to my brother as a birthday gift. Did I really mean to do this, or was I only trying to cheat my conscience ? Who can tell ? I hurried again into Regent Street. There they were, more beautiful than ever. I hovered about the shop for quite half an hour that day. My indecision and vacillation were pitiful. Buttoning up my coat, I would rush from the window, only to find myself back again in five minutes. Sometimes I had my hand on the shop-door. Then I tore it away and hurried into Oxford Street. Then I slunk back again. Self whispered " Buy them—for your brother." Conscience said " Go home." At last I braced myself up for a magnificent effort, and jumped into a bus bound for London Bridge. This saved me for the time.

I now began to calculate how I could become owner of the meerschaums—prior to dispatching them by parcel post to my brother—without paying for them. That was my way of putting it. I calculated that by giving up my daily paper I should save 13s. in six months. After all, why should I take in a daily paper ? To read through columns of public speeches, and police cases, and murders in Paris, is only to squander valuable time. Now, when I left home I promised my father not to waste my time. My father had been very good to me ; why, then, should I do that which I had promised him not to do ? Then, again, there were the theatres. During the past six months

I had spent several pounds on theatres. Was this right ? My mother (who has never, I think, been in a theatre) strongly advised me against frequenting such places. I did not take this much to heart at the time. Theatres did not seem to me to be immoral. But, after all, my mother is older than I am ; and who am I, to set my views up against hers ? By avoiding the theatres for the next six months, I am (already), say, three pounds to the good. I have been frittering away my money, too, on luxuries ; and luxuries are effeminate. Thinking the matter over temperately and calmly in that way, I saw that I should be thoughtfully saving money instead of spending it by buying Romulus and Remus, as I already called them. At the same time, I should be gratifying my father and my mother, and leading a higher and a nobler life.

Even then I do not know that I should have bought the pipes until the six months were up, had I not been driven to it by jealousy. On my life, love for a pipe is very like love for a woman, though they say it is not so acute. Many a man thinks there is no haste to propose until he sees a hated rival approaching. Even if he is not in a hurry for the lady himself, he loathes the idea of her giving herself, in a moment of madness, to that other fellow. Rather than allow that, he proposes himself and so ensures her happiness. It was so with me. Romulus and Remus were taken from the window to show to a black-bearded swarthy man, whom I suspected of designs upon them the moment he entered the shop. Ah, the agony of waiting until he came out. He was not worthy of them. I never knew how much I loved them until I had nearly lost them. As soon as he was gone I asked if he had priced them and was told that he had. He was to call again to-morrow. I left a deposit of a guinea, hurried home for more money, and that night Romulus and Remus were mine. But I never really loved them as I loved my briar.

My Lady Nicotine. 1913.

IN BETHUNE

Lord Dunsany

UNDER all ruins is history, as every tourist knows. Indeed, the dust that gathers above the ruin of cities may be said to be the cover of the most wonderful of the picture-books of Time, those secret books into which we sometimes peep. We turn no more, perhaps, than the corner of a single page in our prying, but we catch a glimpse there of things so gorgeous, in the book that we are not meant to see, that it is worth while to travel to far countries, whoever can, to see one of those books, and where the edges are turned up a little to catch sight of those strange winged bulls and mysterious kings and lion-headed gods that were not meant for us. And out of the glimpses one catches from odd corners of those volumes of Time, where old centuries hide, one builds up part by guesses, part by fancy mixed with but little knowledge, a tale or theory of how men and women lived in unknown ages in the faith of forgotten gods.

Such a people lived in Timgad and left it probably about the time that waning Rome began to call home her outposts. Long after the citizens left the city stood on that high plateau in Africa, teaching shepherd Arabs what Rome had been : even to-day its great arches and parts of its temples stand : its paved streets are still grooved clearly with the wheel-ruts of chariots, and beaten down on each side of the centre by the pairs of horses that drew them two thousand years ago. When all the clatter had died away Timgad stood there in silence.

At Pompeii, city and citizens ended together. Pompeii did not mourn among strangers, a city without a people, but was buried at once, closed like an ancient book.

I doubt if any one knows why its gods deserted Luxor, or Luxor lost faith in its gods, or in itself; conquest from over the desert or down the Nile, I suppose, or corruption within. Who knows? But one day I saw a woman come out from the back of her house and empty a basket full of dust and rubbish right into the temple at Luxor, where a dark green god is seated, three times the size of a man, buried as high as his waist. I suppose that what I saw had been happening off and on pretty well every morning for the last four thousand years. Safe under the dust that that woman threw, and the women that lived before her, Time hid his secrets.

And then I have seen the edges of stones in deserts that might or might not have been cities : they had fallen so long that you could hardly say.

At all these cities, whether disaster met them, and ruin came suddenly on to crowded streets ; or whether they passed slowly out of fashion, and grew quieter year by year while the jackals drew nearer and nearer ; at all these cities one can look with interest and not be saddened by the faintest sorrow—for anything that happened to such a different people so very long ago. Ram-headed gods, although their horns be broken and all their worshippers gone ; armies whose elephants have turned against them ; kings whose ancestors have eclipsed their faces in heaven and left them helpless against the onslaught of the stars ; not a tear is given for one of these to-day.

But when in ruins as complete as Pompeii, as desolate as Timgad amongst its African hills, you see the remnant of a pack of cards lying with what remains of the stock of a draper's shop ; and the front part of the shop and the snug room at the back gape side by side together in equal misery, as though there had never been a barrier between the counter with its wares and the good mahogany table with its decanters ; then in the rustling of papers that blow with dust along long-desolate floors one hears the whisper of Disaster, saying, " See ; I have come." For under plaster shaken down by calamity, and red dust that once was bricks, it is our own age that is lying ; and the little things that lie about the floors are relics of the twentieth century. Therefore in the streets of Bethune the wistful appeal that is in all things lost far off and utterly passed away cries out with an insistence that is never felt in the older fallen cities. No doubt to future times the age that lies under plaster in Bethune, with thin, bare laths standing over it, will appear an age of glory ; and yet to thousands that went one day from its streets, leaving all manner of small things behind, it may well have been an age full of far other promises, no less golden to them, no less magical even, though too little to stir the pen of History, busy with batteries and imperial dooms. So that to these, whatever others may write, the twentieth century will not be the age of strategy, but will only seem to have been those fourteen lost quiet summers whose fruits lie under the plaster.

That layer of plaster and brick-dust lies on the age that has gone, as final, as fatal, as the layer of flints that covers the top of the chalk and marks the end of an epoch and some unknown geologic catastrophe.

It is only by the little things in Bethune, lying where they were left, that one can trace at all what kind of house each was, or guess at the people who dwelt in it. It is only by a potato growing where pavement was, and flowering vigorously under a vacant window, that one can guess that the battered house beside it was once a fruiterer's shop, whence the potato rolled away when man fell on evil days, and found the street, no longer harsh and unfriendly, but soft and fertile like the primal waste, and took root and throve there as its forbears throve before it in another continent before the coming of man.

Across the street, in the dust of a stricken house, the implements of his trade show where a carpenter lived when disaster came so suddenly, quite good tools, some still upon shelves, some amongst broken things that lie all over the floor. And further along the street in which these things are some one has put up a great iron shutter that was to protect his shop. It has a graceful border of painted irises all the way up each side. It might have been a jeweller that would have had such a shutter. The shutter alone remains standing straight upright, and the whole shop is gone.

And just here the shaken street ends and all the streets end together. The rest is a mound of white stones and pieces of bricks with low, leaning walls surrounding it, and the halves of hollow houses ; and eyeing it round a corner, one old tower of the cathedral, as though still gazing over its congregation of houses, a ruined, melancholy watcher. Over the bricks lie tracks, but no more streets. It is about the middle of the town, a hawk goes over, calling as though he flew over the waste, and as though the waste were his. The breeze that carries him opens old shutters and flaps them to again. Old, useless hinges moan ; wall-paper whispers. Three French soldiers trying to find their homes walk over the bricks and groundsel.

It is the Abomination of Desolation, not seen by prophecy far off in some fabulous future, nor remembered from terrible ages by the aid of papyrus and stone, but fallen on our own century, on the homes of folk like ourselves : common things that we knew are become the relics of bygone days. It is our own time that has ended in blood and broken bricks.

Unhappy Far-off Things. 1919.

THE SAMPHIRE GATHERER

W. H. HUDSON

AT sunset, when the strong wind from the sea was beginning to feel cold, I stood on the top of the sandhill looking down at an old woman hurrying about over the low damp ground beneath—a bit of sea-flat divided from the sea by the ridge of sand ; and I wondered at her, because her figure was that of a feeble old woman, yet she moved—I had almost said flitted—over that damp level ground in a surprisingly swift light manner, pausing at intervals to stoop and gather something from the surface. But I couldn't see her distinctly enough to satisfy myself : the sun was sinking below the horizon, and that dimness in the air and coldness in the wind at day's decline, when the year too was declining, made all objects look dim. Going down to her I found that she was old, with thin grey hair on an uncovered head, a lean dark face with regular features and grey eyes that were not old and looked steadily at mine, affecting me with a sudden mysterious sadness. For they were unsmiling eyes and themselves expressed an unutterable sadness, as it appeared to me at the first swift glance ; or perhaps not that, as it presently seemed, but a shadowy something which sadness had left in them, when all pleasure and all interest in life forsook her, with all affections, and she no longer cherished either memories or hopes. This may be nothing but conjecture or fancy, but if she had been a visitor from another world she could not have seemed more strange to me.

I asked her what she was doing there so late in the day,

and she answered in a quiet even voice which had a shadow in it too, that she was gathering samphire of that kind which grows on the flat saltings and has a dull green leek-like fleshy leaf. At this season, she informed me, it was fit for gathering to pickle and put by for use during the year. She carried a pail to put it in, and a table-knife in her hand to dig the plants up by the roots, and she also had an old sack in which she put every dry stick and chip of wood she came across. She added that she had gathered samphire at this same spot every August end for very many years.

I prolonged the conversation, questioning her and listening with affected interest to her mechanical answers, while trying to fathom those unsmiling, unearthly eyes that looked so steadily at mine.

And presently, as we talked, a babble of human voices reached our ears, and half turning we saw the crowd, or rather procession, of golfers coming from the golf-house by the links where they had been drinking tea. Ladies and gentlemen players, forty or more of them, following in a loose line, in couples and small groups, on their way to the Golfers' Hotel, a little further up the coast ; a remarkably good-looking lot with well-fed happy faces, well dressed and in a merry mood, all freely talking and laughing. Some were staying at the hotel, and for the others a score or so of motor cars were standing before its gates to take them inland to their homes, or to houses where they were staying.

We suspended the conversation while they were passing us, within three yards of where we stood, and as they passed the story of the links where they had been amusing themselves since luncheon-time came into my mind. The land there was owned by an old, an ancient, family ; they had occupied it, so it is said, since the Conquest ; but the head of the house was now poor, having no house property in London, no coal mines in Wales, no income from any other source than the land, the twenty or thirty thousand acres let for farming. Even so he would not have been poor, strictly speaking, but for the sons, who preferred a life of pleasure in town, where they probably had private establishments of their own. At all events they kept race-horses, and had their cars, and lived in the best clubs, and year by year the patient old father was called upon to discharge their debts of honour. It was a painful position for so estimable a man to be placed in, and he was much pitied by his friends and neighbours, who regarded him as a worthy representative of the best and oldest family in the county. But he was compelled to do what he could to make both ends meet, and one of the little things he did was to establish golf-links over a mile or so of sand-hills, lying between the ancient coast village and the sea, and to build and run a Golfers' Hotel in order to attract visitors from all parts. In this way, incidentally, the villagers were cut off from their old direct way to the sea and deprived of those barren dunes, which were their open space and recreation ground and had stood them in the place of a common for long centuries. They were warned off and told that they must use a path to the beach which took them over half a mile from the village. And they had been very humble and obedient and had made no complaint. Indeed, the agent had assured them that they had every reason to be grateful to the overlord, since in return for that trivial inconvenience they had been put to they would have the golfers there, and there would be employment for some of the village boys as caddies. Nevertheless, I had discovered that they were not grateful but considered that an injustice had been done to them, and it rankled in their hearts.

I remembered all this while the golfers were streaming by, and wondered if this poor woman did not, like her fellow-villagers, cherish a secret bitterness against those who had deprived them of the use of the dunes where for generations they had been accustomed to walk or sit or lie on the loose yellow sands among the barren grasses, and had also cut off their direct way to the sea where they went daily in search of bits of firewood and whatever else the waves threw up which would be a help to them in their poor lives.

If it be so, I thought, some change will surely come into those unchanging eyes at the sight of all these merry, happy golfers on their way to their hotel and their cars and luxurious homes.

But though I watched her face closely there was no change, no faintest trace of ill-feeling or feeling of any kind ; only that same shadow which had been there was there still, and her fixed eyes were like those of a captive bird or animal, that gaze at us, yet seem not to see us but to look through and beyond us. And it was the same when they had all gone by and we finished our talk and I put money in her hand ; she thanked me without a smile, in the same quiet even tone of voice in which she had replied to my question about the samphire.

I went up once more to the top of the ridge, and looking down saw her again as I had seen her at first, only dimmer, swiftly, lightly moving or flitting moth-like or ghost-like over the low flat salting, still gathering samphire in the cold wind, and the thought that came to me was that I was looking at and had been interviewing a being that was very like a ghost, or in any case a soul, something which could not be described, like certain atmospheric effects in earth and water and sky which are ignored by the landscape painter. To protect himself he cultivates what is called the " sloth of the eye " ; he thrusts his fingers into his ears, so to speak, not to hear that mocking voice that follows and mocks him with his miserable limitations. He who seeks to convey his impressions with a pen is almost as badly off : the most he can do in such instances as the one related, is to endeavour to convey the emotion evoked by what he has witnessed.

Let me then take the case of the man who has trained his eyes, or rather whose vision has unconsciously trained itself, to look at every face he meets, to find in most cases something, however little, of the person's inner life. Such a man could hardly walk the length of the Strand and Fleet Street or of Oxford Street without being startled at the sight of a face which haunts him with its tragedy, its mystery, the strange things it has half revealed. But it does not haunt him long ; another arresting face follows, and then another, and the impressions all fade and vanish from the memory in a little while. But from time to time, at long intervals, once perhaps in a lustrum, he will encounter a face that will not cease to haunt him, whose vivid impression will not fade for years. It was a face and eyes of that kind which I met in the samphire gatherer on that cold evening ; but the mystery of it is a mystery still.

A Traveller in Little Things. 1921.

THE LIFT

Logan Pearsall-Smith

WHAT on earth had I come up for ? I stood out of breath in my bedroom ; I had completely forgotten the errand which had carried me upstairs, leaping two steps at a time. Gloves ! Of course it was my gloves which I had left there. But what did gloves matter, I asked myself, in a world, as Dr. Johnson describes it, bursting with Sin and Misery ?

O stars and garters ! how bored I am by this trite, moralizing way of regarding natural phenomena—this crying of vanity on the beautiful manifestations of mechanical forces. This desire of mine to appear out of doors in appropriate apparel, if it can thus overcome the law of gravitation ; if it can lift twelve stone of matter thirty or forty feet above the earth's surface ; if it can do this every day, and several times a day, is it not quite as remarkable and convenient in the house as a hydraulic lift ?

More Trivia. 1922.

THE IDEAL

Logan Pearsall-Smith

BRIGHT shone the morning, and as I waited (they had promised to call for me in their motor) I made for myself an enchanting picture of the day before me, our drive to that forest beyond the dove-blue hills, the ideal beings I should meet there, feasting with them in the shade of immemorial trees.

And when, in the rainy twilight, I was deposited, soaked, and half-dead with fatigue, out of that open motor, was there nothing inside me but chill and disillusion? If I had dreamed a dream incompatible with the climate and social conditions of these Islands, had I not, out of that very dream and disenchantment, created, like the Platonic Lover, a Platonic and imperishable vision—the ideal Picnic, the Picnic as it might be—the wonderful windless weather, the Watteauish landscape, where a group of mortals talk and feast as they talked and feasted in the Golden Age?

More Trivia. 1922.

HEAT

Robert Lynd

THERE was a time when, for a year or so, I sat in a class-room and studied heat, light, sound and electricity. I never succeeded, unfortunately, in learning much about the nature of any of them, for a number of high-spirited young men with a pronounced anti-scientific bias—with a bias, indeed, against learning of any kind whatsoever—sat in the back benches and devoted their energies on the opening day to the manufacture of paper darts which they hurled at the head of the professor who was lecturing. He was an aged man with jerky movements and a jerky voice and a white beard that streamed like a flag in the wind. Strange that youth should find pleasure in persecuting age in this fashion, but it may be that the young men meant to be merciless, not to the old man, but to the professor. "Gentlemen, gentlemen," he would appeal, and then, with a wave of his tremulous hand, cry, "Put them out, Jackson," to the porter who remained at his side to help him with his apparatus. This, it must be admitted, was not an atmosphere conducive to sober inquiry into the nature of things. Whether it is for this reason or for some other, I am still so ignorant on these matters that I should have to look up in a book before I could explain why it is hotter in summer than in winter or—a still more difficult problem—why it is sometimes colder in summer than in winter. Men of science, I understand, say that these things are governed by law, but those of us who know no science can see no trace of order in a scheme of things that cuts us to the bone with the cold wind one July and melts us like melted butter the next. The days are undoubtedly longer in summer than in winter, but, apart from this, there is no certainty in the seasons. Who could have foretold a month ago that by this time we should be sweltering under a cloudless sky as we used to swelter in the summers of our childhood ? Life is full of surprises, but there is nothing more permanently surprising than the English summer. It surprises us when it is cold ; it surprises us when it is hot ; it surprises us even when it is lukewarm. Whether it bursts upon us in May or in June or in July, it comes on us as unexpectedly as if a millionaire whom we had never met suddenly began to shower his gold on us. It is the genius of the summer to restore us to the Golden Age when men lay lazily under the trees, and crimson-cheeked fruits fell all around them with a plump, so that they had not even to take the trouble to rise out of their lethargy in order to pick them. The anthropologists of our time have attempted to destroy this happy picture of the life of primitive man, and to put in his place a stunted, semi-articulate creature little more enviable in shape or in diet than a baboon. I prefer the evidence of the poets on this point, and I shall continue to think of primitive man as a beautiful and indolent creature in a tennis-shirt and white trousers stretched under a fruit tree by the bank of a purling stream with little crystal waves breaking among the grasses at the bend of the water.

Primitive man, indeed, as the old poets saw, was man before the curse of work fell upon him. He was man as we see him to-day at Henley, young, rich, idle, and happy. How cool it makes one even to think of him in that scene of tree-shadows and running water ! The coloured balloons that float above the punts at Henley—what are they but memories of the lovelier fruits of his lost Paradise ? It is a curious fact that one can think of the

Golden Age only as an age populated by rich young men and rich young women. They may indulge in the energies of sport but not of work. The vulgar servitude of earning one's bread in the sweat of one's brow is the mark of our fallen nature. If, every summer, men and women congregate to Henley, to Goodwood, to Cowes, it is but their make-believe that they are back in the ancient world of green and white and blue, that they have no more duties than children or than angels, and that winds and waters and grassy downs exist but to give them a place of pleasure. Even though I have never been rich and am never likely to be rich so long as the authorities continue to prohibit sweepstakes, I confess that I, too, feel extraordinarily happy in these scenes in which the idle rich take their pleasure. How beautiful is that phrase, " the idle rich " ! It has been used for the most part as a term of abuse, but I will never use it so. Who am I to abuse the idle rich, when to be idle and rich is an amusement in which I would so willingly take part myself ? How charming a man was William Morris to invent a Socialist Utopia in which everybody was idle and rich, or at least in which labour was but a delightful way of making use of leisure, and all the citizens of the nation might have lolled in cushioned punts at Henley !

It is a strange fact, however, that heat is associated in the popular imagination not only with Utopia but with its opposite. Heaven and Hell are, in the thoughts of most people, both hot places. I do not know why this should be except that they both begin with an H. The belief in the heat of Hell, however, is by no means universal. The Hell of the ancient Irish was a cold place where the ice did not melt. They did not squander on the Devil so sacred an element as fire. Even so logical a race as the Irish have, since that time, yielded to the general view of Christendom, as was seen when a Southern Unionist— quoting, I believe, an earlier authority—said that they would fight Home Rule till Hell froze and then they would go on fighting till the ice broke. To him, ice was a contradiction of Hell instead of its conclusive sign. On the other hand, though the picture of Hell has wavered between heat and cold, I do not think there have ever been two opinions about Heaven. In Heaven it is always summer. Every Utopia, every lotus-land, of which men dream is a place of summer fruits and sunny skies. This, it seems to me, is natural. Summer is the time of the fullness of life in fruit and flower. It is probable that we, too, bloom under the auspicious sun. I met a poet during the week who declared that a heat-wave always filled him with energy and that he could work harder at such a time than during any other part of the year. If others of us feel limp instead of buoyant just now, it is, I fancy, because we are engaged in some less heavenly pursuit than writing poetry. Summer fits us for the work we love—writing poetry, playing tennis and such things—and makes the work we hate doubly hateful. The true test of whether we love our work or not is whether we can do it even better in summer than in winter. Winter is an excellent season for routine-work. Even the dull, daily round seems a release from the brutality of the cold outside. Men often tell you that they feel brisk in winter. This only means that in a cold and dismal world they would rather be working than doing anything else. They seek forget-fulness of their miserable surroundings, and there are only two sure means of forgetfulness known to man—work and drink—and, of the two, work is the more economical. I should not like to speak ill of work. I agree with the preachers that it is an excellent discipline for those who need discipline. But, however hard I try and however I picture to myself the activities of Paradise, I cannot imagine any one's being set to clerking or navvying there. Modern spiritualists do, it is true, hint occasionally at a future life in which the workers of this world go on being the workers of the next, but Heaven, in the imaginations of most of us, is a complete change, and in nothing more than in the fact that the angels do no hack-work. It is not, I think, that men wish to be absolutely indolent, but that they wish to be busy as a prince or a poet is busy or as a moderately rich man is busy during a summer holiday.

It is only when the warm summer weather comes that we remember that the object of all civilization should be to make life more and more of a holiday—in other words, to make the activities of all men and women, as far as is possible, enjoyments. If science and invention cannot in a measure take the burden of hack-work off the shoulders of men and women and release them for activities that will make them happy, the men of science and the inventors will have been a doubtful boon. I should not advocate a life of exclusive pleasure—of wine, women and song, in the old phrase—for that, apparently, is the way to melancholy. But, as the perspiration drops from my brow, I do feel that a little more poetry, a little more seaside, and a little more Ascot, should be the portion of the common life of man. Alas ! poor mortals, we are so incapacitated by the long cold of winter that most of us are unable to enjoy the summer sea when we have the chance. We build Brightons and Bournemouths and Margates in order to defend ourselves against the perfect beauty of blue seas. We take shops and chimneys with us down to the edge of the ocean in order that our surroundings may not be too unlike the surroundings of our winter servitude. All the aids to forgetfulness are there—picture-palaces, music-halls, billiard-rooms and bar-rooms—as though in presence of sea and sun there were any need of forgetfulness. We have become such ding-dong slaves that we can no longer enjoy the heat of midsummer, but must continue the habits of the gloomy town even in our holidays. And, in this matter, do not rush to the conclusion that I claim any superiority over the rest of my kind. Do you think that I shall be able to keep out of the casino next month ? Do you think that I shall be able to resist the lure of the picture-palace by the sea in August ? Have I chosen a rustic solitude or an hotel with " good cuisine " as a refuge from the year's drudgery ? Ah ! do not inquire too closely. The cuisine, I trust, will be up to expectations. Good cooking, a blue sea, and a blazing sun—are they not all ingredients of the happiness of a weaker brother ?

The Peal of Bells. 1924.

SWALLOWS

Grace Rhys

When I was born the swifts were screaming about the roofs of my home ; those flying sounds were woven in and out of the first shadowy wakings and tenuous dreams. No summer sound is so wild, not even the wind ; yet when the small screamer is held in the hand, how unbelievably light ! I can remember, too, holding my first swallow ; the scene is all quite plain—the open window, the raising of the quivering house-ladder, the slow ascent of the long-legged pantry-boy, hammer in hand ; the knocking above at the nest ; the long arm at the window and the swallow put in my hand. How light it was ! and polished and warm and clean. What a decorated creature too, grey-blue back, chestnut ear-pieces, breast of salmon-pink, forked tail, and long, pointed wing. Small as I was I felt pity for the half-open beak, the thrilling heart ; sorry for the small sky-haunter. I opened my hand and shrieked too as it shrieked and fled up and away. Even now I feel the same excitement when that sound comes along out of the distance and flashes by. The imagination has the gift of becoming that with which it enters into sympathy. When the screaming bird dashes past on a curve with undulating ribbon-like wings, the spirit darts from the breast, shaped like a swallow, and as mad as he.

Strange that these desert-dwellers, these Arabs of the sky, should so cling to us and our houses. How long ago was it—ten thousand years ? since a swallow of genius

cast an eye on the first house that had a jutting roof-edge.
Fancy the small creature ruminating and conversing with
her mate : " See that nice shelf sticking out ? No burrowing need be done there ; only some good strong plastering.
Burrowing is odious work, cliff dust is choking and makes
my claws sore." So they two fetch their straws and clay
and make their pellets by the water-side (as Israel did in
Egypt), and plastering strongly, fix their nest in its new
shelter. Once the discovery was made, for ever after the
swallows followed the fortunes of man. They built their
nests in Babylon, in Carthage, in Troy ; among the six-
thousand-year-old palaces of Crete. Occasionally in the
earlier hieroglyphics of Egypt you will find the swallow
sitting with folded wings.

Nothing will persuade me but that they like men and
are interested in their doings. They like a warm life and
plenty of it. They like the stout straws of our farmyards,
so easy to nibble into lengths. And of course they like the
clouds of insects that are bred about the home-farm—food
for those fierce, wide-open beaks, those crimson, haired
throats.

This year a pair have built quite near to my window
here in Devon. Leaning far out and looking upward
I have been able to watch the whole performance fairly
at my ease—the plasterers at their work and their ripple
of talk as they clung, flattened to the wall : the completed
nest, a clay purse so closely covered by the eaves that a
round lip like the mouth of a jug has been contrived for
the opening ; the silences when the she-swallow was
sitting ; his visits to her, an arrow-like sweep, a warbling,
and then away. Then the great to-do when the young
were hatched, the squeaking and twittering going on from
four in the morning till sunset. The noisiest time of all is
when the young birds are grown up and about learning to
fly ; what danger ! what excitement ! It was charming
to watch. A gay little black head with chestnut-coloured

cheeks would appear over the lip, the round eyes look out on the sweet gulfs of air, the green waving trees, and lastly at the funny human face smiling so near. "Too deep, too far! Oh, I can't! I daren't!" the little thing would shriek, and then dive back again. There would be a warbling and chattering within, and then another dark head would appear, and so on all day. The father and mother birds, clinging like ornaments of painted bronze to the nest, would twitter exhortations, and all the little ones would be tumbling together at the opening to listen.

In the end, I am quite sure it was the brothers and sisters that handily pushed the biggest out from behind; then, what an uproar! Squeaking frantically, the little thing dropped a foot, the parents flew shrieking round; then the untried wings spread, the forked tail feathered out, the wee creature rose heavily, came round on a wobbling curve and so back home again. For a week after that the fun and the noise went on till all the young ones were slipping out by turns or together, like little swift fishes gliding upon the air.

Now, grown strong, they go off for the whole of the day. But toward evening they still come back to the nest; what a diversion! They are really too big, yet they fit in somehow. They are nearly an hour over packing up, as a rule; darting continually off, as it were, in fits of laughter; and returning again to tumble in a raving heap. Nothing quiets them but the coming of the twilight. Before the first bat appears they are all in, and the nest is silent till dawn.

Each night they return I tell myself: "It is the last"; already we look forward to the shorter day. The light will grow paler as the sun withdraws himself into the south. The swallows will grow more excited, the young ones flying on longer, stronger wings, as daring, as untiring as any. The old ones will be watching the signs and re-membering the way. Each day they will be freshly aware

of the mandate, as they see the pathway of the golden
emperor lower upon the sky. They will have the impulse
to follow his receding glory, shooting straight for the
middle curve of the golden bow, high, high up.

We shall see them getting ready. They will sit and talk
interminably in long rows. You can hear them.

"When ? when ? when ? Joy ! joy ! joy ! Away !
Where ? Far, very far ! Egypt, Africa. Follow the sun !
To-morrow ! To-morrow !"

And when to-morrow comes you may see them lift and
go. Twenty false starts they will make before they are off.
The flocks are waiting by companies together ; now they
whirl up and join together, then settle again. One more
try, and they go ! They rise and rise and then stream out
on the sky in their arrow-shaped formation ; the most
great-hearted swallow of all darts out to the front and leads
alone.

They will cross the seas, by way of France and by the
Netherlands ; they will reach and cross the Pyrenees, the
Alps, the Apennines. Safe in the hollow behind the arrow-
head travel this year's birds, upheld on the whir of the
hosted wings. They disappear on the edge of the sky.

Ah, if I might live again I would choose to be a swallow
and fly with my love to Africa.

A Book of Grace. 1930.

SCIENCE AND RELIGION

Sir Arthur Eddington

If you will look up at the sky in the direction of the constellation Andromeda and spend a few moments scrutinizing the faintest stars you see, you will notice one that is not a sharp point of light like the rest but has a hazy appearance. That star is unique among all that are visible to the naked eye. It is not properly a star; we might rather describe it as a universe. It teaches us that when we have taken together the Sun and all the other naked-eye stars and many hundreds of millions of telescopic stars we have not yet reached the end of things. We have explored only one island—one oasis in the desert of space; in the far distance we discern another island which is that faint patch of light in Andromeda. With the help of a telescope we can make out a great many more, in fact a whole archipelago of island universes stretching away one behind another till our sight fails. That speck of light which any one may see is a sample of one of these islands; it is a world not only remote in space but remote in time. Long before the dawn of history the light now entering our eyes started on its journey across the great gulf between the islands. When you look at it you are looking back 900,000 years into the past.

Amid this profusion of worlds and space and time, where do we come in? Our home, the Earth, is the fifth or sixth largest planet belonging to an inconspicuous middle-grade star in one of the numerous islands of the archipelago. Doubtless there are other globes which are or have been tenanted by beings of similar nature to ourselves ; but we have some reason to think that such globes are uncommon. It seems that normally matter collects in big lumps with terrifically high temperature ; the formation of small cool globes fit for habitation is no part of the normal scheme, though it has happened occasionally by a rare accident. Nature seems to have been intent on a vast scheme of evolution of fiery globes, an epic of milliards of years. As for Man—that was an unfortunate incident which it seems rather ungenerous to refer to. It was only a trifling hitch in the machinery— not a very serious consequence to the universe. No need to be always raking up against Nature her one little inadvertence.

Is that how you and I come in ? To realize the insignificance of our race amid the majesty of the universe is probably healthful. But it brings to us a more alarming thought. For Man is the typical custodian of certain qualities or illusions which make a great difference to the significance of things. He displays purpose in an inorganic world of chance. He *can* represent truth, righteousness, sacrifice. In him there flickers for a few brief years a spark from the divine spirit. Are these as insignificant as he is ?

It may possibly be going too far to say that our bodies are pieces of stellar matter which by a contingency not sufficiently guarded against have taken advantage of the low temperature to assume unusual complication and perform the series of strange antics we call " life." But I do not combat this view ; even if I doubt its tenability, I keep an open mind, and am unwilling to base philosophy or religion on the assumption that it must necessarily break down. But alongside this there is another outlook. Science is an attempt to set in order the facts of experience. Every one will agree that it has met with wonderful success ; and the picture which it draws of the physical universe is its answer to the problem. But it does not start quite at the beginning of the Problem of Experience. The first question asked about facts or theories such as I have been describing is " Are they true ? " I want to emphasize that even more significant than the astronomical results themselves is the fact that this question about them so urgently arises. The question " Is it true ? " changes the complexion of the world of experience—not because it is asked *about* the world but because it is asked *in* the world. If we go right back to the beginning the first thing we must recognize in the world is something intent on truth—something to which it matters intensely that belief should be true. We settle that as the first ingredient of the world of experience, before we invite science to take the problem in hand and put in order other facts of experience. If in its survey of the universe science rediscovers the presence of such an ingredient, well and good ; if not the ingredient remains none the less essential, for otherwise the whole quest is stultified.

What is the truth about ourselves ? We may incline to various answers. We are a bit of a star gone wrong. We are complicated physical machinery—puppets that strut and talk and laugh and die as the hand of time turns the handle beneath. But let us remember that there is one elementary inescapable answer. We are *that which asks the question*. Responsibility towards truth is an attribute of our nature. It is through our spiritual nature, of which responsibility for truth is a typical manifestation, that we first come into the world of experience ; our entry via the physical universe is a re-entry. The strange association of soul and body—of responsibility for truth with a bit of stellar matter that got cold by accident—is a problem in which we cannot but feel intense interest, but not an anxious interest as though the existence and significance of a spiritual side of experience were hanging in the balance. The solution must fit the data ; we cannot alter the data to fit the alleged solution.

I do not regard the phenomenon of living matter (in so far as it can be treated apart from the phenomenon of consciousness) as necessarily outside the scope of physics and chemistry. Arguments that, because a living creature is an organism, it *ipso facto* possesses something which can never be understood in terms of physical science, do not impress me. I think it is insufficiently recognized that modern theoretical physics is very much concerned with the study of organization ; and from organization to organism does not seem an impossible stride. It may happen that some day science will be able to show how from the entities of physics creatures might have been formed which are counterparts of ourselves even to the point of being endowed with life. The scientist will perhaps point out the nervous mechanism of this creature, its powers of motion, of growth, of reproduction, and end by saying " That's you." But remember the inescapable test. " Is it concerned with truth as I am ; then I will acknowledge that it is indeed myself." We demand something more even than consciousness. The scientist might point to motions in the brain and say that these really mean sensations, emotions, thoughts ; and perhaps supply a code to translate the motions into corresponding thoughts. Even if we accept this rather inadequate substitute for consciousness as we intimately know it, we must still protest : " You have shown us a creature which thinks and believes ; you have not shown us a creature to whom it *matters* (in any non-utilitarian sense) what it thinks and believes." The inmost ego, possessing what I have called the inescapable attribute, can never be part of the physical world unless we alter the meaning of the word " physical " to " spiritual "—a change hardly to the advantage of clear thinking. But having disowned our supposed double, we can say to the scientist : " If you will hand over this Robot who pretends to be me, and let it be filled with the attribute at present lacking and perhaps other spiritual attributes which I claim on similar though less indisputable grounds, we may arrive at something that is indeed myself."

An interesting point is that the recent revolutionary changes of science have made this kind of co-operative solution of the Problem of Experience more practicable than it used to be. A few years ago the suggestion of taking the physically constructed man and adapting him to a spiritual nature by casually adding something, would have been a mere figure of speech—a verbal gliding over of insuperable difficulties. In much the same way we talk loosely of building a Robot and then breathing life into him. A Robot is presumably not constructed to bear such last-minute changes of design ; he is a delicate piece of mechanism designed to work mechanically, and to adapt him for anything else would involve wholesale reconstruction. To put it crudely, if you want to fill a vessel with anything you must make it hollow, and the old-fashioned material body was not hollow enough to be a receptacle of spiritual nature. I know that the change in our conception of the material universe and of the aims of physics must be very puzzling to most people ; but I have not time to explain or defend it. I will only say that any of the young theoretical physicists of to-day will tell you that what he is dragging to light as the basis of all the phenomena that come within his province is a scheme of symbols connected by mathematical equations. That is what the physical universe boils down into, when probed by the methods which a physicist can apply. Now a skeleton scheme of symbols is hollow enough to hold anything. It can be—nay it cries out to be—filled with something to transform it from skeleton into being, from shadow into actuality, from symbols into the interpretation of the symbols. And if ever the scientist solves the problem of the living body, he should no longer be tempted to point to his result and say " That's you." He will say rather : " That is how I symbolize you in my description and explanation of those of your properties which I can observe and measure. If you claim any deeper insight into your own nature—any knowledge of what it really is that these symbols symbolize—you can rest assured that I have no rival interpretation of the symbols to propose." The skeleton is the whole contribution of physics to the solution of the Problem of Experience ; from the clothing of the skeleton it stands aloof.

I think we may say that, although the physicist has carried his work to greater perfection than formerly, he now puts it in a form which does not hide its incompleteness. Implicitly, if not explicitly, he advertises for some one to complete it. And we who are interested in the non-material aspects of experience are not butting in ; we are answering his advertisement. But, of course, it does not follow that general opinion among physicists regards us as suitable applicants for the job ; I admit that there are many who would say that it is better to let sound work remain uncompleted than to let it be embellished by incompetent workmen, as they deem us to be.

The scientific conception of the world has come to differ more and more from the commonplace conception, until we have been forced to ask ourselves what really is the aim of this scientific transformation. The doctrine that " things are not what they seem " is all very well in moderation ; but it has proceeded so far that we have to remind ourselves that the world of appearances is the one we have actually to adjust our lives to. That was not always so. At first the progress of scientific thought consisted in correcting gross errors in the commonplace outlook. We learned that the earth was spherical, not flat. That does not refer to some abstract scientific earth, but to the earth we know so well with all its colour, beauty and homeliness. I confess that when I think of a Test Match in Australia I cannot help picturing it as played upside down—so much has the roundness of the earth become part of a familiar outlook. We learned that the earth was rotating. For the most part we give an intellectual assent to this without attempting to weave it into our familiar conception, but we can picture it if we try. In Rossetti's poem the Blessed Damosel looked down from the golden balcony of Heaven through

> The void as low as where this earth
> Spins like a fretful midge.

Looking from the abode of truth, perfect truth alone can enter her mind. She must see the earth as it really is—like a whirling insect. But now let us try something fairly modern. In Einstein's theory the earth, like other matter, is a curvature of space-time, and what we commonly call the spin of the earth is a ratio of two of the components of curvature. What is the Blessed Damosel going to make of that? I am afraid she will have to be a bit of a blue-stocking. Perhaps there is no great harm in that. I am not sure that I would think it derogatory to an angel to accuse him of understanding Einstein's theory. My objection is more serious. If the Blessed Damosel sees the earth in the Einsteinian way she will be seeing truly—I can feel little doubt as to that—but she will be *missing the point*. It is as though we took her to a picture gallery, and she (with that painful truthfulness which cannot recognize anything that is not really there) saw ten square yards of yellow paint, five of crimson, and so on.

So long as physics in tinkering with the familiar world was able to retain those aspects which appeal to the æsthetic side of our nature, it might with some show of reason claim to cover the whole of experience ; and those who claimed that there was another religious aspect of experience had to fight for their claim. But now that its picture omits so much that is obviously essential, there is no suggestion that it is the whole truth about experience. To make such a claim would bring protest not only from those religiously inclined but from all who recognize that man is not merely a scientific measuring machine. If it were necessary I would at this point turn aside to defend the scientist for pursuing the development of a highly specialized solution of one side of the Problem of Experience and ignoring the rest ; but I will content myself with reminding you that it is through his efforts in this direction that my voice is now being heard by you. At any rate there is method in his madness.

Another striking change of scientific views is in regard to determinism—the view that the future is predestined, and that Time merely turns over the leaves of a story that is already written :

> Yea the first Morning of Creation wrote
> What the last Dawn of Reckoning shall read.

Until recently this was almost universally accepted as the teaching of science—at least in regard to the material universe. It is the distinctive principle of the mechanistic outlook which superseded the crude materialistic outlook. But to-day physical theory is not mechanistic, and it is built on a foundation which knows nothing of this supposed determinism. So far as we have yet gone in our probing of the material universe, we find no evidence in favour of determinism. The new theory recognizes a wide domain of phenomena in which the future is for all practical purposes definitely predictable, and explains why this is possible ; but it does not assume the same predictability for all physical phenomena. According to the type of phenomenon studied, forecasts of the future have different degrees of probability ranging from overwhelming odds to even chances. The denial of determinism is not merely qualitative but quantitative ; we have actually a mathematical formula indicating just how far the course of events deviates from complete predictability.

I do not think there is any serious division of opinion as to the decease of determinism. If there is a division among scientists it is between the mourners and the jubilants. The mourners naturally hope that determinism will one day be re-established in its old position in physics ; that is possible, but personally I see no reason to expect that it will return in any shape or form. In any case, our concern is not with prophetic anticipations of what science may be like in future, but with the relations between present-day science and religion. To discuss the extent and consequences of this change would lead to questions too technical to be dealt with here. (To avoid possible misunderstanding I had better say that I do not think it makes any important difference to special theological questions such as miracle, or " direct answer " to prayer.) But I think there is no longer any need to doubt our intuition of free will. Our minds are not merely registering a predetermined sequence of thoughts and decisions. Our purposes, our volitions are genuine ; and ours is the responsibility for what ensues from them. It seems necessary to admit this, for we are scarcely likely to accept a theory which would make the human spirit *more* mechanistic than the physical universe.

I now turn to the question, what must be put into the skeleton scheme of symbols. I have said that physical science stands aloof from this transmutation, and if I say anything positive on this side of the question it is not as a scientist that I claim to speak.

It was by looking into our own nature that we revealed the first failure of the physical universe to be co-extensive with our experience of reality. The " something to which truth matters " must surely have a place in reality, if we are to use the term reality at all. In our own nature, or through the contact of our consciousness with a nature transcending ours, there are other things that claim the same kind of recognition—a sense of beauty, of morality, and finally at the root of all spiritual religion an experience which we describe as the presence of God. In suggesting that these things constitute a spiritual world I am not trying to substantialize them or objectivize them—to make them out other than we find them to be in our experience of them. But I would say that when from the human heart, perplexed with the mystery of existence, the cry goes up, " What is it all about ? " it is no true answer to look only at that part of experience which comes to us through certain sensory organs and reply : " It is about atoms and chaos ; it is about a universe of fiery globes rolling on to impending doom ; it is about tensors and non-commutative algebra." Rather it is about a spirit within which truth has its shrine, with potentialities of self-fulfilment in its response to beauty and right. Shall I not also add that even as light and colour and sound come into our minds from a world beyond, so these other stirrings of consciousness come from something which, whether we describe it as beyond or deep within ourselves, is wider than our own individual personality ?

It is the essence of religion that it presents this side of experience as a matter of everyday life. To live in it, we have to grasp it in the form of familiar recognition and not as a series of abstract scientific statements. Its counterpart in our outward life is the familiar world and not the symbolic scientific universe. The man who commonly spoke of his ordinary surroundings in scientific language would be insufferable ; and if God really has a part in our everyday life, I do not think we need mind if the critic trips us up for speaking and thinking of him un-scientifically.

But perhaps the earnest Christian will say : " I am a plain man and I think of God unscientifically, as you allow. It means a great deal to me to conceive God as the Father, from whom comes power and guidance and to whom I may turn with devotion and trust. But just because it means so much, I have no use for it if it is only a convenient fiction which will not stand close examination. Can you not give some assurance that there is such a God in reality, and that belief in him is not merely a sop to my limited understanding ? " The fear is that when we come to analyse that which we call religious experience, we shall find that the God apparently revealed in it is merely a personification of certain abstract principles. Now I frankly admit that the application of any method which we should call scientific to the examination of our religious experience is likely to work this kind of havoc. But what else could we expect ? Although the method of physical science is inapplicable, the methods of the less exact sciences which are to some extent modelled on it may perhaps be applied. They involve the same kind of abstraction and codifying. If our treatment consists in codifying, what can we possibly get but a code ? The fact that scientific method seems to reduce God to something like an ethical code may throw some light on the nature of scientific method ; I doubt if it throws much light on the nature of God. If the consideration of religious experience in the light of psychology seems to remove from the conception of God every attribute that calls forth our worship or love, it is pertinent to consider whether something of the same sort has not happened to our human friends after psychology has systematized and scheduled them. It does not fall within my scope to give the questioner the assurance he desires ; I doubt whether there is any assurance to be obtained except through the power of the religious experience itself ; but I bid him hold fast to his own intimate knowledge of the nature of that experience. I think that that will take him closer to the ultimate truth than codifying and symbolizing can reach.

I know that my writings have disappointed many because I set aside the question, Is God an objective reality ? Before attempting to answer it, it would be necessary to catechize the questioner as to what meaning —if any—he associates with the word objective. I do not think that it is possible to make the same hard and fast distinction between subjective and objective that we used to make. The theory of relativity has taught us that the subjective element in our experience of the physical universe is far stronger than we had previously suspected. It is true that in relativity theory we continue our attempt to reach purely objective truth. But what results ? A world so abstract that only a mathematical symbol could inhabit it. In the other great modern development of physics—the quantum theory— we have, if I am not mistaken, abandoned the aim, and become content to analyse the physical universe into ultimate elements which are frankly subjective. If it is difficult to separate out the subjective element in our knowledge of the external world, it must be much more difficult to distinguish it when we come to the problem of a self-knowing consciousness, where subject and object— that which knows and that which is known—are one and the same.

I have been laying great stress on *experience* ; in this I am following the dictates of modern physics. But I do not wish to imply that every experience is to be taken at face value. There is such a thing as illusion, and we must try not to be deceived. In any attempt to go deeply into the meaning of religious experience we are confronted by the difficult problem of how to detect and eliminate illusion and self-deception. I recognize that the problem exists, but I must excuse myself from attempting a solution.

The operation of cutting out illusion in the spiritual domain requires a delicate surgical knife ; and the only instrument that I, a physicist, can manipulate is a bludgeon which, it is true, crushes illusion, but at the same time crushes everything of non-material significance and even reduces the material world to a state of uncreatedness. For I am convinced that if in physics we pursued to the bitter end our attempt to reach purely objective reality, we should simply undo the work of creation and present the world as we might conceive it to have been before the Spirit moved upon the face of the waters. The spiritual element in our experience is the creative element, and if we remove it as we have tried to do in physics on the ground that it also creates illusion, we must ultimately reach the nothingness which was in the Beginning.

Reasoning is our great ally in the quest for truth. But reasoning can only start from premises ; and at the beginning of the argument we must always come back to innate convictions. There are such convictions at the base even of physical science. We are helpless unless we admit also (as perhaps the strongest conviction of all) that we have within us some power of self-criticism to test the validity of our own convictions. The power is not infallible, that is to say it is not infallible when associated with human frailty ; but neither is reasoning infallible when practised by our blundering intelligence. I think that this power can be nothing less than a ray proceeding from the light of absolute Truth, a thought proceeding from the absolute Mind. With this guidance we may embark on the adventure of spiritual life, uncharted though it be. It is sufficient that we carry a compass.

Science and Religion (A Symposium).   1931.

ON THE AUTHORSHIP OF
"IN MEMORIAM"

Ronald Knox

WHY Shakespeare more than anybody else ?

The problem " Who wrote *In Memoriam* ? " is one of the most interesting and most complicated in literary history ; and it is safe to say that it has not hitherto received the attention it deserved. Everybody is familiar with the outlines of it. Hallam died in 1833, and the poem which professes to be his epicedium did not see the light until 1850. What is the explanation of this monstrous interval ? Further, when the poem originally appeared, it was accorded a doubtful reception, and was attributed by some critics (a very significant fact) to a feminine hand. Mr. Nicholson has familiarized us with the verdict of one reviewer in particular, who suggested that it was in all probability composed by the widow of some military man. It was only later that Tennyson stepped in, claimed the poem as his own, and gave it the reputation which it holds at present. The question naturally suggests itself, Did Tennyson really write it, or was he screening somebody else ? If we adopt the latter view, it will be necessary to urge some sufficient motive for a literary imposition so audacious and so persistent.

One looks, naturally, for a cryptogram. And here a most impressive fact meets us at the very outset of the inquiry. Give the letters their natural value as Greek numerals : that is, make A=1, E=5, I=10, M=40, N=50, O=70, R=100. The letters of *In Memoriam* thus work out at 10+50+40+5+40+70+100+10+1+40, cyphers which on a careful computation add up to 366, the number of days in the full year ! Scarcely less significant is the result if we take the natural values of the English alphabet, starting with A=0, B=1, C=2, etc. The letters of *In Memoriam* on this reckoning give you 8+13+12+4+12+14+17+8+0+12, and these ten cyphers add up to 100 ! Again, if you give the vowels their natural values as a separate series, this time making A=1, E=2, etc., you find that the vowels IEIOA represent 3+2+3+4+1, cyphers which add up to the mystical number 13. Adding 100 to 13 (for want of anything better to do), you arrive at the number 113, and immediately turn to the 113th canto of the poem to see if it holds any secret for posterity. Is it possible that the cryptographer will have betrayed, by some tiny awkwardness of phrase, some tiny evidence of strained writing, the line in this canto which contains the clue ?

The search is not a difficult one. Few readers of the poem can have failed to note the artificial effect of the 11th line :

A potent voice of Parliament—

why OF Parliament, instead of IN Parliament ? The latter, surely, is what any author would naturally have written. Is not the change from " in " to " of " just such a change as might have been forced on him, not by any demands of literary appropriateness, but by the desire to select two particular letters *which would complete a particular message in cypher* ? It might be a fresh numerical cypher, it might be merely anagrammatical. . . . One has to play with various possibilities, and then an anagram leaps quite suddenly into view. What it is we shall see later. For the present, let us simply note that the 11th line of the 113th canto of *In Memoriam* can be read anagrammatically, and when so read gives a thoroughly sensational message.

It also (as will be seen later) indicates unmistakably that it is the *last* of a series of cryptograms. As an hypothesis, then, it may be worth considering the possibility that it is the last of a series of 11, which will involve verse 1 of canto *x*, verse 2 of canto *y*, and so on. It would be easy to construct an artificial series for the purpose (e.g., 13, 23, etc.), but a natural series is not so easily arrived at. It is here that a certain amount of intricate mathematical thinking is involved, the details of which we spare the reader, giving only the conclusions. It will be seen that the series is a real and natural one, though sufficiently abstruse to be worthy of an accomplished cryptographer such as the poet we are dealing with.

It runs as follows :

$$1 = 1$$
$$\star \qquad \star \qquad \star$$
$$1 \times 2 + 1 = 3$$
$$\star \qquad \star \qquad \star$$
$$2 \times 2 + 2 = 6$$
$$6 \times 2 + 1 = 13$$
$$\star \qquad \star \qquad \star$$
$$3 \times 2 + 3 = 9$$
$$9 \times 2 + 2 = 20$$
$$20 \times 2 + 1 = 41$$
$$\star \qquad \star \qquad \star$$
$$4 \times 2 + 4 = 12$$
$$12 \times 2 + 3 = 27$$
$$27 \times 2 + 2 = 56$$
$$56 \times 2 + 1 = 113$$

Taking the formula as $xy + z$, it will be seen that y is always 2, that z is in turn 1, 2, 1, 3, 2, 1, 4, 3, 2, 1 ; that x is in turn 1, 2, 3, 4, at the beginning of the division, and in the rest of the division is simply a repetition of the last total reached.

On our present hypothesis, then (for it is so far a hypo-thesis) we shall expect to find a cryptogram (in the form of an anagram) in the following lines : line 1 of canto 1, line 2 of canto 3, line 3 of canto 6, line 4 of canto 13, and so on till we get to line 11 of canto 113. Let us give the results of this speculation :

1.	1	I held it truth, with him who sings.
3.	2	O priestess in the vaults of death.
6.	3	And common is the commonplace.
13.	4	Her place is empty, fall like these.
9.	5	So draw him home to those that mourn.
20.	6	And weep the fulness from the mind.
41.	7	Thy changes ; here upon the ground.
12.	8	And leave the cliffs, and haste away.
27.	9	Nor, what may count itself as blest.
56.	10	Such splendid purpose in his eyes.
113.	11	A potent voice of Parliament.

Before we go any farther we may at once comment upon a corroborative symptom. Omit the first two and the last two of these lines, and the intervening lines give us a perfect single acrostic. It runs, " Ah Satan ! " Some-body clearly felt that he or she was being tempted to violate conscience, and registered a protest in this way. We shall see that the seven lines of the acrostic have a common thread running through them.

Anagrams are slow work, and a " Word Making and Word Taking " outfit is recommended to the beginner. The letters of " I held it truth, with him who sings " yield, with a little arrangement, the following rather intriguing result : " Who is writing this ? H.M. luteth hid." It was, no doubt, the word " harp " in the next line of the poem that suggested to the cryptographer the rather fanciful word " luteth." The implication is plain enough : the author of this poem is not its reputed author ;

somebody described as H.M. is really writing the poem but prefers to remain hidden, that is anonymous. So far we have not much to go upon in the way of positive information ; after all, there must have been plenty of people writing in 1850 who would answer to the required initials. We turn on, then, impatiently to canto 3, line 2, and are met with a startling announcement. " O priestess in the vaults of death " reads quite unmistakably " V.R.I. the poetess. Alf T. has no duties." Astounding—impossible ! Yet there it is in black and white ; there is no getting over the documentary evidence. English sovereigns had not yet adopted the imperial title (the Mutiny was yet to come), but already it must have been designed *in petto*. There was only one person in England who could be designated indifferently " H.M." or " V.R.I."

And yet, is it so extraordinary ? Has anybody read Queen Victoria's published diaries without being conscious of a note of domesticity, a note of resignation, a note of common human pathos, which finds its very counterpart in the stanzas of *In Memoriam* ? There was, after all, something to be said for the critic who suspected feminine authorship. But at that period of our history, though a woman might write poetry, a queen might not publish it. It was necessary to conceal the secret as if it had been a guilty one, or the consequences might have been international. The arrangement, then, clearly, was that the work should be published anonymously, but that Tennyson, then a rising poet, should be prepared if necessary to cast veracity to the winds, and shoulder the onus of authorship. It was a patriot's act ; and perhaps something of the moral struggle which it involves is reflected in the next cryptogram, which is in Latin. " And common is the commonplace " (a line which many of us have felt before now to be something less than Elizabethan in its quality) is after all only an ingenious cloak for the Latin motto " Pie hoc nomen clam commodans. T.", that is to say, " Devotedly lending this name in secret. T." The man who wrote thus had faced a moral problem, and had risen superior to it.

It would be necessary for Tennyson to " lend his name " if either of two things happened—if discovery of the real authorship threatened, or if the anonymous appearance of the book should prove injurious to its sales. Which motive in fact became operative ? The next cryptogram leaves us in no doubt, and indeed casts a rather sinister light on the whole proceeding. Tennyson had no doubt been studying Bacon as a master of cryptographic method ; and he will have been struck, as all of us will have been struck, at the singular ease with which you may find cryptograms in the works of the Elizabethans, *because any sort of spelling will do.* Imitating, then, the crude orthography of Gloriana's period, he has delicately indicated the motive which was responsible, at least in part, both for the original publication of the poem and for the invocation of Tennysonian patronage. " Her place is empty, fall like these " can be nothing other than " Her Majesty lacks pelf. I'le help. TE."

It will already have occurred to the ingenious reader that the letter T left over in the third, and the letters TE left over in the fourth cryptogram, are a sort of rudimentary signature, which (by a pretty piece of ingenuity) adds one letter to itself each time it occurs. This is true only of the seven lines which form the acrostic " Ah, Satan," and consequently they stop at " TENNYSO," just short of the complete signature. The fifth and sixth are mere repetitions of the message which the earlier cypher has given us. " So draw him home to those that mourn " is to be read (no doubt in playful allusion to the May Queen) as " O Mother, I'm H.M.'s shadow-author ! TEN." " And weep the fulness from the mind " is meant for a mock warning to the reviewers of the poem, suitably couched in the words, " Who pummels Faith-Defender ?

TENN." One recognizes, in the choice of the verb, Tennyson's own love for vigorous English.

Alas, that our minds should be built on such a mercenary pattern ! We naturally ask, was this generous loan of his name to bring Tennyson no reward from the real authoress of the poem ? History supplies us with a painfully distinct answer—Tennyson became Poet Laureate in 1850, the very year of *In Memoriam's* publication ! It is no doubt to this recognition of his services that he alludes, with what some will think doubtful taste, in the next cryptogram. We have done our best to find some other anagrammatic equivalent for the words " Thy changes ; here upon the ground," but the unfortunate fact defeats us. There can be no doubt that we are to understand it as meaning " Oh hurrah ! Nest-egg pouched ! TENNY." Let us pass hastily over this lapse from dignity, pausing only to admire the characteristically keen appreciation of Nature which the metaphor shows. And, indeed, the recognition was not undeserved, for it appears that the whole conception of the artifice originated with Tennyson : so at least the eighth cryptogram gives us to understand. "And leave the cliffs, and haste away " can hardly stand for anything but " La ! What a safe device Alf had ! TENNYS." He had indeed burrowed deep, but he should not have trusted to the impenetrability of his armour so far as to give way to these regrettable outbursts of exultation.

What, then, was the original purpose of the poem ? Queen Victoria did not know Arthur Hallam, and it is clear that the initials were merely chosen in order to lend plausibility to the story that it was Tennyson's work. Was it, then, some quite imaginary person whose death evoked this touching threnody ? We might have remained in the dark, were it not for one final disclosure of the cypher-lines. The ninth cryptogram is more difficult to read than the others, because more allusively expressed, but there can be no doubt of the true version. " Nor, what may count itself as blest " must be " Let A.H. act for W. Lamb's suit. TENNYSO "—or possibly " Let W. Lamb suit, cast for A. H. TENNYSO." The metaphor will be sartorial on the former supposition, histrionic on the latter ; in any case there can be no doubt as to the hero. William Lamb was the family name of that Lord Melbourne who was Queen Victoria's first and favourite Prime Minister. Mr. Lytton Strachey has given abundant evidence of the warm respect and admiration, something half filial and half romantic, which the young Queen felt for Lord Melbourne. When did he die ? In the November of 1848, a date which exactly suits the circumstances of the poem. It enhances our respect for Queen Victoria's poetic gifts when we reflect that this long and intricate work was the fruit of little more than a year's labour.

The tenth cryptogram raises the question—If Victoria was the authoress of the poem, how was it that Tennyson came to supply the cypher ? There must, it seems, have been collaboration here, and there could be few more generous tributes than that which is paid in the words " Such splendid purpose in his eyes." For these, when read according to the cryptographer's intention, give you : " She lisp'd in sinuous cyphers deep "—the praise is the praise of Victoria, but the voice is the voice of Tennyson. And yet the man who could write such a line as that could take pride in signing himself at the conclusion of his cryptographic message : " A potent voice of Parliament," which, it need hardly be pointed out, stands for " Alf, poet-pen to Victoria. Amen."

The chain of evidence, then, may be summed up as follows :

1.	1	Who is writing this ?	H.M. luteth hid.
3.	2	V.R.I. the poetess.	Alf T. has no duties.
6.	3	Pie hoc nomen clam commodans.	T.
13.	4	Her Majesty lacks pelf ; I'le help.	TE.

9.	5	O Mother, I'm H.M.'s shadow-author !
		TEN.
20.	6	Who pummels Faith-Defender ?
		TENN.
41.	7	Oh, hurrah ! Nest-egg pouched !
		TENNY.
12.	8	La ! What a safe device Alf had !
		TENNYS.
27.	9	Let A.H. act for W. Lamb's suit.
		TENNYSO.
56.	10	She lisp'd in sinuous cyphers deep.
113.	11	Alf, poet-pen to Victoria. Amen.

There is much, no doubt, still to be explained as to the personal allusions of *In Memoriam* ; some, no doubt, deliberately put in as a blind, others referring in a veiled way to incidents in Lord Melbourne's career. But, in the face of evidence such as this, will any one attempt to rack the long arm of coincidence so as to make it cover this extraordinary series of cryptograms ? If so, he has the ostrich-mind that cannot, because it will not, acquiesce in the assured results of modern inquiry.

Why Shakespeare more than anybody else ?

Essays in Satire. 1934.

PHRASES

LOGAN PEARSALL-SMITH

Is there, after all, any solace like the solace and consolation of Language? When I am disconcerted by the unpleasing aspects of existence, when to me, as to Hamlet, this earth seems a sterile promontory, it is not in Metaphysics nor in Religion that I seek for reassurance, but in fine phrases. The thought of gazing on life's Evening Star makes of ugly old age a pleasing prospect; if I call Death mighty and unpersuaded, it has no terrors for me; I am perfectly content to be cut down as a flower, to flee as a shadow, to be swallowed like a snowflake on the sea. These similes soothe and effectually console me. I am sad only at the thought that Words must perish like all things mortal; that the most perfect Metaphors must be forgotten when the human race is dust.

"But the iniquity of Oblivion blindly scattereth her poppy."

More Trivia. 1922.